BUSINESS LAW

Also available:

Smith and Keenan's
ADVANCED BUSINESS LAW

Smith and Keenan's
ENGLISH LAW

Smith and Keenan's
COMPANY LAW FOR STUDENTS

Smith and Keenan's
COMPANY LAW FOR STUDENTS
WITH SCOTTISH SUPPLEMENT

Sixth Edition

BUSINESS LAW

DENIS KEENAN
LLB (Hons) FCIS Cert Ed

of the Middle Temple, Barrister
Formerly Head of Department of Business Studies and Law
at what is now Anglia Polytechnic University

SARAH RICHES
LLB (Hons) PGCE MSc

Dean of Students
Bolton Institute of Higher Education

PEARSON
Longman

Harlow, England • London • New York • Boston • San Francisco • Toronto
Sydney • Tokyo • Singapore • Hong Kong • Seoul • Taipei • New Delhi
Cape Town • Madrid • Mexico City • Amsterdam • Munich • Paris • Milan

Pearson Education Limited
Edinburgh Gate
Harlow
Essex CM20 2JE
England

and Associated Companies throughout the world

Visit us on the World Wide Web at:
www.pearsoneduc.com

First published in Great Britain under the Pitman Publishing imprint in 1987
Second edition published 1990
Third edition published 1993
Fourth edition publishd 1995
Fifth edition published 1998
Sixth edition published under the Longman imprint in 2002

ISBN 0 582 43815 2

British Library Cataloguing-in-Publication Data
A catalogue record for this book is available from the British Library.

10 9 8 7 6 5 4
07 06 05 04 03

Typeset in 9/11 Sabon by 30.
Printed and bound in Great Britain by Ashford Colour Press Ltd, Gosport.

CONTENTS

PREFACE

This book is designed primarily for students studying Business Law at a variety of levels as part of a Business course.

We have assumed that the reader has no previous knowledge of English law; our starting point is basic principles and, when specialist legal terms are used, we have given clear 'jargon free' explanations. The book is designed to give the reader an understanding of the changing legal framework within which modern business organisations must operate. The emphasis is on law in its business context. Thus a range of business documents has been included, enabling the reader to relate the principles of business law to the real world of business.

In this connection our thanks go to the Consumer Credit Trade Association, the Road Haulage Association, Companies House and HMSO for giving us their kind permission to reproduce certain of these documents. The reader should appreciate that the versions of these documents and forms appearing in our text are reduced in size, and also that copyright in them must be respected. This extends also to any alterations or variations in them without the authorisation of the owner of the copyright.

The teaching and learning strategies for vocational courses stress the development of a variety of learning activities. At the end of each chapter we have provided a selection of questions and activities related specifically to the material introduced in that chapter. Further teaching and learning material can be found at the *Business Law* Companion Web Site www.booksites.net/keenan.

The rate of legal change has increased significantly since our last edition. Parliament has been particularly busy, enacting an ambitious legislative programme for the Labour Government and responding to a steady stream of European directives. The courts have been no less active, although the full effect of the changes introduced by incorporation of the European Convention on Human Rights by the Human Rights Act 1998 has yet to be felt.

The text has been thoroughly updated to incorporate changes in business law since the fifth edition, especially the following:

- Access to Justice Act 1999
- Removal of immunity for lawyers from liability in negligence
- Civil justice reforms
- Competition Act 1998
- Contracts (Rights of Third Parties) Act 1999
- Data Protection Act 1998
- Electronic Communications Act 2000
- Employment Relations Act 1999
- Financial Services and Markets Act 2000
- House of Lords reform
- Human Rights Act 1998
- Late Payment of Commercial Debts (Interest) Act 1998
- Limited Liability Partnerships Act 2000
- Public Interest Disclosure Act 1998
- Regulation of Investigatory Powers Act 2000

We have used the new terminology introduced by Lord Woolf's civil justice reforms, popularly known as 'Woolfspeak', throughout the text. For example, we have used the term 'claimant' for all cases to describe the person with a complaint, even though the person was described as 'plaintiff' before the changes in civil procedure on 26 April 1999.

In conclusion, Sarah Riches extends her thanks to Ciaran and Brian McCaughey, who supported her throughout. Denis Keenan wishes to thank Mary Keenan in terms of the organisation of the sources of new material he has required.

Our thanks go to those who were closely involved with this edition, in particular our publisher Pat Bond, and Elizabeth Tarrant and other members of staff at Pearson Education. Our thanks also go to those who set, printed and bound the book. For errors and omissions we are, of course, solely responsible.

Denis Keenan
May 2001   *Sarah Riches*

A Companion Web Site accompanies
BUSINESS LAW

Visit the *Business Law* Companion Web Site at
www.booksites.net/keenan to find valuable teaching and learning material including:

For Students:
- Study material designed to help you improve your results
- Annotated web links relating to the subject of law
- Regular *Updates* to ensure your knowledge of business law is up to date

For Lecturers:
- A secure, password-protected site with teaching material
- Downloadable *Lecturer's Guide*
- Downloadable OHPs

Also: This regularly maintained and updated site will have a syllabus manager and search functions.

LAW REPORT ABBREVIATIONS

The following sets out the abbreviations used when citing the various series of certain Law Reports which are in common use, together with the periods over which they extend

AC	Law Reports, Appeal Cases 1891–(current).
ATC	Annotated Tax Cases 1922–1975.
All ER	All England Law Reports 1936–(current).
All ER Rep	All England Law Reports Reprint, 36 vols 1558–1935.
App Cas	Law Reports, Appeal Cases, 15 vols 1875–1890.
BCLC	Butterworths Company Law Cases 1983–(current).
B & CR	Reports of Bankruptcy and Companies Winding-up Cases 1918–(current).
CLY	Current Law Yearbook 1947–(current).
CMLR	Common Market Law Reports 1962–(current).
Ch	Law Reports Chancery Division 1891–(current).
Com Cas	Commercial Cases 1895–1941.
Fam	Law Reports Family Division 1972–(current).
ICR	Industrial Court Reports 1972–1974; Industrial Cases Reports 1974–(current).
IRLB	Industrial Relations Law Bulletin 1993–(current).
IRLR	Industrial Relations Law Reports 1971–(current).
ITR	Reports of decisions of the Industrial Tribunals 1966–(current).
KB	Law Reports, King's Bench Division 1901–1952.
LGR	Local Government Reports 1902–(current).
LRRP	Law Reports Restrictive Practices 1957–(current).
Lloyd LR or (from 1951) Lloyd's Rep	Lloyd's List Law Reports 1919–(current).
NLJ	New Law Journal.
P	Law Reports, Probate, Divorce and Admiralty Division 1891–1971.
P & CR	Planning and Compensation Reports 1949–(current).
PIQR	Personal Injuries and Quantum Reports.
QB	Law Reports Queen's Bench Division 1891–1901; 1953–(current).
STC	Simon's Tax Cases 1973–(current).
Sol Jo	Solicitors' Journal 1856–(current).
Tax Cas (or TC)	Tax Cases 1875–(current).
WLR	Weekly Law Reports 1953–(current).

TABLE OF STATUTES

TABLE OF CASES

Part 1

INTRODUCTION TO LAW

Chapter 1

THE NATURE OF LAW

The law affects every aspect of our lives; it governs our conduct from the cradle to the grave and its influence even extends from before our birth to after our death. We live in a society which has developed a complex body of rules to control the activities of its members. There are laws which govern working conditions (e.g. by laying down minimum standards of health and safety), laws which regulate leisure pursuits (e.g. by banning alcohol on coaches and trains travelling to football matches), and laws which control personal relationships (e.g. by prohibiting marriage between close relatives).

In this book we are concerned with one specific area of law: the rules which affect the business world. We shall consider such matters as the requirements that must be observed to start a business venture, the rights and duties which arise from business transactions and the consequences of business failure. In order to understand the legal implications of business activities, it is first necessary to examine some basic features of our English legal system. It is important to remember that English law refers to the law as it applies to England and Wales. Scotland and Northern Ireland have their own distinct legal systems.

CLASSIFICATION OF LAW

There are various ways in which the law may be classified; the most important are as follows:

1 Public and private law. The distinction between public and private law is illustrated in Fig 1.1.

(a) *Public law.* Public law is concerned with the relationship between the state and its citizens. This comprises several specialist areas such as:

(i) *Constitutional law.* Constitutional law is concerned with the workings of the British constitution. It covers such matters as the position of the Crown, the composition and procedures of Parliament, the functioning of central and local government, citizenship and the civil liberties of individual citizens.

(ii) *Administrative law.* There has been a dramatic increase in the activities of government during the last hundred years. Schemes have been introduced to help ensure a minimum standard of living for everybody. Government agencies are involved, for example, in the provision of a state retirement pension, income support and child benefit. A large number of disputes arise from the administration

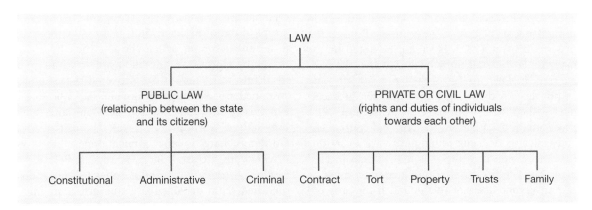

Fig 1.1 The distinction between public and private law

of these schemes and a body of law, administrative law, has developed to deal with the complaints of individuals against the decisions of the administering agency.

(iii) *Criminal law*. Certain kinds of wrongdoing pose such a serious threat to the good order of society that they are considered crimes against the whole community. The criminal law makes such anti-social behaviour an offence against the state and offenders are liable to punishment. The state accepts responsibility for the detection, prosecution and punishment of offenders.

(b) *Private law*. Private law is primarily concerned with the rights and duties of individuals towards each other. The state's involvement in this area of law is confined to providing a civilised method of resolving the dispute that has arisen. Thus, the legal process is begun by the aggrieved citizen and not by the state. Private law is also called civil law and is often contrasted with criminal law.

2 Criminal and civil law. Legal rules are generally divided into two categories: criminal and civil. It is important to understand the nature of the division because there are fundamental differences in the purpose, procedure and terminology of each branch of law.

(a) *Criminal law*. The criminal law is concerned with forbidding certain forms of wrongful conduct and punishing those who engage in the prohibited acts. Criminal proceedings are normally brought in the name of the Crown and are called prosecutions. In 1985 responsibility for the process of prosecution passed from the police to a newly created independent Crown Prosecution Service under the direction of the Director of Public Prosecutions (Prosecution of Offences Act 1985). It should be noted that it may also be undertaken by bodies, such as the trading standards department of the local authority, and by private individuals, e.g. a store detective prosecuting a shoplifter. You have a **prosecutor** who **prosecutes** a **defendant** in the **criminal courts**. The consequences of being found guilty are so serious that the standard of proof is higher than in civil cases: the allegations of criminal conduct must be proved beyond a reasonable doubt. If the prosecution is successful, the defendant is found **guilty** (**convicted**) and may be **punished** by the courts. The

punishments available to the court include imprisonment, fines, or community sentences such as the Community Rehabilitation Order (formerly probation). If the prosecution is unsuccessful, the defendant is found **not guilty** (**acquitted**). A businessman may find himself in breach of the criminal law under such enactments as the Trade Descriptions Act 1968, the Companies Act 1985 and the Health and Safety at Work Act 1974.

(b) *Civil law*. The civil law deals with the private rights and obligations which arise between individuals. The purpose of the action is to remedy the wrong that has been suffered. Enforcement of the civil law is the responsibility of the individual who has been wronged; the state's role is to provide the procedure and the courts necessary to resolve the dispute. In civil proceedings a **claimant** sues a **defendant** in the **civil courts**. The claimant will be successful if he can prove his case on the balance of probabilities, i.e. the evidence weighs more in favour of the claimant than of the defendant. If the claimant wins his action, the defendant is said to be **liable** and the court will order an appropriate remedy, such as damages (financial compensation) or an injunction (an order to do or not do something). If the claimant is not successful, the defendant is found **not liable**. Many of the laws affecting the businessman are part of the civil law, especially contract, tort and property law. The main differences between civil and criminal law are illustrated in Fig 1.2.

The distinction between the criminal and civil law does not depend on the nature of the wrongful act, because the same act may give rise to both civil and criminal proceedings. Consider the consequences of a typical motor accident. Julie is crossing the road at a zebra crossing when she is struck by a car driven by Gordon. An ambulance takes Julie to a local hospital where it is discovered that she has sustained a broken leg. Meanwhile the police have arrived at the scene of the accident and they breathalyse Gordon. The result is positive and Gordon is charged with a criminal offence based on driving with excess alcohol. He appears before the local magistrates' court and is convicted. He is disqualified from driving for 18 months and fined £400. The fine is paid to the court: it does not go to compensate the victim of the criminal act. However,

	Criminal law	Civil law
Concerns	Offences against the state	Disputes between private individuals
Purpose of the action	To preserve order in the community by punishing offenders and deterring others	To remedy the wrong which has been suffered
The parties	A prosecutor prosecutes a defendant	A claimant sues a defendant
Where the action is heard	The criminal courts, i.e. magistrates' court or Crown Court	The civil courts, i.e. county court or High Court
Standard and burden of proof	The prosecutor must prove his case beyond a reasonable doubt	The claimant must establish his case on the balance of probabilities
Decision	A defendant may be convicted if he is guilty and acquitted if he is innocent	A defendant may be found liable or not liable
Sanctions	Imprisonment, fine	Damages, injunction, specific performance, rescission
Examples	Murder, theft, driving with excess alcohol, applying a false trade description to goods	Contract, tort, trusts, property law

Fig 1.2 The differences between criminal and civil law

a criminal court now has a limited power to order an offender to pay compensation for any 'personal injury, loss or damage' caused to the victim of his offence (Powers of Criminal Courts (Sentencing) Act 2000, s 130). Julie must pursue a separate civil action against Gordon to remedy the personal wrong she has suffered. She sues Gordon in the tort of negligence, seeking damages for the injuries she has sustained. The case is heard in the county court where Gordon is found liable. He is ordered to pay £6,000 in damages. Normally the loser in a civil action pays the winner's costs. So Gordon is ordered to pay Julie's costs in bringing the action.

3 Common law and equity. Legal rules may also be classified according to whether they form part of the common law or equity. The distinction between these two systems of law is rooted in history and can only be understood properly by examining the origins of English law. English legal development can be traced back to 1066 when William of Normandy gained the crown of England by defeating King Harold at the Battle of Hastings. Before the arrival of the Normans in 1066 there really was no such thing as English law. The Anglo-Saxon legal system was based on the local community. Each area had its own courts in which local customs were applied. The Norman Conquest did not have an immediate effect on English law; indeed, William promised the English that they could keep their customary laws. The Normans were great administrators and they soon embarked on a process of centralisation, which created the right climate for the evolution of a uniform system of law for the whole country.

THE COMMON LAW

The Norman kings ruled with the help of the most important and powerful men in the land who formed a body known as the Curia Regis (King's Council). This assembly carried out a number of functions: it acted as a primitive legislature, performed administrative tasks and exercised certain judicial powers. The meetings of the Curia Regis came to be of two types: occasional assemblies attended by the barons and more frequent but smaller meetings of royal officials. These officials began to specialise in certain types of work and departments were formed. This trend eventually led to the development of courts to hear cases of a particular kind. The courts which had emerged by the end of the 13th century became known as the Courts of Common Law and they sat at Westminster. The first to appear was the Court of Exchequer. It dealt with taxation disputes but later extended its jurisdiction to other civil cases. The Court of Common Pleas was the next court to be established. It heard disputes of a civil nature between one citizen and another. The Court of King's Bench, the last court to appear, became the most important of the three courts because of its close association with the king. Its jurisdiction included civil and criminal cases and it developed a supervisory function over the activities of inferior courts.

The Normans exercised central control by sending representatives of the king from Westminster to all parts of the country to check up on the local administration. At first these royal commissioners performed a number of tasks: they made records of land and wealth, collected taxes and adjudicated in disputes brought before them. Their judicial powers gradually became more important than their other functions. To begin with, these commissioners (or justices) applied local customary law at the hearings, but in time local customs were replaced by a body of rules applying to the whole country.

When they had completed their travels round the country, the justices returned to Westminster where they discussed the customs they had encountered. By a gradual process of sifting these customs, rejecting those which were unreasonable and accepting those which were not, they formed a uniform pattern of law throughout England. Thus, by selecting certain customs and applying them in all future similar cases, the **common law** of England was created.

A civil action at common law was begun with the issue of a writ which was purchased from the offices of the Chancery, a department of the Curia Regis under the control of the Chancellor. Different kinds of action were covered by different writs. The procedural rules and type of trial varied with the nature of the writ. It was essential that the correct writ was chosen, otherwise the claimant would not be allowed to proceed with his action.

EQUITY

Over a period of time the common law became a very rigid system of law and in many cases it was impossible to obtain justice from the courts. The main defects of the common law were as follows:

(a) The common law failed to keep pace with the needs of an increasingly complex society. The writ system was slow to respond to new types of action. If a suitable writ was not available, an injured party could not obtain a remedy, no matter how just his claim.
(b) The writ system was very complicated, but trivial mistakes could defeat a claim.
(c) The only remedy available in the common law courts was an award of damages. This was not always a suitable or adequate remedy.
(d) Men of wealth and power could overawe a court, and there were complaints of bribery and intimidation of jurors.

It became the practice of aggrieved citizens to petition the king for assistance. As the volume of petitions increased, the king passed them to the Curia Regis and a committee was set up to hear the petitions. The hearings were presided over by the Chancellor and in time petitions were addressed to him alone. By the 15th century the Chancellor had started to hear petitions on his own and the Court of Chancery was established. The body of rules applied by the court was called **equity**.

The early chancellors were drawn from the ranks of the clergy and their decisions reflected their ecclesiastical background. They examined the consciences of the parties and then ordered what was fair and just. At first, each chancellor acted as he thought best. Decisions varied from chancellor to chancellor and this resulted in a great deal of uncertainty for petitioners. Eventually chancellors began to follow previous decisions and a large body of fixed rules grew up. The decisions of the

Court of Chancery were often at odds with those made in the common law courts. This proved a source of conflict until the start of the 17th century when James I ruled that, in cases of conflict, equity was to prevail. For several centuries the English legal system continued to develop with two distinct sets of rules administered in separate courts. Equity is not a complete system of law. Equitable principles were formulated to remedy specific defects in the common law. They were designed to complement the common law rules and not to replace them. Equity has made an important contribution to the development of English law, particularly in the following areas:

1 **Recognition of new rights.** The common law did not recognise the concept of the trust. A trust arises where a settlor (S) conveys property to a trustee (T) to hold on trust for a beneficiary (B). The common law treated T as if he were the owner of the property and B's claims were ignored. The Court of Chancery, however, would require T to act according to his conscience and administer the trust on B's behalf. Thus, equity recognised and enforced the rights of a beneficiary under a trust. The Court of Chancery also came to the aid of borrowers who had mortgaged their property as security for a loan. If the loan was not repaid by the agreed date, the common law position was that the lender (mortgagee) became the owner of the property and the borrower (mortgagor) was still required to pay the outstanding balance. Equity gave the mortgagor the right to pay off the loan and recover his property even though the repayment date had passed. This equitable principle is known as the equity of redemption. It will be considered in more detail in Chapter 4.

2 **Introduction of new remedies.** The new equitable rights were enforced by means of new equitable remedies. In the field of contract law, the Court of Chancery developed such remedies as the injunction, specific performance, rescission and rectification which will be examined in Chapter 7. These remedies were not available as of right like common law remedies: they were discretionary. The Court of Chancery could refuse to grant an equitable remedy if, for example, the claimant had himself acted unfairly.

By the 19th century the administration of justice had reached an unhappy state of affairs and was heavily criticised. The existence of separate courts for the administration of common law and equity meant that someone who wanted help from both the common law and equity had to bring two separate cases in two separate courts. If a person started an action in the wrong court, he could not get a remedy until he brought his case to the right court. The proceedings in the Court of Chancery had become notorious for their length and expense. (Charles Dickens satirised the delays of Chancery in his novel *Bleak House*.) Comprehensive reform of the many deficiencies of the English legal system was effected by several statutes in the 19th century culminating in the Judicature Acts 1873–75. The separate common law courts and Court of Chancery were replaced by a Supreme Court of Judicature which comprised the Court of Appeal and High Court. Every judge was empowered henceforth to administer both common law and equity in his court. Thus, a claimant seeking a common law and an equitable remedy need only pursue one action in one court. The Acts also confirmed that where common law and equity conflict, equity should prevail. These reforms did not have the effect of removing the distinction between the two sets of rules: common law and equity are still two separate but complementary systems of law. A judge may draw upon both sets of rules to decide a case. See, for example, the decision of Denning J in the *High Trees* case (in Chapter 7).

SOME BASIC PRINCIPLES OF LEGAL LIABILITY

Before we consider the specific areas of law governing the activities of business organisations, we must first of all consider the branches of law which are most likely to affect those in business and certain basic principles of liability.

It is a basic function of the law to set out the circumstances in which a person may be required to answer for his actions. Legal liability describes a situation where a person is legally responsible for a breach of an obligation imposed by the law. Such obligations may arise from the operation of either the civil or criminal law. The activities of business organisations are subject to a wide range of potential liability. So, before we consider the specific areas of law governing the formation, operation and dissolution of business organisations, we must first examine in outline the nature and scope of legal liability for wrongful acts.

CIVIL LIABILITY

As we have already seen, the civil law is concerned with the rights and duties which arise between private individuals. The aim of taking legal action is to put right a wrong which has occurred, often by means of an award of compensation. The areas of civil liability which have the greatest impact on businesses are liability in contract and tort.

Contractual liability

Contractual liability arises when two or more persons enter into a legally enforceable agreement with each other. The law of contract is concerned with determining which agreements are binding, the nature and extent of the obligations freely undertaken by the parties and the legal consequences of breaking contractual promises. Every type of business transaction, from buying and selling goods and services to employing staff, is governed by the law of contract. Contractual arrangements are so important to the conduct of business they are examined in more detail in later chapters. (See, in particular, Chapter 7, Introduction to the law of contract; Chapter 8, Types of business contract; Chapter 9, The terms of business contracts; Chapter 10, Contracts for the supply of goods and services; Chapter 16, Employing labour.)

Tortious liability

A tort consists of the breach of a duty imposed by the law. The law of tort seeks to compensate the victims of certain forms of harmful conduct by an award of damages or to prevent harm occurring by granting an injunction. Examples of torts include negligence, nuisance, trespass, defamation (libel and slander) and conversion. These torts, along with others which are relevant to business, will be studied in more detail in Chapter 11.

CRIMINAL LIABILITY

A crime is an offence against the state. The consequences of a criminal conviction are not confined to the punishment inflicted by the court. For example, if a person is convicted of theft, his name will probably appear in the local papers causing shame and embarrassment and he may even lose his job. The sanctions are so severe that the criminal law normally requires an element of moral fault on the part of the offender. Thus, the prosecution must establish two essential requirements: *actus reus* (prohibited act) and *mens rea* (guilty mind). For most criminal offences, both elements must be present to create criminal liability. If you pick someone's umbrella up thinking that it is your own, you cannot be guilty of theft, because of the absence of a guilty mind. There are, however, some statutory offences where Parliament has dispensed with the requirement of *mens rea*. Performance of the wrongful act alone makes the offender liable. These are known as crimes of strict liability. Selling food for human consumption which fails to comply with food safety requirements contrary to the Food Safety Act 1990 is an example of an offence of strict liability. The prosecutor is not required to show that that the seller knew that the food did not comply with food safety requirements. He will secure a conviction by establishing that the food was unsafe and that it was sold. The seller may be able to defend himself by showing that he has taken all reasonable precautions and exercised due diligence to avoid commission of the offence.

LAW OF PROPERTY

The law of property is concerned with the rights which may arise in relation to anything that can be owned. Thus, property covers land, goods and intangible rights such as debts, copyright or the goodwill of a business. The legal implications of acquiring, using and disposing of business property will be studied in more depth in Chapter 15. In order to fully understand other principles of business law which you will encounter before then, it is necessary to consider the relationships which may arise between persons and property, namely, the rights of ownership and possession.

1 Ownership. Ownership describes the greatest rights that a person can have in relation to property. An owner enjoys the fullest powers of use and disposal over the property allowed by law. The owner of this book, for example, has the right to read it, lend it to a friend, hire it out, pledge it as security for a loan, or even tear it into shreds. An owner does not enjoy absolute rights; restrictions may be imposed to protect the rights of other members of the community. The ownership of a house does not entitle the occupants to hold frequent wild parties to the annoyance of neighbours.

2 Possession. Possession consists of two elements: physical control and the intention to exclude others. For example, you have possession of the watch you are wearing, the clothes in your wardrobe at home and your car which is parked while you are at work. Ownership and possession often go hand in hand, but may be divorced. The viewer of a hired TV enjoys possession of the set, but ownership remains with the TV rental firm. If your house is burgled, you remain the owner of the stolen property, but the burglar obtains (unlawful) possession.

QUESTIONS/ACTIVITIES

1 What is law and why is it necessary?

2 What is the 'common law' and how was it created?

3 Why did equity develop and how did it differ from the common law? What is the present relationship between the two systems?

4 Consider the following legal actions and indicate whether civil or criminal proceedings would result:
    (a) Ann decides to divorce her husband, Barry, after ten years of marriage;
    (b) Colin is given a parking ticket by a traffic warden for parking on double yellow lines;
    (c) Diane returns a faulty steam iron to the shop where she bought it, but the shop manager refuses to give her a refund;
    (d) Eamonn drives at 50 mph on a stretch of road where there is a 30-mph limit. He fails to see Fiona who is crossing the road. She is knocked down and sustains severe injuries;
    (e) Graham takes a copy of *Business Law* from the reference section of the library, with the intention of returning it when he has finished his first assignment. He finds the book so valuable that he decides to keep it;
    (f) Hazel returns to England after working abroad for three years. While abroad, she rented her flat to Ian. She now gives him notice to quit, but he refuses to move out.

Chapter 2

THE CHANGING LAW

Over 900 years of history have helped shape the institutions, procedures and body of rules which make up our modern English legal system. The law is a living creation that reflects the needs of the society it serves, each generation leaving its mark on the law.

The rate of legal change has varied greatly down the centuries. English law developed at a relatively gentle pace until the end of the 18th century, but as Britain moved into the industrial age, the pace of legal change quickened. Life at the start of the 21st century is fast moving and the rate of legal change is just as hectic. The law does not stand still long today.

Ideally, business requires a stable environment within which to operate. Yet, the framework of law which governs business activities is subject to constant change. The burden of keeping up to date may be eased slightly by making use of professional people such as an accountant or solicitor to advise on the latest developments in such areas as tax or company law. Nevertheless, the businessman will still need to keep himself informed of general legal changes which will affect his day-to-day running of the business. If he employs others in his business, he will need to keep up to date on such matters as health and safety at work, the rights of his employees and his duties as an employer. If he sells goods direct to the consumer, he must be aware of changes in consumer protection law. Almost every aspect of his business will be subject to legal regulation and the law could always change.

In this chapter we will explore why the law changes and the mechanism by which change takes place.

CAUSES OF LEGAL CHANGE

Legal changes can be divided into two broad categories according to their causes. The first type of legal change is caused by the law responding to changes taking place in society. Political, social and economic changes, technological advancements and changing moral beliefs all lead eventually to changes in the law. Indeed, the law must be responsive to new circumstances and attitudes if it is to enjoy continued respect. The second type of legal change arises from the need to keep the law in good working order. Like any piece of sophisticated machinery, the law machine must be kept in a neat and tidy condition, maintained on a regular basis, with essential repairs undertaken when necessary. We will now examine these two types of legal change in more detail.

LEGAL CHANGE AND THE CHANGING WORLD

Think about the changes that have taken place in our world over the past 100 years. The first to come to mind are probably the spectacular scientific and technological achievements of the past century – motor vehicles, aircraft, the telephone, radio and TV, computers and genetic engineering. Each new development creates its own demand for legal change. Consider, for example, the vast body of law which has grown up around the motor vehicle: there are regulations governing such matters as the construction and maintenance of motor vehicles, the conduct of drivers on the road and even where vehicles may be parked. Indeed, almost half of the criminal cases tried by magistrates' courts are directly related to the use of motor vehicles. The increasing volume of traffic on the roads and the resulting inexorable rise in traffic accidents have also led to developments in the civil law, especially in the areas of the law of tort and insurance. More dramatic changes to the system of compensating the victims of motor accidents have been canvassed over the years, principally by the Royal Commission on Civil Liability in 1978. Its recommendation of a 'no fault' system of compensation financed by a levy on petrol sales has never been implemented.

While science and technology have been taking great leaps forward over the last century, other less dramatic changes have been taking place. The role and functions of the elected government, for example, have altered quite considerably. Nineteenth-century government was characterised by the *laissez-faire* philosophy of minimum interference in the lives of individuals. The government's limited role was to defend the country from external threats, to promote Britain's interests abroad and maintain internal order. In the 20th century, governments took increasing responsibility for the social and economic well-being of citizens. Naturally, the political parties have their own conflicting ideas about how to cure the country's ills. New tactics are tried with each change of government. The law is used as a means of achieving the desired political, economic and social changes. The development of law on certain contentious issues can often resemble a swinging pendulum as successive governments pursue their opposing political objectives. The changes in the law relating to trade union rights and privileges over the past 30 years are a perfect illustration of the pendulum effect. In 1971 the Conservative government introduced the Industrial Relations Act in an attempt to curb what they saw as the damaging power of the unions by subjecting them to greater legal regulation. The changes were fiercely resisted by the trade union movement. The attempt to reform industrial relations law at a stroke was a dismal failure. One of the first tasks of the Labour government, which was elected in 1974, was to dismantle the Industrial Relations Act 1971 and restore the unions to their privileged legal position. When the Conservatives were returned to power in 1979, they did not repeat the mistakes of the previous Conservative government of 1970–74. Instead, they adopted a step-by-step approach to trade union reform and in a series of Acts implemented greater legal control over unions and their activities. Further adjustments to trade union law were made by the Employment Relations Act 1999, following the election of a Labour government in May 1997.

One of the more controversial changes of recent times was the United Kingdom's entry into the European Community (EC) in 1973. The government's motives were clearly directed at the economic and social benefits which it was expected would be derived from joining the EC. But membership also brought great legal changes in its wake: the traditional sovereignty of the Westminster Parliament has been called into question, our courts are now subject to the rulings of the European Court of Justice and parts of our substantive law have been re-modelled to conform to European requirements, e.g. in the field of company law.

Changing moral beliefs and social attitudes are potent causes of legal change. In the past 40 years or so, great changes have taken place in the laws governing personal morality: the laws against homosexuality have been relaxed, abortion has been legalised and divorce is more freely obtainable. Society's view of the role of women has altered greatly over the past century. The rights of women have been advanced, not only by Parliament in measures like the Sex Discrimination Act 1975, but also by the courts in their approach to such matters as rights to the matrimonial home when a marriage breaks down.

The law is an adaptable creature responsive to the complex changes taking place around it. But sometimes in the midst of all this change, the more technical parts of the law, sometimes known as 'lawyers' law', can be ignored. A programme of reform is necessary to ensure that these vitally important, if less glamourous, areas of law do not fall into a state of disrepair.

LAW REFORM

'Lawyers' law' consists largely of the body of rules developed over many years by judges deciding cases according to principles laid down in past cases. One of the great strengths of the system of judge-made law is its flexibility; judges can adapt or re-work the rules of common law or equity to meet changing circumstances. Although modern judges have shown themselves willing to take a bold approach to the task of keeping case law in tune with the times, there is a limit to what can be achieved. Judicial law reform is likely to lead to haphazard, unsystematic changes in the law. Legal change becomes dependent on the chance of an appropriate case cropping up in a court which can effect change. Furthermore, our adversarial trial system is not the best vehicle for investigating the likely consequences of changing the law. Judges cannot commission independent research or consult interested bodies to gauge the effect of the proposed change. The limitations of a system of judge-led law reform led to the setting up of official law reform agencies, which, along with other methods of effecting change in the law, will be considered below.

THE SOURCES OF LEGAL CHANGE

Ideas for changing the law flow from many sources:

1 Official law reform agencies. The main agent of law reform in England and Wales is the Law Commission, which was established by the Law Commission Act 1965. Its job is to keep the law as a whole under review, with a view to its systematic development and reform. The Commission has overall responsibility for planning and co-ordinating the activities of the various law reform agencies, as well as undertaking its own projects. A Law Commission project starts life by appearing as an item in its programme of work which is approved by the Lord Chancellor. The Commission's full-time staff of lawyers then prepare a working paper containing alternative proposals for reform. Following consultations with the legal profession, government departments and other interested bodies, the Commission submits a final report on a firm proposal for reform accompanied by a draft bill. The Law Commission's programme is devised in consultation with the chairmen of the Law Reform Committee and the Criminal Law Revision Committee and specific items may be referred to them for consideration. These part-time standing committees of lawyers, the Lord Chancellor's Law Reform Committee and the Home Secretary's Criminal Law Revision Committee, deal with civil and criminal law reform matters, respectively.

2 Government departments. Each government department is responsible for keeping the law in its own field of interest under constant review. Where issues involving policy consideration rather than technical law reform arise, ministers may prefer to set up a **departmental committee** to investigate the subject, rather than leave it to the Law Commission.

Particularly important or controversial matters may lead to the setting up of a **Royal Commission** by the Crown on the advice of a minister. The dozen or so members of a Royal Commission usually reflect a balance of expert, professional and lay opinion. They work on a part-time basis, often taking several years to investigate a problem thoroughly and make recommendations. Examples of Royal Commissions include the Benson Commission on Legal Services (1979) and the Philips Commission on Criminal Procedure (1981). Royal Commissions and **departmental committees** were notable by their absence during the 1980s. The appointment of a **Royal Commission** on Criminal Justice in 1991, following several well-publicised cases involving miscarriages of justice, marked a departure from the practice of the previous decade.

3 Political parties and pressure groups. At election time, the political parties compete for our votes on the basis of a package of social and economic reforms which they promise to carry out if elected. The successful party is assumed to have a mandate to implement the proposals outlined in its election manifesto. Manifesto commitments, however, form only part of a government's legislative programme. Other competing claims to parliamentary time must be accommodated. For example, legislation may be required in connection with our membership of the EC, or to give effect to a proposal from the Law Commission or a Royal Commission, or simply to deal with an unforeseen emergency. Government claims on Parliament's time will alter during its period in office, as policy changes are made in response to pressures from within Westminster or in the country at large. One of the most significant extra-parliamentary influences on the formulation and execution of government policies is pressure-group activity. Pressure groups are organised groups of people seeking to influence or change government policy without themselves wishing to form a government.

Some pressure groups represent sectional interests in the community. The Confederation of British Industry (CBI), for example, represents business interests, while other pressure groups are formed to campaign on a single issue. The Campaign for Nuclear Disarmament (CND), for example, is concerned solely with the cause of nuclear disarmament. Pressure groups use a variety of techniques to promote their causes, from holding public demonstrations to more direct attempts to gain the support of MPs (known as 'lobbying'). Pressure-group activity may be negative in the sense of mobilising opposition to a proposed government measure, or positive, in seeking to persuade the government to adopt a specific proposal in its legislative programme or to win over a backbench MP, hoping that he will be successful in the ballot for private members' bills.

LAW-MAKING PROCESSES

So far we have considered the main causes of legal change. We will now examine the mechanics of change. The expression 'sources of law' is often used to refer to the various ways in which law can come into being. The main sources of law today are legislation (Acts of Parliament), case law (judicial precedent) and EC law.

Legislation

Legislation is law enacted by the Queen in Parliament in the form of Acts of Parliament or statutes. Parliament is made up of two chambers: the House of Commons and the House of Lords. The Commons consists of 659 elected Members of Parliament (MPs) who represent an area of the country called a constituency. The political party which can command a majority of votes in the Commons forms the **Government** and its leader becomes the **Prime Minister**. Ministers are appointed by the Prime Minister to take charge of the various government departments. The most important ministers form the **Cabinet**, which is responsible for formulating government policy.

The House of Lords, in contrast, is not an elected body. It is currently undergoing reform involving changes to its membership and a review of its role, functions and powers. The first stage of reform involved the removal of the right of most hereditary peers to sit and vote in the House. Following the changes made by the House of Lords Act 1999, the House of Lords is composed of 547 life peers, 92 hereditary peers (75 were elected by their peers

and 17 were royal or elected office holders), 28 law lords and 26 spiritual peers (the Archbishops of Canterbury and York, and 24 bishops of the Church of England). Proposals for the second stage of reform were set out in the report of a Royal Commission, chaired by Lord Wakeham, which was published in January 2000. The Royal Commission made the following recommendations:

- breaking the link between the possession of a peerage and membership of the second chamber;
- the creation of a 550-member chamber;
- membership to be mainly nominated, with no more than 195 elected;
- the establishment of an independent appointment system with a brief to bring in representation from all sectors of society;
- a statutory minimum proportion (30 per cent) of women, and of men;
- fair representation for members of ethnic minority groups;
- a broader range of religious representation, including all Christian denominations and non-Christian faiths;
- a significant minority of regional members chosen on a basis which reflects the views of the regional electorates;
- a statutory minimum (20 per cent) of independent members;
- the overall balance of party political membership to reflect the votes cast in the most recent general election;
- the Lords to retain its current powers in relation to primary legislation, including the power to delay proposed legislation;
- increased powers to challenge secondary legislation, e.g. statutory instruments, and new committees on the constitution and human rights.

At the time of writing the government is undertaking extensive consultation with interested groups about the Royal Commission's proposals and the next stage of reform.

Before leaving the subject of law-making by Parliament, note should be made of the recent progress made towards devolution. The Scotland Act 1998 created the first Scottish Parliament for almost 300 years. There are 129 Members of the Scottish Parliament (MSPs) who are elected by proportional representation every four years. The first elections took place in May 1999. The Parliament has power to pass legislation in all areas where it has 'legislative competence', which includes education, health, transport, local government, the environment and non-statutory Scottish law. Certain matters are reserved for the UK Parliament; they include defence, the UK constitution, foreign affairs and economic policy. The Parliament also has the power to vary the basic rate of income tax in Scotland by 3p.

The Government of Wales Act 1998 provided for the establishment of a Welsh Assembly. There are 60 members of the Welsh Assembly, who are elected every four years by proportional representation. The first elections were held on 6 May 1999. The Act provides for the transfer of the powers and responsibilities from the Welsh Office to the Assembly. Although the Welsh Assembly does not have the power to pass primary legislation, it plays an important role in preparing secondary legislation relating to Wales.

The Northern Ireland Assembly, which was created following a referendum supporting the 1998 'Good Friday Agreement', consists of 108 members elected by proportional representation. The Assembly has legislative and executive authority in respect of matters which were previously within the remit of Northern Ireland government departments, e.g. agriculture, education, the environment, health and social services, economic development and finance.

Parliamentary sovereignty

The supremacy of Parliament in the legislative sphere is known as the doctrine of parliamentary sovereignty. It means that Parliament can make any laws it pleases, no matter how perverse or unfair. Parliament may repeal the enactments of an earlier Parliament; it may delegate its legislative powers to other bodies or individuals. The courts are bound to apply the law enacted by Parliament; the judiciary cannot challenge the validity of an Act of Parliament on the grounds that the legislation is absurd, unconstitutional or procured by fraud (*Pickin* v *British Railways Board* (1974)). However, the courts may challenge the validity of UK legislation if it is in conflict with EC law.

Factortame Ltd v *Secretary of State for Transport (No 2)* *(1991)*
The Merchant Shipping Act 1988 introduced a requirement that 75 per cent of the members of companies operating fishing vessels in UK waters must be resident and domiciled in the UK. The legislation was designed to stop the practice of 'quota hopping' whereby fishing quotas were 'plundered' by vessels flying the British flag but whose real owners had no connection with the UK. The appellants were companies registered in the UK but which were essentially owned or controlled by Spanish nationals. Their fishing vessels failed to meet the new requirements and they were barred from fishing. The appellants argued that the 1988 Act was incompatible with EC law. Since it would take several years to resolve the matter, the appellants asked the court to grant interim relief suspending the 1988 Act until a final ruling could be made. The House of Lords referred the case to the European Court of Justice which ruled that if a rule of national law was the sole obstacle to the granting of interim relief in a case concerning EC law, that rule must be set aside. Applying this ruling, the House of Lords made an order suspending the operation of the disputed provisions of the Merchant Shipping Act 1988 pending final judgment of the issue.

Comment. In 1999 the House of Lords held that the UK's breach of Community law in passing the Merchant Shipping Act 1988 was sufficiently serious to entitle the appellants to compensation. (*R* v *Secretary of State for Transport, ex parte Factortame Ltd (No 5)* (1999).)

R v *Secretary of State for Employment, ex parte the Equal Opportunities Commission* *(1994)*
In this case the House of Lords upheld the right of a statutory body, the Equal Opportunities Commission, to challenge restrictions on part-time workers' rights to redundancy pay and unfair dismissal protection under UK law using the procedure of judicial review (see further, Chapter 3). Their Lordships held that the five-year qualifying period for protection in relation to redundancy and unfair dismissal for those working between eight and 16 hours a week laid down in UK legislation was in breach of EC law (see further, Chapter 16).

Under the Human Rights Act 1998, certain courts may make a 'declaration of incompatibility' if legislation is incompatible with the European Convention on Human Rights. The Human Rights Act will be considered in more detail later in this chapter.

The making of an Act of Parliament

The procedure by which a legislative proposal is translated into an Act of Parliament is long and complicated. Until all the stages in the process have been completed, the embryonic Act is known as a Bill. There are different types of Bill:

1 **Public Bills** change general law or affect the whole of the country. It is assumed that the Bill extends to all of the United Kingdom unless there is a specific provision to the contrary. For example, the Supply of Goods and Services Act 1982 applies to England, Wales and Northern Ireland but not to Scotland.

2 **Private Bills** do not alter the law for the whole community but deal with matters of concern in a particular locality or to a private company or even individuals. Private Bills are mainly promoted by local authorities seeking additional powers to those granted by general legislation.

3 **Government Bills** are introduced by a minister with the backing of the government and are almost certain to become law. Some of the bills are designed to implement the government's political policies, but others may be introduced to deal with an emergency which has arisen or to amend or consolidate earlier legislation.

4 **Private Members' Bills** are introduced by an individual MP or private peer (in the House of Lords) without guaranteed government backing. They usually deal with moral or legal questions rather than with purely party political matters. A private member's Bill is unlikely to become law unless the government lends its support. Some important law reform measures started life as a private member's Bill, including the Murder (Abolition of the Death Penalty) Act 1965 and the Abortion Act 1967.

A Bill must pass through several stages receiving the consent of the Commons and Lords before it is presented for the Royal Assent. A Bill may generally start life in either the Commons or the Lords and then pass to the other House, but in practice most public Bills start in the Commons and then proceed to the Lords: certain kinds of Bill, such as Money Bills, must originate in the Commons. The procedure for a Bill which is introduced in the Commons is illustrated in Fig 2.1.

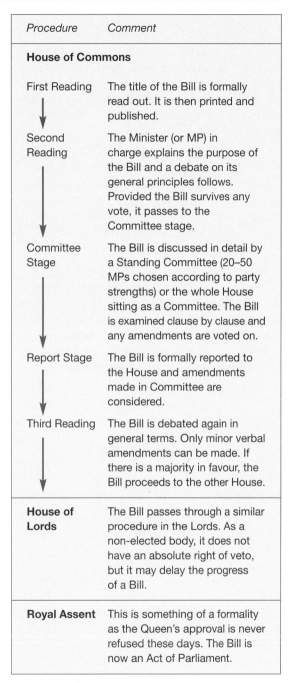

Procedure	Comment
House of Commons	
First Reading	The title of the Bill is formally read out. It is then printed and published.
Second Reading	The Minister (or MP) in charge explains the purpose of the Bill and a debate on its general principles follows. Provided the Bill survives any vote, it passes to the Committee stage.
Committee Stage	The Bill is discussed in detail by a Standing Committee (20–50 MPs chosen according to party strengths) or the whole House sitting as a Committee. The Bill is examined clause by clause and any amendments are voted on.
Report Stage	The Bill is formally reported to the House and amendments made in Committee are considered.
Third Reading	The Bill is debated again in general terms. Only minor verbal amendments can be made. If there is a majority in favour, the Bill proceeds to the other House.
House of Lords	The Bill passes through a similar procedure in the Lords. As a non-elected body, it does not have an absolute right of veto, but it may delay the progress of a Bill.
Royal Assent	This is something of a formality as the Queen's approval is never refused these days. The Bill is now an Act of Parliament.

Fig 2.1 The legislative process

Delegated legislation

The activities of modern government are so varied, and the problems it deals with are so complex and technical, that Parliament does not have sufficient time to deal personally with every piece of legislation required. This difficulty is overcome by passing an enabling Act of Parliament which sets out the basic structure of the legislation but allows other bodies or people to draw up the detailed rules necessary. Rules made in this way are known as delegated legislation. The main forms of delegated legislation are as follows:

1 **Orders in Council.** These are rules made under the authority of an Act by the Queen acting on the advice of the Privy Council (an honorary body descended from the old Curia Regis). In practice, the power to make orders is exercised by the cabinet, whose members are all privy councillors. The Queen's assent is a pure formality.

2 **Rules and regulations.** These are made by a minister in respect of the area of government for which he is responsible, e.g. the power of the Secretary of State for Social Security to make detailed regulations about the income support scheme. (Most orders, rules and regulations are collectively referred to as statutory instruments.)

3 **Byelaws.** These are made by local authorities and certain other public and nationalised bodies to regulate their spheres of activity. This form of delegated legislation requires the consent of the appropriate minister.

Legislation and the judiciary

A Bill which successfully passes through the House of Commons and the House of Lords and has received the Royal Assent becomes an Act of Parliament. The sovereign law-making powers of the Queen in Parliament mean that the validity of a statute cannot be questioned by the courts. Nevertheless, the courts can exercise considerable influence over how the enacted law is applied to practical problems. Sooner or later, every Act of Parliament will be analysed by the judges in the course of cases which appear before them. It is the task of the judge to interpret and construe the words used by Parliament and thereby ascertain the intention of the legislature. The rules of interpretation followed by the judges may be classified according to their origin as either statutory rules or common law rules.

Statutory rules

1 Modern Acts usually contain an interpretation section which defines certain key words used in that Act; e.g. s 61(1) of the Sale of Goods Act 1979 contains definitions of words and phrases used throughout the Act.

2 The Interpretation Act 1978 lays down certain basic rules of interpretation for all Acts, e.g. unless the contrary intention is indicated 'words in the singular shall include the plural and words in the plural shall include the singular' (s 6 of the Interpretation Act 1978).

3 Certain elements of the Act itself may prove useful. These are known as internal or intrinsic aids. The courts may look at the long title of the Act and its preamble (only found in Private Acts and older Public Acts). Headings, side notes and punctuation may also be considered, but only to help clarify the meaning of ambiguous words.

Common law rules

Apart from the limited help provided by Parliament, the judges have been left to develop their own methods of statutory interpretation. A number of approaches to the task of interpretation have emerged, with the judges free to decide which approach is most appropriate to the case in hand. The most important rules of interpretation and various presumptions are explained below.

1 **Literal rule.** According to the literal rule, if the words of the statute are clear and unambiguous, the court must give them their ordinary plain meaning, regardless of the result. Where a literal interpretation produces an absurd or perverse decision, it is up to Parliament to put matters right, and is not the job of non-elected judges. For example, in the case of *Fisher* v *Bell* (1960) it was held that a shopkeeper who had flick knives in his shop window could not be guilty of the offence of offering for sale a flick knife contrary to the Restriction of Offensive Weapons Act 1959, even though it was precisely this kind of conduct that Parliament had intended to outlaw. It is an established principle of contract law that displaying goods in a shop window is not an offer to sell but merely an invita-

tion to treat. The defendant had not offered to sell the flick knives and so could not be guilty of the offence. Parliament closed the loophole by passing amending legislation in 1961.

2 Golden rule. Under the golden rule, where the words of a statute are capable of two or more meanings, the judge must adopt the interpretation which produces the least absurd result. Some judges even argue that the golden rule can be applied where the words have only one meaning, but a literal interpretation would lead to an absurdity. For example, in *Re Sigsworth* (1935) it was held that a man who murdered his mother could not inherit her property even though he appeared to be entitled on a literal interpretation of the Administration of Estates Act 1925. There is a basic legal principle that a person should not profit from his wrongdoing.

3 Mischief rule (rule in *Heydon's* Case). This rule which derives from *Heydon's* Case (1584) lays down that the court must look at the Act to see what 'mischief' or defect in the common law the Act was passed to remedy, and then interpret the words of the Act in the light of this knowledge. In *Gardiner* v *Sevenoaks RDC* (1950), for example, Gardiner claimed that he was not bound by an Act which laid down regulations about the storage of films in premises because he kept his film in a cave. It was held that the cave should be classed as premises because the purpose of the Act was to secure the safety of those working in the place of storage or living close by. The mischief rule is closely associated with the modern purposive approach to interpretation, which says that a judge should adopt the construction which will promote the general aims or purposes underlying the provision.

4 *Ejusdem generis* rule. Where general words follow particular words, the court should interpret the general words as meaning persons or things of the same class or genus, e.g. if the Act referred to 'cats, dogs or other animals', the general words, 'other animals', should be construed in the light of the particular words, 'cats' and 'dogs', as meaning other kinds of domesticated animals and not wild animals.

5 *Expressio unius est exclusio alterius* rule. Under this rule, the express mention of one or more things implies the exclusion of others, e.g. if the Act simply mentioned 'dogs and cats', other kinds of domesticated animals are excluded.

6 *Noscitur a sociis* rule. According to this rule, a word should take its meaning from the context in which it is found. In *Muir* v *Keay* (1875) it was held that a café which stayed open during the night should have been licensed under the provisions of the Refreshment Houses Act 1860. The Act required houses 'for public refreshment, resort and entertainment' to be licensed. The meaning of the word 'entertainment' was gathered from the context of the Act and held to refer to refreshment rooms for the public rather than involving musical or theatrical entertainment.

7 The presumptions. Unless there are clear words to the contrary, the court will make a number of assumptions. They include:

- the Act is not retrospective, i.e. it does not back-date the change in the law;
- the Act does not bind the Crown;
- the Act does not alter the common law;
- the Act does not restrict personal liberty;
- the Act does not create criminal liability unless *mens rea* is present.

8 Use of extrinsic material. Extrinsic materials are sources of information about a piece of legislation apart from the Act itself. The Act may have been prompted by a report of the Law Commission, a Royal Commission or other official committee. The government often sets out proposals for legislation in the form of a Green paper (a discussion document) or a White Paper (firm proposals for legislation). In some cases the legislation is based on an international treaty. The Bill will have been debated in Parliament and the speeches reported in *Hansard* (the official report of proceedings in Parliament). The question arises whether a judge may refer to these materials to help him shed light on the meaning of a statutory provision. Historically, the use of extrinsic aids was severely restricted. In recent years, however, the rule has been relaxed, particularly where the court wishes to apply the 'mischief rule' and is seeking to

discover the 'mischief' which the Act was intended to remedy. The rules at present are as follows:

(a) international conventions and treaties which form the basis of legislation may be consulted especially where the legislation is ambiguous. The court may also consider the preparatory material for such a convention or treaty (*travaux préparatoires*);

(b) reports to the Law Commission, royal commissions and other similar bodies may be referred to but only to discover the 'mischief' the Act was designed to deal with;

(c) the previously strict rule that *Hansard* must not be consulted as an aid to statutory interpretation has now been relaxed. In *Pepper v Hart* (1993) the House of Lords held that, subject to any parliamentary privilege, the rule prohibiting courts from referring to parliamentary materials as an aid to statutory construction should be modified. Reference to parliamentary materials, i.e. *Hansard*, should be permitted where:

  (i) the legislation is ambiguous or obscure or where a literal interpretation would lead to an absurdity;

  (ii) the material referred to consists of statements by a minister or other promoter of the Bill, together with such other parliamentary material as is necessary to understand the statements and their effects;

  (iii) the statements relied on are clear.

Their Lordships held that reference to parliamentary materials did not contravene Art 9 of the Bill of Rights (1688). No other claim to a defined parliamentary privilege was made by the Crown.

The decision of the House of Lords in *Pepper v Hart* marked a new approach to statutory interpretation by the English Courts. The precise scope of the courts' new-found freedom has yet to be clearly and authoritatively established. It was not immediately clear, for example, whether a judge could only refer to *Hansard* where the legislation was ambiguous, obscure or would lead to an absurdity. Their Lordships have subsequently confirmed that the first threshold condition laid down in *Pepper v Hart* must be satisfied before reference is made to *Hansard* (*R v Secretary of State for the Environment, Transport and the Regions, ex parte Spath Holme Ltd* (2001)). In a number of cases the House of Lords has referred to *Hansard* to confirm interpretations already made independently. There is also some doubt about whether the courts are confined to parliamentary material contained in *Hansard*. Can the courts also consider government press releases, briefing notes for ministers and so on? Lord Browne-Wilkinson in *Pepper v Hart* looked at a press release produced by the Inland Revenue.

Case law (judicial precedent)

Despite the enormous volume of legislation produced by parliaments down the ages, statute law remains an incomplete system of law. Large parts of our law still derive from the decisions of judges. This judge-made law is based on a rule known as the doctrine of binding judicial precedent. The principle underlying the doctrine is that a decision made by a court in a case involving a particular set of circumstances is binding on other courts in later cases, where the relevant facts are the same or similar. The idea of the judges making use of previously decided cases dates back to the formation of the common law by the royal justices out of English customary law. But it was not until the 19th century that the general principle of judicial consistency in decision-making developed into a more rigid system of binding precedents. The necessary conditions for such a system did not exist until the standard of law reporting was improved by the creation of the Council of Law Reporting in 1865 and a hierarchy of courts was established by the Judicature Acts 1873–75 and the Appellate Jurisdiction Act 1876.

Precedent in action

Whenever a judge decides a case, he makes a speech, which may last a few minutes in a simple matter but may run to many pages in the Law Reports in a complicated case before the House of Lords. Every judgment contains the following elements:

1 The judge records his findings as to the relevant facts of the case, established from evidence presented in court.

2 He discusses the law which relates to the facts as found; this may involve an examination of the provisions of an Act of Parliament and/or previous judicial decisions.

3 He explains the reasons for his decision; i.e. the rule of law on which his decision is based. This is known as the *ratio decidendi* of a case. It is this part of the judgment which forms a precedent for future similar cases. Other comments by the judge which do not form part of the reasoning necessary to make the decision are referred to as *obiter dicta* (things said by the way); they do not have binding force.

4 The judge concludes his speech by announcing the decision between the parties, e.g. 'I give judgment for the claimant for the amount claimed', or 'I would dismiss this appeal'.

Precedents may be either binding or persuasive. A binding precedent is one which a court must follow, while a persuasive precedent is one to which respect is paid but is not binding. Whether a court is bound by a particular precedent depends on its position in the hierarchy of courts relative to the court which established the precedent. The general rule is that the decisions of superior courts are binding on lower courts. You should refer to Chapter 3 for an outline of the structure of the civil and criminal courts before considering the position of the principal courts which follows.

European Court of Justice

Since joining the EC in 1973, all English courts have been bound by the decisions of the European Court of Justice in matters of European law. The European Court tends to follow its own decisions but is not strictly bound to do so.

House of Lords

As the highest court of appeal in respect of our domestic law, the decisions of the House of Lords are binding on all other English courts. The House of Lords used to be bound by its own previous decisions (*London Street Tramways* v *London County Council* (1898)). In 1966, however, the Lord Chancellor announced by way of a Practice Statement that the House would no longer regard itself absolutely bound by its own precedents. An

example of the use of this freedom is *Miliangos* v *George Frank (Textiles) Ltd* (1976) in which the House overruled its own decision in *Re United Railways of Havana & Regla Warehouses Ltd* (1960) by holding that an English court may award damages in a foreign currency. It should be noted that the freedom to depart from previous precedents has not been exercised very often.

Court of Appeal

The Civil Division of the Court of Appeal is bound by the decisions of the House of Lords and its own previous decisions (*Young* v *Bristol Aeroplane* Co (1944)). There are three exceptions to this general rule:

(a) the Court of Appeal must decide which of two conflicting decisions of its own it will follow;

(b) the Court must not follow one of its own decisions which is inconsistent with a later decision of the House of Lords;

(c) the Court is not bound to follow one of its own decisions which was given *per incuriam*, i.e. where the court has overlooked a relevant statute or case.

Court of Appeal decisions are binding on lower civil courts, such as the High Court and county court. The Criminal Division of the Court of Appeal is bound by House of Lords' decisions and normally by its own decisions but, since it deals with questions of individual liberty, there appears to be greater freedom to depart from its own precedents. Decisions of the Criminal Division of the Court of Appeal are binding on lower criminal courts, e.g. the Crown Court and magistrates' court.

Divisional courts

A Divisional court is bound by the decisions of the House of Lords, the Court of Appeal and its own previous decisions, on the same lines as the Court of Appeal. Its decisions are binding on High Court judges sitting alone and lower courts such as the magistrates' court.

High Court

A High Court judge is bound by the decisions of the House of Lords, Court of Appeal and Divisional courts, but is not bound by another High court judge.

Other courts

Magistrates' courts and county courts are bound by the decisions of higher courts, but their own decisions have no binding force on other courts at the same level.

At first sight, the system of precedent seems to consist of a very rigid set of rules, which have the effect of restricting possible growth in the law. It is certainly true that a court can find itself bound by a bad precedent, the application of which causes great injustice in the particular case before it. However, the system is more flexible in practice.

Since 1966, as we saw earlier, the House of Lords has not been bound by its own precedents, thus creating limited opportunities for the development of new legal principles. Moreover, any court can use a variety of techniques to avoid following an apparently binding precedent. There may be material differences between the facts of the case before the court and the facts of the case setting the precedent, and so the earlier case can be distinguished. It is by avoiding precedents in this way that the judges make law and contribute to the enormous wealth of detailed rules which characterise case law.

EUROPEAN COMMUNITY LAW

On 1 January 1973 the United Kingdom became a member of the EC and thereby subject to a new source of law. Before we examine the nature of Community law and its impact on the English legal system, it is important to understand how the EC has developed and how it functions today.

Historical background

On 18 April 1951 Ministers representing France, West Germany, Italy, Belgium, The Netherlands and Luxembourg took the first step towards the creation of the EC, which the United Kingdom finally joined in 1973. They signed the Treaty of Paris establishing the European Coal and Steel Community (ECSC) with the aim of placing coal and steel production under international control. The same six founding members came together again in March 1957 to sign the two Treaties of Rome which set up the European Economic Community (EEC) and the European Atomic Energy Community (EURATOM).

The EEC was by far the most important of the three communities because its aim was the creation of a common market and harmonisation of the economic policies of member states. For these purposes, the EEC concerned itself with ensuring freedom of movement within the Community for persons, capital and services, devising common agricultural and transport policies and ensuring that competition within the EEC was not restricted or distorted. The constitution of each community is to be found in the Treaty which established it. Since the Merger Treaty of 1965, the three Communities have shared common institutions.

In January 1972 four more European countries agreed to join the EEC by signing the Treaty of Accession in Brussels. Only the United Kingdom, Republic of Ireland and Denmark took their places from 1 January 1973: Norway failed to ratify the Treaty following a negative vote by the Norwegian electorate in a national referendum. In 1981, the nine became ten with the accession of Greece, and membership was increased again when Spain and Portugal joined on 1 January 1986. The former territory of the German Democratic Republic became part of the Community in 1990 on the reunification of Germany.

In 1985 the heads of government of the member states committed themselves to removing all remaining barriers to the creation of a genuine 'common market' by the end of 1992. This commitment was contained in the Single European Act (SEA), which was approved by the European Council in December 1985 and signed in February 1986. The SEA had to be ratified by national Parliaments; this was achieved by the UK Parliament in the form of the European Communities (Amendment) Act 1986. The SEA, which came into force in the Community on 1 July 1987, contained the following elements:

- an agreement to establish an internal (or single) market by 31 December 1992 (the internal market was defined as 'an area without internal frontiers in which the free movement of goods, persons, services and capital is ensured');

- a declaration of the willingness of member states 'to transform relations as a whole among their States into a European Union';
- an acknowledgement of the objective of progressive realisation of economic and monetary union;
- an agreement to develop unrealised policies in the fields of economic and monetary convergence, social policy and the environment;
- a strengthening of the position of the European Parliament in the law-making process by means of a new 'cooperation procedure';
- an extension of the range of matters which could be decided by majority (rather than unanimous) voting by the Council of the European Union.

Further steps towards European integration were taken in December 1991 when the heads of government of the member states, meeting at Maastricht, agreed the details of a Treaty on European Union (TEU). The terms of the TEU include:

- the establishment of a European Union 'founded on the European Communities supplemented by the policies and forms of cooperation created by the TEU';
- the adoption of principles fundamental to the Union including respect for the national identities of the member states, respect for fundamental rights as a principle of Community law and respect for the principle of subsidiarity;
- a new agreement on economic and monetary union, accompanied by a strict timetable for its achievement;
- inter-governmental cooperation on a Common Foreign and Security Policy (CFSP);
- inter-governmental cooperation in the fields of justice and Home Affairs (including asylum and immigration policies and police cooperation in combating terrorism and drug-trafficking);
- expansion of Community powers in a number of economic and social fields, including health protection and overseas development cooperation;
- changes to the balance of power between EC institutions, in particular the strengthening of the role of the European Parliament in the law-making process;
- in a separate protocol all member states (except the UK) subscribed to the Social Chapter which incorporates the social policy objectives of the EC.

The Treaty had to be ratified by all member states before it could come into force. In order for the Treaty to take effect in the UK, Parliament passed the European Communities (Amendment) Act 1993.

On 1 January 1994 the Agreement on the European Economic Area (EEA) came into effect. Under this agreement, the principles and most of the rules of the single market have been extended to five of the seven countries of the European Free Trade Association (EFTA) – Austria, Finland, Iceland, Norway and Sweden. Although these countries obtained the free-trade advantages of the single market, they did not become members and so would have little say in the single market rules to which they are subject. To overcome this drawback, some of the countries have sought EU membership – Austria, Finland and Sweden achieved full membership of the EC from 1 January 1995.

In June 1997, member states concluded negotiations on a new treaty at a European Council held in Amsterdam. The provisions of the Treaty of Amsterdam, which was signed by representatives of member states in October 1997, reflected not only the preoccupations of the Community in relation to, for example, unemployment and public health, but also paved the way for future enlargement of the Union.

The Treaty covers the following areas:

1 Freedom, security and justice

- common action on asylum, visas, immigration and controls at external borders will be brought within Community rules and procedures, although the UK is permitted not to participate in any new measures adopted in relation to visas, asylum and immigration;
- increased cooperation between police forces, customs and other law enforcement agencies in member states to assist the prevention, detection and investigation of criminal offences.

2 Union policies to benefit citizens

- specifying the promotion of a high level of employment as a community objective, introducing a treaty-basis for developing a coordinated strategy for employment and establishing a coordination process for developing employment policies at Community level;

- incorporation into the Treaty of a strengthened Social Chapter applying to all member states, bringing to an end the UK's opt-out negotiated by the former Conservative Prime Minister, John Major, at Maastricht;
- in relation to environmental matters, the achievement of sustainable development becomes one of the objectives of the Community;
- ensuring that Community policies and activities achieve a high level of human health protection;
- measures to enhance the protection of consumers;
- a new Treaty protocol setting out legally binding guidelines on the application of the principles of subsidiarity and proportionality.

3 External policy

- measures to improve the coherence and effectiveness of the Common Foreign and Security Policy.

4 Union's institutions and legislative procedures

- introducing changes to the co-decision procedures and extending the areas where it may be used;
- capping the number of members of the European Parliament at 700;
- extending the areas where qualified majority may be used for adopting the acts of the Council;
- introducing changes to the Commission, e.g. increasing the powers of the President to select Commissioners;
- extending the powers of the Court of Justice in relation to, e.g., safeguarding fundamental rights;
- unofficial consolidation of all treaties, including the Treaty on European Union.

In December 2000 the EC heads of government concluded the Treaty of Nice which paves the way for the future enlargement of the Community from 15 to 27 member states. European states seeking membership include Poland, Romania, Czech Republic, Hungary, Bulgaria, Slovakia, Lithuania, Latvia, Slovenia, Estonia, Cyprus and Malta. The Treaty will make a number of important changes to the organisation and operation of EC institutions to accommodate the expansion of the Community. They include:

- a new voting system for the Council of the European Union which will come into effect on 1 January 2005;

- the European Parliament for 2004–9 will include representation from new member states which have signed accession treaties by the beginning of 2004. The number of MEPs representing each member state will be scaled down, e.g. the number of UK MEPs will fall from 87 to 72. Similar arrangements will be made for the ECSC and the Committee of the Regions;
- the Commission will consist of one Commissioner for each member state from 1 January 2005. (The UK will have to lose one of its two Commissioners.) On accession, a new member state will be entitled to appoint its own Commissioner for one term. However, when the EC consists of 27 members, the number of Commissioners must be less than the number of member states and a rotation system will be put into operation.

The Treaty of Nice will only come into effect when ratified by member states.

European Community or European Union?

It has become fashionable since the ratification of the TEU to refer to the European Union. Technically, the European Union consists of the European Community (the new formal title of what used to be known as the European Economic Community), the European Coal and Steel Community (ECSC), the European Atomic Energy Community (EURATOM), and the new areas of intergovernmental cooperation on foreign and security policy (CFSP), justice and home affairs. The European Community (EC) has not been replaced by the European Union. The EC, along with ECSC and EURATOM, is one 'pillar' of the European Union. The other two 'pillars' are CFSP, and justice and home affairs. Action in respect of these two pillars must be taken on the basis of inter-governmental co-operation: Community law does not apply and the European Court of Justice has no jurisdiction in these areas (although the Treaty of Amsterdam extends the powers of the Court of Justice in relation to action by the Union on asylum and immigration and cooperation on police and judicial matters). However, it should be noted that the Council (see below) now calls itself the Council of the European Union – even when it is enacting EC legislation.

Community institutions

The aims and objectives of the EC are put into effect by four main institutions: the Council of the European Union, the Commission, the European Parliament and the European Court of Justice.

The Council of the European Union

The Council is made up of one minister from each member state, chosen on the basis of the subject under discussion. Thus, meetings of the Council may be attended by the foreign ministers of each country but if, say, the common transport policy is under discussion, the transport ministers of each member state will attend. European Council meetings at head-of-state or government level take place at least twice a year. Each member state acts as President of the Council for six months in rotation. The Council is the supreme law maker for the EC, but this power is restricted by the fact that in most cases it can only legislate in respect of proposals put forward by the Commission. Although few decisions require the approval of all member states, under the Luxembourg Accords, the Council has adopted the practice of unanimity for decisions where vital national interests are at stake. Other decisions may be taken on a simple majority vote or on a qualified majority vote. In the latter case each country has a certain number of votes (France, Germany, Italy and the UK have ten votes each; Spain has eight; Belgium, Greece, The Netherlands and Portugal have five each; Sweden and Austria have four each; Denmark, Finland and Ireland have three each and Luxembourg has two). The qualified majority to take a decision is 62 votes out of a total of 87. The SEA extended the provisions for qualified majority voting to most single-market proposals to help the EC meet the 1992 target for the creation of the single (internal) market.

The Commission

The Commission, which is based in Brussels, comprises 20 members; the larger countries, France, Germany, Italy, the United Kingdom and Spain, are entitled to appoint two Commissioners each, while the ten smaller countries may appoint one Commissioner each. (The Intergovernmental Conference has agreed that when the Union is next enlarged member states with two Commissioners will give up one of their Commissioners.) Of the 20 Commission members, one is the President and two are Vice-Presidents. Commissioners are appointed for a period of five years (previously four years) by mutual agreement between the 15 member states. Once appointed, Commissioners must act with complete independence in the interests of the EC. Each Commissioner is assisted by a Cabinet consisting of six or more officials appointed by the Commissioner and responsible to him. Cabinet members have an important role to play in formulating proposals for approval by the Commission. The *Chefs de Cabinet* meet regularly to coordinate activities and prepare for Commission meetings. The Commission is divided into departments known as Directorates-General, headed by a Director-General who is responsible to a Commissioner. Each Directorate-General is divided into Directorates, which are further divided into Divisions. There are also various specialised services, e.g. a Legal Service.

The Commission plays an important part in the legislative process of the EC. It formulates Community policy, drafts proposed legislation to be laid before the Council, and it can exercise a limited legislative power of its own in some areas, e.g. competition policy and control of government subsidies. The Commission is also responsible for implementing Community legislation and ensuring that treaty obligations are being observed by member states. A new voting system for the Council will come into effect on 1 January 2005 under the Treaty of Nice to accommodate enlargement of the EC.

The Parliament

Originally Members of the European Parliament (MEPs) were nominated by national parliaments from among their own members, but since 1979 MEPs have been directly elected by the citizens of member states. Elections are held every five years. At the June 1999 elections, 626 MEPs were elected: 99 from Germany, 87 each from France, Italy and the UK, 64 from Spain, 31 from The Netherlands, 25 each from Portugal, Belgium and Greece, 22 from Sweden, 21 from Austria, 16 from Denmark and Finland, 15 from Ireland and 6 from Luxembourg. The next elections will be held in June 2004. MEPs tend to sit and vote according to political rather national allegiances. The European Parliament operates in two locations: plenary sessions are held in Strasbourg, while committee meetings take place in Brussels. Despite its name, the European Parliament is an advisory or consultative body rather than a legislative one. It is consulted by the Council and the Commission before certain decisions are taken: it can offer advice and opinions, it monitors the activities of the Commission and the Council and has the power to dismiss the full Commission. Its supervisory powers were extended under the TEU allowing it to set up Committees of Inquiry to investigate contraventions of, or maladministration in, the implementation of Community law. It also has the power to appoint an Ombudsman responsible for investigating complaints of maladministration. It plays an important part in drawing up the Community budget and can reject the entire budget. The SEA strengthened the role of the European Parliament in the legislative process and the TEU extends its powers by allowing it to veto certain proposals in areas such as the single market.

Court of Justice (ECJ)

The Court of Justice, which sits in Luxembourg, is composed of 15 judges, one from each member state. They are assisted by several Advocates-General, whose function is to present an unbiased opinion of the case to the court. Judicial personnel are appointed by unanimous agreement between the governments of member states for terms of six years, which may be renewed. The Court of Justice exercises judicial power within the EC. Its jurisdiction covers the following areas:

1 Preliminary rulings. Under Art 234 (previously Art 177) of the Treaty of Rome, any tribunal in a member state may ask the court to give a preliminary ruling concerning the interpretation of the Treaties or Community legislation enacted under the Treaties. If such a question is raised in a court against whose decision there is no further right of appeal, the ruling of the Court of Justice must be

sought. References to the Court of Justice under Art 234 are not appeals as such. The proceedings of the national courts are suspended while the point of European law is determined by the European Court. The case then resumes in the national court, where the ruling is applied to the facts of the case.

2 Actions against member states. Proceedings may be taken against member states either by the Commission or by another member state in respect of violations of the Treaties or Community legislation. If a case is established, the court will make an order requiring the member state to take the necessary measures to comply with the ECJ's judgment. In the past the ECJ has had to rely on political pressure to secure compliance, but the TEU gives the ECJ the power to impose financial sanctions.

3 Actions against Community institutions. Actions may be brought against Community institutions by other institutions, member states or, in certain circumstances, by corporate bodies and individuals. Such proceedings may be used to annul the acts of the Council and the Commission, to obtain a declaration that the Council or the Commission has failed to act as required by the treaties, to obtain compensation for damage caused by the unlawful actions of Community institutions and their servants and to review penalties imposed by the Commission.

4 Community employment cases. The court also deals with disputes between the EC and its employees.

The SEA provided for the creation of a Court of First Instance (CFI) to help relieve the Court of Justice of some of its workload. The CFI was inaugurated in 1989; its members are appointed for six-year terms by mutual agreement of the governments of the member states. It normally sits in divisions of three or five judges. Members of the court may be asked to perform the role of Advocates-General, in which case they must not participate in the deliberations of the court before judgment. The jurisdiction of the CFI is confined to disputes between the EC and its employees, appeals against implementation of EC competition rules and actions brought by undertakings against the Commission under the ECSC Treaty. Appeal against a decision of the CFI may be made to the Court of Justice, but on a point of law only.

Other institutions

The Court of Auditors. The Court of Auditors, which sits in Luxembourg, is the Community's financial watchdog. Its job is to scrutinise and report on the Community's financial management and oversee the implementation of the budget. It has 15 members, one from each member state, who are appointed every six years by the Council in consultation with the European Parliament.

The Economic and Social Committee (ESC). The ESC consists of representatives from all member states, drawn from various categories of economic and social activity, including employers, workers, professional bodies, consumers, environmentalists, farmers and so on. It is an advisory body whose opinion is sought by the Council and Commission on proposed legislation and other matters.

The Committee of the Regions. This new advisory Committee was established by the TEU. It consists of representatives from each member state, drawn from regional and local bodies. The Committee is consulted on proposed legislation in such areas as education, culture and public health to ensure that regional interests are considered.

The European Investment Bank (EIB). The EIB, which is based in Luxembourg, is the Community's bank. It lends money to finance capital investment projects.

The EC Ombudsman. This position was created by the TEU. The EC Ombudsman, who is appointed by the European Parliament for a five-year term of office, has the task of receiving and dealing with complaints from citizens of member states concerning maladministration by any Community institution or body, except the European Court of Justice. The EC Ombudsman may receive complaints direct from aggrieved individuals and there is no limitation period on complaints. The EC Ombudsman may also receive complaints from MEPs or mount an investigation on his own initiative. Like his UK counterpart, the EC Ombudsman has no power to impose sanctions on institutions found guilty of maladministration. He must rely on adverse publicity and political pressure to secure an appropriate remedy. He must submit an annual report to the European Parliament and a report in each case where maladministration is found.

Sources of Community law

The nature and effect of Community law are summarised in Fig 2.2. The main sources of EC law are as follows:

1 The Treaties. The Treaties are the primary source of EC law. The foundations of the Community legal system were laid in the original Treaties of Paris and Rome and have been added to by further Treaties, such as the Treaty of Accession and the TEU. These Treaties have not been revised by the Amsterdam Treaty.

Some Treaty provisions are so specific that they take direct effect in member states and give rise to enforceable Community rights. Article 141 (previously Art 119), which establishes the principle of 'equal pay for equal work', for example, is directly effective (*Defrenne* v *Sabena* (1976)). Any employee, irrespective of whether they work in the public or private sector, can rely on Art 141 against his or her employer in an action for equal pay in domestic courts. Article 141 is an example of a Community provision which gives an individual rights against other individuals or undertakings. Such a provision is said to have horizontal direct effect. (Provisions which create individual rights against a member state are said to have vertical direct effect.) Some Treaty provisions are insufficiently precise or, by their nature, are incapable of conferring rights on individuals. Member states are expected to give effect to these provisions by enacting specific legislation in their own parliaments.

2 Secondary law. The Treaties empower the Council and Commission to make three types of legislation:

(a) Regulations are designed to achieve uniformity of law among the member states. They are of general application and usually have direct force of law in all member states without the need for further legislation, i.e. they are directly effective (horizontally and vertically). However, a regulation may provide that some of its provisions are to be implemented by member states. In this case, the provision does not have direct effect.

An example of a regulation is reg 1436/70, which requires tachographs to be fitted in commercial vehicles. The Commission brought enforcement proceedings against the UK for failure to implement Art 21 of the regulation (*EC Commission* v *UK* (*Re Tachographs*) (1979)).

(b) Directives seek to harmonise the law of member states. They are instructions to member states to bring their laws into line by a certain date. The states themselves are free to choose the methods by which the changes are implemented, e.g. by Act of Parliament or statutory instrument. Directives, unlike Regulations, are therefore not directly applicable. However, provisions of a Directive may take direct effect (vertically) if not duly implemented by a member state. An example of a Directive is Directive 93/13/EEC on unfair terms in consumer contracts (see further, Chapter 9). The Directive, which introduced a general requirement of fairness in consumer contracts, was implemented in the UK by means of delegated legislation (the Unfair Terms in Consumer Contracts Regulations).

If a Directive is not implemented by the required date:

- the state in default may find itself subject to enforcement proceedings brought by the Commission. In 1982 the UK was found to be in breach of its Community obligations for failing to comply with the requirements of 'equal pay for work of equal value' set out in the Equal Pay Directive (*EC Commission* v *United Kingdom* (1982));
- public employees may be able to rely on the directive as against the state in its capacity as an employer (*Marshall* v *Southampton & SW Hampshire AHA* (*Teaching*) (1986) – see later). In *Foster* v *British Gas PLC* (1991) the Court of Justice defined 'the state' in broad terms so that in certain circumstances it might include newly privatised industries;

- individuals who have suffered loss as a result of failure to implement a Directive may be able to sue the state for damages, provided that: (a) the result required by the Directive involved conferring rights on individuals; (b) the content of the rights can be determined from the Directive; and (c) there is a causal link between the failure to implement the Directive and the damage suffered by those affected (*Francovich* v *Italian Republic* (1992));

(c) Decisions may be addressed to a state, a company or an individual and are binding on the addressee. Some decisions may have direct effect in the sense that third parties may be able to rely on the decision in an action against the addressee. An example of a Decision is Council Decision 89/469 'concerning certain protective measures relating to bovine spongiform encephalopathy in the United Kingdom', which was adopted in the wake of the discovery of 'mad cow' disease.

3 Decisions of the Court of Justice. Judgments of the Court of Justice on matters of European law are binding on courts within the member states.

The law-making process

Regulations, directives and decisions come into effect by a number of different procedures. The procedure to be followed in each case is determined by the relevant Treaty article.

1 Consultation procedure. Before the amendment of the EEC Treaty by the SEA, this was the only procedure which operated. Under this procedure, the Commission formulates proposals which are submitted to the Council for consideration. The European Parliament has a right to be consulted and to give an opinion. A final decision is then taken by the Council on the proposal in accordance with the appropriate voting procedures. Although other procedures now predominate, the consultation procedure has been retained for some matters, e.g. the Common Agricultural Policy (CAP).

2 Cooperation procedure. This procedure, which was introduced by the SEA, involves the European Parliament more fully in the decision-making process. Parliament has the opportunity to give its opinion and propose amendments on two occasions: the first occasion is when the Commission

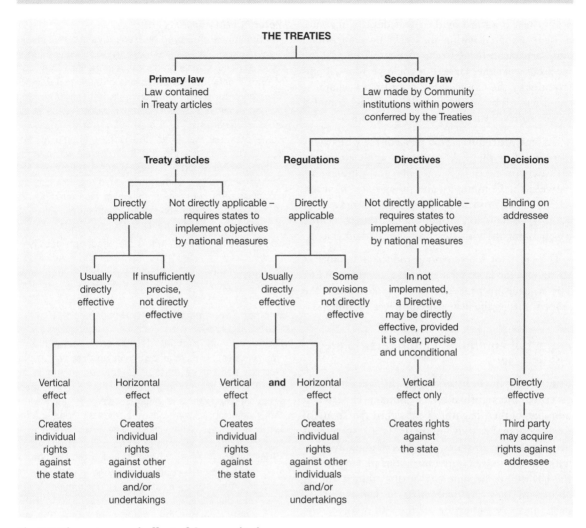

Fig 2.2 The nature and effect of Community law

proposal is submitted to the Council and the second is after the Council has considered Parliament's opinion and reached a 'Common Position'. Parliament has more opportunity to influence a proposal under this procedure but does not have a right of veto. This procedure now only applies to articles concerning economic and monetary union (EMU), as a result of changes made at Amsterdam.

3 Co-decision procedure. This procedure was introduced by the TEU and will apply to most single-market proposals, consumer protection, culture and public health. The procedure follows the cooperation procedure up to the point where Parliament considers the Common Position adopted

by the Council. If Parliament approves the proposal, the Council adopts the measure. If Parliament indicates its intention to reject the Common Position, a Conciliation Committee, consisting of 12 representatives of the Council and an equal number of MEPs, is convened with a view to reaching an agreement acceptable to both sides. If the Conciliation Committee is unable to reach an agreement or the agreement it does reach is unacceptable to Parliament, the proposal lapses. If Parliament proposes amendments to the Common Position, then, following further consideration by the Commission and the Council, the Council may adopt the measure provided it approves all the amendments. If it does not, then the Conciliation Committee is convened. If a joint text is agreed by the two sides, the measure must be adopted within six weeks by the Council and Parliament. If the Committee fails to agree, the proposal will either lapse or it could be adopted unilaterally by the Council; but even then Parliament could reject it by an absolute majority. This complex procedure gives Parliament a power of veto.

4 Assent procedure. This procedure, which was introduced by the SEA, applies to applications for membership to the Community and agreements between the Community and other states or international organisations. The Council may only adopt a Commission proposal under this procedure by obtaining the formal approval of Parliament.

The Treaty of Amsterdam introduced a number of changes to the law-making processes within the EC. The co-decision procedure was simplified and the scope for using the new procedure was extended.

Impact of Community membership on English law

Britain's application to join the EC was formally accepted and signified on 22 January 1972 when ministers of the UK government signed the Treaty of Accession in Brussels. A treaty is an agreement between sovereign states, which is binding in international law only. Treaty obligations undertaken by the UK do not become law in this country unless and until they are embodied in legislation by Parliament. Membership of the EC involved the acceptance of Community law as part of English law. This could only be achieved by passing an Act of Parliament: the European Communities Act 1972.

Section 2(1) of the 1972 Act provides that Community law which is intended to take direct effect within member states (i.e. provisions of the Treaties and Regulations) shall automatically form part of the law of the UK. Under s 2(2) Community legislation which requires some act of implementation by member states (i.e. Directives) may be brought into force by Orders in Council or ministerial regulations. Certain measures, such as the creation of major criminal offences, must be implemented by Act of Parliament. English courts are required to take note of the Treaties and the decisions of the European Court. The supremacy of Community law over English law is illustrated by the following cases.

Macarthys Ltd v Smith (1979)

Mrs Smith was employed by Macarthys Ltd as a stockroom manager. She claimed that she was entitled to the same pay as her male predecessor in the job. The Court of Appeal held that the provisions of the Equal Pay Act 1970 only applied to comparisons between men and women employed by the same employer at the same time. However, Art 119 (now Art 141) of the Treaty of Rome provides that 'men and women should receive equal pay for equal work'. Mrs Smith's case was referred to the European Court of Justice, which ruled that Art 119 applied to cases of a woman following a man in a job. The provisions of Art 119 took priority over the Equal Pay Act 1970 by virtue of the European Communities Act 1972. Mrs Smith succeeded in her action for equal pay.

Comment. This case illustrates the direct applicability of Treaty articles and their horizontal direct effect. Article 119 conferred rights on Mrs Smith, which were enforceable against her private-sector employer in the UK courts.

Marshall v Southampton & S W Hampshire AHA (Teaching) (1986)

The Area Health Authority (AHA) had a policy that its employees should retire at the age at which social security pensions became payable, i.e. 60 for women and 65 for men. The AHA was prepared to waive the policy in respect of certain employees and in fact allowed Miss Marshall, a senior dietician, to work past the normal retiring age for female employees. When she was dismissed at the age of 62, Miss Marshall claimed she had been discriminated against on the grounds of her sex since if she had been a man she would have continued working until the age of 65. She based her claim on the Sex Discrimination Act 1975 and the EC Equal Treatment Directive. Both the industrial tribunal and the Employment Appeal Tribunal dismissed her claim on the Sex Discrimination Act because arrangements in relation to death and retirement are excluded from the Act's prohibition of discrimination. The Court of Appeal referred Miss Marshall's case to the European Court of Justice to determine whether her dismissal breached the Equal Treatment Directive and, if it did, whether she could rely on the Directive in the English courts. Miss Marshall succeeded on both points.

Comment. (i) The European Court of Justice found that, as the UK had failed to implement fully the EC Equal Treatment Directive, Miss Marshall could rely on the Directive against the state in its capacity as her employer, i.e. the Directive had a vertical direct effect. Directives do not have a horizontal direct effect and do not create rights which individual workers can enforce against their private-sector employers.

(ii) The decision in the *Marshall* case prompted a change in the law. The Sex Discrimination Act 1986 now requires employers to set a common retirement age for their employees, irrespective of their sex.

(iii) Miss Marshall returned to the European Court of Justice to challenge the statutory limit on awards made under the Sex Discrimination Act 1975. The European Court agreed with her argument that such a limit was in breach of the Equal Treatment Directive (*Marshall* v *Southampton & SW Hampshire Area Health Authority (No 2)* (1993)). The statutory limits have now been removed in respect of claims made under both the Sex Discrimination Act 1975 and the Race Relations Act 1976.

By enacting the European Communities Act 1972, the UK Parliament has relinquished part of its sovereignty. Certain forms of Community law automatically take precedence over English law without reference to Parliament. Nevertheless, the 1972 Act is a statute like any other and could be repealed by a future Parliament and full sovereignty would be restored.

HUMAN RIGHTS

The UK is very unusual in having no written constitution, which sets out the powers of the Crown, Parliament, the Government and the judiciary, and the rights of citizens. In the UK, a person is free to do anything which is not specifically prohibited by the law. However, there is no statement of basic civil rights and no mechanism to prevent Parliament passing legislation which restricts civil rights. Most other countries have written constitutions which incorporate a statement of fundamental civil rights guaranteed by the state and the courts.

In 1950 the Council of Europe adopted a European Convention on Human Rights (ECHR) which was based on the United Nations' Universal Declaration on Human Rights. The UK ratified the ECHR in 1951. The rights and freedoms protected by the ECHR and subsequent amendments (known as protocols) ratified by the UK are set out in Fig 2.3.

Unlike the Universal Declaration on Human Rights, the ECHR established institutions and procedures for protecting the rights enshrined in the Convention. The European Court of Human Rights, which sits at Strasbourg, adjudicates on petitions brought by individual citizens against a state and cases brought by one state against another. Individual petitions may only be brought

The European Convention on Human Rights	
Article	*Rights and Freedoms*
2	The right to life.
3	Freedom from torture or inhuman or degrading treatment.
4	Freedom from slavery and forced labour.
5	The right to liberty and security of the person.
6	The right to a fair trial.
7	Protection from any retrospective effect of the criminal law.
8	Right to respect for private and family life.
9	Freedom of thought, conscience and religion.
10	Freedom of expression.
11	Freedom of assembly and association.
12	The right to marry.
14	The enjoyment of Convention rights without discrimination on the grounds of sex, race, colour, language, religion, political or other opinion, national or social origin, association with a national, minority, property, birth or other status.
The First Protocol	
1	The right to peaceful enjoyment of one's possessions.
2	The right to education.
3	The right to free elections.

Fig 2.3 The European Convention on Human Rights

to the court if the relevant state has accepted the rights of its citizens to bring a petition and all domestic remedies have been exhausted. The European Commission on Human Rights is responsible for ensuring that the individual petition is admissible and in all cases trying to help the parties to resolve the dispute. If an out-of-court settlement cannot be reached, the case may be referred to the court. If the court decides that a state is in breach of the ECHR, it can award compensation or other 'just satisfaction' of the case. The court has no powers of enforcement and in practice it relies on the goodwill of states to implement its judgments.

Although the UK ratified the ECHR, and from 1966 allowed UK citizens to bring individual petitions to the court, the provisions of the ECHR had not been incorporated into UK law. As with other treaties, UK judges in domestic courts could take the ECHR into account in interpreting UK legislation and in applying the rules of common law. However, if the legislation was clear but in conflict with the ECHR, judges had to apply the UK legislation. Individuals were forced to exhaust all rights of appeal in UK courts, at great expense, before being allowed to take the case to the European Court of Human Rights. About half of the other signatory states had incorporated the ECHR into their domestic law. Their citizens could rely on the ECHR in their domestic courts and any legislation in conflict with the ECHR could be declared invalid.

In 1997 the Labour government indicated its intention to incorporate the European Convention on Human Rights (ECHR) into UK law. The Human Rights Act 1998, which came fully into force on 2 October 2000, enables people to enforce their Convention rights in UK courts rather than having to exhaust all domestic remedies before bringing a case to the European Court of Human Rights in Strasbourg. UK legislation must now be interpreted as far as possible by the courts in a way which is compatible with Convention rights. If a provision of UK legislation is incompatible with Convention Rights, specified courts are able to make a 'declaration of incompatibility'. The courts specified include the House of Lords, the Judicial Committee of the Privy Council, the Court of Appeal and the High Court. The incompatible provision remains in force until it is amended by ministerial order. Where the legislation emanates from the Scottish Parliament or the Assemblies in Wales and Northern Ireland, the courts have the power to overrule provisions which are incompatible with the ECHR. It is unlawful for a public authority to act in a way which is incompatible with the ECHR. Individuals who are affected by the unlawful act are entitled to take proceedings and seek an award of damages if their case is upheld. A minister in charge of a Bill is required to make a written statement that he believes the Bill is compatible with the ECHR or, if he is unable to make such a statement, that he nevertheless wishes the House to proceed with the Bill.

The first 'declaration of incompatibility' was made by the High Court in December 2000 in respect of the role of the Secretary of State for the Environment, Transport and the Regions in planning decisions (*R v Secretary of State for the Environment, Transport and the Regions, ex parte Holding and Barnes plc* (2001)). The court held that involvement of the Secretary of State (a member of the executive) in making planning decisions was incompatible with Art 6, which states that 'everyone is entitled to a fair and public hearing ... by an independent and impartial tribunal established by law'. The Secretary of State could not be said to be impartial because he was acting both as a policy-maker and decision-taker.

QUESTIONS/ACTIVITIES

1 Every year the government announces its programme for legislation by way of the Queen's Speech at the State Opening of Parliament in October or November. Select one proposal for legislation. Find out why this legal change is being proposed. Keep a diary to record its progress through the legislative procedure. What changes are made to the Bill during its passage through Parliament?

2 Describe the relationship between Parliament and the judiciary in respect of Acts of Parliament.

3 What are the advantages and disadvantages of the doctrine of judicial precedent?

4 How has Britain's membership of the European Community affected the English legal system?

5 Explain the differences between the following pairs:
 (a) MP and MEP;
 (b) *ratio decidendi* and *obiter dicta*;
 (c) a Bill and a statute;
 (d) ECSC and EEC;
 (e) the Law Commission and the Law Reform Committee;
 (f) Orders in Council and byelaws;
 (g) a binding precedent and a persuasive precedent;
 (h) the golden rule and the mischief rule;
 (i) the Council of the European Union and the Commission;
 (j) a regulation and a directive;
 (k) the European Community and the European Union.

Chapter 3

LEGAL SERVICES AND DISPUTE SETTLEMENT

Every facet of modern business life is governed by the law. Today's businessman needs to be alert to the legal implications of his activities. He will require a basic understanding of the principles of business law so that legal considerations can be built into the planning and decision-making process. At some stage, however, professional legal advice and help are likely to be needed – to advise on the implications of a recent change in the law or to draft a legal document or to assist in resolving a dispute. In this chapter we will consider the sources of legal advice and information available to business and the various methods of settling disputes.

LEGAL SERVICES

The question of who is allowed to provide particular types of legal service is in the process of change as a result of reforms instituted by the Courts and Legal Services Act 1990 and more recently by the Access to Justice Act 1999.

THE LEGAL PROFESSION

The legal profession in England and Wales is divided into two distinct branches: barristers and solicitors. These two types of lawyer fulfil different functions, although there is a certain amount of overlap in their activities.

Solicitors

Solicitors are the general practitioners of the legal profession, providing an all-round legal service. Solicitors may practise alone but usually they operate in partnership with other solicitors. The solicitor is often the first port of call for anyone with a legal problem; consequently, his work is enormously varied. The workload associated with personal or private clients includes drafting wills, conveyancing (the legal formalities of buying and selling a house), winding-up a deceased person's estate, dealing with claims for compensation arising from accidents or matrimonial problems. Business clients generate a different kind of work: for example, forming companies or drafting partnership agreements, applying for licences, drawing up contracts, advising on tax changes or new legal obligations in respect of employees. When the legal problem involves court proceedings, the solicitor deals with the preparatory stages, such as gathering evidence and interviewing witnesses. A solicitor is entitled to appear in court on behalf of his client, although until relatively recently rights of audience were limited to the magistrates' court and the county court. (if the case necessitated an appearance in a higher court, then the services of a barrister had to be obtained.) The Courts and Legal Services Act 1990, however, introduced new arrangements for determining advocacy rights, which has led to suitably qualified solicitors enjoying more extensive rights of audience in the higher courts. Solicitors without full rights of audience are now also allowed to appear in the higher courts in limited circumstances, e.g. in criminal appeals from the magistrates' court to the Crown Court and reading out formal unchallenged statements in the High Court.

The opportunity for a solicitor to become a judge used to be limited to appointment as a circuit judge. However, the introduction of increased rights of audience for some solicitors following the Courts and Legal Services Act 1990 has opened the way for solicitors to obtain higher judicial office.

The Law Society is the governing body for solicitors. It controls the education and examination of students, issues 'practising certificates' which solicitors wishing to practise must obtain, sets standards of professional conduct and deals with complaints about solicitors.

Barristers

If solicitors are the 'GPs' of the legal world, barristers are the consultant specialists. They specialise in advocacy (i.e. representing a client in court) and have a right to appear in any court or tribunal. They used to enjoy exclusive rights of audience in the higher courts, such as the House of Lords, Court of Appeal and High Court. However, the Courts and Legal Services Act 1990 dismantled this monopoly and introduced new arrangements for deciding who may act as an advocate in the courts. A barrister's work is not confined to advocacy. Indeed, some barristers spend most of their time on paperwork – writing opinions on specialised and difficult areas of law for solicitors or drafting documents.

There are two types of barrister: QCs (Queen's Counsel) and juniors. After 15–20 years' practice, a barrister may apply to become a QC or to 'take silk'. Queen's Counsel (or 'silks') are appointed by the Queen on the advice of the Lord Chancellor. They represent the top 10 per cent of the barristers' profession. There are several advantages to taking silk: QCs enjoy a higher status, they command higher fees and can concentrate on advocacy and giving opinions rather than poorly remunerated 'paperwork'. They are known as 'leaders' because they normally only appear in court accompanied by a junior barrister.

Barristers are not allowed to form partnerships; they must practise on their own account. Nevertheless, groups of barristers share chambers (rooms in an office) and collectively employ a barrister's clerk who acts as their office manager. The Courts and Legal Services Act 1990 abolished any common law rule which prevented barristers from forming multi-disciplinary practices with other professions, but the Act preserved the right of the General Council of the Bar to make rules prohibiting such arrangements.

The General Council of the Bar, which was established in 1987, is the governing body of barristers. Admission to the Bar is controlled by the four Inns of Court (the Inner Temple, the Middle Temple, Gray's Inn and Lincoln's Inn). The education and examination of students for the Bar is the responsibility of the Council of Legal Education.

The relationship between solicitors and barristers

Together, solicitors and barristers provide a comprehensive legal service. A person with a legal problem starts by consulting a solicitor and in so doing will enter into a contract for legal services. The solicitor will be competent to deal with most of the matters brought to him but in some cases he will need to retain the services of a barrister. The barrister's brief may be to give an opinion on a difficult point of law or to represent the client in court. A solicitor may approach any barrister to undertake the brief and, according to the 'cab rank' principle, the barrister must accept the work subject to his availability and the negotiation of a proper fee. Traditionally, barristers have not stood in a contractual relationship with the solicitors who briefed them. The fee was regarded as an 'honorarium', and as a result barristers could not sue solicitors who were reluctant to pay, although the same solicitors could bring an action against recalcitrant clients. Section 61 of the Courts and Legal Services Act 1990 abolished any common law rule preventing a barrister from entering into a contract for the provision of his services, although the General Council may continue to make rules prohibiting barristers from entering into contracts.

Until recently both solicitors and barristers were immune from actions in negligence arising from the conduct of a case in court or work immediately preparatory to such a case. However, in *Arthur Hall and Co v Simons* (2000) the House of Lords decided that the immunity could no longer be justified. Both branches of the legal profession can be liable in negligence now for all aspects of their work.

In the past a barrister could only be instructed by a solicitor. Clients did not have direct access to the barrister's services. The rules have now been relaxed to allow members of professional bodies, such as accountants and surveyors, direct access to a barrister, and since 1996, members of the public whose cases have been prepared by trained Citizens' Advice Bureaux staff.

OTHER LEGAL PERSONNEL

Public notaries

A notary public is an officer of the law who is authorised, among other things, to draw up, attest and certify deeds and other documents, to prepare wills and probate documents, to administer oaths and take a statement of truth. Most notaries are also solicitors.

Legal executives

Most firms of solicitors employ staff who are not qualified as lawyers to deal with some of the more routine work of the legal office, such as conveyancing. Legal executives, as they are known, have achieved professional recognition with the establishment of the Institute of Legal Executives (ILEX) in 1963. Unadmitted clerks may now qualify for membership by combining practical experience with success in the Institute's examinations. In 1997, ILEX received approval from the Lord Chancellor and four designated senior judges for an application to grant limited rights of audience in the courts to suitably qualified Fellows of the Institute.

Licensed conveyancers

Up until the mid-1980s, solicitors enjoyed a statutory monopoly over conveyancing work. (The monopoly extended to barristers as well, but as a rule of practice, they do not carry out conveyancing work.) It was a criminal offence for an unqualified person to prepare documents relating to the transfer of title to property for gain. Many solicitors were heavily dependent on conveyancing work but there were growing criticisms of the level of charges and standard of service provided. A small measure of competition for conveyancing work was introduced with the creation of a new profession of 'licensed conveyancers' by Part II of the Administration of Justice Act 1985. The Council for Licensed Conveyancers is responsible for the admission, training, professional standards and discipline of licensed conveyancers.

Lawyers in industry, commerce and public service

The vast majority of qualified lawyers work in private practice providing legal services to a wide range of clients. A growing number of organisations, however, are setting up their own legal departments staffed by solicitors and barristers. The functions of these 'in-house' lawyers depend on the type of organisation they work for. Banks, insurance companies and building societies employ lawyers to fulfil their specialist legal requirements. Central government departments and local authorities employ their own lawyers to help them discharge their statutory functions. The legal department of a private company undertakes legal work of a general nature, i.e. conveyancing, drawing up contracts, providing advice on employment matters, company administration and so on.

OTHER SOURCES OF INFORMATION AND ADVICE

1 Information and advice for business

The legal profession is not the only source of information and advice on legal matters which a businessman can turn to. Accountants are well versed in the intricacies of tax laws and the complex requirements of company law. Some of the large firms of accountants have established business and management consultancy services. Government departments are a fruitful source of information for those in business: e.g. the Department of Trade and Industry on employment legislation; the Inland Revenue on tax; Customs and Excise on VAT regulations. There is also a large number of government-sponsored organisations providing information and advice: the Equal Opportunities Commission, the Commission for Racial Equality, the Health and Safety Commission, the Office of Fair Trading and the Small Business Service, to name a few. A businessman may also benefit from joining a trade association. The Consumer Credit Trade Association, for example, produces a quarterly journal which reports changes in the law. It also runs a Legal Advisory Bureau for its members. Professional associations (e.g. the Chartered Institute of Personnel and Development) perform a similar service for its members employed in business.

2 Information and advice for citizens and consumers

Many people are deterred from seeking legal advice and taking legal action because of fear of what it will cost them. However, there are schemes and organisations which aim to provide low cost legal help.

(a) Community Legal Service Fund

Unlike businessmen, private individuals may be able to obtain financial help in legal matters from the Community Legal Service Fund, which is administered by the Legal Services Commission, as established by the Access to Justice Act 1999. The help available includes:

(i) **Civil legal aid** – available for individuals requiring help in relation to civil matters. A solicitor may provide **legal help** (previously referred to as 'advice and assistance') with problems which fall within the scope of the scheme, such as housing problems, clinical negligence, credit and debts, contract disputes, welfare benefits and financial claims arising from divorce. The scheme does not cover defamation and malicious falsehood, conveyancing, company or partnership law, neighbour or boundary disputes. Eligibility for immediate help is based on a means test carried out by the solicitor. Applicants will qualify for help if they are receiving certain state benefits or are on a low income. If the application is successful, the solicitor will be able to carry out two hours' worth of work (three hours in the case of divorce work). If more work is required, the solicitor must apply to the Legal Services Commission for permission to carry on. Permission will only be granted if the case satisfies a 'merits' test, i.e. the applicant has a good enough case to justify further support. If court proceedings become necessary, a Legal Representation Certificate must be obtained.

(ii) **Criminal legal aid** – available for defendants in criminal proceedings in the Crown Court and magistrates' court. Eligibility is based on the applicant's means and the requirements of justice.

(iii) The **duty solicitor scheme** – under this solicitors are available in police stations and magistrates' courts to give free legal advice.

Under the Access to Justice Act 1999, criminal legal aid, including the duty solicitor scheme, will eventually be operated by a Criminal Defence Service.

(b) Conditional fees

The Courts and Legal Services Act 1990 introduced conditional fee arrangements. Advocates or litigators can enter into agreements with their clients whereby they receive their normal fee plus an uplift in the event of success but nothing if unsuccessful. The percentage of any uplift must be specified in the agreement and is subject to a maximum percentage determined by the Lord Chancellor in consultation with the designated judges, the Bar, the Law Society and other appropriate authorised bodies. The maximum uplift permitted is 100 per cent. The scheme, which became available in 1995, was originally limited to cases involving personal injury, insolvency and the European Court of Human Rights. However, in 1998 conditional fee arrangements were extended to all civil cases, other than family proceedings. The Access to Justice Act 1999 made a number of changes to the scheme. It allows the uplift payable in successful cases to be recovered from the losing side and for the cost of any insurance premiums to be similarly recoverable. Conditional fee arrangements are now an important method of funding civil actions, particularly as the Access to Justice Act 1999 removed personal injury cases (with the exception of clinical negligence) from eligibility for legal aid.

There is a range of voluntary organisations which provide legal advice and assistance to private individuals. Citizens' Advice Bureaux provide free advice on many legal matters including housing, social security entitlement, consumer complaints and employment rights. Some inner-city areas are served by law centres. Law centres are staffed by lawyers and tend to provide more specialised advice and assistance on social welfare matters, including immigration, landlord and tenant, debt and social security benefits. There are also specialised advice centres available in the areas of housing and consumer problems. Over time the Community Legal Service will develop its role in co-ordinating the activities of these organisations with the aim of ensuring a comprehensive system of advice and other legal services to match local needs.

Trade unions often offer free legal advice and assistance on employment matters to their members. Legal advice and assistance may form part of a person's insurance cover. Motoring organisations, such as the AA and RAC, provide legal advice and help for their members.

METHODS OF DISPUTE SETTLEMENT: THE COURTS

The courts are the focal point of our legal system. They provide a formal setting for the final settlement of many of the disputes that occur in our society. The conflict may be between individuals or, where a breach of the criminal law has been alleged, between the state and one of its citizens. It is the function of the court to establish the facts of the case, identify the legal rules to be applied and to formulate a solution. The decision of the court not only has an immediate impact on the parties concerned, but it also affects similar cases which may arise in the future as a result of the operation of the doctrine of judicial precedent. Our present-day system of courts and tribunals can be classified in a number of different ways:

1 **Civil and criminal courts.** Some courts deal exclusively with either civil or criminal matters, but the majority hear both civil and criminal cases, e.g. magistrates' courts.

2 **First instance and appeal courts.** A court which hears a case for the first time is known as a court of first instance or a court of original jurisdiction. These courts can make mistakes, so there is provision for cases to be reheard by an appeal court. Some courts hear cases both at first instance and on appeal, e.g. the High Court.

3 **Courts and tribunals.** In addition to the ordinary courts, Parliament has created a large number of special courts and tribunals to administer various aspects of social and welfare legislation. Social Security Appeal Tribunals, for example, deal with disputed claims to income support.

In this part of the chapter we will consider an outline of the existing criminal and civil court systems. We will also briefly explain the role of tribunals, arbitration, conciliation, mediation and ombudsmen as means of resolving disputes.

Classification of criminal offences

If a person is charged with a criminal offence, he will be tried by either the magistrates' court or Crown Court. Cases are distributed between these two courts according to principles laid down in the Magistrates' Courts Act 1980. The seriousness of the offence determines the kind of trial a person receives. Minor offences, for example most motoring offences, are tried summarily in the magistrates' court, while more serious offences, such as murder and robbery, are tried on indictment by a judge and jury in the Crown Court. The system of appeals from the decisions of these two courts is illustrated in Fig 3.1 (less serious offences) and Fig 3.2 (more serious offences).

CRIMINAL COURTS

Magistrates' courts

Magistrates' courts have been part of the legal scene for over 600 years. Today their importance lies in the fact that magistrates' courts handle over 95 per cent of all criminal cases. There are two kinds of magistrate, or justices of the peace, as they are also known. There are over 30,000 part-time, unpaid amateur judges, known as lay magistrates. They are appointed by the Lord Chancellor on the recommendation of local committees from among the 'great and good' of a local community. (In Greater Manchester, Lancashire and Merseyside, appointments are made by the Chancellor of the Duchy of Lancaster.) Since legal knowledge is not a qualification for the position, a new magistrate must undergo an initial course of training. In court, the justices are given guidance on points of law by a legally qualified justices' clerk. A minimum of two lay magistrates is required to try a case, but usually three sit together. There are approximately 95 full-time, paid, professional district judges (magistrates' court), formerly known as stipendiary magistrates. District judges (magistrates' court) are appointed from persons having a seven-year general advocacy qualification within the meaning of the Courts and Legal Services Act 1990. (A person has a general advocacy qualification if he has a right of audience

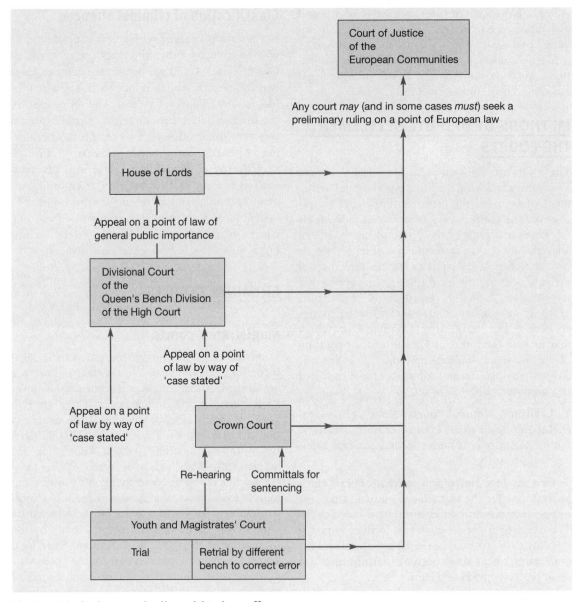

Fig 3.1 Criminal courts dealing with minor offences

in relation to any proceedings in the Supreme Court, or all proceedings in county courts or magistrates' courts.) They work in London and other big cities, such as Birmingham and Manchester, and sit alone to try a case.

The appointment and removal of magistrates and the organisation and management of the Magistrates' Courts Service is governed by the Justices of the Peace Act 1997.

Jurisdiction

As well as their civil jurisdiction, which will be discussed later in this chapter, the magistrates deal with the following criminal matters.

1 Trial of minor offences. The magistrates are responsible for deciding both the verdict and the sentence. Their sentencing powers are limited to six months' imprisonment or a £5,000 fine in

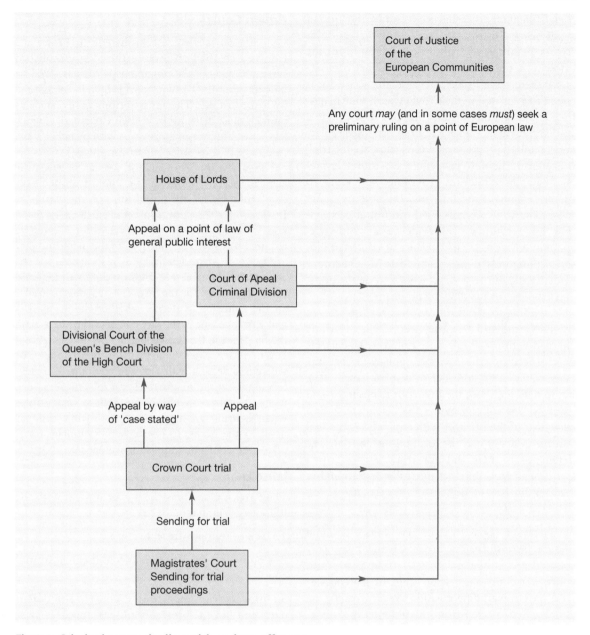

Fig 3.2 Criminal courts dealing with serious offences

respect of any one offence. The maximum sentence they can impose is 12 months' imprisonment, where a person is convicted of two or more offences. However, in some cases they have the power to send a convicted person to the Crown Court for sentencing.

Under the Magistrates' Courts Act 1980, as amended by the Criminal Appeals Act 1995, the magistrates have the power to rectify an error by means of a retrial by a different bench.

2 Sending for trial and committal proceedings. Traditionally, a person could not be tried by the Crown Court unless the evidence had been examined by the magistrates' court to see whether the prosecution has a good enough case to justify a

trial. Committal proceedings either took the form of a full hearing of the evidence, known as an 'old-style' committal, or without consideration of the evidence, a procedure known as a 'paper committal'. If there was a *prima facie* case, the accused was committed for trial in the Crown Court. One magistrate could sit alone for this purpose. The Criminal Justice and Public Order Act 1994 proposed replacing committal proceedings with a 'transfer for trial' procedure. The new procedure was never implemented and the relevant provisions were repealed by the Criminal Procedure and Investigations Act 1996. The 1996 Act modified committal proceedings by excluding oral evidence at 'old-style' committal hearings. The evidence at contested old-style committals is now limited to documentary evidence, i.e. written statements and depositions, and exhibits presented by the prosecution.

A 'sending for trial procedure' was introduced by the Crime and Disorder Act 1998 for adults charged with indictable only offences. Under this new procedure, the accused appears before the magistrates' court in order to resolve issues relating to bail, legal aid, the taking of depositions and exhibits. The court provides the defendant with a statement of the offences with which he is charged and the evidence and the location of the trial. The defendant is then sent for trial at the Crown Court. The procedure became fully operational in January 2001 on a pilot basis in selected areas.

3   Youth courts. If a child (aged 10 to 13) or young person (aged 14 to 17) commits a criminal offence, he or she can be brought before a specially selected group of magistrates sitting as a youth court. The court has a wide range of sentences at its disposal, including custodial measures. Young people are protected from the potentially damaging effects of a court appearance in a number of ways. The less formal proceedings must be held separately from an adult court, the public is not admitted and there are strict controls on what the press can report.

4 Criminal administration. Magistrates issue summonses, warrants of arrest and search, and they grant bail to people awaiting trial.

Crown Courts

Crown Courts were established in 1972 by the Courts Act 1971 to replace the long established system of quarter sessions and assize courts. Trial on indictment in the Crown Court is by a judge assisted by a jury of 12. The most serious cases, such as murder, must be heard by a High Court judge, while less serious matters may be dealt with by either a circuit judge or a recorder (a part-time judge).

The jury comprises men and women between the ages of 18 and 70, drawn at random from the electoral roll. Under the provisions of the Criminal Justice Act 1988, a person between the ages of 65 and 70 is eligible for jury service but cannot be required to serve. The functions of the judge and jury are quite distinct. The judge is responsible for the conduct of the trial. He rules on points of law and sums up the case for the jury. The jury must consider all the evidence to decide whether the accused is guilty or innocent. If the jury convicts, the judge plays the final part in the proceedings by passing sentence.

When the Crown Court is hearing an appeal, or where it is dealing with a person committed for sentencing from the magistrates, there is no jury. The judge sits with between two and four lay magistrates when hearing an appeal but, following changes made by the Access to Justice Act 1999, magistrates no longer sit on committals for sentencing.

Jurisdiction

The Crown Court has the power to deal with the following criminal matters:

1 Trial of serious offences.

2 Committals for sentencing from the magistrates' courts.

3 Appeals from magistrates' courts. The defendant (but not the prosecution) may appeal against conviction and/or sentence. The appeal takes the form of a complete rehearing of the case. The Crown Court can confirm or reverse or vary the decision of the magistrates or return the case to them with an expression of its opinion. The court can impose any sentence which the magistrates' court could have passed. This means that the defendant faces the danger that he may receive a more severe sentence on appeal.

High Court

The High Court is split into three divisions: Queen's Bench, Family and Chancery. In the past when the court was hearing an appeal or, in the case of the Queen's Bench Division, exercising its supervisory jurisdiction, a minimum of two High Court judges sat together and it became known as a 'Divisional Court'. Under the Access to Justice Act 1999, however, a single judge of the High Court will now be able to hear judicial review applications, appeals by way of case stated and applications for *habeas corpus* in criminal cases, which were previously only heard by a Divisional Court.

Jurisdiction

The jurisdiction of the High Court in criminal matters is as follows:

1 **Appeals from magistrates' courts.** An appeal may be made by way of 'case stated' by either the prosecution or the defence, but only on a point of law. This form of appeal requires the magistrates to provide a 'case' for the opinion of the High Court. The 'case' consists of a statement containing the magistrates' findings of fact, the arguments put forward by the parties, the decision and the reasons for it. The Divisional Court has the power to confirm, reverse or amend the decision of the magistrates' court or it can send the case back with an expression of its opinion.

2 **Appeals from Crown Court.** The Divisional Court also hears appeals by way of case stated from the Crown Court, in respect of all criminal cases dealt with by that court.

3 **Judicial review.** The Divisional Court of the Queen's Bench plays an important role in monitoring abuse of power when it deals with applications for judicial review. As part of this general supervisory power, it can quash the decision of a magistrates' court which has exceeded its powers or failed to observe the rules of natural justice.

Court of Appeal (Criminal Division)

The Court of Appeal consists of two Divisions. The Criminal Division is composed of the Lord Chief Justice, a maximum of 35 Lords Justices of Appeal and any High Court judge who is asked to sit. Normally, three judges sit to hear a case, but if a difficult or important point of law is involved, a court of five or seven may be convened.

Jurisdiction

The Court of Appeal deals with the following criminal cases:

1 **Appeals from trials on indictment in the Crown Court.** The defence (but not the prosecution) may appeal against the conviction and/or sentence. In an appeal against conviction, the court may confirm or quash the conviction or order a new trial. Where there is an appeal against the sentence, the court may confirm or reduce the sentence or substitute one form of sentence for another.

2 **References by the Attorney-General.** There are two kinds of reference which may be made by the Attorney-General. The first is where a person has been acquitted following trial on indictment in the Crown Court. The Attorney-General may refer any point of law which has arisen in the case to the Court of Appeal for its opinion. The decision of the court does not affect the outcome of the original trial. The second kind of reference is where a person has been sentenced by the Crown Court but the Attorney-General considers the sentence to be unduly lenient. The Court of Appeal may impose any sentence which the Crown Court could have imposed. Thus, the defendant could be dealt with more severely by the Court of Appeal.

3 **References by the Criminal Cases Review Commission.** The Criminal Appeals Act 1995 established an independent body to investigate and, where appropriate, refer to the Court of Appeal cases involving possible wrongful conviction or sentence. The Criminal Cases Review Commission, which started work in April 1997, consists of 14 Commissioners. One-third of the commissioners must be legally qualified and the remaining two-thirds must have knowledge of some aspect of the criminal justice system. The Commission may only refer a case to the Court of Appeal if a new issue by way of argument or evidence is raised and there is a 'real possibility' that the conviction, verdict, finding or sentence will not be upheld.

House of Lords

The House of Lords is not only the second chamber of our Parliament, but also acts as a final court of appeal in both civil and criminal matters for both England and Northern Ireland, and in civil matters for Scotland. The judges are drawn from the Lord Chancellor, Lords of Appeal in Ordinary (Law Lords) and peers who have held or are holding high judicial office. A minimum of three is required, but in practice five normally sit to hear an appeal. Decisions are by majority judgment.

Jurisdiction

The House of Lords hears the following criminal appeals:

1 Appeals from the Court of Appeal (Criminal Division).

2 Appeals from the Divisional Court of the Queen's Bench Division. In both cases, either the prosecution or defence may appeal, provided a point of law of general public importance is involved. Permission must be obtained from the House of Lords or the Court of Appeal or the Divisional Court, as appropriate.

Criminal courts review

In December 1999, Lord Justice Auld, a senior Court of Appeal judge, was appointed to undertake a review of the criminal courts. The terms of reference of the review included:

- the structure and organisation of, and distribution of work between, courts;
- the composition of the courts, including the use of juries and magistrates;
- case management, procedure and evidence, including the using of information technology;
- service to, and treatment of, those using or attending the courts;
- liaison between the courts and other agencies within the criminal justice system;
- management and funding of the system;
- the organisation and procedures of the Court of Appeal Criminal Division.

CIVIL COURTS

Reform of civil litigation

In 1994 the then Lord Chancellor, Lord MacKay, invited Lord Woolf to undertake a review of the rules and procedures of the civil courts in England and Wales. Lord Woolf produced an interim report in 1995 and his final report, Access to Justice, in July 1996. Lord Woolf identified the following problems with the civil justice system:

- a lack of equality between wealthy powerful litigants and their under-resourced opponents;
- the system was too expensive, the costs of bringing a case often exceeding the value of the claim;
- it was difficult to estimate how long the litigation would last and how much it would cost;
- the system was very slow;
- civil procedure was too complicated;
- the system was fragmented; no one had overall responsibility for the administration of civil justice;
- the system was too adversarial; the parties set the pace of litigation, rather than the courts.

Some of the proposals in Lord Woolf's interim report were implemented before the publication of the final report. The financial limit for small claims cases was increased from £ 1,000 to £3.000 (except for personal injury cases), from January 1996 (since then the limit has been raised again to £5,000). The Vice-Chancellor of the Chancery Division, Sir Richard Scott, was appointed the Head of Civil Justice in January 1996.

The main changes recommended in Lord Woolf's final report were given effect by the Civil Procedure Act 1997 and new Civil Procedure Rules, which came into effect in 1 April 1999. The main changes are as follows:

1 New terminology. The new rules are expressed in more modern language – sometimes referred to as 'Woolfspeak'. For example, 'plaintiffs' are now known as 'claimants', and 'writs' are called 'claim forms'. A summary of some of the more important changes to legal terminology is set out in Fig 3.3.

2 Encouraging settlement. The new rules contain a number of features which are designed to encourage the parties to settle their dispute.

Civil justice reforms – a new language	
Old term	*New term*
Plaintiff	Claimant
Writ, originating summons, petition	Claim form
Pleading (the reason for the claim)	Statement of case
Minor/infant (person under the age of 18)	Child
Affidavit	Statement of truth
In chambers or in camera	In private
Ex parte	Without notice
Subpoena	Witness summons
Discovery (of documents)	Disclosure
Anton Piller orders (a pre-trial order empowering a plaintiff to enter the defendant's property to search for and seize documents and articles relating to the cause of action)	Search orders
Interlocutory injunction	Interim injunction
Mareva injunction (granted by a court to prevent the defendant transferring assets abroad)	Freezing injunction
Next friend (adult who acts on behalf of child in litigation)	Litigation friend

Fig 3.3 New terminology following the Woolf reforms

(a) *Alternative dispute resolution (ADR).* The parties will be actively encouraged at various stages to use ADR (see later).

(b) *Pre-action protocols.* Cases will be managed in accordance with pre-action protocols, which operate like codes of practice, with which the parties must comply at the pre-trial stage. The protocols include timetables for the exchange of information and use of expert witnesses, e.g. the parties will be encouraged to instruct a single expert witness, rather than each side mustering their own expert witnesses. The effect of the protocols is that there will be more work, and costs, which must be paid for up front.

(c) *Costs and payments into court.* The judge now has greater discretion about the award of costs. The criteria to be considered include the conduct of the parties at the pre-trial stage, whether it was reasonable to raise a particular issue and the way in which the parties have pursued their cases. It has always been the case that the defendant can make a payment into court so as to reduce costs if the claimant's award does not exceed the amount paid in. It is now possible for the claimant to make an offer to settle with a similar effect on the matter of costs.

3 A single jurisdiction. The High Court and county courts become a single jurisdiction operating to a common set of procedural rules. Proceedings are commenced in the same way in any court. Cases are then allocated to the most appropriate court.

4 Case management. Cases will be allocated to one of three tracks, depending on their value and complexity.

(a) A *fast track* for claims between £5,000 and £15,000. These cases will be heard by the county court within 30 weeks. The judge will set a timetable to ensure that the case can be tried on time. The normal hearing time will be three hours but with an absolute maximum of one day.

(b) A *small claims track* for all cases up to £5,000, except personal injury and housing cases, where the limit is £1,000. These cases will be dealt with.

(c) A *multi-track* for all claims over £15,000 and for complex cases of less than £15,000. Judges will manage the cases, setting and monitoring the timetable to be followed by the parties. Estimates of the costs will be published by the court or agreed by the parties and approved by the court. The High Court will deal with multi-track cases.

Appeals – Access to Justice Act 1999

The Access to Justice Act 1999 makes provision for reform of the system of appeals in civil and family cases. The main changes in relation to civil appeals are as follows:

- Provision for permission to be required to exercise a right of appeal in civil cases at all levels.
- Limits to the right to bring a second appeal, unless the appeal would raise an important point of principle or practice, or there is some other compelling reason.
- Giving the Lord Chancellor power to prescribe the routes of appeal within county courts, the High Court and the Civil Division of the Court of Appeal. The following appeal routes have now been prescribed:

(a) appeals from county courts other than in family proceedings will lie to the High Court;

(b) appeals from the decisions of masters, registrars and district judges of the High Court will lie to a judge of the High Court;

(c) appeals from district judges in county courts will lie to a judge of a county court;

(d) in multi-track proceedings, appeals of final orders or where the decision itself was made on appeal, the appeal will lie to the Court of Appeal irrespective of who heard the case in the first place.

- Provision for the Master of the Rolls or a lower court to direct that an appeal which would normally be heard by either the county court or the High Court should instead be heard by the Court of Appeal.

The structure of the civil courts is set out in Fig 3.4.

County courts

County courts were established in 1846 to provide a cheap and speedy method for the settlement of small civil disputes. Today, the vast majority of civil proceedings are dealt with by these local courts.

The county courts are staffed by circuit judges. They usually sit alone to hear a case, but a jury of eight may be called where, for example, fraud has been alleged. The judge is assisted by a district judge, appointed from persons having a seven-year advocacy qualification within the meaning of the Courts and Legal Services Act 1990. He also has limited jurisdiction to try cases where the claim does not exceed £5,000 or, with the consent of both of the parties, any action within the general jurisdiction of the court.

Jurisdiction

The jurisdiction of the county courts is governed by the County Courts Act 1984, the Courts and Legal Services Act 1990, the Civil Procedure Act 1997 and the Civil Procedure Rules. The types of action which the court can deal with are as follows:

1 *Actions in contract and tort* (including defamation if the parties agree). The county court deals with all small claims track and fast track actions, and some multi-track cases.

2 *Actions for the recovery of land* or concerning title or rights over land.

3 *Actions in equity* where the amount involved does not exceed £30.000. This category includes proceedings involving mortgages and trusts.

4 *Bankruptcies*. The jurisdiction is unlimited in amount, but not all county courts have bankruptcy jurisdiction.

5 *Company winding-ups* where the paid-up share capital of the company does not exceed £120,000. The court must have a bankruptcy jurisdiction.

6 *Contested probate proceedings* where the amount of the deceased person's estate does not exceed £30,000.

7 *Family matters*, e.g. undefended divorce. The court must have divorce jurisdiction. The jurisdiction of the courts in respect of the financial maintenance of children whose parents live apart is being phased out with responsibility for such matters being transferred to the Child Support Agency.

8 *Consumer credit*, landlord and tenant, and racial discrimination cases.

9 *Patents*. Following the recommendation of the Oulton Committee, the Copyright, Designs and Patents Act 1988 made provision for the establishment of a patents county court with countrywide jurisdiction to deal with cases relating to patents and designs.

Actions which exceed the limits of the county court are normally heard by the High Court. However, the parties may agree to such an action being dealt with by the lower court.

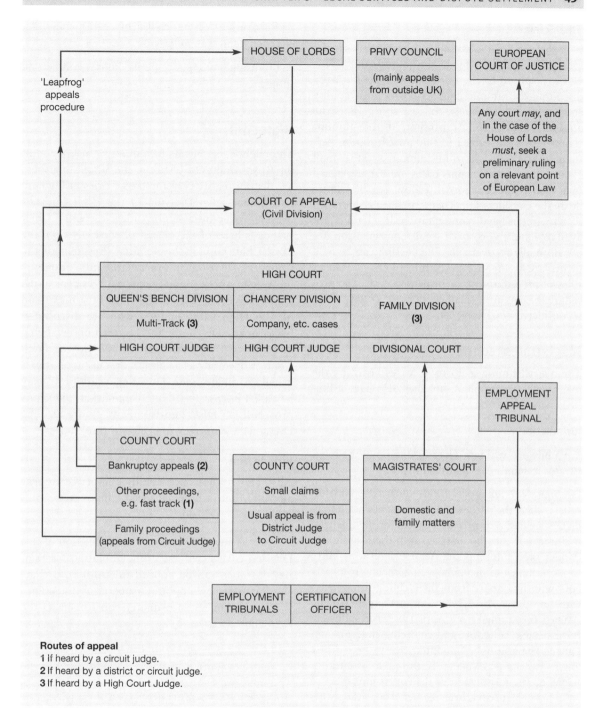

Routes of appeal

1 If heard by a circuit judge.

2 If heard by a district or circuit judge.

3 If heard by a High Court Judge.

Fig 3.4 **System of courts exercising civil jurisdiction**

Small claims

In 1973, the Lord Chancellor introduced a special scheme for small claims in the county court. This was a response to the criticism that people were discouraged from pursuing actions because county court justice was likely to cost more than the amount in dispute. At present, if the amount claimed does not exceed £5,000 (or £1,000 for personal injury), the case will be allocated to the small claims track. Small claims cases are usually heard by a district judge who will follow any procedure he or she considers fair. The parties are encouraged to do without legal representation: legal aid is not available and the costs of legal representation are not normally recoverable. The hearing can be held in private in an informal atmosphere and strict rules of procedure can be dispensed with. The procedure for making a small claim in the county court is considered in Chapter 14.

Magistrates' courts

The overwhelming majority of cases heard by the magistrates are criminal, but they also have a limited civil jurisdiction.

Jurisdiction

1 Family proceedings. The jurisdiction of the magistrates in family law matters includes:

(a) *matrimonial proceedings*, such as separation orders where the parties to a marriage are not immediately seeking a divorce and orders for the financial maintenance of the parties and their children. (Under the Child Support Act 1991 responsibility for securing child maintenance payments from parents who live apart from their children has been transferred to the Child Support Agency. The Agency, operational from April 1993, is responsible for assessing, collecting and enforcing child maintenance. The amount of maintenance to be paid by absent parents is calculated according to a statutory formula. The jurisdiction of the courts in respect of child maintenance has been restricted accordingly.);

(b) *child care proceedings*, including the power to make contact orders (replacing access orders) and residence orders (replacing custody orders);

(c) *care proceedings*, whereby a child can be taken into the care of a local authority.

2 Recovery of certain civil debts, e.g. income tax, electricity and water charges.

3 Licensing matters, e.g. public houses and betting shops.

High Court

The High Court has its headquarters in London at the Royal Courts of Justice in the Strand, but there are district registries in the larger cities in England and Wales. Each Division of the High Court is presided over by a senior judge: the Lord Chief Justice is head of the Queen's Bench Division; the Lord Chancellor is the nominal President of the Chancery Division (in practice the job is done by the Vice-Chancellor); and there is a President of the Family Division. They are assisted by a maximum of 106 High Court judges, who are distributed between the Divisions, the largest number being attached to the Queen's Bench. When the High Court is operating as a court of first instance, trial is usually by judge alone. However, a jury of 12 may be called in cases involving defamation, malicious prosecution, false imprisonment or fraud. The Divisional Courts consist of two or three judges.

Jurisdiction

All three Divisions are equally competent to hear any case, but in practice specific matters are allocated to each Division.

1 Queen's Bench Division. The jurisdiction of this Division covers civil and criminal matters, cases at first instance and on appeal. In addition, it exercises an extremely important supervisory function.

When sitting as an ordinary court, it hears the following cases:

(a) *Actions in contract and tort*. The High Court will normally deal with cases allocated to the multi-track procedure.
(b) *Judicial review*. Under the Access to Justice Act 1999, judicial review applications may now be heard by a single judge sitting alone.
(c) A *Commercial Court* deals with disputes concerning insurance, banking and the interpretation of commercial documents.

(d) An *Admiralty Court* deals with admiralty actions arising out of, for example, collisions at sea and salvage.

(e) A *Technology and Construction Court* (formerly known as the Official Referee's Court) deals with cases involving technical issues, such as construction and engineering disputes.

The Divisional Court of the Queen's Bench Division hears the following matters:

(a) *Civil appeals* (other than in matrimonial proceedings) by way of case stated from the magistrates' court and from the Crown Court.

(b) *Judicial review* of the actions of inferior courts, tribunals and administrative bodies. For this purpose, the court may make orders of **mandamus, prohibition** and *certiorari*. If someone has been unlawfully detained, for example in a mental hospital, he or she may apply to the Divisional Court for a writ of *habeas corpus*.

2 Chancery Division. The Chancery Division hears the following actions:

(a) *Equity matters*, which were dealt with by the old Court of Chancery before 1875 and other cases allocated to it since then. These include actions involving trusts, mortgages, partnerships, specific performance of contracts, rectification of deeds, companies, bankruptcies and taxation.

(b) A *Court of Protection* deals with actions involving the management of the property and affairs of mental patients.

(c) A *Patents Court* deals with patents and related matters outside the jurisdiction of the patents county court.

(d) *Appeals from the Commissioners of Inland Revenue* on income tax matters.

The Divisional Court of the Chancery Division hears appeals from the county courts in bankruptcy matters.

3 Family Division. The first-instance jurisdiction of the Family Division includes:

(a) *Matrimonial matters*, e.g. defended divorces.

(b) *Actions involving children*, e.g. adoption and legitimacy.

The Divisional Court of the Family Division hears appeals from magistrates' courts and county courts in matters relating to the family.

Crown Court

Like the magistrates' court, the Crown Court is mainly a criminal court, but it too has a civil jurisdiction, hearing appeals from the magistrates in affiliation and licensing matters.

Court of Appeal (Civil Division)

The Civil Division of the Court of Appeal is headed by the Master of the Rolls, who is assisted by the Lord Justices of Appeal. Normally three judges sit to hear an appeal, although in important cases a full court of five may be assembled. The decisions are made by a simple majority. Since 1982, some cases have been heard by two judges, in an attempt to reduce the waiting time for hearings. Under the Access to Justice Act 1999, the Master of the Rolls, with the agreement of the Lord Chancellor, is allowed to give directions about the minimum number of judges required for various types of proceedings, and the Master of The Rolls will be able to decide how many judges should hear any particular appeal. The Civil Division of the Court of Appeal now has much greater flexibility in its operation by being able to operate in courts of one, two or more judges.

Jurisdiction

The court hears appeals from the High Court, county courts (except in bankruptcy cases) and various tribunals, such as the Lands Tribunal and the Employment Appeal Tribunal. It may uphold or reverse the decision of the lower court, or change the award of damages. In certain situations, it may order a new trial.

House of Lords

The House of Lords is the final court of appeal in civil matters. Its composition was discussed earlier in this chapter.

Jurisdiction

The Law Lords hear civil appeals from the following sources:

1 **The Court of Appeal**, with the permission of the Court of Appeal or the House of Lords.

2 **The High Court**, under the 'leapfrog' procedure introduced by the Administration of Justice Act 1969. This form of appeal goes straight to the House of Lords, 'leapfrogging' the Court of Appeal. The trial judge must certify that the case is suitable for an appeal direct to the House of Lords because it involves a point of law of general public importance relating wholly or mainly to a statute or statutory instrument (often concerned with taxation); the House must grant leave to appeal and the parties must consent.

OTHER IMPORTANT COURTS

Court of Justice of the European Community

On joining the European Community in 1973, the United Kingdom agreed to accept the rulings of the European Court of Justice in matters of European law (see further Chapter 2). The House of Lords continues to be the final court of appeal in respect of purely domestic law, but where a dispute has a European element, any English court or tribunal may (and in some cases must) seek the opinion of the European Court in Luxembourg on the point of European law in question.

Judicial Committee of the Privy Council

The Judicial Committee of the Privy Council is not a formal part of our court structure, yet it has had a considerable influence on the development of English law. The Committee advises the Queen on criminal and civil appeals from the Isle of Man, the Channel Islands, British Colonies and Protectorates and from certain independent Commonwealth countries. The Committee's decisions are very influential because cases are usually heard by the Lord Chancellor and Lords of Appeal in Ordinary with the addition of senior Commonwealth judges, where appropriate.

European Court of Human Rights

The European Court of Human Rights, which sits at Strasbourg, deals with claims that the European Convention on Human Rights has been breached. Cases may be brought either by individuals, provided that the relevant state has accepted the right to bring an individual petition, or by one state against another.

The European Court of Human Rights comprises 21 judges, one from each state which has ratified the Convention. Cases are usually heard by seven judges sitting together.

The decisions of the Court are binding on governments in international law but do not bind UK courts. However, UK courts must take the judgments of the Court of Human Rights into account when deciding a question in relation to a Convention right, following the incorporation of the European Convention on Human Rights into UK law by the Human Rights Act 1998.

TRIBUNALS

The work of the ordinary courts is supplemented by a large number of tribunals set up by Act of Parliament to hear and decide upon disputes in specialised areas. As the lives of ordinary people have been affected more and more by the activities of government, particularly since the advent of the welfare state, so there has been a considerable growth in the number and jurisdiction of tribunals. They deal with a wide range of subjects, such as social security, employment and mental health. The attraction of tribunals is that they operate cheaply and quickly with a minimum of formalities. Although the chairman is usually legally qualified, other members are drawn from non-legal experts in the subject under consideration. Legal representation is discouraged as generally legal aid is not available and costs are not awarded. The work of tribunals is subject to scrutiny by the courts. An appeal from the decision of a tribunal can normally be made to the ordinary courts on a point of law but not on the facts. The Divisional Court of the Queen's Bench Division ensures that a tribunal acts fairly, according to its powers.

One of the best known tribunals is the employment tribunal (formerly known as the industrial tribunal). When it was established in 1964, it had a very limited jurisdiction, but now it is one of the busiest tribunals. It sits locally to hear complaints by employees about contracts of employment; unfair dismissal; redundancy; sex, race and disability discrimination in employment; and equal pay. Since 1994 employment tribunals have also been able to hear claims for breach of a contract of employment where the amount claimed does not exceed £25,000. The breach must arise from or be outstanding at the termination of the employment. Previously these claims could only be heard in the ordinary courts. Personal injury claims and claims relating to living accommodation, intellectual property and restraint of trade are not included in the transfer of jurisdiction and will continue to be heard in the civil courts. The tribunal normally consists of a legally qualified chairman aided by two lay members, one representing employers and the other representing employees. However, changes introduced in 1993 enabled employment tribunal chairmen to sit alone to hear certain cases. The proceedings are fairly informal, especially as the strict rules of evidence are relaxed. Employees may receive 'legal help' from the Community Legal Service Fund to help them prepare for the hearing by, e.g., drafting documents. Legal aid to cover the cost of representation at the tribunal hearing is not available, although applicants can be represented by a trade union official or a friend. Normally each side pays its own costs. The tribunal's powers include being able to make awards of compensation totalling thousands of pounds. An appeal lies to the Employment Appeal Tribunal and from there to the Court of Appeal. The Employment Rights (Dispute Resolution) Act 1998 introduced changes to the law relating to the resolution of individual employment rights disputes.

In May 2000 the Lord Chancellor appointed Sir Andrew Leggatt to undertake a review of the tribunal system and to report by 31 March 2001.

ALTERNATIVE DISPUTE RESOLUTION

In recent years, potential litigants have been encouraged to resolve their differences without resorting to formal legal action in the courts. Mechanisms of alternative dispute resolution (ADR) include arbitration, conciliation and mediation.

Arbitration

A court appearance can be a very costly and public way of resolving a dispute. Many in the commercial world seek to avoid the possibility by agreeing at the outset that any dispute will be referred to arbitration. Such clauses are often contained in contracts of insurance and partnership. Arbitration schemes have also been set up by trade bodies, such as the Association of British Travel Agents, to deal with complaints involving their members. Arbitration allows the parties to present their arguments to an arbitrator of their choice, in private and at their own convenience. The arbitrator may be legally qualified but usually he has special knowledge or experience of the subject matter. Both sides agree to be bound by the decision of the arbitrator, which can be enforced as if it were the judgment of a court.

The Arbitration Act 1996 now provides a comprehensive statutory framework for the conduct of arbitration.

Conciliation

In this chapter we have examined formal methods of settling disputes by means of legal action in a court or tribunal. In practice, only a relatively small number of disputes are resolved in this way. The vast majority are settled by more informal means before they reach the door of the court. There are many good reasons why the parties may prefer an 'out-of-court' compromise to courtroom conflict: e.g. fear of spoiling an otherwise satisfactory relationship, the cost of legal action, the amount of money at stake, difficulty in predicting the outcome of the case, the likelihood of bad publicity. The drawbacks of pursuing a court action act as a powerful incentive for the parties to settle out of court. In some cases, however, the initiative for a settlement comes not from the parties themselves, but from an outside agency; for example, the Advisory, Conciliation and Arbitration Service (ACAS) tries to resolve both collective and individual disputes between employers and employees by means of conciliation. ACAS receives a copy of all employment tribunal applications. A conciliation officer will then offer his services to the parties to help them reach a settlement. Many claims are settled at this stage with the parties avoiding the ordeal of a tribunal hearing.

Mediation

Another alternative to litigation in the civil courts is mediation. This form of alternative dispute resolution consists of using a neutral third party (mediator) to help the parties to a legal dispute to reach a common position. The advantages of mediation compared to litigation include reduced costs and a reduction in conflict, making it particularly suitable for divorce cases. Mediation was an important part of the reforms to divorce proceedings introduced by the Family Law Act 1996, although the results of trial schemes are reported to be disappointing.

OMBUDSMAN

The Swedish term 'ombudsman' describes an official or commissioner who acts as an independent referee between a citizen and his government and its administration. The first ombudsman to be appointed in the UK was the Parliamentary Commissioner for Administration (PCA) in 1967. The job of the PCA is to investigate complaints of maladministration by government departments and various other public bodies, such as the Charity Commission and the English Tourist Board. Maladministration means poor or failed administration and can include unreasonable delay, bias or unfairness, failure to follow proper procedures, mistakes in handling claims and discourtesy. The PCA will not normally deal with matters which could be resolved through a court or tribunal. Complaints can only be brought by someone with a specific interest in the matter, i.e. it affects him or the organisation to which he belongs, and should not relate to events more than 12 months old. The PCA can investigate complaints received directly from the public. The powers of the PCA are confined to conducting an investigation into a complaint and, if the complaint is justified, recommending a remedy. The PCA has no power to order a specific remedy and there is no right of appeal from the decisions of the PCA. The ombudsman method of dealing with complaints has found favour in many areas of official and commercial activity. Ombudsmen now operate in the following areas:

- local government;
- the health service;
- institutions of the European Community;
- prisons;
- legal services;
- building societies;
- pensions;
- banking;
- insurance;
- investment;
- estate agents.

QUESTIONS/ACTIVITIES

1. For each of the actions listed below state:
   - (a) Which court or tribunal would hear the case?
   - (b) What type of lawyer could represent the parties?
   - (c) Who would try the action?
   - (d) To which court or tribunal would an appeal lie?
     - (i) in a prosecution for murder;
     - (ii) in an undefended divorce;
     - (iii) in a claim for damages of £75,000 for negligence causing personal injury;
     - (iv) in an application for a late extension by the licensee of a public house;
     - (v) in a claim by an employee that he has been unfairly dismissed;
     - (vi) in a bankruptcy petition where the debts are £20,000;
     - (vii) in a claim by a resident that his local authority has failed to produce accounts for public inspection as required by law;
     - (viii) in a claim for damages of £200 for breach of contract;
     - (ix) in an application by a social services department to take a child into care.

2. What part do laymen take in the administration of the legal system? Should they be replaced by professionals?

3. Our legal system often allows for two levels of appeal. Is this a wasteful use of resources?

4. What are the advantages and disadvantages of using tribunals rather than the ordinary courts to decide disputes?

5. What alternatives to litigation in the ordinary courts are available? What are the advantages and disadvantages of these alternative methods of dispute resolution compared to litigation in the courts?

Part 2

BUSINESS ORGANISATIONS

Chapter 4

CLASSIFICATION AND SURVEY OF TYPES OF BUSINESS ORGANISATION

CLASSIFICATION OF BUSINESS ORGANISATIONS

The private sector

A business can be run in what is called the private sector of commerce and industry through any one of three types of business organisation. These are given below.

The sole trader

This means going it alone with a one-person business. You can take all the profits of the business but suffer all its losses and have all the problems and worries.

The partnership

You can share the losses (if any) and the problems and worries with a partner or partners but of course the profits must also be shared. It is normally necessary for the partners to make a contract called a partnership agreement which is often in writing because it then provides a good record of what was agreed about the business. However, writing is not necessary; a verbal agreement will do and, indeed, a partnership can in some cases be inferred from conduct. For example, if A acts as if he were the partner of B he may become one in law, at least to a creditor who has relied on the apparent situation, even though there is no contract, verbal or written, between them. Partnership by estoppel, as it is called, and other forms of non-contractual partnership are more fully explained in Chapter 5.

The company

A business may be incorporated as a **registered company**. This is created by following a registration procedure carried out through the Registrar of Companies in Cardiff. He is an official of a government department called the Department of Trade and Industry.

A registered company can be formed by two or more people who become its shareholders. Directors must be appointed to manage the company and act as its agents. A company secretary must also be appointed either from the shareholders or from among those advising the business, such as an accountant (provided he is not also the company's auditor, who cannot hold an office of profit within the company) or solicitor. Since the implementation of an EC directive by SI 1992/1699, a private company limited by shares or guarantee may be formed with one member only or allow its membership to fall to one. This and its ramifications are explained in Chapter 6.

If the business is large enough an appointment as company secretary may be made after public advertisement of the post. No special qualifications are required for secretaries of private companies but qualifications are laid down for secretaries of public companies. These are explained in Chapter 6.

In the past trading companies were incorporated by **Royal Charter**. However, incorporation by registration was set up in 1844 by the Joint Stock Companies Act of that year, and it is most unlikely that incorporation by Royal Charter would be used today to incorporate a commercial business. Charters are still used to incorporate certain organisations, such as professional bodies which control the professions, e.g. the Chartered Institute of Secretaries and Administrators, and for incorporating certain bodies in the public sector, such as the British Broadcasting Corporation.

As to how you get a charter, the organisation wanting one sends what is called a petition to the Privy Council. The Privy Council consists of members of the current Cabinet who become members of the Council when they first take office, former members of the Cabinet, and others appointed by the Queen on the recommendation of the Prime Minister as an honour for service in some branch of public affairs at home or overseas. There are also what are called *convential members* who become members by reason of holding another office, e.g. the Speaker of the House of Commons and the Lords of Appeal in Ordinary (the Law Lords). The petition asks for the grant of a charter and sets out the powers required. If the Privy Council considers that it is appropriate to grant a charter, the Crown will be advised to do so.

The public sector

At the end of the Second World War the then Labour government thought it right to bring into the public sector certain organisations providing goods or services to the public on a national basis with a complete or partial monopoly, e.g. the mining of coal. Public corporations were formed to manage these organisations. These organisations have now been returned to the private sector through the medium of public limited companies with shareholders. The commercial public corporations are for all practical purposes non-existent, though an example in the social services area is the Health and Safety Executive set up by the Health and Safety at Work Act 1974 to supervise and enforce health and safety through inspectors (see further, Chapter 16).

NATURAL AND JURISTIC PERSONS

Natural persons

These are human beings who are known to the law as natural persons. An adult human being has in general terms the full range of legal rights and a

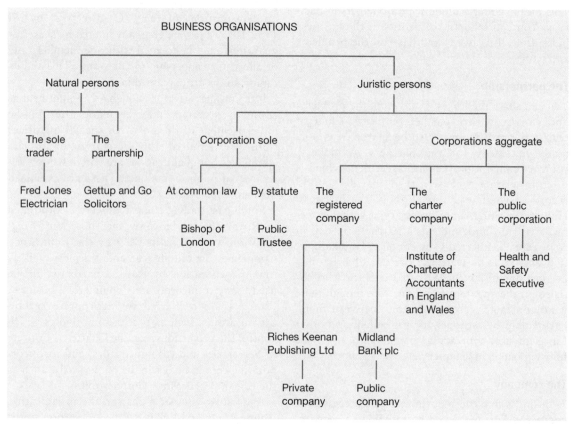

Fig 4.1 **Business organisations in terms of natural and juristic persons**

full range of legal duties. Thus, if A makes a contract with B and B fails to perform it, A has a right, e.g. to damages, because B failed to perform a duty. A similar situation would occur if A failed in his duty to perform the contract thus denying B his right to have it performed.

However, the law distinguishes between certain classes of human beings and gives them a **status** which means that they have more limited rights and duties than are given to other persons. Examples are minors (persons under the age of 18), and persons of unsound mind.

Some contracts of minors are not binding on them and they cannot be sued for damages for breach of contract if they fail to perform them. Persons of unsound mind can refuse to perform their contracts where the other party was aware of the mental state when the contract was made. These matters are more fully dealt with in Chapter 7.

Non-human creatures are not legal persons and do not have those rights and duties which a human being gets at birth. However, animals may be protected by the law for certain purposes, such as conservation. For example, s 9 of the Wildlife and Countryside Act 1981 protects certain wild animals by making it a criminal offence for a person intentionally to kill, injure or take any animal included in Sch 5 to that Act, e.g. bats.

Juristic persons

Legal personality is not given only to human beings. Persons can form a corporation, that corporation having a legal personality with similar rights and duties to human beings. As we have seen, these corporations are formed by Royal Charter, Act of Parliament, or by registration under the Companies Act 1985 or previous Acts. There are also corporations sole, which were introduced by lawyers under common law.

Charter companies and those formed by Act of Parliament have their own legal personalities and act through human agents. This is also true of the registered company, which is allowed by law through the agency of its directors to make contracts, hold property, and carry on business on its own account, regardless of the particular persons who may happen at the particular time to hold its shares.

Thus, if A and B form a registered company, AB Ltd, the separate legal personality of AB Ltd is created on formation. A and B can now, if as is likely they have been appointed as directors of the company, make contracts on behalf of AB Ltd as its agents. The rights and duties under those contracts will belong to AB Ltd and not to A and B as individuals. The rule of corporate personality is illustrated by the following.

Salomon v *Salomon & Co* (1897)

Mr Salomon carried on business as a leather merchant and boot manufacturer. In 1892 he formed a limited company to take over the business. Mr Salomon was the major shareholder. His wife, daughter and four sons were also shareholders. They had only one share each. The subscribers to the company's memorandum met and appointed Mr Salomon and his two elder sons directors and, therefore, agents of the company (see further Chapter 6). The company gave Mr Salomon 20,000 shares of £1 each in payment for the business and he said that a further £10,000 of the purchase price could be regarded as a loan to the company which it could repay later. Meantime the loan was secured on the assets of the company. This charge on the assets made Mr Salomon a secured creditor who, under the rules of company law, would get his money before unsecured (or trade) creditors if the company was wound up. The company fell on hard times and a liquidator was appointed. The assets were sufficient to pay off the debentures but in that event the trade creditors would receive nothing. The unsecured creditors claimed all the remaining assets on the ground that Mr Salomon and the company were one. Thus he could not lend money to himself or give himself a security over his own assets. Eventually, the House of Lords held that the company was a separate and distinct person. The loan and the security were valid transactions between separate individuals, i.e. Mr Salomon and the company, and therefore Mr Salomon was entitled to the remaining assets in payment of the secured loan.

Comment. The creditors of Mr Salomon's original business had been paid off. The unsecured creditors were creditors of the company and the House of Lords said that they must be deemed to know that they were dealing with a limited company whose members, provided they had paid for their shares in full, could not be obliged to meet its debts.

Looking behind the corporate personality

This idea of corporate personality can lead to abuse and where, for example, it has been used to avoid legal obligations, the courts have been prepared to ignore the separate personality of the company (or draw aside the corporate veil or curtain) and treat the business as if it was being run by its individual members. An illustration of this appears in the following case.

Gilford Motor Co Ltd v Horne (1933)

Mr Horne had been employed by Gilford. He had agreed to a restraint of trade in his contract under which he would not approach the company's customers to try to get them to transfer their custom to any similar business which Mr Horne might run himself.

Mr Horne left his job with Gilford and set up a similar business using a registered company structure. He then began to send out circulars to the customers of Gilford inviting them to do business with his company.

Gilford asked the court for an injunction to stop Mr Horne's activities and Horne said that he was not competing but his company was and that the company had not agreed to a restraint of trade. An injunction was granted against both Mr Horne and his company to stop the circularisation of Gilford's customers. The corporate structure could not be used by Mr Horne to evade his legal contractual duties.

Corporations sole

All the forms of corporation which have been discussed so far have one feature in common which is that they are corporations aggregate, having more than one member. However, English law also recognises the idea of the corporation sole which is a corporation having only one member.

A number of such corporations were created by the common lawyers in early times because they were concerned that land did not always have an owner and that there could be a break, however slight, in ownership.

Church lands, for example, were vested in the vicar of the particular area and at higher levels in other church dignitaries, such as the bishop of the diocese. When such persons died, the land had no legal owner until a successor was appointed to the job so the common lawyers created the concept of the corporation sole under which the office of vicar or bishop was a corporation and the present vicar or bishop the sole member of that corporation. The land was then transferred to the corporation and the death of the particular vicar or bishop had thereafter no effect on the landholding because the corporation did not die and

continued to own the land. The Bishop of London is a corporation sole and the present holder of the office is the sole member of the corporation. The Crown is also a corporation sole.

It does not seem likely that any further corporations of this sort will be created by the common law but they can still be created by Act of Parliament. For example, the Public Trustee Act 1906 sets up the office of Public Trustee as a corporation sole. The Public Trustee will act as an executor to administer a person's estate when that person dies, or as a trustee, to look after property for beneficiaries such as young children, and a lot of property is put into his ownership for the benefit of others from time to time. It would be very difficult to transfer all this property to the new holder of the office on the death or retirement of the civil servant who is in fact the Public Trustee. So the person who holds the office of Public Trustee is the sole member of a corporation called the Public Trustee and the property over which he has control is transferred to that corporation and not to the individual who is the holder of the office.

The Public Trust Office was abolished with effect from 1 April 2001. The function has been combined with that of the Official Solicitor, who is an officer of the Supreme Court and acts also for persons suffering a disability, such as mental incapacity. Apart from this change, the principles stated above remain valid.

SURVEY OF TYPES OF BUSINESS ORGANISATIONS: ADVANTAGES AND DISADVANTAGES

The major advantages and disadvantages of the various forms of business organisations in the private sector will now be looked at under the headings set out below.

COMMENCEMENT OF BUSINESS

Sole traders and partnerships

These organisations can commence business merely by opening the doors of the premises. It is usual to register for Value Added Tax, though this is not compulsory unless the turnover of the business is at registration level (currently £54,000 or more), and of course the premises which are being used must, under planning and other regulations, be available for business purposes. Planning requirements are considered later in this chapter.

If the organisation is not using the name of its proprietor(s), but using a business name, as where Freda Green trades as 'London Fashions' (the business name), or Fred and Freda Brown trade as 'Paris Fashions' (the business name), then the organisation must comply with the requirements of the Business Names Act 1985. This will be dealt with in more detail in later chapters, e.g. Chapter 5, but it contains provisions restricting the choice of the business name. For example, a name must not be chosen which suggests a connection with central and local government unless the Department of Trade and Industry consents. This is to prevent the public getting a possibly false sense of security because these government authorities get a regular and safe income from taxes and Council Tax and business rates. There are also requirements regarding disclosure of the name during the lifetime of the business.

Companies

A private company cannot trade until its application for registration has been dealt with by the Registrar of Companies and he has given the company a certificate of incorporation.

The Companies Act 1985 requires public companies to have an authorised and issued share capital of at least £50,000 in nominal value, of which at least one-quarter has been paid plus the whole of any premium. This is essential so that the company can trade and/or borrow.

If, therefore, a public company does have an authorised capital of £50,000 and the shares are £1 each but are sold for £1.50, that is at a premium of 50p, the company must have a paid-up share capital of £37,500 before it can trade and/or borrow.

All business is carried out in the name of the company which will normally register for VAT. The choice of the corporate name and a business name, if the company uses one, is controlled by the Companies Act 1985 and the Business Names Act 1985, and these Acts provide also for publicity to be given to the name. These matters will be dealt with in Chapter 6.

RAISING BUSINESS FINANCE – GENERALLY

Sole traders and partnerships

All businesses need money to begin trading: some kind of start-up finance. Sole traders must either put in enough of their own money if they have it or put in what they have and try to borrow the rest. Partners are in the same position. Certainly, a bank will not lend 100 per cent of the finance.

Usually the best place to try for a loan is one of the large banks. The bank will want some security for its money and this may mean giving the bank a mortgage on the house of the sole trader, or houses of the partners. It should be borne in mind that lenders such as banks will not advance the full market value of the property offered as a security. For example, a lender may lend up to, say, 70 per cent of the value of freehold land and buildings. The figures for borrowing are less than the asset value because of the impact on that value of the forced sale that takes place when a lender calls in the security, if the loan cannot be repaid.

Interest rates can differ according to the deal given by the bank. Interest may be variable and change with the base rate, as is the case where the bank allows the organisation to overdraw a bank account up to a certain amount. The alternative is a loan at a fixed rate of interest. These are usually more expensive but may be better than an overdraft facility if the loan is taken at a time of low interest rates.

A partnership can, of course, attract more capital by admitting new partners. There is, however, a limit to this because the Companies Act 1985 restricts a partnership to a maximum of 20 people; but some professions, e.g. accountants and solicitors, are exempt and can have partnerships of unlimited size.

Companies

Here the capital structure is more complicated. If two people wishing to form a private company and be its directors contribute £10,000 each to form the company, which has what is called a nominal (or authorised) capital of £40,000, each of the two members taking 20,000 shares of £1 each, then:

1 all the company's capital is **issued**;

2 the £20,000 cash received by the company is its **paid-up capital**;

3 the balance of £20,000 remaining is the **uncalled capital**. This can be called up for payment at any time in accordance with what is said in the company's articles as to the length of notice to be given.

A company may also raise money by borrowing, often from a bank, either by way of a loan at fixed interest or, more commonly, by the granting of an overdraft facility.

The lender does not become a member of the company and if the company falls on hard times and is wound up the lender, being a creditor, is entitled to recover his loan before the shareholders get anything for their shares.

A lending bank will take a security (called a debenture) over the company's assets for its loan and will usually ask the directors to give another security by guaranteeing the loan so that if the company does not repay it they will have to. This takes away some of the advantages of limited liability.

Once again, the bank will not advance the full value of the property offered as a security by the company for the reasons stated above.

There is no limit on the number of shareholders which a company may have and so it can raise as much capital as it wishes if it can sell its shares to outsiders. A public company can offer its shares to the public, but a private company must negotiate personally with outsiders who might buy its shares.

RAISING BUSINESS FINANCE – SECURITIES

We have already given some consideration to the methods of financing business organisations (see above). We have noted the advantage of forming a limited company because of the ability within the company structure to issue **share capital**. If required, share capital can be issued with a variety of different rights in terms, for example, of voting. It can be preference with a fixed dividend and/or ordinary on which dividend will be paid only if and when distributable profits are made.

However, in other forms of business organisation, for example the sole trader and the partnership, it is also necessary, as it is in the company structure, to consider in more detail the raising of **loan capital** and the method by which some sort of security, over and above the contractual promise of the borrower to repay the loan, can be given.

As regards loan capital, a company has a great advantage in that it can give a floating charge over its assets to a substantial lender, e.g. a bank. Partnerships and sole traders cannot do this because they are subject to bills of sale legislation which in effect stops it; however, the Law Commission has issued a consultation paper prepared at the request of the Department of Trade and Industry in which it invites views from business as to whether partnerships should be allowed to grant floating charges by making changes in the law. (See *Partnership Law*, Law Commission, Autumn 2000; and see later in this chapter.)

A sole trader or a firm can only mortgage its business premises and fixed plant and give personal guarantees from the sole proprietor or the partners. Sole traders and partners can also mortgage their own private property. These forms of security are also quite common in the private limited company where directors will normally be asked to give guarantees of the company's major debts and mortgage their private property to secure, for example, bank lending to the company. All of this makes something of a mockery of limited liability so far as directors of private companies are concerned.

We shall now consider these securities in more detail.

CHARGES

A charge is a type of security by which a person who borrows money gives the lender rights over his (the borrower's) assets to support the duty of the borrower to repay what is owed under the contract of loan. The lender thus has two rights:

1 to sue the borrower on the contract of loan; and

2 to sell the assets which the borrower has charged in order to recover what is owed to him but no more. Any surplus on sale, less the costs of selling the property, must be returned to the borrower. The charge may be fixed or floating (see below).

A mortgage, which will be considered below, is a term most often used to mean a fixed charge over land. However, the term 'mortgage' may be used to describe any type of fixed (but not a floating) charge over any item of land or other property such as a mortgage by a shareholder who uses his shares, which are personal property, as security for a loan.

Fixed charges

A fixed legal charge can be given over **identified property** belonging to the borrower. This property may be either real property, e.g. land and buildings, or personal property, e.g. machinery and equipment.

If real property is being used, there is no need for the borrower to transfer his ownership in the land to the lender. The Law of Property Act 1925 allows the lender who has taken the fixed legal charge over, say, land and buildings, to sell it on his own without any assistance from the borrower, even though the lender has not taken a transfer of the ownership from the borrower by what is called a conveyance.

If personal property, such as machinery and equipment, were to be used as security, the borrower would have to transfer, by a method called assignment, the ownership in the machinery and equipment to the lender. Unless this was done, the lender could not give a good title to a buyer of the machinery and equipment if he decided to sell it, which he would want to do if the borrower did not repay the loan.

The great benefit of the fixed legal charge is that once it has been given, the lender can sell the property charged by himself. The contract of loan will, of course, end his right to do this once the loan has been repaid.

Furthermore, if the company becomes insolvent the preferential creditors (e.g. those owed wages or salaries up to £800 for a period of four months, or Revenue and VAT payments owing) do *not count for payment before the fixed charge*. Therefore, a creditor, such as a bank with a fixed charge, will get more than it would under a floating charge, as preferential creditors do rank before a floating charge. Thus, if the directors have given a personal guarantee of the company's overdraft, they will have less to pay on the overdraft to the bank if the bank holds a fixed charge.

Floating charges

1 Generally. This is a charge which is not attached to any particular asset when the charge is made. Instead it applies to the assets of the borrower as they are at the time the charge crystallises, as it will, for example, if the borrower fails to make repayment of the loan as agreed. The borrower is in the meantime free to sell the assets he has and any new assets which his business acquires are available to be sold by the lender if they were in the ownership of the borrower when the charge crystallised. When the charge crystallises it becomes in effect a fixed charge over the assets which the borrower then has. The lender can then sell them to recoup his loan.

2 Floating charges restricted to companies. In theory, a floating charge could be used by a sole trader or partnership but because of legislation relating to bills of sale such a charge is not viable except in the case where the borrower is a company.

A floating charge gives the lender an interest in the personal property, e.g. stock in trade, of the borrower, and yet those goods are left in the borrower's possession. This may make him appear more creditworthy to another trader who sees the borrower's assets but does not realise that these are already charged to secure a loan.

If such a charge is to be valid there must be the registration of a bill of sale listing the items charged, e.g. the stock, in the Bills of Sale Registry. The floating charge does not lend itself to the listing of the property charged in this way because its essential feature is that the assets charged are always changing. If the borrower sold a tin of beans from his stock, he would have to amend the bill of sale; if he bought four dozen jars of jam, it would also have to be amended. The Bills of Sale Acts 1878 and 1882 do not apply to charges given by companies and so companies do not have to follow this particular registration procedure. However, as we shall see in Chapter 6, the registration procedures of the Companies Act 1985 must be carried out.

GUARANTEES

Generally

If a bank lends money to a business it will normally want, in addition to a charge over the assets, a guarantee from the sole trader or partner, or the directors of the company. These persons promise to meet the business debt from their personal resources if the business cannot.

Partners' and directors' bank guarantees are usually joint and several. This means that any partner or director is obliged to pay the whole debt and may then sue his co-partners or co-directors for a contribution. The nature of this liability is explained in Chapter 5 and the formalities necessary for a guarantee in Chapter 7.

Guarantees can be open, that is to cover whatever figure a loan or overdraft may reach, or be limited to a fixed amount.

Independent advice

A special problem has arisen in business law in relation to the giving of guarantees and other securities, e.g. charges over land, by third parties to support the business borrowing of another. The major examples relate to the giving of guarantees and other securities by a spouse or elderly parent to a bank to support the business borrowing of the other spouse or a son or daughter.

The lender should, as a matter of good practice, advise the spouse or parent to take legal advice from a solicitor who is independent of the lender. This should accompany the security document when it is sent to the spouse or parent for signature – a lender should not simply entrust the security to the debtor to obtain the surety's signature. The lawyer who gives the independent advice should act as a witness to the guarantor's signature on the guarantee (or charge) and confirm that he has fully explained to the guarantor or person giving the charge the nature and content of the guarantee (or charge). An appropriate form of words for a guarantee appears in the box in Fig 4.2.

However, although it is good practice for the lender, e.g. a bank, to give independent advice, it is not a legal requirement that it does so. Even in the absence of such advice, the security is enforceable by

Signed and delivered as a deed by the said Joseph Jones in my presence after the contents of this guarantee had been fully explained by me to him.

Signed

John Adams

Solicitor

Fig 4.2 An appropiate form of words for a guarantee

the bank because in these cases the House of Lords decided that there is no presumption of undue influence (see *National Westminster Bank plc v Morgan* (1985)). The proper way to deal with these cases was through the law of negligence, said the Court of Appeal in *Cornish v Midland Bank* (1985), but only if an employee of the bank **actually gives** negligent advice or fails to properly explain the consequences of the transaction to the person giving the security, e.g. that if the business fails the bank will require the person giving the security to pay off the overdraft of the company and this may mean selling his home. If the bank employee does not intend to give advice, then at least he should advise the taking of independent legal advice. If he does not do so, the bank will be able to enforce the security but may be liable in damages to the person giving the security under the ruling in *Hedley Byrne v Heller & Partners* (1963). This will, in appropriate cases, make the security of little use to the bank though it depends on the amount of damages which the court awards to the person who gave the charge.

The House of Lords used a different approach in *Barclays Bank plc v O'Brien* (1993) where a wife acted as guarantor in regard to a loan made to her husband and not to the couple jointly. The husband told his wife that she was acting as guarantor for a loan of £60,000 whereas it was £135,000. The loan was not repaid and the bank tried to enforce the guarantee against the wife. The House of Lords held that the bank failed. Lord Browne-Wilkinson approached the problem as follows:

● a person (such as Mrs O'Brien) who has been induced by another person's legal wrong (such as her husband's misrepresentation) to act as guarantor for that other person has a right in equity to set aside the transaction as against that person;

- the right to set aside the transaction will also be available against the lender if the lender has actual or *constructive* notice of the facts giving rise to the above mentioned equity.

Applying the above two principles to the facts of *O'Brien*, Lord Browne-Wilkinson said that:

- where one of two cohabitants (marriage is not essential) offers to provide a guarantee or other security for the other's debts:
  - (a) the lender has *constructive* notice that the proposed surety may not have properly consented; therefore,
  - (b) the lender must take reasonable steps to satisfy himself that the consent has been properly obtained; and
- the taking of 'reasonable steps' involves 'bringing home' to the guarantor the risks that are being run by providing the security and advising the taking of legal advice. The judge said that the best way of dealing with this was to hold a private meeting with the guarantor at the bank. So the bank must act as counsellor. Of course, in doing so it may fall foul of *Cornish* in that unless the official doing the counselling is absolutely accurate in the advice given, the bank may be liable in negligence.

The House of Lords did not apply this rule in *CIBC Mortgages plc v Pitt* (1993) where the husband misled the wife as to the purpose of the loan which was not to pay off the existing mortgage on their home and buy a holiday home. It was used by the husband for speculation on the Stock Exchange with disastrous results. Lord Browne-Wilkinson, in holding the wife's guarantee enforceable by the lenders, said that what distinguished a joint advance from the mere guarantor situation was that in the latter there is not only the possibility that undue influence was being exercised but also the increased risk that it was in fact exercised because at least on its face the guarantee by a wife of her husband's debts is not for her financial benefit. It is the combination of these two factors that puts the creditor on enquiry and leads to constructive notice of possible wrongdoing by the principal debtor.

The amount of litigation that involves attempts by occupiers such as wives and co-habitees to avoid eviction by relying on *O'Brien* shows no sign of declining, and this despite very clear statements of policy by the courts that move away from the 'counselling' principles of *O'Brien*, and which are *more protective of institutional lenders such as banks*.

Examples are to be found in *Barclays Bank plc v Boulter* (1999) where the House of Lords stated that, as a general rule, in seeking to rely on the *O'Brien* principle the burden of proving *constructive notice* of undue influence is on the person claiming such influence. In the absence of adequate proof of the extent of the bank's knowledge of the circumstances, therefore, the wife or co-habitee will fail. The House of Lords stated that to put a burden on the bank to show that it had no notice of relevant circumstances could operate very unreasonably towards the bank. Furthermore, in *Woolwich plc v Gomm* (1999) the loan was a remortgage of the matrimonial home for a further loan that was used by the husband for his sole benefit. The bank obtained a possession order on the property when the loan was not repaid, the Court of Appeal stating that a lender such as the bank in this case is only obliged to act with reasonable caution and is not bound to be unduly suspicious that the wife or co-habitee has been subject to undue influence. The court felt that in a remortgage situation there was no need to make further enquiries. *Royal Bank of Scotland v Etridge (No 2)* (1998) also shows a retreat from *O'Brien* in that the Court of Appeal ruled that a lender was entitled to assume that a solicitor who had been asked to advise a wife had discharged his duties fully and competently.

The above cases do not apply, of course, where it can be shown that the bank was on *actual notice* of undue influence. They do show, however, that it is increasingly difficult to show that lenders have *constructive notice*.

MORTGAGES

Generally

A mortgage is a type of loan. It is special because the borrower (called the mortgagor) has not just promised to repay the loan to the lender (called the mortgagee) but has given him also a charge on his (the borrower's) property. If the borrower fails, for example, to repay the loan, the lender can sell the property and pay himself from the sale price. Alternatively, if the lender thinks he can get his money back from the rents, if any, which the property is producing he can ask the court for the appointment of a receiver who will collect the rents until the loan is paid off.

A person when buying a house often gets a loan in the form of a mortgage from a bank or building society and charges the house as security.

Legal mortgages of land

If Alan Brown wishes to borrow money from the Barchester Bank by giving the bank a legal mortgage of his (Alan's) private house, he will normally create a charge by way of legal mortgage over the house. This is done by means of a short deed stating that a charge on the land is created.

An example of a suitable deed for Alan Brown to sign is given in the Law of Property Act 1925. The deed may be expanded to include other matters which the borrower agrees to do, e.g. to insure the property charged, but the basic provisions are set out below (Fig 4.3). Alan Brown will then sign the deed and his signature will be witnessed.

The mortgage deed usually provides that the money is to be repaid six months after the date of the deed. However, the borrower is not expected to repay the loan by this date. It is only put in so that the lender has all his remedies from that date since he can regard himself as being owed the principal sum. There is no particular reason to have six months as the repayment date and in fact it is not uncommon for mortgage deeds to be drafted to provide that the mortgage money is due immediately on the signing of the deed.

The contract of loan (or in some cases the mortgage itself) will state the time within which the loan must be repaid, but if the borrower is in breach of that arrangement the charge is fully effective for use by the lender after six months.

This form of charge could also be used by Alan Brown to give as security any leases which he had, as where he was only renting business premises under a 25-year lease and wished to give a legal mortgage of that lease.

Equitable mortgages of land

An equitable mortgage can arise where the lender and borrower do not follow the procedures set out in the section above. Where a customer wanted an overdraft from his bank, he could formerly just leave the title deeds of his house with the bank. This created an equitable mortgage. However, the law relating to equitable mortgages and charges has been changed by *United Bank of Kuwait plc* v *Sahib and Others* (1996). The bank had obtained a charging order against the debtor's interest in his jointly-owned home in Hampstead, London. Before the charging order was made an organisa-

---

THIS LEGAL CHARGE, is made the first day of June 2001 between Alan Brown of 14 River Street, Barchester of the one part and the Barchester Bank of the other part.

WHEREAS Alan Brown is seised of the hereditaments hereby charged and described in the Schedule hereto for an estate in fee simple in possession free from encumbrances;

NOW IN CONSIDERATION, of the sum of £100 000 now paid by Barchester Bank to Alan Brown (the receipt whereof Alan Brown doth hereby acknowledge) this Deed witnesseth as follows;

1. Alan Brown hereby covenants with Barchester Bank to pay on the first day of December next the sum of £100 000 with interest thereon at the rate of 10 per cent per annum.

2. Alan Brown as beneficial owner hereby charges by way of legal mortgage All and Singular the property mentioned in the Schedule hereto with the payment to Barchester Bank of the principal money and interest hereby covenanted to be paid by Alan Brown.

Fig 4.3 A mortgage deed

tion called SoGenAl had made a loan to the debtor who orally agreed to hold his title deeds in the property to the order of SoGenAl. The court was asked whether there was an equitable charge or mortgage in favour of SoGenAl which took priority over the interest of the bank. The answer was no because the old rule that a mere deposit or oral agreement about title deeds created for the purpose of securing a debt operated, without more, as an equitable mortgage or charge had not survived s 2 of the Law of Property (Miscellaneous Provisions) Act 1989. This section requires that 'A contract for the sale *or other disposition* of an interest in land can only be made in writing and only by incorporating all the terms which the parties have expressly agreed in one document, or where contracts are exchanged in each.' (Emphasis is added.) Therefore, such a written document must accompany the deposit of title deeds. (See further, Chapter 7.)

The position of the lender is not so strong where the mortgage is equitable. The lender cannot sell the property but must first apply to the court for an order for sale or if he thinks he can get his money back from the rents, if any, which the property is producing he can ask the court for an order appointing a receiver.

It is worth noting briefly at this point that when considering the words 'writing', 'signature' and 'deed' the passing of the Electronic Communications Act 2000 should be borne in mind. Section 7, which is already in force, allows electronic signatures to be adduced and acceptable as evidence of a signature. However, delegated legislation is required to make changes in legislation such as the Law of Property (Miscellaneous Provisions) Act 1989 to eliminate 'paper' requirements. The writing and signature requirements of the Act will come to cover electronic methods.

The borrower's right of redemption

Lawyers call this the 'equity of redemption' and, as we have seen, the mortgage deed provides when the money is to be repaid. It is usual to say 'after six months' in order that the lender's range of remedies is available after that period. Originally at common law the land used as a security became the property of the lender as soon as the date for repayment had passed unless the loan had been repaid by then, even if only a small amount was still owed. However, equity allowed and still allows the borrower the right to redeem the land and free it from its position as a security even though the contractual date for repayment has passed and even though it has not yet arrived.

If a person wants to repay a mortgage early, he will normally have to give notice, say, of six months, that he intends to do this or be prepared to pay interest for, say, six months ahead after he has repaid the loan, so that the lender can find another investment.

Thus, if A repays his loan on 30 June (ahead of time), he will probably, according to the agreement, have given notice not later than 31 December in the previous year. If not, he will, according to the agreement, pay off the capital plus the interest due to date on 30 June but also interest until 31 December next.

A mortgage is also subject to the rule of restraint of trade (see Chapter 7). It may also sometimes happen that a mortgage may prevent repayment for a reasonable time as regards the rule as to equity of redemption and yet redemption may be allowed before that time because while the mortgage term lasts unreasonable restrictions are placed on the freedom of a person to pursue his trade or profession.

Thus, in *Esso Petroleum Co Ltd* v *Harper's Garage (Stourport) Ltd* (1967) (see also Chapter 7) an agreement not to repay a mortgage on a garage for 21 years was probably not an unreasonable time in terms of the equity of redemption rule. However, during that time the garage owner had to sell only Esso fuels. It was decided that the restraint on fuel sales was unreasonable and that the mortgage could be repaid earlier, leaving the owner of the garage free to sell other fuels.

A further right of the borrower on repayment of the loan is that on redemption the property must be returned to him free of any conditions which applied while the loan was unpaid and the mortgage was in existence. Restrictions applicable before redemption are more likely to be upheld by the court than those which are stated to survive redemption.

Noakes and Co Ltd v Rice (1902)

Mr Rice wanted to buy a public house. He borrowed the money from Noakes and Co Ltd who were brewers and owners of the pub. The brewers lent Mr Rice the money but he had to agree to sell only Noakes' beer. After Mr Rice had repaid his mortgage, Noakes said he must still sell only their beer. The court decided that he was not bound to do so. During the mortgage Mr Rice was bound to sell only Noakes' beer but not after repayment of the loan.

Comment. Much depends upon the bargaining power of the parties. In mortgage arrangements between large companies what is called a collateral advantage may be allowed to continue after repayment of the loan. For example, in *Kreglinger* v *New Patagonia Meat & Cold Storage Co Ltd* (1914) Kreglinger had lent money to New Patagonia and New Patagonia gave Kreglinger a mortgage of its property. The mortgage said that for five years New Patagonia should not sell sheepskins to anyone without offering them first to Kreglinger. New Patagonia repaid the loan after two years but the House of Lords decided that New Patagonia was still bound to offer the sheepskins first to Kreglinger.

The possibility of using the rules of restraint of trade to attack restraints during the period of the mortgage is considered above. (See *Esso Petroleum Co Ltd* v *Harper's Garage (Stourport) Ltd* (1967).)

Consumer Credit Act

A mortgage term relating, for example, to interest, must not be an extortionate credit bargain under the Consumer Credit Act 1974. If it is the court may change the mortgage arrangements to do justice between the parties. The borrower must be an individual, a partnership or another unincorporated body.

The other provisions of the 1974 Act relating to loans are directed at second mortgages and apply only to loans of £25,000 or under which are not made by building societies, local authorities, insurance companies or friendly societies.

MORTGAGES OF PERSONAL PROPERTY

Just as land can be used as a means of securing debts, so also can personal goods. The main way in which this can be done is by mortgage.

In this case the person who borrows the money retains the business assets, e.g. office equipment, but transfers the ownership of them to the lender to secure the loan.

As we have seen, this raises a problem because, since the borrower keeps the assets, those who do business with him, perhaps on credit, may be misled as to his creditworthiness, because the assets displayed are owned by a lender and not by the borrower who has them.

To stop this happening the security is void and the lender cannot sell the goods mortgaged unless a bill of sale is made out and registered in the Central Office of the Supreme Court under the Bills of Sale Acts 1878–82. These bills must be re-registered every five years if they are still in operation. This Register is open to public examination and therefore those who do business with the borrower can find out whether he has mortgaged his goods.

MORTGAGES OF CHOSES IN ACTION

As we have seen, personal property (i.e. property other than land) is divided into two kinds known as choses in possession and choses in action. Choses in possession are goods such as jewellry and furniture which are tangible things and **can be physically used and enjoyed** by their owner. Choses in action are intangible forms of property which are **not really capable of physical use or enjoyment**. Their owner is normally compelled to bring an action at law if he wishes to enforce his rights over property of this sort. A contrast is provided by a fire extinguisher and a fire insurance policy. The extinguisher is a **chose in possession**. If you had a fire **you could use the extinguisher** to put it out – the insurance policy would not be much use for this. However, it is a valuable piece of property because although, **as a chose in action, it has no physical use** it gives a right to require the insurance company to make good any loss caused by the fire. Other examples of choses in action are debts, patents, copyrights, trade marks, shares, negotiable instruments such as cheques, and the goodwill of a business.

It is possible to use a chose in action as security for a loan and lenders frequently take life assurance policies as security. A bank would do this in the case of an overdraft. However, shares in companies are perhaps the commonest chose in action to be used as security.

Shares can be made subject to a legal mortgage but the shares must actually be transferred to the lender and his name is in fact entered on the company's share register. An agreement is made out in which the lender agrees to retransfer the shares to the borrower when the loan is repaid.

You can also have an equitable mortgage of company shares and this is in fact often the method used. The share certificate is deposited with the lender, together with a blank transfer. This means that it is signed by the registered holder, i.e. the borrower, but the name of the person to whom the shares are to be transferred is left blank. The shares are not actually transferred, but the agreement which accompanies the loan allows the lender to sell the shares by completing the form of transfer and registering himself or someone else as the legal owner if the borrower fails to repay the loan. The shares can then be sold and transferred as required.

LIABILITY OF THE PROPRIETORS

Sole traders

A sole trader is liable for the debts of the business to the extent of everything he owns. Even his private possessions may be ordered to be sold to pay the debts of the business. There is no such thing as limited liability. A sole trader can make a free transfer of personal assets to a husband or wife (spouse) or other relative, but the transfer can be set aside and the assets returned to the sole trader and then used to pay the business creditors if the court is satisfied the transfer was to defeat creditors. Also, if property is transferred to a spouse, it is lost to the sole trader if the marriage ends in divorce and the spouse refuses to give it up.

Partnerships

In the case of a partnership governed by the Partnership Act 1890, partners are jointly and severally liable for the debts and other liabilities of the firm, such as negligence liability, even though the negligence results from the work of one only of the partners. The problem is made more acute for these firms and the partners because there is

unlikely to be full insurance cover on offer for professional liability claims.

They can be sued together by a creditor who has not been paid. They can also be sued individually (or severally). Thus, if A, B and C are partners and the firm owes X £3,000 but this cannot be paid from the partnership funds, then, for example, X may sue A for the whole £3,000 and A may then try to get a contribution of £1,000 from B and £1,000 from C. If they are insolvent, he will not get the contribution, or at least not all of it.

The liability extends to the private assets of the partners. Even the estate of a deceased partner is liable for the debts of the firm incurred while he was a partner if there is anything left in his estate after paying his private debts.

There is also liability for the debts of the firm incurred after retirement unless the firm's existing customers are informed of the retirement and public notice of retirement is given in *The London Gazette*, which is a daily publication obtainable from the Stationery Office.

There may be a limited partnership and those who want to put a limit on their liability for the debts of a partnership firm may become limited partners. This is provided for by the Limited Partnerships Act 1907.

However, at least one partner must have unlimited liability for all the debts of the firm. A limited partner is not liable for the debts of the firm, though if the firm fails and is dissolved, his capital may be used to pay its debts as far as required before any of it is returned to him.

A limited partnership is, however, unsatisfactory because the limited partner has no right to take part in the management of the firm. If he does, he becomes liable with the other partners for the debts and liabilities of the firm during the period for which he was involved in management.

Limited liability partnerships (LLPs)

These can be registered under the Limited Liability Partnerships Act 2000. The provisions of this legislation are considered more fully in Chapter 5. However, on the matter of liability the Act goes some way to meeting the concerns of partners regarding unlimited liability. The LLP is a separate person like a company. The LLP and not its members is liable to third parties. However, a negligent member's personal assets are at risk since in the case of professional negligence the assets of the LLP are at the risk as are the personal assets of the negligent member, *but not the personal assets of the other non-negligent members.*

Companies

The rule of limited liability which says that a shareholder in a company who has once paid for his shares in full cannot be required to pay any more money into the company even if it cannot pay its debts, does allow the shareholders in a company to leave the company's creditors unpaid.

However, directors, and in some cases members, may have personal liability. As far as directors are concerned, this applies most commonly if they have continued to trade and incur debts when the company was unable to pay its existing debts. These matters will be dealt with further in Chapter 6.

Also, company directors are, as we have seen, often asked to give their personal guarantees of certain debts of the company – for example, a bank overdraft. This makes limited liability a bit of an illusion for them since, if the company does not pay, they can be required to do so.

CONTINUITY

Sole traders

The death of a sole trader brings the organisation to an end and the executors who are in charge of the sole trader's affairs will either have to sell the business as a going concern to someone else or sell the assets one by one to other businesses. Of course, if the assets of the business have been left to a person by the will the executors have a duty to transfer those assets to that person as part of the winding-up of the estate, unless it is necessary to sell them to pay the deceased's debts.

If a sole trader becomes bankrupt, there is no way in which he can legally continue in business because if he obtains credit beyond a prescribed amount (currently £250) either alone or jointly with someone else, without telling the person who gives the credit that he is an undischarged bankrupt, he commits a criminal offence.

Partnerships

The death, bankruptcy or retirement of a partner in an ordinary 1890 Act partnership can lead to the firm closing down business, but it is usual for the partnership agreement to provide that the business shall continue under the remaining partner or partners. However, the continuing partners or sole partner (as he is perhaps strangely called) will have to find the money to buy out the share of the deceased, bankrupt or retiring partner. Unless the firm has provided for this, it can cause difficulties in terms of raising the necessary funds.

As regards *limited liability partnerships*, clearly the firm, being a *persona* at law, is not dissolved by the death, bankruptcy or retirement of a member of the firm, but the personal representatives or the former member on retirement are entitled to receive any amount, e.g. by way of repayment of capital, to which the former member was entitled. This would, of course, involve the raising of the necessary funds and the same would be true of the new ordinary partnership that is envisaged by the Law Commission, which would also have a separate legal personality.

Companies

A company has what is called perpetual succession. Thus, if A and B are the members of AB Ltd and A dies or becomes bankrupt, the executors or trustee in bankruptcy, as the case may be, must sell A's shares to a purchaser if they wish to realise the cash paid for them. The company's capital is unaffected and the company is not dissolved. A company can purchase its own shares under the Companies Act 1985 but it is not forced to do so.

PUBLICITY AND EXTERNAL CONTROL OF THE UNDERTAKING

Sole traders and ordinary partnerships

Little, if any, publicity attaches by law to the affairs of these organisations. Their paperwork and administration is a matter for them to decide, subject, in a partnership, to anything that the partnership agreement may say about this. These organisations can keep their accounts on scraps of paper in a shoebox if they wish to, though obviously they should keep proper accounts. However, subject to satisfying the Revenue as to the genuineness of their accounts, usually through an independent accountant, there are no legal formalities and no filing of documents or accounts for the public to see.

Limited liability partnerships

Section 15 of the Limited Liability Partnerships Act 2000 gives the Secretary of State for Trade and Industry power to make regulations that apply any law relating to companies to LLPs. These regulations will impose a disclosure and filing requirement in terms of accounts and reports similar to that of registered companies (see below). Thus, as is usual, the acquisition of limited liability will involve public disclosure of profits and the distribution among the partners.

Companies

A considerable amount of publicity attaches to companies – even small private ones.

Unless the members of the company have unlimited liability – which is a possible form of corporate organisation – the company must file its accounts annually together with the reports of its directors and auditors. These items are kept by the Registrar and are available for inspection by the public on request from Companies House.

In the past all companies whether public or private were required to appoint auditors, which was an expense forced on them but not upon sole traders and partnerships. However, there are now audit exemptions as described below.

The Companies Act 1985 (Audit Exemption) (Amendment) Regulations 2000 came into effect on 1 August 2000. This means that the accounts of all eligible companies (i.e. those with turnovers of not more than £1 million) do not have to be audited. However, any member or members holding not less than one-tenth of the issued share capital can require the company to obtain an audit for its accounts for that year. A company is not

entitled to the exemption if at any time during its financial year it was:

(a) a public company;
(b) a banking or insurance company;
(c) an organisation authorised to conduct investment business under the Financial Services Act 1986; or
(d) a member of a group of companies, unless it is an exempt group under the 1997 regulations as where the turnover of the group as a whole is not more than £1 million.

In order to qualify for the exemption, the company must be an eligible company and the balance sheet must include a statement by the directors that:

(a) in the year in question the company was entitled to the exemption;
(b) no member or members have deposited with the company a notice requesting an audit;
(c) the directors acknowledge their responsibility to ensure that the company keeps accounting records complying with s 221 of the Companies Act 1985 and for preparing accounts which give a true and fair view of the affairs of the company as at the end of the accounting reference period and of its profit and loss as required by s 226 of that Act and which in other respects comply with the Companies Act 1985 in relation to the accounts. The regulations amend Part VII of the Companies Act 1985 by amending sections in that Part.

The Companies Act 1985 allows **small companies** to avoid certain publicity in regard to the accounts. A small company is one which has satisfied two of the following conditions for the current financial year and the one before:

1 Turnover, i.e. gross income before deducting the expenses of running the business, not exceeding £2.8 million.
2 Balance sheet total, which is in effect the total assets, not exceeding £1.4 million.
3 Employees, not exceeding 50 as a weekly or monthly average throughout the year.

A small company is allowed to file just an abbreviated version of its balance sheet with the Registrar instead of a copy of the full accounts required by the Companies Act 1985. The members of the company, however, are entitled to a copy of fuller accounts. In particular, the *abbreviated* accounts do not have to show details of the salaries of directors, nor is it necessary to file a directors' report or a profit and loss account.

As regards the fuller accounts to which members are entitled, these need not be full Companies Act 1985 accounts. There are regulations in force which provide that a small company will comply with the law if it provides what are called *shorter form financial statements* to the members. A number of items may be left out of the shorter form statements, e.g. details of any debentures issued in the course of the year.

The Companies Act 1985 also allows **medium companies** to avoid certain publicity in regard to the accounts but to a lesser degree. A medium company is one which has been within the limits of *two* of the following thresholds for the current year and the one before:

1 **Turnover:** not exceeding £11.2 million.
2 **Balance sheet total:** not exceeding £5.6 million.
3 **Employees:** not exceeding 250 as a weekly or monthly average throughout the year.

Shareholders are entitled to *full* Companies Act 1985 accounts. The modifications in regard to the filed accounts are:

(a) the profit and loss account may commence with 'gross profit or loss' which combines 'turnover', 'cost of sales information' and 'other operating income' which would otherwise require separate disclosure;
(b) there is no need to give, in the notes to the accounts, the analyses of turnover and profit according to the branches of the company's business in which they were made.

The directors' report and balance sheet are required in full. The reason for the modification is that details of turnover and profit were used, sometimes to the unreasonable disadvantage of medium companies, by competitors who could identify the most profitable and the most unprofitable areas of the medium company's business.

The directors must state in the accounts that the company satisfies the conditions for a small or medium company and this must be supported by a report by the auditors giving an opinion confirming this. The auditors' report on the full accounts must accompany the modified accounts, even though the full accounts are not sent to the Registrar. The references to reports of auditors do not apply where the company is exempt from the obligation to appoint auditors.

In this connection, the government has announced that it intends to raise the thresholds for small and medium companies to the maximum allowed under EU law, after taking into account the Company Law Review Steering Group's view on small company accounts. The Steering Group is undertaking a thorough review of company law, but legislation is at least two/three years away, so that implementation may be seen by 2003.

The current maximum thresholds allowed under EU law are:

Small company

Turnover	not more than £4.8 million
Balance sheet total	not more than £2.4 million
Number of employees	not more than 50

Medium-sized company

Turnover	not more than £19.2 million
Balance sheet total	not more than £9.6 million
Number of employees	not more than 250

When these thresholds are raised, the audit exemption threshold will also be raised to £4.8 million from the existing £1 million in terms of turnover.

All companies must file with the Registrar of Companies an annual return showing, for example, who the company's directors and its secretary are and the interests of the directors as directors in other companies. The return also shows the changes in the company's membership over the year and a full list of members must be given every three years. However, the Companies Registration Office (CRO) has a system under which CRO produces a document for the annual return listing all the relevant information which CRO has on the company. The company secretary merely confirms that it is correct or amends it as required. The 'shuttle system', as it is called, is designed to save a significant amount of form filling by company administrators. The form of the shuttle document appears at the end of Chapter 6 but it is worth noting here that under changes made in the Autumn of 2000 for companies with 20 or fewer members Companies House will give a list of members from previous records it holds so that the company will have only to correct the list if necessary. This will mean, in effect, that these companies, i.e. 98 per cent of the Register of Companies, will be able to submit a full list of members annually.

In addition, formal company meetings, called annual general meetings, must be held by a company at specified intervals so that shareholders are kept informed of corporate activities. However, private companies may opt out of this requirement by what is called an elective resolution (see further, Chapter 6).

In conclusion, therefore, those who run companies and limited liability partnerships will have to spend some time in ensuring that the business is carried on in such a way as to comply with relevant legislation. The sole trader and ordinary partner have a much less complicated legal environment which can be to their advantage. However, the administrative burden on companies, particularly small companies, may be significantly reduced if deregulation proceeds.

In this connection, under regulations made under the Limited Liability Partnerships Act 2000 small LLPs will automatically qualify for audit exemption in the same way as companies limited by shares.

TAXATION AND NATIONAL INSURANCE

Once a business is running the question of the taxation and national insurance (NIC) arises. The subject is one of extreme complexity and so only an outline of the system can be given.

Income tax – the system of schedules

In the UK different types of income are taxed under what are known as Schedules. This dates back to the days when different departments of the Inland Revenue dealt with the different kinds of income which a wealthy person might have. Its purpose was to achieve secrecy as to total income. These days one inspector of taxes deals with all parts of a taxpayer's income and the word 'Schedule' no longer has any significance. It simply means a 'type' of tax.

Income tax – generally

Income tax is the main tax which is paid by people who have earnings either from an occupation or from investment income. Employees pay income tax under Schedule E. They pay weekly or monthly by deduction from pay. The self-employed pay income tax under Schedule D and are responsible for making the relevant payment to the Collector of Taxes. For this reason the self-employed should keep full and accurate records of all transactions of the business.

Taxation and the self-employed sole trader

Sole traders should ideally draw up annual accounts, though it is not necessary to do so. The trader's annual tax return (see below) provides space for a return of business income and expenses in a standard format which may in some cases be regarded as enough and do away with the need for annual accounts. However, if accounts are drawn up, the question of what accounting date to use will arise. In other words, what is to be the year end for the relevant financial statements? Accounts can be made up to the end of the first year's trading or to the end of the calendar year, i.e. 31 December, or to the end of the tax year on 5 April. Where calendar year or tax year is chosen, the accounts may represent income for less than 12 months but the following year and subsequent years will cover a full 12 months' trading.

The method of taxation

Assessments of income tax are made for tax years which run from 6 April in each year. Thus, the tax year 2000/2001 runs from 6 April 2000 to 5 April 2001. In broad terms the assessment will be based on the profits of the business for the accounting year which ends in the same tax year. Thus, if the year end of the business is 30 September 1998, the 1998/99 assessment will be based on the profits of the business for the year ended 30 September 1998.

Payment of tax – method of assessment

This is based upon a tax return, which will be received by the sole trader in April of each year. The return requires the trader to give all the information required to calculate income tax and capital gains tax (see below) due for the year. Under the system of self-assessment, the trader can calculate what is due and there are explanatory notes on the return to assist in this. However, the trader may supply the relevant figures and ask the Revenue to calculate the tax bill or, alternatively, if the trader has an accountant, the accountant may do it. The method is entirely a matter for the trader. The tax return also explains how to calculate any national insurance contributions (see below) that may be due. These are paid to the Collector at the same time as the income tax.

The trader will then be required to make the two payments towards the tax bill: one on 31 January and the other on 31 July (but see below).

If the business makes a loss, this may be set against any other taxable income or may be carried forward to offset profits in subsequent years.

Payment of tax – timing

In an attempt to bring the self-employed more into line with the PAYE system for employed persons, the Revenue has devised a system of payment that involves estimating the income of the self-employed. An illustration appears below:

John is a freelance journalist. His payment position is:

Tax year 1999/2000: The year ends on 5 April 2000 and John's tax liability from earnings and, e.g., interest and income from investments is calculated as £10,000. His tax bill for 1999/2000 is payable in two instalments of £5,000, the first on or before 31 January 2001 and the second on or before 31 July 2001.

However, this is not the end of the matter. With John's first payment on 31 January 2001 *the Revenue will require one-half of the tax John will owe for the tax year 2000/2001 that ends on 5 April 2001.* This is estimated on John's earnings during the 1999/2000 tax year, i.e. a liability of £10,000. Therefore, the payment on 31 January 2000 will be £10,000 and the payment on 31 July £5000 as before.

If when the *actual figures for the tax year 2000/2001* are available John has not earned enough to require payment of £15,000 in tax, he will get a refund. If he has earned more, a third payment will be required before 31 January 2002.

Where accounts are prepared

An accountant should normally be employed to draw up the business accounts. Nevertheless, the trader is still responsible for the accuracy of the records on which they are based and therefore for the accuracy of the accounts and for correctly declaring the amount of profit.

Under the rules of self-assessment it is not necessary to send the accounts with the tax return. The relevant information can instead be included as indicated in the tax return. However, it should be borne in mind that the Tax Office can ask to see the accounts (if any) and the business records in order to check the figures given in the return. These powers will be used more often and include random checks because where the trader or his accountant computes the tax payable there must be a more rigorous check on records and computation.

Employing labour

If the trader employs someone for the first time, the local Tax Office must be informed. The employee's Tax Office may not be the same as the trader's but the trader's local Tax Office will send the information to the correct office. The Tax Office will send the trader a New Employer's Starter Pack which includes the necessary instructions, tables and forms.

The trader will then be responsible for deducting income tax and Class 1 national insurance contributions from the employee's pay in accordance with the 'Pay As You Earn' system (PAYE). The tax and NIC which the trader has deducted must be sent to the Inland Revenue Accounts Office each month, though this can be done quarterly if the average monthly payments of tax and NIC are below £1,500. The trader must also tell the Tax Office, at the end of each tax year, how much each employee has earned and the amount of deductions for tax and NIC together with any benefits paid, e.g. car allowance. The employees must also be given a statement showing their earnings for the year, the tax and NIC deductions paid, and any benefits provided.

National insurance

Most people who are in work pay national insurance contributions. The class of contribution paid depends upon whether the person concerned is employed or self-employed.

Those who are self-employed pay two kinds of NIC: Class 2 which all self-employed people pay and Class 4 which becomes payable if profits are above a certain limit.

Class 2 contributions must be paid by self-employed earners unless they have a certificate of exemption on the ground that their income is below a certain level, i.e. £3,825 in 2000/1. Expenses are deducted when calculating earnings. Class 2 contributions are payable at a flat rate; this is £2.00 a week for 2000/1. Class 2 contributions can be paid by a bank direct debit or under other billing arrangements provided by the Inland Revenue national insurance contributions office, the old Contributions Agency having been merged with the Inland Revenue.

Class 2 contributions do not count for the payment of unemployment benefit, but they do count for incapacity benefit, basic retirement pension, widow's benefit and maternity allowance. Application can be made for repayment of Class 2 contributions if the earnings in the relevant year are low enough to entitle the earner to exception.

Class 4 contributions are paid by self-employed earners. They are levied as a percentage of profits, i.e. for 2000/1 it is payable on earnings between £ 4,585 and £27,820 at the rate of 7 per cent. The maximum is therefore £1,947.40 even where profits are more than the maximum in the band.

The profits are those chargeable to income tax under Schedule D, and Class 4 contributions are usually collected by the Inland Revenue with the income tax. Class 4 contributions do not give the trader any additional benefits.

Schedule D – advantages

A major advantage with Schedule D is the trader's ability to deduct expenses which would not be allowable to employed persons. For example, the trader may use a room in his home as a study from which to write and a partner may use another room as an office from which to help with the work. If so, a proportion of the heating and lighting and other costs of the home may be allowable against tax, whereas they would not be allowable to an employee who brought work home to complete in a study. There are also capital allowances available to the trader in regard, for example, to plant and machinery, such as a new word processor which has been purchased during the year.

Partnerships

The trading and professional income of a partnership is charged to tax under Schedule D which applies the current year basis of assessment to this income as in the case of sole traders.

To a large extent a partnership is treated as a separate entity for tax purposes in that assessments are made jointly on the partnership. The profits assessed for the tax year in question are allocated among the partners according to the partnership agreement, e.g. in the profit-sharing ratio. The tax assessment for each partner is then calculated separately taking into account personal circumstances, e.g. whether they are married or single and whether they are entitled to mortgage relief and so on. The individual assessments are then aggregated and the total bill is a liability of the firm. Because partners are 'jointly and severally' liable for the debts of the firm (see further, Chapter 5) any of the partners could be liable for the whole bill if the other partners were insolvent.

As to settling the bill, there are two main ways as follows:

- each partner pays his share of the liability into the partnership account and the partnership pays the bill; or
- the partnership pays the full amount and the current accounts of the individual partners are charged with each one's share.

Capital allowances are allowed as deductions from the profits of the firm for expenditure on, for example, plant and machinery and motor vehicles.

Salaried partners will normally be regarded as employees and pay income tax under Schedule E by the PAYE system.

The profits of a limited liability partnership will be taxed as if the business was carried on by individuals in an ordinary partnership and not as if the business was carried on by a company.

Companies

Companies pay what is called corporation tax. The tax is also levied on unincorporated associations but not partnerships. It is thus payable by companies which are limited or unlimited and extends to many clubs. The tax is payable on profits of a UK resident company whether these profits arise in the UK or abroad. The tax is therefore 'residence' based. Relief is given in respect of any foreign tax paid on profits earned abroad. The tax is charged on the profits of the company and this includes income from all sources including capital gains. The basis of assessment is the accounting period of the company. Rates of tax are settled for each financial year, i.e. the 12 months ended 31 March. If a company's accounting period straddles two 31 March periods, profits are apportioned and the tax is charged on each part of the year at the rate applicable to that part.

Capital allowances are deducted as part of adjustment of total business profits but appropriations of profit such as dividends and transfers to reserves are not allowable as deductions. Directors' emoluments are allowed so long as they appear reasonable.

Large companies pay their corporation tax by quarterly instalments. Broadly these are companies with profits of over £1.5 million. For other companies the whole of the tax is due on the date following the expiry of nine months from the end of the company's accounting period (or year end).

Traders who consider changing from a sole trader or partnership regime usually do so for tax purposes, but all the implications should be considered. Corporate status involves giving more publicity to the affairs of the business in terms of the need to file documents, such as the annual return with the Registrar of Companies, and to prepare statutory accounts under the Companies Act 1985. These must be filed, at least in an abbreviated version. A small company will not require an audit, as we have seen, but since an accountant will normally prepare the business accounts, the trader will find that the charge will increase for statutory accounts.

The tax advantages depend upon the trader's circumstances. Those who commonly draw all the profits from the business will find that the company faces higher national insurance since a charge of 12.2 per cent is levied on directors' pay but not on sole traders' or partners' drawings. Dividends escape national insurance, but the effective tax rate for any dividends withdrawn after taking into account corporation tax is 40 per cent, i.e. the same as if the income had been earned as a sole trader or partner.

If it is intended to leave profits in the business, there may be an advantage. Corporation tax on company profits is 10 per cent for the first £10,000 and then 20 per cent up to £300,000 compared with the 40 per cent rate. In addition, the transfer of assets from a sole trader's or partnership business can result in an assessment for capital gains tax, though it is possible to follow methods that allow some deferment of payment of this tax. These matters are beyond the scope of this book and are not considered further.

Capital Gains Tax

So far as 'business' is concerned, the taxation implications of this tax are likely to arise in a situation outside the scope of this book, i.e. business transfers. If we assume that a sole trader or a partnership is to transfer the business and its assets to a limited company with the sole trader or partners becoming the major shareholders in the new company, then in so far as certain of the assets may have been purchased some years ago, e.g. land and buildings, and are now valued at a higher price than when purchased, a charge to capital gains tax may arise on the transfer. There are somewhat complicated provisions called tapering under which account is taken of the fact that some of the gain may be merely inflation and this element is deducted from the gain.

As a broad indication, from 5 April 2000 as regards an asset held from 0–1 year the percentage of gain chargeable is 100 per cent at a rate of 40 per cent. There is then a sliding scale until we reach assets held for over four years where the percentage of gain chargeable is 25 per cent at a rate of 10 per cent.

PLANNING

One of the features of the operation of a business, no matter which vehicle is chosen, may be the need to obtain at some stage planning permission in connection with a business development.

To obtain planning permission it is necessary to apply to the relevant local authority. Permission should be granted unless there are clear-cut reasons for refusal. The authority has in general to decide applications in accordance with the development plan for the area. Matters such as road safety and congestion, and adequacy of water supply and sewage disposal, are also relevant. It should also be borne in mind that most building work is subject to building regulations regarding health and safety, energy conservation and arrangements for the disabled.

A check should be made with the relevant authority to see whether planning permission is required. Internal alterations do not generally require it unless they in some way affect the exterior. Repair and maintenance of existing buildings does not normally require permission but you will need it if you are putting up a new building. Extensions up to 1,000 square metres or 25 per cent of the volume of the original building and not exceeding the height of the original building do not require permission. Permission is not required if the premises were previously used for broadly the same purpose, but it is if they are to be used for a different purpose.

The time taken

From the time of application, it can take anything from about four weeks to three months or more for a decision to be made, depending on the size and complexity of the scheme.

Outline planning permission

It is possible to make an application for outline planning permission to see whether permission will be given in principle. This has the advantage that detailed drawings are not required though as much information as possible should be given. This can then be followed with an application for full planning permission. There is a fee involved and the relevant authority will give the necessary information.

Appeals

If the relevant authority refuses planning permission, an appeal can be made to the Secretary of State for the Environment. An appeal may also be made on the ground that the authority has imposed conditions which the applicant cannot or does not wish to accept. Failure to reach a decision within a time limit of eight weeks or such longer period agreed with the authority is also a ground for appeal. Appeals can be made at any time within six months of the authority's decision or six months from the date when it ought to have been made. There is no charge for the appeal itself, but there are bound to be some legal and other expenses. Most appeals are dealt with within 20 weeks.

How long does permission last?

Both outline and detailed planning permission will normally include a condition that the development must be begun within five years. How soon it is completed is a matter for the developer.

It is also worth remembering that planning permission runs with the land and is not personal to the owner or occupier. This means that land or buildings can usually be sold or let with the benefit of planning permission, which should encourage and assist a sale or letting and the price or rental.

Going ahead without permission

If the authority thinks the development is unacceptable, it may make an enforcement notice to put matters right. This may even involve the demolition of any building work carried out. It is possible to appeal against an enforcement notice to the Secretary of State, but if the appeal is dismissed and the enforcement notice becomes effective, it is an offence not to comply with it and could lead to a prosecution in a magistrates' court.

Planning and environmental considerations

In addition to problems of business development in terms of planning, a business may also fall foul of laws relating to the environment and the two may clash. If so, the business may ask the High Court for judicial review of the offending restriction as in *R v Kennet District Council, ex parte*

Somerfield Stores (1999) where in terms of noise being emitted from refrigeration equipment the council planning authority placed a restriction of a lower number of decibels on the planning permission than the environment authorities had in an abatement order served under the Environmental Protection Act 1990. The High Court ruled in favour of the planning authority.

QUESTIONS/ACTIVITIES

1 Which of the following business organisations have been formed by registration?
   (a) Wilkinson-Brown & Co, Chartered Accountants
   (b) Mammoth plc
   (c) The United Kingdom Atomic Energy Authority
   (d) Small Ltd.

2 'A registered company is a juristic or legal person and is therefore a legal entity distinct from its members.'
   Explain this statement and state two advantages of incorporation showing how these advantages depend upon corporate personality.

3 The court will not allow the theory of corporate personality to be used as a means of fraud or sharp practice – the judge has the power to 'draw aside the corporate veil'.
   Explain what happens when the court does draw aside the veil and describe a situation in which the court has exercised its power.

4 In relation to a company, what is:
   (a) its authorised share capital?
   (b) its issued share capital?
   (c) its paid-up capital?
   (d) its uncalled capital?

5 A and B are partners in an ordinary partnership. The firm is insolvent. Joe, a creditor, has successfully sued A for a debt of £2,000. What rights, if any, has A against B?

6 A, B, C and D wish to form a partnership in which all of them will be limited partners. Advise them.

7 What is the maximum number of employees allowed to a company which wishes to qualify as a 'small' company?

8 Outline the provisions under which companies can dispense with the audit requirement.

9 Explain the regime of taxation which applies to:
   ● sole traders; and
   ● companies.

10 Give a short account of ways in which mortgages of real and personal property may be created. Explain what is meant by the 'equity of redemption'.

11 Discuss the importance in securities transactions of the Bills of Sale Acts.

12 When is it important for a person giving a guarantee or other security to be advised by an independent solicitor? State with reasons whether or not the guarantee or other security will be unenforceable if independent advice is not received.

13 Fred Jones is a sole trader who wishes to expand his business premises. Explain the basic planning procedures to be followed.

Chapter 5

NON-CORPORATE ORGANISATIONS – SOLE TRADERS AND PARTNERSHIPS

THE SOLE TRADER

Having introduced the various business organisations, we will now consider, in more detail, the legal environment in which sole traders operate.

FORMATION OF THE BUSINESS

Name of the organisation

Business names

(a) Generally. The main formality facing the sole trader on commencement of business is the Business Names Act 1985. Even this does not apply if he trades in his own name. If, however, a business name is chosen, then the 1985 Act must be complied with. For example, a business name occurs where the organisation is run in a name which does not consist **only** of the surname of the sole trader. Forenames or initials are allowed in addition.

Therefore, if Charlie Brown is in business as 'Brown', or 'C Brown', or 'Charlie Brown', the name of the organisation is not affected by the Act. The names are not business names. Recognised abbreviations may also be used, such as 'Chas Brown', and still the name is not a business name.

However, if Charlie Brown is in business as 'High Road Garage', or 'Chas Brown & Co', 'C Brown & Co', 'Brown & Co', he is using a business name and the 1985 Act must be complied with as regards choice of the name and disclosure of the name of the true owner.

The rules regarding disclosure do not apply where the only addition to the name of the sole trader is an indication that the business is being carried on in succession to a former owner.

Often a sole trader will want to use the name of the previous owner of the business so that he can use the goodwill attached to it. Goodwill is the probability that customers will continue to use the old business for their requirements. It may also be a reputation for a certain class of article, such as a Rolex watch. If Charlie Brown bought a business called 'The Village Stores' from Harry Lime, the new business could be called 'Charlie [Chas or C] Brown (formerly Harry Lime's)' and would not be affected by the Act. However, if Charlie Brown went further than merely including his own name and that of the previous owner as if he traded as 'Charlie ['Chas' or 'C'] Brown Village Stores (formerly Harry Lime's)' or 'Village Stores', he would have a business name and would have to comply with the Act.

(b) Restriction on choice of business name. As we have seen, the **main** controls are that a sole trader's business must not be carried on in Great Britain:

(i) under a name which leads people to believe that it is connected with a central or local government authority unless the Department of Trade and Industry agrees. This is to prevent a possibly false sense of security in the public who deal with the business because these authorities get regular income from the enforced payment of taxes and Council Tax. Thus, trading under a name such as 'County Council Supplies' would require the permission of the DTI.

Also in this category, and requiring the consent of the DTI, are names which imply a national or international connection, such as 'The International Metal Co', and names which imply that the organisation is in some way distinguished, e.g. 'Society' or 'Institute'. Words which imply the carrying on of a specific function also require DTI permission, e.g. 'Insurance' and 'Building Society'. This will not be obtained unless those functions are the ones which the organisation carries out.

(ii) under a sensitive name unless the relevant body agrees. These are set out in regulations issued by the Department of Trade and Industry. Examples are that if the word 'Royal' is to be used, the Home Office must agree.

The use of the word 'Charity' requires the permission of the Charity Commissioners. Regulations in 1992 have made it clear that plural or possessive forms of sensitive names are included. So 'Charities' and 'Charities'' are controlled.

(iii) under obscene names such as 'Hookers & Co' or names obtained by deception, as where a person is using the word 'charity' having got permission from the Charity Commissioners following the submission of false or misleading information about the functions of the organisation.

(c) **Disclosure of true owner's name: what must be disclosed?** A user of a business name must disclose his or her name together with a business or other address in Great Britain. This is to enable documents, such as claim forms to commence a legal claim, to be served at that address.

(d) **Where must the information be disclosed?**

(i) In a clear and readable way on all business letters, written orders for the supply of goods or services, invoices and receipts issued by the business, and written demands for the payment of money owed to the business.

(ii) Prominently, so that it can be easily seen and read in any premises where the business is carried on, but only if customers or suppliers of goods or services go on to those premises.

(iii) Disclosure must also be made immediately and in writing to anybody with whom business is being done or discussed if the person concerned asks for the information. This would mean, for example, giving the information on, say, a business card, to a salesman to whom an order was being given or discussed if the salesman asks for the names of the owners of the business.

(e) **What happens if an owner does not comply with the law?** A sole trader who does not obey the law commits a **criminal offence** and is liable to a fine. On the **civil side** he may not be able to enforce his contracts, for example to sue successfully for debts owed to him. This will be so where, for instance, the other party to the contract can show if he is sued that he has been unable to bring a claim against the business because of lack of knowledge of the name and address of the owner.

Suppose that Freda Green trades as 'Paris Fashions' in Lancashire and supplies Jane Brown with dresses for her boutique in Yorkshire, but without giving Jane Brown any idea that she, Freda Green, owns Paris Fashions. Suppose, further, that Freda moves her business to Kent and Jane Brown finds that the dresses are sub-standard and wants to return them, but cannot because she does not know where 'Paris Fashions' has gone. If Jane is sued for non-payment by Freda, the court may refuse Freda's claim, though the judge has a discretion to enforce it if in the circumstances he thinks it is just and equitable to do so.

Protection of business names

The fact that there is no registration of business names places businesses that use them in a more difficult position in terms of protecting the name than companies that trade in their corporate names (see further, Chapter 6). As we shall see, the Registrar keeps an index of company names and a company cannot be registered in a name that is the 'same' as a name already on the index. In addition, the Secretary of State can direct a company to change its name within 12 months of registration if it is 'too like' the name of a company on the index. The above provisions do not apply to business names and a passing off action would have to be brought (see below). This is a difficult and often expensive claim. However, if the name is in the nature of a trade mark it can be registered and protected more easily. The Trade Marks Act 1994 has extended this possibility particularly in allowing registration of geographical locations, e.g. 'The Barbican Tandoori'. Thus, persons trading in a name which includes a geographical location, as where J Singh does in fact trade under the name of 'The Barbican Tandoori', the name can be registered under the 1994 Act and will be easier to protect (see further, Chapter 15).

Passing off

A sole trader must not run his business under a name which is so like that of an existing concern that the public will confuse the two businesses. Similarity of name is not enough; usually the two concerns must also carry on the same or a similar business.

If this does happen, the sole trader will be liable to a civil action for the tort of passing off and the existing concern can ask the court for an injunction to stop the use of its name. If it is successful in getting the injunction and the new organisation still carries on business under the confusing name, its owner is in contempt of court and may be fined or imprisoned until he complies and changes the name of his business.

However, a sole trader may do business in his own name even if this does cause confusion, provided that he does not go further and advertise or manufacture his goods in such a way as to confuse his products with those of the existing concern.

DISSOLUTION

Our sole trader, whom we shall call Fred Smith, may decide at any time to retire from the business and dissolve it by selling off the assets of the business to other tradespeople. Alternatively, the business may be sold as a going concern to another trader and continue under him.

Apart from the legal formalities involved in selling and transferring assets, for example conveying shop premises to a new owner, there are no special legal difficulties provided all the debts of the business are paid in full. However, if Fred cannot pay his debts, he may be forced to dissolve his business by his creditors under a process called bankruptcy.

DEBT RECOVERY

Before proceeding to look at insolvency procedures it is worth noting what is available to recover debts before taking the ultimate step which is to put insolvency procedures in train.

If Fred's creditors have tried all the usual ways of recovering their debts, e.g. statements, solicitor's letters and so on, they may think about suing Fred in the county court. The jurisdiction and procedure of that court have already been described in Chapter 3.

Interest on debt

As regards the payment of interest on debt that the court can award as part of the judgment, we must first look at the contract to see whether there is any provision for interest. If there is, the court will follow the provision in making its award. However, since the enactment of the Late Payment of Commercial Debts (Interest) Act 1998, small businesses have, even in the absence of a contractual provision, been able to charge big businesses with interest on overdue bills. The Act contains a default credit period of 30 days from delivery of either the invoice for the payment or the goods or services, whichever is later.

Statutory Instrument 1998/2479 provides that a business is a small business if the number of full-time employees is 50 or fewer. A large business is a business in which the number of full-time employees is more than 50. The instrument gives further details in terms, e.g., of counting part-time employees as fractions of full-time employees and averaging provisions for the relevant figure of 50.

Statutory Instrument 1998/2765 sets the rate of interest at bank rate plus 8 per cent per annum, while SI 2000/2740 brings into force those parts of the 1998 Act that allow small businesses to claim interest against other small businesses which fail to pay their bills on time.

A further phase of the Act is scheduled to be introduced in 2002 that will allow businesses, big or small, to charge each other interest on overdue bills where the contract does not deal with the matter of interest.

Where the customer still does not pay

Let us assume that one of Fred's creditors has obtained a judgment against him and that he still will not pay. The judgment itself orders Fred to pay direct to his creditor. The creditor will therefore know quite quickly whether he needs to consider further action (called enforcement) to try to get the money.

If Fred has not paid, the creditor can try to get the money by asking the county court for any of the following:

- a warrant of execution;
- a garnishee order; or
- a charging order.

The court can, in an appropriate case, make an attachment of earnings order under which an employer deducts money from wages or salary through the court until the judgment is paid. This is not available in Fred's case because he is self-employed and an earnings order is not available against Fred's profits. It is necessary to pay a fee for any of the above procedures but the amount paid by the creditor will be added to the money he is already owed. The fee is not refunded if the enforcement does not succeed. If Fred has no money or assets (which is unlikely), it will fail and there is nothing the court can do by way of enforcement.

Warrant of execution

This gives the bailiffs, who work out of the office of the sheriff of the county, the authority to visit Fred's home or business. The bailiff(s) will try either:

- to collect the money owed; or
- to take goods to sell at auction to pay the debt.

It is worth noting that there may be some activity in this area under the Human Rights Act 1998. Article 1 of the First Protocol of the Human Rights Convention deals with property rights and, since the bailiff service is an emanation of the state, the Convention applies. Property taken in execution is sold at very cheap prices at sheriffs' sales and makes less contribution than it might in paying off the debtor's debts. This provides an imbalance between the rights of the creditor and the debtor that may lead to cases and changes on the basis of a breach of the 'fair balance' test implicit in the Protocol.

Garnishee order

If a creditor knows that Fred is owed money by a third party as where, for example, there is a credit balance on Fred's bank account or building society account, the creditor may wish to divert the payment away from Fred to himself. This can be done by the creditor applying to the court for a garnishee order *nisi*, as it is called. The order is addressed to the bank or building society forbidding it to pay the debt to the debtor Fred and requiring a representative of the bank or building society to attend before the court to show why the money in the account (or according to the order perhaps part of it) should not be paid to the creditor. The order is served at least seven days before the next court hearing on the matter and, if at that

hearing no reason has been shown as to why the payment should not be made to the creditor, the court may make the garnishee order absolute requiring payment by the bank or building society to the creditor. The creditor, in order to use the garnishee proceedings, must be a person who has obtained a judgment from the court that the relevant debt is owed to him.

Charging order

This order prevents Fred from selling property over which it is made, e.g. a house, land, business premises and any shares Fred may hold, until the creditor is paid. The creditor will have to wait for the money until the property is sold but can ask the court for an order to force Fred to sell.

Getting a garnishee order or a charging order can be complicated and the creditor would normally require the help of a solicitor.

We will now consider the situation where for some reason or another the creditor has been unable to get his money and turns to the ultimate procedure – to make Fred bankrupt.

BANKRUPTCY PROCEDURE – GENERALLY

Bankruptcy procedure is set out in the Insolvency Act 1986. Bankruptcy proceedings, which involve asking the court for a bankruptcy order, may be taken against Fred by creditors. Fred may also take proceedings to make himself bankrupt if he cannot pay his debts. His affairs will then be taken over by an insolvency practitioner, who is usually an accountant.

This may be a great relief to Fred if, as is likely, he is being pressed and harassed to pay debts he cannot meet. On bankruptcy his creditors will have to press the insolvency practitioner to pay. He is, of course, an independent person and a lot of the nastiness goes out of the situation once he takes over from Fred.

In particular, those who supply services to Fred's home – such as electricity, gas, water and telephone – must treat him as a new customer from the date of the bankruptcy order and cannot demand settlement of outstanding bills as a condition of continuing supply. They can, however, require a deposit as security for payment of future supplies.

THE PETITION

A petition to the court for a bankruptcy order may be presented by a creditor or creditors only if:

1   The creditor presenting it is owed £750 or more (called the bankruptcy level) by Fred. Two or more creditors (none of whom is individually owed £750) may present a **joint petition** if together they are owed £750 or more by Fred, as where A is owed £280 and B £600.

2   The debt is defined as a debt **now due** which Fred appears to be unable to pay, or a **future debt** which Fred has no reasonable prospect of being able to pay.

3   The creditor, to show that this is so, and if the debt is now due, sends Fred a further demand asking for payment. If the demand is not complied with within three weeks, the court will accept that Fred cannot pay the debt.

4   The debt is a **future debt**, such as a loan repayable in the future. The creditor(s) must send Fred a demand asking him to give evidence that he will be able to pay it. If Fred does not provide satisfactory evidence within three weeks of the demand that he will be able to meet the debt when it is due, the court will accept that there is no reasonable prospect that it will be paid.

5   The debt is not secured, as by a charge on Fred's property. A secured creditor cannot present a petition unless he is, for example, prepared to give up his security. In any case, secured creditors, such as banks who have taken a security in return, say, for giving Fred an overdraft facility, will normally get their money by selling that property of Fred's over which they have a charge. Any surplus of the sale price, after payment of the debt to the bank and the cost to the bank of selling the property, is returned to Fred's estate for distribution among his other creditors. If there is a shortfall in the sale price, the bank will have to prove in the bankruptcy as an unsecured creditor for the balance but will only receive the same dividend, as it is called, as other unsecured creditors on this balance, e.g. 25p in the £.

SCHEMES OF ARRANGEMENT UNDER THE DEEDS OF ARRANGEMENT ACT 1914

This is an alternative procedure to bankruptcy under which Fred would not become bankrupt at all. Deeds of arrangement are unaffected by the Insolvency Act 1986. Such a deed has advantages in that no applications to the court are required **but** creditors who do not accept it may petition the court within one month of it being made asking that Fred be made bankrupt. The fact that the deed has been entered into is the ground for the petition. A possible practical scenario appears below.

1   Fred may wish to put a proposal to his creditors under which he will hand over his business to a trustee for the benefit of his creditors. The trustee will be an independent person such as an accountant who may be able to deal more expertly with the sale of Fred's business or the running of it and so pay the creditors off. If the creditors are willing to go along with this, Fred will not be made bankrupt.

2   Alternatively, Fred may wish to put up a scheme of arrangement by way of compromise of his debts. This would involve the creditors accepting final payment of, say, 50p in the £, which they may feel will be a better deal than bankruptcy, particularly if the cost of the bankruptcy proceedings is likely to be high.

3   These schemes need the consent of a majority in number and value of the creditors. For example, if there are 100 creditors and A is owed £901 and the other 99 are owed £1 each, the rest cannot force a scheme on A because he has the majority in value, although the others have a majority in number. Equally, A plus 49 of the rest cannot force the scheme on the others. A plus 49 creditors have a majority in value but not in number. However, A plus 50 of the rest could force the scheme on the others; they have a majority in number of 51 per cent and a clear majority in value.

However, as we have seen, dissentients can petition the court for a bankruptcy order so really all of the creditors need to be happy with the scheme, or at least too apathetic to petition.

THE INTERIM ORDER AND VOLUNTARY ARRANGEMENT UNDER THE INSOLVENCY ACT 1986

This is another alternative to bankruptcy. It involves an application to the court but once accepted by 75 per cent in value of the creditors it is binding on the dissentients who cannot petition for a bankruptcy order. A possible practical scenario appears below.

1 It would, of course, be difficult for Fred to make proposals for a scheme if a particular creditor (or creditors) had presented a petition to bankrupt him and was proceeding with it.

2 Therefore, if Fred wants breathing space to try a scheme to prevent his bankruptcy, he may, when a creditor presents a petition (or, indeed, if he thinks a scheme might be acceptable after he has presented a petition against himself), apply to the court to make what is called an interim order.

3 This protects his property and stops the proceedings for a bankruptcy order from carrying on. Also, secured creditors are prevented from selling that property of Fred's on which the security has been taken, though any scheme which is accepted cannot take away the rights of secured creditors to be paid before unsecured creditors. Still, an interim order will keep Fred's property together while a scheme is considered.

4 As part of obtaining an interim order, Fred must give the name of a qualified insolvency practitioner (called a 'nominee') who is willing to act as a supervisor for the proposed scheme. The court must be satisfied that:

(a) the nominee is properly qualified as an insolvency practitioner and has stated in his report that he considers that the arrangement has a reasonable prospect of success; and

(b) Fred has not made a previous application for an interim order in the last 12 months. Obviously, a debtor cannot keep asking for these orders so as, perhaps artificially, to put off bankruptcy proceedings. The nominee will report to the court on the proposals in Fred's voluntary arrangement and if the court thinks that they are reasonable it will direct the holding of a meeting of creditors which the nominee will call. If 75 per cent in value of the creditors entitled to vote attending the meeting in person or by proxy approve the proposals by voting for them, they will be binding on all creditors.

Under Sch 3 of the Insolvency Act 2000 an individual voluntary arrangement binds *all* the debtor's creditors *including unknown creditors* and they are only entitled to the dividends under the arrangement and cannot sue for the full debt or commence bankruptcy proceedings. They may, however, apply to the court for relief on the ground that their interests are unfairly prejudiced by the arrangement.

The nominee, or another practitioner chosen by the creditors, will supervise the arrangement. If it is honoured the debtor, Fred, avoids bankruptcy and all the restrictions and publicity which go with it.

Under Sch 3 of the Insolvency Act 2000 an individual may put a proposal for a voluntary arrangement to his creditors without having to obtain an interim order.

THE EFFECT OF A BANKRUPTCY ORDER – GENERALLY

1 If a scheme is either not put forward or, if put forward, not accepted, the bankruptcy proceedings will, if successful, end in the court making a bankruptcy order.

2 Once the order is made and Fred becomes bankrupt, his property is automatically transferred to the control of the Official Receiver. He is a civil servant dealing with bankruptcy with the aid of a staff of suitably qualified people. If Fred had put up a scheme of arrangement which had failed to get acceptance, the 'supervisor' of that scheme could have been appointed as trustee to Fred instead of the Official Receiver.

The office of the Official Receiver, being part of the insolvency service, is an emanation of the state and therefore subject to the direct application of the Human Rights Convention. Thus, in *Foxley* v *United Kingdom* (2000) the Official Receiver had obtained a court order under s 371 of the Insolvency Act 1986 directing F's post to the

Official Receiver as trustee in F's bankruptcy. F was serving a prison sentence of four years for corruption. The trustee opened letters and copied them, some being the subject of legal professional privilege. He was held to be in breach of Art 8 of the Convention (right to respect for family life, home and correspondence). No compensation was awarded but there will no doubt be more claims against insolvency procedures now that these claims can be heard, under the Human Rights Act 1998, in UK courts.

3   The transfer of Fred's property to the control of the Official Receiver does not apply to such tools, books, vehicles, and other items of equipment as are necessary to Fred to be used personally by him in his job as in the case of a sole trader plumber. Nor does it apply to such clothing, bedding, furniture, household equipment and provisions as are necessary for the basic domestic needs of Fred and his family. These items are retained in Fred's ownership and control unless their individual value is more than the cost of a reasonable replacement. Thus, very expensive tools and/or household items may have to be sold to swell Fred's estate for his creditors and be replaced by viable but cheaper lines.

4   Fred is required to submit a statement of affairs to the Official Receiver within 21 days of becoming bankrupt, i.e. 21 days from the day on which the bankruptcy order was made. This statement is the starting point of the taking over of Fred's affairs by someone else. The statement will help in this.

5   The main contents of the statement of affairs are:

(a) particulars of Fred's assets and liabilities;
(b) the names, residences, and occupations of his creditors;
(c) the securities, if any, held by them, plus the dates on which these securities were given.

The debtor's income

There is no reason why Fred should not continue to receive money from his trade or profession. However, the trustee may apply to the court for an **income payments order** under which a specified sum from Fred's earnings will be paid to the trustee either by the debtor or the person making the payment, e.g., in the case of an author, by the publisher paying a sum from annual royalties to the trustee. The court will not, however, make an income payments order if it reduces the debtor's income to below the sum regarded by the court as necessary to meet the reasonable needs of the debtor and his family. In this connection, it was held in *Kilvert* v *Flackett* (1998) that a tax-free lump sum of £50,504 paid to a bankrupt on retirement was to be regarded as income and could be made the subject of an income payments order for the benefit of the creditors of the estate of the undischarged bankrupt to whom it was paid.

Credit and other disabilities

An undischarged bankrupt is disqualified from sitting in Parliament or as a magistrate and from any elective office in local government. Under s 360 of the Insolvency Act 1986 an undischarged bankrupt is guilty of a criminal offence punishable by a maximum of two years' imprisonment or an unlimited fine if either alone or jointly with any other persons the bankrupt obtains credit to the extent of £250 or more without disclosing to the person from whom he obtains it information about his bankrupt status *or* if he engages directly or indirectly in a business, other than the one in which he was made bankrupt, without disclosing to all persons with whom he does business, whether they give him credit or not, the name in which he was made bankrupt. Under s11 of the Company Directors Disqualification Act 1986 an undischarged bankrupt commits a criminal offence if he acts as a company director or takes part in the management of a company unless the court gives permission.

Pensions

The Welfare Reform and Pensions Act 1999 provides that where a bankruptcy order is made against any person, any rights that he or she has in a Revenue-approved pension scheme are to be excluded from the estate for the purposes of bankruptcy proceedings. The Act covers occupational schemes, personal pensions and the government's new stakeholder pensions.

Reform

As we have seen, individuals who are undischarged bankrupts are barred from some public offices, such as that of a magistrate or a local councillor. The government is considering reducing some of these bans with the object of encouraging commercial risk-taking by removing social stigma, but only where honest individuals have suffered business misfortune. At the moment, however, the law remains unchanged.

COMMITTEE OF CREDITORS

1 If someone other than the Official Receiver is appointed as Fred's trustee, the creditors may at a general meeting set up a committee of creditors of at least three and not more than five creditors to keep an eye on the way in which the trustee deals with the assets. The trustee must take into account any directions given to him by the committee or of a general meeting of creditors. If there is a difference of view between the committee and the general meeting, the general meeting decision is followed.

2 The trustee is not bound to set up a committee of creditors unless a majority in value of creditors present and voting in person or by proxy resolve to do so. However, it can be helpful to the trustee because the creditors, or some of them, may well have experience in Fred's area of trade. Thus, if Fred's debts are £50,000, a creditor, or more likely creditors, owed at least £25,001 must want a committee of creditors.

THE PUBLIC EXAMINATION

1 Once a bankruptcy order has been made against Fred, the Official Receiver (even if he is not the trustee) or the trustee may apply to the court for the public examination of Fred. One-half in value of Fred's creditors may require the Official Receiver to make the application to the court for a public examination. This is not a majority but literally one-half, i.e. in the example given above, £25,000.

2 At the public examination Fred can be questioned by the Official Receiver or the trustee (where this is a different person from the Official

Receiver), or by any creditor on the subject of his business affairs and dealings in property and the causes of business failure.

3 The main purpose of the public examination is to help the Official Receiver to find out why Fred's business failed and whether he has been guilty of some misconduct which could lead to his prosecution for a criminal offence, e.g. fraud.

THE FAMILY HOME

1 The family home is likely to be Fred's most valuable asset. If it is in Fred's name only, it vests in (is owned in law by) the trustee on his appointment. If it is in the joint names of Fred and another, e.g. his wife, then only Fred's half vests in the trustee.

2 In any event the trustee will be keen to sell the property so that Fred's creditors can have the benefit of what Fred owns in the property, usually after repayment of a mortgage.

3 However, the trustee must honour rights of occupation of the home. Fred will have rights of occupation only if persons under 18 (e.g. his children) reside with him at the commencement of his bankruptcy. His wife will have rights of occupation in her own right whether she is a joint owner or not. These rights arise under the Matrimonial Homes Act 1983. The trustee will therefore want an order for sale and Fred and his family will want to continue in occupation. If they do, the trustee cannot sell with vacant possession, which gives the best price.

4 Under the Insolvency Act 1986 the order for sale, if asked for, can be postponed for 12 months from the date of the bankruptcy order so that Fred and his family can find somewhere else to live. In the meantime the trustee can, if he wishes, ask the court for a charge on the proceeds of sale, if any, of the property. If the court grants this charge, the ownership of the property goes back to Fred who could sell it, but if he did so the proceeds of sale would belong to the trustee under his charge.

5 Finally, if the trustee applies for an order for sale after 12 months from the bankruptcy order, the rights of the creditors will become paramount and he will normally get the order, and Fred and

his family will have to move out. The court may still delay the order for sale further if there are special circumstances, as where the property is specially adapted for the use of the bankrupt, or a member of his family who is disabled.

PROOF OF DEBT

1   Fred's creditors will send details of their debts to Fred's trustee. These details may be unsworn claims or may be sworn claims, which means that the creditor has gone to a solicitor and said to him on oath that the debt is really due.

2   Both unsworn and sworn claims are called proofs of debt. The trustee will normally accept an unsworn claim unless he is doubtful about it and is going to challenge it, possibly before the court. If this is so, he would probably ask the creditor to submit a sworn claim.

MUTUAL DEALINGS – SET OFF

1   Any mutual dealings between Fred and any of his creditors are important. Say Fred is owed £20 by a customer, Sid, but Fred owes Sid £10. The trustee will ask Sid to pay the £20 to him but Sid will be able to set off (as it is called) the £10 Fred owes him against the £20 he owes the trustee, and pay only £10 to Fred's trustee.

2   This way Sid gets in fact a dividend of £1 in the £1 on the debt Fred owes him. If there was no law allowing set off, Sid would have to pay £20 to Fred's trustee and then prove for his debt of £10 in Fred's bankruptcy. If Fred's trustee had only sufficient assets from Fred's business to pay Fred's creditors 50p in the £1, then Sid would have had to pay £20 but would have got only £5 back. As it is he has had the whole £10 in value.

CARRYING ON THE BUSINESS AND DISCLAIMER

1   Fred's trustee may, with the permission of the committee of creditors or the court, carry on Fred's business for a while (but not for too long) if it will bring more money in for the creditors.

2   As we have seen, when the court makes the bankruptcy order Fred's property comes into the ownership and control of his trustee for the benefit of his creditors. One result of this is that in the case of an interest in land, such as a lease, say, for 20 years, the trustee becomes in effect the owner of the lease and the landlord can ask the trustee, quite legally, to pay the rent. If, as is likely, the trustee is an accountant with a good practice, he will obviously be in a position to pay the rent and cannot really defend himself if he does not do so. The trustee may find, additionally, that the lease has repairing clauses which Fred has not carried out and the landlord may call upon the trustee to put the premises in good order.

3   The trustee will therefore write to the landlord **disclaiming the property.** He then has no personal liability, nor has Fred any personal liability. The landlord is left to prove for his lost rent and perhaps the fact that Fred has not kept the premises in good order as damages in the bankruptcy. The landlord will get such payment as Fred's assets will allow. He is therefore by disclaimer put in the same position as the other creditors in the bankruptcy and loses any personal claim he may have made against the trustee or Fred.

TRANSACTIONS AT AN UNDERVALUE AND PREFERENCES

1   Fred's trustee may swell the amount of assets available to the creditors by using those provisions of the Insolvency Act 1986 which deal with two problems:

(a)   Cases where Fred might have decided to transfer his property to his wife receiving little or nothing in return. This is called a transaction at an undervalue. However, the matter is not simply one of money paid for property. In the case of *Agricultural Mortgage Corporation plc v Woodward and Another* (1994) the Court of Appeal decided that a tenancy of a farm granted by an insolvent farmer to his wife (to ensure that his creditors did not get vacant possession of the property and to discourage its sale to repay a loan they had made to him) was a transaction at undervalue and could be set aside, even though the wife agreed to pay an annual rent of £37,250, which was a proper market rent. This was because the wife had received substantial bene-fits over and above the specific rights of the tenancy agreement. She had safeguarded the family home, enabling her to acquire and carry on the family farm, and acquired a surrender value for the ten-ancy. Even more significantly, she could hold the mortgage corporation to ransom since it would have to negotiate with her and pay a high price to get vacant possession before selling the farm and repaying the debt owed to it.

(b) Cases where Fred has decided to pay certain of his creditors in full and prefer them to others. He might, for example, have decided to pay in full a debt to a person who had been particularly helpful to him in business or a debt which he owed a relative. This is not a transaction at undervalue because the person concerned is paid in full but it is a preference.

2 Fred's trustee can recover property or money passing in a transaction at undervalue or as a pref-erence as follows:

(a) if the bankrupt was a party to any transactions at undervalue in the five years before the presenta-tion of the petition (this is before he was made bankrupt by the bankruptcy order), the trustee can apply to the court to have the transaction set aside, provided that the trustee can show that the debtor was insolvent at the time of the transaction or became insolvent as a result of it;

(b) if the transaction at an undervalue took place within two years before the bankruptcy, insolvency of the debtor (Fred) at the time or as a result is not a requirement and the transaction can be set aside;

(c) where the transaction at undervalue is in favour of an 'associate' (e.g. a close relative), there is a presumption of insolvency, though the debtor can bring proof to show that this was not so;

(d) the trustee can make an application to have set aside any preference made within six months before the petition or within two years if the preference is in respect of an associate, e.g. a spouse or children.

The trustee must prove that in our case Fred was insolvent at the time of the preference or became insolvent as a result of it, and where the preference is in favour of an associate, there is a presumption that our debtor Fred intended to prefer the associ-ate, although this may be refuted by Fred providing evidence to the contrary.

Transactions defrauding creditors

Section 423 of the Insolvency Act 1986 applies. The section is designed to operate in conjunction with the above provisions regarding transactions at under-value and preferences. The above, as will have been noted, have time limits after which the transaction cannot be set aside. The value of s 423 is that it is not subject to specific time limits, though obviously it will be difficult to show that an old transaction was intended to defraud more recent creditors.

Protection of innocent third parties

It should be noted that a transaction cannot be set aside under any of the above provisions against a person who acquired property *from a person other than the bankrupt* for value and in good faith with-out knowledge of the undervalue or preference. Thus, if Fred disposes of his property at an under-value to person A, the transaction can be set aside as against A. However, if A sells the property to B, who takes it in good faith for value and without knowledge of the nature of the transaction between Fred and A, B can retain the property.

PAYMENT OF THE CREDITORS – PREFERENTIAL PAYMENTS

1 As the trustee gets in money from Fred's busi-ness, either as income or from the sale of assets, he will pay Fred's creditors in a set order of priority laid down in Sch 6 to the Insolvency Act 1986 after providing money for his own fees and expenses.

2 The main preferential debts are:

(a) PAYE deductions from pay, i.e. income tax and national insurance, which were made or ought to have been made and paid over in the 12 months before the bankruptcy;

(b) value added tax and car tax for six months and 12 months respectively before the bankruptcy;

(c) sums due in respect of general betting duty, gaming licence duty or bingo duty within 12 months before the bankruptcy;

(d) wages or salaries of employees due within four months before the bankruptcy up to a maximum of £800 for each employee;

(e) all accrued holiday pay of employees.

If the above debts come in total to £5,000 and Fred's assets raise only £2,500, each claimant will get half of what is claimed and other creditors will get nothing.

PROTECTION OF EMPLOYEES

1 Under ss 189–190 of the Employment Rights Act 1996 an employee who loses his job when his employer (in this case Fred) becomes bankrupt can claim through the Department of Trade and Industry (DTI) the arrears of wages, holiday pay and certain other payments which are owed to him rather than rely on the preferential payments procedure.

2 Any payments made must be authorised by the DTI and the right to recover the sums payable are transferred to the DTI so that it can try to recover from the assets of the bankrupt employer the costs of any payments made, but only up to the preferential rights the actual employees would have had. What can be recovered from the DTI may, in fact, be a higher sum than the preferential payments in bankruptcy allow.

3 Major debts covered are as follows:

(a) arrears of pay for a period not exceeding eight weeks up to a rate prescribed annually by statutory instrument and currently £240 per week. Persons who earn more than £240 per week can only claim up to £240;

(b) pay in respect of holidays which has not been paid in respect of holidays actually taken and holidays due but not taken up to a rate again of £240 per week with a limit of six weeks;

(c) payments promised to an employee instead of giving him notice but not paid at a rate not exceeding £240 per week;

(d) any payment which Fred may not have made in regard to an award by an employment tribunal of compensation to an employee for unfair dismissal.

4 Claims on the DTI will not normally be allowed if the trustee can satisfy the Department that the preferential payments will be paid from funds available in the bankruptcy and without undue delay.

TRADE CREDITORS

If all the preferential creditors have been paid in full, payments can then be made to the ordinary unsecured or trade creditors. If these claims come in total to, say, £12,000 and the trustee has only £4,000, each trade creditor will get one-third of what is claimed and the deferred creditors will get nothing.

DEFERRED CREDITORS

If all the unsecured creditors can be paid, the deferred creditors come next. These are, for example, debts owed by Fred to, say, his wife. They are not paid until all other creditors have received payment in full.

DISCHARGE OF THE BANKRUPT

1 Fred, if a 'first timer', will be automatically discharged three years after he became bankrupt unless the Official Receiver satisfies the court that Fred is not complying with his obligations, as where he is concealing assets. The period is two years where the debts are less than £20,000. 'Old hands', i.e. those who have been undischarged bankrupts in the last 15 years, are not automatically discharged but must apply to the court, and this cannot be done in the first five years following a bankruptcy order.

2 Any money owed by Fred which has not been paid at the date of discharge is in general no longer payable at law. Fred can then go back into business legally free of his old debts and with no restrictions on obtaining credit. However, damages awarded against the debtor Fred for personal injury caused by negligence or nuisance, money payable under maintenance and other matrimonial orders, fines and debts incurred by fraud, are not discharged and remain payable.

Bankruptcy reform

The government has issued a consultation document entitled *Bankruptcy: A Fresh Start* that it hopes will help those people who go bankrupt through no fault of their own but rather by commercial misfortune,

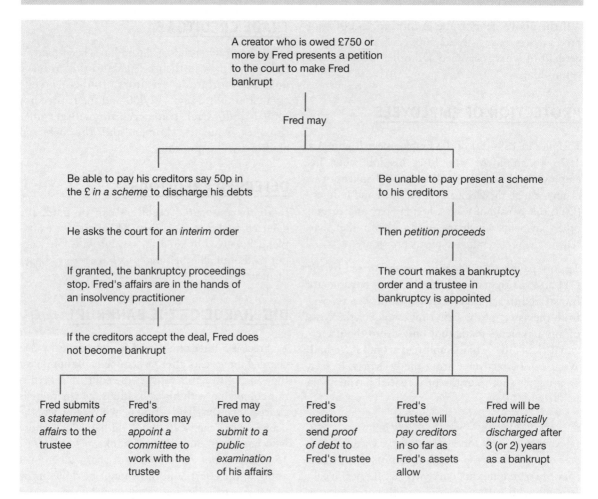

A creator who is owed £750 or more by Fred presents a petition to the court to make Fred bankrupt

Fred may

Be able to pay his creditors say 50p in the £ *in a scheme* to discharge his debts

He asks the court for an *interim* order

If granted, the bankruptcy proceedings stop. Fred's affairs are in the hands of an insolvency practitioner

If the creditors accept the deal, Fred does not become bankrupt

Be unable to pay present a scheme to his creditors

Then *petition proceeds*

The court makes a bankruptcy order and a trustee in bankruptcy is appointed

Fred submits a *statement of affairs* to the trustee

Fred's creditors may *appoint a committee* to work with the trustee

Fred may have to *submit to a public examination* of his affairs

Fred's creditors send *proof of debt* to Fred's trustee

Fred's trustee will *pay creditors* in so far as Fred's assets allow

Fred will be *automatically discharged* after 3 (or 2) years as a bankrupt

Fig 5.1 The personal insolvency of Fred Smith: an outline of the main Insolvency Act 1986 procedures

while retaining stringent sanctions for those who set out to mislead and deceive. For our purposes, the most important proposals are:

- an early discharge for the 'honest' bankrupt. Bankrupts will be discharged within six months of a bankruptcy order being made against them, but there are no proposals to remove the disabilities in terms of, e.g., credit and the holding of public office while undischarged;
- the setting up of post-bankruptcy individual voluntary arrangements (IVAs). At present, IVAs are only available *prior* to the making of a bankruptcy order as a means of preventing bankruptcy if the requisite approval of the creditors is obtained. Post-bankruptcy IVAs would help a bankrupt to apply future income in pay-

ment of bankruptcy debts under the supervision of the Official Receiver;
- financial counselling would be made available to bankrupts;
- where the bankrupt had put money into the failed business as capital and had been subject to honest commercial failure, he would retain a pound for pound equivalent right in the value of the family home. Thus, if the family home was worth £150,000 and the bankrupt had invested £50,000 in the business, only £100,000 of value in that home would be available to creditors. This is intended as fresh start-up capital.

It is worth noting that the post-bankruptcy IVA provisions closely resemble the 'Chapter 13 procedure' in the United States.

THE ORDINARY PARTNERSHIP

Having considered the legal position of sole traders, we now turn to the legal environment of the ordinary partnership. The provisions relating to limited liability partnerships will be considered later in this chapter.

DEFINITION AND NATURE OF A PARTNERSHIP

The Partnership Act 1890 sets out the basic rules which apply to this type of business organisation. All section references in this chapter are to that Act unless reference is given to some other Act.

In addition, the 1890 Act codified the case law on partnership which there had been up to 1890. Some of the cases we quote are earlier than the 1890 Act. We use them because the 1890 Act was based upon them and they are, therefore, examples of what the Act was trying to achieve and presumably has achieved. The cases after 1890 are interpretations of the words used in the Act following its being passed by Parliament.

The legal environment of the ordinary partnership is much more complex than that of the sole trader and the two environments have little in common except that in both cases the corporate structure is not used. There are similar restrictions on the choice of name, but since a partnership is an association of persons and a sole trader regime is not, there are much wider rules to consider in partnership. For example, the ability of a sole trader to contract on behalf of the business, i.e. himself, is obvious, but in the partnership situation where there are two or more individuals involved questions such as to what extent one partner, particularly if not authorised by the others, can make a contract with an outsider which will bind the firm and himself and the other partners arise. Bearing this in mind, we can now proceed to consider the law of the ordinary partnership.

Definition

An **informal** partnership is defined as 'The relation which subsists between persons carrying on a business in common with a view of profit' (s 1).

It should be borne in mind that if the parties have agreed to be partners, then they will be. All the definition is saying is that any persons who carry on a business in common with a view of profit are partners, even if they have not expressly agreed to be. This is what we mean by an 'informal partnership'. The definition and what follows should be understood in that light – it is a definition of the facts required to make an informal partnership.

Explanation and consequences of the definition

1 The relation which subsists is one of contract. A partnership is a contract based on being **in a business which has started.**

Thus, if Jane and John decide that they **will** run a shop, they are not partners in the informal sense until the shop is actually operating. While they are preparing to open, as by ordering goods and starting a bank account, they are not partners and contracts in the 'preparing' stage are not partnership contracts. If they are made, they are made only by the person who actually enters into them.

Spicer (Keith) Ltd v Mansell (1970)

Mr Mansell (M) and Mr Bishop (B) lost their jobs. They agreed to go into business together and form a limited company to run a restaurant. While they were forming the company and before it had received its certificate of incorporation from the Registrar, Mr B ordered some goods from Spicer's for the business. They also opened a bank account in the name of the company.

The company was eventually formed but was not bound by the contract which Mr B had made because it was not in existence at the time. It was a pre-incorporation contract. These contracts do not bind the company when it comes into being.

Mr B went bankrupt before Spicer's had been paid. So, rather than prove in a bankruptcy, Spicer's sued M on the basis that he was a partner of Mr B and since partners are jointly and severally liable for the debts of the firm, M, they said, should pay and then get a contribution from B (though it was not too likely that he would).

The Court of Appeal decided that B and M were not partners. They were not carrying on a business together in partnership. They were preparing to carry on a business as a company as soon as they could. They were company promoters, not partners.

Comment. (i) The case illustrates the importance of the relationship of partners and, indeed, its possible terrible consequences. Each partner makes the other his agent for the purpose of making contracts for him and, provided those contracts were within the scope of the partnership business, he is liable to perform all such contracts as if he had made them himself. Fortunately for Mr Mansell, in this case the court did not accept that the parties were partners so that Mr Bishop was liable on his own for the debt to Spicer.

(ii) The two persons in this case had agreed to engage in business activities, but all they had done was to open a bank account, and one had ordered goods for the restaurant. The court did not regard these two activities as enough to constitute being 'in business'. Also, **intention** is important in these cases and clearly here Mansell and Bishop did not intend to trade as partners. The intention appeared to be to promote a company.

(iii) A more recent illustration that eventually involved a change in the law is provided by *Khan* v *Miah* (1998) where three persons agreed to set up an Indian restaurant, the finance being provided almost entirely by one of them. Prior to the restaurants' opening, furniture and equipment were purchased, a laundry contract entered into, press advertisements were placed and the freehold of premises was acquired by the person who supplied the money. The parties then fell out and the business did not proceed as planned, but who owned the assets provided by one person's money since, in the absence of a contrary agreement, partnership capital is owned equally by the partners regardless of how much each has put in? The Court of Appeal ruled that the person who provided the finance owned them. There was no partnership because the business never began. There was an appeal to the House of Lords (see *Khan* v *Miah* (2000)) where the House of Lords allowed an appeal from the Court of Appeal by ruling that parties who agree on a joint venture to find, acquire and fit out premises for business purposes become partners in the business from the time when they embark upon those agreed activities, and it is irrelevant whether or not the business has commenced trading. In other words, *partnership begins on a joint venture, not on trade.*

2   A partnership is 'between persons', but a company, being a legal person, can be a partner with a human person, provided that its memorandum of association gives the necessary power. The members of the company may have limited liability while the human person has not. Two or more limited companies can be in partnership, forming a consortium as an alternative to merging one with the other. It should not be assumed that a limited company is a limited partner. The company is liable for the partnership debts to the limit of its assets. It is the liability of the company's members which is limited – a very different thing.

3   Partners must be carrying on a business, and for this reason a group of people who run a social club would not be an informal partnership.

Under s 45 a business includes 'every trade, occupation, or profession', but this does not prevent a particular profession from having rules forbidding members to be in partnership, e.g. a barrister is not allowed to be in partnership with another barrister, at least for the purpose of practice at the Bar.

The importance of being in a joint business venture as partners is also shown by *Khan* v *Miah* (2000).

4   Partners must act in common, and the most important result of this is that unless the agreement says something different, every general partner must be allowed to have a say in management, as s 24(5) also provides. A partner who is kept out of management has a ground to dissolve the firm unless there is something in the agreement which limits the right to manage.

The specimen ordinary partnership agreement which appears at the end of this chapter should be looked at to see how management rights have been dealt with.

5   There must be a view of profit, and so it is unlikely that those groups of persons who have got together to run railway preservation societies are informal partnerships.

6   The sharing of gross returns by A and B will not normally indicate a partnership between A and B. Partners share net profits, i.e. turnover less the outgoings of the business. Section 2 says that the sharing of gross returns does not, of itself, provide evidence of partnership, as the following case shows.

Cox v Coulson (1916)

Mr Coulson had a lease of a theatre. A Mr Mill was the employer/manager of a theatre company. Mr Coulson and Mr Mill agreed to present a play called 'In time of war'. Mr Coulson was to provide the theatre and pay for the lighting and advertising and get 60 per cent of the money which came in at the box office – the gross takings. Mr

Mill paid those taking part in the play and provided the scenery and the play itself and got 40 per cent of the gross takings.

Mrs Cox paid to see the play. As part of the performance an actor had to fire a revolver with a blank round in it. Because of alleged negligence a defective cartridge was put in the revolver and when the actor fired it Mrs Cox, who was sitting in the dress circle, was shot and injured. She wanted to succeed in a claim for damages against Mr Coulson. He had more money than Mr Mill. However, the actor was employed by Mr Mill and he alone was liable vicariously for the actor's negligence unless Mrs Cox could convince the court that Mill and Coulson were partners. The court decided that they were not; they were merely sharing the gross returns. Only the actor and Mr Mill were liable.

Comment. (i) The sharing of profits suggests a partnerlike concern with the expenses of the business and its general welfare. Sharing gross returns does not produce an **implied agreement** of partnership.

(ii) If there is an **express agreement**, oral or written, and in it the partners agree to share gross returns, then there would be a partnership.

7 **Joint ownership** according to s 2 does not of itself make the co-owners partners. That means that there is no joint and several liability for debt between the co-owners, say, A and B. So if A and B are joint owners of 12 Acacia Avenue and A cannot pay a debt, say, for a carpet which he has had fitted in his bedroom, B cannot be made liable as a partner. Co-owners are not agents one of the other as partners are. It should not be thought from this that the joint owners of property can never be partners. If A and B are left a row of houses in a will and collect and spend the rents, their relationship will not be one of implied partnership because English law does not recognise joint ownership of property as a business and s 2 affirms this. However, if the joint owners enter into a partnership contract, written or oral, sharing the rents, say 50/50, and appear to **intend** a partnership, then a partnership there will be. But, if the only evidence of partnership is joint ownership of property, this is not enough to establish a partnership. This is the true meaning of s 2.

8 **Formalities,** that is, writing, are not required for a partnership agreement. In fact, there need not be a contract at all. If the definition in s 1 is complied with and the parties seem to intend a partnership, there will be one, and the Partnership Act 1890 will then set down the rules that will govern the arrangement if nothing else is agreed. These are only a fallback position imposed on the partners and the most would-be partners would want to change some of them, hence the desirability of an agreement. In addition, and to make quite sure what has been agreed by the partners, there should be a written agreement.

A model form of partnership deed suitable for an ordinary partnership is provided later in this chapter. This shows what is normally dealt with by such agreements.

THE SHARING OF PROFITS AS EVIDENCE OF PARTNERSHIP

At one time the sharing of profits was almost conclusive evidence of informal partnership. During this period a number of everyday business transactions could give rise to a partnership, though the parties did not want this because of the possibility of incurring liability for another's debts. The position was eventually clarified in regard to certain business transactions, some of which are set out below, by s 2(3) of the Act of 1890.

(a) **Partners can pay off a creditor by instalments out of the profits of the business.** This comes from the following case which was decided before the 1890 Act.

Cox v Hickman (1860)

A trader had got into debt and his creditors decided that instead of making him bankrupt and getting only a proportion of what he owed them, they would let him keep the business but supervise him in the running of it and take a share of the profits each year until their debts were paid in full.

An attempt was made in this case to make one of the supervising creditor/trustees liable for the trader's debts as a partner. But was he a partner? The court said he was not. He was a creditor being paid off by a share of profits.

Comment. (i) There was, in addition, no mutual participation in trade here, but a mere supervision of the business. Of course, if creditors assume an active role in management they may well become informal partners.

(ii) The more modern approach would be for the creditors to ask the court for the appointment of a receiver to run the business. Obviously, he would not be regarded as a partner since that would hardly be his **intention**.

(b) **Partners can pay their employees or agents by a share of profits.** It has long been the practice of some organisations to pay employees in part by some profit-sharing scheme. The Act makes this possible without putting the employees at risk of being regarded as partners and liable for the debts of the firm if the true partners run into money trouble.

The provision is also important to the true partners because the giving of labour is sufficient to form a partnership: the putting in of money by way of capital is not essential. So this provision makes sure that the employees themselves cannot claim to be partners just because they are sharing profits under an employees' scheme.

(c) **Partners can pay interest on a loan by a share of net profits provided that the contract of loan is in writing and signed by all the parties to it.** This provision will protect a lender if a creditor tries to make him liable for the debts of the firm he has lent the money to, as where the creditor argues that the lender is really a dormant partner.

However, the lender must not take part in the running of the business. Remember also that the lender will not need the protection of this provision if he is paid a fixed rate of interest on his loan, e.g. 8 per cent per annum instead of 8 per cent per annum of the profit. If he is paid 8 per cent per annum interest, he is clearly a creditor and not a partner.

Do not think, because there is no written contract, that a lender will always be a partner. It is still a matter for the court to decide if it is argued that he is. Normally a properly drafted written contract should persuade the court that the lender is not a partner.

Deferred creditors

Under s 3 those receiving money from the firm under heading (c) above are deferred creditors if the partners go bankrupt during their lifetime or die insolvent.

Lenders will not get any of the money owed to them until all other creditors have been paid £1 in the £.

Thus, lenders of money do not get the best of both worlds. Section 2 provides that they do not become partners and liable for debts, but s 3 makes them deferred creditors if the partners are insolvent.

TYPES OF PARTNERS

Partners are of different types in law as set out below.

The general partner

This is the usual type of partner who, under s 24, has the right to take part in the management of the business unless there is an agreement between himself and the other partner(s) that he should not. For example, the partnership agreement may say that some junior partners are not to order goods or sign cheques. We shall see, however, that in spite of restrictions of this kind, if a junior partner ordered goods on behalf of the firm, though he had no authority to do so, the contract would be good and the seller could sue the partners for the price if they did not pay.

However, by ignoring the partnership agreement and making unauthorised contracts in this way, the junior partner could give his co-partners grounds to dissolve the firm, on the grounds that he was in breach of the partnership agreement, and exclude him from their future business operations.

The dormant partner

The 1890 Act does not mention this type of partner but in fact he is a partner who puts money (capital) into the firm but takes no active part in the management of the business. If he does take part in management, he would cease to be a dormant partner and become a general partner.

The salaried partner

It is quite common today, at least in professional practices of, for example, solicitors and accountants, to offer a young assistant a salaried partnership without the assistant putting any money into the firm as the general (or equity) partners do.

Normally, these salaried partners are paid a salary just as an employee is with tax and national insurance being deducted from it. They are not partners for the purpose of dissolving the firm. If they want to leave they do so by serving out their notice or getting paid instead.

However, because they usually appear on the firm's letterheading as partners, or on the list of partners for inspection under the Business Names Act 1985 (see later), they could, according to the decision in Stekel v Ellice (1973), be liable to pay the debts of the firm as a partner if the outsider has relied on their status as such.

Because of this case a salaried partner should get a full indemnity, as it is called, from the general partners in case he is made to pay the firm's debts or meet its liability to its clients. In practice this will not happen unless the firm has not paid its debts or satisfied its liability to clients. Liability as a partner is joint and several so that if A is a full partner and B a salaried partner, and the debt £2,000, either A or B could be made to pay it all and then claim only a contribution, which would often be one half, from the other partner. Thus, if B pays the £2,000, he is entitled to £1,000 from A. However, if B gets an indemnity from A, then if B has to pay the £2,000, he can recover all of it from A.

There is no real problem for the salaried partner in the large firm with its massive insurances and extensive assets, but the practice has spread to medium and small firms of, e.g., accountants and solicitors where problems could arise in terms of partner liability.

An illustration involving a small law firm appears below.

Nationwide Building Society v *Lewis* (1998)
Bryan Lewis & Co, a two-partner law firm, was sued by the building society for alleged negligence in connection with advice given to the society on a mortgage application. The second defendant was a Mr Williams who was a salaried partner described as a partner on the firm's letterhead. Mr Lewis wrote the relevant report which allegedly contained negligent advice but was bankrupt and the society pursued its claim for damages against Mr Williams. He was found initially to be jointly and severally liable with Mr Lewis and required to pay any damages awarded without much hope of getting a contribution from Mr Lewis, and this even though Mr Williams did not write the relevant report and played no part in its preparation. On appeal he was held not liable. The Society had not **relied** on him as a partner.

The partner by holding out (or by estoppel)

The usual way in which this happens in practice is where a person allows his or her name to appear on the firm's letterheading, or on the list of partners for inspection under the Business Names Act 1985 whether that person is or is not a full partner. (See *Stekel* v *Ellice* (1973) and *Nationwide Building Society* v *Lewis* (1998).) It can also happen on the retirement of a partner if the partner retiring does not get his name off the letterheading or list.

Under s 14 everyone who by words, spoken or written, or by conduct, represents himself, or knowingly allows himself to be represented, as a partner in a particular firm, is liable as a partner to anyone who has, because of that, given credit to the firm or advanced money to it.

Thus, although such a person is not truly a partner, he may be sued by a client or creditor who has **relied** on the fact he was a partner.

However, to become a partner by holding out (or estoppel, as it is also called) the person held out must **know** that he is being held out as a partner and if he knows it must also be shown that he **consents**. The following case is an example.

Tower Cabinet Co Ltd v *Ingram* (1949)
In January 1946 Ingram and a person named Christmas began to carry on business in partnership as household furnishers under the name of 'Merry's' at Silver Street, Edmonton, London. The partnership lasted until April 1947 when it was brought to an end by mutual agreement. After the dissolution of the firm, Christmas continued to run 'Merry's' and had new notepaper printed on which Ingram's name did not appear. In January 1948 Christmas was approached by a representative of Tower Cabinet and eventually ordered some furniture from them. The order was confirmed on letterheading which had been in use before the original partnership was dissolved and Ingram's name was on it, as well as that of Christmas. Ingram had no knowledge of this and it was contrary to an agreement which had been made between him and Christmas that the old letterheading was not to be used. Tower Cabinet obtained a judgment for the price of the goods against 'Merry's' and then tried to enforce that judgment against Ingram as a member of the firm. The court decided that since Ingram had not knowingly allowed himself to be represented as a partner in 'Merry's' within s 14 of the Partnership Act 1890, he was not liable as a partner by holding out (or estoppel).

Comment. As the case shows, a partner who has retired will not be liable if after retirement his name appears on the firm's letterheading if the other partners agree before he retires that the stock of old letterheading will be destroyed, or that his name will be crossed out. If old notepaper is used in spite of the agreement, the ex-partner is not liable: there is no duty in law to stop people telling lies! However, something should be done to show lack of consent if it is known that old letterheading is being used. This could be, for example, a recorded delivery letter to the continuing partners expressing dissent.

A partner who intends to work with the firm, perhaps part time, after retirement, can avoid the above problems by describing himself on the firm's letterheading as a 'consultant'.

The person who is held out is liable to a client or creditor who has relied on him being a partner. That is all s 14 says. However, in *Hudgell, Yeates & Co v Watson* (1978), the court said that the true or actual partners could also be liable to such a client or creditor if they themselves were responsible for the holding out or knowingly allowed holding out to take place.

Section 14 provides that the continued use of a deceased partner's name will not make his estate (that is, the property he has left on death) liable for the debts of the firm.

It is worth noting that the 'holding out' provisions of s 14 are applied by the court when making a salaried partner liable.

MEMBERSHIP OF THE FIRM

As we have seen, for most partnerships, the maximum number of partners allowed is 20 but this limit does not apply, for example, to partnerships of solicitors, accountants, and members of the Stock Exchange, and other businesses and professions, such as medical practitioners, which may be permitted by statutory instruments issued from time to time and where there may be partnerships of unlimited size. We have seen, also, that practising barristers cannot be in partnership.

These are negative rules but there are some positive provisions to try to help people become partners in the Sex Discrimination Act 1975 and the Race Relations Act 1976. The sex discrimination provisions are extended to all partnerships (Sex Discrimination Act 1986) but in the case of race discrimination only if there are six or more partners. This covers failure to offer a person a partnership on sex or race grounds, or to offer it but on worse terms, or to refuse or give inferior benefits, facilities and services to a partner on the grounds of sex or race, for example to refuse a cheap loan for house purchase or the use of a firm's car.

The restrictions on race discrimination to firms with six or more partners does in fact allow race discrimination in the smaller firms, but not, for example, in the major accounting or law firms.

A minor may become a member of a partnership (*Lovell and Christmas v Beauchamp* (1894)) but can avoid (get out of) the contract at any time while he is under 18 or for a reasonable period of time afterwards.

The law in practice prohibits a partnership with a person of unsound mind who does not understand the nature of the partnership arrangement he has made. These capacity problems are also dealt with in Chapter 7.

THE FIRM AND THE FIRM NAME

Generally

In English law the ordinary partnership firm is not an artificial person separate from the partners. In other words, it is not a person (or *persona*) at law as a company is.

If there are ten partners in 'Snooks, Twitchett & Co', then the firm name, that is 'Snooks, Twitchett & Co', is only a convenient short form for (or a collective designation of) all the partners. It saves reeling off all their names when business is done. Thus, a contract can be made in the firm name.

If the firm wishes to sue, or if it is sued by a creditor, the Rules of the Supreme Court (which are rules made by the judges to deal with procedure in court) do give a sort of personality to the firm in that they allow:

(a) actions by and against outsiders in the firm name; 'Snooks, Twitchett & Co' can sue or be sued in that name;
(b) enforcement of judgments and orders against the assets of the firm, as by taking and selling those assets to pay the judgment creditor;

(c) the Revenue to make an assessment to taxation on the firm as such in respect of the profits (see further, Chapter 4).

A judgment against the firm can also be enforced in the same way against the private property of any partner if the assets of the firm are not enough.

So, although in legal theory a partnership firm is not a *persona* at law, for some practical purposes, e.g. contracting, suing and being sued, and taxation, the firm is regarded as a sort of independent entity.

Choice of name

Restrictions on the name chosen for the firm are set out below.

Passing off at common law

As far as the common law is concerned, partners, say A and B, can trade in any name that suits them so long as the name does not suggest that their business is the same as that of a competitor. It must not deceive or confuse the customers of some other person or persons, say, C and D.

If it does, the court will, if asked, give an injunction and/or damages against A and B to protect the business of C and D.

However, people can carry on business in their **own names,** even if there is some confusion with another person's business, unless it is part of a scheme deliberately to deceive the public as the following case shows.

Croft v *Day* (1843)

A firm called Day & Martin were well-known makers of boot polish. The original Mr Day and Mr Martin had been dead for some time but Mr Croft had bought the business and carried it on in the 'Day & Martin' name. A real Mr Day and a real Mr Martin went into the manufacture of boot polish and adopted the Day & Martin name for the fraudulent purpose of representing to the public that they were the old and widely known firm of that name. Mr Croft went to court and was given an injunction to stop the real Mr Day and the real Mr Martin from trading in their own names in the circumstances of this case.

Business names and company legislation

Under the **Business Names Act 1985** the names of all the members of a partnership and their addresses in Great Britain where documents can be served must be stated in a notice which must be prominently displayed so that it can be easily read at all the firm's business premises. The names must also be stated in readable form on all business letters and documents. However, this requirement is relaxed in the case of a firm which has more than 20 partners. If there are more than 20 partners, the firm may choose not to list the names of the partners on the relevant documents but have instead a statement on the business letters and documents of the firm's principal place of business with an indication that a list of partners' names can be obtained and inspected there. If this choice is made, no partner's name shall appear on the relevant documents except in the text of a letter or by way of signature. The Act also requires every partnership to provide to anyone with whom it is doing or discussing business a note of the partners' names and addresses on such information being asked for by that person.

In some cases official approval is required for the use of certain partnership names. For example, the use of the word 'Royal' in a firm's name requires the approval of the Home Office. These matters were more fully considered in Chapter 4.

Under the **Companies Act 1985** the use of the descriptions 'Company' or 'and Company' are allowed for partnerships even though they suggest that they are companies. However, the Companies Act 1985 makes it an offence to use a firm name which ends with the expression 'Public Limited Company' or 'plc' or 'Limited' or 'Ltd' for associations such as partnerships, whether ordinary partnerships or limited partnerships. Failure to comply with this rule results in liability to a fine for every day it goes on.

THE RELATIONSHIP BETWEEN PARTNERS AND OUTSIDERS

The power of a partner, including a salaried partner, to make himself and his other partners liable for transactions which he enters into **on behalf of the firm** (not on his own behalf) is based on the law of agency. Each partner is the agent of his co-partners.

Section 5 makes this clear. It says that every partner is the agent of the firm and of his co-partners for the purpose of the business of the partnership.

PARTNERS' POWERS

A partner's authority to enter into transactions on behalf of the firm and his co-partners may be set out under the following headings.

Actual authority

If a partner is asked by his co-partners to buy a new van for the firm's use and makes a contract to purchase one, the firm is bound. Section 6 deals with authorised acts and says that the firm will be liable for the authorised acts of partners and also of employees of the firm.

Apparent or 'ostensible' authority

If a partner enters into a transaction on behalf of the firm without authority, the person he deals with may, if he does not know of the lack of authority, hold the firm bound under the provisions of s 5 which gives partners some apparent authority.

However, s 5 says that **the transaction must be connected with the business.** If there is a dispute about this, the court will decide what can be said to be 'connected', regardless of what the partnership agreement may say.

Mercantile Credit Co Ltd v Garrod (1962)
Mr Parkin and Mr Garrod had entered into an agreement as partners for the letting of garages and the carrying out of motor repairs, but the agreement expressly excluded the buying and selling of cars. Parkin, without Garrod's knowledge, sold a car to Mercantile for the sum of £700 but the owner of the car had not consented to the sale. The finance company did not, therefore, become the owner of the car and wanted its money back. The court held that the firm was liable and that Mr Garrod was liable as a partner to repay what the firm owed to Mercantile. The judge dismissed the argument that the transaction did not bind the firm because the agreement excluded the buying and selling of cars. He looked at the matter instead from 'what was apparent to the outside world in general'. Parkin was doing an act of a like kind to the business carried on by persons trading as a garage.

Comment. The point of the case is that although the buying and selling of cars was expressly forbidden by the partnership agreement, the firm was bound. This is a correct application of s 8, which provides that internal restrictions on the authority of partners will have effect only if the outsider deals with a partner, but with actual notice of the restrictions. In this case Mercantile had no such knowledge of the restrictions.

Also the transaction must be carried out **in the usual way of business.** In other words, it must be a **normal** transaction for the business.

An example can be seen in *Goldberg v Jenkins* (1889) where a partner borrowed money on behalf of the firm at 60 per cent interest per annum when money could be borrowed at between 6 per cent and 10 per cent per annum. He had no actual authority to enter into such a transaction and the court held that the firm was not bound to accept the loan. The firm did borrow money but it was not usual or normal to borrow at that high rate.

Finally, s 5 says that **the outsider must know or believe that he is dealing with a partner in the firm.** Because of the requirements of the Business Names Act 1985 as regards the display of the names of the owners of the firm on various documents and in various places which we have already considered, a **dormant partner** is now more likely to be known as a partner to an outsider. So if a dormant partner makes an unauthorised contract in the ordinary course of business in the usual or normal way, the outsider should now be able to say that he knew or believed the dormant partner to be a partner. If so, a dormant partner can enter into an unauthorised transaction which will bind the firm under s 5. If the outsider does not know the dormant partner is a member of the firm, as where the 1985 Act is not being complied with, then the firm will not be bound. The dormant partner would be liable to compensate the outsider for any loss following upon his failure to get a contract with the firm.

Examples of apparent authority as laid down by case law

Section 5 does not say what acts are 'in the usual course of business'. However, the courts have, over the years, and sometimes in cases heard before the 1890 Act was passed codifying the law, decided that there are a number of definite areas in which a partner has apparent authority. These are set out below.

1 All partners in all businesses. Here there is apparent authority to sell the goods (but not the land) of the firm, and to buy goods (but not land) on behalf of the firm; to receive money in payment of debts due to the firm and give valid receipts. So if A pays a debt due to the firm to B, a partner, who gives A a receipt and then fails to put the money into the firm's funds, A is nevertheless discharged from payment of the debt. There is also a power to pay debts owed by the firm including a power to draw cheques for this purpose. Partners can also employ workers, but once they are set on they are employees of **all** the partners so that one partner cannot discharge an employee without the consent of the others. Partners also have an insurable interest in the firm's property and can insure it. They may also employ a solicitor to defend the firm if an action is brought against it. The authority of an individual partner to employ a solicitor to bring an action on behalf of the firm seems to be restricted to actions to recover debts owing to the firm.

2 All partners in trading partnerships. Partners in trading firms have powers **which are additional** to those set out in **1** above. Thus partners in a firm of grocers have more powers than partners in a professional practice of, e.g., law or accountancy. There does not seem to be any good reason for this, but it has been confirmed by many cases in court and cannot be ignored.

In *Wheatley* v *Smithers* (1906) the judge said in regard to what was meant by the word 'trader': 'One important element in any definition of the term would be that trading implies buying or selling.' This was applied in *Higgins* v *Beauchamp* (1914) where it was decided that a partner in a business running a cinema had no implied power to borrow on behalf of the firm. The partnership agreement did not give power to borrow and because the firm did not trade in the *Wheatley* v *Smithers* sense, there was no implied power to borrow. If a firm is engaged in trade, the main additional implied powers of the partners are:

(a) to borrow money on the credit of the firm even beyond any limit agreed on by the partners unless this limit is known to the lender. Borrowing includes overdrawing a bank account;

(b) to secure the loan, which means giving the lender a right to sell property belonging to the firm if the loan is not repaid.

Situations of no apparent authority

No partner, whether in a trading firm or not, has apparent authority in the following situations:

1 He cannot make the firm liable on a deed. He needs the authority of the other partners. This authority must be given by deed. In English law an agent who is to make contracts by deed must be appointed as an agent by a written document which states that it is a deed.

2 He cannot give a guarantee, e.g. of another person's debt, on which the firm will be liable.

3 He cannot accept payment of a debt at a discount by, e.g., accepting 75p instead of £1, nor can he take something for the debt which is not money. He cannot, therefore, take shares in a company in payment of a debt owed to the firm.

4 He cannot bind the firm by agreeing to go to arbitration with a dispute. Going to arbitration with a dispute and having it heard by, say, an engineer, if the dispute relates, for example, to the quality of engineering work done under a contract, is a sort of compromise of the right to go first to a court of law and have the case heard by a judge. A partner cannot compromise the legal rights of the firm.

5 As we have seen, a partner has no apparent authority to convey or enter into a contract for the sale of partnership land.

A partner's liability for debt and breach of contract by the firm

If, because of actual or apparent authority, a partner (or for that matter another agent such as an employee) makes the firm liable to pay a debt or carry out a contract, as where goods are ordered and the firm refuses to take delivery, the usual procedure will be to sue the firm in the firm name. If the court gives the claimant a judgment and the firm does not have sufficient assets to meet it, the partners are liable to pay it from their private assets. Under s 3 of the Civil Liability (Contribution) Act 1978 each partner is liable to pay the amount of the judgment in full. He will then have a right to what is called a contribution from his co-partners.

Before the 1978 Act contribution was equal. Thus, if A paid a partnership debt of £300, he could ask his partners, B and C, for a contribution of £100 each.

This rule of equal contribution was taken away by s 2 of the 1978 Act, which provides that the amount of any contribution which the court may give is to be what it thinks is 'just and equitable' so that it need not in all cases be equal, but most often will be.

The effect of the above rules is that a partner can be required to pay the firm's debts from his private assets. From this we can see that only if **all** the partners are unable to pay the firm's debts will the firm be truly insolvent (decided most recently in *Secretary of State for Trade and Industry* v *Forde* (1997)).

Under s 9 the estate of a deceased partner is also liable but **only** for the debts of the firm which were incurred while the deceased was a partner.

Torts

Under s 10 the firm is liable for the torts of partners which they commit in the ordinary course of business, but not where the partner acts outside the scope of the firm's usual activities.

Therefore, a partner in an accountancy practice who prepares the financial statements of a company negligently in the course of the firm's business will not only be liable to the client and possibly to others who he knows will rely on those statements, say, to invest in the company, but will also make his fellow partners liable.

This is not the case in a limited liability partnership under the Act of the same name passed in 2000. In such a case only the firm's assets and the private assets of the negligent partner are at risk. The Act of 2000 is further considered at the end of this chapter.

At common law the firm is also liable for the torts of its employees committed in the course of their employment. So if the firm's van driver injures a pedestrian by negligent driving, both he and the firm would be liable under the common law rule of vicarious liability.

The words of s 10 make it clear that there is no action by one partner against the firm's assets for injuries caused by torts in the course of business. Thus, in *Mair* v *Wood* (1948) fishermen operated a trawler in partnership. One partner was injured when he fell because another partner had failed to replace an engine hatch properly. The court held that the injured partner had no claim in negligence against the firm and its assets but only against the negligent partner in his personal capacity, a successful claim resulting in the payment of damages from the negligent partner's personal assets and not from those of the firm.

LIABILITY OF INCOMING AND OUTGOING PARTNERS

Now we shall deal with the period during which the partner is liable for the firm's debts, or to put it in another way, from what date do his co-partners become his agents and when does that agency come to an end?

There are four things to look at as set out below.

1 Admission as a partner. Under s 17 a person does not simply by becoming a partner take on liability for debts or torts incurred by the firm before he joined it. He can if he wishes take on this liability by a process called novation (see below).

The position of incoming partners, or joiners as they are sometimes called, was affirmed by the High Court in *HF Pension Scheme Trustees Ltd* v *Ellison* (1999) where it was decided that since the relationship of partners was based on agency, an incoming partner could not be liable as a principal in terms of his personal capacity for the negligence of a co-partner that took place before he joined the firm, because the negligent acts could not have been done on his behalf.

2 Retirement as a partner. Also under s 17 a person does not, by retiring, cease to be liable for the debts and obligations of the firm incurred before he retired. The law is not likely to allow a partner to avoid his liabilities simply by retiring from the firm.

A retiring partner is not liable for future debts or liabilities unless, as we have seen, he is held out under s 14 or under s 36 because he has not given proper notice of his retirement. (See below.)

The date on which the contract was made or order given decides the matter of liability. So in a contract for the sale of goods, A, a retired partner, will be liable if the contract or order was made or given when he was a partner, even if the goods were delivered after he had retired.

3 Novation and indemnity. Under s 17 a retiring partner may be discharged from liabilities incurred before retirement if an agreement to that effect, called a **novation**, is made with the following people as parties to it:

(a) the partners who are to continue the business;
(b) the creditor concerned; and
(c) the retiring partner.

The agreement releases the retiring partner from his liabilities and accepts in his place the liability of the continuing partners, either alone or with the addition of any new partners.

The use of a novation is rare except perhaps in the case of banks which may well release an outgoing partner if they have enough cover from the other partners including any new partner in terms of a guarantee of the firm's indebtedness.

Creditors are not forced to accept or take part in novation and may continue to regard the retiring partner as liable for debts incurred while he was a partner. If this is so, the retiring partner should get an **indemnity** from the continuing partners. This will not release him from liability to the creditors but if he does have to pay a pre-retirement debt, he can recover what he has paid in full under the indemnity, and not just a contribution which is all he could recover without the indemnity.

The indemnity approach is much more common than the novation approach. It is in any case impractical to use a novation where there are a considerable number of creditors. It would be a lengthy and difficult process to get, say, 100 trade creditors to join in a novation. In fact, the indemnity is often found in the partnership agreement which may have a clause such as 'In the event of retirement the remaining partners shall take over the liabilities of the firm'.

4 Notifying retirement. The law requires a retiring partner to notify his retirement. The reason for this is that people who deal with the firm are entitled, in all fairness, to assume when they do business with it that all the partners are the same unless there has been notice of a change.

The rules are set out in s 36 which states, in effect, that if X, who was a partner in Y & Co, leaves the firm and the firm contracts with Z who knew that X was a member of the firm but does not know that he has left, X will be liable to Z (along with other partners of course) if the firm does not meet its obligations. To avoid this liability there must have been adequate notice of X's retirement.

In order to indicate what adequate notice is, the law divides creditors into three classes as follows:

1 Creditors who have previously dealt with the firm and who knew X was a partner. In this case it is necessary to show that the creditor received actual notice of the retirement. This may be by a letter from the firm, or by receiving a letter from the firm on which X's name is deleted, or by seeing the notice of retirement in *The London Gazette* (see below), **but only if he actually reads the *Gazette*.**

2 Creditors who have not had previous dealings with the firm but who knew or believed X to be a partner before he retired. As far as these people go, X will not be liable for post-retirement debts:

(a) If they had for some reason actual knowledge of X's retirement; or
(b) X's retirement was published in *The London Gazette*, **whether it was seen or not.**

The London Gazette is published daily by the Stationery Office and contains all sorts of public announcements: for example, bankruptcies, company liquidations and partnership dissolutions.

3 Creditors who have not had previous dealings with the firm and do not know that X was ever a partner. These people cannot hold X liable for post-retirement debts even if no notice has been received by them and even though no notice has been put in the *Gazette*. X could only be liable to these people if he was knowingly held out as a partner under s 14.

In *Tower Cabinet Co Ltd* v *Ingram* (1949), which was dealt with earlier in this chapter, no notice of Mr Ingram's retirement was put in the *Gazette*, but he was not liable to Tower Cabinet under s 36 because they did not know or believe him to be a partner prior to his retirement. He was not liable either under s 14 (holding out) for reasons already given.

Section 36 states that the estate of a deceased or bankrupt partner is not liable for debts incurred after death or bankruptcy, as the case may be, even if no advertisement or notice of any kind has been given.

Just as a written partnership agreement is to be recommended at the beginning of the relationship, so it is very sensible to address the matters that arise when a partner leaves by retirement and record them in a binding deed of retirement.

RELATIONSHIP OF PARTNERS WITHIN THE PARTNERSHIP

We shall now deal with the relation of partners to one another. It is governed by ss 19–31 of the 1890 Act, the provisions of which are set out below.

The ability to change the partnership agreement

Section 19 states that partners can change the business of the firm but because of the provisions of s 24 **all** the partners must be in agreement about this.

Partners can also change the provisions of the 1890 Act which the Act puts into partnership agreements unless the partners have dealt with the matter in the agreement themselves. For example, the Act provides in s 24 that profits and losses are to be shared equally but the partners may provide for a different share, e.g. one-third/two-thirds, in their agreement.

The provisions of the Act which deal with the relationship of the partners and outsiders cannot be changed in this way. Section 8 says that internal restrictions on the authority of partners, for example in the partnership agreement, have no effect on an outsider unless he has **actual** notice of the restriction.

This was illustrated by the case of *Mercantile Credit Co Ltd* v *Garrod* (1962) where the partnership agreement said that there was to be no buying or selling of cars. This did not prevent the sale of a car to Mercantile by a partner being good, since Mercantile had no knowledge of the restriction.

A written partnership agreement may be varied by attaching a written and signed indorsement to the original agreement. However, even where the original agreement is written (and obviously if it is oral) the partners may, either orally or by the way they deal with one another, vary the agreement. This is not surprising since the original agreement of partners does not have to be in writing.

The case which follows is an example of partners agreeing to one thing but sliding into a different way of going on. The books of the firm were kept and the accounts prepared from them in a way which was different from the original agreement.

Pilling v *Pilling* (1887)

A father took his two sons into partnership with him. The partnership agreement provided that the assets of the business were to remain the father's and that he and his sons should share profits and losses in thirds. Each son was to have, in addition to a one-third share of the profits, £150 a year out of the father's share of profit, and repairs and expenses were to be paid out of profits. It was also agreed that the father **only** should have four per cent on his capital per annum and that the depreciation of the mill and machinery, i.e. the major assets, was to be deducted before the profit was calculated.

The partnership lasted for ten years and no depreciation was charged on the mill and machinery. The £150 per annum was paid to the sons but it was charged against the profits of the business and not against the father's share. Each partner was credited with interest on capital, not merely the father, but, as it happens, the profit was divided into thirds. Later on the court was asked to decide whether the assets of the business still belonged to the father or whether they belonged to the firm as partnership property. The court decided that the way in which the partners had dealt with each other was evidence of a new agreement. The assets were therefore partnership property, even though the articles had said that they were to continue to belong to the father.

Comment. The major change here was to allow each partner interest on capital although only the father brought any in. From this the court presumed that the father's capital had become partnership property and had not remained his personal property, as was the original intention in the agreement.

Partnership property

Whether property becomes partnership property or remains in the separate ownership of a particular partner depends upon the intention of the partners. Ideally this intention should be made absolutely clear in the partnership agreement if there is one. If property is treated as partnership property, it becomes an asset of the firm and is transferred to all the partners as co-owners.

Under ss 20 and 21, and in the absence of an express agreement to the contrary, property will be regarded as partnership property if:

- it is purchased with partnership money, as by a cheque drawn on the firm's account;
- it is brought into the firm by a partner who has the value of it credited to his capital account, which clearly indicates the intention to bring it in;
- it is treated as an essential part of the firm's property by the partners; but the mere fact that the property is used in the business is not enough to transfer that property to the firm. This statement is supported by the following case.

Miles v *Clarke* (1953)

Mr Clarke wished to start a photography business and he took a lease of premises for the purpose. He was not a skilled photographer and employed other people to do the photography work. The business made a loss but after some negotiations Mr Miles, who was a successful freelance photographer, decided to join in with Mr Clarke. Miles brought in his customers and there were a large number of these. The agreement made between Miles and Clarke provided that the profits were to be shared equally and that Miles was to draw £153 per month on account of his profits. The business did well but Miles and Clarke quarrelled and it had to be wound up. In this action the court was asked to decide the ownership of the assets and Miles was claiming a share in all the assets of the business. The court decided that there was no agreement except as to the way profits were to be divided and so the stock in trade of the firm and other consumable items, such as films, must be considered as part of the partnership assets, even though they were brought in by Clarke. However, the lease and other plant and equipment should be treated as belonging to the partner who brought them in – that was Clarke. The personal goodwill, i.e. customers, belonged to the person who brought them in, so Miles retained the value of his customers and Clarke retained the value of his.

In normal circumstances there is no doubt about the ownership at least of the major assets of the firm. For example, a lease of premises from which to conduct business would be bought with the firm's money and transferred into the names of some or all of the partners to hold as trustees for themselves and others as partners. The device of the trust is required because, as we know, an ordinary partnership is not a *persona* at law. The problems outlined above arise when, say, the lease is used as business premises but is held in the name of one partner who has allowed its use within the firm. Does he hold it on an implied trust for himself and the others or not? That is the question which a court may have to decide.

The commercial importance of identifying partnership property

The ability to identify partnership property is important in the business world:

1 To the partners themselves, because any increase in value of partnership property belongs to the firm (i.e. all the partners), but if the property belongs to only one partner the increased value belongs to him alone. Also, a decrease in value is suffered by the firm if it is partnership property but if it belongs to only one partner all the loss is his.

2 To the creditors of the firm and the creditors of the partners individually, since this affects what property is available to pay their debts if the business fails. If a firm goes out of business and all the partners are also insolvent, then the firm's creditors can have the firm's assets sold to pay their debts before the private creditors of the partners have access to those assets. Also, private creditors have first right to sell private assets before the firm's creditors have access to them.

3 Because dealings with partnership property must be only for partnership purposes in accordance with the partnership agreement. If the property is owned personally by a partner, he can do what he likes with it unless the firm has some contractual rights over it, as where the firm is renting it from the partner. Obviously, the contract must be complied with or an action for damages would be available to the firm against the partner.

Implied financial terms

These are set out below.

Profits and losses

Section 24 says that unless there is some other agreement between the partners, all the partners are to share equally in the capital and profits of the business and must contribute equally towards losses of capital or otherwise.

This is regardless of capital contributed. If those who have contributed more capital are to get more of the profit, the partnership agreement must say so.

Interest on capital

Section 24 also says that, unless the partners agree, no partner is to get interest on the capital he puts into the firm. In practice, where partners do not make equal contributions of capital it is often agreed that those who contributed more are to get interest on capital at an agreed rate per annum. This interest is taken away from profits before they are distributed to the partners.

Interest on advances (loans)

If a partner helps to finance the firm by making it a loan on top of contributing capital, then s 24 provides that he is entitled to 5 per cent per annum on the advance (or loan) from the date when it was made. There is no rule that an advance by a partner to the firm carries any higher interest. This has to be specially provided for.

Indemnity

Section 24 also requires the firm to indemnify every partner who makes payments from his own funds in the ordinary conduct of the business. Thus, if while a partner is negotiating an insurance for the firm he is told by the broker that a premium on an existing policy is due that day and he pays it with his own private cheque, the firm must pay him back.

Implied management powers

Management powers are normally written out in the partnership agreement. If not, the following rules apply:

1 **Under s 24(5) every partner may take part in the management of the business.** This is not surprising because a partnership is defined as the carrying on of business 'in common'. The right is also a fair one because a partner may find himself saddled with the debts of a firm, and if this is so, he should at least have the chance of managing it.

Any unjustified exclusion of a partner from the management of the firm will almost certainly enable him to petition to dissolve the firm on the just and equitable ground in s 35.

This right to manage concept has also been applied to small companies which are essentially partnerships in all but legal form. Cases illustrating this, such as *Ebrahimi* v *Westbourne Galleries* (1972) will be looked at in Chapter 6.

2 **Section 24(6) says that a partner is not entitled to a salary.** Partners share profits, but if the firm has some partners who are more active in the business than others it is usual for the partnership agreement to provide for a salary for the active partners which is paid in addition to a share of profit. A further exception is, as we have seen, the salaried partner where there is an entitlement to salary to the exclusion of any share of profits.

Apart from that, a partner who has had to work harder than usual because his fellow partner has failed to work as he should in the business is not entitled to an extra amount from the firm's assets. In the absence of agreement, the court will not make an award of remuneration while the firm is a going concern. The partner who is failing to work properly in the business is, however, in breach of a term which requires him to do so and this is a ground for the dissolution of the firm. The term may be found stated expressly in the partnership agreement but will in any case be implied.

3 **Under s 24(7) and (8) no new partners can be brought in and no change may be made in the business of the firm unless all the partners consent.** It should be noted, however, that a retiring partner's consent is not required.

This is a fair provision. New partners ought not to be thrust upon the old partners by a majority vote. Mutual confidence is essential.

As regards what are called 'ordinary matters', these are to be settled by a majority of the partners regardless of capital contributed, provided the decisions are made in good faith and after proper consultation with all of the partners. The Act makes no attempt to define 'ordinary matters'. There is no case law to help us. Much will depend upon the circumstances of the case.

4 Under s 24(9) every partner is entitled to access to, and may also inspect and copy, the firm's books. These books must be kept at the place where the business is run or, if there is more than one place, at the main place of business.

The court will make an order (an injunction) preventing a partner from exercising the above rights if he is, e.g., taking the names of customers from the books to try to get them to use his own separate business instead of that of the firm.

Inspection may be through an agent (*Bevan* v *Webb* (1901)), so that a partner who was not able himself to assess financial information could employ an accountant to inspect the books.

5 Although the 1890 Act says nothing about it, it is implied by law that every partner shall attend at, and work in, the business. If he does not, the other partners have a ground to dissolve the firm. However, there is normally no claim for damages for breach of contract, these being a common law remedy and partnership, being based on equity, has no remedy of damages for breach of duty between partners.

Expulsion of a partner

Section 25 says that no majority of partners can expel any other partner unless a power to do so appears in the partnership agreement.

If an expulsion is challenged in the courts, the judge will be most concerned to see that a majority expulsion clause has not been abused.

It must be shown:

1 That the complaint which is said to allow expulsion is covered by the expulsion clause. For example, in *Snow* v *Milford* (1868) the court decided that the 'adultery of a banker all over Exeter' was not a ground for his expulsion because it was not within the wording of the expulsion clause. This dealt only with financial frauds which would discredit a banking business.

2 That the partner expelled was told what he had done wrong and given a chance to explain. An illustration is to be found in *Barnes* v *Youngs* (1898) where a partner who was living with a woman to whom he was not married continued to do so after becoming a partner. There was nothing to show that this was damaging to the firm's business. Even so, he was expelled by his fellow partners who refused to tell him why they were doing so. The court held that his expulsion was unlawful and ineffective.

3 That those who exercised the power of expulsion did so in all good faith. For example, in *Blisset* v *Daniel* (1853) a partner was expelled. He had done nothing wrong to hurt the firm, but the partnership agreement said that a majority of the partners could buy out another. The motive of the other partners was just to get a bigger share of the property and profits. The court said that the expulsion was not effective. It was done in bad faith.

However, if **1** to **3** above are satisfied, the court will regard the expulsion as valid. For example, in *Greenaway* v *Greenaway* (1940), the partnership agreement provided for expulsion in the event of conduct contrary to the good faith required of partners or prejudicial to their general interest. After several years of quarrelling, one partner assaulted another. The offender was given notice of expulsion. The court later said that although quarrelling by itself was not enough, the assault was inexcusable. Another reason for the expulsion was the fact that the offending partner had made disapproving remarks about a fellow partner to the firm's employees. This was not in line with the good faith rule. The expulsion was valid.

Of course, the expelled partner is entitled to his share of the firm's assets, as he would be if he retired. However, provision is often made to pay him out over a period of time and not immediately so that he cannot demand his total share of the assets as soon as he is expelled.

Relationship of utmost good faith

It is a basic principle of partnership law that each partner must treat his co-partners with utmost fairness and good faith. An example of bad faith in this context is, as we have seen, *Blisset* v *Daniel* (1853), above.

The principle of utmost good faith is not set out as a general proposition in the 1890 Act. The Act does, however, set out certain areas to which the good faith principle is applied. They are as follows:

1 The duty to account. Section 28 requires every partner to give true accounts and full information regarding all things affecting the firm to any partner.

This is a **positive duty** to disclose facts. It is not merely a **negative duty** not to misrepresent facts.

As the following case shows, silence can amount to misrepresentation as between partner and partner.

Law v Law (1905)

Two brothers, William Law and James Law, were partners in a woollen manufacturers' business in Halifax. William lived in London and did not take a very active part in the business and James offered to buy William's share for £10,000. After the sale William discovered that certain partnership assets, that is money lent on mortgage, had not been disclosed to him by James. William brought an action against James for misrepresentation. The court decided that there was a duty of disclosure in this sort of case and the action was settled by the payment of £3,550 to William, which he accepted in discharge of all claims between him and his brother.

Under s 29 each partner must also account to the firm for any benefit he has had without the consent of the other partners from any transaction concerning the firm or from any use by him of the partnership name or customer connection. An illustration is to be found in the following case.

Bentley v Craven (1853)

Mr Bentley carried on business in partnership with the defendants, Messrs Craven, Prest and Younge, as sugar refiners at Southampton. Craven was the firm's buyer and because of this he was able to buy sugar at a great advantage as to price. He bought supplies of sugar cheaply and sold it to the firm at the market price. The other partners did not realise that he was selling on his own account and Bentley, when he found out, brought this action, claiming for the firm a profit of some £853 made by Craven. The court decided that the firm was entitled to it.

Comment. Those who wish to make comparisons with other fiduciaries will note that a partner, like a trustee, may not make a private gain out of his membership of the firm. There is also a comparison with directors' secret profits and benefits, which will be dealt with in Chapter 6.

2 Duty not to compete with the firm. Section 30 provides that if a partner without the consent of his co-partners carries on any business of the same kind as his firm so as to compete with it, he must account for and pay over to the firm all the profits he has made from that competing business.

Section 30 is in fact no more than an extension of the duty to account because a partner cannot be prevented from competing by the use of s 30. The section actually allows him to compete but requires him to hand over all the profits of the competing business.

A particular partnership agreement may expressly provide that there shall be no competing business. If this is so, the other partners can get an injunction from the court to stop the competing business from being carried on.

DISSOLUTION

A partnership is usually dissolved without the help of the court, though sometimes the court is brought in.

Non-judicial dissolution

Any of the following events will normally bring about a dissolution of a partnership.

1 The ending of the period for which the partnership was to exist. Section 32(a) states that a partnership for a fixed term is dissolved when the term expires. A partnership for the joint lives of A, B and C ends on the death of A or B or C.

2 The achievement of the purpose for which the partnership was formed. By reason of s 32(b) a partnership for a single undertaking is dissolved at the end of it. In *Winsor v Schroeder* (1979), S and W put up equal amounts of cash to buy a house, improve it, and then sell it at a profit which was to be divided equally. The court decided that they were partners under s 32(b) and that the partnership would end when the land was sold and the profit, if any, divided.

If in partnerships of the types set out in 1 and 2 above, the firm continues in business after the period has expired, without any settlement of their affairs by the partners, an agreement not to dissolve will be implied. Unless there is a new agreement to cover the continuing partnership, it is a partnership at will. Section 27 applies to it so that the rights and duties of the partners are the same as before the original partnership ended. However, since it has now become a partnership at will, any partner can give notice to end it.

3 By the giving of notice. Under s 32(c) a partnership which is not entered into for a period of time or for a particular purpose can be dissolved by notice given by **any partner,** but not a limited partner.

The notice must be in writing if the partnership agreement is in the form of a deed (s 26(2)). If not, oral notice will do.

The notice takes effect when all the partners know of it or from any later date which the person giving the notice states as the date of dissolution (s 32(c)). No particular period of notice is required. Withdrawal of the notice requires the consent of all the partners (*Jones* v *Lloyd* (1874)), otherwise the dissolution goes ahead and the court will, if asked by a partner, order the other partners to wind up the firm with him. The court said in *Peyton* v *Mindham* (1972) that it could and would declare a dissolution notice to be of no effect if it was given in bad faith as where A and B dissolve a partnership with C by notice in order to exclude C from valuable future contracts.

Dissolution by notice depends on what the partnership agreement says. If, as in *Moss* v *Elphick* (1910), the partnership agreement says that dissolution is only to be by mutual consent of the partners, s 32(c) does not apply.

4 Death of a partner. Under s 33(1) the death of a partner (but not a limited partner) dissolves the firm. The share of the partner who has died goes to his personal representatives who are usually appointed by his will. They have the rights of a partner in a dissolution. Partnership agreements usually provide that the firm shall continue after the death of a partner so that the dissolution is only a technical one. A deceased partner's share is paid out to his personal representatives, although partnership agreements do sometimes provide for repayment of capital by instalments, or by annuities, e.g. to a spouse or other dependant. Of course, there is bound to be a true dissolution of a two-partner firm when one partner dies since if the other carries on business, it is as a sole trader.

5 Bankruptcy of a partner. By reason of s 33(1) the bankruptcy of a partner (not a limited partner) dissolves the firm. The partnership agreement usually provides that the business shall continue under the non-bankrupt partners, which means that the dissolution is again only a technical one, and the bankrupt partner's share is paid out to his trustee in bankruptcy. The agreement to continue the business must be made before the partner becomes bankrupt. (*Whitmore* v *Mason* (1861).)

6 Illegality. Under s 34 a partnership **is in every case** dissolved by illegality. There can be no contracting-out in the partnership agreement.
There are two types of illegality –

(a) *Where the business is unlawful;* for example, where the objects are unlawful because, as in *Stevenson & Sons Ltd* v *AG für Cartonnagen Industrie* (1918) the English company, Stevenson, was in partnership with a German company as a sole agent to sell the German company's goods. This would obviously involve day-to-day trading with an enemy in wartime and the partnership was therefore dissolved on the grounds of illegality. The classic case is *Everet* v *Williams* (1725). This was a claim by one highwayman against another to recover his share of profits derived from a partnership covering activities as a highwayman. The claim was dismissed because the partnership was illegal, being to commit crime, and the 'partners' were sentenced to be hanged!

(b) *Where the partners cannot legally form a partnership to carry on what is otherwise a legal business,* as in *Hudgell, Yeates & Co* v *Watson* (1978) where a firm of solicitors was regarded as dissolved when one partner had made himself unqualified to practise as a solicitor by mistakenly failing to renew his annual practising certificate.

Judicial dissolution

Dissolution by the court (normally the Chancery Division of the High Court) is necessary if there is a partnership for a fixed time or purpose and a partner wants to dissolve a firm before the time has expired or the purpose has been achieved and there is nothing in the partnership agreement which allows this to be done.

There must be grounds for dissolution. These are set out below.

(a) **Partner's mental incapability.** This a ground under the Mental Health Act 1983. The petition for dissolution is in this case heard by the Court of Protection which sits to look after the property of people who are of unsound mind or under some other disability. The partner concerned must be incapable, because of mental disorder, of managing his property and affairs.

A petition may be presented on behalf of the partner who is under the disability or by any of the other partners.

(b) **Partner's physical incapacity.** This is a ground under s 35(b). The incapacity must be permanent. In *Whitwell* v *Arthur* (1865) a partner was paralysed for some months. He had recovered when the court heard the petition and it would not grant a dissolution.

Partnership agreements often contain express clauses which allow dissolution after a stated period of incapacity. In *Peyton* v *Mindham* (1972) a clause allowing a fixed-term partnership to be dissolved after nine months' incapacity was enforced. (See the model partnership deed, clause 16(g) on pp 111–12.)

Section 35(b) states that the incapacitated partner cannot petition. It is up to his co-partners to do so, otherwise he continues as a partner.

(c) **Conduct prejudicial to the business.** Section 35(c) provides for this. The conduct may relate to the business, as in *Essell* v *Hayward* (1860) where a solicitor/partner misappropriated £8,000 of trust money in the course of his duties as a partner. This was a ground for dissolving a partnership for a fixed term, i.e. the joint lives of the partners.

It may, of course, be outside conduct. This will usually justify a dissolution if it results in a criminal conviction for fraud or dishonesty.

Moral misconduct is not enough unless, in the view of the court, it is likely to affect the business. In *Snow* v *Milford* (1868) where the matter of dissolution was also considered, as well as the matter of expulsion, 'massive adultery all over Exeter' was not regarded by the court as sufficient

grounds for dissolution under s 35(c). There was no evidence that the adulterous conduct had affected the business of the bank.

Section 35(c) forbids a petition by the partner in default.

(d) **Wilful or persistent breach of the agreement or conduct affecting the relationship.** This is covered by s 35(d). It includes, for example, refusal to meet on business or keep accounts, continued quarrelling and very serious internal disagreements. However, as the court said in *Loscombe* v *Russell* (1830), the conduct must be 'serious'. Thus, occasional rudeness or bad temper would not suffice.

'Wilful' means a serious breach inflicting damage on the firm. Less serious breaches are enough if 'persistent'. In *Cheesman* v *Price* (1865) a partner failed 17 times to enter small amounts of money he had received in the firm's books. The court ordered dissolution. The essential trust between the partners had gone.

Again, s 35(d) forbids a petition by the partner in default. No partner can force a dissolution by his own default.

(e) **The business can only be carried on at a loss.** This is provided for by s 35(e). It is hardly surprising as a ground for dissolution in view of the fact that partners are in business together with a view to profit, as s 1 states. Therefore, they must have a means to release themselves from loss.

Section 35(e) is not available if the losses are temporary. In *Handyside* v *Campbell* (1901) a sound business was losing money because a senior managing partner was ill. He asked the court for a dissolution. The court would not grant it. The other partners could manage the firm back to financial prosperity.

The court will not, however, expect the partners to put in more capital. (*Jennings* v *Baddeley* (1856).)

Any partner may petition.

(f) **The just and equitable ground.** Under s 35(f) the court may dissolve a partnership if it is just and equitable to do so. Although there is no direct authority on s 35(f), it appears to give the court wide powers to hear petitions which could not be made under the other five heads that we have considered.

In *Harrison* v *Tennant* (1856) a judicial dissolution was ordered where a partner was involved in long and messy litigation which he refused to settle. A similar order was made in *Baring* v *Dix* (1786) where the objects of the firm could not be achieved. The partnership was to further a patent device for spinning cotton which had wholly failed but Dix would not agree to dissolution. The court dissolved the firm.

It appears from *Re Yenidje Tobacco Co Ltd* (1916), a company dissolution based upon the fact that the company was in reality a partnership, that deadlock between the partners is enough for dissolution, even though the business is prospering.

Any partner may petition. The court is unlikely, however, to dissolve a firm on the petition of a partner committing misconduct unless the other partners are doing so as well.

The power of creditors to seek the dissolution of a partnership is considered under the heading 'The insolvent partnership' (see later in this chapter).

Effect of dissolution

Realisation and distribution of the assets

(a) *Realisation.* If it is not intended to bring the business to an end (i.e. wind it up) following a dissolution by reason, e.g., of death or retirement, the partnership agreement usually provides that the deceased or retiring partner's share in the firm's assets shall go to the remaining partners and that they shall pay a price for it based on the last set of accounts.

If this is not to be done, the assets of the firm will be sold on dissolution.

Section 39 gives each partner on dissolution the right to insist that the assets of the firm be used to pay creditors in full and that any surplus be paid to the partners according to their entitlement. For this purpose each partner has what is called a lien over the assets. It becomes effective only on dissolution. It is enforceable by the partner concerned applying to the court for the appointment of a receiver under his lien who will make the appropriate distribution.

(b) *Sale of goodwill.* If the assets are sold one of them may well be goodwill. It is unlikely these days that goodwill will appear on the balance sheet of the partnership accounts, but that does not mean that it does not exist. There are varying definitions of goodwill, e.g. 'the probability of the old customers resorting to the old place' (Lord Eldon, a famous Lord Chancellor); 'the public approbation which has been won by the business' (Sir Arthur Underhill – an authority on partnership law); and 'the benefit arising from connection and reputation' (Lord Lindley – one of our greatest equity lawyers, and later a judge who was the first author of the standard practitioners' work *Lindley on Partnership*).

Goodwill is in financial terms the excess of the price you pay for a business over the net tangible assets, such as plant and machinery, which you acquire.

When goodwill is sold, the seller and buyer usually agree by the contract of sale to restrictions to stop the seller from, for example, setting up in the same business again next door to the one he has just sold and taking back the goodwill of that business.

If there is no agreement as to restrictions on the seller, the position is as set out below:

- the purchaser may represent himself as continuing the business of the seller (*Churton* v *Douglas* (1859)), but he must not hold out the seller as still being in the business;
- the seller may, however, carry on a similar business and compete with the buyer (*Trego* v *Hunt* (1896)); this can decrease the value of partnership goodwill;
- the seller must not, however, compete under the name of the former firm or represent himself as continuing the same business;
- the seller may advertise his new business but may not actually circularise or otherwise canvass customers of his old firm.

(c) *Final account.* When the firm is dissolved and the property sold there is a final account between the partners and then a distribution of the assets. This account is a record of transactions from the date of the last accounts to the date of the winding-up.

(d) *Distribution of assets*. Section 44 applies and if the assets when realised are sufficient to satisfy all claims, payment is made first to outside creditors, both secured and unsecured. Then each partner is paid what is due to him as advances or loans, as distinct from capital. The costs of the winding-up are then paid (*Potter* v *Jackson* (1880)). Then each partner is paid the amount of capital due to him; any surplus is divided between the partners in the profit-sharing ratio.

If there are insufficient assets to pay outside creditors and the partners' entitlements, s 44(a) applies and the partners have to make good the deficiency in the profit and loss-sharing ratio.

The insolvent partnership

The Insolvent Partnerships Order 1994 (SI 1994/2421) came into force on 1 December 1994. It revokes and replaces the Insolvent Partnerships Order 1986 (SI 1986/2142). It provides a code for the winding-up of insolvent partnerships and introduces two new procedures, i.e. voluntary arrangements and administration orders for insolvent partnerships. The main provisions appear below. References to Articles and Schedules are references to Articles and Schedules in the Order.

Voluntary arrangements

Article 4 and Sch 1 introduce the rescue procedure of a voluntary arrangement into partnership insolvency. The members of an insolvent partnership make a proposal to the firm's creditors for the settlement of its debts by a binding voluntary arrangement. Part I of the Insolvency Act 1986 (company voluntary arrangements) is applied with appropriate modifications as set out in Sch 1.

Insolvent members of the firm may under Art 5 make use of the voluntary arrangement provisions of Part I of the 1986 Act (if corporate members of the firm) or Part VIII (if individuals).

Administration orders

Article 6 and Sch 2 provide for the appointment by the court of an administrator who can put proposals to creditors for the survival of the firm or a more advantageous realisation of its assets by applying Part II of the 1986 Act (Administration orders) with appropriate amendments for partnerships as set out in Sch 2. An application to the court must be presented by the members of the insolvent partnership or by a creditor or creditors or by all of those parties together or separately.

Winding-up by the court

Under Art 7 any insolvent partnership may be wound up by the Court (there is no provision for voluntary winding-up) under Part V of the 1986 Act (as modified by Sch 3) where no concurrent petition is presented against the partners. They become contributories to the full amount of the firm's debts. Before the court has jurisdiction, the firm must have carried on business in England and Wales at some time within the period of three years ending with the day on which the winding-up petition was presented.

A petition against the firm may be presented by a creditor or creditors and also by the liquidator or administrator of a corporate member of the firm or former corporate member. Also included are the administrator of the firm, a trustee in bankruptcy of a partner or former partner and the supervisor of a relevant voluntary arrangement.

The grounds are set out in s 221 of the 1986 Act as modified and set out in Sch 3. Of these, inability to pay debts will be the usual creditor ground but there are others, e.g. cessation of business and just and equitable ground, but in all cases the firm must be insolvent. Inability may be proved under s 222 of the 1986 Act (as modified and set out in Sch 3) by serving a written demand on the firm requiring it to pay a debt or debts exceeding £750 then due and the firm does not pay, secure or compound the debt within three weeks of service.

Application of Company Directors Disqualification Act 1986

Where there is a winding-up of the firm by the court, each partner is deemed an officer and director of the firm. If the court is satisfied that they have not run the firm responsibly, the partners could be disqualified as unfit to act as a director or in the management of a company for up to 15 years. Article 16 and Sch 8 apply.

ORDINARY LIMITED PARTNERSHIPS

Generally

The Limited Partnerships Act 1907 provides for the formation of limited partnerships in which one or more of the partners has only limited liability for the firm's debts. These partnerships are not common because in most cases the objective of limited liability can be better achieved by incorporation as a private company.

A limited partnership is not a legal entity and must not have more than 20 members, though this provision does not apply to limited partnerships of solicitors, accountants, or stockbrokers, among others. There must also be one general partner whose liability for the debts of the firm is unlimited. A body corporate may be a limited partner.

Registration

Every limited partnership must be registered with the Registrar of Companies. The following particulars must be registered by means of a statement signed by the partners:

(a) the firm name;
(b) the general nature of the business;
(c) the principal place of business;
(d) the full name of each partner;
(e) the date of commencement of the term of the partnership, if any;
(f) a statement that it is a limited partnership;
(g) the particulars of each limited partner and the amount contributed by him, whether in cash or otherwise.

Any change in the above particulars or the fact that a general partner becomes a limited partner must be notified to the Registrar within seven days. Failure to register means that the limited partner is fully liable as a general partner. When a general partner becomes a limited partner, the fact must be advertised in *The London Gazette* if the transaction is to be effective in law.

The Register of Limited Partnerships is open to inspection by the public who may also obtain certified copies of, or extracts from, any registered statement.

Rights and duties of a limited partner

A limited partner is not liable for the debts of the firm beyond his capital, but he may not withdraw any part of his capital and, even if he were to do so, he would still be liable to the firm's creditors for the amount he originally subscribed.

A limited partner has no power to bind the firm and may not take part in its management. If he does manage the firm, he becomes liable for all the liabilities incurred by the firm during that period. Nevertheless, he may give advice on management to the other partners and he may also inspect the books.

The death, bankruptcy or mental disorder of a limited partner does not dissolve the partnership and a limited partner cannot dissolve the partnership by notice.

In addition, any question arising as to ordinary business matters may be decided by a majority of general partners, and a new partner can be introduced without the consent of the existing limited partners.

LIMITED LIABILITY PARTNERSHIPS

We have now completed our study of the ordinary partnership and the ordinary limited partnership. Quite a lot of material is involved and the reader may wonder whether in view of the changes to be introduced by the new limited liability partnership it is worth looking at the older forms of business organisation. The answer has to be yes because the newer limited liability arrangements are designed mainly for the professional firms of lawyers and accountants who have for so long been liable to the full extent of their capital in the firm and personal property in meeting claims for negligence even though full indemnity insurance is not normally available. There are in the field of UK business many other partnerships consisting of trading firms which, of course, can use the limited liability regime. However, many may feel that registration and the filing of accounts for public inspection and other central controls are not worth a measure of limited liability. These trading partners are not really at risk of the major claims for damages faced by professional firms. This plus sheer inertia will mean that a large number of somewhat informal partnerships will continue to exist and that those embarking on a career in business will need to be familiar with all three structures, i.e. the ordinary partnership, the ordinary limited partnership, and the more recent limited liability partnership which may be used mainly by the firms of those in professional practice of one sort or another.

The Limited Liability Partnerships Act

The Limited Liability Partnerships Act 2000 received the Royal Assent on 20 July 2000. It effects a radical change in the liability of the firm and its partners, for those who adopt this new form of business organisation. The Partnership Act 1890 and the Limited Partnerships Act 1907 remain in force and the law relating to them is unchanged.

The main purpose of the Act is to create a new form of legal entity known as a limited liability partnership (LLP). An LLP combines the organisational flexibility and tax status of a partnership with limited liability for its members. The LLP and not its members will be liable to third parties, but a negligent member's personal assets will be at risk.

Section 1. This states that an LLP is a legal person with unlimited capacity. Its members may be liable to contribute to its assets on winding up.

Section 2. This deals with incorporation and requires at least two people to subscribe to an incorporation document to be sent to the Registrar of Companies. The contents of the incorporation document are dealt with – in particular, the situation of the registered office and the members on incorporation and whether some or all of them are to be 'designated members' (see below).

Section 3. This deals with the issue of a certificate of incorporation by the Registrar and provides that it is conclusive evidence that all requirements have been complied with.

Section 4. This deals with membership and provides that the members are those who sign the incorporation document or who become members by agreement with the other members. Cessation of membership is also by agreement.

Section 5. This is concerned with the relationship of the members, which is to be governed by any agreement between them or, failing such agreement, is to be governed by any provision in regulations to be made by the Secretary of State.

Section 6 states that each member of the LLP is an agent of it, unless he has no authority to act in a particular matter, although there are ostensible authority provisions, in that the outsider must, for example, be aware that there is no authority to act.

Of particular importance in terms of liability is s 6(4), which provides that where a member of an LLP is liable to any person (other than another member of the LLP) as a result of a wrongful act or omission of his in the course of the business of the LLP or with its authority, the LLP is liable to the same extent as the member. *This provision does not make other members liable.*

Thus, if in a firm of accountants one partner negligently prepares accounts for a client that to the knowledge of the firm are to be relied on, for example, by a person intending to make a bid for the business, the firm's assets will be liable to pay damages for negligence, but only the negligent partner's assets will be liable if the firm's assets are insufficient. The other partners may, therefore, lose their capital in the firm but no more. They are, however, liable to contribute to the assets of the firm if it is wound up because of non-payment of business debts. The extent of that liability has yet to be decided by regulations.

Section 7 gives a member's representatives, e.g. executors or trustee in bankruptcy, a right to receive amounts due to the member (or former member) but with no power to interfere in management.

Section 8. This deals with designated members who achieve such status by being specified as such on the incorporation document or by agreement with members. These members are required for certain compliance functions under the Act, e.g. notification to the Registrar of a name change.

Section 9 provides for the registration of membership changes.

Sections 10 to 13 are concerned with taxation. These clauses are expressed in broad terms to apply in general existing rules for partnerships and partners.

Sections 14 to 17 are concerned with regulation-making powers, and *s 18* deals with interpretation.

The Schedule is concerned with names and situation of registered office. These provisions are similar to those applying to companies.

REFORM: A PARTNERSHIP WITH LEGAL PERSONALITY

The Law Commission has issued a *Consultation Paper on Partnership Law* in response to a request from the DTI. There are also proposals regarding partnerships in Scotland made by the Scottish Law Commission that are not considered here. The review is being conducted in respect of the provisions of the Partnership Act 1890, many but not all of which operate as default provisions in the absence of a contrary agreement of the partners, and the Limited Partnerships Act 1907. The Limited Liability Partnerships Act 2000 (see above) is not involved. The reforms would, however, if implemented, narrow the present distinction between ordinary partnerships and the new limited liability partnership.

The three main proposals are:

1 Proposals to introduce separate legal personality. There are two sub-proposals here:

(a) to confer legal personality on all partnerships without registration. There would be a transitional period to allow the parties to a partnership agreement to organise their affairs or to opt out of the continuing aspect of separate personality of the firm;

(b) to make legal personality depend on registration. Under this sub-proposal only a registered partnership would have legal personality capable of continuing regardless of changes in the membership of the firm. Under this option non-registered partnerships would not have legal personality.

The Commission feels that having a system of registration would create a more complex situation in which there would be a legal environment for registered partnerships and another for non-registered firms. The Commission also feels that many small firms would not register and so lose the benefits of legal personality.

On balance, therefore, the provisional view of the Commission is the first option, i.e. continuity of legal personality without registration, and views are invited on this. The creation of a registered partnership regime would bring partnership law in the UK closer to those legal systems in Europe in which legal personality is conferred by registration.

2 Proposals to avoid the unnecessary discontinuance of business caused by the dissolution of the firm under the 1890 Act default rules when one person ceases to be a partner.

3 Proposals to provide a more efficient and cheaper mechanism for the dissolution of a solvent partnership.

Other reform proposals

The following suggestions for reform are, according to the Commission, intended to clarify some of the uncertainties in the 1890 Act, to update provisions which are outdated or spent, and to propose adaptations of existing provisions if in the event consultees support the separate and continuing legal personality of the firm.

(a) *Partnership and agency*. With the concept of legal entity the partners would be agents of the firm but not of each other.

(b) *Ownership of property*. With separate personality the firm would be able to hold property in its own name. It would not be necessary, as now, to use the device of the trust. Also, the firm and not the partners would have an insurable interest in partnership property.

(c) *Partners' liability for the obligations of the firm*. As a result of separate personality, the firm would be primarily liable.

A partner's liability would be subsidiary but unlimited. Creditors would normally need to get a judgment against the firm before enforcing the claim against the assets of the firm or the partners. The liability of partners would be joint and several for the debts and obligations of the firm.

(d) *Partners' duties*. Partners have a duty to act in good faith in equity already. The Commission proposes to include the duty in a reformed statute and possibly also a duty of skill and care in negligence.

There is a suggestion that partners be relieved of the duty of good faith when, on the break-up of a firm, they are competing for its client base, provided that they act honestly and reasonably.

(e) *Litigation*. A partnership with a separate legal personality would be sued in its own name and the partners could be sued in the same action.

(f) *Information about the firm*, including former partners who may have subsidiary liability at the time of a claim, would be available if the partnership was registered. If this is not so, the Commission proposes an extension to the Business Names Act 1985 requiring display of such information by the firm administratively.

(g) *Floating charges*. Currently partnerships cannot grant floating charges over the firm's assets. The Commission makes no proposals on this but has invited views.

MODEL FORM OF ORDINARY PARTNERSHIP DEED

AN AGREEMENT made this *4th* day of *June* two thousand

and *one* between *John Jones*

of *Bleak House, Barchester; Chartered Accountant*

and *Jane James*

of *12 Acacia Avenue, Barchester; Chartered Accountant*

and *William Pitt*

of *55 Low Terrace, Barchester; Chartered Accountant*

IT IS HEREBY AGREED AND DECLARED AS FOLLOWS:

Duration and objects

1. The said *John Jones, Jane James and William Pitt* shall become and remain partners in the business of Chartered Accountants for a term of *five* years from the date of this deed if they shall so long live.

Comment   The period of five years ensures that it is not a partnership at will. We do not want a partnership at will because it can be terminated by notice at any time thus allowing a partner to leave the firm with ease so that years of work are brought to an end at the will of one partner.

2. Although the partnership constituted by this Deed is for a period of *five* years nevertheless it is the intention of the parties hereto to continue in partnership from *five*-year period to *five*-year period subject only to the incidence of death or retirement.

Comment   Since a fixed term has been agreed, there should be provision for it to be continued upon the same terms on the expiry of the fixed term. It is better to include this in the deed so that there is no doubt what will happen at the end of each term of five years. In any case, of course, s 27 would apply and the partnership would be at will but on the same terms as the fixed partnership which had just expired.

3. The death retirement expulsion or bankruptcy of a partner shall not determine the partnership between the partners but without prejudice to the generality of this clause the parties hereto shall review the provisions of this deed whenever the admission of a new profit-sharing partner into the partnership is being contemplated.

   Comment This clause is inserted to make sure, for example, that the death of a partner does not cause a dissolution as between those partners who remain and that the business continues under the remaining partners. If this clause was not included, there would be an automatic dissolution under s 33(1) on the death of a partner.

Firm name

4. The partners shall practise in partnership under the firm name of *Jones, James, Pitt & Co.*
   (or such other name as the partners may hereafter agree).

Location of practice

5. The business of the partnership shall be carried on at
   10 Oak Buildings, Barchester
   and/or such other place or places as the partners may from time to time decide.

Bankers and application of partnership money

6. (i) The bankers of the firm shall be the *Barchester* Bank plc or such other bankers as the partners shall agree upon both for the moneys of clients for the time being in the keeping of the partnership and for the moneys of the partnership.

   (ii) All partnership money shall be paid to the bankers of the partnership to the credit of the partnership and the partners shall make such regulations as they may from time to time see fit for opening operating or closing the bank accounts of the partnership and for providing the money required for current expenses.

   (iii) All outgoings incurred for or in carrying on the partnership business and all losses and damages which shall happen or be incurred in relation to the business are to be paid out of the moneys and profits of the partnership and if there is a deficiency shall be contributed by the partners in the shares in which they are for the time being respectively entitled to the profits of the partnership.

   Comment Clause 6(ii) gives the partners power to make regulations as to who may draw cheques in the name of the firm. In many cases this will be each partner alone, though where there are more than two partners it is usual to provide that all cheques over a certain amount are to be signed by at least two of the partners.

Capital

7. (i) The initial capital of the partnership shall be a sum of *£30,000* to be contributed by the partners in equal shares together with such further cash capital (if any) as the partners may from time to time agree to be required (in addition to any loan capital) for the purposes of the partnership and which shall be provided (except as may from time to time be otherwise agreed by the partners) in the proportion in which the partners are for the time being entitled to share in the profits of the partnership.

   (ii) *Five thousand pounds (£5,000)* being the agreed value of the goodwill of the business carried on at *10 Sandy Lane, Barchester* by the said *John Jones* which will be taken over by the said partnership and which shall be credited in the books of the firm as part of the capital brought in by the said *John Jones.*

   (iii) The said sum of *£30,000* and any further capital provided by the partners shall carry interest at the rate of *ten (10)* per cent per annum to be payable *half-yearly in arrears on 30th June and 31st December* or at such other rate and payable at such other times as the partners shall from time to time decide.

Comment   Unless there is a specific provision, such as the one in (iii) above, interest on capital is not payable.

Profits

8. The partners shall be entitled to the net profits arising from the business in *equal shares* or such other shares as may from time to time be agreed by the partners. Such net profits shall be divided among the partners immediately after the settlement of the annual accounts in the manner hereafter provided.

Comment   Oddly enough, although the 1890 Act says that partners are in business with a view of profit, it says nothing about dividing profit. This special provision makes the matter of division clear.

Management and control of the partnership

9. The control and management of the partnership shall remain in the hands of the partners and salaried partners (if any) shall not be entitled to take part therein.

Circulation of agendas and other information

10. All agendas and minutes of partners' meetings and balance sheets and profit and loss accounts shall be circulated to all partners.

Partnership accounts and partners' drawings

11. At the close of business on the *31st May* in the year two thousand and two and on the same day in each succeeding year the accounts of the partnership shall be made up.

Each partner may draw on account of his share of profit to such extent as may be decided by the partners from time to time.

Comment   The partners may agree, for example, that £1,000 per month as a maximum be drawn. It is usually also provided that, if on taking the annual account the sums drawn out by any of the partners are found to exceed the sum to which that partner is entitled as his share of the year's profits, the excess shall be refunded immediately.

Conduct of the partnership business

12. Each partner shall diligently employ himself in the partnership business and carry on and conduct the same for the greatest advantage of the partnership.

Holidays

13. Each partner shall be entitled to *five* weeks holiday in aggregate in each year of the partnership.

Comment   It may sometimes be found that the agreement states that some or all of this holiday must be taken between certain dates in the year.

Restrictions

14. No partner shall without the previous consent of the others:

(a)   hire or dismiss any employee or take on any trainee;

(b)   purchase goods in the name or on behalf of the firm to an amount exceeding *one thousand (£1,000) pounds*;

(c)   compound release or discharge any debt owing to the partnership without receiving the full amount therefor;

(d)   be engaged or interested whether directly or indirectly in any business or occupation other than the partnership business;

(e)   advance the moneys of or deliver on credit any goods belonging to the partnership;

(f)   make any assignment either absolutely or by way of charge of his share in the partnership;

(g)   give any security or undertaking for the payment of any debt or liability out of the moneys or property of the partnership;

(h)   introduce or attempt to introduce another person into the business of the partnership;

(i)   enter into any bond or become surety for any persons or do or knowingly permit to be done anything whereby the capital or property of the partnership may be seized attached or taken in execution.

Comment   This clause can be extended as required. However, since partners have considerable apparent authority under s 5 of the 1890 Act and case law, the above prohibitions will in many cases not prevent an outsider who has no knowledge of them from claiming against the firm.

They do provide grounds for dissolution of the firm if a partner is in wilful or persistent breach of them or the partnership agreement in general.

It is generally unwise to have a very large number of prohibitions because this is likely to restrict the activities of the firm and its individual partners unduly.

Partners' debts and engagements

15.   Every partner shall during the partnership pay his present and future separate debts and at all times indemnify the other partners and each of them and the capital and effects of the partnership against his said debts and engagements and against all actions suits claims and demands on account thereof.

Expulsion of partners

16.   If any partner shall:

(a)   by act or default commit any flagrant breach of his duties as a partner or of the agreements and stipulations herein contained; or

(b)   fail to account and pay over or refund to the partnership any money for which he is accountable to the partnership within 14 days after being required so to do by a partner specifically so authorised by a decision of the partners; or

(c)   act in any respect contrary to the good faith which ought to be observed between partners; or

(d)   become subject to the bankruptcy laws; or

(e)   enter into any composition or arrangement with or for the benefit of his creditors; or

(f)   be or become permanently incapacitated by mental disorder, ill-health, accident or otherwise from attending the partnership business; or

(g)   except with the consent of the other partners absent himself from the said business for more than **six** calendar months in any one year or for more than **ninety** consecutive days (absence during the usual holidays or due to temporary illness or as agreed not being reckoned);

then and in any such case the other partners may by notice in writing given to him or (in the case of his being found incapable by reason of mental disorder of managing and administering his property and affairs for the purposes of Part VII of the Mental Health Act 1983) to his receiver or other appropriate person or left at the office of the partnership determine the partnership so far as he may be concerned and publish a notice of dissolution of the partnership in the name of and as against such partner whereupon the partnership will so far as regards such partner immediately cease and determine accordingly but without prejudice to the remedies of the other partners for any antecedent breach of any of the stipulations or agreements aforesaid and any question as to a case having arisen to authorise such notice shall be referred to arbitration.

Dissolution 17. Upon the dissolution of the partnership by the death of a partner or by a partner retiring, the other partners shall be entitled to purchase upon the terms hereinafter specified the share of the partner (including goodwill) so dying or retiring: provided that written notice of intention to purchase shall be given to the retiring partner or to the personal representatives of the deceased partner within *two* calendar months after the date of the dissolution.

18. The purchase money payable under clause 17 hereof shall be the net value of the share of the deceased or retiring partner as at the date of the dissolution after satisfying all outstanding liabilities of the partnership with interest at the rate of *ten (10)* per cent per annum as from the date of dissolution: provided that if the value of the said share cannot be agreed upon the same shall be submitted to arbitration in the manner hereinafter provided.

The purchase money shall be paid by *six equal* instalments the first instalment to be paid at the end of *three months* after the date of the dissolution and thereafter at the end of each succeeding period of *three months* with interest at the rate of *ten (10)* per cent per annum upon so much of the purchase money as shall remain unpaid for the time being and such purchase money shall if required be secured by the bond of the surviving partners with not fewer than two sureties.

Goodwill 19. For the purposes of the foregoing clauses the goodwill of the partnership shall be deemed to be valued at *three years'* purchase of the average net profits of the partnership for the preceding *five* years or the average of the whole period if the partnership shall have subsisted for less than *five* years.

Comment Any other basis of assessment which the partners may decide upon could, of course, have been included or the matter of goodwill could have been omitted entirely.

20. In the event of one of the partners retiring and the other partners purchasing his share the retiring partner shall not during the unexpired residue of the term of the partnership carry on or be interested either directly or indirectly in any business similar to that of the said partnership and competing therewith within a radius of *one mile* of *10 Oak Buildings, Barchester* or of any other place of business belonging to the partnership at the date of the notice of retirement.

21. Upon the determination of the partnership any partner or his personal representative shall have power to sign in the name of the firm notice of the dissolution for publication in the Gazette.

Arbitration 22. Should any doubt or difference arise at any time between the said partners or their personal representatives with regard to the interpretation or effect of this agreement or in respect of the rights duties and liabilities of any partner or his personal representatives whether in connection with the conduct or winding-up of the affairs of the partnership, such doubt or difference shall be submitted to a single arbitrator to be appointed by the President for the time being of the Institute of Chartered Accountants in England and Wales.

Comment Without an arbitration clause it is open to any partner to pursue a dispute through the courts. Nothing injures a business more than an open dispute between partners. Arbitration, which may be quicker and sometimes cheaper than court litigation and certainly more private, should always be considered. Also, it should be less confrontational than legal proceedings and so do less damage to the relationship between the partners, though the fact that even an arbitration is necessary means that some damage has already been done.

```
            IN WITNESS whereof the parties hereto have hereunto set
            their hands and seals the day and year first above-mentioned.

            Signed as a deed by the
              above-named John Jones in the
              presence of,

            George Blake,                    George Blake        John Jones
                42 Hill Top,
                  Barchester.

            Signed as a deed by the
              above-named Jane James in the
              presence of,

                George Blake.                George Blake        Jane James

            Signed as a deed by the
              above-named William Pitt in the
              presence of,

                George Blake.                George Blake        William Pitt
```

Note Partnership deeds also usually contain complex provisions relating to life assurance for retirement, annuities for partners' dependants in the case of death, and annuities to partners in the event of permanent incapacity. There are often, also, much more complex provisions relating to payments to be made to any partner on death or retirement and the continuation of the partnership for tax purposes. However, these do not assist in the understanding of the Partnership Act 1890 and involve knowledge of matters not dealt with in this text. They have accordingly been omitted.

QUESTIONS/ACTIVITIES

1 Joseph David Soap wishes to set up in business on his own as a carpenter, having acquired a small business connection from John Smith. Which of the following trading names, if any, would require Joe to comply with the provisions of the Business Names Act 1985?
   (a) David Soap
   (b) J D Soap & Co
   (c) Joe Soap
   (d) Joe Soap Carpentry (formerly John Smith's)
   (e) J D Soap
   (f) Chipaway
   (g) Dave Soap

2 Your friend, Fred, intends to go into business on his own as a timber merchant under the name of 'County Council Supplies'. What could happen to Fred if he does this?

3 Old John Brown has been in business as a furniture remover in Barchester since 1975. Last year young John Brown moved to Barchester and has started up a furniture removal business in his own name. Can old John Brown stop him?

4 Adam Smith, a grocer, comes to you for advice on his finances. What advice would you give him in terms of each of the following questions which he asks you?
   (a) 'Times have been very hard for me lately. I owe so many people so much money. I could probably pay my creditors, say, half of what I owe them but no more. Is there a way of doing this, given that I understand that a builder to whom I owe £1,000 appears to have gone to court to make me bankrupt?'
   (b) 'Anyway, I have tried to make my family safe. Last week I gave my wife the family home and on

the same day sold her two terraced houses in Barchester worth £40,000 for £500. Yesterday I also paid my brother off. I owed him £1,000 from when I started up so he should have it. My creditors can't upset these deals, I take it.'

(c) 'I have not paid John, my driver, for a month and I doubt whether I can now. I wish I could have helped him but I guess he will have to go down with all the other creditors. That's the position, isn't it?'

(d) 'Of course, even if they make me bankrupt I shall rent another shop and go on trading. Nothing can be done about that, can it?'

5 Joe is a solicitor employed by Bloggs & Co. There are two partners, Harry and Ian. Ian is intending to retire and it has been decided that Joe should replace Ian as a partner, with Harry carrying on as a partner.

Explain to each of Joe, Harry and Ian what steps each should take to protect himself as a result of the changeover.

6 Cliff has been asked by his friends, Don and Eric, to help them set up an antiques business. Don and Eric want Cliff to lend them £5,000 and they say they will give Cliff one-third of the profits instead of interest on the loan.

What are the dangers to Cliff in such an arrangement and how can he overcome them?

7 Fred is a new partner in Gee & Co, a firm of surveyors. In discussion at a recent meeting of the partners Fred was told that the office building at which the firm is based is not partnership property. Explain to Fred:

(a) what is meant by the expression 'partnership property';

(b) what effect it will have on him if the office building is not partnership property;

(c) how it can be that an asset which is used in the firm's business is not in fact partnership property.

8 You have been appointed as partnership secretary in the firm of Jones, James & Pitt, Chartered Accountants. The partnership articles appear on pp 108–13. The following problems emerge over a number of partners' meetings:

(a) John Jones soon became unhappy about his future prospects. He retired from the firm last month and has taken a partnership with Snooks & Co, Chartered Accountants, whose office is two doors away from the offices of Jones, James & Pitt. Jane James and William Pitt, the remaining partners, are anxious to stop John from competing with them.

(b) Before he left, John Jones contracted to buy a microcomputer system for the practice from Scroggs Ltd, although at an earlier partners' meeting it was decided that the purchase should be deferred for one year. The system cost £5,000. Jane and William have so far refused to take delivery of the system or pay for it.

(c) Scroggs Ltd have written to the firm saying that unless the debt is paid they will petition the court to wind up the firm.

Having read the partnership articles thoroughly:

(i) prepare as part of your answer a memorandum for the next partners' meeting outlining the legal position of the firm in the three cases described above.

(ii) if you think there is a claim under (a) above, draft as part of your answer a letter to the firm's solicitors, Weeks & Co, for the signature of the partners, stating what has happened and describing the relevant provisions of the partnership articles.

(iii) draft as part of your answer a letter to Scroggs Ltd to deal with whatever you think the legal position is under (b) and (c) above.

Chapter 6

COMPANIES

In Chapter 4 we made a general survey of the different types of business organisation – the sole trader, the partnership, and the corporation. In particular, we considered the role of the corporation as a business organisation in the public and private sectors.

This chapter is concerned only with one type of corporation – the registered company – because this is the basic form of corporate business organisation. The law relating to registered companies is to be found mainly in the Companies Act 1985 (as amended by the Companies Act 1989) and case law. All section references in this chapter are to the Companies Act (CA) 1985 unless otherwise indicated.

We have also included the provisions of the Companies Act 1985 (Electronic Communications) Order 2000. This order which is made under ss 8 and 9 of the Electronic Communications Act 2000 modifies certain provisions of the Companies Act 1985 for the purpose of authorising or facilitating the use of electronic communications between companies and their members, debenture holders and auditors and between companies and the registrar of companies. Reference is made to the relevant provisions at appropriate places in the text. We refer to the order as the 'Electronic Communications Order 2000'.

TYPES OF REGISTERED COMPANIES

Registered companies may be limited or unlimited and public or private.

Limited companies

Most registered companies are limited by shares. This means that the liability of the members of the company is limited. The company's liability is not limited. It must pay its debts so long as it has any funds from which to do so.

Where the liability of the members of the company is limited by shares, it means that once the members have paid the full nominal value of their shares, plus any premium that may have been payable on them, they cannot be asked to pay any more even if the company is wound up and cannot pay its creditors in full from the funds that are left.

If, therefore, John Green owns 100 shares issued at £1 each by Boxo plc, then once he has paid £100 to Boxo plc for them neither he nor anyone else who buys them from him can be required to pay more. If the shares had been issued at a premium of 50p, then once John had paid £150 to Boxo, neither he nor anyone else who bought the shares from him could be required to pay more. If John transferred the shares before he had paid for them in full, then the person who bought them from him would have to pay the balance if called upon to do so by Boxo plc.

Companies may also be limited by guarantee. Only brief mention needs to be made of them in a book on business law since they are mostly formed for charitable, social, political or other *non-trading purposes*. However, the members are liable only to the amount they have agreed upon in the memorandum. (A specimen memorandum for a company limited by shares appears at the end of this chapter.) There is a separate clause in the memorandum of a guarantee company which might say, for example:

> Every member of the company undertakes to contribute such amount as may be required (not exceeding £100) to the company's assets if it should be wound up while he is a member or within one year after he ceased to be a member, for payment of the company's debts and liabilities contracted before he ceased to be a member and of the costs charges and expenses of winding-up.

Obviously, this liability arises only if the company is wound up. Guarantee companies cannot be registered with a share capital as well so they will normally get their income from members' sub-scriptions, as in the case of a club.

Furthermore, guarantee companies cannot have a share capital, so they must be formed as private companies since the definition of a public company is in part based upon the state of its share capital.

Unlimited companies

Companies may be registered in which the liability of members is unlimited. Not many of these exist because of the personal liability of their members, which is unpopular. However, some organisations are prepared to put up with the fact that the liability of their members is unlimited in view of certain privileges available (see below).

Also, there is some advantage over an ordinary partnership in that there is a separate company *persona* for making contracts and holding property plus perpetual succession so that, for example, the death of a member does not cause a dissolution. A limited liability partnership is, of course, a legal person.

The main advantage over the limited company is that unlimited companies do not have to file accounts with the Registrar so that the public has no access to their financial statements. However, the price of financial secrecy is unlimited liability. The above provisions do not apply if the company concerned is a subsidiary or holding company of a limited company.

The memorandum of an unlimited company does not contain any clause stating that the liability of its members is limited. This achieves the unlimited liability.

These companies may also have a share capital, in which case the members must pay for their shares in full plus any premium, and even then they have personal liability for the company's debts if it is wound up and does not have sufficient funds to pay its debts. These companies are always private companies. Public companies must be limited by shares.

PUBLIC AND PRIVATE COMPANIES

The Companies Act 1985 defines a public company and leaves private companies largely undefined other than by the fact that they are companies which do not satisfy the public limited company (PLC) definition, and s 170 of the Financial Services Act 1986 generally prohibits the issue by private companies of advertisements offering their securities.

A public company is a company limited by shares. Its memorandum of association has a separate clause stating that it is a public company.

Two members are required for a public company. Also, a public company cannot start trading or borrow money until it has received a certificate from the Registrar of Companies under s 117.

This certificate will not be given unless the issued share capital of the company is at least £50,000 and not less than one-quarter of the nominal value of each share and the whole of any premium has been received by the company.

Therefore, at least £50,000 in nominal value of shares must have been purchased in the company and £12,500 paid up on them. If the shares were of a nominal value of £1 and issued at a premium of 50p, then a company would have had to receive £12,500 plus £25,000 = £37,500. This is to stop public companies starting up in business without enough capital and then possibly being wound up quickly leaving the creditors unpaid.

If a company does trade or borrow without a s 117 certificate, the company and its directors commit a criminal offence. However, transactions such as contracts for the supply of goods and loans can be enforced against the company. Also, if the company is asked to pay, say for goods supplied, and does not do so within 21 days of the demand, the company's directors become jointly and severally liable to pay the debts.

As we have seen under SI 1992/1699 (see Chapter 4), a private company may be formed with or allow its membership to drop to one person. The consequences of having a single member private company limited by shares or guarantee will be referred to as the text proceeds. Single member status is not available to unlimited private companies.

Incidentally, there are no re-registration requirements to convert to single-member status. Conversion is achieved by transferring all the shares to the single member. No resolutions are required and there are no filing requirements at Companies House. However, a statement must appear on the Register of Members at the side of the name and address of the sole member in the following form: 'The company became a single-member company on (date) (month) (year)'. A similar statement must be made if the company goes back to more than one member, recording when it did so on the lines set out above.

Companies House
—— *for the record* ——

Please complete in typescript,
or in bold black capitals.

CHFP000

12

Declaration on application for registration

Company Name in full RICHES KEENAN PUBLISHING LIMITED

I, DENIS KEENAN

of 2 LOW STREET, BARCHESTER

† Please delete as appropriate.

do solemnly and sincerely declare that I am a † [solicitor engaged in the formation of the company][person named as director or secretary of the company in the statement delivered to the Registrar under section 10 of the Companies Act 1985] and that all the requirements of the Companies Act 1985 in respect of the registration of the above company and of matters precedent and incidental to it have been complied with.

And I make this solemn declaration conscientiously believing the same to be true and by virtue of the Statutory Declarations Act 1835.

Declarant's signature A. J. Keenan

Declared at 14 HIGH STREET, BARCHESTER

Day	Month	Year
0 5	0 3	2 0 0 1

On

❶ Please print name.

before me ❶ H. MIDDLETON

Signed H Middleton **Date** 5 MARCH 2001

† A Commissioner for Oaths or Notary Public or Justice of the Peace or Solicitor

Please give the name, address, telephone number and, if available, a DX number and Exchange of the person Companies House should contact if there is any query.

DARLTON & CO. CHARTERED ACCOUNTANTS

120. HIGH STREET, BARCHESTER

BB26 0YE   Tel 10040-660-894

DX number   DX exchange

Companies House receipt date barcode

This form has been provided free of charge by Companies House.

Form revised June 1998

When you have completed and signed the form please send it to the Registrar of Companies at:
Companies House, Crown Way, Cardiff, CF14 3UZ   DX 33050 Cardiff
for companies registered in England and Wales
or
Companies House, 37 Castle Terrace, Edinburgh, EH1 2EB
for companies registered in Scotland   **DX 235 Edinburgh**

Fig 6.1 Company registration declaration

Companies House
— for the record —

*Please complete in typescript,
or in bold black capitals.*
CHFP000

10

First directors and secretary and intended situation of registered office

Notes on completion appear on final page

Company Name in full   RICHES KEENAN PUBLISHING LIMITED

Proposed Registered Office   140, HIGH STREET
(PO Box numbers only, are not acceptable)

Post town   BARCHESTER

County / Region   BARCHESTERSHIRE   Postcode   BB26 OYE

If the memorandum is delivered by an agent for the subscriber(s) of the memorandum mark the box opposite and give the agent's name and address.   X

Agent's Name   DALTON & CO CHARTERED ACCOUNTANTS

Address   120 HIGH STREET

Post town   BARCHESTER

County / Region   BARCHESTERSHIRE   Postcode   BB26 OYE

Number of continuation sheets attached   14

Please give the name, address, telephone number and, if available, a DX number and Exchange of the person Companies House should contact if there is any query.

DALTON & CO. CHARTERED ACCOUNTANTS
120. HIGH STREET, BARCHESTER
BB26 OYE   Tel 10040-660-894
DX number   DX exchange

Companies House receipt date barcode

This form has been provided free of charge by Companies House.

Form revised July 1998

When you have completed and signed the form please send it to the Registrar of Companies at:
Companies House, Crown Way, Cardiff, CF14 3UZ   DX 33050 Cardiff
for companies registered in England and Wales
or
Companies House, 37 Castle Terrace, Edinburgh, EH1 2EB
for companies registered in Scotland   **DX 235 Edinburgh**

Fig 6.2 First directors, secretary and intended situation of registered office

Company Secretary (see notes 1-5)

Company name	RICHES KEENAN PUBLISHING LIMITED	
NAME *Style / Title	MS	*Honours etc
Forename(s)	JANE MAY	
Surname	WILLIAMS	
Previous forename(s)		
Previous surname(s)		
Address	25 MIDDLE STREET	

Voluntary details

Usual residential address
For a corporation, give the registered or principal office address.

Post town	BARCHESTER	
County / Region	BARCHESTERSHIRE	Postcode BB26 9AM
Country	ENGLAND	

I consent to act as secretary of the company named on page 1

Consent signature J. M. Williams.   **Date** 5 MARCH 2001

Directors (see notes 1-5)

Please list directors in alphabetical order

NAME *Style / Title	MR	*Honours etc
Forename(s)	DENIS JOSEPH	
Surname	KEENAN	
Previous forename(s)	–	
Previous surname(s)	–	
Address	2 LOW STREET	

Usual residential address
For a corporation, give the registered or principal office address.

Post town	BARCHESTER	
County / Region	BARCHESTERSHIRE	Postcode BB26 0BG
Country	ENGLAND	

Day	Month	Year	
1 2	0 8	1 9 4 6	**Nationality** BRITISH

Date of birth

Business occupation AUTHOR/JOURNALIST

Other directorships DODGY FINANCE LIMITED

I consent to act as director of the company named on page 1

Consent signature D. J. Keenan   **Date** 5 MARCH 2001

Fig 6.2 (*continued*)

Directors (continued)   (see notes 1-5)

NAME	*Style / Title	M S	*Honours etc
* Voluntary details	Forename(s)	SARAH	
	Surname	RICHES	
	Previous forename(s)	–	
	Previous surname(s)	–	
	Address	1 HIGH STREET	

Usual residential address
For a corporation, give the registered or principal office address.

Post town	BARCHESTER	
County / Region	BARCHESTERSHIRE	Postcode BB26 0YE
Country	ENGLAND	

	Day	Month	Year		
Date of birth	1 6	0 4	1 9 6 0	Nationality	BRITISH

Business occupation	AUTHOR/LECTURER
Other directorships	DODGY TRAINING LIMITED

I consent to act as director of the company named on page 1

Consent signature	*Sarah Riches*	Date	5 MARCH 2001

SPECIMEN

This section must be signed by
Either

an agent on behalf of all subscribers	Signed		Date

Or the subscribers

(*i.e those who signed as members on the memorandum of association).*

	Signed	A.J.Keenan	Date 5/3/01
	Signed	*Sarah Riches*	Date 5/3/01
	Signed		Date
	Signed		Date
	Signed		Date
	Signed		Date

Fig 6.2 (*continued*)

Notes

1. Show for an individual the full forename(s) NOT INITIALS and surname together with any previous forename(s) or surname(s).

   If the director or secretary is a corporation or Scottish firm - show the corporate or firm name on the surname line.

   Give previous forename(s) or surname(s) except that:

   - for a married woman, the name by which she was known before marriage need not be given,

   - names not used since the age of 18 or for at least 20 years need not be given.

   A peer, or an individual known by a title, may state the title instead of or in addition to the forename(s) and surname and need not give the name by which that person was known before he or she adopted the title or succeeded to it.

   Address:

   Give the usual residential address.

   In the case of a corporation or Scottish firm give the registered or principal office.

   Subscribers:

   The form must be signed personally either by the subscriber(s) or by a person or persons authorised to sign on behalf of the subscriber(s).

2. Directors known by another description:

   - A director includes any person who occupies that position even if called by a different name, for example, governor, member of council.

3. Directors details:

   - Show for each individual director the director's date of birth, business occupation and nationality. **The date of birth must be given for every individual director.**

4. Other directorships:

   - Give the name of every company of which the person concerned is a director or has been a director at any time in the past 5 years. You may exclude a company which either **is** or at **all times during the past 5 years** when the person was a director, **was**:

   - dormant,

   - a parent company which wholly owned the company making the return,

   - a wholly owned subsidiary of the company making the return, or

   - another wholly owned subsidiary of the same parent company.

   If there is insufficient space on the form for other directorships you may use a separate sheet of paper, which should include the company's number and the full name of the director.

5. Use Form 10 continuation sheets or photocopies of page 2 to provide details of joint secretaries or additional directors.

Fig 6.2 (*continued*)

FORMATION

A company, whether public or private, is formed (or incorporated) by applying for registration with the Registrar of Companies in Cardiff. The people who want the company to be formed (who are called the promoters) must send certain documents to the Registrar. The main ones are set out below.

(a) Memorandum of association.

(b) Articles of association. These documents are dealt with in more detail at the end of this chapter.

(c) Form 12 (see Fig 6.1), being a statutory declaration of compliance with the requirements of the Companies Act 1985 as regards registration which is required by s 12.

This declaration may be given by a solicitor who has been assisting in the formation of the company or by a person named as a director or the secretary of the company in Form 10 (see Fig 6.2).

The declaration is usually made before a commissioner for oaths (a solicitor) and false statements made in the declaration could result in the person making them being prosecuted for the crime of perjury.

(d) Form 10 (see Fig 6.2), which is a statement of the company's first directors and secretary required by s 10.

Those persons named in the statement are, just by being named in it, appointed as the first directors and secretary of the company.

If the Registrar is satisfied with the contents of the above documents, he will issue a certificate of incorporation. (See Fig 6.3.)

The Electronic Communications Order 2000 makes changes in the law to allow the electronic filing of the above documents. Where this is done, the order removes the need for witnesses to electronic signatures and statutory declarations, the latter being replaced by an electronic statement by a solicitor engaged in the formation or a person named as a director or secretary.

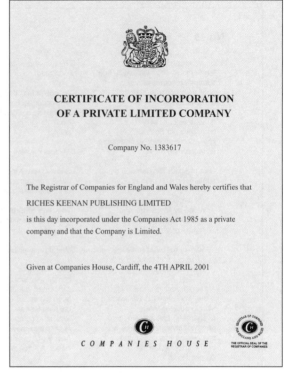

Fig 6.3 Certificate of incorporation

COMPANIES HOUSE – CROWN COPYRIGHT reproduced with the permission of the Controller of Her Majesty's Stationery Office

PRE-INCORPORATION CONTRACTS

Generally

A company cannot make contracts until it has been incorporated. This takes place on the first moment of the day of the date on its certificate of incorporation.

Transactions entered into by the company's promoters and others in connection with its business before that time are not binding on the company when it is incorporated and the company cannot adopt these contracts after its incorporation. Thus, if the company's directors, who are its agents, were to write to a seller of goods and say that the company was now formed and would take over a pre-incorporation contract, the company would not be bound by it.

However, the company's promoters or other persons who may act for it at the pre-incorporation stage do incur personal liability to the other party to the contract under s 36C.

Phonogram Ltd v *Lane* (1981)

Phonogram lent £6,000 for the business of a company to be called Fragile Management Ltd. Mr Lane, who was not a promoter of Fragile, signed 'for and on behalf of' the company a letter promising repayment by Fragile. The company was never formed and Phonogram sued Mr Lane personally for repayment of the sum of £6,000 under what is now s 36C. The Court of Appeal decided that Mr Lane was personally liable.

Comment. (i) The case shows that although s 36C is usually discussed in the context of making promoters personally liable, anyone acting on the company's business at the pre-incorporation stage is covered by s 36C. Also, the section says that a person acting for the company can avoid personal liability by an express agreement in the pre-incorporation contract that he is not to be liable. This case decides that the words 'for and on behalf of' the company were not enough. They do not amount to a specific agreement to prevent personal liability.

(ii) The *Phonogram* case made it clear that s 36C can apply to make a promoter or other purported agent liable even though the company has not actually begun the process of formation. However it was held in **Cotronic (UK) Ltd** v **Dezonie** (1991) that there must at least be a clear intention to form the company as there was in *Phonogram*. In the *Cotronic* case a contract was made by Mr Dezonie on behalf of a company which had been struck off the register at a time when nobody concerned with its business had even thought about re-registering it. The Court of Appeal held that the contract was a nullity and Mr Dezonie was not liable on it under s 36C.

Solutions to the problem of personal liability of promoters

A promoter or other person conducting the company's business prior to its incorporation can overcome the difficulties facing him as regards personal liability in the following ways.

1 By incorporating the company before any business is done so that there are no pre-incorporation transactions.

2 By agreeing a draft contract with the other party and making it an object of the company that the company shall enter into it on formation. Nevertheless, if the company does not in fact enter into it, through the agency of its directors, there is no binding agreement either on the promoter or on the other party or the company.

3 By making a binding contract between the promoter and the other party and a draft contract on the same terms with the company. The binding contract must provide that once the company is formed and signs the draft contract through its agents, the promoter is released from the first contract which was binding on him.

This is a simple solution for most promoters who, after all, are usually promoting their own businesses as companies. They are normally in charge of the company and the board following incorporation and can easily arrange that the company signs through its agents the draft contract, thus releasing the promoter from his first binding contract.

4 By making a pre-incorporation contract with a specific clause saying that the promoter is not liable on it, as s 36C allows. There would seem to be little point in a third party signing such a contract since neither the company nor the promoter would be bound.

It is possible to purchase from company registration agents a company which is already formed, sometimes called a 'shelf' company because the agent takes it off his shelf and hands it over in terms, at least, of its essential documents. In such a case problems relating to pre-incorporation contracts do not arise because the company is in existence when the contract is made. It should, however, be noted that it will be necessary to change the directors and secretary of the shelf company since these will be the agents who formed it; also, the name may not suit and may need to be changed.

Contracts (Rights of Third Parties) Act 1999

Under this Act the promoter and the third party are able to give the company, when it is incorporated, the right to sue and be sued upon a pre-incorporation contract. The Act makes clear that a party given such rights in a contract (in this case the particular pre-incorporation contracts(s)) does not have to be in existence when the original contract is made.

THE MEMORANDUM OF ASSOCIATION

We shall learn about this document by dealing with the clauses it must contain and in the context of the specimen memorandum which appears on pp 177–9.

The company's name (Clause 1)

A company is only a legal person but, like a human being, it must have a name. The Companies Act 1985 and the Business Names Act 1985 together contain a system for controlling the names and business names of companies. The main rules are set out below.

On registration

The following rules apply.

1 The final words of the name – generally. A private company, whether limited by shares or guarantee, must end its name with the word 'limited' (s 25). A public company must end its name with the words 'public limited company' (s 25). The short forms – 'Ltd' and 'plc'– are allowed by s 27. These words, or their short forms, must not appear elsewhere in the name (s 26). There are criminal penalties on the company and its officers for wrongful use under ss 33 and 34.

2 The final words of the name – an exemption. Section 30 allows private companies limited by guarantee to apply for exemption in the sense of leaving off the word 'limited' from the name. The section gives automatic exemption if the conditions are satisfied. The company simply sends to the Registrar of Companies what is called a statutory declaration, which is a statement made before a commissioner for oaths that certain facts are true. The declaration is signed by a director and the secretary of the company. The facts that it declares to be true are the ones which s 30 requires for exemption, that is that:

- the objects of the company are to promote commerce, art, science, education, religion, charity, or any profession, and anything that would help that;
- the company's profits or income will be applied to the promotion of those objects;
- the payment of dividends is prohibited;
- all surplus assets on a winding-up will be transferred to another body with similar or charitable objects.

If the company at any time does not satisfy the above requirements, the Registrar may direct it to include 'limited' in its name again.

The exemption is not fully effective because, although the company need not use the word limited in its name, s 351 says that despite the exemption, all business letters and order forms of the company must include a statement that it is limited. However, the company at least avoids the need to use the word 'limited' **as part of its name.** The word 'limited' generally connotes a commercial profit-orientated organisation which a s 30 company is not.

The Electronic Communications Order 2000 allows, in place of the statutory declaration, an electronically communicated statement made *on formation of the company* by a solicitor engaged in the formation, or by a person named as a director or secretary or, *in the case of a company changing its name to omit the word 'limited',* by a director or secretary of the company.

3 Same, similar, and offensive names. Under s 26 a name will not be accepted by the Registrar if it is the same as one already on the Index of Names which he is required to keep by s 714. **Similar** names will be registered. So if there is a company called Widgets Ltd on the Index the Registrar would register a new company called Widgets (Holdings) Ltd.

However, a company may be required by the Trade Secretary to change its name within 12 months of registration if it is 'too like' that of a company already on the Index (s 28). It is up to other companies to ascertain this, e.g. by purchasing daily extracts from the Register of the names of companies which have gone on it. There are firms which will supply these.

If a period of 12 months has passed, the Trade Secretary can do nothing under s 28 but Widgets Ltd could bring an action at common law for passing off. For example, in *Société Anonyme des Anciens Etablissements Panhard et Lavassor v Levassor Motor Co Ltd* (1901) (which we can call the *Panhard* case) the claimant was a French company whose cars were sold in England. The French company wished to set up an English company to act as an agent in England to improve the sales of its cars here.

To try to stop this, the defendant English company was registered, the hope being that the French company could not then register an English company in its name in England because a company with that name would already be on the Register.

The court said that the name of the English company must be taken off the Register. The members of the English company were told that they must change the name of their company or wind it up.

Finally, a name will not be registered if it is in the opinion of the Trade Secretary offensive or if its publication would be a criminal offence. Offensive words will not often be met with in business but the Registrar of Companies turned down the names 'Prostitutes Ltd' and 'Hookers Ltd' when application was made for the registration of the business of a prostitute. The expression 'Personal Services' was eventually accepted but the registration was later cancelled because the company had been formed for an immoral purpose contrary to public policy. (See *Attorney-General* v *Lindi St Clair (Personal Services) Ltd* (1981)).

4   Connection with the government. A name which is likely to suggest a connection with the government or a local authority, e.g. 'District Council Supplies Ltd', will be registered only if the Trade Secretary approves (s 26).

5   Sensitive names. A name which includes any word or expression which is to be found in regulations made by the Trade Secretary under s 29 will not be registered as a company or business name unless the Trade Secretary approves.

The list of these sensitive names (which all imply some connection of prestige) also states the name of a government department or other organisation which can object to the use of the name and which must be approached and say that it does not disapprove before the Trade Secretary can give his approval.

Examples under regulations already issued are that for the use of 'Prince', 'Princess', 'Queen', approval of the Home Office is required, and for 'Bank', 'Banking', approval of the Bank of England is necessary. For the use of 'Charity' or 'Charitable' the approval of the Charity Commission is required.

Change of name

A company can change its name and have one which is different from the name it was registered in.

1   Voluntary change. A company may by special resolution change its name at any time.

A special resolution is an important form of resolution which will be looked at again later, but for now it will be enough to say that if it is passed at a meeting, as where it is not a written resolution (see later in this chapter), the meeting at which it is passed must be called by at least 21 days' notice and that the resolution must be passed by a majority of at least three-quarters of those present at the meeting in person or by proxy (i.e. a person appointed to attend and vote for the shareholder) **and** voting. Thus, if the company has members attending the meeting in person or by proxy who between them have 100 votes, then at least 75 votes must be cast for the resolution.

A private company is allowed by s 381A to use a unanimous written resolution which is effective without a meeting of the members. Further details of these resolutions appear later in the chapter but wherever a special, extraordinary or ordinary resolution is referred to in this text a private company can use the written resolution procedure except, so far as this text is concerned, for an ordinary resolution to remove a director from office.

The new name must comply with the same requirements as on first registration which are listed above. The Registrar issues a new certificate of incorporation and the change does not take effect until that has been done.

2   Compulsory change. The Trade Secretary may (as we have seen) within 12 months of registration direct a change if the name in which the company has been registered is too like (or the same as) one which appears on the Registrar's Index of Names (s 28(2)).

The Trade Secretary may also within five years of the date of registration direct a company to change its name if he believes that misleading information was provided at the time of its registration (s 28(3)).

There is no appeal to the court in this case.

A company might, for example, have misled the Registrar as to the nature of its business in order to obtain registration in a particular name. This would cover the obtaining of a sensitive name by deception where false information has been given to the approving authority. Thus, the use of the word 'Charity' requires the approval of the Charity Commissioners and if promoters gave false information to the Commissioners in order to get permission to use, say, 'Barchester Charities' which they intended to use for personal gain, the name would have been obtained by deception and be subject to s 28(3).

Furthermore, the Trade Secretary may direct a company to change its name **at any time** if the registered name gives so misleading an indication of its activities as to be likely to cause confusion and harm to the public (s 32).

In this case the company may appeal to the court against the direction. Section 32 can apply where a company called, say, 'Prosperous Investments Trust' went through a genuine form of registration but was later acquired and used for the making of cheap home computers. These companies are called 'shell' companies and what goes on behind the shell is deceptive in terms of the name of that shell.

Directions under s 32 are rare but such a direction was given by the Secretary of State in regard to the Association of Certified Public Accountants of Britain which the Secretary of State considered was a registered name that was likely to mislead the public. The direction was based on the use of the word 'certified' – it could lead to confusion with other accounting bodies such as the Association of Chartered Certified Accountants.

An application to the court to set aside the direction was dismissed. (See *Association of Certified Public Accountants of Britain* v *Secretary of State for Trade and Industry* (1997)).

Publication of name

Sections 348 and 349 provide that the company's full name must be shown in an obvious place and in readable form outside the registered office and all places of business, and on all business letters, notices, and official publications, and in all bills of exchange, cheques, promissory notes, orders for money or goods, receipts and invoices, signed or issued on its behalf.

Fines can be imposed on the company and its officers for failure to comply with the sections and also the officers of the company may incur personal liability for any amount due unless it is paid by the company (s 349(2), (3), and (4)). Thus, in *Hendon* v

Adelman (1973) a cheque signed on behalf of L & R Agencies Ltd omitted the ampersand (&) in the company's name, which appeared as L R Agencies Ltd. It was held that the directors who had signed the cheque had not complied with what is now s 349 and so they were personally liable on it.

However, according to a more recent decision, it seems that so long as the outsider knows that he is dealing with a company and that the liability of its members is limited, trifling errors in the name will not trigger the liability. Thus, in *Jenice Ltd and Others* v *Dan* (1993) the defendant who was a director of Primekeen Ltd signed a cheque incorrectly printed by the bank in the name of 'Primkeen Ltd'. The company went into liquidation and did not meet the cheque. Nevertheless, Mr Dan was not liable on it. There was no doubt that outsiders would have known that they were dealing with a limited company and no mischief had been done. Some judges have interpreted the section strictly, as the *Hendon* case shows, and regarded it as requiring that every part of the name be correct. The interpretation used in *Jenice* seems more sensible.

Business names

If a company has a place of business in Great Britain and carries on business here in a name which is not the corporate name – for example, Boxo Ltd carrying on business as 'Paris Fashions' – then the business name (Paris Fashions) must not suggest a connection with government or a local authority or contain sensitive words without the approval of the Trade Secretary, and in the case of sensitive names, also the approval of the body listed in the Regulations referred to above (Business Names Act 1985, ss 2 and 3).

A company which is using a business name has to state its corporate name in readable form on all business letters, orders for goods and services, invoices, receipts, and written demands for payment of business debts, and must also give an address in Great Britain where the service of documents will be effective. This is normally the registered office.

A notice giving the same information must be shown in a prominent place in any premises where the business is carried on and to which customers and suppliers have access. Furthermore, the corporate name and address for service of documents must be given straight away and in writing on request to anyone who is doing or negotiating business with the company (Business Names Act 1985, s 4).

The criminal sanction consists of default fines on the company if it does not comply and also on its directors and other officers such as a secretary (Business Names Act 1985, s 7). The civil sanction is that the company may not be able to enforce its contracts (Business Names Act 1985, s 5). The rules on this are the same as for partners and sole traders who are operating under a business name but have not followed the Business Names Act 1985. (The sanction is explained in Chapter 5.)

So far as our specimen memorandum is concerned, we have chosen to form our company in the personal names of the shareholders and directors. Those who form companies often have to do this because all the made up names they want, e.g. City Publishing Ltd, are already on the Index. If this is so, personal names will be registered even though a company with that name is already on the Register, provided that the names are at the time of registration those of directors of the business.

Use of e-mail and faxes

For the purposes of the Companies Act 1985 and the Business Names Act 1985, it is considered that external e-mail and faxes are to be regarded in the same way as letters so that the rules relating to the publication of names applies to them. The Civil Evidence Act 1995 confirms that documents that are computer-generated are to be treated in the same manner as paper documents. The same Act dealing with business records defines records as 'records in whatever form' so business letters and order forms sent by fax are to be treated in the same way as conventional written or typed documents and the name provisions apply.

Abuse of names by Internet users

Persons can select any name for their Internet address, provided it has not already been registered with Nominet UK, the body responsible for allocating UK domain names. A decision of the High Court indicates that if, by error, the same Internet domain name is allocated to two or more organisations, the court is prepared to resolve a dispute. The case *Pitman Training Ltd* v *Nominet UK* (1997) decided that a genuine registration of a name to which the organisation applying is entitled will be protected. The case confirms that the rule of 'first come, first served' applies. In the case Pitman Publishing registered the name *Pitman.co.uk* and later when the publisher tried to use the name it discovered that the name had been allocated and was in use by Pitman Training. Nominet restored the domain name to the publisher and a claim by the training company to establish its right to the name failed. The case is reported on the Lord Chancellor's Department website: *http://www.open.gov.uk/lcd/ scott.htm.*

An additional problem which has arisen because of the rapid growth of the Internet and its use by business organisations for e-mail and commerce generally, is the parallel growth of a breed of speculators who register domain names which form a crucial part of a particular business Website and e-mail address, in the hope, for example, of offering it for sale to the business concerned with the possibility of receiving a high price for exclusivity. In *BT plc* v *One in a Million* (1997) the High Court granted injunctions to restrain defendants who had registered company names and/or trade marks as domain names on the Internet on the basis of passing off and trade-mark infringement. The court also said that since the names were now of no use to the defendants, they should be assigned to the claimants. The decision means that, at least in the UK, it should be easier to protect Internet domain names.

Registered office (Clause 2)

As will be seen from the specimen memorandum, there is only a statement that the registered office is situated in England. The actual address is not given but, as we have seen, it is filed with the Registrar when applying for registration. (See Form 10 earlier in this chapter.)

The actual address can be changed by an ordinary resolution of the members. This requires a 51 per cent majority. Alternatively, the directors may change it if, as is usual, they are given this power by the articles. A company whose memorandum states that its registered office is to be situated in 'England' or 'England and Wales' may change its registered office to somewhere else in England and Wales since 'England' includes Wales for this purpose. In spite of the fact that the law of England and Wales is the same, a company which has chosen to have its registered office in Wales either initially or by change cannot change its registered office to a place in England. In any case an English or a Welsh company cannot change its registered office to a place in Scotland since the law is different there. In addition, if a company is to have its registered office in Scotland, it must be registered in Edinburgh.

A major purpose of the registered office is to keep various statutory registers, such as the register of members and records, for the purpose of inspection. In addition, it is the company's address where legal documents, notices and other communications can be served.

Objects (Clause 3)

Generally

This clause lists the things which the company can do. If it enters into a transaction which is not included in the clause, that transaction will at common law be *ultra vires* (that is, beyond its powers) and void (that is, of no effect).

Ashbury Railway Carriage & Iron Co v *Riche* (1875)
The company was formed for the purposes of making and selling railway waggons and other railway plant. It got a contract to build a railway system in Belgium and entered into an agreement under which Riche was to be a subcontractor in this exercise. The company later ran into difficulties and the directors told Riche that his contract was at an end. He sued for breach of that contract. The House of Lords decided that he had no claim because the contract which the company had made to construct the railway system and of which he was a subcontractor was *ultra vires* and void. On a proper reading of the objects, the company had power to supply things for railways but had no power actually to make them.

By way of explanation of the decision of the above case, it should be said that the *ultra vires* rule was brought in by the courts to protect shareholders. It was thought that if a shareholder, X, bought shares in a company which had as its main object

publishing and allied activities (see specimen memorandum clause 3(a) at the end of this chapter), then X would not want the directors of that company to start up a different kind of business because he wanted his money in publishing.

In more recent times it has been noted that shareholders are not so fussy about the kind of business the directors take the company into so long as it makes money to pay dividends and raises the price of the company's shares on the stock market.

The people most affected by the *ultra vires* rule in more recent times were creditors who had supplied goods or services to a company for a purpose not contained in its objects clause. If the company was solvent, no doubt such creditors would be paid, but if it went into insolvent liquidation they would not even be able to put in a claim. Other creditors might get some part of their debts if the company had any funds but the *ultra vires* creditors would get nothing.

For this reason it became usual to put in the objects clause a large number of objects and powers, as is the case with our specimen memorandum, and also to say, as the final paragraph of our clause 3 which follows 3(w) does, that each clause contains an independent main object which can be carried on separately from the others. The House of Lords decided in *Cotman* v *Brougham* (1918) that this type of clause was legal.

If this clause did not appear, the court would regard our clause 3(a), which contains our main object, as our only business activity and say that all the other clauses contained only powers to be used to achieve the end of publishing.
Therefore, our power of investment set out in clause 3(h) would be restricted to investment in the activities set out in clause 3(a). However, we have an independent main objects clause and may therefore invest in other activities, for example in the shares of oil companies.

Also, the decision of the Court of Appeal in *Bell Houses Ltd* v *City Wall Properties Ltd* (1966) states that an objects clause can be drafted in such a way as to allow the company to carry on any additional business which the members or directors choose. Our clause 3(b) is an example and allows the members ('the company') by ordinary resolution (not the directors, as in *Bell Houses*) to resolve to carry on another business in addition to publishing. This type of clause is often referred to as a 'subjective objects clause'.

In this way the limitations which are placed by the common law on a company's business activities by the *ultra vires* rule have been much reduced, though, of course, the control over the activities of the directors by the members has also been lessened. In fact, with a large number of clauses in the objects clause, as our typical memorandum has, together with an independent objects sub-clause as in *Cotman* and a type of *Bell Houses* clause, the modern company's contractual capacity approaches that of a natural person. The *ultra vires* rule as a method of controlling the activities of the board has been largely abandoned. In addition, there has, during the last few years, been massive statutory intervention to make the *ultra vires* rule ineffective. (See below.)

Companies Act 1985

Sections 35 and 35A as inserted by the Companies Act 1989 now represent the United Kingdom's response to Article 9 of the First Directive (No 68/151) issued by the European Economic Community for the harmonisation of company law in the member states of the EC.

They are intended to largely eliminate the effect of the *ultra vires* rule on the claims of creditors, though it has less relevance today since fewer transactions are likely to be *ultra vires* at common law.

However, on the assumption that the narrow scope of a particular company's memorandum may still allow for this, a review of the provisions of the section may be worthwhile.

Section 35 deals with the *ultra vires* rule as it relates to the company's **capacity** to enter into the transaction. The authority and power of its directors and other officers to make, say, a contract on its behalf are considered later in this chapter.

Section 35 does not abolish the rule but reforms it, and as far as trade creditors of a company are concerned little should now be heard of it. There is a continuing relevance of the rule in other areas, which are considered below.

1 The company's capacity. Section 35 provides that the validity of an act of a company shall not be called into question by reason of anything in the company's memorandum. Thus, in the *Ashbury* case the **contents** of the objects clause only allowed the company to make things for railways. The contract with Mr Riche which was part of a scheme to build a whole railway system would now have been enforceable by him because the contents of (what is in) the memorandum do not affect the validity of a transaction in terms of the company's capacity to enter into it.

2 The rights of members. Under s 35 any member can ask the court for an injunction to prevent the directors from **entering into an *ultra vires* transaction** but not if the members have ratified it by special (or written) resolution. If the directors have actually entered into an *ultra vires* transaction, an injunction is not available, but it is if they are contemplating such a transaction. If the situation is such that an action for an injunction can go ahead, the contents of the memorandum and the special clauses referred to above will continue to be relevant in deciding whether or not the intended transaction can be restrained. Thus, the rule is reformed but not abolished.

3 Transactions with the directors of the company or its holding company. Under s 322A transactions with the directors of the company or its holding company are voidable (capable of being made legally ineffective) by the company if they are *ultra vires*, and once again the contents of the objects clause and not s 35 will be relevant. A holding and subsidiary relationship exists where one company (the holding company) controls the other (the subsidiary company) because, for example, the holding company owns more than 50 per cent of the shares in the subsidiary. Transactions with a director's connected persons are included, e.g. the spouse or minor child of a director. The above transactions are not voidable by the company where the problem is that they are beyond the objects of the company if the members have ratified them by a special resolution. The position where the directors have exceeded their own powers but not those of the company is considered later in this chapter.

4 Liability of directors. Directors have in the past been liable to pay damages to the company if they entered into an *ultra vires* transaction which caused the company loss, which of course it may not do.

This is still the position and the objects clause is relevant in deciding the liability of the directors. However, s 35(3) allows the members to relieve the directors of this liability by passing a special resolution. This must be a separate resolution; a resolution ratifying the transaction is not enough.

5 **Charities.** There is a special regime for charities which obviously need separate treatment, because people give not so much to the charity as to its objects which should therefore be kept to. Under s 64 of the Charities Act 1993, s 35 is not available to protect a transaction by a person dealing with a charity unless:

(a) he has given full consideration to the charity in money or money's worth, which simply means that it is a deal in which the charity has received the proper value in terms, say, of goods it has received under a contract; **and**

(b) he is unaware that the transaction was beyond the company's objects; **or**

(c) he was unaware that the company was a charity.

The various forms of ratification referred to above do not apply.

6 **Ordinary creditors.** So far as the company's capacity is concerned, there should be no problems and their transactions should be enforceable against the company by reason of s 35. Also of assistance are the following:

(a) there is now no constructive notice of the company's objects as there was before. Mr Riche had not read the *Ashbury* objects but was deemed to know what they were. Now s 711A applies and provides that there is no deemed knowledge that a particular transaction is not within the objects;

(b) there is no duty to enquire as to the capacity of the company, nor under s 35A as to the authority of its agents such as the directors to make a particular transaction;

(c) transactions are enforceable against the company even by those who have actual knowledge that they are not within the company's objects. Section 35A(2)(b) applies so that even if a creditor had read the memorandum and realised that a transaction was not within the objects he could still enforce it against the company.

Authority of directors as agents

It is convenient to consider here the authority of the directors to bind the company to a transaction as agents. A transaction will not necessarily be enforceable because it is within the company's capacity in terms of the provisions in its objects clause or because of s 35, if the directors do not have authority as agents to enter into it on behalf of the company. Table A to the CA 1985 gives wide powers to the directors in reg 70. They can exercise all the powers of the company unless, for example, company legislation requires the members to act. Thus, for example, the directors cannot alter the articles because this requires a resolution of the members. However, some articles may restrict the powers of the directors much more than this by, for example, restricting their power to borrow. Thus, we may have a situation in which the company has unlimited power to borrow but the directors can borrow only up to, say, one-half of the company's paid-up capital. What is the position of a lender whose loan exceeds this amount? There is some protection in case law, which is considered later in this chapter, but for most practical purposes the matter is covered by s 35A. The section provides that in favour of a person dealing with the company in good faith, the power of the board of directors to bind the company or authorise others to do so shall be deemed free of any limitation under the company's constitution.

A person is not to be regarded as acting in bad faith just because he knows that the act is beyond the powers of the directors, and under s 35B there is no duty to enquire, nor as we have seen is there constructive notice. Provided the above requirements are met, a transaction entered into by the board acting together as a board will bind the company.

In addition, the section deals with a situation where the directors authorise other persons to make contracts on behalf of the company. This is to overcome the common law rule that a company can only act through 'organs' of the company. At common law the board of directors is an organ of the company but only if acting collectively as a board. Section 35A overcomes this by making it clear that an act done by a person authorised by the board is in effect an act of the board and therefore an act by an 'organ' of the company. Thus, if the board authorises the company's purchasing officer to buy materials from outsiders for use in the company's manufacturing process, each purchase will in effect be a transaction decided on by the directors. There is no longer an assumption, as there was in previous and to some extent defective legislation, that all commercial decisions are made at boardroom level. If, therefore, the board collectively make a decision to enter into a transaction which is beyond their powers, s 35A will make the transaction enforceable against the company. The same is true if an individual director or other person authorised by the board to act exceeds the powers of the board in respect of a transaction on behalf of the company which he as an authorised person has made. Our lender should therefore be able to enforce his loan against the company, though the following points should be borne in mind.

1   **Good faith.** Under s 35A a person is to be regarded as acting in good faith unless the contrary is proved. Thus, the burden of proof will be on the company if it wishes to avoid a transaction on the 'bad faith' ground. Section 35A also provides that a person is 'dealing with' a company even though the transaction is gratuitous in that no consideration has been provided to the company. This protects, for example, charitable donations by the directors beyond their powers.

2   **Member injunctions.** A member is not prevented by s 35A from asking the court for an injunction to stop the directors from acting beyond their powers but this cannot be done if the transaction has been entered into, nor if the members have ratified the directors' lack of authority by ordinary resolution.

3   **Director liability.** The directors are liable to compensate the company as they always have been if they cause the company loss by acting outside their powers. Relief from this liability can be given by the members by special resolution.

4   **Charities.** Once again, there are special rules for charities. Section 35A will not protect a person dealing with a charity unless he has given full consideration and did not know that the transaction was beyond the directors' powers or did not know he was dealing with a charity.

Altering the objects clause

Under s 4 the objects clause can be freely changed or amended by a special (or written) resolution. This type of resolution has already been explained in dealing with changing the company's name.

Furthermore, a company may alter its objects (or be registered with objects) which merely state that it is to carry on business as a general commercial company. This means that it can carry on any trade or business whatsoever. The company will also have powers to do all such things as are incidental or conducive to that end without listing them in the objects clause.

If a company does register with, or change its objects clause to, this new formula it will have effectively opted out of the *ultra vires* rule even for internal purposes of shareholder injunctions. However, in the case of an existing company the change will have to be approved by a special (or written) resolution of the members. The new formula has been quite popular with company formation agents when forming companies for clients. However, since the use of the new formula is at the moment confined largely to private companies, we have left our memorandum (which appears at the end of this chapter) in what might be described as the old form since this is likely to be met with by those working with PLCs, though admittedly our company is private. It is also necessary to explain cases such as *Cotman v Brougham* (1918).

Companies which adopt the 'one line' objects clause will require to add to it if they wish to make charitable or political donations since these would not appear to be included in the phrase 'general commercial company'. Failure to include extra objects could involve problems of applications by a member or members to the court for an injunction.

Once a special resolution to alter the objects clause has been passed it stands unless within 21 days of it being passed the holder(s) of 15 per cent of the company's issued share capital or, if the company's share capital is divided into classes, say A ordinary and B ordinary, 15 per cent of the holders of any class, apply to the court to cancel it. Those who apply must not have voted for the resolution.

The court need not cancel the resolution but may instead, under s 5(5), order the purchase of the dissentients' shares from the company's funds, thus reducing its capital. Alternatively, the other members may buy the shares, in which case capital is not reduced.

There can, of course, be no dissentient rights where the unanimous written resolution procedure is used.

Limitation of liability (clause 4)

This, as can be seen from the specimen memorandum, simply states: 'The liability of the members is limited' – unless of course the company is unlimited, when this clause is not put in.

The clause cannot be altered so as to make the company an unlimited one. However, the company may be re-registered as unlimited under s 49. All unlimited companies must be private companies and public companies cannot apply for re-registration under s 49, but must convert to private companies first.

An unlimited company may re-register as a limited company under s 51. This does not apply to a company which was previously a limited company but re-registered as an unlimited one. In this case there is no going back.

It will be recalled that an unlimited company is in general not required to file accounts with the Registrar and so there can be no going backwards and forwards between limited and unlimited status because this could lead to selective filing of accounts: e.g. if the accounts are bad, re-register as unlimited; if they improve, re-register as limited and file them and so on. The CA 1985 prevents this.

Capital (clause 5)

This clause must state the amount of the company's authorised capital and its division into a fixed nominal (or par) value. In our case the authorised capital is £10,000 divided into 10,000 shares of £1 each.

The main result of this clause is that English companies cannot have what are called 'no par' value shares. In the case of no par shares, the company would decide to issue, say, 100 shares and receive, say, £200. This £200 would appear in the balance sheet as 'stated capital'. In this country if the shares had a nominal value of £1 each the bal-

ance sheet would have to show called-up share capital as £100 and share premium account £100.

The share premium account is like capital and is a rather clumsy way of indicating that the whole £200 the company has received is capital. With no par value shares this is obvious. The whole £200 is shown in the balance sheet as stated capital and it is clear what it is.

As we have already seen, the authorised share capital of a PLC must be at least £50,000 divided into shares of a fixed nominal (or par) value.

Association clause

Finally, there is an association clause which states that the subscribers wish to be formed into a company and that they agree to take the shares opposite their names.

Only one subscriber is required where the intention is to form a one-member company.

ARTICLES OF ASSOCIATION

The second major document governing the company is the articles of association. A specimen set of articles appears at the end of this chapter. Reference will be made to these as required in the rest of this chapter.

Companies which do not wish to draft their own articles may adopt Table A of the Schedule to the Companies (Tables A–F) Regulations 1985, or they may have adopted earlier Tables A in previous company legislation.

We have not done this. Our articles have been specially drafted, largely to show that in dealing with companies we must always be prepared to find articles which are specially drafted.

Those who learn Table A and assume that no other form of articles exists will be in some trouble in dealing with companies. It will be of interest to see, where appropriate, how our own articles differ from Table A.

For the moment it would be advisable for the reader to look at the major headings of our model and see in broad terms what the articles cover. As will be seen, they regulate the rights of the members of the company and the manner in which the business of the company shall be done.

The articles must be printed, divided into paragraphs numbered consecutively, and signed by each subscriber to the memorandum in the presence of at least one witness (s 7(3)).

Electronic communication

It should be noted that the Electronic Communications Order 2000 amends Table A to allow the electronic appointment of proxies and the sending of notices. We have made similar changes in our own articles accordingly.

Legal effect of the articles

The articles (together with the memorandum) when registered are a contract which binds the company and the members as if signed and sealed by each member; so says s 14(1).

It follows from this that:

1 The members are bound to the company by the provisions of the articles. This is illustrated by the following case.

Hickman v *Kent or Romney Marsh Sheep Breeders' Association* (1915)

The articles of the Association provided that any dispute between a member and the company must be taken first to arbitration. H, a shareholder, who was complaining that he had been wrongfully expelled from the company, took his case first to the High Court. The court decided that the action could not continue in the High Court. H was contractually bound by the articles to take the dispute to arbitration first.

2 The company is also bound to the members in respect of their rights as members. Again, the following case is an illustration of this point.

Pender v *Lushington* (1877)

The articles of the Direct United States Cable Co gave its members voting rights but fixed a maximum amount of votes (100) which each member could cast no matter how many shares he held. The Globe Telegraph and Trust Co held a large number of shares in Direct United and to evade the 100 votes rule and increase its voting power it transferred some of its shares to P who agreed to be a nominee of Globe and vote with it. L, who was the chairman of Direct United, refused to allow P to cast his votes

and a resolution supported by Globe and P was lost. P asked the court for an injunction to restrain the company and L from declaring that P's votes were bad. The court granted the injunction. P had a contractual right to vote given to him by the articles and he could enforce this right. His votes must be accepted.

3 Each member is bound to the other members. This is illustrated by the following case.

Rayfield v *Hands* (1958)

A clause in the articles of a company provided that: 'Every member who intends to transfer shares shall inform the directors who will take the said shares equally between them at a fair value.' Rayfield, a member, told the defendant directors that he wanted to transfer his shares. The directors refused to take and pay for them, saying that they had no liability to do so.

The court decided that the word 'will' indicated an obligation to take the shares and that the clause imposed a contractual obligation on the directors to take them. This was in the nature of a collateral contract. When a member bought shares he made a contract with the company but also a collateral contract with the other members to observe the provisions of the articles. Thus, the members could sue each other and there was no need for the company, with whom the main contract was made, to be a party to the action.

Comment. Although the article placed the obligation to take shares **on the directors**, the judge construed this as an obligation falling upon the directors in their capacity as **members**. Otherwise the contractual aspect of the provision in the articles would not have applied. The articles are not a contract between the company and the directors who, in their capacity as directors, are outsiders for this purpose. (See below.)

4 Neither the company nor the members are bound to outsiders. This is illustrated by the following case.

Eley v *The Positive Government Security Life Assurance Co Ltd* (1876)

The articles of the company appointed Mr Eley as solicitor of the company for life. During the course of this employment he became a member of the company. Later he was dismissed and brought an action against the company for damages for breach of the contract which he said was contained in the articles. The court decided that his action failed. There was no contract between the company and Mr Eley. He was an outsider in his capacity as a solicitor. The articles gave him rights only in his capacity as a member.

It should be noted that the Contracts (Rights of Third Parties) Act 1999 does not apply to the statutory contract set out in s 14. The 1999 Act specifically excludes it to prevent third-party rights from arising. Thus, the legal decisions set out above continue to apply and are not affected by the 1999 Act.

Alteration of the articles

The company may alter or add to its articles by a special (or written) resolution (s 9), subject to certain restrictions of which the following are the most important.

1 The court will not allow an alteration to be enforced if it is not for the benefit of the members as a whole, as where the company takes a power of expulsion of members for no particular reason.

Brown v British Abrasive Wheel Co Ltd (1919)
The majority shareholders (98 per cent) in a company agreed to provide more capital for the company on condition that the two per cent minority (who were not prepared to put more money in) would sell their shares to the majority. Negotiations having failed, the articles were altered to include a clause under which a shareholder was forced to transfer his shares to the other members at a fair value if requested to do so in writing. The court decided that the alteration could not be allowed. The clause could be used to deprive any minority shareholder of his shares without any reason being given and it was not for the benefit of the company (i.e. the members) as a whole that any one or more of their number should be expelled for no good reason.

However, expulsion is allowed if it does benefit the members as a whole as where the member expelled is competing with the company.

Sidebottom v Kershaw Leese & Co Ltd (1920)
Mr Sidebottom, who was a minority shareholder in the company, carried on a business which competed with the company. Because of this the articles were altered to include a clause under which any shareholder who competed with the company had to transfer his shares at a fair value to persons nominated by the directors. The Court of Appeal decided that the alteration was valid. Although it only applied to a particular member at the time, it could be applied in the future to any member who competed with the company (but not, of course, to members who did not). This would always be for the benefit of the company in that its members would have power to exclude a competitor.

2 A company cannot justify breach of a contract outside of the articles by showing that the breach resulted from an alteration of the articles.

Southern Foundries Ltd v Shirlaw (1940)
Mr Shirlaw, who was a director of Southern Foundries, was appointed managing director of that company for ten years by a contract outside the articles. The company was taken over by Federated Industries. With their voting power they altered the articles to provide that Federated Industries had power to remove any director of Southern Foundries and that the managing director of Southern Foundries must also be a director. Mr Shirlaw was subsequently removed from his directorship and therefore could no longer qualify as managing director and his contract was terminated while it still had some years to run. The House of Lords decided that the company was liable in damages. Although a company always had a legal right to change its articles, if by doing so it caused a breach of an outside contract then, while the alteration could not be prevented, the company was liable in damages if there was a breach of a contract outside of the articles as a result of the alteration.

3 Shareholders' rights are contained in the articles. Obviously, these rights can be changed by a special resolution of the company in general meeting. There would seem to be no objection to the use of the unanimous written resolution by private companies here since if there was unanimity there would, by definition, be no dissentients (see below); in the absence of unanimity the company would have to proceed by a special resolution of three-quarters in general meeting. However, if the company has more than one class of shares, e.g. A Ordinaries and B Ordinaries, then the special resolution is not enough.

Under s 125 a special resolution is not effective unless holders of three-quarters of the issued shares of each class consent in writing, e.g. by returning a tear-off slip on a letter to indicate their agreement or not, or by means of an extraordinary resolution at a class meeting. A private company cannot insist on unanimous objection by the unanimous written resolution approach because objection by only three-quarters is enough.

In addition, s 127 applies; under this 15 per cent of the class who did not vote for the variation may apply to the court within 21 days of the resolution which altered the articles. Once such an application has been made, the variation will not take effect unless and until it is confirmed by the court.

So if under our specimen Art 3 we had created shares of different classes all of which had one vote per share on a poll, as Art 52 provides, then any special resolution of the company in general meeting to change that article, e.g. to one vote per share to the holders of A Ordinaries as before, and one vote per two shares to the holders of B Ordinaries, would need also the approval of the holders of shares in Class B.

The point of this is that those holding the A Ordinary shares may well be able to get a special resolution in general meeting and so weaken the position of the B Ordinary shareholders, but they cannot do so without the necessary class consent of the B Ordinary shareholders. The changes do not need the consent of those holding A Ordinary shares because their rights have not been varied, each A Ordinary shareholder having one vote per share as before.

FINANCING THE COMPANY

We shall now deal with the raising of money for the company.

Share capital

The capital of a company may be divided into preference and ordinary shares. In addition, both of these classes of shares may, under s 159, be issued as redeemable by the company at a future date.

Preference shares

These shares have the right to payment of a fixed dividend, e.g. 10 per cent of the nominal value, before any dividend is paid on the other shares. However, there is no right to such dividend unless the company has sufficient distributable profits to pay it. This is why preference shares differ from loan capital. Interest on loan capital must be paid whether the company has distributable profits or not. If it has no profits, it must be paid from capital as by a sale of assets or the raising of a further loan.

Once the preference dividend has been paid in full, the preference shareholders have no right to share in surplus profit with the ordinary shareholders unless, as is rare, the preference shares are participating preference shares. Preference shares may be cumulative or non-cumulative. If they are cumulative and in any one year there are insufficient profits to pay the preference dividend, it is carried forward and added to the dividend for the following year and is paid then if there are sufficient profits.

So if Eric is the holder of 100 preference shares of £1 each, carrying a preference dividend of 10 per cent, then if in year one the dividend cannot be paid, the £10 to which Eric is entitled is carried forward to year two and if there are sufficient profits in that year Eric will receive £20. If the shares are non-cumulative, Eric would not receive the £10 lost in year one, but only £10 for year two and subsequently.

Ordinary (or equity) shares

These rank for dividend after the preference shares and sometimes also the terms of issue provide that the preference shares shall have a right to claim repayment of capital before the ordinary shares if the company is wound up.

Ordinary shares, therefore, carry most risk. Generally they have most of the voting rights in general meetings and therefore control the company, it being common to provide that the preference shares shall not have a vote at all unless their dividend is in arrear. Ordinary shares receive a fluctuating dividend which depends upon distributable profits left after the preference dividend has been paid.

Redeemable shares

Under s 159 a company with a share capital may, if authorised by its articles (as our company is in Art 3), issue redeemable shares, whether ordinary or preference. Redeemable shares may be made redeemable between certain dates. The holder thus knows that his shares cannot be redeemed before the earlier of the two dates, which is usually a number of years after the issue of the shares in order to give him an investment which will last for a reasonable period. He also knows that the shares are bound to be redeemed by the later of the two dates mentioned. However, there are no legal provisions requiring a company to fix the time of redemption at the time of issue, and a company may wish to leave the date of redemption to be decided by the board when financially convenient.

Redeemable shares may be issued only if there are in issue other shares which cannot be redeemed. It is not therefore possible for a company to redeem all its share capital and end up under a board of directors with no members. The shares must be cancelled after redemption. The company cannot hold and trade in redeemed shares.

The power to issue redeemable equity shares is useful in the expansion of the small business. Outside investors often like ordinary share capital with its greater potential returns in the way of dividend and capital gain, but the smaller businessman may wish to buy them out after the business has developed. He can do this by issuing redeemable ordinary shares. Redeemable preference shares are less attractive to the speculative investor. They are safe but carry only a fixed dividend no matter how high the profits.

Purchase of own shares

Sections 162–178 apply and any company may by following the procedures laid down in these sections purchase its own shares, including any redeemable shares – as where the date for redemption has not arrived. The shareholder(s) concerned must of course be willing to sell the shares and the company must want to buy them. The company cannot be forced to buy them, nor can a shareholder be forced to sell.

The important legal considerations are set out below.

1 The company's articles must allow the purchase, as ours do (see Art 4).

2 The shares must be fully paid. The Companies Act 1985 does not allow the purchase (or for that matter, redemption) of partly-paid shares.

3 Under s 165 a company cannot purchase its shares if as a result of the purchase there would no longer be any member of the company holding shares other than redeemable shares. There must be a member or members holding non-redeemable shares.

4 A public limited company must have allotted share capital of at least £50,000.

5 The shares must be cancelled following purchase. The company cannot hold and therefore trade in its own shares.

Reform

The government sought consultation of changes to the law set out in 5 above and following the consultation has decided, when legislative time allows, to amend the present law to allow companies to purchase their own shares and hold them in what is called treasury for resale at a later date. The maximum allowed to be held will be 10 per cent of share capital and voting rights and dividend rights on the shares will be suspended to accord with EU law. Initially, the reform will apply only to companies listed on the Stock Exchange, but consultation will continue in terms of an extension to other companies.

Market purchase

Public companies may make a market purchase on, for example, the Stock Exchange or the Alternative Investment Market (AIM) (see below), or an off-market purchase from an individual shareholder.

Before a Stock Exchange or AIM purchase can be made by the directors the members must approve by ordinary resolution. The resolution must state the maximum number of shares which the directors can acquire and the maximum and minimum prices which they can pay. The minimum price is often specified, but the maximum price is usually according to a formula, for example one based upon the Daily Official List of the Stock Exchange on a day or days preceding the day on which the share is contracted to be purchased, e.g. an amount equal to 105 per cent of the average of the upper and lower prices shown in the quotation for ordinary shares of the company in the daily list of the Stock Exchange on the three business days immediately preceding the day on which the contract to purchase is made.

The duration of the authority to purchase must be stated in the resolution by stating the date on which it expires.

A copy of the resolution must be filed with the Registrar of Companies within 15 days after it is passed.

Off-market purchase

These provisions are mainly for private companies but can be used, as we have seen, by PLCs whose shares are not listed on the Stock Exchange or quoted on the AIM, which is regulated by the Stock Exchange for the smaller PLCs which cannot or who do not wish to comply with the conditions for a full listing on the Stock Exchange.

The procedure is as follows:

1 A special (or, in private companies, written) resolution of the members is required before the contract is entered into. **The contract must therefore be approved in advance.** So far as PLCs are concerned (but not private companies), the resolution must specify the duration of authority to make the contract being a period not longer than 18 months.

2 The special resolution is **not** effective unless the draft contract is made available for inspection by the members at the registered office during the 15 days immediately preceding the meeting and at the meeting. Where the unanimous written resolution procedure is used there will not, of course, be a meeting and so the draft contract will have to be circulated to the members with their copy of the resolution for signature. **This applies wherever in this text it is stated that documents must be available at a meeting.**

3 The special resolution is invalid if passed by the votes of the member whose shares are being purchased. Thus there must be sufficient other shareholders' votes to give the necessary majority of 75 per cent of those voting in person or by proxy. The member whose shares are being purchased can vote other shares he may have which are not being purchased on a poll but he cannot in any event vote on a show of hands. The above provisions might appear to rule out the use by private companies of the unanimous written resolution procedure since the member whose shares were being purchased would, by implication, appear to be voting for the purchase in respect of all his shares. However, the provisions inserted by the 1989 Act solve this by saying that the person whose shares are being purchased is not to be regarded as a person who is entitled to vote. So the resolution must be unanimously agreed to by the other members and the one whose shares are being purchased is not included.

Off-market contingent contracts

All companies may make contingent purchase contracts. These are contracts by the company to buy its own shares on the happening of a future event, for example a contract to buy the shares of an employee on retirement. This is permitted if the procedures for an off-market purchase set out above are followed.

It should be noted that the company cannot assign its right to buy the shares to someone else. This is to prevent a market developing in contingent purchase contracts.

The company cannot release, i.e. give up, its right to buy except by authorisation of a special resolution of the members.

Purchase of own shares: miscellaneous provisions

When a company has purchased its own shares it must within 28 days disclose the fact to the Registrar, giving the number and nominal value of the shares purchased and the date they were delivered to the company. Furthermore, the contract of purchase must be kept at the registered office for ten years and can be inspected by members. In a PLC it can be inspected also by any other person without charge.

If a company fails to purchase the shares when it has agreed to do so there is no action by the member for damages. However, he can bring an action for specific performance but the court will not make such an order unless the company can pay for the shares from its distributable profits.

Purchase (or redemption) partly from capital – private companies only

This provision is intended for private companies who have some distributable profits **but these are not enough** to purchase or redeem the shares and the company is either unwilling or unable to raise money from a fresh issue of shares. In such a case it can purchase or redeem its shares partly from capital.

It is in effect an easier procedure for private companies to reduce their share capital or to satisfy the claims of a retiring member or the estate of a deceased member in respect of shares in the company which might not be easily saleable elsewhere.

As regards the conditions, the articles must authorise a purchase from capital, as ours do. (See Art 4.) The 'permissible capital payment' (PCP) is the shortfall after taking into account distributable profits or the proceeds of a fresh issue of shares, which the company must utilise first. If there are no distributable profits or proceeds of a fresh issue of shares, there can be no purchase or redemption wholly from capital. This restricts the advantages of the section to some extent.

There must be a statutory declaration of solvency by the directors. This says that the company will be solvent immediately after making the purchase (or redemption) and for one year afterwards. The statutory declaration states the PCP and the declaration itself is based on accounts prepared within three months before the statutory declaration, taking into account any distributions (e.g. dividends) which may have been made between the accounts and the statutory declaration.

A report by the auditors must be attached to the statutory declaration stating that the PCP has been properly calculated **and** that the directors' opinion as to solvency is reasonable in terms of the facts of which the auditors are aware.

A special (or written) resolution of the members is also required and the statutory declaration and auditors' report must be available for inspection **at the meeting.** The position regarding voting and circularisation of documents in the case of a unanimous written resolution has already been described. In spite of the audit exemption provisions, the requirement for an auditors' report when purchasing shares from capital is retained. This means that very small companies can exempt themselves from the requirement to appoint an auditor unless and until it becomes necessary for some purpose other than the audit of annual financial statements. If it becomes necessary, an auditor will have to be appointed unless the relevant regulations say otherwise. This is indicated as required throughout this chapter.

The resolution must be passed within one week of the date of the statutory declaration. It is invalid if passed with the votes of the shares of the person whose shares are being bought. Such persons may vote other shares on a poll but not on a show of hands. (The position in regard to written resolutions has already been explained.)

The capital payment must be made not earlier than five weeks (to allow for objections) and not later than seven weeks from the resolution. If an indefinite period was allowed for the capital payment the statutory declaration would be getting outdated, so seven weeks is the maximum time.

Publicity must be given in order to protect creditors. A notice in writing may be given to all the company's creditors stating the fact and the date of the special (or written) resolution, the amount of the PCP, that the statutory declaration and auditors' report can be inspected at the registered office and that any creditor may seek to restrain the payment by applying to the court to cancel the special resolution during the period of five weeks from the special resolution. The statutory declaration and auditors' report must be kept at the registered office for inspection by any member or creditor until the end of the fifth week following the special resolution.

Alternatively, an advertisement may be put in *The London Gazette* and one national newspaper giving the same information as listed above.

At the date of the notice or advertisement copies of the statutory declaration and auditors' report must have been sent to the Registrar so that they are available for inspection by a company search.

Dissentient shareholders or creditors may also apply to the court, within five weeks of the resolution, to cancel it, for example if available profits have not been utilised. The court may order the purchase of the dissentient shares or the payment of creditors. This provision is obviously inapplicable, so far as members are concerned, where there is a written resolution,

If the company goes into insolvent winding-up within 12 months of a payment from capital, then the seller of the shares and the directors giving the statutory declaration are each liable to repay the money in full with a right of contribution against the others involved.

Transfer of purchased shares

A transfer form is not required on completion of the purchase. The seller merely hands over his share certificate to the company for cancellation.

Loan capital

Trading companies have an implied power to borrow and charge their assets as security for a loan, i.e. to give the lender a right to appoint, for example, a receiver to sell the company's assets in order to repay the loan if the company does not otherwise repay it, or, where practicable, to run the business for a while in order to sell it as a going concern (see below).

Even so, the memorandum usually gives an express power to borrow and details of the extent to which the company can charge its assets as security. (See clause 3(j) of the specimen memorandum.)

Section 117 puts restrictions on borrowing by newly-formed PLCs. Such companies cannot commence business or borrow until they have received a certificate allowing them to do this from the Registrar of Companies.

The certificate will not be issued until at least £50,000-worth of the company's capital has been allotted (sold) and at least one-quarter of the nominal value of each share and the whole of any premium has been received by the company.

Debenture and debenture stock

When a lender makes a loan to a company he will obviously require some evidence of that fact. This is usually a written document in the form of a deed which is called a debenture, a term which has its origin in the Latin word for 'owing'.

A **single debenture** evidences a loan from a person where the lender is in privity of contract with the company and is a creditor of it. Its modern use is to secure a loan or overdraft facility from a bank. In this context it is the document by which the company charges in favour of the bank all its assets and undertakings, thus giving the bank the right to appoint an administrative receiver if the company does not pay what it owes. The administrative receiver (unlike a receiver who merely collects rent and/or sells assets to pay the lender) is given management powers by the

Insolvency Act 1986 and can run the company while he is realising money from the company's assets to pay the bank. If the company is a going concern when he has done this – and sometimes his management will have cured the company's ills – the running of the company is handed back to its board of directors. It should be said, however, that in many receiverships the assets of the company and its goodwill, where it is a going concern, are transferred to another organisation which is interested in it and believes it can run the ailing company profitably.

This is in contrast to a liquidator of a company in a winding-up. He is really an undertaker and his job is to sell what assets the company has to pay the creditors as far as he can and then see that the company is removed from the Register.

Debenture stock is found where the loan is to come from the public, those who subscribe for the debenture stock receiving a stock certificate rather like a share certificate. The company keeps a register of debenture holders and the stock certificates can be transferred from one person to another in a similar way to shares. However, unlike shares, which cannot be issued at a discount (s 100), debentures can be so issued. It would, for example, be unlawful to issue, say, a £1 share at 75p, but this would be legal in the case of a debenture.

When debentures are issued for public subscription, the company enters into a trust deed with trustees for the debenture holders. The trustees are often an insurance company. The insurance company has the charge over the assets and the power to appoint a receiver or an administrative receiver and the trustees are the creditors of the company on trust for the individual stock holders who are not in privity of contract with the company.

From a commercial point of view this is necessary because the holders of debenture stock are widely dispersed and need some central authority, such as the trustees, to look after their interests with the company.

Our company could not make an issue of debenture stock since, under s 75 of the Financial Services and Markets Act 2000, a private company cannot offer its shares or debentures to the public. We could, however, issue a debenture to a bank for the purpose of securing an overdraft facility since this would not be a public issue.

Registration of charges

The much revised provisions relating to company charges contained in the Companies Act 1989 have still not been implemented. There is opposition from some quarters in the business world and it is now uncertain whether they will be implemented at all. In fact, the government-appointed Company Law Review Steering Group has issued a consultation document entitled *Registration of Charges* and it may be some time before we see any change. In consequence, instead of dealing with the old and revised rules, we think it better to restrict ourselves to the old and still existing rules as follows.

Under s 395 particulars of a charge to secure a debenture or an issue of debentures must be registered with the Registrar of Companies. The object of this is to show those doing business with the company, who may inspect the Register, what charges there are affecting the company's property.

In addition, copies of the documents creating charges must be kept at the company's registered office and be available for inspection by members and creditors without charge (s 407).

The company must also keep a register of charges affecting its property (s 407). This may also be inspected by members and creditors without charge (s 408).

Failure to register a charge

Failure to register particulars of a charge with the Registrar within 21 days of its creation means that the charge will be void if the company is wound up and a liquidator appointed, or if an administrator is appointed. The charge is **not** void if an administrative receiver is appointed. (As to the nature of these offices see later in this chapter.) The lender would then become an unsecured creditor and would have no rights over the property which the company had charged to secure his loan. Nevertheless, the money intended to be secured, if not on demand, becomes immediately repayable. In addition, an unregistered charge is not void while the company is a going concern.

It is because the security may be lost that the law allows a secured creditor to register the charge himself and to claim the costs from the company (s 399).

However, in practice, banks, which commonly lend money or give overdraft facilities to companies on a secured debenture, get the signatures of the appropriate officers of the company on the document registering the charge and then post it to the Registrar in Cardiff themselves. Thus, the company registers the charge but the bank ensures that this is done.

Failure to register the charge in the company's register leads to a default fine on the company's officers at fault, but the charge is still valid.

There are also provisions allowing the court to approve the registration of particulars of a charge delivered after 21 days. The charge will be valid from the date of its registration but has no priority over persons who took charges over the company's property while it was not registered.

THE ISSUE OF SHARES AND DEBENTURES

Generally

Under s 80 the directors of public and private companies cannot issue shares without the express authority of the members. This is usually given by the members by ordinary resolution at a general meeting of the company. The authority may be given for a particular allotment of shares or it may be a general power, though if it is it can be given only for a maximum period of five years and then it must be renewed. The authority once given may be taken away or varied by the members by ordinary resolution insofar as it has not been exercised.

Under s 80A private companies may elect by an elective resolution (see later in this chapter) that the authority given to the directors to allot shares can be given for an indefinite period or a fixed period of longer than five years. The fixed period is renewable, and further renewable, by the company in general meeting. The authority may also be varied or revoked by the company in general meeting. The authority must in all cases state the maximum number of relevant securities that may be allotted, e.g. the whole of the company's un-issued share capital.

Similar permission to allot debenture stock is not required unless the debentures can, by the terms of issue, be converted at some time in the future to shares.

Under s 89, when public and private companies wish to offer shares where the members have given them power under s 80, they must offer them to existing members first in proportion to their present holdings, e.g. one new for three existing shares, or whatever formula covers the number of shares being issued.

This requirement to issue to existing members may be excluded. A **private company** can add to its articles by a special (or written) resolution a clause stating that these pre-emption rights, as they are called, shall not apply to the company and this will last unless and until the articles are altered by special resolution or the company ceases to be a private company. It may in fact be permanent.

A **public company** (and a private company which does not adopt the above approach) can disapply the pre-emption rights by special (or, in the case of a private company, written) resolution of its members which may be for a particular issue or a general disapplication which can only be for five years and then must be renewed. Alternatively, a public company and a private company may disapply pre-emption rights temporarily by a provision in the articles, but this must be renewed every five years and is not the permanent alteration referred to above.

The provisions of ss 80 and 89 prevent the directors from using the power of allotment to issue shares to persons favourable to themselves in order to keep their position on the board and thus their control of the company. This did happen in the past but now the consent of the members is required, both to allot the shares in the first place and then to issue them outside to persons other than existing members.

Even in a private company which has given the directors a power of allotment for an indefinite period the members must still approve the disapplication of pre-emption rights. This assumes that the private company has not opted out of the pre-emption provisions altogether (see above).

THE PROSPECTUS

Generally

A private company cannot issue a prospectus because, as we have seen, it cannot offer its shares or debentures to the public. It must sell its securities by private negotiation with individuals interested.

However, a public company, provided it has the necessary member authority under s 80 and the members have disapplied their pre-emption rights under s 89, may issue shares by means of a prospectus. This is a document explaining the nature of the investments which a would-be subscriber to the issue will be taking.

Offer for sale

A public company which intends to issue shares or debentures to the public could, in law, do so directly itself. However, such issues require considerable expertise and experience in those who make them and the method used is normally an offer for sale.

Under an offer for sale the securities (shares or debentures) are offered to the public by an issuing house, e.g. a merchant bank, instead of being offered by the company direct to the public. Just before the offer the issuing house will have agreed to buy the securities concerned and is, in effect, offering its own shares to the public. Nevertheless, the relevant legislation (see below) applies to the offer and the prospectus issued under the offer for sale must comply with it.

The issuing house is paid by the fact that it pur-chases the shares at one price from the company and offers them at a slightly higher price to the public.

Allotment of shares under a prospectus

The company, being by definition a public company, must obtain one-quarter of the nominal value of each share issued plus the whole of any premium on it before it can allot shares to those members of the public who want to take them (s 101).

It is also most important in a contract to take shares in a public company that the shares shall be quoted on a recognised stock exchange. If they are not so quoted, they have no market and there is some difficulty in selling them.

In this connection there are two major controls: i.e. the approval of the company for listing and the listing particulars for issue to the buying public are subject to the requirements of the Financial Services Authority, while permission to *trade the securities* issued is a matter for the London Stock Exchange.

REGULATION OF THE SECURITIES MARKET AND OF ADMISSION TO IT

European Union law requires each member state to nominate and create a Competent Authority to maintain an Official List (or market) of securities which is to regulate the admission of securities to the Official List and to monitor those who issue shares in terms of adherence to the listing rules. This function is carried out here by the Financial Services Authority (FSA) under the Financial Services and Markets Act 2000. The FSA's Listing Rules are contained in what is known as 'The Purple Book' because of its colour. The details of these rules are beyond the scope of this book. Permission to actually trade the securities in the market is a matter for the London Stock Exchange.

The FSA can refuse an application for listing where it considers that granting it would be detrimental to the interests of investors. It can also suspend a listing as where, for example, a company has failed to comply with reporting requirements in the Listing Rules so that investors and potential investors do not have sufficient information on which to make informed decisions about the company's securities in order to deal in them.

General duty of disclosure in listing particulars

The Financial Services and Markets Act (FSMA) 2000 in s 80 makes statutory only 'financial condition' information. This, according to the section, is information which investors and their professional advisers would reasonably require in order to make an informed assessment of the company's financial position, its assets and liabilities and

prospects. Less information may be given to sophisticated investors, e.g. professional advisers (s 80(4)(c)).

You will find that company prospectuses appear, for example in the *Financial Times*, *The Times*, the *Daily Telegraph* and the *Independent* – you will find it instructive to read these to see in more detail what is required.

Supplementary listing particulars

Section 81 of the FSMA 2000 provides that where there is any significant change following the submission of listing particulars to the Financial Services Authority, but before dealings in the securities have started, supplementary particulars must be approved and published.

Exemptions from disclosure

Section 82 of the FSMA 2000 gives the Financial Services Authority power to authorise the omission of material from the listing particulars which would otherwise be required. The discretion is limited to particular grounds, e.g. discretion is given for international securities which are only dealt in by those who understand the risks. This will, for example, preserve the informality and speed which is vital to the Eurobond market (s 82(1)(c)).

Compensation for false or misleading particulars

Section 90 gives express liability to those responsible for the listing particulars for material misstatements, material omissions, and misleading opinions. The remedy given is for persons suffering loss to sue for a money compensation.

However, under s 90(6) any liability, civil or criminal, which a person may incur under the general law continues to exist. Thus, a claimant could still sue for fraud or misrepresentation under the Misrepresentation Act 1967, or for a negligent misstatement under the rule in *Hedley Byrne & Co v Heller & Partners* (1963). (See further, Chapter 11.)

As regards who can sue, s 90(1) states that 'any person responsible for the listing particulars is liable to pay compensation to a person who has – (a) acquired securities to which the particulars apply; and (b) suffered loss in respect of them ...'. This would seem to include all subscribers whether they have relied on the prospectus or not. Materiality in terms of loss appears to be the test and not reliance. It seems, therefore, that a subscriber need not be aware of the error or even have seen the listing particulars.

Section 90(1) would seem also to cover subsequent purchases in the market. However, such a purchaser could presumably only sue if he bought while the particulars were the only source of information affecting the price of the securities. Once the company issues new information, e.g. supplementary particulars, or other new material has been published, e.g. the loss of a major contract, then it would presumably be unreasonable to allow a claim.

Persons responsible

As regards civil claims, regulations made under s 79(3) set out those who can be regarded as responsible for all or some part of the listing particulars. These include the issuing company and its directors and anyone who expressly takes responsibility for a part or parts of the particulars, e.g. an expert who authorised the contents of the particulars or part of them.

Exemption is given for those who merely give advice in a professional capacity but who do not give specific reports for inclusion as experts.

As regards criminal liability, there is, under s 397 of the Financial Services and Markets Act 2000, a sanction of up to seven years' imprisonment and/or a fine for those who make false statements in the particulars.

Section 91 of the FSMA 2000 gives the Financial Services Authority power to impose financial penalties on issuers who have breached the listing rules. In addition, the Authority may issue public or private censures and suspend or cancel the listing of the securities.

Defences

Section 151 provides that a person responsible for non-compliance with or a contravention of s 150 shall not be liable if he can prove:

(a) that he had a reasonable belief in the truth of the statement or that it was reasonable to allow the relevant omission;

(b) that the statement was by an expert and that he had reasonable belief in the expert's competence and consent to inclusion of his statement; and

(c) if (a) and (b) above cannot be proved, that he published a correction or took reasonable steps to see that one was published and he reasonably believed it had been.

There is also exemption if the relevant statement is from an official document and also if the person who acquired the securities knew of the defect in the particulars.

OFFERS OF UNLISTED SECURITIES

Offers of securities on the Alternative Investment Market are governed by the Public Offers of Securities Regulations 1995. These are not considered in any detail in this text which is intended for students and not would-be specialists in the field of company flotations. In any case, there are no great differences between the form and contents of a prospectus under the regulations and under the Financial Services and Markets Act 2000. In addition, the main learning requirement in general business law – who is responsible for the prospectus and what happens if it is misleading? – is covered by provisions in the regulations which again show no great difference from the rules applying to a Stock Exchange prospectus (or listing particulars as it may be called) which we have already described.

THE REMEDY OF RESCISSION

The main remedy for loss resulting from a misstatement in a prospectus is, as we have seen, damages based either on breach of a statutory duty under the Financial Services and Markets Act 2000 (or the Public Offers of Securities Regulations 1995) or the Misrepresentation Act 1967, or at common law under the case of *Hedley Byrne* which laid down the principles of liability for negligent misstatements.

The remedy of rescission involves taking the name of the shareholder off the register of members and returning money paid to the company by him. This is against the modern trend because it goes contrary to the principle of protection of the creditors' buffer which is the major purpose of the many statutory rules relating to capital maintenance.

The modern trend is to leave the shareholder's capital in the company but allow him a remedy for money compensation if the shares are less valuable because of the misstatement against those who were responsible for the misstatement such as directors or experts.

The cases which are illustrative of the remedy of rescission are rather old and are not referred to here. Suffice it to say that in order to obtain rescission the shareholder must prove a material misstatement of fact not opinion (the principles in the *Hedley Byrne* case cover actions for damages for opinions), and that the misstatement induced the subscription for the shares. The action can only be brought by the subscriber for the shares under the prospectus. It is thus less wide than the claim for money compensation under s 90(1) which, as we have seen, seems to extend to subsequent purchasers in the market.

The right to rescind is a fragile one, being lost unless the action is brought quickly; or if the contract is affirmed, as where the shareholder has attended a meeting and voted the shares; or where the company is in liquidation or liquidation is imminent.

MEMBERSHIP

Becoming a member

A person may become a member of a company:

1 **By subscribing** the memorandum of association. Membership commences from the moment of subscription. On registration of the company the names of the subscribers (or subscriber in the case of a one-person company) must be entered in the register of members (s 22). They are, however, members without such an entry.

2 **By agreeing** to become a member and having his name entered on the register of members. Actual entry on the register is essential for membership, which commences only from the date of entry. A person may show agreement to become a member:

(a) by obtaining shares from the company, by applying for them as a result of a prospectus (public company), or following private negotiation (private company);

(b) by taking a transfer from an existing member following a purchase or a gift of the shares.

Minors

A minor may be a member unless the articles forbid this. The contract is voidable, which means that the minor can repudiate his shares at any time while a minor and for a reasonable time after becoming 18. He cannot recover any money paid on the shares unless there has been total failure of consideration. Since being a member of a company appears in itself to be a benefit regardless of dividends, the minor is unlikely to be able to use this 'no consideration' rule.

Personal representatives

The personal representatives of a deceased member do not become members themselves unless they ask for and obtain registration. However, s 183 gives them the right to transfer the shares.

Bankrupts

A bankrupt member can still exercise the rights of a member. He may, for example, vote or appoint a proxy to vote for him. However, he must exercise his rights and deal with any dividends he receives in the way in which his trustee in bankruptcy directs. The trustee in bankruptcy has the same right as a personal representative to ask for registration as the holder of the shares.

Shareholders' rights

The main rights given by law to a shareholder are as follows:

1 **A right to transfer his shares.** This is subject to any restrictions which may be found in the articles. Private companies may restrict the right to transfer shares, for example by giving the directors in the articles a right to refuse registration of the person to whom they have been transferred. Public companies listed on the Stock Exchange or quoted on the AIM cannot have restrictions of this kind in their articles because the agreement with the relevant regulatory authority forbids it.

2 Meetings. A member is entitled to receive notice of meetings and to attend and vote or appoint a proxy to attend and vote for him.

The Electronic Communications Order 2000 modifies the CA 1985 to enable notices of company meetings to be sent electronically to those entitled to receive them. It also modifies the CA 1985 to enable a member to appoint a proxy electronically by communicating with an electronic address supplied by the company for the purpose.

3 Dividends. A shareholder's right to dividend depends on the company having sufficient distributable profits out of which to pay the dividend.

Although dividend is declared by the members in general meeting, the members cannot declare a dividend unless the directors recommend one. Furthermore, they can resolve to reduce the dividend recommended by the directors but cannot increase it.

4 Accounts. A shareholder is entitled to a copy of the company's accounts within seven months of its accounting reference date (i.e. the end of its financial year) in the case of a public company and ten months in the case of a private company. The accounts must be filed with the Registrar of Companies at Companies House at or before the end of the above periods according to the type of company involved.

Listed companies can, however, provide their shareholders with a summary financial statement giving merely key information from the full accounts. Nevertheless, those shareholders who want a copy of the full accounts are entitled to one on request. This is designed to alleviate the problems faced by certain of the privatised industries such as British Telecom and British Gas which have large numbers of shareholders who, formerly, had all to receive very bulky and expensive copies of the full accounts. The full (or shorter form) accounts of private companies must be circulated to members but those members can, by unanimous agreement, called an elective resolution, dispense with the requirement to lay the accounts before a general meeting. A member and, where the company has one, the auditor can require them to be laid and can call a general meeting for the purpose if the directors will not do so.

The matter of the alteration of shareholders' rights has already been considered.

The Electronic Communications Order 2000 modifies the CA 1985 to enable copies of the annual accounts and reports including the summary financial statements to be sent electronically to those entitled to receive them.

Shareholders' duties

A shareholder is under a duty to pay for his shares when called upon to do so but is not in general liable for the company's debts beyond the amount (if any) outstanding on his shares. There are some exceptional cases; for example, where, to the member's knowledge, the membership of the company falls below two and the company carries on business with that reduced number for more than six months, the liability of the existing member for debts incurred after the expiration of the six months is joint and several with the company (s 24).

Thus, the member is treated as if he were a partner with the company and if the debt is, say, £2,000, the remaining member can be asked to pay the full amount and seek a contribution of £1,000 from the company. The member is not, of course, likely to be sued unless the company is insolvent, in which case he has little chance of getting the contribution.

Section 24 does not apply to the one-person company or indeed under the single-member company regulations to any private company.

Cessation of membership

The most usual ways in practice that a person may cease to be a member of a company are by:

1 transfer of his shares to a purchaser or as a gift;
2 rescission of the contract under a misleading prospectus, though the more likely and acceptable remedy today would be to remain a member but receive monetary compensation;
3 redemption or purchase of shares by the company;
4 death or bankruptcy;
5 winding-up of the company.

MEETINGS, RESOLUTIONS AND ANNUAL RETURN

Shareholders' meetings

There are two kinds of company general meeting: the annual general meeting and an extraordinary general meeting.

Annual general meeting

Section 366 states that an annual general meeting must be held in every calendar year and not more than 15 months after the last one. So if a company held an annual general meeting on 30 March 2001 it must hold the next one in 2002, and on or before 30 June 2002.

However, if a company holds its first annual general meeting within 18 months of its incorporation, it need not hold one in its year of incorporation or the following year. Thus, if a company was incorporated on 1 November 2000, it would have until 30 April 2002 to hold its first annual general meeting.

The notice of the meeting must say that it is the annual general meeting. A specimen notice appears below.

A private company can elect to dispense with the requirement to hold the AGM. However, any member may, by giving notice to the company not later than three months before the end of the year in which an AGM should have been held but for the opting out, require an AGM to be held in that year. For example, Boxo Ltd holds an AGM in 2000 at which all the members entitled to be present and vote agree to opt out of the AGM requirement. No AGM is to be held in 2001 and thereafter, but if a member thinks one should be held in 2001, he can achieve this by giving notice to the company not later than 30 September 2001.

Extraordinary general meetings

All general meetings other than the annual general meeting are extraordinary general meetings. They may be called by the directors at any time.

Section 368 gives holders of not less than one-tenth of the paid-up share capital on which all calls due have been paid the right to requisition an extraordinary general meeting. The requisition must state the objects of the meeting, be signed by the requisitionists, and deposited at the registered office of the company. If the directors do not call a meeting within 21 days of the date of depositing the requisition, the requisitionists, or the majority in value of them, may call the meeting within three months of the date of the deposit of the requisition.

To prevent the directors from convening (i.e. calling) the meeting to be held on a long distant date so that the members' desire to discuss urgent matters is defeated, s 368 provides that the directors are not deemed to have duly convened a meeting if they convene it for more than 28 days after the date of the notice convening the meeting. So if they called it to be held, say, six months after the date of the notice they would not have complied with the Act and the requisitionists could call it. It should be noted that the above provisions refer to 'holders' of shares and 'requisitionists'. One member with one-tenth or more of the paid-up share capital cannot therefore ask for an EGM to be held. Two members holding at least one-tenth of the paid-up share capital are required. This is to ensure that there will be a quorum at any meeting which is called and the provision of the Interpretation Act 1978 that the singular includes the plural and vice versa does not apply because of this (see *Morgan* v *Morgan Insurance Brokers Ltd* (1993).

Notice of meetings

This must be given in accordance with the provisions of the articles. Our Art 43 requires 21 clear days' notice (i.e. excluding the day of service of the notice and the day of the meeting) of the annual general meeting and for a meeting to pass a special resolution or appoint a director, and 14 clear days in other cases.

The articles usually provide, as our Art 43 does, that a meeting shall not be invalid because a particular member does not receive notice, unless of course this is deliberate as distinct from accidental.

In order to work out the clear days' notice, we also need a provision like the one in our Art 95 which says that notice is deemed (or assumed) to be served 24 hours after posting. Thus, if we post

RICHES KEENAN PUBLISHING LIMITED

NOTICE IS HEREBY GIVEN THAT THE FIRST ANNUAL GENERAL MEETING of the company will be held at 140 High Street, Barchester on the 5th day of January 2001 at 10:30 am to transact the ordinary business of the company.*

A member entitled to attend and vote at the meeting is entitled to appoint a proxy to attend and vote instead of him. A proxy need not also be a member.

By order of the board

J.M. WILLIAMS

....

Secretary

140 High Street
Barchester

1 December 2000

* Article 44 of our articles states the ordinary business of our AGM and no notice of it is required. If the articles do not include references to ordinary business (and the current Table A does not), the items of business set out in our Art 44 would have to be set out in the notice.

Fig 6.4 Specimen notice of an Annual General Meeting

the notice of an extraordinary general meeting on, say, 1 February, it is deemed served on 2 February and we can hold the meeting on 17 February at the earliest. Table A to the CA 1985 deems service 48 hours after posting.

Quorum at general meetings

Under our Art 45 no business may be validly done at a general meeting unless a quorum (i.e. minimum number) of members is present when the meeting begins. This means in effect that there need not be a quorum throughout the meeting so long as there is one at the beginning.

Article 45 also provides that **two members personally present** (not by proxy) shall be a quorum. As regards single-member companies the regulations add s 370A to the CA 1985. This provides that notwithstanding any provision in the articles (so that no changes in our Art 45 are required), one member present in person or by proxy shall be a quorum. Section 382B is also added under which if a sole member takes any decision which could have been taken in general meeting he shall (unless it is a written resolution) provide the company with a written record of it. It is desirable that he should sign the written record though the regulations are silent on this.

If the resolution is one which must be filed with the Registrar of Companies, as where the sole member alters the articles, then the filing requirements apply.

Voting

This may be by a show of hands in which case, obviously, each member has one vote, regardless of the number of shares or proxies he holds. However, the articles usually lay down that the chairman or a certain number of members may demand a poll; Table A and our Art 49 provide for two. If a poll is successfully demanded, each member has one vote per share and proxies can be used. (See our Art 52.)

Proxies

If the articles so provide, voting on a poll may be by proxy (see our Art 52). A proxy is a written authority given by the member to another person to vote for him at a specified meeting. The company may require these authorities to be deposited at the company's office before the meeting. However, under s 372 the articles cannot require them to be deposited more than 48 hours before the meeting. Our Art 57 requires 48 hours.

Minutes

A company must keep minutes of the proceedings at its general and board meetings. Members have a right to inspect the minutes of general meetings but not those of directors' meetings.

Resolutions – generally

There are four main kinds of resolution passed at company meetings as set out below.

1 An ordinary resolution, which may be defined as 'a resolution passed by a majority (over 50 per cent) of persons present and voting in person or by proxy at a general meeting'.

Any business may be validly done by this type of resolution unless the articles or the Companies Acts provide for a special or extraordinary resolution for that particular business.

An example of the use of an ordinary resolution is for the members to give their permission for the directors to allot the company's unissued share capital under s 80.

2 An extraordinary resolution, which is one passed by a majority of not less than three-quarters of the members who, being entitled to vote, do so whether in person or by proxy at a general meeting of which notice has been given specifying the intention to propose a resolution as an extraordinary resolution (s 378(1)). Under s 369 14 days' notice of the meeting must be given or seven days in the case of an unlimited company.

The company may resolve by an extraordinary resolution to wind up if it cannot by reason of its liabilities continue in business. This will put the company into a creditors' voluntary winding-up (see later in this chapter).

3 A special resolution, which is one passed by the same majority as is required for an extraordinary resolution at a general meeting of which at least 21 days' notice has been given stating the intention to propose the resolution as a special resolution (s 378(2)).

The distinction between a special and extraordinary resolution lies, therefore, in the period of notice of the meeting. A special resolution requires 21 days, whereas an extraordinary resolution requires only 14. The majorities are the same. It will be appreciated that if an extraordinary resolution is to be proposed at the annual general meeting 21 days' notice will have to be given because that is the requirement for the AGM.

A special resolution is required, for example, to alter the objects clause, to change the company's name, or the articles, or for the company to approve in advance a contract to make an off-market purchase of its shares. Section 380 provides that within 15 days of the passing of an extraordinary or special resolution a copy of the resolution must be forwarded to the Registrar of Companies. Some ordinary resolutions must be sent to the Registrar but by no means all. An example of one which requires filing is the ordinary resolution to allow the directors to exercise a power of allotment under s 80.

The copy sent to the Registrar may be printed or be in any form approved by the Registrar (s 380). He will accept a typewritten copy.

4 Ordinary resolutions after special notice. Section 379 requires that for certain ordinary resolutions, for example one removing a director before his period of office is ended, special notice must be given.

Where special notice is required it must be given to the company secretary not less than 28 days before the meeting at which the resolution is to be proposed and by the company to the members not less than 21 days before that meeting.

This means that if, for example, a member wishes to propose the removal of a director by this procedure under s 303, then when he stands up at the meeting to propose that removal, the company secretary must have been on notice of his intention to do so for 28 days at least and the members for 21 days at least.

The purpose of the notice of 28 days is so that the company secretary can as s 304 requires alert the director concerned to the possibility of his removal so that the director can circulate members with his reasons why he should not be removed or, that failing, prepare an oral statement to be given at the meeting at which his removal is proposed.

Before leaving the topic of resolutions passed at meetings, it should be noted that resolutions can be passed by a small number of members. For example, if a company has 5,000 members but only 30 attend the meeting and 70 appoint proxies, a special, or extraordinary, or ordinary resolution can be validly passed by three-quarters or at least 51 per cent, as the case may be, taken from those present at the meeting and voting in person or by proxy.

Members' resolutions at the AGM

Under s 376, a member (or members) representing not less than one-twentieth of the total voting rights of all the members can by making a written requisition to the company compel the directors:

1 to give to members who are entitled to receive notice of the next AGM notice of any resolution which may be properly moved and which they intend to move at that meeting; and

2 to circulate to the members any statement of not more than 1,000 words with respect to the matter referred to in any proposed resolution or the business to be dealt with at the meeting.

The requisition must be made not later than six weeks before the AGM if a resolution is proposed and not less than one week before if no resolution is proposed.

It should be noted that since s 376 uses the expression 'member or members' the section can be used by one member with the required shareholding.

Written resolutions of private companies

As part of the deregulation of private companies the Companies Act 1985 provides for written resolutions which can be passed by the members of a private company without the need to call or hold a meeting. The 1985 Act provides that anything which can be done by a private company by a resolution in general meeting or in a class meeting (as where a class of shareholders is being asked to vary their rights and they are unanimous in wishing to approve the variation, in the absence of unanimity there would have to be a class meeting), can be done without a meeting, and without any previous notice being required, by a resolution signed by or on behalf of **all** the members of the company who at the date of the resolution were entitled to attend and vote at meetings of the company. The signatures need not be on a single document so that the resolution may, for example, be typed on separate sheets of paper and circulated to the members for signature. The date of the resolution is the date on which it is signed by, or on behalf of, the last member to sign.

There are some cases where the written resolution procedure cannot be used, e.g. the removal of a director by ordinary resolution after special notice to the company (see above). The ordinary resolution must be passed at a meeting of the company because the director concerned is allowed to make representations as to why he should not be removed, either in writing with the notice of the meeting or orally at the meeting.

The company is required to keep a record of written resolutions and the signatures of those members who signed them in a record book which is, in effect, a substitute for what would, in the case of a meeting, be the minutes.

Involvement of auditors

The Deregulation (Resolutions of Private Companies) Order 1996 deals with the involvement of the company's auditors (if any) in the written resolution procedure, as follows:

1 Article 3 repeals the pre-existing provisions of the CA 1985, i.e. ss 381B and 390(2), and substitutes a new s 381B (duty to notify auditors of proposed written resolutions). The new section imposes a duty on the directors and secretary of a company to send the company's auditors (if any) a copy of, or otherwise inform them of the contents of, any written resolution proposed under s 381A (written resolutions of private companies) at or before the time that resolution is supplied to a member for signature. Breach of the duty will result in a criminal offence but will not affect the validity of any resolution passed under s 381A.

As regards the criminal offence, it is a defence for the accused to prove:

(a) that the circumstances were such that it was not practicable for him to comply with the requirements; or

(b) that he believed on reasonable grounds that a copy of the resolution had been sent to the company's auditors or that they had otherwise been informed of its contents.

2 Since s 381B is repealed, the auditors have no right to require the company to call a meeting rather than use the written resolution procedure nor need the company wait seven days to see whether the auditors state whether the resolution does or does not concern them as auditors.

So far as the auditors are concerned, the regulations operate merely to give them information as to resolutions being passed by the company bearing in mind that had the company passed the resolution at a general meeting the auditors would have received notice of it and have been entitled to attend and be heard on any part of the business which concerns them as auditors (s 390(1)).

Finally, Art 4 amends s 381C(1) to make it clear that the statutory written resolution procedure under s 381A may be used notwithstanding any provision in the company's memorandum or articles but does not prevent the use of any power conferred by such a provision instead.

Elective resolutions of private companies

Again, as part of the deregulation of private companies, the Companies Act 1985 allows a private company to opt out of, for example, the requirement of member approval for allotment of shares by the directors, the laying of accounts and reports before a general meeting, and to dispense with the holding of the annual general meeting.

The resolution required to achieve the opting out is called an elective resolution and can be passed at a meeting of the company. Such a resolution is not effective unless:

1 at least 21 days' notice in writing is given of the meeting at which it is to be proposed, the terms of the resolution being stated; and
2 the resolution is agreed to at the meeting, in person or by proxy, by all the members entitled to attend and vote at the meeting.

An elective resolution may be revoked by an ordinary resolution of the company and an elective resolution ceases to have effect if the company is re-registered as a public company.

The law allows the written resolution procedure to be used for the passing of an elective resolution.

Impact of the Electronic Communications Order 2000 on meetings and resolutions

- *Notices of meetings* can be sent electronically to those entitled to receive them. Either notices can be sent directly to an electronic address supplied for the purpose by the recipient or they can be published on a Website and the recipient notified of their availability in a manner agreed with him. In the latter case, the notice must be published on the Website for at least the period for which notice of the meeting must normally be given.
- *As regards proxies*, a member may appoint a proxy electronically by communicating with an electronic address supplied by the company for the purpose.
- *As regards the filing of resolutions* and other documents with the Registrar of Companies, the order enables the Registrar to direct that any document required to be delivered to him under the Companies Act 1985 and the Insolvency Act 1986 may be delivered electronically in a form and manner directed by him. In practice, Companies House gives guidance on these matters.
- *The relevant articles of Table A are changed* or added to in order to accommodate the above electronic procedures. Special articles, such as ours are overriden and do not require amendment, but we have done so in line with best practice.

The annual return

Under s 363 a company must file an annual return with the Registrar of Companies. It must be made up to a date of 12 months after the previous return or, in the case of the first return, 12 months after incorporation. The company may move the date of its next annual return by indicating the new date on the current annual return. The new date then governs future annual submissions. The return must be delivered to the Registrar within 28 days of the make up date.

The shuttle concept

Under a procedure introduced by the Registrar of Companies, companies are issued with a shuttle document (Form 363s) containing all the information relevant to the annual return which the Register already holds on the company's file. The company is merely required to confirm or amend the shuttle document and return it. There is no need as formerly to complete a blank form.

If the return is not made, the company and every officer in default is liable to a fine, and in addition the directors may become disqualified by the court.

An example of an annual return appears at the end of this chapter.

The electronic shuttle

We have noted that the Electronic Communications Order allows the Registrar of Companies to direct that documents to be delivered to Companies House may be so delivered by electronic means. In this connection, Companies House is looking at the feasibilty of introducing an e-shuttle for submission of annual returns. Instead of sending a company a pre-printed from as now, it would send the information by e-mail. The company would then reply to the e-mail either to confirm that the information remains correct and current or to give details of changes. The annual return filing fee would be paid electronically and the returned e-shuttle would be authenticated by the company quoting a unique PIN number previously agreed with Companies House. An 'image' of the returned e-shuttle would be made and be accessible on-line from Companies House.

PROTECTION OF MINORITY INTERESTS

The rule in *Foss* v *Harbottle* (1843)

The rule in *Foss* is that the majority of the members, by which we mean those who can command more than 50 per cent of the votes in general meeting, will be able to get the company to do what they want it to do, even if this does not suit the other members. It is in other words a principle of majority rule.

In that sense it is very hard on the minority, so when we consider minority rights it is the **exceptions** to *Foss* that we are looking at. The rule has not been allowed to ride roughshod over all minority rights.

In addition, there are some situations of wrongs to the minority which **fall outside the rule** in *Foss* and to which that decision does not apply.

Foss v *Harbottle* (1843)
The claimants, Foss and Turton, were shareholders in a company called 'The Victoria Park Company' which was formed to buy land to use as a pleasure park. The defendants were the other directors and shareholders of the company. The claimants alleged that the defendants had defrauded the company in various ways and, in particular, that certain of the defendants had sold land belonging to them to the company at a very high price without disclosing this to the members of the company. The claimants now sued on behalf of the company and asked the court to order that the defendants make good the losses to the company. The court decided that since the members of the company had not been consulted and that since it was possible that a simple majority of them in general meeting might resolve to allow the defendants to keep the alleged profits, the court would not give a remedy to the company at the request of the minority.

The rule does not apply where the wrong is not to the company but to the member personally.

One of the major cases which illustrates this has already been considered in the section on the articles. It is *Pender* v *Lushington* (1877). Mr Pender did not challenge the principle of majority rule but merely complained that an individual, the chairman of the company, was refusing to allow him to exercise his voting rights which were given to him in the articles. The court said that his votes must be accepted. There was no question of majority rule in this case. It was merely a claim for a personal wrong by an individual within the company. In such a situation *Foss* did not apply.

Exceptions to Foss

The main exceptions appear below.

1 **Where the act is *ultra vires*.** Section 35(2) of the 1985 Act gives a statutory right to ask the court for an injunction to restrain the directors from entering into *ultra vires* transactions, but not if the members of the company have ratified a particular transaction by special resolution.

2 **Fraud on the minority.** This is a wide category and only the main examples can be given here. Fraud in this context means some sort of improper behaviour by the majority which amounts to an abuse of their voting control.

There are three main areas in which this rule is applied:

(a) *Where the minority itself is defrauded*. Here we find cases of expulsion of members without reason. Thus, in *Brown* v *British Abrasive Wheel Co Ltd* (1919), the facts of which have already been considered, the rule in *Foss* did not prevent Brown going to court and complaining that the majority intended to insert a provision in the articles containing a power of expulsion without reason because the majority could not use their voting power in this improper fashion.

However, a power to expel members who compete against the company is not an improper use of voting power by the majority, as the decision in *Sidebottom* v *Kershaw Leese & Co Ltd* (1920) (considered above) illustrates.

These cases are not examples of wrongs to members personally but to members of the company generally. The claimant represents not only himself, as in *Pender*, but also all other members who might in future be affected by the fraud, i.e. expelled without reason. *Foss* is potentially a bar here because a minority shareholder is challenging on behalf of himself and other shareholders in a representative action the right of the majority to rule the company in the future. In *Pender* the claimant was merely challenging the right of an individual, i.e. the chairman, to refuse him (and not other members) the right to cast his votes. However, as we have seen in *Brown*, *Foss* will not be a bar where the court finds that the majority are acting in an improper manner.

(b) *The proper purpose rule.* If the directors use, or propose to use, their *intra vires* powers, or those of the company, for an improper purpose, then a minority shareholder can bring a representative claim on behalf of himself and the other shareholders asking that the transaction in question be set aside or stopped. Suppose that an hotel company is the subject of a take-over bid by a property developer who wishes to convert the hotels into offices. Suppose again that to keep themselves in control of the company and to keep it as an hotel company the directors lease the hotels to a friendly company with which they do business, which in turn leases them back to the hotel company with the condition that the premises are only to be used as hotels.

This will frustrate the bid; the bidder will not go ahead and the change of use of the property from hotels to offices, which might have given a better dividend to the shareholders of the hotel company, will not take place.

In such a situation a member of the hotel company could bring a representative action on behalf of himself and the other shareholders to stop or set aside the leasing arrangements.

However, it is very important to note that the rule in *Foss* will prevent such a claim unless the claimant can show that the 'wrongdoers', i.e. the directors, are also in control of the voting in general meeting. If they are not, the action cannot proceed because a simple majority in general meeting can, and may, approve the action of the directors.

It is not necessary in (a) above for the claimant to show that the 'wrongdoers' are in control of the voting in general meeting because a simple majority cannot ratify an act which is fraud on the minority anyway. A simple majority can ratify the acts of directors for an improper purpose short of fraud on the minority.

(c) *Where the company is defrauded.* Actions here are of an entirely different nature. The member sues here to put right **a wrong done to the company** and not (except indirectly) a wrong to its members. The action is not representative, but **derivative**. The claimant gets his right to sue from the company.

In these cases the company is never the claimant. A company can only be brought into court as a claimant by its directors or a simple majority of its members.

However, the company must appear in the action, otherwise the court cannot give it a remedy. This is done by the claimant bringing the company into court as a defendant, but it is only a nominal defendant; in reality it is the claimant in the case.

The decision in *Foss* will prevent a derivative action unless the claimant can show that the 'wrongdoers' are also in control of the voting in general meetings. If they are not, the action cannot proceed because a simple majority can and may approve of the action of the directors and even if this is unlikely, in view of the circumstances of the case, the attitude of the majority must be tested.

An illustration is provided by the following case.

Cook v Deeks (1916)

The directors of a construction company negotiated for a construction contract on behalf of the company and then took the contract in their own names and for their own benefit. In other words, they misappropriated a corporate opportunity, which is a breach of duty by a director. A meeting of the company was called and the directors, by their votes as holders of three-quarters of the shares, passed a resolution declaring that the company had no interest in the contract. Mr Cook brought a derivative claim on behalf of the company against the directors and the court decided that the benefit of the contract belonged to the company and the directors must account to the company for any profits that they made on the contract.

Can damage by negligence be a fraud on the minority?

It would seem that a minority shareholder may bring a claim where the directors use their powers negligently and that negligent conduct causes loss to the company, at least so long as the negligence has resulted in a benefit to the wrongdoers. This sort of conduct can apparently be brought under the head of 'fraud on the minority'.

Daniels v Daniels (1978)

A husband and wife were two directors of a company and also its majority shareholders. They caused the company to sell to the wife (Mrs Beryl Daniels) some land owned by the company. Four years later she resold the land for over 28 times what she paid for it. The claimants, who were minority shareholders, sought a remedy for the company on the basis that the negligence of the defendants had caused the company loss because they had sold its property at an undervalue. No fraud was alleged.

The court was asked whether there was a claim in law on these facts and the court said that there was. In particular, the judge said that there would be a claim 'where the directors used their powers, intentionally or unintentionally, fraudulently or negligently, in a manner which benefits themselves at the expense of the company'.

Comment. Whether such a claim can be brought for negligent mismanagement of the company causing loss, but without benefit to the wrongdoer, is not clear. In *Pavlides v Jensen* (1956) the court said that there was no claim for pure negligence without profit.

In such a case, however, it would appear that the minority can petition under s 459 for 'unfair prejudice' (see below).

Once again, it is essential if a claim is to be brought for negligence with benefit that the wrongdoers are in control of the voting at general meetings. Negligence, with or without benefit to the wrongdoers, can, so far as the **common law** is con- cerned, be ratified by the members in general meeting, provided the wrongdoers are not in control of the voting. Member ratification of an act alleged to be unfairly prejudicial under s 459 will not prevent this **statutory claim** from being brought.

Statutory protection of the minority

In addition to the protection available to the minority by reason of the **exceptions** to *Foss*, various minority rights are given by statute.

The most far-reaching is the right of a minority shareholder to petition the court for relief under s 459 where the shareholder believes that his interests are being 'unfairly prejudiced' by the way in which the company's affairs are being carried on. This section will be looked at separately.

Other main examples of statutory protection are:

(a) the right given to 15 per cent to object to the courts in regard to a proposed variation of class rights;

(b) the right given to 15 per cent to object to the court regarding a proposal to change the company's objects;

(c) the right given to any shareholder to apply to the court to cancel the special resolution under which a private company proposes to make a purchase of shares partly from capital;

(d) the right of a member of a solvent company to petition the court for a compulsory winding-up on the just and equitable ground;

(e) the right given to one-tenth of the members to require the convening of an extraordinary general meeting;

(f) the right given to a member or members with a one-twentieth interest to get an item up for discussion at the AGM.

Relief from unfair prejudice

Under s 459 any member may petition the court on the grounds that the affairs of the company are being conducted in a manner which is unfairly prejudicial to the interests of its members generally or of some part of its members (including the petitioner himself) or that any actual or proposed act is so unfairly prejudicial.

A summary of the main points arising from case law and other sources appears below.

Unfair prejudice

The circumstances leading to 'unfair prejudice', according to the Jenkins Committee, which was set up to consider company law reform and reported in 1962, were as follows:

1 directors paying themselves excessive salaries, thus depriving members who are not directors of any dividends or of adequate dividends.

This was the scenario in Re Sam Weller (1989) and the High Court decided that minority shareholders whose only income from the company was dividends could be regarded as unfairly prejudiced under s 459 by low dividend payments;

2 refusal of the board of a private company to put the personal representatives of a deceased shareholder on the register, thus preventing the shares from being voted and leading sometimes to the personal representatives selling the shares to the directors at an inadequate price;

3 the issue of shares to directors on advantageous terms;

4 the refusal by the board to recommend payment of dividends on non-cumulative preference shares held by a minority.

It may also be that negligent mismanagement by the directors causing loss to the company is unfairly prejudicial conduct, though this is as yet uncertain in view of the absence of definitive case law.

According to the court in *Re a Company* (1983), it is not unfairly prejudicial for the directors to refuse to purchase the company's shares under s 162. In that case the executors of a deceased shareholder in a private company wanted to cash in the shares to provide a trust fund for the education and maintenance of the deceased shareholder's minor children. This fund would have yielded more than the company was paying in dividends on the shares. In the event the directors would not buy the shares, though they were prepared to approve a sale to an outsider if one could be found. This conduct was not unfairly prejudicial, said the court.

However, it seems that removal from the board as in *Ebrahimi* v *Westbourne Galleries* (1972), or other exclusion from management, is covered. This has, in fact, been the basis of the majority of cases brought under the section since it came into law. The section talks about conduct unfairly prejudicial **to the interests** of some part of the members, and in a private company a substantial shareholder can expect to be a director: it is an interest of his membership.

The court said that this was the case in *Re London School of Electronics* (1985) where a director was excluded from management. The court made an order for the purchase of his shares by the majority shareholders. Thus he got his capital out and could go into another business. It will be seen that this is a better remedy than *Westbourne*, i.e. winding-up under the just and equitable ground. The person excluded from management gets his capital out without the need to wind up a solvent company when the directors have merely fallen out with each other.

Nevertheless, it was held in *Re a Company (No 001363 of 1988)* (1989) that a petition for winding-up on the just and equitable ground can still be made if that is the petitioner's choice.

Finally, it should be noted that the House of Lords ruled in *O'Neill* v *Phillips* (1999) that, provided a member of a company has not been excluded from management as a director, he cannot demand that his shares be purchased under s 459 simply because he feels that the company is not being managed properly. The decision makes clear that the s 459 remedy is not a 'cure-all' for shareholders who, for a variety of reasons, are not satisfied with the way in which a company is being run. This is particularly true where they are also in management.

Relief available

Section 461 gives the court a power to make any order it sees fit to relieve the unfair prejudice, including in particular an order:

(a) *to regulate the future conduct* of the company's affairs. This could include the making of a court order altering the articles as in the following case decided under earlier minority protection law.

Re H R Harmer (1959)

Mr H senior, formed a company through which to deal in stamps. He gave his two sons shares in the company but kept voting control himself. Mr H senior was 'governing director' and his sons were also directors. Mr H senior ignored resolutions of the board; he set up a branch abroad which the board had resolved should not be set up; he dismissed trusted employees, drew unauthorised expenses; and engaged a private detective to watch the staff, presumably because he thought they might steal valuable stamps (imagine the effect on industrial relations!). Eventually the sons petitioned the court.

The court found, in effect, unfair prejudice. In giving relief the court ordered Mr H senior to act in accordance with the decisions of the board and ordered that he should not interfere in the company's affairs otherwise than as the board decided. The company's articles were altered by the court order to this effect.

Comment. Once the articles have been altered by the court order, a special resolution is not enough to change the articles affected by the court order. The court itself must give permission for the change.

(b) *to restrain the doing or continuance of any act* complained of by the petitioner. Under this the court could make an order directing the reduction of directors' remuneration found to be excessive and preventing the payment of dividends to the minority.

(c) *to authorise civil proceedings* to be brought in the name of the company by such persons and on such terms as the court directs. This provision is of particular interest in that the court may authorise the bringing of civil proceedings by the company, seemingly without any of the restrictions of Foss on derivative claims. It should be noted that the claim would not be derivative. The company would be the claimant under the court order and there would be no need for the nominal defendant procedure.

(d) *to provide for the purchase* of a member's shares by the company or its other members and if the former is chosen, reduce the company's share capital as required. This provision was, of course, applied in *Re London School of Electronics* (1985) where the order was that the majority shareholders should buy the shares of the member/director who had been excluded from management. This has been the remedy most frequently asked for and obtained in s 459 claims.

Reform

The Law Commission has published a consultation document entitled *Shareholders' Remedies* outlining proposals for change in the law and procedure concerning the remedies available to shareholders to enforce their companies' rights and their personal rights.

The document states that the existing derivative claims are 'unclear and old-fashioned'. It recommends that the circumstances in which a shareholder can sue on behalf of a company be set out in rules of court which are easy to find, clearly expressed and flexible to operate.

The document also looks at the statutory remedy designed for use by a shareholder who has been unfairly prejudiced by the conduct of the company's management. Among the recommendations is a new more streamlined statutory remedy created to deal with the most common allegations of unfairly prejudicial conduct. These have already been outlined above in the reference to the Jenkins Committee.

DIRECTORS AND SECRETARY

The management of a company is usually entrusted to a small group of people called directors. The main control of the shareholders lies in their power to appoint or remove directors. The company secretary is an important officer of the company in terms of its day-to-day administration.

Every public company must have at least two directors and every private company at least one (s 282). Every company must have a secretary and a sole director cannot also be the secretary (s 283).

This means that a one-person company must have at least two officers since the one member/director cannot also be the secretary. The new law makes no change to s 283.

Appointment

The first directors are usually named in the articles. The first directors in our company were named in that way (see Art 60). If no appointment is made in the articles, the subscribers of the memorandum, or a majority of them, may make the appointment in writing.

Neither of these methods of appointment, as we saw at the beginning of this chapter, is effective unless the person concerned is named and gives consent in the statement of first directors, etc. (Form 10, which is required by s 10(2)).

Subsequently directors are usually appointed by the members of the company in general meeting by ordinary resolution. The board of directors is normally allowed to fill casual vacancies (see our Art 72), that is, vacancies which come about because, e.g., a director dies, or resigns his directorship before his term of office has come to an end, or to appoint additional directors up to the permitted maximum. Our maximum is five (see Art 59), and so if we have only two directors the board could appoint up to three more under our Art 72. Directors approved as additional or to fill casual vacancies usually hold office until the next AGM (see Art 72) when the members decide by ordinary resolution whether they are to continue in office.

At this point we should perhaps note that an elective resolution to dispense with the holding of the AGM cannot be considered in isolation. Changes to the articles may well have to be made because they may require the holding of an AGM as ours do (see Art 40). The retirement by rotation of directors is also triggered by the AGM in many articles, including our own (see Arts 67–73). So amendments would have to be made if we had this particular piece of deregulation in our company. We could remove the requirement to hold an AGM and all reference to it in the articles and have no provision for retirement by rotation, or trigger retirement by rotation by a date, e.g. 31 March in each year when one-third of the board retires by rotation.

Generally, one or more full-time directors is appointed a **managing director**. The articles must provide for the appointment (see our Art 74) and articles normally enable the board to confer on the managing director any of the powers exercisable by the board and to vary these powers (see Art 77).

Many of the provisions of company law, e.g. the rules relating to directors' loans and the disclosure of those loans in the accounts, apply to 'shadow directors'. These are, under s 741, people in accordance with whose directions or instructions the board of the company is accustomed to act but excluding professional advisers such as lawyers and accountants who may give the board professional advice on which they usually act.

However, those who give advice other than purely in a professional capacity in the sense of legal and accounting advice may be included. The Court of Appeal ruled – in a case that appears to extend the definition of shadow director – that the concepts of **direction** and **instruction** in the definition did not exclude the giving of advice. The company concerned was in the travel business. It went into liquidation owing creditors an estimated £4.46 million. Disqualification proceedings were brought successfully against three of its directors and two of its advisers who were consultants with experience in the travel business (see *Secretary of State for Trade and Industry* v *Deverell* (2000)). It should be noted that such a disqualification also prevents the holding of directorships in other companies.

The above provisions are intended to stop the evasion of the law relating to directors by a major shareholder who can control the company without being on the board. Such a person cannot, for example, get around the law relating to directors' loans by resigning temporarily from the board in order to allow the company to make him a loan. He would be covered because he would be a 'shadow director'.

Remuneration – generally

If a director is to receive remuneration, his contract of service (if he is an employee, executive director (e.g. sales director)) or the articles (in the case of a fee-paid non-executive director) must provide for it (see our Art 61). As regards an executive director's service contract, s 318 says that the company must keep a copy of it, normally at the registered office, and that this copy is to be open to the inspection of members. While this may be of general interest, it is vital where a member or members intends to try to remove a director from the board before his term of office has expired. A director who is removed in this way has a right to sue for damages if he has a contract which has still some time to run.

Members can look at the contract and see what their act in removing the director might cost the company.

The notes to the accounts of the company must under Sch 6 disclose the salaries or fees of the directors and the chairman. This is not required in the 'abbreviated' accounts which small companies may file with Companies House.

The Greenbury Code of Practice on remuneration

As regards non-statutory developments, the Greenbury Committee, which was appointed and reported following public concern regarding the apparently excessive salaries being paid to executive directors (particularly those of the privatised public utilities), recommended a Code of Practice which requires the setting up of a remuneration committee of non-executive directors only to decide the policy to be adopted on executive directors' remuneration, pension rights and compensation for loss of office and the actual remuneration of each individual director. Admittedly the Code only specifically applies to listed companies and the only sanction is against listed companies since the Financial Services Authority and the Stock Exchange have agreed to enforce the Greenbury recommendations through the Listing Rules. But the principles underlying the Code apply to all companies and so a mention of the rules of the Code is relevant. The sanction for non-listed companies is basically bad publicity arising from excessive remuneration for directors, in terms of their relationship with their shareholders rather than the public at large. So far as legislation was concerned, there was no requirement to disclose the actual package being received by directors (but see below).

Members do have a right to inspect a copy of a contract of service between a director and the company or its subsidiary. The contract must, under s 318 CA 1985, be available at the registered office or principal place of business – not convenient for all shareholders – unless the contract is one that the company can terminate within the next 12 months without compensation. It is also worth noting again that a director can be given a service contract of up to five years without member approval: this does not assist in the matter of high severance payments when the company terminates the contract before it is due to expire.

The Greenbury Code contains a number of provisions to assist disclosure. Importantly the remuneration committee's report is to be attached to the annual report and accounts or incorporated therein. The report will in particular disclose full details of the package to be received by each named director, e.g. basic salary, benefits in kind, annual bonus and long-term incentive schemes including share options.

The Code does not require that the report be voted upon by the shareholders but states that the remuneration committee should give annual consideration to whether it should be and minute their conclusions. A vote is required on long-term incentive schemes on the basis that they may lead to a dilution of capital. In addition, the chairman of the committee is to report to the shareholders at the AGM accounting for the relevant decisions on the packages disclosed and answering questions on them.

In order to avoid large payments when a director leaves, the Code recommends one year or less as the normal notice period in service contracts. It accepts that this may initially at least lead to insecurity, so a two-year period may be acceptable and even three years for a newly-appointed director with the term reducing after that.

The Hampel Committee

A further committee on corporate governance under the chairmanship of Sir Ronald Hampel issued a final Report in January 1998. Its recommendations on remuneration are supportive of Greenbury.

DTI reform proposals – building on Greenbury and Hampel

The DTI has issued a consultative document entitled *Directors' Remuneration* containing proposals on directors' remuneration. These are set out below. They are likely to form part of the wider review and amendment of company law currently being pursued. The proposals are:

- notice or contract periods for executive directors to be limited to one year in the absence of exceptional reasons;
- contract termination arrangements to be agreed before recruitment and then explained to shareholders in remuneration reports;
- directors to provide a clear explanation to shareholders of any compensation arrangements after an executive director's departure;

- greater links between company performance and directors' pay and greater shareholder involvement with the issue of directors' pay, such as requiring shareholders to vote on the remuneration of the board as set out in the remuneration report each year; and
- to require annual shareholder approval of remuneration policy. Current thinking within the DTI, following representations from the Institute of Directors and others, suggests that only this level of shareholder involvement will be allowed, at least as a first stage.

Statutory requirements on disclosure of remuneration

New requirements for the disclosure of directors' remuneration were introduced by the Company Accounts (Disclosure of Directors' Emoluments) Regulations 1997. They apply to all companies listed and unlisted for accounting periods ending on or after 31 March 1997.

The regulations amend provisions in Part I of Sch 6 to the Companies Act 1985 relating to the disclosure of directors' emoluments or other benefits in the notes to a company's annual accounts in respect of any financial year.

Under the regulations:

- companies will be required to show aggregate details of directors' remuneration under four headings – emoluments (i.e. basic salary and annual bonuses); gains made on the exercise of share options; gains made under long-term incentive schemes; and company contributions to money purchase pension schemes. Small companies' full and shorter form accounts can show merely the total of the aggregate amounts;
- where the aggregate remuneration exceeds or is equal to £200,000, companies will be required to show also the figures attributable to the highest paid director and the amount of his or her accrued retirement benefits if he or she is a member of a defined benefit pension scheme, i.e. a pension scheme in which the rules specify the benefits to be paid, and the scheme must be financed accordingly;
- companies are no longer required to show the number of directors whose emoluments fell within each band of £5,000.

For listed companies, the regulations bring the Companies Act into line with Greenbury and the Listing Rules. For unlisted companies they streamline the former disclosure requirements.

Exceptions for unlisted companies

The above requirements apply to companies listed on the Stock Exchange and on the Alternative Investment Market. Unlisted companies, must comply with the requirements with two important exceptions:

- unlisted companies do not have to disclose the amount of gains made when directors exercise share options. They have merely to disclose the number of directors who have exercised their share options;
- unlisted companies do not have to disclose the net value of any assets that comprise shares which would otherwise be disclosed in respect of assets received under long-term incentive schemes. Instead they disclose the number of directors in respect of whose qualifying service shares were received or receivable under long-term incentive schemes.

Enforcement of fair dealing by directors

Duration of contracts of employment

Under s 319 contracts of employment with directors which are for a period of more than five years and cannot be terminated by the company by notice, must be approved by the members by ordinary resolution in general meeting. If this is not done the contract can be terminated by reasonable notice, which is not defined by the Act but which at common law would be at least three months. (*James v Kent & Co Ltd* (1950).)

This provision is also useful to those who want to remove a director from office. In the past boards of directors have given themselves long contracts without consulting the members. This has made it difficult to remove them because the compensation payable under a long service contract which had been broken by removal of the director concerned was sometimes more than the company could afford. It can still be costly.

Substantial property transactions

Section 320 requires the approval of the members by ordinary resolution in general meeting (or written resolution) of any arrangement to transfer to, or receive from, a director (or connected person, see below) a non-cash asset, e.g. land, exceeding £100,000 or exceeding 10 per cent of the company's net assets, whichever is the lower. The section does not apply, however, to non-cash assets of less than £2,000 in value.

Thus, a company whose assets less its liabilities amounted to £200,000 would have to comply with s 320 in respect of a transaction with a director for a non-cash asset worth more than £20,000.

Section 320 is designed to prevent directors (at least without member approval) from buying assets from the company at less than their true value or transferring their own property to the company at more than market value.

Transfers to and from connected persons are regarded as transfers to and from a director himself. The main category of connected persons is a director's wife or husband and children under 18, plus companies in which the director, together with his connected persons, holds one-fifth or more interest in the equity share capital. A director's partner is also included (s 346).

Sections 319 and 320 apply to all companies and shadow directors are included.

It should be noted that the 1985 Act refers to 'arrangements' rather than contracts and this will catch transactions where they are not to be carried out under legally binding agreements.

Loans, quasi-loans and credit taken by directors

Sections 330–347 deal with the above matters. The rules are more strict for 'relevant' companies than they are for 'non-relevant' companies.

Relevant companies are all public companies and private companies which are part of a group containing at least one public company. Free-standing private companies, i.e. those which are not members of a group, are non-relevant companies. Our own company is therefore a non-relevant company and under this heading we shall consider fully only the restrictions on free-standing private companies, though some comparison will be made with the position in relevant companies.

First, a description of loans, quasi-loans, and credit.

1 Loans and quasi-loans. Basically, a quasi-loan occurs when a director incurs personal expenditure but the company pays the bill. The director pays the company back later. In a loan the company would put the director in funds; he would buy, e.g. personal goods, and then repay the loan.

Examples of quasi-loans are:

(a) the company buys a yearly railway season ticket for a director to get to work; he repays the company over 12 months;

(b) a director uses a company credit card to pay for personal goods, e.g. a video. The company pays the credit card company and the director repays his company over an agreed period;

(c) the company purchases an airline ticket for a director's wife who is accompanying him on a business trip at the director's expense. The director repays the company over an agreed period.

It should be noted that the director's own expenses for the trip which would be paid by the company are not affected. It is only **personal** and not business transactions which are controlled.

2 Credit. Examples of credit are:

(a) a furniture company sells furniture to a director on terms that payment be deferred for 12 months;

(b) the company services a director's personal car in its workshops and the director is given time to pay;

(c) the company sells a Rolls-Royce to the wife of one of its directors under a hire-purchase agreement.

Control over loans, quasi-loans and credit

The position is as follows:

1 There is no restriction on quasi-loans and credit on the directors or connected persons of our non-relevant company. Just by way of comparison, in a relevant company quasi-loans to directors and connected persons would be restricted to £5,000 outstanding at any one time and repayment to the company of any quasi-loan incurred must be made within two months. Credit to a director or connected person would be restricted to £10,000, but there is no particular time for repayment.

2 There is no bar on transactions with connected persons in our non-relevant company. In a relevant

company transactions with connected persons are controlled as if they were with the director himself.

3 Loans to directors and shadow directors. In our non-relevant publishing company we can make a loan to a director only if it would assist in his duties. Although loans to shadow directors are controlled it is unlikely that control in that capacity would ever be used. If a shadow director has 'duties', he would be regarded as a *de facto* (in fact) director and the loan would be controlled as a director's loan.

There is no limit to the amount which we can lend but the loan must be approved either:

(a) by an ordinary resolution of the members before it is made; or
(b) by an ordinary resolution after it is made. The members must pass this ordinary resolution at or before the next AGM. If the loan is by contract repayable within six months after the next AGM it is not necessary to have the approval of the members.

A private company which has dispensed with the requirement to hold an AGM would have to get the members to approve the loan by ordinary resolution before it was made.

This is a very restrictive provision because we must be able to show that the loan was to assist in duties. If, for example, one of our directors was being moved to another part of the country to run a branch office, we could provide a bridging loan to finance the purchase of a house in the area while he was selling his present home. Unless we can do this we can only lend up to £5,000 maximum. All companies can do this for any purpose whatsoever and without the approval of the members or repayment within six months of the next AGM.

If we were a relevant company we could again lend to assist in duties, by following the above procedures, but this time the loan would be limited to £20,000.

Non-relevant moneylending companies are better off. They can lend to one of their directors for any purpose and without limit, provided the loan is on ordinary commercial terms, e.g. no better rate of interest or repayment terms than a member of the public would get if he was of the same financial standing as the director concerned. The above provisions apply also to relevant companies which are in the business of moneylending except that the maximum which can be lent is £100,000.

Moneylending companies can also lend money to a director for the purpose of the purchase or improvement of his principal residence up to a maximum of £100,000, provided it is on the same terms as are available to the company's employees for house purchase and improvement loans. This sum does not aggregate with the general loan nor with the small loan of £5,000 above and so a director could be lent £205,000 in all: £100 000 for housing plus £100,000 as a general loan for other purposes and a small loan of £5,000.

Disclosure in accounts

All transactions involving loans, quasi-loans and credit to directors and their connected persons in all companies, relevant and non-relevant, must be disclosed in notes to the company's accounts. There is an exemption in the case of credit, provided the credit did not at any time during the year in question exceed £5,000. Even though the credit limit is raised to £10,000 for relevant companies, the disclosure limit is retained at £5,000.

Even though, as in our company, there is no control over quasi-loans and credit, if any such transaction is entered into with a director or his connected person during the period covered by the accounts it must be disclosed. Thus, the credit transaction in 2(c) above is not controlled in a non-relevant company but must be disclosed in its accounts. The wife is a connected person and the credit for a Rolls-Royce is bound to exceed £5,000.

Disclosure is done by stating in the note to the accounts the name of the director concerned and the opening position in regard to a loan, quasi-loan or credit, the highest point reached in the year covered by the accounts and the closing position together with the amount of interest due and not paid (if any).

If the directors refuse to disclose these matters in the company's accounts, the auditors **must** do so in their report.

The relevant regulations dealing with audit exemption do not deal with the application of the above provisions where the company does not have auditors. Presumably, if the company does not have auditors, there will be no audit report in which to make the disclosure so that the provisions cannot take effect.

Material interests

Material interests of directors and their connected persons must also be disclosed in a note to the accounts. A material interest could be, for example, a contract to build a new office block which the company had entered into with a building firm run by a director, or by the spouse of a director.

It might also be a loan to the brother of a director. A brother is not a connected person but the loan might be a material interest.

The Companies Act 1985 states that the board of directors will decide whether a transaction is material, though the auditors must disclose it in their report if the directors fail to disclose it in the accounts and the auditor thinks it is material.

The position where the company has no auditors is considered above.

There are exemptions from disclosure for material interests of £1,000 or less. Material interests exceeding £5,000 must always be disclosed. Between these two figures it depends on the net assets of the company. Disclosure is required if the value of a material interest exceeds 1 per cent of the net assets of the company. Thus, a company with net assets of £400,000 would have to disclose material interests of £4,000 and above.

The above figures (or thresholds) are subject to change by statutory instrument but at the time of writing remain as stated.

Disclosure by a director of any interest in contracts with the company **to the board** is considered below.

Contracts with a sole member/director

The single-member company regulations add a new s 322B to the CA 1985. This provides that the terms of a contract with a sole member/director must either be set out in a written memorandum or recorded in the minutes of the next board meeting. This does not apply if the contract is in writing or is entered into in the ordinary course of business as where the company buys raw materials from the sole member/director.

Disclosing interests in contracts

Section 317 provides that every director who has an interest whether direct or indirect (as through a connected person) in a contract or proposed contract with the company must disclose his interest either at the board meeting at which the contract is first discussed or if the interest has not arisen at that time then at the first board meeting after the interest arises. In *Guinness* v *Saunders* (1990) the House of Lords decided that disclosure had to be made at a full meeting of the board and not at a meeting of a committee of the board. The section provides for a general notice procedure under which a director may give notice that he is a member of a specified company or a partner in a specified firm and is to be regarded as interested in any contract which may, after the date of the notice, be made with that company or firm. This general notice procedure is not available unless the interest arises only because the director is a member of a company or partner in a firm. Thus, if the interest arises because the director is a director of the other company but not a member of it, disclosure should be made in relation to each transaction as it arises.

A director who fails to make disclosure as required is liable to a fine. In addition, the contract can in appropriate circumstances be regarded as cancelled (or rescinded) but this must be done quickly and preferably before any performance has taken place. The company's articles may waive the right to rescind (Table A does not) or the members by ordinary or unanimous written resolution can do so.

There can be no waiver by the board. However, the director concerned can vote in favour of adopting it under the written resolution procedure or at a general meeting and even in the latter case if he controls the voting at the meeting. This is because the director is not in breach of duty in terms of the making of the contract but only in breach of the duty of disclosure.

The above disclosures should be made by new directors at the first board meeting in so far as they apply to then existing contracts.

The provisions of s 317 extend to any transaction or arrangement set out in s 330, i.e. loans, quasi-loans and credit to a director or connected persons such as a spouse or minor child of the director. The principle of disclosure also applies whether or not the arrangement is a valid and enforceable contract so that the disclosure provisions cannot be avoided by including in, e.g., a loan arrangement a clause to the effect that it is not intended to create legal relations (see s 317(5)).

The principles of disclosure are also applied to shadow directors by s 317(8). But the interest of a shadow director must be declared by notice in writing to the directors and not at a meeting of the board. The notice may state a specific interest and be given before the date of the meeting at which the shadow director would have been required to declare his interest if he had been a director or it may be a general one (s 317(8)(a) and (b)).

In *Re Neptune (Vehicle Washing Equipment) Ltd* (1995) the High Court held that even a sole director must declare and record his interest in a contract with the company at a board meeting. The sole director concerned had resolved to pay himself £100,000 as severance pay on the termination of his employment and the shareholders caused the company to sue to recover it on the grounds that he had not disclosed his interest in the contract at a board meeting under the CA 1985, s 317. Therefore, the company claimed the contract could be avoided. In deciding preliminary matters prior to the trial, it was decided that he should have made disclosure at a board meeting, even though he was a sole director. The court said he could have a meeting on his own, or perhaps with the company secretary present, so that the declaration could be made and recorded in the minutes. However, the declaration need not be made aloud: the director could silently declare it while thinking about any conflicts of interest there might be. Obviously, to record it in the minutes is the important point.

Removal

Under the provisions of s 303 every company has power to remove any director before the end of his period of office.

The removal is carried out by an ordinary resolution of the members in general meeting. A written resolution cannot be used. Special notice of 28 days must be given to the company secretary that the resolution will be moved. The meeting at which the removal of a director under s 303 is to be considered must be called by at least 21 days' notice.

The director is entitled to have a written statement in his defence, as it were, sent with the notice of the meeting. That failing, he can make an oral statement at the meeting.

As we have seen, the removal of a director does not affect any right he may have to claim money compensation for the dismissal.

Retirement

The company's articles generally provide that a certain number of directors shall retire annually. This is called retirement by rotation. Our article provides for one-third to retire annually (see Art 67). Those retiring are usually eligible for re-election (see Art 68).

Resignation

The articles usually provide that a director vacates office when he notifies his resignation to the company (see Art 64).

Disqualification

The grounds for disqualification of directors in our company are set out in Art 64. This is a usual type of article which companies have.

In addition, the court may disqualify directors. For example, under s 3 of the Company Directors Disqualification Act 1986 the court can disqualify a director following persistent default in filing returns, accounts and other documents with the Registrar. Persistent default is conclusively proved by the fact that the director has had three convictions in a period of five years for this kind of offence. The maximum period of disqualification in this case is five years.

Another ground for disqualification, which is increasingly coming before the courts, is to be found in s 10 of the 1986 Act. It occurs when a company goes into liquidation and the evidence shows that the directors have negligently struggled on for too long with an insolvent company in the hope that things would get better but which has in the end gone into insolvent liquidation. This is called wrongful trading and the maximum period of disqualification is 15 years. The directors are also jointly and severally liable for such of the company's debts as the court thinks fit. The court is not restricted to making an order relating only to debts incurred during the period of wrongful trading.

A director may also be disqualified if he or she is held by the court to be 'unfit' to hold the office of director. The company must be insolvent, generally as a result of serious management failures, and often involving failure to pay NIC and taxes. There is no personal liability for the debts of the company but disqualification can be for a period of up to 15 years and there is a minimum period of two years. Sections 6, 7 and 8 of the 1986 Act apply.

A register of disqualification orders made by the court is kept by the Registrar of Companies. The public can inspect that register and see the names of those currently disqualified from acting as directors. Obviously, the name is removed at the end of the period of disqualification.

Disqualification – some case law

The High Court decided in *Re Seagull Manufacturing Co (No 2)* (1994) that a disqualification order may be made against a director regardless of his or her nationality and current residence and domicile. Furthermore, the conduct leading to the disqualification need not have occurred within the jurisdiction. In other words, you can run an English company badly from abroad. The director concerned was a British subject but at all material times he was resident and domiciled in the Channel Islands. Nevertheless, he could be disqualified under s 6 for unfitness. The relevant legislation contained no express jurisdiction requirement or territorial distinction.

The High Court also decided in *Re Pamstock Ltd* (1994) that a director who was also the secretary of the company could be disqualified as much for failure to perform his duties as secretary as those of a director. The company had two directors and one was also the company secretary. It traded beyond the point at which it should have ceased to do so and went into insolvent liquidation. The judge said that as the company secretary one of the directors had failed to ensure that accounts and returns were filed on time and that an adequate system of management was put in place. These were serious defaults which must be

taken into account when dealing with the period of disqualification. This implies that it was the director's failure to carry out his duties as secretary that were at the root of his disqualification for two years. There is, of course, no power to disqualify a company secretary from acting as such.

POWERS OF DIRECTORS

The Act requires certain powers to be exercised by the members, e.g. alteration of the memorandum and articles. Apart from this the distribution of powers between the board and the members depends entirely on the articles (see Arts 62 and 63).

DUTIES OF DIRECTORS

The relationship between a company and its directors is that of principal and agent and as agents the directors stand in a **fiduciary relationship** to their principal, the company. In addition, directors owe **a duty of care at common law not to act negligently** in managing the company's affairs.

Fiduciary duties

Examples of these duties are as follows:

(a) **Directors must use their powers for the proper purpose**, that is, for the benefit of the company. If they do not do so, the transactions they have entered into can be avoided by the company, **provided that the person with whom the directors dealt was aware of the improper use of the power.**

Rolled Steel Products (Holdings) Ltd v *British Steel Corporation* (1985)
A Mr Shenkman was the majority shareholder in Rolled Steel and held all the issued share capital in another company called Scottish Steel apart from some purely nominal holdings. Scottish Steel owed a lot of money to BSC and Mr Shenkman had given his personal guarantee of that debt. BSC wanted more security and Mr S caused Rolled Steel to enter into a guarantee of the Scottish Steel debt as well. There was no benefit to Rolled Steel in this and BSC knew there was not.

Rolled Steel went into liquidation, as did Scottish Steel, and the court was asked to decide whether BSC could prove in the liquidation of Rolled Steel on the guarantee.

Eventually the Court of Appeal decided that they could not. The transaction was not *ultra vires* Rolled Steel because the objects clause contained a paragraph giving an express power to enter into guarantees. Rolled Steel also had an independent objects clause, as in *Cotman* v *Brougham* (1918), so the giving of guarantees was an object of the company which it could exercise whether there was any benefit to it or not. However, Mr S and the other directors of Rolled Steel had exercised a power to give guarantees for an improper purpose, i.e. a purpose which was of no benefit to the company. The guarantee could, therefore, be avoided by the liquidator of Rolled Steel, provided that those to whom it was given were aware of the improper purpose. Since BSC knew that there was no benefit to Rolled Steel in the guarantee, they could not enforce it and prove in the liquidation.

Comment. (i) Sections 35 and 35A would not seem to affect the proper purpose rule, as applied in the *Rolled Steel* case, because the proper purpose rule is not concerned with *ultra vires* problems as ss 35 and 35A are.

(ii) Under s 35 the company is deemed to have the *capacity* to carry out an act, whether covered by the objects clause or not, and under s 35A the directors are deemed to have *power as agents* to enter into it on behalf of the company, whether they have or not.

Actual knowledge of the contents of the company's memorandum and articles by an outsider, who therefore knows the company does not have the capacity, or if it has, the directors do not have power to make it on the company's behalf, does not affect the validity of the transaction between the company and the outsider.

This seems, however, to assume that the directors were acting properly, i.e. for the benefit of the company. If they were not and the outsider (as in the case of BSC) knew they were not and, indeed, even persuaded the directors to act improperly, then the transaction will, as in *Rolled Steel*, be unenforcable against the company.

It is possible for the shareholders to ratify an improper purpose act by the directors unless this amounts to fraud. The Court of Appeal in the *Rolled Steel* case referred throughout to ratification by *unanimous* resolution of the shareholders by referring to cases where ratification had been unanimous, there having been no meeting of the shareholders but merely an informal agreement, as in *Re Horsley & Weight Ltd* (1982). However, in principle, an ordinary resolution passed in general meeting should be enough to ratify. So Mr Shenkman could have ratified his improper act because he was a majority shareholder though he had not done so. It was held in *North-West Transportation* v *Beatty* (1887) that director/shareholders are under no duty to abstain from voting.

(b) **Directors must not take secret profits and benefits from the company.** This is illustrated by the following case.

Industrial Development Consultants Ltd v *Cooley* (1972)
Mr Cooley, an architect, was the managing director of Industrial Development Consultants Ltd which carried on business as building and development consultants. He represented the company in negotiations with the Eastern Gas Board which were intended to get contracts for the company to design four large depots for the EGB.

The Board did not give the contracts to the company but soon afterwards asked Mr C whether he would take on the contracts in his private capacity. He told the company he was suffering from a nervous breakdown and got released from his service contract and was then given the EGB contracts. The company sued him for the profit on the four contracts. The court decided that since Mr C got the chance to make the profit while he was managing director of the company he must account to the company for all the profit received on the four contracts.

Duty of skill and care, i.e. not to act negligently

There is nothing in the Companies Act which sets out the standard of skill and care which a director must bring to his work. We must therefore turn to case law where the position is as set out below.

1 Non-executive directors without business qualifications or experience, e.g. a doctor of medicine who has recently joined the board of his family company which makes steel castings.

The standard of care here is by reason of the decision in *Re City Equitable Fire Insurance Co* (1925) **subjective** in that the director is only required to do his best. He is bound only to show such skill and care in the conduct of the company's business as may be expected from a person of his actual knowledge or experience (or lack of it). Also, he is not required to give all his attention to the company's business, nor to attend all board meetings. He can rely on the advice of the company's officials unless he has reason to suspect their competence.

2 Non-executive directors with relevant qualifications and/or experience in business. The standard here is **objective**. This means that a director of, say, an insurance company who is not an employee/executive director but who is professionally qualified in the field of insurance or has experience in that area must exercise such reasonable skill and care as may be **expected** from a person of his professional standing and/or experience.

This was made clear in the decision of the High Court in *Dorchester Finance v Stebbing* (1977) where a chartered accountant and a non-qualified, but experienced, accountant were held liable along with a chartered accountant executive director for loss to the company caused by the making of loans which could not be recovered by the company because they infringed what is now the Consumer Credit Act 1974.

The two non-executive directors had facilitated the illegal lending by signing blank cheques, but had acted with good faith throughout. They had, however, failed to attend board meetings, leaving the running of the company to the executive director, Mr S. The court said that non-executive directors who were qualified or experienced could not rely on the subjective standard in the *Re City Equitable* case. They must assist in the management of the company.

It ought to be said at this point that the judge in the *Dorchester* case said that in the Companies Act the duties of directors were the same so that the fact that he was dealing with accountants was not crucial to his decision. However, he did not specifically distinguish *Re City Equitable*, which was another High Court decision, and so in the absence of higher resolving authority we are left with the possibility that a non-executive director without business qualifications or experience may only be required to meet a subjective test.

3 Executive directors. Directors such as finance directors are normally employed for their expertise in company matters and under contracts of service. Here the decision in *Lister v Romford Ice and Cold Storage Co Ltd* (1957) applies. This states that there is an implied term in the contract of service that the director will exercise the reasonable skill and care which a person in his position **ought** to have. Thus the test is objective and the *City Equitable* case does not apply.

The above duties, both fiduciary and of skill and care, are owed to the company. If loss is caused, it is the company which must sue and which will be compensated. The duties are not owed directly to individual shareholders, even though the price of their shares might have fallen as a result of the breach of duty (*Prudential Assurance Co Ltd v Newman Industries Ltd (No 2)* (1982)).

Duties to employees

Until 1980 directors owed no duties to employees but this was provided for in the Companies Act 1980. The current provision is s 309 of the Companies Act 1985, which states that the matters to which the directors of a company are to have regard in the performance of their duties is to include the interests of the company's employees in general as well as the interests of its members.

The duty cannot be enforced directly by the employees since it is owed to the company (or, in other words, the shareholders). It means that in, say, a scheme of reconstruction of the company, the directors could be required by the shareholders to show that they had considered the position of employees who might be made redundant even though the general body of UK shareholders, particularly the institutional shareholders such as the major insurance companies, would be unlikely to do this.

However, s 309 would not allow the directors to put the interests of the employees entirely before those of the company. For example, s 309 would provide a justification for directors (if challenged by the shareholders) who carried out a reconstruction in such a way as to save jobs. It would not be within s 309 for the directors to carry on the company's business at a loss and put it at risk of liquidation in order to save jobs.

All s 309 means is that the directors cannot be accused by the shareholders of being in breach of their duty if they consider the interests of the employees. There is no positive duty to do anything for them.

Section 719 provides that the powers of a company are to be assumed to include the power to make provisions for its own or its subsidiary's employees, or former employees, when the company or its subsidiary ceases to carry on the whole or part of its business or transfers the whole or part of its business to someone else. This means that redundancy payments on a scale more generous than the state requires can be paid in the liquidation, or on a transfer of the business to those who lose their jobs.

Unless there are different provisions in the memorandum or articles, an ordinary (or written) resolution of the members is required to approve the exercise of this section. Once such a resolution has been passed, the power can be exercised by a liquidator. However, the payment can only come from surplus assets which would otherwise have gone to shareholders. There must be no reduction in the funds available to creditors.

Relief from liability

As we have seen, a director may be relieved from liability by ratification of improper purpose acts by ordinary resolution or unanimous resolution of the members. In addition, although under s 310 the company's memorandum or articles cannot validly contain a clause exempting directors from liability for breach of duty, the section does provide that a company may indemnify its directors against **liability to the company** (but not breaches to others) and also pay the costs of any criminal or civil proceedings if these are **successfully** defended. The court can grant relief under s 727 so that the director is not liable if it thinks that the director concerned has acted 'honestly and reasonably'. This applies to any proceedings at civil law.

Section s 310 also permits the company to purchase insurance for its directors against liability to the company (but not to others) and if it does so it must state the fact in the directors' annual report to the shareholders.

The provisions of s 310 were considered in *Burgoine* v *London Borough of Waltham Forest* (1997) where the High Court ruled that the prohibition on indemnities in regard to directors and other officers applies only to indemnities given by the company and not to indemnities given by others, e.g. insurance companies. Thus, it does not affect indemnities by way of liability insurance taken out by a director *himself* in respect of his liabilities, or by the company on his behalf for claims by the company. A director's own policy will normally cover liability to outsiders.

Directors' duties to outsiders

Directors' duties are not in general owed to outsiders, i.e. those who are not shareholders or employees. However, where the directors make a contract with an outsider on behalf of a company, the directors may be liable, as other agents are, for

breach of warranty of authority. The basis of this action is that an agent warrants to the third party that his principal has the capacity to make the contract and that he, the agent, is authorised to make it. Thus, if the contract is beyond the company's powers or those of the directors and does not bind the company, there may be an action against the directors for breach of warranty of authority. This will be for money compensation.

It will be noted, however, that, in view of the provisions of ss 35 and 35A, it is most unlikely that a transaction will not bind the company and the action for breach of warranty against directors is, subject to judicial interpretation of ss 35 and 35A, likely to largely disappear from the law. It might be used where the directors made an *ultra vires* contract with a connected person which the members did not ratify. The contract would not bind the company and the connected person might bring a claim for breach of warranty against the directors.

Directors' meetings

Notice of board meetings must be given to all directors unless they are out of the United Kingdom. Unless the articles otherwise provide, any director can call a board meeting (see our Art 78).

Quorum

Table A provides that the quorum necessary for the valid transaction of business by the directors may be fixed by the directors themselves and unless it is so fixed then the quorum is two directors personally present (see our Art 78).

Voting

Unless the articles say differently, each director has one vote and resolutions of the board require a majority of only one. If there is an equality of votes the resolution is lost unless the chairman has and exercises a casting vote in favour of the resolution (see our Art 78).

Directors as agents

If the board acting together (or collectively), or one director acting on his own, has **actual authority** to make a particular contract on behalf of the company and that contract is within their powers and the company's powers (or, if not, is protected by s 35) then the contract when made will be binding on the company.

However, where the directors act together, or as individuals, beyond their powers the position is as set out below.

Collective acts of the board

There are the following possibilities:

1 Companies Act 1985 (as amended). As we have seen, s 35A provides that in favour of a person dealing with a company in good faith, the power of the board of directors to bind the company shall be deemed to be free of any limitation under the company's constitution, and a person shall not be regarded as acting in bad faith just because he knows that an act is beyond the powers of the directors. Therefore, if the above requirements are met, a transaction entered into by the board beyond its powers will bind the company.

2 The rule in *Turquand*'s case. This rule is best explained by looking straightaway at the facts of the case.

Royal British Bank v *Turquand* (1856)

The articles of the company gave the directors the power to exercise the company's borrowing powers if they first obtained approval of the members by ordinary resolution in general meeting.

The directors borrowed money for the company but did not get the ordinary resolution and the question whether the loan was valid or not arose.

The court said it was. The bank could sue the company to recover its loan even though the directors were not, as it happened, authorised to borrow. The bank was an outsider and was entitled to assume that an ordinary resolution in general meeting had been passed.

Comment. This case succeeded because the ordinary resolution involved did not have to be filed with the Registrar of Companies. Therefore, there was no constructive notice of it. During the period when there was constructive notice of a company's memorandum and articles and the contents of its file at the Registry it was decided that *Turquand* could not apply where the resolution required was a special or extraordinary resolution because these had to be filed and an outsider would have constructive notice that they had not been. The relevant decision is *Irvine* v *Union Bank of Australia* (1877).

Since the 1985 Act (as amended) in general abolishes the rule of constructive notice, *Turquand*'s case should now apply to situations where special and extraordinary resolutions are required. The effect is to widen the rule.

3 Relationship between s 35A and the rule in *Turquand*'s case. Section 35A gives the same protection as *Turquand* where correct internal procedures were not followed.

On the other hand, *Turquand*'s case would appear to be wider in some respects than s 35A because it was applied in *Mahoney* v *East Holyford Mining Co* (1875) where the directors who made the transaction had never been appointed at all, and in *Davis* v *R Bolton & Co* (1894) where the directors made a transfer of shares without a quorum at the meeting. The transfer was held valid.

Although s 35A has not been fully interpreted by the courts, it seems logical to suppose that it would not apply in the circumstances of *Mahoney* and *Davis* because the court will presumably expect that when an English statute says 'the power of the board of directors to bind the company' it means directors who are properly appointed and have a quorum at the relevant meeting. If so, Turquand is still a valuable decision.

4 The proper purpose rule. As we have seen, directors must use their agency powers for the proper purpose, that is for the benefit of the company. If they do not do so, the transactions they have entered into, while not *ultra vires* themselves or the company, can be avoided by the company provided that the person with whom the directors dealt was aware of the improper use of the power. (See again the *Rolled Steel* case.)

Acts of individual directors and other officers of the company

To what extent will a company be bound by a transaction entered into by an individual director or other officer, e.g. the company secretary, who has no actual authority to enter into it?

There are the following possibilities:

1 Companies Act 1985 (as amended). Section 35A states that in favour of a person dealing with a company in good faith the power of the board to authorise other persons to bind the company shall be deemed free of any limitation under the company's constitution. Therefore, an individual director, company secretary, employee or other agent authorised by the board to bind the company will do so even if he exceeds the powers given to the board or other agents of the company by the articles. Once again, knowledge of lack of power is not bad faith.

2 The rules of agency law – usual (or ostensible) authority. Where a director or other officer of a company has no actual authority or authorisation under s 35A to enter into a transaction, an outsider may be able to regard the company as bound by it if it is usual in the company context for a director or officer to be able to enter into a transaction of the kind in question. Since it is usual to delegate wide powers to a managing director and executive directors, an outsider will normally be protected if he is dealing with a person who is a managing director or other executive directors, e.g. sales director or who has been held out as such by the company.

Thus, in *Freeman & Lockyer* v *Buckhurst Park Properties Ltd* (1964), a managing director without express authority of the board, but with its knowledge, employed on behalf of the company a firm of architects and surveyors for the submission of an application for planning permission which involved preparing plans and defining boundaries. It was held that the company was liable to pay their fees. The managing director had bound the company by his acts which were within the usual authority of a managing director.

Where, however, the outsider deals with a non-executive director or officer who has not been authorised under s 35A, his position is much less secure. An ordinary director and other officers of the company have little usual authority to bind the company.

Once one gets below the director level, the position becomes even more of a problem. There is little, if any, usual authority in the executive of a company to make contracts on its behalf without actual authority, though it would appear that a company secretary has authority to bind the company in contracts relating to day-to-day administration.

Thus, in *Panorama Developments* v *Fidelis Furnishing Fabrics* (1971), the secretary of a company ordered cars from a car hire firm representing that they were required to meet the company's customers at London Airport. Instead he used the cars for his own purposes. The company did not pay the bill, so the car hire firm claimed from the secretary's company. It was held that the company was liable, for its secretary had usual authority to make contracts such as the present one which was concerned with the administrative side of the business.

It is worth noting here that lawyers sometimes use a different expression for 'usual' authority and call it 'ostensible' authority, and so the reader should be prepared for this. We prefer 'usual' since the authority arises because it is what a person holding an office can *usually* do. The expressions are used indiscriminately by the courts.

The secretary

Every company must have a secretary and a sole director cannot also be the secretary (s 283). A corporation may be a secretary to a company, but a company, X, cannot have as secretary a company, Y, if the sole director of company Y is also the sole director or secretary of company X (s 283).

Section 284 provides that a provision requiring or authorising a thing to be done by or to a director and the secretary shall not be satisfied by its being done by or to the same person acting both as director and secretary. By s 288 the register of directors includes particulars of the secretary. This means that the single-member company may have only one member but must have at least two officers since the sole member/director cannot also be the secretary.

It is usual for the secretary to be appointed by the directors who may fix his term of office and the conditions upon which he is to hold office. Our Art 63(c) confers such a power upon the board. The secretary is an employee of the company. He is regarded as such for the purpose of preferential payments in a winding-up.

As we have seen, the secretary enjoys the power to make contracts on behalf of the company even without authority. This is, however, restricted to contracts in the administrative operations of the company, including the employment of office staff and the management of the office, together with the hiring of transport. (See the *Panorama* case.)

His authority is not unlimited. He cannot, without authority, borrow money on behalf of the company (*Re Cleadon Trust Ltd* (1939)). He cannot, without authority, commence an action in the courts on the company's behalf (*Daimler Co Ltd* v *Continental Tyre and Rubber Co Ltd* (1916)). He cannot summon a general meeting himself (*Re State of Wyoming Syndicate* (1901)), nor register a transfer of shares without the board's approval (*Chida Mines Ltd* v *Anderson* (1905)). These are powers which are vested in the directors.

Certain duties are directly imposed on the secretary by statute. The most important of these includes the submission of the annual return. The CA 1985 authorises the company secretary to sign forms prescribed under the Act.

COMPANY INSOLVENCY AND CORPORATE RESCUE

Section references are to the Insolvency Act 1986 unless otherwise indicated.

Types of insolvency procedures and practitioners

A corporate insolvency may lead to the appointment of an administrator, a receiver, an administrative receiver or a liquidator. There are often joint appointments of, say, two partners from the same firm to cope with the work involved.

Administration (or corporate rehabilitation)

Only the court can initiate the administration procedure. It does so by an administration order. Before the order can be made the court must be satisfied:

1 that the company concerned is, or is likely to become, unable to pay its debts; and

2 that at least one of the purposes set out in s 8(3) will, **more probably than not**, be achieved if an order is made. *Re Consumer and Industrial Press Ltd* (1988) (see below) decides that **probability** and not mere **possibility** is required.

The two main purposes are:

(a) that the order will promote the survival of the company as a going concern in terms of the whole or part of the business; or

(b) that the assets will be more advantageously realised than they would be in a sale during liquidation.

Re Consumer and Industrial Press Ltd (1988) gives an example of (b) above. The company had, since 1949, published a magazine. Net liabilities were adjudged by accountants to be too great to trade out of trouble. The Inland Revenue petitioned for a winding-up. The company asked for an administration order. The court made the order. Administrators were appointed to manage the company so that at least the next issue of the magazine could be published. The company might be saved by an arrangement with creditors, but even if not it would get a better price for the title if publication continued than if it were sold in a liquidation.

The management powers of an administrator are extensive; they appear in Sch 1.

Receivership

Where property has been used as a security for a loan, the lender usually takes power to appoint a receiver out of court under a fixed charge on the property (see Chapter 4). Such a receiver is not a manager of the property as an administrative receiver is. (See below.) A receiver need not be qualified as an insolvency practitioner, so, for example, the common practice of appointing surveyors to collect the income of charged property to pay what is owed continues. Further details of this type of receivership are unlikely to be required in an examination and so no more will be said about it.

Administrative receivership

Administrative receivership arises where a secured creditor – often a bank – appoints an administrative receiver **out of court** under power in a debenture securing a loan. The debenture gives fixed charges over, e.g., the company's land and buildings together with a floating charge (see Chapter 4) over the undertaking.

Powers of management are usually given to the administrative receiver in the debenture but in any case wide powers to run the company are given in Sch 1. Even so, the overriding duty of an administrative receiver is to realise the security for the benefit of the secured creditor appointing him (*Re B Johnson & Co Ltd* (1955)).

If the administrative receiver does decide to run the business, he owes a duty of care to its owners to run it as profitably as possible and is liable for negligent mismanagement. The duties go beyond mere good faith. Honesty is not enough. Proper management is required. The Court of Appeal so ruled in *Medforth* v *Blake* (1999) where the administrative receivers had failed to ask for and obtain discounts on foodstuffs in the course of managing the business of pig farming. The owner of the company had frequently reminded the administrative receivers of the availability and importance of such discounts.

Liquidation

This procedure brings the company's life to an end, generally because its financial position dictates this. Exceptions occur where solvent companies are wound up in mergers and reconstructions.

Where the company is insolvent, creditors are entitled to appoint the liquidator (s 100) and form a committee to work with him (s 101). Where the company is solvent, the liquidator is appointed by the members in general meeting (s 91(1)).

A liquidator has as a basic function the duty to sell the company's assets and distribute the proceeds of sale to the company's creditors. However, he may allow the company to continue its business for a limited purpose, i.e. for what is called beneficial winding up, as where he allows the completion of work in progress for a more beneficial sale of the product. He has no statutory or other managerial powers.

Qualifications of insolvency practitioners

To safeguard the public by ensuring that those who take over companies in the capacity of insolvency practitioner of whatever kind are appropriately qualified, the Insolvency Act 1986 requires that insolvency practitioners be authorised by, for example, the Institute of Chartered Accountants in England and Wales, or of Scotland or in Ireland; the Chartered Association of Certified Accountants; the Insolvency Practitioners Association or the Law Society.

The professional bodies concerned must have applied successfully to the Department of Trade and Industry (DTI) for recognition.

The Act also provides for an individual application to the DTI. This is intended for those who do not belong to professional bodies recognised for this purpose by the DTI.

In both cases the professional body and the DTI must be satisfied that the education, training and experience requirements for the office are complied with.

Authorisation is for the period stated in the authorisation, e.g. 12 months, and may be withdrawn. Insolvency practitioners must also show that they have made proper bonding arrangements with an insurance company to deal with any loss which might happen to the company because of their maladministration of its affairs.

In addition to membership of an approved professional body, insolvency practitioners are usually members of the Insolvency Practitioners Association.

Appointment of insolvency practitioners

Administrator

The person petitioning the court for an administration order will also ask the court to appoint one or more administrators. Their names will usually be before the court and they will have consented to act. The order must name the administrator(s) and identify the purpose or purposes to be achieved.

Under s 9 a petition for an administration order may be made:

(a) by the company (following an ordinary resolution of the members);
(b) by the directors (presumably not all of them but following a board resolution);
(c) by a creditor (secured or unsecured).

Contingent creditors, e.g. guarantors of the company's debts, may apply. The holder of a floating charge, e.g. a bank, can block the appointment. Notice of presentation of a petition must be given to holders of a floating charge (s 9(2)(a)). Such holders being *secured* creditors may then appoint an administrative receiver. If so, the court will dismiss the petition for an administration unless those appointing the administrative receiver then consent (s 9(3)(a)).

The fact that *ordinary* creditors object to the making of an administration order is not necessarily a bar, as where the directors make the application that is not supported by the creditors. In *Structures and Computers Ltd* v *Ansys Inc* (1997) the High Court ruled that where it is satisfied that there is a real prospect of an administration order achieving one or more of its purposes, the court has a discretion to make the order even though in this case the application was opposed by more than half the creditors.

Administrative receiver

Of major importance is the appointment out of court. The debenture containing the floating charge will also give grounds for appointment of an administrative receiver. The most usual ground is found in appointments by banks in respect of an overdraft which is payable on demand. The bank has merely to call it in knowing that it cannot be repaid and appoint an administrative receiver.

In other cases, e.g. where a loan is not repayable on demand, failure to pay interest or the principal monies as required will give grounds for an appointment. Since modern debentures (or trust deeds in the case of a public issue of loan stock) set out a variety of grounds for an appointment, it is rarely necessary to ask the court to do so in a corporate situation but it has power under s 37 of the Supreme Court Act 1981.

Liquidators

These appointments depend upon the type of liquidation involved. The two basic types are:

1 Voluntary liquidation set in motion by a resolution of members (s 84); and

2 Compulsory liquidation where the court orders winding-up, most commonly following a petition by a creditor (or creditors) on the ground that the company cannot pay its debts (s 122). That ground is sometimes satisfied under s 123(1) by a creditor to whom the company owes more than £750 serving a demand for payment and the company does not pay, secure or compound the debt within three weeks of the demand. A further ground appears in s 123 which is: 'if it is proved to the satisfaction of the court that the company is unable to pay its debts as they fall due'. This ground has been used more frequently in recent times because of the waiting period of three weeks which is required in the statutory demand procedure. Some think that this is too long to wait, particularly in the case of severe insolvencies where assets are being dissipated rapidly. Under s 123 a creditor can petition straightaway for a winding-up order and submit proof of inability to pay by the company at the same time. Thus, in *Taylors Industrial Flooring Ltd* v *M & H Plant Hire (Manchester) Ltd* (1990) goods were supplied in December 1998 and, in spite of subsequent billings, nothing had been paid by the debtor by April 1999 when the petition was presented and a winding-up order made.

Voluntary liquidation may be further divided into:

(a) a members' voluntary, which occurs when a declaration of solvency has been given by a majority of the directors before the special resolution to wind up has been passed; and

(b) a creditors' voluntary, which occurs where a special resolution is passed not preceded by a declaration of solvency or where the voluntary winding-up was commenced by an extraordinary resolution stating that the company cannot, by reason of its liabilities, continue its business (s 84).

The declaration states that the directors are of the opinion that the company will be able to pay its debts plus interest at the official rate in full within a stated period not exceeding 12 months (s 89(1) and s 89(4)). It must be made not more than five weeks before the special resolution is passed.

It is not in practice necessary that every debt be paid within the stated period. Commonly, for example, the Revenue has not completed its assessments and cannot be paid. Nevertheless, if funds are available to pay such debts when ascertained, the members' winding-up continues and there is no need to convert to a creditors' voluntary, nor are the directors liable for a false declaration.

In a members' voluntary, the liquidator is appointed by ordinary (or written) resolution of the members and the creditors are not involved. In a creditors' voluntary, a liquidator is appointed by ordinary (or written) resolution of the members.

The creditors also have a right to appoint a liquidator, though if they do not the person appointed by the members will act (s 100). Under the Winding-Up Rules the creditors' appointment is by a majority in value, so small creditors have little, if any, say. If there is a conflict, in terms of the person appointed, the creditors' choice prevails. The creditors may also appoint, under s 101, a liquidation committee to assist the liquidator.

In a compulsory liquidation the court may appoint a provisional liquidator (normally the official receiver) between petition and order (s 135(1)), for example, to protect the assets if they are being or might be misappropriated. In any case the official receiver becomes liquidator when the order is made. The creditors then consider at a meeting whether to appoint another insolvency practitioner. If so, that person takes office.

In a creditors' voluntary the 1986 Act corrects a former abuse of procedure called 'Centrebinding'. Formerly, when the members appointed a liquidator he could be immediately active and, if dishonest (as some were before authorised practitioners were required), dispose of the company's property before the creditors had a chance to nominate a liquidator at a subsequent meeting. In *Re Centrebind Ltd* (1967) the court held that the members' liquidator was legally entitled to act. Now s 166 provides that the members' nominee cannot, before the creditors' meeting, validly exercise any of his powers without court sanction, except to take property into his custody and control, protect the assets, as by ensuring that the directors no longer have the company's cheque books in their possession, and dispose, e.g., of perishable goods.

Legal effect of the various procedures and appointments

Administration – suspension of rights

Presentation of a petition for administration 'freezes' creditors' rights and prevents the company from being put into liquidation (s 10(1)). A secured creditor can, however, appoint an administrative receiver, and if this is done the administration cannot proceed (s 10(2)(b)). Hire-purchase creditors cannot repossess property, nor can court proceedings or executions or distress continue unless the administrator consents or court gives leave. Hire-purchase includes chattel leasing and retention of title arrangements (s 10(4)).

These restrictions continue after the order is made. After that there can, in addition, be no effective appointment of an administrative receiver.

The Court of Appeal has ruled that the consent of the administrator or leave of the court is necessary to commence or continue *criminal* as well as *civil* proceedings against a company in administration (see *Rhondda Waste Disposal Ltd (in administration)* (2000), where the Environmental Agency wished to prosecute for failure by the company to comply with one of the conditions of a waste management licence. The Court of Appeal agreed that because the administrator would not consent, leave was required. The court gave that leave because the pollution was serious. Consent or leave is also required even if a *civil* action is not being brought by a creditor but by a claimant suing for an alleged breach of a patent (see *Biosource Technologies Inc v Axis Genetics PLC (in administration)* (2000).

Administration – charged property and goods on hire-purchase (HP)

Section 15 gives administrators wide powers to deal with assets subject to a charge or hire-purchase agreement. The section is designed to prevent, for example, the inhibition of a company rescue scheme where the insolvency practitioner cannot negotiate successfully with a particular chargeholder or owner and so cannot sell the property concerned to a purchaser of the business as part of a rescue package.

There are two categories. As regards assets subject to a floating charge (see Chapter 4), the administrator can deal with them as if no charge existed. However, the proceeds of realisation are subject to the same priority in the lender as before, though they can be used to meet expenses if the administration order is rescinded. Nevertheless, the administrator can use the proceeds in the business.

All other property on HP may be disposed of if the court is satisfied that the disposition will facilitate the administration (s 15(2)). The court order will, however, specify that the proceeds *must* go to pay off the chargeholder or owner and the administrator must make up any difference, if any, between the sale price and the market price from the company's funds (s 15(5)(b)).

The general right given to aggrieved creditors by s 27(1) to complain to the court about the administration applies to give a right to complain about the above activities.

Administrative receiver – charged property

An administrative receiver may apply to the court for an order to dispose of property subject to a charge (there is no reference to goods on hire-purchase) which ranks in priority to the one under which he has been appointed (s 43(1) and (2)). The court must be satisfied that the disposal would be likely to promote a more advantageous realisation than would otherwise be achieved (s 43(1)). The rights of the prior secured creditors are transferred to the proceeds of sale which must be applied towards discharging the sums secured by the various securities. Even so, the administrative receiver has been able to dispose of the property. There are similar provisions relating to the making up of any difference in sale price and market price.

Insolvency practitioners as agents

An administrator is an agent of the company (s 14(5)). In addition, protection is given to outsiders who deal with him; under s 14(6) they need not enquire whether he is acting within his powers provided they act in good faith.

An administrative receiver appointed out of court is an agent also (s 44(1)(a)). A liquidator is not a general agent. He can only continue the business so far as necessary for a beneficial winding-up (s 81(1) and Sch 4, para 5). Thus, a liquidator may continue the business, e.g. to complete work in progress, so as to get a better price for the finished goods. He is obviously able to sell the assets and, indeed, the business, the contract being between the purchaser and the company 'acting by its liquidator'.

The effect of the above is that in an administration directors are not dismissed but their powers are suspended and, indeed, the administrator may remove and replace directors (s 14(2)). Employees are not dismissed. An administrator

(who is not liable on pre-existing contracts) contracts on behalf of the company which is therefore liable. In contrast to an administrative receiver, there is no statutory provision that he contracts with personal liability also.

An administrative receiver is not liable on pre-existing contracts. He contracts as an agent for the company but he is also personally liable on the contracts, subject to the right to be indemnified out of the assets of the company (s 44(1)(b) and (c)). Directors are not dismissed but their management powers are suspended. Employees are not dismissed unless continuance in post is inconsistent with the receivership, as could be the case, for example, with a managing director.

The absence of a general agency in a liquidation means that the powers of the directors cease (*Fowler v Broads Patent Night Light Co* (1893)). Employees are dismissed (*Chapman's Case* (1866)).

As regards administrators and administrative receivers, there are provisions in s 37 and s 44 respectively under which they will adopt contracts of employment after 14 days from appointment. The effect of this is that under s 19 if liabilities under contracts of employment are outstanding when the administrator vacates office, they are payable equally with other claims outstanding, including the administrator's fees and expenses.

This means that if the administrator's fees and expenses outstanding are £1,000 and wages and salaries outstanding are £1,000 and only £500 is left, the administrator takes £250 and wages and salaries take £250 towards payment.

This gave practitioners an incentive to contract out of this liability though the Act does not specifically allow this. It nevertheless became the practice based on statements made in the High Court in *Re Withall and Conquest and Specialised Mouldings* (1987) to send a letter to employees within the first 14 days of the administration disclaiming adoption of employment contracts. It was assumed that the effect of this would be that during an administration (or administrative receivership) remuneration including holiday pay and payments due under occupational pension schemes would be paid, as is usual practice anyway, but no more. Payments in lieu of notice were not paid nor was redundancy pay.

However, in *Powdrill v Watson* (1994) the Court of Appeal held that the letter was of no effect and that practitioners could not contract out. This could have wrecked rescue operations since practitioners would not take on the duties faced with losing their fees and expenses to employees. In response the government rushed through Parliament the Insolvency Act 1994 restricting liability under employment contracts in an administration or administrative receivership to 'qualifying liabilities', i.e. wages or salaries including sickness and holiday pay and contributions to occupational pensions schemes. These will rank *equally* with the administrator's fees and expenses, and other outstanding claims. Other liabilities under employment contracts, e.g. redundancy pay and payments in lieu of notice, will remain but will be treated as unsecured claims against the company.

Duties of insolvency practitioners

The main duty of an administrator is to prepare a plan to achieve the purpose(s) of the administration order. He is given three months to do this – extendable by the court. The proposals are put before a meeting of creditors, which must approve them. If they do not, the administration order may be discharged (s 24(5)). If the proposals are approved, the administration proceeds. If eventually it fails, the court has power to discharge the administration order. Normally the administrator would apply under s 18(3). If the administration succeeds, the administrator can be released under s 20.

The main duties of an administrative receiver are to apply income from the business or sale of assets to pay:

(a) his fees and expenses and outstanding claims for wages and salaries (see above);
(b) preferential creditors (see below);
(c) the secured creditor appointing him (with interest); and
(d) any surplus to the company or to a liquidator if the unsecured creditors have put the company into liquidation.

The main duties of a liquidator are to realise the company's assets to pay:

(a) his own fees and expenses;
(b) preferential creditors, e.g. PAYE deductions and NIC for 12 months next before the commencement of the winding-up, VAT for six months,

wages and salaries for four months up to a maximum of £800 per employee, and accrued holiday pay of employees. Assessed taxes are no longer preferential. It should be noted that if a bank has provided funds to pay wages and salaries **before, but not after**, the onset of insolvency proceedings to try to save the company by assisting it to trade, that debt becomes preferential under the rule of subrogation;

(c) secured creditors (see below);
(d) unsecured creditors;
(e) deferred debts, e.g. dividends declared but not paid. Any surplus will be returned to the shareholders pro rata to shareholding.

It should be noted that if a bank has provided funds to pay wages and salaries *before* the liquidation (or receivership for that matter), the debt becomes preferential under what is called the rule of subrogation. The reason for this rule is that it may encourage banks to advance further money for the payment of wages at a critical time in the debtor company's affairs so as to enable it to continue trading and possibly avoid collapse leading to the appointment of a receiver or liquidator.

A secured creditor may rely on his security and not prove in the liquidation. Any surplus on sale of the security over and above his debt must be returned to the liquidator less the cost of sale. He may, alternatively, give up his security and prove for the whole debt, or value his security and prove for the balance as an unsecured creditor. If he takes the latter course, the liquidator can within six months buy the security at the valuation or insist on a sale by public auction. If the liquidator does not exercise either of these rights, the creditor owns the security and may prove for the balance as an unsecured creditor.

Swelling the assets

The assets available to the liquidator or administrator (not an administrative receiver) can be increased where prior to the administration or liquidation there have been transactions at undervalue (s 238) and preferences (s 239) (as where a creditor has been preferred over the others). An example is to be found in *Re Kushler* (1943), a case decided under previous legislation.

In that case ordinary creditors were ignored but the company paid some £700 into its bank account merely to clear the overdraft which the directors had personally guaranteed. Repayment by the bank was ordered.

A further and common example of a preference concerns the repayment of directors' loan accounts. In many smaller companies the directors may have lent money to the company and it will repay these loan accounts so as to avoid problems relating to repayment once an insolvency practitioner takes over. If the relevant repayment is made within two years of the insolvency practitioner's appointment, as is often the case, it is recoverable by him from the directors concerned and may be used to pay the company's debts in the prescribed order. A major authority for this is the ruling of the court in *Re Exchange Travel (Holdings) Ltd* (1996).

Under s 241 the court can set these transactions aside and allow the liquidator to recover money or property for the company. Preferences made in the six months prior to administration or liquidation can be recovered. If the preference is to a person connected or associated with the company, e.g. a director or a relative of a director (see s 435), the period is two years (see *Re Exchange Travel (Holdings) Ltd* (1996)). Transactions at under value made up to two years before can be set aside, whether the recipient was connected or associated with the company or not. The company must have been insolvent at the time of such transaction or have become insolvent as a result of it.

Voluntary arrangements

Provision for company voluntary arrangements exists on the lines of the rules relating to insolvent sole traders which were considered in Chapter 5.

Once again, the aim of a voluntary arrangement is to avoid insolvency proceedings by substituting a satisfactory settlement of the company's financial difficulties. For example, a composition may be made between the company and its creditors under which the creditors accept, say, 60p in the £1 in full settlement of their debts.

The directors must draw up proposals assisted by an insolvency practitioner, called a **nominee**, who will give a professional assessment as to the feasibility of the composition and report to the court as to whether the members and creditors should meet to consider the proposals. If the court agrees, the nominee will call the relevant meetings.

The composition is approved if a simple majority of members are in favour and 75 per cent in value of the unsecured creditors agree. If the composition is approved as required that approval is reported to the court by the nominee who becomes the **supervisor** of the arrangement and implements it. The arrangement becomes binding on any person who had notice of the meeting and was entitled to attend and vote. Creditors cannot sue for payment or petition for winding-up. The rights of secured and preferential creditor are not affected. At any stage *any* creditor may challenge a decision of the supervisor in court.

Company voluntary arrangements – the disadvantages

The main disadvantages of company voluntary arrangements (CVA) are that they cannot be made binding on a secured or preferential creditor in terms of priority of payment without the creditor's consent, and that there is no provision for obtaining a moratorium to hold off actions by hostile creditors while the proposal for a CVA is being drawn up and considered, unless the CVA proposal is being combined with the appointment of an administrator when the law relating to administrations applies and provides protection. Administration is costly and time-consuming and in any case the making of an administration order can always be blocked by a secured creditor who may appoint an administrative receiver. Although the company moratorium was left out of the Insolvency Act 1986, it will have been noted that the 'interim order' is available in the insolvency of individuals under the 1986 Act. (See further, Chapter 5.)

For the above reasons, the government announced in 1995 that it would introduce the 28-day moratorium proposal set out below. In fact, it was not enacted at that time. In outline, the new procedure was set out s follows:

- the company must receive five days' notice of the intention to appoint an administrative receiver;
- the directors, and only they, can propose a moratorium;

- a nominee is appointed to consider the viability of a company voluntary arrangement – during the moratorium the directors would remain in control of the company but supervised by the nominee;
- the 28-day moratorium comes into effect. The creditors can extend it for a further two months. They can also approve a CVA;
- during the moratorium there can be no enforcement of a security or other creditor action;
- the company cannot dispose of charged assets but suppliers may cease supplies and rights of set-off (see Chapter 5) are not affected;
- the moratorium does not crystallise floating charges;
- if at the end of the moratorium the creditors reject a CVA, the company is regarded as insolvent but the nominee cannot be appointed as administrative receiver;
- if a CVA is approved or the company continues to trade after the moratorium, there can be no repeat moratorium within the next 12 months and during that time no five-day notice is required for the appointment of an administrative receiver.

Funding during the moratorium will be a major issue and adequate funding must be available to satisfy the nominee.

Reform – the Insolvency Act 2000

The Insolvency Act 2000 received the Royal Assent on 1 December 2000. It follows the broad outline given above *but the 28-day moratorium is available only to small companies and no notice is required before the appointment of an administrative receiver*, the banks having agreed to co-operate by not doing so unless there is, for example, fraud.

In addition, the Act allows the Secretary of State for Trade and Industry to accept undertakings that have the same legal effect as a disqualification order. The undertaking will be initiated by the DTI where the Secretary of State considers a director to be unfit. Such a director may consent to a stated period of disqualification by giving a disqualification undertaking to the DTI. A person so disqualified may subsequently apply to the court to vary the undertaking he has given. Another important change in regard to individual insolvency covers the situation where a deceased debtor was the joint tenant of property, usually with his wife. It was ruled by the Court of Appeal in *Re Palmer (A Debtor)* (1994) that since under real property law a joint interest passed by survivorship at the moment of death, in this case to the widow, it did not form part of the deceased's estate in bankruptcy. This meant that in some cases what was the main asset, namely the deceased debtor's interest in the matrimonial home, was beyond the reach of his creditors. The Act, therefore, amends s 421 of the Insolvency Act 1986 by providing that the deceased's interest in property which he held on a joint tenancy on the day he died becomes part of his estate and may be dealt with accordingly.

Finally, the Insolvency Act 2000 amends s 219 of the 1986 Act that allowed answers obtained under powers of compulsion derived from the Companies Act 1985 (offences in a winding-up) to be used as evidence against the person concerned. This contravened the European Convention on Human Rights and was not compatible with the judgment of the European Court of Human Rights in *Saunders v United Kingdom* (1994). The Act therefore amends s 219 to make it compatible with the Convention by stating that this evidence shall not be adduced or questions asked about it.

SPECIMEN MEMORANDUM OF ASSOCIATION

The Companies Act 1985
COMPANY LIMITED BY SHARES

Memorandum of Association of

RICHES KEENAN PUBLISHING LIMITED

1. The name of the company is Riches Keenan Publishing Limited.
2. The registered office of the company will be situated in England.
3. The objects for which the company is established are:

(*a*) To carry on business as authors, editors, proprietors, printers and publishers of newspapers, journals, pamphlets, circulars, magazines, books and other literary and advertising works and undertakings, and to carry on all or any of the businesses of printers, stationers, lithographers, stereotypers, electrotypers, photographic printers, chromo lithographers, photo lithographers, photo process, steel and copper plate engravers, die sinkers, typefounders, photographers, dealers in parchment, advertising agents, designers, draughtsmen, publishers and dealers in or manufacturers of any other articles or things of a character similar or analogous to the foregoing or any of them, or connected therewith and to establish and carry on, as may from time to time by the company be thought fit, a tutorial and lecturing system, college, school, or colleges and schools, where students may receive tuition in economics, sciences, arts, industry, languages, commerce, journalism, and all or any other branches of knowledge, or endeavour to provide for the giving and holding of lectures, scholarships, exhibitions, classes and photographic and recording disc and tape media for the promotion or advancement of education.

(*b*) To carry on any other business (whether manufacturing or otherwise) which may seem to the company capable of being conveniently carried on in connection with the above objects, or calculated directly or indirectly to enhance the value of or render more profitable any of the company's property.

(*c*) To purchase or by any other means acquire any freehold, leasehold, or other property for any estate or interest whatever, and any rights, privileges, or easements over or in respect of any property, and any buildings, offices, factories, mills, works, wharves, roads, railways, tramways, machinery, engines, rolling stock, vehicles, plant, live and dead stock, barges, vessels, or things, and any real or personal property or rights whatsoever which may be necessary for, or may be conveniently used with, or may enhance the value of any other property of the company.

(*d*) To build, construct, maintain, alter, enlarge, pull down, and remove or replace any buildings, offices, factories, mills, works, wharves, roads, railways, tramways, machinery, engines, walls, fences, banks, dams, sluices, or watercourses and to clear sites for the same, or to join with any person, firm, or company in doing any of the things aforesaid, and to work, manage, and control the same or join with others in so doing.

(*e*) To apply for, register, purchase, or by other means acquire and protect, prolong and renew, whether in the United Kingdom or elsewhere, any patents, patent rights, brevets d'invention, licences, trade marks, designs, protections, and concessions which may appear likely to be advantageous or useful to the company, and to use and turn to account and to manufacture under or grant licences or privileges in respect of the same, and to expend money in experimenting upon and testing and in improving or seeking to improve any patents, inventions, or rights which the company may acquire or propose to acquire.

(*f*) To acquire and undertake the whole or any part of the business, goodwill, and assets of any person, firm, or company carrying on or proposing to carry on any of the businesses which this company is authorised to carry on, and as part of the consideration for such acquisition to undertake all or any of the liabilities of such person, firm, or company, or to acquire an interest in, amalgamate with, or enter into partnership or into any arrangement for sharing profits, or for cooperation, or for limiting competition, or for mutual assistance with any such person, firm or company, or for subsidising or otherwise assisting any such person, firm or company, and to give or accept, by way of consideration for any of the acts or things aforesaid or property acquired, any shares, debentures, debenture stock or securities that may be agreed upon, and to hold and retain, or sell, mortgage, and deal with any shares, debentures, debenture stock, or securities so received.

(g) To improve, manage, cultivate, develop, exchange, let on lease or otherwise, mortgage, charge, sell, dispose of, turn to account, grant rights and privileges in respect of, or otherwise deal with all or any part of the property and rights of the company.

(h) To invest and deal with the moneys of the company not immediately required in such shares or upon such securities and in such manner as may from time to time be determined.

(i) To lend and advance money or give credit to such persons, firms, or companies and on such terms as may seem expedient, and in particular to customers of and others having dealings with the company, and to give guarantees or become security for any such persons, firms, or companies.

(j) To borrow or raise money in such manner as the company shall think fit, and in particular by the issue of debentures or debenture stock (perpetual or otherwise), and to secure the repayment of any money borrowed, raised, or owing, by mortgage, charge, or lien upon the whole or any part of the company's property or assets (whether present or future), including its uncalled capital, and also by a similar mortgage, charge, or lien to secure and guarantee the performance by the company of any obligation or liability it may undertake.

(k) To draw, make, accept, endorse, discount, execute, and issue promissory notes, bills of exchange, bills of lading, warrants, debentures, and other negotiable or transferable instruments.

(l) To apply for, promote, and obtain any Act of Parliament, provisional order, or licence of the Department of Trade and Industry or other authority for enabling the company to carry any of its objects into effect, or for effecting any modification of the company's constitution, or for any other purpose which may seem expedient, and to oppose any proceedings or applications which may seem calculated directly or indirectly to prejudice the company's interests.

(m) To enter into any arrangements with any governments or authorities (supreme, municipal, local, or otherwise), or any companies, firms, or persons that may seem conducive to the attainment of the company's objects or any of them, and to obtain from any such government, authority, company, firm, or person any charters, contracts, decrees, rights, privileges, and concessions which the company may think desirable, and to carry out, exercise, and comply with any such charters, contracts, decrees, rights, privileges, and concessions.

(n) To subscribe for, take, purchase, or otherwise acquire and hold shares or other interests in or securities of any other company having objects altogether or in part similar to those of this company or carrying on any business capable of being carried on so as directly or indirectly to benefit this company.

(o) To act as agents or brokers and as trustees for any person, firm, or company, and to undertake and perform sub-contracts, and also to act in any of the businesses of the company through or by means of agents, brokers, sub-contractors, or others.

(p) To remunerate any person, firm, or company rendering services to this company, either by cash payment or by the allotment to him or them of shares or securities of the company credited as paid up in full or in part or otherwise as may be thought expedient.

(q) To pay all or any expenses incurred in connection with the promotion, formation, and incorporation of the company, or to contract with any person, firm or company to pay the same, and to pay commissions to brokers and others for underwriting, placing, selling, or guaranteeing the subscription of any shares, debentures, debenture stock or securities of this company.

(r) To support and subscribe to any charitable or public object, and any institution, society, or club which may be for the benefit of the company or its employees, or may be connected with any town or place where the company carries on business; to give or award pensions, annuities, gratuities, and superannuation or other allowances or benefits or charitable aid to any persons who are or have been directors of, or who are or have been employed by, or who are serving or have served the company, and to the wives, widows, children, and other relatives and dependants of such persons; to make payments towards insurance; and to set up, establish, support, and maintain superannuation and other funds or schemes (whether contributory or non-contributory) for the benefit of any such persons and of their wives, widows, children, and other relatives and dependants.

(s) To promote any other company for the purpose of acquiring the whole or any part of the business or property and undertaking any of the liabilities of this company, or of undertaking any business or operations which may appear likely to assist or benefit this company or to enhance the value of any property or business of this company, and to place or guarantee the placing of, underwrite, subscribe for, or otherwise acquire all or any part of the shares or securities of any such company as aforesaid.

(*t*) To sell or otherwise dispose of the whole or any part of the business or property of the company, either together or in portions, for such consideration as the company may think fit, and in particular for shares, debentures, or securities of any company purchasing the same.

(*u*) To distribute among the members of the company in kind any property of the company, and in particular any shares, debentures, or securities of other companies belonging to this company or of which this company may have the power of disposing.

(*v*) To procure the company to be registered or recognised in any part of the world.

(*w*) To do all such other things as may be deemed incidental or conducive to the attainment of the above objects or any of them.

It is hereby expressly declared that each sub-clause of this clause shall be construed independently of the other sub-clauses hereof, and that none of the objects mentioned in any sub-clause shall be deemed to be merely subsidiary to the objects mentioned in any other sub-clause.

4. The liability of the members is limited.

5. The share capital of the company is £10,000 divided into 10,000 shares of £1 each.

WE, the several persons whose names, addresses and descriptions are subscribed are desirous of being formed into a company in pursuance of this Memorandum of Association, and we respectively agree to take the number of shares in the capital of the company set opposite our respective names.

Names, addresses and descriptions of subscribers	Number of shares taken by each subscriber
Sarah Riches 1 High Street, Barchester AUTHOR/LECTURER *Sarah Riches*	ONE
Dennis Keenan 2 Low Street, Barchester AUTHOR/LECTURER *Denis Keenan*	ONE
Total Shares Taken	TWO

Dated the 5 March 2001
Witness to the above signatures:
John Green
3 Middle Street,
Barchester *John Green*

Note: Under the Electronic Communications Order 2000 where the memorandum is delivered to the Registrar otherwise than, as here, in legible form and is authenticated by each subscriber in such manner as is directed by the Registrar, the requirement for signature in the presence of at least one witness and for attestation of (witness of) the signatures is not required.

SPECIMEN ARTICLES OF ASSOCIATION

The Companies Act 1985

COMPANY LIMITED BY SHARES

Articles of Association of

RICHES KEENAN PUBLISHING LIMITED

Preliminary

1. The Regulations contained in Table A in the Schedule to the Companies (Tables A–F) Regulations 1985, shall not apply to this Company.
2. In these Articles, unless the context otherwise requires –
'The Act' shall mean the Companies Act, 1985 and every other Act incorporated therewith, or any Act or Acts of Parliament substituted therefor; and in case of any such substitution the references in these presents to the provisions of non-existing Acts of Parliament shall be read as referring to the provisions substituted therefor in the new Act or Acts of Parliament.
'Communication' means the same as in the Electronic Communications Act 2000.
'Electronic communication' means the same as in the Electronic Communications Act 2000.
'The Register' shall mean that Register of Members to be kept as required by Section 352 of The Companies Act 1985.
'Month' shall mean calendar month.
'Paid up' shall include 'credited as paid up'.
'Secretary' shall include any person appointed to perform the duties of Secretary temporarily.
'In writing' shall include printed, lithographed, and typewritten.
Words which have a special meaning assigned to them in the Act shall have the same meaning in these presents.
Words importing the singular number only shall include the plural, and the converse shall also apply.
Words importing males shall include females.
Words importing individuals shall include corporations.

Share capital

3. Subject to the provisions of the Act and without prejudice to any rights attached to any existing shares, any share may be issued with such rights or restrictions as the company may by ordinary resolution determine. Subject to the provisions of the Act shares may be issued which are to be redeemed or are to be liable to be redeemed at the option of the company or the holder on such terms and in such manner as may be provided by the terms of issue.

Shares and certificates

4. Subject to the provisions of the Act the company may purchase its own shares (including any redeemable shares) and make a payment in respect of the redemption or purchase of its own shares otherwise than out of distributable profits of the company or the proceeds of a fresh issue of shares.
5. The directors may make arrangements on the issue of shares for a difference between the holders of such shares in the amount of calls to be paid and in the time of payment of such calls.
6. The company shall be entitled to treat the person whose name appears upon the register in respect of any share as the absolute owner thereof, and shall not be under any obligation to recognise any trust or equity or equitable claim to or interest in such share, whether or not it shall have express or other notice thereof.
7. Every member shall be entitled without payment to one certificate under the common seal of the company, specifying the share or shares held by him, with the distinctive numbers thereof (if any) and the amount paid up thereon. Such certificate shall be delivered to the member within two months after the allotment or registration of the transfer, as the case may be, of such share or shares.

8. If any member shall require additional certificates he shall pay for each such additional certificate such reasonable sum as the directors shall determine.

9. If any certificate be defaced, worn out, lost, or destroyed, it may be renewed on payment of such reasonable sum as the directors may prescribe, and the person requiring the new certificate shall surrender the defaced or worn-out certificate, or give such evidence of its loss or destruction and such indemnity to the company as the directors think fit.

Joint holders of shares

10. Where two or more persons are registered as the holders of any share they shall be deemed to hold the same as joint tenants with benefit of survivorship, subject to the provisions following –

(a) The company shall not be bound to register more than three persons as the holders of any share.

(b) The joint holders of any share shall be liable, severally as well as jointly, in respect of all payments which ought to be made in respect of such share.

(c) On the death of any one of such joint holders the survivor or survivors shall be the only person or persons recognised by the company as having any title to such share; but the directors may require such evidence of death as they may deem fit.

(d) Any one of such joint holders may give effectual receipts for any dividend, bonus or return of capital payable to such joint holders.

(e) Only the person whose name stands first in the register of members as one of the joint holders of any share shall be entitled to delivery of the certificate relating to such share, or to receive notices from the company, or to attend or vote at general meetings of the company, and any notice given to such person shall be deemed notice to all the joint holders; but any one of such joint holders may be appointed the proxy of the person entitled to vote on behalf of the said joint holders, and as such proxy to attend the vote at general meetings of the company.

Calls on shares

11. The directors may from time to time make calls upon the members in respect of all moneys unpaid on their shares, provided that no call shall be payable within one month after the date when the last instalment of the last preceding call shall have been made payable; and each member shall, subject to receiving fourteen days' notice at least, specifying the time and place for payment, pay the amount called on his shares to the persons and at the times and places appointed by the directors. A call may be made payable by instalments.

12. A call shall be deemed to have been made at the time when the resolution of the directors authorising such call was passed.

13. If a call payable in respect of any share or any instalment of a call be not paid before or on the day appointed for payment thereof, the holder for the time being of such share shall be liable to pay interest for the same at such rate as the directors shall determine from the day appointed for the payment of such call or instalment to the time of actual payment; but the directors may if they shall think fit waive the payment of such interest or any part thereof.

14. If by the terms of the issue of any shares, or otherwise, any amount is made payable at any fixed time or by instalments at any fixed times, whether on account of the amount of the shares or by way of premium, every such amount or instalment shall be payable as if it were a call duly made by the directors, and of which due notice had been given; and all the provisions hereof with respect to the payment of calls and interest thereon, or to the forefeiture of shares for nonpayment of calls, shall apply to every such amount or instalment and the shares in respect of which it is payable.

Transfer of shares

15. The instrument of transfer of any share in the company shall be in writing, and shall be executed by or on behalf of the transferor and unless the share is fully paid by or on behalf of the transferee, and the transferor shall be deemed to remain the holder of such share until the name of the transferee is entered in the register in respect thereof.

16. No fee shall be charged for the registration of any instrument of transfer.

Transmission of shares

17. On the death of any member (not being one of several joint holders of a share) the executors or administrators of such deceased member shall be the only persons recognised by the company as having any title to such share.

18. Any person becoming entitled to a share in consequence of the death or bankruptcy of a member shall, upon such evidence being produced as may from time to time be required by the directors, have the right either to be registered as a member in respect of the share or, instead of being registered himself, to make such transfer of the share as the deceased or bankrupt person could have made; but the directors shall in either case have the same right to decline or suspend registration as they would have had in the case of a transfer of the share by the deceased or bankrupt person before the death or bankruptcy.

19. Any person becoming entitled to a share by reason of the death or bankruptcy of the holder shall be entitled to the same dividends and other advantages to which he would be entitled if he were the registered holder of the share, except that he shall not, before being registered as a member in respect of the share, be entitled in respect of it to exercise any right conferred by membership in relation to meetings of the company.

Forfeiture of shares and lien

20. If any member fail to pay any call or instalment of a call on the day appointed for payment thereof the directors may, at any time thereafter during such time as any part of the call or instalment remains unpaid, serve a notice on him requiring him to pay so much of the call or instalment as is unpaid, together with interest accrued and any expenses incurred by reason of such nonpayment.

21. The notice shall name a further day (not being earlier than the expiration of fourteen days from the date of the notice) on or before which such call or instalment and all interest accrued and expenses incurred by reason of such nonpayment are to be paid, and it shall also name the place where payment is to be made, such place being either the registered office or some other place at which calls of the company are usually made payable. The notice shall also state that in the event of nonpayment at or before the time and at the place appointed the shares in respect of which such call or instalment is payable will be liable to forfeiture.

22. If the requisitions of any such notice as aforesaid be not complied with, any shares in respect of which such notice has been given may at any time thereafter, before payment of all calls or instalments, interest, and expenses due in respect thereof has been made, be forfeited by a resolution of the directors to that effect.

23. Any shares so forfeited shall be deemed to be the property of the company, and, subject to the provisions of the Act, may be sold or otherwise disposed of in such manner, either subject to or discharged from all calls made or instalments due prior to the forfeiture, as the directors think fit; or the directors may at any time before such shares are sold or otherwise disposed of, annul the forfeiture upon such terms as they may approve.

24. Any person whose shares have been forfeited shall cease to be a member in respect of the forfeited shares, but shall, notwithstanding, remain liable to pay to the company all moneys which at the date of the forfeiture were presently payable by him to the company in respect of the shares, together with interest thereon at such rate as the directors shall appoint, down to the date of payment; but the directors may, if they shall think fit, remit the payment of such interest or any part thereof.

25. When any shares have been forfeited an entry shall forthwith be made in the register of members of the company recording the forfeiture and the date thereof, and so soon as the shares so forfeited have been disposed of an entry shall also be made of the manner and date of the disposal thereof.

26. The company shall have a first and paramount lien upon all shares (not fully paid up) held by any member of the company (whether alone or jointly with other persons) and upon all dividends and bonuses which may be declared in respect of such shares, for all debts, obligations, and liabilities of such member to the company: Provided always that if the company shall register a transfer of any shares upon which it has such a lien as aforesaid without giving to the transferee notice of its claim, the said shares shall be freed and discharged from the lien of the company.

27. The directors may, at any time after the date for the payment or satisfaction of such debts, obligations, or liabilities shall have arrived, serve upon any member who is indebted or under obligation to the company, or upon the person entitled to his shares by reason of the death or bankruptcy of such member, a notice requiring him to pay the amount due to the company or satisfy the said obligation, and stating that if payment is not made or the said obligation is not satisfied within a time (not being less than fourteen days) specified in such notice, the shares held by such member will be liable to be sold, and if

such member or the person entitled to his shares as aforesaid shall not comply with such notice within the time aforesaid, the directors may sell such shares without further notice.

28. Upon any sale being made by the directors of any shares to satisfy the lien of the company thereon the proceeds shall be applied: first, in the payment of all costs of such sale; next, in satisfaction of the debts or obligations of the member to the company; and the residue (if any) shall be paid to the person entitled to the shares at the date of the sale or as he shall in writing direct.

29. An entry in the minute book of the company of the forfeiture of any shares, or that any shares have been sold to satisfy a lien of the company, shall be sufficient evidence, as against all persons entitled to such shares, that the said shares were properly forfeited or sold; and such entry, and the receipt of the company for the price of such shares, shall constitute a good title to such shares, and the name of the purchaser shall be entered in the register as a member of the company, and he shall be entitled to a certificate of title to the shares, and shall not be bound to see to the application of the purchase money, nor shall his title to the said shares be affected by any irregularity or invalidity in the proceedings in reference to the forfeiture or sale. The remedy (if any) of the former holder of such shares, and of any person claiming under or through him, shall be against the company and in damages only.

Alteration of share capital

30. The directors may, with the sanction of an Ordinary resolution of the company previously given in general meeting, increase the capital by the issue of new shares, such aggregate increase to be of such amount and to be divided into shares of such respective amounts as the resolution shall prescribe.

31. Subject to the provisions of the Act the new shares shall be issued upon such terms and conditions and with such rights, priorities, or privileges as the resolution sanctioning the increase of capital shall prescribe.

32. Any capital raised by the creation of new shares shall, unless otherwise provided by the conditions of issue, be considered as part of the original capital, and shall be subject to the same provisions with reference to the payment of calls and the forfeiture of shares on nonpayment of calls, transfer and transmission of shares, lien, or otherwise, as if it had been part of the original capital.

33. The company may by ordinary resolution –

(a) subdivide its existing shares or any of them into shares of smaller amount than is fixed by the memorandum of association: provided that in the subdivision of the existing shares the proportion between the amount paid and the amount (if any) unpaid on each share of reduced amount shall be the same as it was in the case of the existing share from which the share of reduced amount is derived;

(b) reduce its capital subject to the provisions of the Act;

(c) consolidate and divide its capital into shares of larger amount than its existing shares;

(d) cancel any shares which, at the date of the passing of the resolution, have not been taken or agreed to be taken by any person.

Borrowing powers

34. The directors may, with the consent of the company in general meeting, raise or borrow for the purposes of the company's business such sum or sums of money as they think fit. The directors may secure the repayment of or raise any such sum or sums as aforesaid by mortgage or charge upon the whole or any part of the property and assets of the company, present and future, including its uncalled or unissued capital, or by the issue, at such price as they may think fit, of bonds or debentures, either charged upon the whole or any part of the property and assets of the company or not so charged, or in such other way as the directors may think expedient.

35. Any bonds, debentures, debenture stock or other securities issued or to be issued by the company shall, subject to the provisions of the Act, be under the control of the directors, who may issue them upon such terms and conditions and in such manner and for such consideration as they shall consider to be for the benefit of the company.

36. The company may, upon the issue of any bonds, debentures, debenture stock or other securities, confer on the creditors of the company holding the same, or on any trustees or other persons acting on their behalf, a voice in the management of the company, whether by giving to them the right of attending and voting at general meetings, or by empowering them to appoint one or more of the directors of the company, or otherwise as may be agreed.

37. If the directors or any of them, or any other person, shall become personally liable for the payment of any sum primarily due from the company, the directors may execute or cause to be executed any mortgage, charge, or security over or affecting the whole or any part of the assets of the company by way of indemnity to secure the directors or persons so becoming liable as aforesaid from any loss in respect of such liability.

38. The register of charges shall be open to inspection by any creditor or member of the company without payment, and by any other person on payment of such reasonable sum as the directors may determine.

39. A register of the holders of the debentures of the company shall be kept at the registered office of the company, and shall be open to the inspection of the registered holders of such debentures and of any member of the company, subject to such restrictions as the company in general meeting may from time to time impose. The directors may close the said register for such period or periods as they may think fit, not exceeding in the aggregate thirty days in each year.

General meetings

40. The annual general meeting of the company shall be held in the month of March in each year at such time and place as the directors shall appoint. In default of an annual meeting being so held an annual meeting may be convened, to be held at any time during the next succeeding month, by any three members in the same manner as nearly as possible as that in which meetings are to be convened by the directors.

41. The directors may whenever they think fit, and they shall upon a requisition made in writing by members in accordance with the Act, convene an extraordinary general meeting of the company. If at any time there shall not be present in England and capable of acting sufficient directors to form a quorum, the directors in England capable of acting, or if there shall be no such directors then any two members, may convene an extraordinary general meeting of the company in the same manner as nearly as possible as that in which meetings may be convened by the directors, and the company at such extraordinary general meeting shall have power to elect directors.

42. In the case of an extraordinary meeting called in pursuance of a requisition, unless such meeting shall have been called by the directors, no business other than that stated in the requisition as the objects of the meeting shall be transacted.

43. An annual general meeting and an extraordinary general meeting called for the passing of a special resolution or a resolution appointing a person as a director shall be called by at least twenty-one clear days' notice. All other extraordinary general meetings shall be called by at least fourteen clear days' notice but a General Meeting may be called by shorter notice if it is so agreed –
(a) in the case of an annual general meeting by all the members entitled to attend and vote thereat; and
(b) in the case of any other meetings by a majority in number of the members having a right to attend and vote being a majority together holding not less than ninety-five per cent in nominal value of the shares giving that right. The notice shall specify the time and place of the meeting and the general nature of the business to be transacted and in the case of an annual general meeting shall specify the meeting as such.
Subject to the provisions of the Articles and to any restrictions imposed on shares, the notice shall be given to all the members, to all persons entitled to a share in consequence of the death or bankruptcy of a member and to the directors and auditors.
Clear days in relation to the period of notice means that period excluding the day when the notice is given or deemed to be given and the day for which it is given or on which it is to take effect.
The accidental omission to give notice of a meeting to, or the non-receipt of notice of a meeting by, any person entitled to receive notice shall not invalidate the proceedings at that meeting.

Proceedings at general meetings

44. The business of an annual general meeting shall be to receive and consider the accounts and balance sheets and the reports of the directors and auditors, to elect directors in place of those retiring, to elect auditors and fix their remuneration, and to sanction a dividend. All other business transacted at an annual general meeting, and all business transacted at an extraordinary meeting, shall be deemed special.

45. No business shall be transacted at any general meeting except the declaration of a dividend or the adjournment of the meeting, unless a quorum of members is present at the time when the meeting proceeds to business; and such quorum shall consist of not less than two members personally present.

46. If within half an hour from the time appointed for the meeting a quorum be not present the meeting, if convened upon the requisition of members, shall be dissolved. In any other case it shall stand adjourned to the same day in the next week at the same time and place, and if at such adjourned meeting a quorum be not present, those members who are present shall be deemed to be a quorum, and may do all business which a full quorum might have done.

47. The chairman (if any) of the board of directors shall preside as chairman at every general meeting of the company. If there be no such chairman, or if at any meeting he be not present within fifteen minutes after the time appointed for holding the meeting, or is unwilling to act as chairman, the members present shall choose one of the directors present to be chairman; or if no director be present and willing to take the chair the members present shall choose one of their number to be chairman.

48. The chairman may, with the consent of any meeting at which a quorum is present, adjourn the meeting from time to time and from place to place; but no business shall be transacted at any adjourned meeting other than the business left unfinished at the meeting from which the adjournment took place. When a meeting is adjourned for twenty-one days or more, notice of the adjourned meeting shall be given as in the case of an original meeting. Save as aforesaid, it shall not be necessary to give any notice of an adjournment or of the business to be transacted at an adjourned meeting.

49. At any general meeting every question shall be decided in the first instance by a show of hands; and unless a poll be (on or before the declaration of the result of the show of hands) demanded by at least two members entitled to vote, or directed by the chairman, a declaration by the chairman that a resolution has been carried or not carried, or carried or not carried by a particular majority, and an entry to that effect in the minutes of the meeting, shall be conclusive evidence of the facts, without proof of the number or proportion of the votes recorded in favour of or against such resolution.

50. If a poll be demanded or directed in the manner above mentioned it shall (subject to the provisions of the next succeeding article hereof) be taken at such time and in such manner as the chairman may appoint, and the result of such poll shall be deemed to be the resolution of the meeting at which the poll was so demanded. In the case of an equality of votes at any general meeting, whether upon a show of hands or on a poll, the chairman shall be entitled to a second or casting vote. In case of any dispute as to the admission or rejection of any vote the chairman shall determine the same, and such determination made in good faith shall be final and conclusive.

51. A poll demanded upon the election of a chairman or upon a question of adjournment shall be taken forthwith. Any business other than that upon which a poll has been demanded may be proceeded with pending the taking of the poll.

Votes of members

52. Upon a show of hands every member present in person shall have one vote only. Upon a poll every member present in person or by proxy shall have one vote for every share held by him.

53. A member in respect of whom an order has been made by any court having jurisdiction (whether in the United Kingdom or elsewhere) in matters concerning mental disorder may vote, whether on a show of hands or on a poll, by his receiver, *curator bonis* or other person authorised in that behalf appointed by that court and any such receiver, *curator bonis* or other person may, on a poll, vote by proxy. Evidence to the satisfaction of the directors of the authority of the person claiming to exercise the right to vote shall in the case of an instrument in writing be deposited at the office, or such other place as is specified in accordance with the Articles for the deposit of appointments of proxy, not less than forty-eight hours before the time appointed for holding the meeting or adjourned meeting at which the right to vote is to be exercised and in default the right to vote shall not be exercisable. Where the appointment of the proxy is contained in an electronic communication, the procedure in Article 58 of these Articles is in all respects to be followed and the appointment is to be received at the address used for the purposes of such communication, and in default the right to vote shall not be exercisable.

54. No member shall be entitled to vote at any general meeting unless all calls or other sums presently payable by him in respect of the shares held by him in the company have been paid, and no member shall be entitled to vote in respect of any shares that he has acquired by transfer at any meeting held after the expiration of three months from the incorporation of the company unless he has been possessed of the

shares in respect of which he claims to vote for at least three months previous to the time of holding the meeting at which he proposes to vote.

55. On a poll votes may be given either personally or by proxy.

56. The appointment of a proxy shall be executed by the appointer or his attorney duly authorised, or if such appointer be a corporation by an authorised officer or attorney. Provided always that a corporation being a member of the company may appoint any one of its officers or any other person to be its proxy, and the person so appointed may attend and vote at any meeting and exercise the same functions on behalf of the corporation which he represents as if he were an individual shareholder.

57. The appointment of a proxy and the power of attorney or other authority (if any) under which it is signed, or a notarially certified copy of such power or authority, shall, in the case of an instrument in writing, be deposited at the registered office of the company not less than forty-eight hours before the time fixed for holding the meeting at which the person named in such instrument is authorised to vote, and in default the instrument of proxy shall not be treated as valid.

58. The appointment of a proxy shall be in the following form, or in any other form of which the directors shall approve –

RICHES KEENAN PUBLISHING LIMITED

I,   , of   , being a member of Riches Keenan Publishing Limited hereby appoint   , of
     , as my proxy to vote for me and on my behalf at the annual (*or* extraordinary, *as the case may be*) general meeting of the company to be held on the   day of   20   and at any adjournment thereof. Signed on this   day of   20

In the case of an appointment contained in an electronic communication where the address has been specified for the purpose of receiving electronic communications:

1 in the notice convening the meeting, or

2 in any instrument of proxy sent out by the company in relation to the meeting, or

3 in any invitation contained in an electronic communication to appoint a proxy issued by the company in relation to the meeting,

the communication be received at such address not less than 48 hours before the time for holding the meeting or adjourned meeting at which the person named in the appointment proposes to vote.

Directors

59. The number of directors shall not be less than two nor more than five.

60. The following persons shall be the first directors of the company:

SARAH RICHES
DENIS KEENAN

61. The directors shall be entitled to such remuneration as the company may by ordinary resolution determine and unless the resolution provides otherwise, the remuneration shall be deemed to accrue from day to day.

Powers of directors

62. The business of the company shall be managed by the directors, who may pay all expenses incurred in the formation and registration of the company, and may exercise all such powers of the company as are not by the Act or by these Articles required to be exercised by the company in general meeting, subject, nevertheless, to any regulations of these Articles, to the provisions of the Act, and to such regulations, not being inconsistent with the aforesaid regulations or provisions, as may be prescribed by the company in General Meeting; but no regulation made by the company in General Meeting shall invalidate any prior act of the directors which would have been valid if such regulation had not been made.

63. Without prejudice to any of the powers by these Articles or by law conferred upon the directors, it is hereby declared that they shall have the following powers –

(a) To pay all the preliminary expenses incurred in or about the formation, promotion, and registration of the company and the procuring its capital to be subscribed.

(b) To purchase or otherwise acquire on behalf of the company any property, rights, or things which the company may purchase or acquire.

(c) To appoint, remove, or suspend any managers, secretaries, officers, clerks, agents, or servants, and to direct and control them, and fix and pay their remuneration.

(d) To enter into negotiations and agreements or contracts (preliminary, conditional, or final), and to give effect to, modify, vary, or rescind the same.

(e) To appoint agents and attorneys for the company in the United Kingdom or abroad, with such powers (including power to subdelegate) as may be thought fit, and to provide, if necessary, for the management of the affairs of the company by any other company or any firm or person.

(f) To enter into any arrangement with any company, firm, or person carrying on any business similar to that of this company for mutual concessions, or for any joint working or combination, or for any restriction upon competition, or for any pooling of business or profits that may seem desirable, and to carry the same into effect.

(g) To give, award, or allow any pension, gratuity, or compensation to any employee of the company, or his widow or children, that may appear to the directors just or proper, whether such employee, his widow or children, have or have not a legal claim upon the company.

(h) To commence and carry on, or defend, abandon, or compromise any legal proceedings whatsoever, including proceedings in bankruptcy, on behalf of the company, or to refer any claims or demands by or against the company to arbitration, and to observe and perform the awards, and to accept compositions from or give time to any debtor or contributor owing money or alleged to owe money to the company.

(i) To give receipts, releases, and discharges on behalf of the company.

(j) To invest and deal with any of the moneys of the company not immediately required for the purposes of its business in such manner as they may think fit, and to vary such investments or realise the amount invested therein.

(k) To give indemnities to any director or other person who has undertaken or is about to undertake any liability on behalf of the company, and to secure such director or other person against loss by giving him a mortgage or charge upon the whole or any of the property of the company by way of security.

(l) To remunerate any person rendering services to the company, whether in its regular employment or not, in such manner as may seem fit, whether by cash, salary, bonus, or shares or debentures, or by a commission or share of profits, either in any particular transaction or generally, or howsoever otherwise.

Disqualification of directors

64. The office of a director shall be vacated if –

(a) he ceased to be a director by virtue of any provision of the Act or he becomes prohibited by law from being a director; or

(b) he becomes bankrupt or makes any arrangement or composition with his creditors generally; or

(c) he is, or may be, suffering from mental disorder and either –

    (i) he is admitted to hospital in pursuance of an application for treatment under the Mental Health Act 1983; or

    (ii) an order is made by a court having jurisdiction (whether in the United Kingdom or elsewhere) in matters concerning mental disorder for his detention or the appointment of a receiver, *curator bonis* or other person to exercise powers with respect to his property or affairs; or

(d) he resigns his office by notice to the company; or

(e) he shall for more than six consecutive months have been absent without permission of the directors from meetings of directors held during that period and the directors resolve that his office be vacated.

65. A director shall not be disqualified by his office from entering into contracts, arrangements, or dealings with the company, nor shall any contract, arrangement, or dealing with the company be voided, nor shall a director be liable to account to the company for any profit arising out of any contract, arrangement, or dealing with the company by reason of such director being a party to or interested in or deriving profit from any such contract, arrangement, or dealing, and being at the same time a director of the company, provided that such director discloses to the board at or before the time when such contract, arrangement, or dealing is determined upon his interest therein, or, if his interest be subsequently acquired, provided that he on the first occasion possible discloses to the board the fact that he has acquired such

interest. But, except in respect of any indemnity to a director under Article 63*(k)* hereof, no director shall vote as a director in regard to any contract, arrangement, or dealing in which he is interested, or upon any matter arising thereout, and if he shall so vote his vote shall not be counted, nor shall he be reckoned in estimating a quorum when any such contract, arrangement, or dealing is under consideration.

66. The continuing directors may act notwithstanding any vacancy in their body, but if and so long as the number of directors is reduced below the number fixed by or pursuant to the regulations of the company as the necessary quorum of directors, the continuing directors may act for the purpose of increasing the number of directors to that number, or of summoning a general meeting of the company, but for no other purpose.

Rotation of directors

67. At the first annual general meeting, and at the annual general meeting in every subsequent year, one third of the directors for the time being, or if their number is not three or a multiple of three then the number nearest to but not exceeding one third, shall retire from office, the directors to retire in each year being those who have been longest in office since their last election, but as between persons who became directors on the same day those to retire shall (unless they otherwise agree among themselves) be determined by lot.

68. A retiring director shall be eligible for re-election.

69. The company at the annual general meeting at which any director retires in manner aforesaid shall fill up the vacated office, and may fill up any other offices which may then be vacant, by electing the necessary number of persons, unless the company shall determine to reduce the number of directors. The company may also at any extraordinary general meeting, on notice duly given, fill up any vacancies in the office of director, or appoint additional directors, provided that the maximum hereinbefore mentioned be not exceeded.

70. If at any meeting at which an election of directors ought to take place the places of the vacating directors be not filled up, the vacating directors, or such of them as have not had their places filled up, shall continue in office until the annual general meeting in the next year, and so on from time to time until their places have been filled up.

71. The company may from time to time in general meeting increase or reduce the number of directors, and may also determine in what rotation such increased or reduced number is to go out of office.

72. The directors shall have power at any time and from time to time to appoint any other qualified person to be a director of the company either to fill a casual vacancy or as an addition to the board, but so that the total number of directors shall not at any time exceed the maximum number hereinbefore fixed. Any director so appointed shall hold office only until the next following annual general meeting, when he shall retire, but shall be eligible for re-election.

73. Seven days' previous notice in writing shall be given to the company of the intention of any member to propose any person other than a retiring director for election to the office of director. Provided always that, if the members present at a general meeting unanimously consent, the chairman of such meeting may waive the said notice, and may submit to the meeting the name of any person duly qualified.

Managing directors

74. The directors may from time to time appoint one or more of their body to be a managing director or manager of the company, and may fix his or their remuneration either by way of salary or commission or by conferring a right to participation in the profits of the company, or by a combination of two or more of those modes.

75. Every managing director or manager shall be liable to be dismissed or removed by the board of directors, and another person may be appointed in his place. The board may, however, subject to the provisions of the Act, enter into any agreement with any person who is or is about to become a managing director or manager with regard to the length and terms of his employment, but so that the remedy of any such person for any breach of such agreement shall be in damages only, and he shall have no right or claim to continue in such office contrary to the will of the directors or of the company in general meeting.

76. A managing director or manager shall not, while he continues to hold that office, be liable to retire by rotation, and he shall not be taken into account in determining the rotation in which the other directors shall retire (except for the purpose of fixing the number to retire in each year), but he shall be subject to the same

provisions as regards removal and disqualification as the other directors, and if he cease to hold the office of director from any cause he shall *ipso facto* cease to be a managing director.

77. The directors may from time to time entrust to and confer upon the managing director or manager all or any of the powers of the directors that they may think fit. But the exercise of all powers by the managing director or manager shall be subject to such regulations and restrictions as the directors may from time to time make or impose, and the said powers may at any time be withdrawn, revoked, or varied.

Proceedings of directors

78. The directors may meet together for the dispatch of business, adjourn, and otherwise regulate their meetings as they think fit, and determine the quorum necessary for the transaction of business. Until otherwise determined two directors shall constitute a quorum. Questions arising at any meeting shall be decided by a majority of votes. In case of an equality of votes the chairman shall have a second or casting vote. A director may, and the secretary on the requisition of a director shall, at any time summon a meeting of the directors. Notice of every meeting of directors shall be given to every director who is in the United Kingdom.

79. The directors may elect a chairman of their meetings, and determine the period for which he is to hold office; but if no such chairman be elected, or if at any meeting the chairman be not present within five minutes after the time appointed for holding the same, the directors present shall choose some one of their number to be chairman of such meeting.

80. The directors may delegate any of their powers to committees, consisting of such member or members of their body as they think fit. Any committee so formed shall in the exercise of the powers so delegated conform to any regulations that may be imposed on him or them by the directors. The regulations herein contained for the meetings and proceedings of directors shall, so far as not altered by any regulations made by the directors, apply also to the meetings and proceedings of any committee.

81. All acts done by any meeting of the directors or of a committee of directors, or by any persons acting as directors, shall, notwithstanding that it be afterwards discovered that there was some defect in the appointment of any such directors or persons acting as aforesaid, or that they or any of them were disqualified, be as valid as if every such person had been duly appointed and was qualified to be a director.

Minutes

82. The directors shall cause minutes to be made in books provided for the purpose –
   (a) of all appointments of officers made by the directors;
   (b) of the names of the directors present at each meeting of the directors and of any committee of the directors;
   (c) of all resolutions and proceedings at all meetings of the company and of the directors and of committees of directors.

The seal

83. The seal shall be used only by the authority of the directors or of a committee of directors authorised by the directors. The directors may determine who shall sign any instrument to which the seal is affixed and unless otherwise so determined it shall be signed by a director and by the secretary or by a second director.
Comment
It is no longer necessary for a company to use the procedure of sealing in order to make a deed (see CA 1985, s 36A). However, there is nothing to prevent the use of a seal by the company if the directors so wish and s 36A provides for this. Where the company has retained its seal and intends to use it from time to time the above article will govern its use.

Dividends

84. Subject to the provisions of the Act, the company may by ordinary resolution declare dividends in accordance with the respective rights of members, but no dividend shall exceed the amount recommended by the directors.

85. Subject to the provisions of the Act, the directors may pay interim dividends if it appears to them they are justified by the profits of the company available for distribution. If the share capital is divided into different classes, the directors may pay interim dividends on shares which confer deferred or non-preferred

rights with regard to dividend as well as on shares which confer preferential rights with regard to dividend. No interim dividend shall be paid on shares carrying deferred or non-preferred rights if, at the time of payment, any preferential dividend is in arrear. The directors may also pay at intervals settled by them any dividend payable at a fixed rate if it appears to them that the profits available for distribution justify the payment. Provided the directors act in good faith they shall not incur any liability to the holders of shares conferring preferred rights for any loss they may suffer by the lawful payment of an interim dividend on any shares having deferred or non-preferred rights.

86. Except as otherwise provided by the rights attached to shares, all dividends shall be declared and paid according to the amounts paid up on the shares on which the dividend is paid. All dividends shall be apportioned and paid proportionately to the amounts paid up on the shares during any portion or portions of the period in respect of which the dividend is paid; but, if any share is issued on terms providing that it shall rank for dividend as from a particular date, that share shall rank for dividend accordingly.

87. A general meeting declaring a dividend may, upon the recommendation of the directors, direct that it shall be satisfied wholly or partly by the distribution of assets and, where any difficulty arises in regard to the distribution, the directors may settle the same and in particular may issue fractional certificates and fix the value for distribution of any assets and may determine that cash shall be paid to any member upon the footing of the value so fixed in order to adjust the rights of members and may vest any assets in trustees.

88. Any dividend or other moneys payable in respect of a share may be paid by cheque sent by post to the registered address of the person entitled or, if two or more persons are the holders of the share, or are jointly entitled to it by reason of the death or bankruptcy of the holder, to the registered address of that one of those persons who is first named in the register of members or to such person and to such address as the person or persons entitled may in writing direct. Every cheque shall be made payable to the order of the person or persons entitled or to such other person as the person or persons entitled may in writing direct and payment of the cheque shall be a good discharge to the company. Any joint holder or other person jointly entitled to a share as aforesaid may give receipts for any dividend or other moneys payable in respect of the share.

89. No dividend or other moneys payable in respect of a share shall bear interest against the company unless otherwise provided by the rights attached to the share.

90. Any dividend which has remained unclaimed for twelve years from the date when it became due for payment shall, if the directors so resolve, be forfeited and cease to remain owing by the company.

Accounts

91. No member shall (as such) have any right of inspecting any accounting records or other book or document of the company except as conferred by statute or authorised by the directors or by ordinary resolution of the company.

Notices

92. Any notice to be given to or by any person pursuant to the Articles (other than a notice calling a meeting of the directors) shall be in writing or shall be given using electronic communications to an address for the time being notified for that purpose to the person giving the notice.

93. No member shall be entitled to have a notice served on him at any address not within the United Kingdom; and any member whose registered address is not within the United Kingdom may, by notice in writing or electronically, require the company to register an address within the United Kingdom, which, for the purpose of the service of notices, shall be deemed to be his registered address. Any member not having a registered address within the United Kingdom, and not having given notice as aforesaid, shall be deemed to have received in due course any notice which shall have been displayed in the company's office and shall remain there for the space of forty-eight hours, and such notice shall be deemed to have been received by such member at the expiration of twenty-four hours from the time when it shall have been so first displayed.

In this Article and in Article 92 'address' in relation to elecronic communications includes any number or address used for the purpose of such communications.

94. It shall not be necessary to give notice of general meetings to any person entitled to a share in consequence of the death or bankruptcy of a member unless such person shall have been duly registered as a member of the company.

95. Any notice if served by post shall be deemed to have been served at the expiration of twenty-four hours after it has been posted; or in the case of a notice contained in an electronic communication at the expiration of 24 hours after the time it was sent; and in proving such service it shall be sufficient to prove that the envelope containing the notice was properly addressed prepaid and posted. Proof that a notice contained in an electronic communication was sent in accordance with guidance issued by the Institute of Chartered Secretaries and Administrators shall be conclusive evidence that the notice was given.

Arbitration

96. If and whenever any difference shall arise between the company and any of the members or their respective representatives touching the construction of any of the Articles herein contained, or any act, matter, or thing made or done, or to be made or done, or omitted, or in regard to the rights and liabilities arising hereunder, or arising out of the relation existing between the parties by reason of these presents or of the Statutes, or any of them, such differences shall be forthwith referred to two arbitrators – one to be appointed by each party in difference – or to an umpire to be chosen by the arbitrators before entering on the consideration of the matters referred to them, and every such reference shall be conducted in accordance with the provisions of the Arbitration Acts.

Winding-up

97. With the sanction of an extraordinary resolution of the members and any other sanction required by the Act any part of the assets of the company, including any shares in other companies, may be divided between the members of the company *in specie*, or may be vested in trustees for the benefit of such members, and the liquidation of the company may be closed and the company dissolved, but so that no member shall be compelled to accept any shares whereon there is any liability.

Names, Addresses and Descriptions

SARAH RICHES
1 High Street,
Barchester

AUTHOR/LECTURER

DENIS KEENAN
2 Low Street,
Barchester

AUTHOR/LECTURER

Dated 3 March 1998
Witness to the above signatures:
    John Green
    3 Middle Street,
    Barchester

Note: Under the Electronic Communications Order 2000 where the Articles are delivered to the Registrar otherwise than, as here, in legible form and are authenticated by each subscriber in such manner as is directed by the Registrar the requirement for signing in the presence of at least one witness and for attestation of (witness of) the signature is not needed.

SPECIMEN ANNUAL RETURN

Companies House has obviously not issued a shuttle document in regard to our fictitious company. However, since a company may as an alternative make the annual return on Form 363a, as where it wishes to change the date of submission before the receipt of the shuttle document, we have used that instead. Form 363a does not involve preparation and issue by Companies House but contains the same information about the company as Form 363s.

Companies House
— for the record —

363a

Please complete in typescript,
or in bold black capitals.

CHFP000

Annual Return

Company Number | 138 3617

Company Name in full | RICHES KEENAN

PUBLISHING LIMITED

SPECIMEN

| | Day | Month | Year |

Date of this return
The information in this return is made up to

0 4 / 0 4 / 2 0 0 2

Date of next return
If you wish to make your next return
to a date earlier than the anniversary
of this return please show the date here.
Companies House will then send a form
at the appropriate time.

| | Day | Month | Year |

3 1 / 0 3 / 2 0 0 3

Registered Office
Show here the address **at the date of
this return.**

140 HIGH STREET

*Any change of
registered office*
must *be notified
on form 287.*

Post town | BARCHESTER

County / Reg. | BARCHESTERSHIRE

UK Postcode | BB2 6 0YE

Principal business activities

Show trade classification code number(s)
for the principal activity or activities.

2211

If the code number cannot be determined,
give a brief description of principal activity.

Companies House receipt date barcode

When you have completed and signed the form please send it to the
Registrar of Companies at:
Companies House, Crown Way, Cardiff, CF14 3UZ   DX 33050 Cardiff
for companies registered in England and Wales
or
Companies House, 37 Castle Terrace, Edinburgh, EH1 2EB
for companies registered in Scotland   **DX 235 Edinburgh**

Form revised September 1999

Page 1

Fig 6.5 Specimen annual return

Comment The number 2211 is the Standard Industrial Classification (SIC) Code for the principal business activity of a company. Our business is the publishing of books and 2211 is the relevant classification.

Register of members

If the register of members is not kept at the registered office, state here where it is kept.

DALTON & CO

CHARTERED ACCOUNTANTS, 120 HIGH STREET

Post town BARCHESTER

County / ~~Region~~ BARCHESTERSHIRE UK Postcode B B 2 6 0 Y E

Register of Debenture holders

If there is a register of debenture holders, or a duplicate of any such register or part of it, which is not kept at the registered office, state here where it is kept.

DALTON & CO

CHARTERED ACCOUNTANTS, 120 HIGH STREET

Post town BARCHESTER

County / ~~Region~~ BARCHESTERSHIRE UK Postcode B B 2 6 0 Y E

Company type

Public limited company	
Private company limited by shares	X
Private company limited by guarantee without share capital	
Private company limited by shares exempt under section 30	
Private company limited by guarantee exempt under section 30	
Private unlimited company with share capital	
Private unlimited company without share capital	

Please tick the appropriate box

Company Secretary

Details of a new company secretary must be notified on form 288a.

(Please photocopy this area to provide details of joint secretaries).

* Voluntary details.

If a partnership give the names and addresses of the partners or the name of the partnership and office address.

Usual residential address must be given. In the case of a corporation or a Scottish firm, give the registered or principal office address.

Name * Style / Title MS

Forename(s) JANE MARY

Surname WILLIAMS

Address 25 MIDDLE STREET

Post town BARCHESTER

County / ~~Region~~ BARCHESTERSHIRE UK Postcode B B 2 6 9 A N

Country ENGLAND

Page 2

Fig 6.5 *(continued)*

Directors

Details of new directors must be notified on form 288a

Please list directors in alphabetical order.

Name * Style / Title | M S

Directors In the case of a director that is a corporation or a Scottish firm, the name is the corporate or firm name.

| | Day | Month | Year |

Date of birth | 1 6 / 0 4 / 1 9 6 0

Forename(s) | SARAH

Surname | RICHES

Address | 1 HIGH STREET

Usual residential address must be given. In the case of a corporation or a Scottish firm, give the registered or principal office address.

Post town | BARCHESTER

County / Region | BARCHESTERSHIRE UK Postcode | B B 2 6 O Y E

Country | ENGLAND **Nationality** | BRITISH

Business occupation | AUTHOR/LECTURER

* Voluntary details.

Name * Style / Title | MR

Directors In the case of a director that is a corporation or a Scottish firm, the name is the corporate or firm name.

| Day | Month | Year |

Date of birth | 1 2 / 0 8 / 1 9 4 6

Forename(s) | DENIS JOSEPH

Surname | KEENAN

Address | 2 LOW STREET

Usual residential address must be given. In the case of a corporation or a Scottish firm, give the registered or principal office address.

Post town | BARCHESTER

County / Region | BARCHESTERSHIRE UK Postcode | B B 2 6 O Y E

Country | ENGLAND **Nationality** | BRITISH

Business occupation | AUTHOR/JOURNALIST

Page 3

Fig 6.5 *(continued)*

	Class *(e.g. Ordinary/Preference)*	Number of shares issued	Aggregate Nominal Value *(i.e Number of shares issued multiplied by nominal value per share, or total amount of stock)*
Issued share capital Enter details of all the shares in issue at the date of this return.			
	ORDINARY	10,000	10,000
	Totals	10,000	10,000

List of past and present shareholders
(Use attached schedule where appropriate)
A full list is required if one was not
included with either of the last two
returns.

There were no changes in the period ✓

        paper   in another format

A list of changes is enclosed ☐ ☐

A full list of shareholders is enclosed ✓ ☐

Certificate

I certify that the information given in this return is true to the best of my knowledge and belief.

Signed | J. M. Williams. | **Date** | 10 APRIL 2002

† Please delete as appropriate.

† a director /secretary

When you have signed the return send it with the fee to the Registrar of Companies. Cheques should be made payable to **Companies House.**

This return includes | ONE | continuation sheets.
(enter number)

Please give the name, address, telephone number, and if available, a DX number and Exchange, for the person Companies House should contact if there is any query.

JANE MARY WILLIAMS
140 HIGH STREET BARCHESTER
BB26 9AN   Tel | 0122921 4066 EXT 20

DX number | DX exchange |

Page 4

Fig 6.5 *(continued)*

List of past and present shareholders
Schedule to form 363a

CHFP000

Company Number 1 3 8 3 6 1 5

Company Name in full RICHES KEENAN PUBLISHING LTD

➤ Changes to shareholders particulars or details of the amount of stock or shares transferred must be completed each year
➤ You must provide a "full list" of all the company shareholders on:
  ● The company's first annual return following incorporation;
  ● Every third annual return after a full list has been provided
➤ List the company shareholders in alphabetic order or provide an index
➤ List joint shareholders consecutively

Shareholders' details	Class and number of shares or amount of stock held	Shares or amount of stock transferred *(if appropriate)*	
		Class and number of shares or amount of stock transferred	Date of registration of transfer
Name SARAH RICHES Address 1 HIGH STREET BARCHESTER UK Postcode B B 4 0 Y E	6,000		
Name DENIS JOSEPH KEENAN Address 2 LOW STREET BARCHESTER UK Postcode B B 2 6 0 B 6	4,000		
Name Address UK Postcode L L L L L L L			

9/99

Fig 6.5 *(continued)*

1 Able and Ben are the promoters of Wye Ltd and are the two subscribers to the memorandum. The documents required to be sent to the Registrar of Companies in order to obtain the incorporation of Wye Ltd are ready to go. One of Wye Ltd's objects is to acquire the business of John Wye. John is getting difficult and insists that a contract for the sale of his business shall be signed now or the deal is off.

Advise Able and Ben, who do not want to lose the opportunity to acquire John Wye's undertaking.

2 The articles of association of Trent Ltd state that Cyril and David are appointed until aged 60 as Company Secretary and Chief Accountant respectively at salaries of £30,000 per annum. Cyril and David took up their posts five years ago, when they were 35 and 40 respectively.

(a) Cyril has received a letter from the Chairman of Trent Ltd discharging him from the post of Company Secretary. Cyril would like to retain the job;

(b) David has given his resignation to the Board of Trent Ltd but the Board will not accept it.

Advise Cyril and David.

3 Derwent Ltd has suffered declining profits for four years. The directors have not declared a dividend for three years and in order to avoid facing the shareholders did not call an AGM last year.

Eric, who holds shares in Derwent, has got together with some of his fellow shareholders to form a group to see what can be done to get the company better managed.

Write a letter to Eric advising him and telling him how the group should proceed in practical terms.

4 Severn Ltd runs a very successful business and makes a good profit. However, over the past few years the controlling directors have increased their remuneration so that it absorbs all the profits. Jane, who is a minority shareholder not on the board, gets no dividends and wishes to do something about this state of affairs.

Explain to Jane what action she should take.

5 As Secretary of Ouse Ltd write a memorandum for the Board explaining the differences between raising finance –
(a) by an issue of shares;
(b) by an issue of unsecured loan stock;
(c) by an issue of debentures secured by a floating charge over the company's asets; and
(d) by an issue of preference shares.

6 (a) How is the voluntary winding-up of a company brought about?
(b) What decides whether a voluntary winding-up is controlled:
(i) by the members, or
(ii) by the creditors?

7 In relation to corporate insolvency distinguish between an administrator and an administrative receiver.

Part 3

BUSINESS TRANSACTIONS

Chapter 7

INTRODUCTION TO THE LAW OF CONTRACT

BUSINESS CONTRACTING – GENERALLY

Once the businessman has decided on the particular form of business organisation that suits his needs, he can concentrate on his main purpose: establishing and building up the business. This will involve acquiring premises and equipment, taking on employees, buying raw materials and stock, marketing the product or service and meeting orders. Underpinning all these business transactions is the presence of a contract.

Most people think that a contract is a formal written document which has been signed by the parties in the presence of independent witnesses. If all contracts took this form there would be little room for argument about whether the parties had entered into a legally binding agreement, the obligations they had undertaken or the consequences of failing to carry out the terms of the agreement. In practice, however, few contracts are like this. The vast majority of contracts are entered into without formalities. The parties may even be unaware of the legal significance of their actions. Think about the agreements you have made over the past week:

- buying a newspaper;
- taking the bus or train into work or college;
- agreeing to complete an assignment by a particular date;
- getting a cup of coffee at breaktime;
- arranging to meet a friend for lunch.

Can all these transactions be classed as contracts? You probably feel that some of them were never intended to have legal consequences. So, what then is a contract? When is a contract formed? What are the obligations of the parties to a contract? What happens if either party breaks the agreement? The answers to these questions are provided by the law of contract.

The foundations of the present-day law of contract were laid in the 19th century. This period in our history saw the rapid expansion of trade and industry, and, inevitably, an increase in the volume of commercial disputes. Businessmen turned to the courts for a solution. Gradually, the judges developed a body of settled rules which reflected both the commercial background of the disputes from which they arose and the prevailing beliefs of the time. The dominant economic philosophy of the 19th century was *laissez-faire* individualism – the view that the state should not meddle in the affairs of business and that individuals should be free to determine their own destinies. This philosophy was mirrored in the law of contract by two assumptions: freedom of contract and equality of bargaining power. The judges assumed that everyone was free to choose which contracts they entered into and the terms on which they did so. If negotiations could not produce an acceptable basis for agreement, the parties were, in theory, free to take their business elsewhere. The parties were deemed to be of equal bargaining strength. The judges' assumptions produced an acceptable legal framework for the regulation of business transactions. Parliament, too, played its part by codifying parts of the common law of particular relevance to the businessman; for example, the law relating to contracts for the sale of goods became the Sale of Goods Act 1893 (now the Sale of Goods Act 1979). However, the same basic rules were applied in situations where one of the parties was in a weak bargaining position. Employees, consumers and borrowers, for example, found themselves without adequate protection from the law. It has been necessary for Parliament to intervene to redress the balance between employers and employees, businessmen and consumers, lenders and borrowers. In these areas, the concept of freedom of contract has been modified.

This section is concerned with the legal framework governing the supply of goods and services. It explores the nature and extent of any liability which may be incurred as a consequence of a business transaction, whether between one businessman and another, or between a businessman and a consumer. In order to understand these specific areas of business law, it is necessary first to look at the basic ground rules of the law of contract.

NATURE OF A CONTRACT

A contract has been defined as a legally binding agreement or, in the words of Sir Frederick Pollock: 'A promise or set of promises which the law will enforce'. However, not all promises or agreements give rise to contracts. If you agreed to keep the house tidy while your parents were away on holiday, you would not expect to find yourself in the county court being sued for breach of contract if you failed to do so. So what kinds of agreements does the law recognise as creating enforceable rights and duties?

TYPES OF CONTRACT

Contracts may he divided into two broad classes:

1 Speciality contracts. These formal contracts are also known as deeds. Formerly, these contracts had to be in writing and 'signed, sealed and delivered'. However, the Law of Property (Miscellaneous Provisions) Act 1989 abolished the requirement for a seal on a deed executed by an individual. The formalities now are that the signature of the person making the deed must be witnessed and attested. (Attestation involves making a statement to the effect that the deed has been signed in the presence of a witness.) It must be clear on the face of the document that it is intended to be a deed. The previous rule that a deed must be written on paper or parchment has also been abolished. The use of seals by corporate bodies is unaffected by the Act. Certain contracts, such as conveyances of land, must be made in the form of a deed, but these are relatively few in number.

2 Simple contracts. Contracts which are not deeds are known as simple contracts. They are informal contracts and may be made in any way – orally, in writing, or they may be implied from conduct.

ESSENTIALS OF A VALID CONTRACT

The essential ingredients of a contract are:

1 Agreement. An agreement is formed when one party accepts the offer of another.
2 Consideration. The parties must show that their agreement is part of a bargain; each side must promise to give or do something for the other.
3 Intention. The law will not concern itself with purely domestic or social arrangements. The parties must have intended their agreement to have legal consequences.
4 Form. In some cases, certain formalities must be observed.
5 Capacity. The parties must be legally capable of entering into a contract.
6 Genuineness of consent. The agreement must have been entered into freely and involve a 'meeting of minds'.
7 Legality. The purpose of the agreement must not be illegal or contrary to public policy.

A contract which possesses all these requirements is said to be valid. If one of the parties fails to live up to his promises, he may be sued for a breach of contract. The absence of an essential element will render the contract either void, voidable or unenforceable.

1 Void contracts. The term 'void contract' is a contradiction in terms since the whole transaction is regarded as a nullity. It means that at no time has there been a contract between the parties. Any goods or money obtained under the agreement must be returned. Where items have been resold to a third party, they may be recovered by the original owner. A contract may be rendered void, for example, by some forms of mistake.

2 Voidable contracts. Contracts founded on a misrepresentation and some agreements made by minors fall into this category. The contract may operate in every respect as a valid contract unless and until one of the parties takes steps to avoid it. Anything obtained under the contract must be

returned, in so far as this is possible. If goods have been resold before the contract was avoided, the original owner will not be able to reclaim them.

3 Unenforceable contracts. An unenforceable contract is a valid contract but it cannot be enforced in the courts if one of the parties refuses to carry out its terms. Items received under the contract cannot be reclaimed. Contracts of guarantee are unenforceable unless evidenced in writing. The essential elements of a valid contract will now be considered in more detail. Remember – just as a house must have sound foundations, walls and a roof, so must a contract have all its essentials to be valid.

Agreement

The first requisite of any contract is an agreement. At least two parties are required; one of them, the **offeror**, makes an offer which the other, the **offeree**, accepts.

Offer

An offer is a proposal made on certain terms by the offeror together with a promise to be bound by that proposal if the offeree accepts the stated terms. An offer may be made expressly – for example, when an employer writes to a prospective employee to offer him a job – or impliedly, by conduct – for example, bidding at an auction.

The offer may be made to a specific person, in which case it can only be accepted by that person. If an offer is made to a group of people, it may be accepted by any member of the group. An offer can even be made to the whole world, such as where someone offers a reward for the return of a lost dog. The offer can be accepted by anyone who knows about it, and finds the dog.

Carlill v Carbolic Smoke Ball Co (1893)
The company inserted advertisements in a number of newspapers stating that it would pay £100 to anyone who caught 'flu after using its smoke balls as directed for 14 days. The company further stated that to show its sincerity in the matter it had deposited £1,000 at the Alliance Bank to meet possible claims. Mrs Carlill bought one of the smoke balls, used it as directed but still caught 'flu. She claimed the £100 reward but was refused, so she sued the company in contract. The company put forward a number of arguments in its defence: (a) it claimed that it had attempted to contract with the whole world, which was clearly impossible. The Court of Appeal held that the company had made an offer to the whole world and it would be liable to anyone who came forward and performed the required conditions. (b) The company further submitted that the advertisement was in the nature of a trade 'puff' and too vague to be a contract. The court dealt with this argument by asking what ordinary members of the public would understand by the advertisement. The court took the view that the details of use were sufficiently definite to constitute the terms of a contract and that the reference to the £1,000 deposited at a bank was evidence of an intention to be bound. (c) The company also argued that the claimant had not provided any consideration in return for its promise. The court held that the inconvenience of using the smoke ball as directed was sufficient consideration. (d) Finally, the company submitted that there was no notification of acceptance in accordance with the general rule. The court held that in this kind of contract, which is known as a unilateral contract, acceptance consists of performing the requested act and notification of acceptance is not necessary.

The court concluded that Mrs Carlill was entitled to recover the £100 reward.

It is important to identify when a true offer has been made because once it is accepted the parties are bound. If the words and actions of one party do not amount to an offer, however, the other person cannot, by saying 'I accept', create a contract. A genuine offer must, therefore, be distinguished from what is known as an 'invitation to treat'.

An invitation to treat

This is where a person holds himself out as ready to receive offers, which he may then either accept or reject. The following are examples of invitations to treat.

1 The display of goods with a price ticket attached in a shop window or on a supermarket shelf. This is not an offer to sell but an invitation for customers to make an offer to buy.

Fisher v Bell (1960)
A shopkeeper had a flick-knife on display in his shop window. He was charged with offering for sale an offensive weapon contrary to the provisions of the Restriction of Offensive Weapons Act 1959. His conviction was

quashed on appeal. The Divisional Court of the Queen's Bench Division held that the display of goods with a price ticket attached in a shop window is an invitation to treat and not an offer to sell. (The Restriction of Offensive Weapons Act 1961 was passed soon after this case to close the loophole in the law.)

Pharmaceutical Society of Great Britain v *Boots Cash Chemists (Southern) Ltd* (1953)

Boots operated a self-service, 'supermarket' system at their Edgware branch in which their merchandise, including drugs on the Poisons List, was laid out on open shelves around the shop. Customers selected their purchases from the shelves, placed them in a wire basket and paid for them at a cash desk which was supervised by a registered pharmacist. The Pharmaceutical Society claimed that by operating this system Boots had committed an offence contrary to s 18 of the Pharmacy and Poisons Act 1933, which requires that the sale of drugs included on the Poisons List must take place in the presence of a qualified pharmacist. The Pharmaceutical Society argued that the sale took place when a customer placed his purchase in the basket, which was not supervised by a pharmacist. The Court of Appeal held that the display of drugs on the open shelf constituted an invitation to treat. The customer made the offer to buy at the cash desk and the sale was completed when the cashier accepted the offer. Since the cash desks were supervised by a registered pharmacist, the requirements of the Act had been fulfilled and, therefore, Boots had not committed an offence.

Thus, it is a clearly established principle of civil law that if goods are displayed for sale with an incorrect price ticket attached to them, the retailer is not obliged to sell at that price. Under the criminal law, however, the retailer may find himself facing a prosecution for a breach of the provisions of the Consumer Protection Act 1987.

2　Advertisements, catalogues and brochures. Many businesses make use of the press, TV, commercial radio and, in more recent times, the Internet, to sell their products direct to the public. Even if the word 'offer' is used, the advertisement is still an invitation to treat.

Partridge v *Crittenden* (1968)

Partridge placed an advertisement in the *Cage and Aviary Birds* magazine, which read ''Bramblefinch cocks, bramblefinch hens, 25s each'. A Mr Thompson replied to the advertisement and was sent a bramblefinch hen. Partridge was charged with 'offering for sale' a wild bird contrary to the provisions of the Protection of Birds Act 1954 and was convicted at the magistrates' court. His conviction was quashed on appeal to the Divisional Court of the Queen's Bench Division. The Court held that since the advertisement constituted an invitation to treat and not an offer to sell, Partridge was not guilty of the offence with which he had been charged.

Comment. It should be noted that the word 'offer' did not appear in the advertisement in this case. However, in *Spencer* v *Harding* (1870) a circular containing the word 'offer' was held to be an invitation to treat.

An advertisement placed in a newspaper or magazine by a mail order firm constitutes an invitation to treat: the customer makes the offer, which may be accepted or rejected by the mail order firm.

Similar principles apply to electronic trading via the Internet, otherwise known as e-commerce. Posting advertisements on a website amounts to an invitation to treat; by selecting the products and services required, the customer is making an offer to buy, which may be accepted or rejected by the seller. So if a company by mistake advertises on its website £200 video recorders for sale at £2, it could refuse to sell the goods at the advertised price.

Although most advertisements will be treated as invitations to treat, there are some situations where an advertisement may be regarded as a definite offer, e.g. as in *Carlill* v *Carbolic Smoke Ball Co* (1893).

3　Company prospectuses. When a company wishes to raise capital by selling shares to the public, it must issue a prospectus (an invitation to treat). Potential investors apply for shares (the offer) and the directors then decide to whom to allot shares (the acceptance).

4　Auctions. At an auction sale the call for bids by an auctioneer is an invitation to treat. The bids are offers. The auctioneer selects the highest bid and acceptance is completed by the fall of the hammer.

Payne v *Cave* (1789)

The defendant made the highest bid for the claimant's goods at an auction sale, but he withdrew his bid before the fall of the auctioneer's hammer. It was held that the defendant was not bound to purchase the goods. His bid amounted to an offer which he was entitled to withdraw at any time before the auctioneer signified acceptance by knocking down the hammer. The common law rule laid down in this case has now been codified in s 57(2) of the Sale of Goods Act 1979.

Advertising a forthcoming auction sale does not amount to an offer to hold it.

Harris v Nickerson (1873)

The defendant, an auctioneer, advertised in the London papers that a sale of various goods including office furniture would take place in Bury St Edmunds. The claimant travelled from London to attend the sale, but the items of furniture he had been commissioned to buy were withdrawn from the sale. It was held that the defendant auctioneer was not obliged to compensate the claimant for a wasted journey. Advertising that a sale of certain items will take place is a mere declaration of intention. It does not create a binding contract with anyone who acts on the advertisement by attending the sale.

However, advertising that an auction will be 'without reserve' amounts to an offer by the auctioneer that once the auction has commenced the lot will be sold to the highest bidder however low the bids might be (*Warlow v Harrison* (1859) and more recently *Barry v Heathcote Ball & Co (Commercial Auctions) Ltd* (2000)).

5 Tenders. Large undertakings, such as public authorities, often place contracts by inviting interested firms to tender (offer) for the business. An invitation to tender can give rise to a binding obligation on the part of the inviter to consider tenders submitted in accordance with the conditions of the tender.

Blackpool and Fylde Aero Club Ltd v Blackpool Council (1990)

The defendant council invited the claimant club, together with six other parties, to tender for the concession to offer pleasure flights from the council-owned airport. The invitation to tender required tenders to be submitted in accordance with an elaborate procedure and stated that tenders received after 12 noon on 17 March 1983 would not be considered. The club's tender was delivered by hand and placed in the letterbox in the Town Hall at 11 am on 17 March. Unfortunately, the letterbox was not cleared until the next day. The club's tender was marked late and was not considered by the council. The concession was awarded to another tenderer. The club sued for breach of a contract to consider tenders which conform with the requirements specified by the council. The Court of Appeal held that by adopting a formal tendering procedure the council impliedly undertook to consider all conforming tenders. The council's invitation to tender was an offer to consider all qualifying tenders and the submission by the club of a tender within the time limit was an acceptance. The club was entitled to damages for breach of contract.

The acceptance of a tender has different legal consequences, depending on the wording of the original invitation to tender. There are two possibilities:

Example 1

The Metropolitan Borough of Newtown invites tenders for the supply of 100 tons of potatoes for the use of the School Meals Service in the Borough from 1 January to 31 December. The acceptance of a tender creates a legally binding contract. The successful supplier must deliver 100 tons of potatoes which the Borough must pay for.

Example 2

The Metropolitan Borough of Newtown invites tenders for the supply of potatoes, not exceeding 100 tons, for the period 1 January to 31 December as and when required by the School Meals Service. The acceptance of a tender in this situation has the effect of creating a standing offer on the part of the supplier to deliver potatoes if and when orders are placed by the School Meals Service. Each time an order is placed by the School Meals Service it constitutes an acceptance which creates an individual contract. If the supplier refuses to fulfil the order, he will be in breach of contract (*Great Northern Rly Co v Witham* (1873)). This form of tender does not prevent the supplier giving notice that he will not supply potatoes in the future or the School Meals Service from not placing orders, if they decide to cut potatoes from the school dinner menu.

The process of competitive tendering came under scrutiny in the following case.

Harvela Investments Ltd v Royal Trust Co of Canada Ltd (1985)

The first defendants decided to dispose of shares in a company by sealed competitive tender. They sent identical telexes to two prospective purchasers, the claimants and the second defendants, inviting tenders and promising to accept the highest offer. The claimants bid $2,175,000, while the second defendants bid '$2,100,000 or $100,000 in excess of any other offer'. The first defendants accepted the second defendants' offer. The House of Lords held that the second defendants' 'referential bid' was invalid. The decision was a practical one. The purpose of competitive tendering is to secure a sale at the best possible price. If both parties had submitted a referential bid, it would have been impossible to ascertain an offer and no sale would have resulted from the process.

6 Statements of price in negotiations for the sale of land. Where the subject matter of a proposed sale is land, the courts are reluctant to find a definite offer to sell unless very clearly stated.

Harvey v Facey (1893)

Harvey sent a telegram to Facey. 'Will you sell us Bumper Hall Pen? Telegraph lowest cash price ...' Harvey telegraphed his response: 'We agree to buy Bumper Hall Pen for £900 asked by you. Please send us your title deeds.' The Judicial Committee of the Privy Council held that there was no contract. Facey's reply to Harvey's initial enquiry was not an offer to sell but merely a statement of the price he might be prepared to sell at if he wished to sell. As Facey had not made an offer, Harvey's second telegram could not amount to an acceptance.

Clifton v Palumbo (1944)

In the course of negotiations for the sale of a large estate, the claimant wrote to the defendant: 'I am prepared to offer my Lytham estate for £600,000. I also agree that sufficient time shall be given to you to complete a schedule of completion.' The Court of Appeal held that these words did not amount to a firm offer to sell, but rather a preliminary statement as to price.

Gibson v Manchester City Council (1979)

In 1970 the Council adopted a policy of selling its council houses to tenants. The City Treasurer wrote to Mr Gibson in February 1971 stating that the council 'may be prepared to sell' the freehold of his house to him at a discount price. The letter invited Mr Gibson to make a formal application which he duly did. In May 1971 control of the council passed from the Conservatives to Labour and the policy of selling council houses was reversed. Only legally binding transactions were allowed to proceed. The council did not proceed with Mr Gibson's application. The House of Lords held that the City Treasurer's letter was an invitation to treat and not an offer to sell. Mr Gibson's application was the offer and, as this had not been accepted by the council, a binding contract had not been formed.

Termination of the offer

An offer can end in a number of ways:

1 **By acceptance.** An offer which has been accepted constitutes a contract. That offer is no longer available for acceptance.

2 **By rejection.** An offer is rejected if:

(a) the offeree notifies the offeror that he does not wish to accept the offer;

(b) the offeree attempts to accept subject to certain conditions;

(c) the offeree makes a counter-offer.

Hyde v Wrench (1840)

Wrench offered to sell his farm to Hyde for £1,000. Hyde replied with a 'counter-offer' of £950, which was refused. Hyde then said that he was prepared to meet the original offer of £1,000. It was held that no contract had been formed. The 'counter-offer' of £950 had the effect of rejecting Wrench's original offer.

Sometimes it is difficult to decide whether the offeree is making a counter-offer or simply asking for more information about the offer. A request for more information will not reject the offer.

Stevenson v McLean (1880)

The defendant offered to sell a quantity of iron to the claimants for cash. The claimants asked whether they could have credit terms. When no reply to their enquiry was forthcoming, the claimants accepted the terms of the original offer. Meanwhile, the defendant had sold the iron elsewhere. It was held that the enquiry was a request for more information, not a rejection of the offer. The defendant was liable for breach of contract.

3 **By revocation before acceptance.** An offer may be revoked (withdrawn) at any time before acceptance but it will only be effective when the offeree learns about it.

Byrne v Van Tienhoven (1880)

The defendants posted a letter in Cardiff on 1 October to the claimants in New York, offering to sell them 1,000 boxes of tinplates. On 8 October the defendants posted a letter withdrawing the offer, which was received by the claimants on 20 October. However, on 11 October the claimants telegraphed their acceptance which they confirmed by letter posted on 15 October. It was held that a revocation takes effect only when communicated to the offeree. The contract in this case came into existence when the defendants' offer was accepted by the claimants on 11 October. The letter of revocation was ineffective as it was received after the acceptance was complete.

It is not necessary that the offeror himself should tell the offeree that the offer has been revoked; the information may be conveyed by a reliable third party.

Dickinson v Dodds (1876)
The defendant, on Wednesday, offered to sell some property to the claimant, the offer to be left open until 9 am, Friday. On Thursday, the claimant heard from a Mr Berry that the defendant had sold the property to someone else. Nevertheless, the claimant wrote a letter of acceptance which was handed to the defendant at 7 am on the Friday morning. The Court of Appeal held that as the claimant had heard about the revocation from Berry, who was a reliable source, the offer was no longer available for acceptance. No contract had been formed.

In *Dickinson v Dodds* the offer was expressed to be open until Friday at 9 am. Such an offer may be revoked before the end of the time limit, unless it has already been accepted.

Routledge v Grant (1828)
The defendant offered to buy the claimant's house, giving the claimant six weeks to consider the proposal. It was held that the defendant could withdraw the offer at any time before acceptance, even though the deadline had not yet expired. The claimant's attempt to accept the offer after it had been withdrawn was ineffective.

A promise to keep an offer open will be binding if it can be enforced as a separate contract. A legally binding option will be created if the offeree provides some consideration in return for the offeror's promise to keep the offer open.

Mountford v Scott (1975)
The purchaser of a house paid the seller £1 for an option to buy, exercisable within six months. The Court of Appeal held that the seller could not withdraw the offer before the option expired.

The Law Revision Committee recommended in 1937 that a promise to keep an offer open for a definite period of time or until the happening of a specific

event should be binding even if there is no consideration for the promise. In 1975 the Law Commission made a similar recommendation but limited to promises made 'in the course of a business'.

The effect of revocation in the case of a potentially 'unilateral' contract, such as in *Carlill*'s case, is not straightforward. Where the offer has been made to the whole world, as, for example, where a reward has been offered in a newspaper for the return of a lost dog, a revocation will probably be effective as against anyone who has yet to start looking for the dog, provided it is given the same publicity as the original offer of the reward. However, if someone has started to perform the act requested in the offer, the offer cannot be revoked.

Errington v Errington (1952)
A father bought a house for his son and daughter-in-law to live in. The father paid a deposit of one-third of the purchase price and borrowed the balance from a building society. He told his son and daughter-in-law that if they paid the mortgage he would convey the house to them when all the instalments had been paid. The Court of Appeal held that the father's offer could not be revoked provided the son and daughter-in-law continued to make the mortgage payments.

4 **If the offer lapses.** The offeror may stipulate that the offer is only open for a limited period of time. Once the time limit has passed, any acceptance will be invalid. Even if no time limit is mentioned, the offer will not remain open indefinitely. It must be accepted within a reasonable time.

Ramsgate Victoria Hotel Co v Montefiore (1866)
The defendant offered to buy shares in the claimant's company in June. The shares were eventually allotted in November. The defendant refused to take them up. The Court of Exchequer held that the defendant's offer to take shares had lapsed through an unreasonable delay in acceptance.

What is a reasonable time will vary with the type of contract.

5 **Death.** If the offeror dies after having made an offer and the offeree is notified of the death, any acceptance will be invalid. However, where the offeree accepts in ignorance of what has happened,

the fate of the offer seems to depend on the nature of the contract. An offer which involves the personal service of the offeror clearly cannot be enforced, but other offers may survive, be accepted and carried out by the deceased's personal representatives. If the offeree dies, there can be no acceptance. The offer was made to that person and no one else can accept.

6 Failure of a condition attached to the offer. An offer may be made subject to conditions. Such a condition may be stated expressly by the offeror or implied by the courts from the circumstances. If the condition is not satisfied, the offer is not capable of being accepted.

Financings Ltd v *Stimson* (1962)
The defendant saw a car at the premises of a dealer on 16 March. He wished to obtain the car on hire-purchase. He signed a form provided by the claimant finance company which stated that the agreement would be binding only when signed by the finance company. The defendant took possession of the car and paid the first instalment on 18 March. However, being dissatisfied with the car, he returned it to the dealer two days later. On the night of 24–25 March the car was stolen from the dealer's premises, but was recovered badly damaged. On 25 March the finance company signed the hire-purchase agreement, unaware of what had happened. The defendant refused to pay the instalments and was sued for breach of the hire-purchase agreement. The Court of Appeal held that the hire-purchase agreement was not binding because the defendant's offer to obtain the car on hire-purchase was subject to an implied condition that the car would remain in substantially the same state until acceptance. Since the implied condition had not been fulfilled at the time the finance company purported to accept, no contract had come into existence.

Acceptance

Once the presence of a valid offer has been established, the next stage in the formation of an agreement is to find an acceptance of that offer. The acceptance must be made while the offer is still open. It must be absolute and unqualified.

Unconditional acceptance

If the offeree attempts to vary the terms offered, this will be treated as a counter-offer. As we have already seen in *Hyde* v *Wrench* this has the effect

of rejecting the original offer. A similar problem exists in 'battle of forms' cases. This is where the offeror makes an offer on his own pre-printed standard form which contains certain terms, and the offeree accepts on his own standard form which contains conflicting terms.

Butler Machine Tool Co v *Ex-Cell-O Corp (England)* (1979)
The claimants offered to supply a machine tool to the defendants for £75,535. However, the quotation included a term which would entitle the sellers to increase this price (price-variation clause). The defendants accepted the offer on their own standard terms which did not provide for any variation of their quoted price. The claimants acknowledged the order. When the machine was delivered, the claimants claimed an extra £2,892 which the defendants refused to pay. The Court of Appeal held that the defendants had not unconditionally accepted the original offer. They had made a counter-offer which had been accepted by the claimants. The defendants' terms governed the contract. The claimants' action to recover the increase in price, therefore, failed.

One form of conditional acceptance is the use of the phrase 'subject to contract' in negotiations involving the sale of land. These words usually mean that the parties do not intend to be bound at that stage. However, if there is clear evidence of a contrary intention, a court may be prepared to find that a contract has been concluded despite the use of the customary words 'subject to contract' (*Alpenstow Ltd* v *Regalian Properties plc* (1985)). The advantage of 'subject to contract' agreements is that they allow either party to withdraw from the agreement at any time and for any reason without facing an action for breach of contract. The problem is that the parties may incur considerable expense on negotiations which do not ultimately result in a contract being formed. Some legal systems overcome this problem by imposing a duty to negotiate in good faith. English law, however, does not recognise such a duty and an agreement to negotiate will not be binding.

Walford v *Miles* (1992)
The defendants owned a photographic processing business, which they wished to sell. In 1985 there were unsuccessful negotiations with a company. In 1986, the claimants heard that the business was for sale for about

£2 million. The claimants were keen to buy at this price because they thought that the business had been considerably undervalued. In March 1987, the claimants and defendants reached a 'subject to contract' agreement for the sale of the business. The defendants asked for a letter, known as a 'comfort letter', from the claimants' bankers confirming that they would provide the finance for the deal and in return the defendants promised to terminate negotiations with any third parties. The comfort letter was provided as agreed but the defendants sold the business to the company which had made the unsuccessful offer in 1985. The claimants sued for breach of an implied term to negotiate in good faith. The House of Lords held that an agreement to negotiate is unenforceable because it lacks the requirement of certainty. In this case no time limit was given for exclusive negotiations. Their lordships indicated, however, that it would be possible to enter into a binding 'lock-out' agreement, i.e. an agreement to deal exclusively with one party and not to consider other offers for a limited period. The Court of Appeal upheld such an agreement in *Pitt* v *PHH Asset Management Ltd* (1993) (discussed later in this chapter).

Method of acceptance

An acceptance may take any form. It can be given orally or in writing but silence cannot normally amount to an acceptance.

Felthouse v Bindley (1862)

The claimant had been negotiating to buy his nephew's horse. He eventually wrote to his nephew: 'If I hear no more about him, I shall consider the horse is mine at £30 15s.' The nephew did not reply to this letter but he did ask the auctioneer, who had been engaged to sell all his farming stock, to keep the horse out of the sale, as he had sold it to his uncle. The auctioneer by mistake included the horse in the sale and was sued by the uncle in the tort of conversion. The basis of the uncle's claim was that the auctioneer had sold his property. The court held that the uncle had no claim. Although the nephew had mentally accepted the offer, some form of positive action was required for a valid acceptance. Since there was no contract between the uncle and nephew, ownership of the horse had not passed to the uncle.

Comment. This case established the principle that the offeree's silence or failure to act cannot constitute a valid acceptance. The rule has a particularly useful application to the problem of 'inertia selling'. This is where a trader sends unsolicited goods to a person's home, stipulating that if he does not receive a reply within a specified time, he will assume that his offer to sell the goods has been accepted and the indicated price is payable. The *Felthouse* rule makes it clear that a recipient of goods in these circumstances is not obliged to pay, because his silence or inaction cannot amount to an acceptance. Many people, however, have paid up in ignorance of the law.

More effective control of 'inertia selling' was introduced in the form of the Unsolicited Goods and Services Act 1971, which has now been updated and extended by the Consumer Protection (Distance Selling) Regulations 2000. The regulations outlaw the supply of unsolicited goods and services to consumers. The recipient of unsolicited goods may treat them as an unconditional gift. It is also an offence to make a demand for payment from a consumer for unsolicited goods or services.

Felthouse v *Bindley* would seem to suggest that only an oral or written acceptance will be valid. However, acceptance may be implied from a person's conduct.

Brogden v Metropolitan Railway Co (1877)

Brogden had supplied the railway company with coal for many years without the benefit of a formal agreement. Eventually the parties decided to put their relationship on a firmer footing. A draft agreement was drawn up by the company's agent and sent to Brogden. Brogden filled in some blanks, including the name of an arbitrator, marked it as 'approved' and returned it to the company's agent who put it in his drawer. Coal was ordered and supplied in accordance with the terms of the 'agreement'. However, a dispute arose between the parties and Brogden refused to supply coal to the company, denying the existence of a binding contract between them. The House of Lords held that a contract had been concluded. Brogden's amendments to the draft agreement amounted to an offer which was accepted by the company either when the first order was placed under the terms of the agreement or at the latest when the coal was supplied. By their conduct the parties had indicated their approval of the agreement.

Examples of acceptance by conduct include returning a lost dog in a reward case, or using a smoke ball in the prescribed manner in *Carlill* v *Carbolic Smoke Ball Co*. The offeror may state that the acceptance must be in a particular form. It follows that the offeror's wishes should be respected. So if he asks for an acceptance in writing, a verbal acceptance by telephone will not be valid. Sometimes the offeror may say 'reply by return post', when he really means 'reply quickly' and a telephone call would be acceptable. Provided that the chosen method of acceptance fulfils the intentions of the offeror, it will be binding.

Yates Building Co Ltd v R J Pulleyn & Sons (York) Ltd (1975)

The vendors of a piece of land stated that an option to buy it should be exercised by 'notice in writing . . . to be sent registered or recorded delivery'. The acceptance was sent by ordinary post. The Court of Appeal held that the vendor's intention was to ensure that they received written notification of acceptance. The requirement to use registered or recorded delivery was more in the nature of a helpful suggestion than a condition of acceptance.

Communication of acceptance

The general rule is that an acceptance must be communicated to the offeror, either by the offeree himself or by someone authorised by the offeree. The contract is formed at the time and place the acceptance is received by the offeror. If the post, however, is the anticipated method of communication between the parties, then acceptance is effective immediately the letter of acceptance is posted. Provided the letter is properly stamped, addressed and posted, the contract is formed on posting, even if the letter is delayed or never reaches its destination. This special rule was established in 1818.

Adams v Lindsell (1818)

On 2 September 1817 the defendants who were wool traders based in Huntingdon wrote to the claimants, who were woollen manufacturers in Bromsgrove, offering to sell them some wool and asking for an answer 'in course of post'. This letter was wrongly addressed and as a result it did not reach the claimants until 5 September. The same day the claimants posted a letter of acceptance which reached the defendants on 9 September. The evidence was that if the offer letter had been correctly addressed a reply 'in course of post' could have been expected by 7 September. On 8 September the defendants sold the wool to someone else. It was held that the contract was formed when the claimants posted their letter of acceptance. In reaching this conclusion the court may have been influenced by the fact that it was the defendants' misdirection of the offer letter which led to the delayed acceptance.

Household Fire Insurance Co v Grant (1879)

Grant applied for shares in the claimant company. A letter of allotment was posted but Grant never received it. When the company went into liquidation, Grant was asked, as a shareholder, to contribute the amount still outstanding on the shares he held. The Court of Appeal held that Grant was a shareholder of the company. The contract to buy shares was formed when the letter of allotment (acceptance) was posted.

The 'postal rules' have been applied to acceptances by telegram but not to more instantaneous methods of communication such as telex and telephone.

Entores v Miles Far East Corp (1955)

The claimants, a London company, made an offer to the defendants' agents in Amsterdam by means of a Telex message. The Dutch agents accepted the offer by the same method. The claimants later alleged that the defendants had broken their contract and wished to serve a writ (now claim form) on them, which they could do if the contract was made in England. The Court of Appeal held in favour of the claimants. The decision of the court was expressed by Parker LJ in the following terms: 'So far as Telex messages are concerned, though the despatch and receipt of a message is not completely instantaneous, the parties are to all intents and purposes in each other's presence just as if they were in telephonic communication, and I can see no reason for departing from the general rule that there is no binding contract until notice of the acceptance is received by the offeror. That being so, and since the offer . . . was made by the [claimants] in London and notification of the acceptance was received by them in London, the contract resulting therefrom was made in London.' The approach of the Court of Appeal was confirmed by the House of Lords in *Brinkibon v Stahag Stahl* (1982).

Acceptances sent by electronic means are likely to be treated in the same way as telephone or telex acceptances; the seller's acceptance will only be effective when received by the customer. The problem of applying this approach to e-commerce is that if a seller is doing business with customers based in different countries, the contract will be formed in the country (and jurisdiction) where the customer is based. E-traders can avoid these difficulties by confirming customers' orders by e-mail and asking the customer to confirm the purchase by clicking on a confirmation button. The effect of these precautions is that the contract will be concluded at the seller's place of business.

Clearly, the 'postal rules' are a potential problem for an offeror: if the letter of acceptance is lost in the post, he may be unaware that a binding contract has been formed. An offeror can protect himself by specifically stating that the acceptance is only complete when received on or before a certain date.

Holwell Securities v Hughes (1974)

Dr Hughes had agreed to grant Holwell Securities Ltd an option to buy his premises. The option, which would constitute the acceptance, was exercisable 'by notice in writing' to the doctor within six months. The company posted a letter of acceptance but it was never delivered. The Court of Appeal held that no contract had been formed. Since Dr Hughes had stipulated actual 'notice' of the acceptance, the postal rules did not apply. The acceptance would only be effective when received by the doctor.

Note that the postal rules only apply to the communication of acceptances: offers and revocations of offers must be communicated to be effective.

Consideration

On the previous pages we have seen how an agreement is formed – the requirements of offer and acceptance – but the mere fact of an agreement alone does not make a contract. The law concerns itself with bargains. This means that each side must promise to give or do something for the other. The element of exchange is known as 'consideration' and is an essential element of every valid simple contract. A promise of a gift will not be binding unless made in the form of a deed. Consideration can take two forms: executed or executory. What is the difference between them?

1 Executed consideration is where one party promises to do something in return for the act of another, e.g. reward cases.

Promise	Act
£10 reward offered for the return of 'Lucky' – black and white cat. Ring Mrs Smith (01308 215 8793).	David sees the advert in the local paper. He finds the cat, returns it to Mrs Smith and claims the reward.

'Cash with order' terms are an example of executed consideration.

2 Executory consideration is where the parties exchange promises to perform acts in the future, e.g. 'cash on delivery' terms.

Promise	Act
Jones & Co Ltd promises to pay £950 when a new computer is delivered.	Fastype Ltd promises to deliver the computer within six weeks.

Rules governing consideration

1 Consideration must not be in the past. If one party voluntarily performs an act, and the other party then makes a promise, the consideration for the promise is said to be in the past. Past consideration is regarded as no consideration at all.

Act	Promise
John gives Susan a lift home in his car after work.	On arrival, Susan offers John £1 towards the petrol but, finding that she has not any change, says she will give him the money the next day at work.

In this example, John cannot enforce Susan's promise to pay £1 because the consideration for the promise (giving the lift) is in the past. John would have given Susan the lift home without expecting payment and so there was no bargain between the parties.

Re McArdle (1951)

Mr McArdle died leaving a house to his wife for her lifetime and then to his children. While Mrs McArdle was still alive, one of the children and his wife moved into the house. The wife made a number of improvements to the house costing £488. After the work had been completed, all the children signed a document in which they promised to reimburse the wife when their father's estate was finally distributed. The Court of Appeal held that this was a case of past consideration. The promise to pay £488 to the wife was made after the improvements had been completed and was, therefore, not binding.

The rule about past consideration is not strictly followed. If, for example, a person is asked to perform a service, which he duly carries out, and later a promise to pay is made, the promise will be binding.

Re Casey's Patents, Stewart v Casey (1892)

Casey agreed to promote certain patents which had been granted to Stewart and another. (A patent gives the holder exclusive rights to profit from an invention.) Two years later Stewart wrote to Casey promising him a one-third share of the patents 'in consideration' of Casey's efforts. It was held that Stewart's original request raised an implication that Casey's work would be paid for. The later letter merely fixed the amount of the payment.

2 Consideration must move from the promisee. If A (the promisor) makes a promise to B (the promisee), the promise will only be enforceable (unless made in the form of a deed) if B can show that he has provided consideration in return for A's promise.

Tweddle v Atkinson (1861)

John Tweddle and William Guy agreed that they would pay a sum of money to Tweddle's son, William, who had married Guy's daughter. William Guy died without paying his share and William Tweddle sued his late father-in-law's executor (Atkinson). His claim failed because he had not provided any consideration for the promise to pay.

The rule that consideration must move from the promisee is closely related to the doctrine of privity of contract. This doctrine states that a person cannot be bound by or take advantage of a contract to which he was not a party. The doctrine of privity of contract and the exceptions to the rule, including the recent changes contained in the Contracts (Rights of Third Parties) Act 1999, will be examined in more detail later in this chapter. It should be noted at this point, however, that the 1999 Act does not change the requirement that the promisee must show consideration to enforce any promise not made in the form of a deed.

3 Consideration must not be illegal. The courts will not entertain an action where the consideration is contrary to a rule of law or is immoral. The question of legality will be considered in more detail later in this Chapter.

4 Consideration must be sufficient but need not be adequate. It must be possible to attach some value to the consideration but there is no requirement for the bargain to be strictly commercial. If a man is prepared to sell his Jaguar car for £1, the contract

will not fail for lack of consideration. The courts will not help someone who complains of making a bad bargain. The following are examples of cases where the consideration was of little value, but, nevertheless, it was held to be sufficient.

Thomas v Thomas (1842)

After the death of her husband, Mrs Thomas agreed to pay rent of £1 a year in order to continue living in the same house. It was held that the payment of £1 was valid consideration.

Chappell & Co Ltd v Nestlé Co Ltd (1959)

Nestlé was running a special offer whereby members of the public could obtain a copy of the record 'Rockin' Shoes' by sending off three wrappers from Nestlé's sixpenny chocolate bars, plus 1s 6d. The records had been made by Hardy & Co but the copyright was owned by Chappell & Co Ltd, which claimed that there had been breaches of its copyright. The case turned round whether the three wrappers were part of the consideration. The House of Lords held that they were – even though they were thrown away when received. In the words of Lord Somervell, 'A peppercorn does not cease to be good consideration if it is established that the promisee does not like pepper and will throw away the corn.'

A person who promises to carry out a duty which he is already obliged to perform is in reality offering nothing of value. The 'consideration' will be insufficient. However, if a person does more than he is bound to do, there may be sufficient consideration. The promise may involve a public duty imposed by law.

Collins v Godefroy (1831)

Collins was subpoenaed to give evidence in a case in which Godefroy was a party. (A subpoena is a court order which compels a person's attendance at court.) Godefroy promised to pay 6 guineas for Collins' loss of time. Collins' action to recover this money failed because he was already under a legal duty to appear in court. He had not done anything extra.

Glasbrook Bros Ltd v Glamorgan County Council (1925)

Glasbrook Bros were the owners of a strike-hit mine. They asked for police protection for the safety men whose presence was necessary to prevent the mine flooding. They were unhappy with the arrangements originally offered by the local police. Eventually it was agreed that 70 policemen would be stationed in the colliery and that

Glasbrook Bros would pay for this extra security. The House of Lords held that, since the police had provided more protection than they thought necessary, this constituted consideration. They were entitled to payment.

Note: *Glasbrook* v *Glamorgan* was considered by the Court of Appeal in upholding a claim by a police authority for £51,699 against Sheffield United Football Club for special police services provided at the club's home matches between August 1982 and November 1983 (*Harris* v *Sheffield United Football Club* (1987)).

Similar principles apply where a person is bound by a pre-existing contractual duty.

Stilk v Myrick (1809)

During the course of a voyage from London to the Baltic and back, two of a ship's crew deserted. The captain promised to share the wages of the deserters amongst the remaining crew. It was held that this promise was not binding as the sailors were already contractually bound to meet such emergencies of the voyage. They had not provided consideration.

The decision in *Stilk* v *Myrick* was reconsidered by the Court of Appeal in the following case.

Williams v Roffey Bros & Nicholls (Contractors) Ltd (1990)

The defendant building contractors had a contract to refurbish a block of 27 flats. They had sub-contracted the carpentry work to Williams for £20,000. After the contract had been running some months, during which time Williams had completed nine flats and received some £16,200 on account, it became apparent that Williams had underestimated the cost of the work and was in financial difficulties. The defendants, concerned that the carpentry work would not be completed on time and that as a result they would fall foul of a penalty clause in their main contract, agreed to a further £575 per flat. Williams completed eight more flats but did not receive full payment. He stopped work and brought an action for damages. The defendants argued that they were not obliged to pay as they had promised Williams extra pay for something he was already contractually bound to do, i.e. complete the work. Williams in turn submitted that the defendants obtained a benefit in that they had avoided a penalty for late completion and did not have the expense of engaging another contractor. The Court of Appeal held that Williams was entitled to the extra payments. Where A promises additional payments to B in return for B's prom-

ise to complete work on time, and by giving this promise A obtains a benefit by avoiding a penalty clause, for example, then B's promise may constitute sufficient consideration to support A's promise of extra pay, provided A's promise has not been obtained as a result of fraud or economic duress (see p 230).

Hartley v Ponsonby (1857)

When almost half of the crew of a ship deserted, the captain offered those remaining £40 extra to complete the voyage. In this case, the ship was so seriously undermanned that the rest of the journey had become extremely hazardous. It was held that this fact discharged the sailors from their existing contract and left them free to enter into a new contract for the rest of the voyage.

A slightly different problem arises where a person agrees to accept a smaller sum of money as full payment under a contract to pay a larger amount. For example, what is the legal position if Derek owes Graham £100, but Graham says that he will accept £90 in full settlement? Can Graham change his mind and sue for the outstanding £10? The long-established common law rule, known as the rule in *Pinnel's Case* (1602), is that an agreement to accept a lesser sum is not binding unless supported by fresh consideration.

Foakes v Beer (1884)

Mrs Beer had obtained judgment for a debt against Dr Foakes. She agreed that she would take no further action in the matter, provided that Foakes paid £500 immediately and the rest by half-yearly instalments of £150. Foakes duly kept to his side of the agreement. Judgment debts, however, carry interest. The House of Lords held that Mrs Beer was entitled to the £360 interest which had accrued. Foakes had not 'bought' her promise to take no further action on the judgment. He had not provided any consideration.

The decision in *Foakes* v *Beer* was reconsidered by the Court of Appeal in the following case.

Re Selectmove Ltd (1995)

Selectmove owed the Inland Revenue large sums of tax and national insurance. In July 1991, Selectmove's managing director suggested to a collector of taxes that the company should pay future income tax and national insurance contributions as they became due and clear the arrears at £1,000 per month from 1 February 1992. The collector said that he would have to obtain approval for this proposal and that he would come back to the company if it was not acceptable. Selectmove heard no more from the Inland Revenue until 9 October 1991, when the Revenue demanded payment of the arrears in full and threatened to present a winding-up petition. The question was whether the proposal made by Selectmove's managing director in July had become a binding agreement. It was argued on behalf of Selectmove that the decision in *Williams* v *Roffey Bros* was authority for the proposition that a promise to perform an existing obligation can amount to good consideration provided that there are practical benefits to the promisee. The Court of Appeal held that the *Williams* principle, which related to a case involving the supply of services, should not be extended to a situation involving an obligation to make a payment which is clearly governed by the authority of the House of Lords in *Foakes* v *Beer*. The court concluded that if there was an agreement between Selectmove and the Inland Revenue, it was unenforceable because of the absence of consideration.

There are some exceptions to the rule.

1 If the smaller payment is made, at the creditor's request, at an earlier time, at a different place, with an additional item or by a different method, consideration has been shown. (Note that since the decision in *D & C Builders Ltd* v *Rees* (1965), discussed later, payment by cheque rather than by cash does release a debtor from his obligation to pay the full amount.)

2 The rule does not apply to a composition agreement. This is where a debtor agrees with all his creditors to pay so much in the £ of what he owes. Provided that the debtor honours the agreement, a creditor cannot sue for any outstanding sum.

3 A promise to accept a smaller sum in full satisfaction will be binding on a creditor where the part-payment is made by a third party on condition that the debtor is released from the obligation to pay the full amount (*Hirachand Punamchand* v *Temple* (1911)).

4 The final exception is provided by equity. You will remember from Chapter 1 that equity is a system of law based on the idea of fairness and doing right according to conscience. The rule about part-payment would seem an ideal candidate for intervention by equity. It seems very unfair that a court will support a person who has gone back on his word, especially where the agreement

to accept a lesser amount has been relied upon. The equitable rule of promissory estoppel which was developed by Denning J in the *High Trees* case may provide some assistance.

Central London Property Trust Ltd v High Trees House Ltd (1947)

In 1937 the claimants granted a 99-year lease on a block of flats in London to the defendants at an annual rent of £2,500. Owing to the outbreak of war in 1939, the defendants found it very difficult to get tenants for the flats and so in 1940 it was agreed that the rent should be reduced to £1,250. By 1945 the flats were full again and the claimants sued to recover the arrears of rent as fixed by the 1937 agreement for the last two quarters of 1945. Denning J held that they were entitled to recover this money, but if they had sued for the arrears from 1940–45, the 1940 agreement would have defeated their claim. The defendants had relied upon the reduction in rent and equity would require the claimants to honour the promises contained in the 1940 agreement.

Thus, it seems that if a person promises that he will not insist on his strict legal rights, and the promise is acted upon, then the law will require the promise to be honoured even though it is not supported by consideration. The following points should be noted about promissory estoppel:

1 The rule can only be used as a defence and not as a cause of action. In the words of Birkett LJ in *Combe* v *Combe* (1951), promissory estoppel must be 'used as a shield and not as a sword'. Consideration is still an essential requirement for the formation of a contract.

2 The rule will only operate if the promisee has relied upon the promise so that it would be inequitable to allow the promisor to insist on his strict legal rights. At first it was thought that the promisee must have acted to his detriment. However, Lord Denning MR argued that detrimental reliance is not essential and that it is sufficient that the promisee has altered his position by acting differently from what he otherwise would have done.

3 It is a principle of equity that whoever seeks the help of equity must himself have acted equitably or fairly. Thus, the promisee must have acted according to his conscience if he is to rely on promissory estoppel as a defence.

D & C Builders v Rees (1965)

D & C Builders, a small building company, had completed some work for Mr Rees for which he owed the company £482. For months the company, which was in severe financial difficulties, pressed for payment. Eventually, Mrs Rees, who had become aware of the company's problems, contacted the company and offered £300 in full settlement. She added that if the company refused this offer they would get nothing. The company reluctantly accepted a cheque for £300 'in completion of the account'. The company later sued for the balance. The Court of Appeal held that the company was entitled to succeed. Mr Rees could not rely on promissory estoppel to resist the claim because his wife had held the company to ransom and could not be said to have acted equitably. Moreover, the different method of payment, i.e. by cheque rather than by cash, did not release Mr Rees from the obligation to pay the full amount owed.

4 The rule does not as yet extinguish rights: it only suspends the rights of the promisor. So if the promise refers to a particular period of time or a state of affairs (e.g. war conditions), the promisor can revert to the original position at the end of the stated time or when conditions change by giving notice to the promisee.

Tool Metal Manufacturing Co Ltd v Tungsten Electric Co Ltd (1955)

Tool Metal granted a licence to Tungsten Electric to deal in products protected by patents owned by Tool Metal. Tungsten Electric agreed to pay 'compensation' if they manufactured more than a specific amount. In 1942 Tool Metal indicated that they wished to prepare a new licence agreement and in the meantime they would not claim compensation. Tool Metal later gave notice that they wished to resume their claim to compensation. The House of Lords held that Tool Metal were entitled to claim compensation after giving reasonable notice of their intention to do so.

Privity of contract

The common law doctrine of privity of contract states that a person cannot be bound by, or take advantage of, a contract to which he is not a party. The doctrine, which had been developed by the common law judges by the middle of the 19th century, was reaffirmed by the House of Lords in 1915.

Dunlop Pneumatic Tyre Co Ltd v Selfridge & Co Ltd (1915)

The claimants, Dunlop, sold a quantity of tyres to Dew and Co, dealers in motor accessories, on the basis that Dew & Co would not sell the tyres below the claimants' list price and they would obtain a similar undertaking from anyone they supplied with tyres. Dew and Co sold tyres to the defendants, Selfridge, which agreed to observe the restrictions and to pay Dunlop £5 for each tyre sold below the list price. Selfridge sold some of the tyres below list price and Dunlop sued for breach of contract. Selfridge argued that they were not a party to a contract with Dunlop. The House of Lords held that, as there was no contract between Dunlop and Selfridge, Dunlop could not enforce the penalty of £5 for every tyre sold below Dunlop's list price. Viscount Haldane based his decision on two principles: first, that only a person who is party to a contract can sue on it; and second, in order to enforce a simple contract a person must provide consideration.

Note. The agreement between Dunlop and Dew and Co is known as a resale price maintenance agreement. Such agreements are now outlawed by s 2(2)(a) of the Competition Act 1998. The Competition Act will be considered in more detail later in this chapter.

If A enters into a contract with B for the benefit of C, the common law doctrine of privity prevents C from suing B on the contract. There is nothing to stop A from suing on behalf of C, but the question arises whether A is limited to recovering damages only for his own loss, or can he also recover for losses suffered by C?

Jackson v Horizon Holidays Ltd (1975)

Mr Jackson entered into a contract with Horizon for a four-week family holiday to Ceylon for £1,200. The holiday was a disaster. Mr Jackson was awarded £1,100 for breach of contract by the Court of Appeal. The damages covered not only his own distress and disappointment but also that suffered by his wife and children. Although the outcome in this case can be justified by saying that the damages were compensation for his own distress because his family's holiday had been ruined, Lord Denning made it clear that the award was designed to cover not only Mr Jackson's loss but also the loss suffered by his wife and children.

The House of Lords expressed disapproval of Lord Denning's reasoning in the *Jackson* case in *Woodar Investment Development Ltd v Wimpey*

Construction UK Ltd (1980), but gave its support for the level of damages awarded. More recently the House of Lords has shown that it is prepared in limited circumstances to allow a party to a contract to recover damages which represent a third party's loss.

Linden Garden Trust Ltd v *Lenesta Sludge Disposals Ltd* (1993)

The owner of land entered into a building contract with a contractor to develop a site for shops, offices and flats. The parties envisaged that the site would subsequently be transferred to a third party. It was alleged that the third party had suffered financial loss as a result of the contractor's poor workmanship which amounted to a breach of contract. The owner of the site brought an action for breach of contract but was met by the defence that as the site had been transferred to a third party he had only suffered nominal loss. The House of Lords rejected this argument and upheld the right of the owner to recover full damages on behalf of the third party.

Although privity of contract has been regarded as a fundamental principle of English law, there is a large number of exceptions to the rule. Where an exception applies, a person who is not a party to a contract may be able to take legal action.

1 **Assignment of contractual rights.** It is possible for a party to a contract to transfer the benefit of a contract to another person. For example, A may agree to sell B his CD collection for £2,000. A may transfer his right to payment under the contract to a third party, C. This process is known as assignment. Provided the assignment is absolute, in writing and notice is given to the debtor, it will take effect as a statutory assignment under s 136 of the Law of Property Act 1925. This means that the assignee (C in the example above) can sue the debtor (B) in his own name. The assignee gets the same rights as the assignor (A) had. The burden of a contract cannot be assigned unless the other party consents.

2 **Agency.** An agent is a person who is employed by a principal to make contracts on his behalf with third parties. A principal will be bound by contracts made by the agent with the third party even if the existence of the agency is not revealed. This is known as the doctrine of the undisclosed principal.

3 **Land law.** There are many situations in land law where the doctrine of privity of contract does not apply. For example, a lease of property often contains a number of covenants by the landlord and the tenant. If the tenant assigns the lease to a third party, either party, landlord or new tenant, may enforce a covenant in the original lease against each other.

4 **Trusts.** The doctrine of privity does not apply to the law of trusts. If X and Y by contract create a trust for the benefit of B, B can enforce his rights under the trust even though he was not a party to the contract.

5 **Collateral contract.** A collateral contract may arise where one party makes a promise to another, the consideration for which is that the promisee will enter into a contract with a third party. The device of a collateral contract was often used to enforce a promise made by car dealers before a purchaser entered into a hire-purchase agreement with a finance company.

Andrews v *Hopkinson* (1956)

The defendant car dealer recommended a car to the claimant saying: 'It's a good little bus. I would stake my life on it.' The claimant entered into a hire-purchase agreement with a finance company and when the car was delivered he was asked to sign a delivery note which said that he was satisfied with its condition. This was the first opportunity the claimant had to examine the vehicle. The claimant was seriously injured when a week later the car suddenly swerved into a lorry. The car was completely wrecked. A subsequent examination revealed that the steering mechanism was faulty at the time of delivery. As the law then stood, the delivery note may have barred the claimant from suing the finance company. The claimant successfully sued the defendant for breach of the promise made before he entered into the hire-purchase agreement. The defendant was also liable in the tort of negligence.

6 **Other causes of action.** The doctrine of privity of contract means that a person who is not a party to a contract cannot bring an action in contract. He may have some other cause of action on which to base a claim. If a husband enters into a contract with a garage to have his wife's car serviced, she will not be able to sue the garage in contract if the

service is carried out badly. However, if she is injured in an accident caused by a defective service to the car's brakes, she may be able to sue the garage in the tort of negligence (see later).

Beswick v *Beswick* (1961)

Peter Beswick was a coal merchant. He agreed to sell the business to his nephew, John, provided that John paid him £6.50 per week for the rest of his life and if his wife survived him she would receive an annuity of £5 per week. John took over the business and paid the agreed sum to Peter until Peter died. John paid Peter's widow for one week but then refused to make any more payments. Peter's widow sued John for specific performance of the contract and arrears of the annuity. She sued in her personal capacity and as administratrix of her husband's estate. The House of Lords held that she was entitled to succeed in her capacity as administratrix but privity of contract would prevent her from succeeding in her personal capacity.

7 Contracts (Rights of Third Parties) Act 1999. In 1996 the Law Commission recommended that the doctrine of privity be relaxed to allow a person who is not a party to a contract to sue on it, provided that the contract contains an express term to that effect and it purports to confer a benefit on the third party. These recommendations have now been implemented by the Contracts (Rights of Third Parties) Act 1999.

The 1999 Act institutes reform of the doctrine of privity by recognising the right of third parties to enforce contracts which have been made for their benefit. It should be noted that the Act only applies to contracts for the **benefit** of third parties and does not affect the established principle that **burdens** cannot be imposed on a third party without his consent.

The main provisions of the Contract (Rights of Third Parties) Act 1999 are set out below.

Right of a third party to enforce a term of a contract (s 1)

A third party will have the right to enforce a term of a contract:

● where the contract expressly so provides;
● where the term purports to confer a benefit on the third party, unless it appears that the con-

tracting parties did not intend him to have the right to enforce the term.

The third party must be expressly identified in the contract either by **name**, e.g. Fred Smith; **class**, e.g. Fred Smith's employees; or **description**, e.g. Fred Smith's son. It is not necessary, however, for the third party to be in existence when the contract is made. This provision allows the contracting parties to confer enforceable rights on, for example, a company which, although in the process of formation, has not yet been incorporated.

The right of a third party to enforce a contract is subject to the terms and conditions of the contract. It is, therefore, open to the contracting parties to limit or impose conditions on the rights of the third party to enforce the contract.

The third party is entitled to all the remedies for a breach of contract which would have been available to him if he had been a party to the contract. The rules relating to damages (including the duty to mitigate loss), injunctions, specific performance and other types of remedy will all apply.

Although the Act is primarily designed to enable third parties to enforce positive rights, it also allows third parties to take advantage of any exclusion or limitation clauses in the contract. The effect of the Act on exemption clauses will be examined further in Chapter 9.

For the purposes of the Act, the 'promisor' is defined as the party to the contract against whom the contractual term is enforceable by the third party, while the 'promisee' is the party to the contract by whom the term is enforceable against the promisor. So if A makes a contract with B, by which B agrees to confer a benefit on C, B is the 'promisor', A is the 'promisee', and C is the 'third party'.

Applying the provisions of the Act to the facts of *Beswick* v *Beswick* (above), it is probable that if the case arose today Mrs Beswick would have the right to enforce John Beswick's promise to pay her an annuity. The contract between Peter Beswick and his nephew John purported to confer a benefit (the payment of an annuity) on Mrs Beswick, who was expressly named. Under s 1 of the 1999 Act, a presumed right of enforceability by Mrs Beswick would be created, which could only be rebutted if

John Beswick could show 'on a proper construction of the contract that the parties did not intend the term to be enforceable by a third party'.

Variation and rescission of the contract (s 2)

The effect of this section is to restrict attempts by the contracting parties to alter (vary) the contract or cancel (rescind) it without the agreement of the third party. Where a third party has a right under s 1 to enforce a term of a contract, the contracting parties may not, by agreement, rescind or vary the contract in such a way as to extinguish or alter the third party's entitlement, without the third party's consent if:

- the third party has communicated to the promisor his acceptance of the term, or
- the promisor is aware that the third party has relied on the term;
- the promisor can reasonably be expected to have foreseen that the third party would rely on the term and the third party has in fact relied on the term.

Acceptance may be in the forms of words or conduct, but if the acceptance is sent by post, the 'postal rules' will not apply and the acceptance will only be effective when received by the promisor.

The principle that variation or rescission of the contract can only be made with the third party's consent will not apply in the following circumstances:

- where there is an express term in the contract allowing the contracting parties to vary or rescind without the third party's consent;
- where, on the application of the contracting parties, a court dispenses with the requirement of consent because the third party's whereabouts are unknown or he is incapable of giving consent because of mental incapacity or it cannot be ascertained whether he has relied on the contractual term. This power is exercisable by either the High Court or county court.

Defences, set-off or counterclaims available to the promisor (s 3).

This section applies where the third party is seeking to enforce a contractual term against the promisor. It sets out the defences, set-offs and counterclaims available to the promisor in any proceedings by the third party. The following principles apply:

1 The third party's claim will be subject to all the defences and set-offs which would have been available to the promisor in an action by the promisee arising from or in connection with the contract and relevant to the term the third party is seeking to enforce (s 3(2)).

Example 1
The contract is void because of mistake or illegality, or has been discharged because of frustration, or is unenforceable because of a failure to observe necessary formalities. In these circumstances the third party will not be able to enforce the term because the promisee would not have been able to enforce the contract.

Example 2
A and B enter into a contract for the sale of goods, whereby the purchase price is to be paid to C. B delivers goods which are not of satisfactory quality in breach of the statutory implied term contained in s 14 of the Sale of Goods Act 1979. In an action for the price of the goods brought by C, A will be entitled to reduce or extinguish the price because of the B's breach of contract.

2 The contracting parties may include an express term in the contract to the effect that the promisor may have available to him any matter by way of defence or set-off in proceedings brought by the third party or the promisee (s 3(3)).

Example
A agrees to buy B's car for £3,000, with the purchase price to be paid to C. B owes A money under a completely unrelated contract. A and B agree to an express term in the contract for the sale of the car that allows A to raise in any claim brought by C any matter which would have given A a defence or set-off in a claim brought by B. So if C brought a claim for the purchase price, A would be able to set off the money owed by B.

3 The promisor will also have available to him any defence or set-off, or any counterclaim not arising from the contract, but which is specific to the third party (s 3(4)).

Example 1
A enters into a contract with B whereby A will pay C £1,000. C already owes A £400. A has a set-off to a claim by C and need only pay £600.

Example 2

C induces A to enter into a contract with B by misrepresentation, but B is unaware of the misrepresentation. A may have a defence (or a counterclaim for damages) if sued by C, which would not have been available if the action had been brought by B.

4 The contracting parties may include an express provision to the effect that the promisor cannot raise any defences, set-offs or counterclaims that would have been available to the promisor had the third party been party to the contract (s 3(5)).

Example

B agrees to buy a painting from A, an art dealer, for his daughter C's birthday. C is expressly given the right to enforce delivery of the painting. B already owes a considerable amount of money for other works of art he has purchased. B is concerned that C's right to enforce the contract is unaffected and so A and B agree that A cannot raise against C any defences or set-offs which would have been available to A in any action by B.

Enforcement by the promisee (s 4)

This section makes it clear the rights given to third parties under the Act are in addition to any rights that the promisee has to enforce the contract. This means that in a contract between A and B for the benefit of C, B can sue on behalf of C.

Protection against double liability (s 5)

This section provides that where the promisee has already recovered damages from the promisor in respect of the third party's loss, in a claim against the promisor by the third party, any award will be reduced to take into account sums already recovered. This section is designed to protect the promisor against double liability.

Exceptions (s 6)

This section excludes certain kinds of contracts from the operation of the Act. Third parties acquire no rights of enforcement in relation to the following contracts:

- contracts on a bill of exchange, promissory note or other negotiable instruments;
- contracts under s 14 of the Companies Act 1985, by which the memorandum and articles

are deemed to constitute a contract between the company and its members;
- contracts of employment: without this provision, employees taking lawful industrial action would be at risk of being sued for breach of their contracts of employment by customers of any employer;
- contracts for the carriage of goods by sea; however, third parties will be able to take advantage of any exclusion or limitation clauses made for their benefit in such contracts.

The application of the Act to exemption clauses will be discussed in more detail in Chapter 9.

Supplementary provisions (s 7)

The section clarifies that any existing rights or remedies available to a third party are not affected by the Act.

It also prevents a third party from invoking s 2(2) of the Unfair Contract Terms Act 1977 to contest the validity of an exemption clause which purports to exclude or limit liability for negligently caused loss and damage (other than death or personal injury). The Unfair Contract Terms Act will be considered in more detail in Chapter 9.

Intention

So far we have established two requirements for a binding contract: agreement and consideration. The law demands, in addition, that the parties intended to enter into a legal relationship. After all, if you invite a friend round for a social evening at your house, you would not expect legal action to follow if the occasion has to be cancelled. So how does the law decide what the parties intended? For the purpose of establishing the intention of the parties, agreements are divided into two categories: business/commercial and social/domestic agreements.

Business/commercial agreements

In the case of a business agreement, it is automatically presumed that the parties intended to make a legally enforceable contract. It is possible, however, to remove the intention by the inclusion of an express statement to that effect in the agreement.

Rose and Frank Co v Crompton (J R) & Brothers Ltd
(1923)
The defendants, English paper tissue manufacturers, entered into an agreement with the claimants, an American company, whereby the claimants were to act as sole agents for the sale of the defendants' tissues in the USA. The written agreement contained the following 'Honourable Pledge Clause'.

> This arrangement is not entered into ... as a formal or legal agreement and shall not be subject to legal jurisdiction in the law courts ... but it is only a definite expression and record of the purpose and intention of the parties concerned to which they honourably pledge themselves that it will be carried through with mutual loyalty and friendly co-operation.

The claimants placed orders for tissues which were accepted by the defendants. Before the orders were sent, the defendants terminated the agency agreement and refused to send the tissues. The House of Lords held that the sole agency agreement was not binding owing to the inclusion of the 'honourable pledge clause'. In so far as orders had been placed and accepted, however, contracts had been created and the defendants, in failing to execute them, were in breach of contract.

When the parties enter into an agreement subject to contract, they are expressly stating that they will not be bound unless and until a formal contract is drawn up.

There are situations where it would appear at first sight that the parties had entered into a commercial arrangement, but, nevertheless, a contract is not created.

1 **Collective agreements.** Employers and trade unions regularly enter into collective agreements about rates of pay and conditions of employment. Section 179 of the Trade Union and Labour Relations (Consolidation) Act 1992 states that such agreements are not intended to be legally enforceable unless they are in writing and expressly affirm that they are to be binding. It should be noted, however, that the Employment Relations Act 1999 inserted a new s 70A in the 1992 Act, which deals with recognition of trade unions. Under s 70A agreements between an employer and a trade union about the method by which they will conduct collective bargaining (or if not agreed by the parties, specified by the Central Arbitration Committee) will take effect as if they were contained in a legally enforceable contract. The only remedy for breach is specific performance.

2 **Advertisements.** Generally speaking, vague promises or guarantees given in the course of promoting a product are not intended to be taken seriously. By contrast, more specific pledges such as, 'If you can find the same holiday at a lower price in a different brochure, we will refund you the difference', are likely to be binding. (See *Carlill v Carbolic Smoke Ball Co.*)

3 **Public bodies.** Where one of the parties is a public body which is bound by Act of Parliament to supply a particular service, there is no intention to enter into a contract with customers. For example, if you post a letter by ordinary first class mail and it is delayed or lost, you cannot sue the Post Office for breach of contract.

4 **Letters of comfort.** A comfort letter is a document supplied by a third party to a creditor, indicating a concern to ensure that a debtor meets his obligations to the creditor. Comfort letters are sometimes provided as an alternative to a formal guarantee in respect of a loan but are usually carefully worded so as to avoid the creation of any legal obligation. In *Kleinwort Benson Ltd v Malaysian Mining Corporation Bhd* (1989) the Court of Appeal held that despite the commercial nature of the transaction which gave rise to a presumption of an intention to create legal relations, the comfort letter provided by Malaysian Mining merely stated its current policy and did not amount to a contractual promise to meet the liabilities of its subsidiary.

5 **Letters of intent.** A letter of intent is a device by which one person indicates to another that he is likely to place a contract with him, but is not yet ready to be contractually bound. A typical example of a situation where a letter of intent might be provided is where a main contractor is preparing a tender and he plans to subcontract some of the work. He would need to know the cost of the subcontracted work in order to calculate his own tender, but would not want to be committed to that subcontractor until he knows whether his tender has been successful. In these circumstances, the main contractor writes to tell the subcontractor that he has been chosen. Normally the letter is

carefully worded so as to avoid any legal obligations. However, if the letter of intent invites the subcontractor to begin preliminary work an obligation to pay for the work will arise even though a formal contract may never be concluded (*British Steel Corporation* v *Cleveland Bridge and Engineering Co Ltd* (1984)).

Social/domestic arrangements

Social arrangements between friends do not usually amount to contracts because the parties never intend their agreement to be legally binding. You might agree to meet someone for lunch or accept an invitation to a party, but in neither case have you entered into a contract. If it can be shown, however, that the transaction had a commercial flavour, the court may be prepared to find the necessary intention for a contract.

Simpkins v *Pays* (1955)
The claimant, Simpkins, lodged with the defendant, Mrs Pays, and her granddaughter. Each week all three ladies jointly completed a competition run by a Sunday newspaper. The entries were sent off in the defendant's name. One entry won a prize of £750 which the defendant refused to share with the claimant. It was held that the parties had embarked on a joint enterprise, expecting to share any prize money. There was an intention to enter into a legal relationship and the claimant was entitled to one-third of the winnings.

Most domestic arrangements within families are not intended to be legally binding. An agreement between husband and wife or parent and child does not normally give rise to a contract. That is not to say that there can never be business contracts between members of a family. Many family businesses are run as partnerships; a wife can be employed by her husband.

If the husband and wife are living apart, they can make a binding separation agreement.

Merritt v *Merritt* (1970)
Mr Merritt had left his wife to live with another woman. He agreed that if his wife completed the mortgage repayments on the matrimonial home, he would transfer the house to her. Mrs Merritt duly completed the repayments but her husband refused to convey the house to her. The Court of Appeal held that, as the parties were living apart, the agreement was enforceable.

Form

If you ask someone what a contract is you will probably he told that it is a written document. Some contracts are indeed in writing but the majority are created much more informally either orally or implied from conduct.

Generally, the law does not require complex formalities to be observed to form a contract. There are, however, some types of contract which are exceptions to this rule.

1 Contracts which must be in the form of a deed. Certain transactions involving land require the execution of a deed, i.e. conveyances, legal mortgages and leases for more than three years. A promise of a gift is not binding unless in this form.

2 Contracts which must be in writing. The Law of Property (Miscellaneous Provisions) Act 1989 provides that a contract for the sale or other disposition of land can only be made in writing and by incorporating all the terms which the parties have expressly agreed in one document, or where the contracts are exchanged, in each. The document must be signed by or on behalf of each party to the contract.

In the following case the Court of Appeal considered whether the formalities required for the sale of land under the 1989 Act applied to a so-called 'lockout' agreement, i.e. an agreement to deal exclusively with one party and not to consider other offers for a limited period.

Pitt v *PHH Asset Management Ltd* (1993)
The claimant, Mr Pitt, and a Miss Buckle were both interested in purchasing a cottage in Suffolk from the defendants, PHH Asset Management. Every time Mr Pitt made an offer for the property, he was gazumped by Miss Buckle. On the occasion of Mr Pitt's third offer for the property, it was agreed orally that PHH would not consider any further offers, provided that Mr Pitt exchanged contracts within two weeks. PHH sold the cottage to Miss Buckle at a higher price before the two-week period had expired. Mr Pitt sued PHH for breach of the 'lock-out' agreement. PHH argued that the agreement was unenforceable on three grounds: (i) the agreement formed part of the continuing negotiations for the sale of the property and as such was 'subject to contract'; (ii) the agreement was a contract for the sale of an interest in land and was, therefore, only enforceable if the formalities required by the Law of Property

(Miscellaneous Provisions) Act 1989 were observed; and (iii) Mr Pitt had given no consideration for the agreement. The Court of Appeal held that PHH was in breach of contract and was liable to pay damages. The court said that the lock-out agreement was capable of existing independently of any agreement to sell the cottage and was, therefore, not 'subject to contract'. The 1989 Act did not apply either, for the same reason. The court found that Mr Pitt had provided consideration in the form of removing a threat to make difficulties for Miss Buckle and in promising to exchange contracts within two weeks.

Under the Bills of Exchange Act 1882, bills of exchange, cheques and promissory notes must be in writing. Similarly, the transfer of shares in a limited company must be in writing. Regulations introduced under the Consumer Credit Act 1974 lay down requirements about the form and content of regulated consumer credit and hire agreements. The Employment Rights Act 1996 requires that employees are given a written statement of the terms and conditions of employment within two months of starting work. Failure to provide a written statement does not affect the validity of a contract of employment, although it does entitle an employee to refer the matter to an employment tribunal. The tribunal can decide on the particulars which should have been included in the written statement. An example of a possible form of written statement may be seen in Chapter 16.

3 **Contracts which must be evidenced in writing.** There is only one type of contract which must be evidenced in writing: a contract of guarantee. If you borrow money or buy goods on credit, you may be asked to find someone who will guarantee the debt. This means that if you do not or cannot repay the money, the guarantor will pay your debt for you. The requirement of written evidence does not affect the formation of such contracts. The absence of writing does not make the agreement void, so if any money or property has changed hands it can be kept. However, if one of the parties wishes to enforce the contract in the courts, the necessary note or memorandum must be produced.

Formalities and electronic communications

As we enter the third millennium, we find ourselves in the midst of a new industrial revolution.

It is widely predicted that the rapid development of electronic communication technology will revolutionise the way in which business is conducted in the future. Although e-commerce currently accounts for a very small proportion of transactions in the UK, the government recognises the enormous potential for electronic trading and has set itself the ambitious target of making the UK the best place in the world to trade electronically. The Electronic Communications Act 2000 is designed to facilitate the development of electronic commerce by providing for:

- a voluntary registration system for organisations providing cryptography support services, such as electronic signature and confidentiality services;
- legal recognition of electronic signatures;
- the removal of obstacles in other legislation to the use of electronic communication and electronic storage in place of paper. (It should be noted that the Law of Property (Miscellaneous Provisions) Act 1989 has already abolished the requirement that a deed must be written on paper.) The power to modify legislation to facilitate the use of electronic communications or electronic storage will be exercisable by ministerial order.

Capacity

If there is one thing which more than another public policy requires it is that men of full age and competent understanding shall have the utmost liberty of contracting and their contracts when entered into freely and voluntarily shall be held sacred and shall be enforced by courts of justice. (Sir George Jessel, 1875)

This classic statement of freedom of contract by a 19th century Master of the Rolls still essentially holds good today – it is assumed that everyone is capable of entering into a contract. There are, however, some groups of people who are in need of the law's protection either because of their age or inability to appreciate their own actions. The groups which are covered by special rules are those under the age of 18 (minors), mental patients and drunks.

Minors

Before 1970 anyone under the age of 21 was known as an infant. The age of majority was lowered to 18 on 1 January 1970 and 'infants' were renamed 'minors'. The rules relating to contractual capacity are designed to protect the minor from exploitation by adults. A minor is free to enter into contracts and enforce his rights against an adult. The adult's rights will depend on the way in which the contract is classified.

1 Valid contracts. There are two types of contract which will bind a minor: contracts for necessary goods and services and beneficial contracts of service. A minor must pay a reasonable price for 'necessaries' sold and delivered to him. Section 3 of the Sale of Goods Act 1979 defines 'necessaries' as 'goods suitable to the condition in life of the minor and to his actual requirements at the time of sale and delivery'. Clearly, luxury goods are excluded. Expensive but useful items may be necessaries if they are appropriate to the social background and financial circumstances of the minor. If the minor is already adequately supplied, the goods will not be classed as necessaries.

Nash v Inman (1908)
A Saville Row tailor sued an infant Cambridge student for the price of clothes (including 11 fancy waistcoats) he had supplied. The tailor failed in his action because the student was already adequately supplied with clothes.

A minor is also bound by contracts of employment, apprenticeship and education, which, taken as a whole, are for his benefit.

Roberts v Gray (1913)
The infant defendant had agreed to go on a world tour with the claimant, a professional billiards player. After the claimant had spent much time and some money organising the tour, the infant changed his mind and refused to go. The claimant sued for breach of contract. The Court of Appeal held that this was essentially a contract to receive instruction. Since this was for the infant's benefit, the contract was valid. The claimant was awarded £1,500 damages.

If the minor sets himself up in business, he will not be bound by his trading contracts, even though they are for his benefit. The minor can, none the less, sue on these contracts.

Cowern v Nield (1912)
Nield was an infant hay and straw dealer. He refused to deliver a quantity of hay which had been paid for by Cowern. It was held that, provided the infant had not acted fraudulently, he was not liable to repay Cowern.

2 Voidable contracts. There are three kinds of contract which are voidable: leases of land, partnerships and the purchase of shares. Voidable means that the contract is binding on the minor until he decides to reject it. He must repudiate the contract before becoming 18 or within a reasonable time of reaching 18. The main effect of repudiation is to relieve the minor of all future liabilities, but he can be sued for liabilities which have already accrued, such as arrears of rent.

3 Other contracts. Before looking at how the law deals with other contracts made by minors, we will consider the effect of changes introduced by the Minors' Contracts Act 1987 (MCA). The law concerning contracts made by minors used to be governed mainly by the Infants Relief Act 1874. Section 1 of the 1874 Act provided that contracts for the repayment of money lent or to be lent, contracts for the supply of non-necessary goods and accounts stated were 'absolutely void'. Section 7 placed a bar on enforcement proceedings against a minor who ratified a contract on reaching 18 unless the ratification was contained in a new contract for which fresh consideration had been provided.

The MCA implements the recommendations of the Law Commission contained in its 1984 Report on Minors' Contracts. Section 1 disapplies the Infants Relief Act 1874 to contracts made in England and Wales after 9 June 1987. (It should be noted that the 1874 Act was not repealed and it still applies to Northern Ireland.) The result is to restore the application of the common law rules to such contracts. In particular, a contract made by a minor, which is later ratified by him on reaching 18, is now enforceable against the minor without the need for a fresh contract. Section 2 makes any guarantee supporting a loan to a minor enforceable against the adult guarantor, thus reversing the position established in *Coutts* v *Browne-Lecky* (1946). Section 3 improves the remedies available to an adult who has contracted with a minor. We shall now examine in more detail the combined effect of the common law and the MCA.

Contracts which are neither valid nor voidable do not bind the minor but are binding on the other party. As has been noted above, a minor may be bound by such a contract if he ratifies it, either expressly or impliedly, on reaching 18. Although the minor can enforce the contract against the other party, his remedies are limited since he will not be able to obtain an order of specific performance because of lack of mutuality.

Once the contract has been performed by the minor, he cannot recover money paid or property transferred under the contract except in the same circumstances in which such a remedy would be available to an adult, i.e. where there has been a total failure of consideration. The case of *Stocks* v *Wilson* (1913) and s 3(1) of the MCA support the view that a minor acquires title (rights of ownership) to any property transferred to the minor under such a contract. Similarly, a minor can transfer title in property under a non-binding contract. A minor may be liable to restore certain benefits which he has received under a contract which does not bind him. Section 3(1) of the MCA provides that where a contract has been made with a minor which is unenforceable against him, or he has repudiated it, because he was a minor, the court may, if it thinks it just and equitable to do so, require him to return the property or any property representing that which he has acquired. The scope of the statutory remedy is as follows:

(a) The minor can be made to return the goods and money which he still has in his possession. So if Sebastian, age 17, acquires a case of champagne on credit and fails to pay he can be required to return the goods to the seller.

(b) If the minor has exchanged the original goods for other property, the court may require him to hand over the goods received in exchange. So if Sebastian, in the example above, has bartered a bottle of champagne for a dozen quail's eggs, the seller of the champagne may be able to recover the quail's eggs.

(c) If the minor has sold the original goods for cash, he can be ordered to hand over the sale proceeds. So if Sebastian sold the case of champagne for cash, he could be required to hand over the money to the seller.

(d) If the minor has consumed or disposed of the goods, or the proceeds of any sale of the goods, he cannot be made to compensate the other party. So if Sebastian drank the champagne or used the proceeds of any sale of the champagne to pay for an evening at a night-club, he could not be required to compensate the unpaid seller.

Section 3(2) of the MCA expressly preserves the remedies which were available before the MCA was passed. The equitable doctrine of restitution allows an adult to recover money or property acquired by a minor as a result of fraud. The remedy is confined to restitution of the actual property acquired. Thus, if a minor has parted with the goods or the precise notes and coins, this remedy is not available. In practice, adults seeking restitution are likely to base their claims on the statutory remedy contained in s 3(1) since it is not subject to the same limitations which apply to the equitable remedy.

Drunks and mental patients

Section 3 of the Sale of Goods Act 1979 provides that they are required to pay a reasonable price for necessaries in the same way as minors. Other kinds of contract are governed by common law. If a person is suffering from mental disability or drunkenness at the time of making the contract, he will be able to avoid his liabilities if he can show that he did not understand what the agreement was about and the other person was aware of his disability.

The judges of the Court of Protection may exercise wide powers over the property and affairs of mental patients placed in their care under the Mental Health Act 1983. They can make contracts on behalf of the patient and carry out contracts already made by him.

GENUINENESS OF CONSENT

The most basic requirement of a contract is the presence of an agreement. It must have been entered into voluntarily and involved 'a genuine meeting of minds'. The agreement may be invalidated by a number of factors – mistake, misrepresentation, duress and undue influence.

Mistake

The general rule of common law is that a mistake does not affect the validity of a contract. The guiding principle is *caveat emptor*, which means 'let the buyer beware'. So if a person agrees to pays £1,000 for a car, when in reality it is only worth £500, the contract is valid and he must stand the loss.

Leaf v *International Galleries* (1950)
Mr Leaf bought a painting of 'Salisbury Cathedral' from International Galleries for £85. The Gallery attributed the painting to John Constable. When Leaf tried to sell the painting five years later, he was informed that it was not by Constable. Both the buyer and seller had made a mistake about the quality and value of the painting but this did not affect the validity of the contract.

It should be noted that a mistake of law will not invalidate a contract since every one is presumed to know the law.

There are, however, some kinds of mistake which so undermine the agreement that the contract is void. If this is the case, no rights of ownership can pass and any goods which have changed hands can be recovered. A mistake will invalidate the contract in the following situations:

1 Mistakes as to the subject matter of the contract. The parties may be mistaken as to the identity of the subject matter. If a seller makes an offer in respect of one thing and the buyer accepts, but is thinking of something else, the parties are clearly talking at cross-purposes and there is no contract.

Raffles v *Wichelhaus* (1864)
The defendant agreed to buy cotton which was described as 'arriving on the Peerless from Bombay'. There were two ships called the Peerless sailing from Bombay: one in October and the other in December. It was held that there was no binding contract between the parties as the defendant meant one ship and the claimant the other.

When the parties contract in the mistaken belief that a particular thing is in existence, but in fact it

has ceased to exist, the contract is void. These situations are known as cases of *res extincta*.

Couturier v *Hastie* (1852)
A contract was made for the sale of Indian corn which the parties believed to be on board a ship bound for the UK. Unknown to the parties, the corn had overheated during the voyage and been landed at the nearest port and sold. The House of Lords held that the agreement was void.

The common law *res extincta* rules are reflected in the provisions of the Sale of Goods Act 1979. Section 6 provides: 'where there is a contract for the sale of specific goods and the goods without the knowledge of the seller have perished at the time when the contract is made, the contract is void'. In some situations, the non-existence of the subject matter will not render the contract void. A court may be prepared to place responsibility for non-existence on one of the parties.

McRae v *Commonwealth Disposals Commission* (1951)
The Commission contracted to sell to McRae the wreck of an oil tanker which was described as lying on Jourmand Reef off Papua. McRae incurred considerable expenditure in preparation for the salvage operation. In fact, there was no tanker anywhere near the specified location and no place known as Jourmand Reef. The High Court of Australia awarded damages to McRae for breach of contract. It was held that the contract contained an implied promise by the Commission that there was a tanker at the stated location.

2 Mistake as to the identity of one of the parties. If one party makes a mistake about the identity of the person he is contracting with, this may invalidate the contract. Where the identity of the party contracted with is material to the contract, a mistake will result in the contract being void.

Cundy v *Lindsay* (1878)
Lindsay & Co, Belfast linen manufacturers, received an order for a large quantity of handkerchiefs from a rogue called Blenkarn. The rogue had signed his name in such a way that it looked like 'Blenkiron & Co', a well-known, respectable firm. Lindsay & Co despatched the goods on credit to Blenkarn who resold 250 dozen to Cundy. Blenkarn did not pay for the goods and was later convicted of obtaining goods by false pretences. Lindsay &

Co sued Cundy for conversion. The House of Lords held that the contract between Lindsay & Co and Blenkarn was void for mistake. Lindsay & Co intended to deal with Blenkiron & Co, not the rogue, Blenkarn. Cundy was liable in conversion.

Where the identity of the other party is not material, the contract will be valid until the mistaken party realises that he has been misled and avoids the contract for misrepresentation.

Phillips v Brooks Ltd (1919)

A man entered the claimant's shop to buy some jewellery. He selected various items of jewellery and offered to pay by cheque. While writing the cheque the man said, 'You see who I am, I am Sir George Bullough.' He gave an address in St James's Square. The claimant knew of a Sir George Bullough and after checking in a directory that Sir George had an address in St James's Square, he asked if the man would like to take the jewellery with him. The man replied that the jeweller had better let the cheque clear first but he would like to take the ring as it was his wife's birthday the following day. The cheque was dishonoured. The man, who was in fact a rogue called North, pledged the ring with the defendant pawnbrokers. The claimant sued the defendants for the return of the ring or its value. It was held that the contract between the claimant and the rogue North was not void for mistake but voidable for fraud. At the time the contract was made the claimant intended to deal with the person physically in his shop and his identity was immaterial. As the claimant had not rescinded the contract by the time North pledged the ring, the defendants obtained good title (rights of ownership).

Lewis v Averay (1971)

Lewis sold his car to a man who claimed he was Richard Greene, the star of a popular television series, 'Robin Hood'. The man paid by cheque, producing a pass to Pinewood Studios as proof of his identity. He resold the car to Averay. The cheque had been taken from a stolen cheque book and was later dishonoured. Lewis sued Averay in the tort of conversion. The Court of Appeal held that Lewis intended to deal with the man actually in front of him, despite his fraudulent claim to be Richard Greene. The contract between Lewis and the rogue was not void for mistake, but rather voidable for a fraudulent misrepresentation. Since Lewis had not avoided the contract by the time the rogue sold the car to Averay, Averay acquired good rights of ownership. He was not liable in conversion.

3 **Mistaken signing of a written document.** As a general rule, a person who signs a document is assumed to have read, understood and agreed to its contents. Exceptionally, a person may be able to plead *non est factum* – 'It is not my deed'. Three elements must be present if the contract is to be avoided: the signature must have been induced by fraud, the document signed must be fundamentally different from that thought to be signed, and the signer must not have acted negligently.

Saunders v Anglia Building Society (1971)

Mrs Gallie was a 78-year-old widow. In June 1962 she was visited by her nephew, Walter Parkin, and a Mr Lee. Lee asked her to sign a document, which he told her was a deed of gift of her house to her nephew Walter. Mrs Gallie had broken her spectacles and, as she could not read without them, she signed the document without reading it through. The document which Mrs Gallie signed was in fact an assignment of her leasehold interest in the house to Lee. The Anglia Building Society advanced £2,000 to Lee on the strength of the deed. Mrs Gallie brought an action against Lee and the building society claiming that the deed was void. She pleaded *non est factum*. She succeeded at first instance against both Lee and the building society. However, the building society won on appeal to the Court of Appeal. Then Mrs Gallie died and an appeal to the House of Lords was brought by Mrs Saunders, the executrix of her estate. The House of Lords held that the plea of *non est factum* must fail. Although her signature had been induced by fraud, the document she signed was not fundamentally different from that which she thought she had signed. Moreover, persons wishing to plead *non est factum* must show that they exercised reasonable care in signing. Mrs Gallie had not taken the trouble to read the document.

The principles set out in *Saunders* will apply to a person who signs a blank form (*United Dominions Trust Ltd* v *Western* (1975)).

Mistake in equity

At common law, mistake only rarely invalidates a contract. It may, nevertheless, be possible for the court to apply equitable principles to achieve a measure of justice in the case. A court may grant the following forms of equitable relief.

1 **Rescission on terms.** The court may be prepared to set aside an agreement, provided the parties accept the conditions imposed by the court for a fairer solution to the problem.

Grist v *Bailey* (1966)

Bailey agreed to sell a house to Grist for £850. The price was based on both parties' belief that the house had a sitting tenant. The value of the house with vacant possession would have been about £2,250. Unknown to the parties, the tenants had died and their son did not stay on in the property. The judge held that the contract was not void at common law but he was prepared to set the contract aside provided Bailey offered to sell the property to Grist for the proper market price of £2,250.

2 **Rectification.** If a mistake is made in reducing an oral agreement into writing, the court may rectify the document so that it expresses the true intention of the parties.

3 **Specific performance.** A court may refuse to grant an order of specific performance against a party who made a mistake, if it would be unfair to enforce the contract against him.

MISREPRESENTATION

The formation of a contract is often preceded by a series of negotiations between the parties. Some of the statements made may later turn out to be false. The nature of the statement will determine whether a remedy is available and, if it is, the type of remedy (see Fig 7.1).

A false statement, which is not incorporated into the contract, is known as a misrepresentation. A misrepresentation is a false statement made by one party which induces the other to enter into a contract. As a general rule, a positive statement must be made; keeping quiet about something does not normally amount to misrepresentation. Gestures, smiles and nods can amount to a statement. A course of conduct can also amount to a representation.

Spice Girls Ltd v *Aprilia World Service BV* (2000)

The claimant, SGL, was a company formed to promote the Spice Girls pop group. At the beginning of May 1998, SGL entered into a contract with the defendant, AWS, an Italian company which manufactures motorcycles and scooters, to film a TV commercial to be shown until March 1999. When the contract was signed, the Spice Girls consisted of five members. However, a month earlier Geri Halliwell had announced to the other members of the group and its management that she intended to leave the group at the end of September 1998. It had been decided to keep this information confidential and AWS was not informed when the contract was signed. In an action by SGL for money allegedly due under the agreement, the High Court held that by participating in the 'shoot' of the TV commercial, SGL represented by conduct that it did not know or had no reasonable grounds to believe that any of the members of the group intended to leave. As the members of the group knew Ms Halliwell intended to leave during the period when the commercial was to be used, this amounted to a misrepresentation.

There are certain situations where a failure to speak will amount to an actionable misrepresentation:

1 where there is a relationship of good faith between the parties, e.g. between partners;
2 where the contract is one of utmost good faith, e.g. proposals for insurance cover;
3 where a half-truth is offered. In one case a solicitor stated that he was not aware of any restrictive covenants on a piece of land, which was literally true, but if he had bothered to read relevant documents, he would have discovered that there were indeed restrictive covenants (*Nottingham Patent Brick and Tile Co* v *Butler* (1886));
4 where there has been a change in circumstances between the time of the negotiations and the conclusion of the contract.

With v *O'Flanagan* (1936)

The defendant was a doctor who wished to sell his medical practice. In January 1934, during the course of

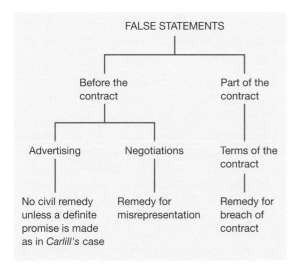

Fig 7.1 Remedies for false statements

negotiations with the claimant, he stated (correctly) that the practice was worth £2,000 a year. Unfortunately, the defendant then fell ill and the practice was run by other doctors. By the time the contract of sale to the claimant was signed in May, receipts had fallen to £5 per week. It was held that the defendant's failure to inform the claimant of the change of circumstances between initial negotiations and the conclusion of the contract was a misrepresentation.

The misrepresentation must involve a statement of fact and not a statement of law, opinion or intention. A statement of law cannot amount to a misrepresentation since everyone is presumed to know the law. A statement of intention will not normally amount to a misrepresentation because a representation is a statement about existing facts or past events. However, if a person misrepresents what he intends to do in the future, he may be liable for misrepresentation.

Edgington v *Fitzmaurice* (1885)
The directors of a company invited members of the public to lend money to the company. The directors stated that the money would be used to improve the company's buildings and extend the business. The directors' real intention was to pay off the company's existing debts. It was held that the directors' statement was a fraudulent misrepresentation. As Bowen LJ put it: 'There must be a misstatement of an existing fact: but the state of a man's mind is as much a fact as the state of his digestion. It is true that it is very difficult to prove what the state of a man's mind at a particular time is, but if it can be ascertained it is as much a fact as anything else. A misrepresentation as to the state of a man's mind is, therefore, a misstatement of fact.'

A statement of opinion will not normally be actionable as a misrepresentation because an opinion is a statement of belief which is not capable of proof.

Bissett v *Wilkinson* (1927)
During the course of negotiations for the sale of a farm in New Zealand to Wilkinson, Bissett stated that the land would support 2,000 sheep. The farm had not previously been used for grazing sheep and Wilkinson knew this. It was held that Bissett was merely expressing his opinion. There was no misrepresentation.

There are occasions when a statement of opinion may amount to a representation of fact. If it

can be established that the person making the statement did not hold that opinion or that he was in a position to know the facts on which his opinion was based, there may be an actionable misrepresentation.

Smith v *Land and House Property Corporation* (1884)
The vendors of a hotel stated that it was 'let to a Mr Frederick Fleck (a most desirable tenant)'. In fact, Mr Fleck was in arrears of rent. It was held that the description of Mr Fleck was not a mere expression of opinion. The vendors were in a position to know the facts about their tenant. Their opinion that he was a desirable tenant was not supported by facts within their knowledge.

It must be shown that the statement has induced the person to whom it was made to enter into the contract. If the person attempts to check the truth of what has been said, he clearly has not relied on the statement.

Attwood v *Small* (1838)
The seller of a mine made exaggerated claims about its earning capacity: The buyer appointed expert agents to investigate the mine. The agents reported that the seller's claims were true and the sale went ahead. The House of Lords held that an action by the buyer to rescind the contract must fail because the buyer had relied on his agents' report rather than the seller's statements.

Comment. If a person is given an opportunity to test the accuracy of a statement, but he does not take it, he can still bring a claim (*Redgrave* v *Hurd* (1881)).

Kinds of misrepresentation and their effects

There are three kinds of misrepresentation: fraudulent, negligent or innocent. In each case, the contract is voidable.

1 Fraudulent misrepresentation. A person will be liable for fraud if he makes a statement which he knows to be false, or he has no belief in its truth or he is reckless, careless whether it is true or false (*Derry* v *Peek* (1889)). The injured party may rescind the contract and also sue for damages for the tort of deceit. The assessment of damages for a fraudulent misrepresentation was discussed by the House of Lords in the following case.

Smith New Court Securities Ltd v Scrimgeour Vickers (1996)

The claimant, Smith New Court, was induced by a fraudulent misrepresentation made by the defendants' employee to buy shares in Ferranti at 82.25p per share. At the time of purchase, the shares were trading at about 78p per share. Unknown to either party, the shares were grossly overvalued because Ferranti was the victim of a fraud totally unconnected with the current case. When the fraud became known, the price of the shares slumped. The question for the court was whether the claimant could recover the difference between the price it had paid (the contract price) and the market price (4.25p per share) or the difference between the contract price and the value of the shares had it known of the fraud (44p per share). The House of Lords held that the claimant was entitled to recover for all the damage resulting from the transaction. The loss suffered by the claimant was £10,764,005, which represented the difference between the contract price and the value of the shares with knowledge of the fraud.

2 Negligent misrepresentation. This is where the person making the false statement has no reasonable grounds for believing the statement to be true. Damages may be awarded in tort for a negligent misstatement under the principle established in *Hedley Byrne & Co Ltd v Heller and Partners Ltd* (1963) (discussed in Chapter 11).

Esso Petroleum Co Ltd v Mardon (1976)

Mardon entered into a three-year tenancy agreement with Esso in respect of a newly developed petrol filling station. During the negotiations an experienced dealer representative employed by Esso told Mardon that the station would have an annual throughput of 200,000 gallons by the third year. Despite Mardon's best efforts, the throughput only reached 86,000 by the third year. Mardon lost a considerable sum of money and was unable to pay for petrol supplied by Esso. Esso sued for money owed and possession of the petrol station. Mardon counterclaimed for rescission of the tenancy agreement and damages for negligence. The Court of Appeal applied the principle established in *Hedley Byrne & Co Ltd v Heller and Partners Ltd*. When Esso's representative forecast the station's potential as part of the pre-contractual negotiations, a duty of care arose. Esso intended that their forecast would be relied upon by Mardon. Esso was in breach of the duty of care because of the error made by its representative. Esso was liable in damages for its negligence.

Comment. Although this case was decided in 1976, the events to which the decision relates took place in the early 1960s, before the introduction of the Misrepresentation Act 1967.

Damages may now also he awarded under s 2(1) of the Misrepresentation Act 1967.

Howard Marine and Dredging Co Ltd v A Ogden & Sons (Excavations) Ltd (1978)

The defendants won a contract to carry out excavation work for the Northumbrian Water Authority. The work involved dumping the spoil at sea, for which purpose the defendants needed to charter seagoing barges. The defendants approached the claimants who were the owners of two suitable barges. During the course of negotiations, the claimants' marine manager stated that the payload of the barges was 1,600 tonnes. This was based on the deadweight figure of 1,800 tonnes given in the Lloyd's Register. However, the Register was wrong. The shipping documents, which the marine manager had seen, gave the true deadweight as 1,195 tonnes, and this gave a payload of 1,055 tonnes. The contract to charter the barges did not mention these figures.

The defendants fell behind schedule because of the shortfall in the capacity of the barges. They ceased to pay the charter hire and were sued by the claimants. The defendants counterclaimed for damages under the Misrepresentation Act 1967 and in negligence at common law. The Court of Appeal held the claimants were liable under s 2(1) of the Misrepresentation Act 1967 for the misrepresentation of the barges' capacity. The claimants were unable to prove that their marine manager had reasonable grounds for relying on the capacity figures given in the Register in preference to the figures contained in the shipping documents. The court did not reach a firm conclusion about the claimants' liability for negligence at common law.

Comment. The Court of Appeal in this case was concerned only with the question of liability and not the measure of damages. There had been some uncertainty as to whether the basis of damages under s 2(1) of the Misrepresentation Act 1967 was contractual or tortious. However, in *Sharneyford Supplies Ltd v Edge* (1987) the Court of Appeal held that it should be tortious. The effect of this is that the representee can only recover loss which he has incurred through reliance on the misrepresentation. However, the damages will be assessed in the same way as for fraud so that the misrepresentee can recover for all losses flowing from the misrepresentation (*Royscot Trust Ltd v Rogerson* (1991)).

The injured party is more likely to be successful under the Act, because it reverses the normal burden of proof. Thus, the defendant will only escape liability if he can prove that the statement was made innocently. The judge may also award rescission as well as damages.

3 **Innocent misrepresentation.** An innocent misrepresentation is a false statement made by a person who had reasonable grounds to believe that it was true, not only when it was made, but also when the contract was entered into. The basic remedy is rescission of the contract: under s 2(2) of the Misrepresentation Act 1967, the court may in its discretion award damages instead. There was some uncertainty about whether damages could be awarded under s 2(2) if rescission was no longer available because, for example, a third party had acquired rights in the subject matter of the contract (see below). In *Thomas Witter Ltd* v *TBP Industries Ltd* (1996) the Court of Appeal decided that damages could be awarded under s 2(2), provided that the right to rescind had existed at some time, but it was not necessary for the right to rescind to exist at the time the court gave judgment.

RESCISSION

Rescission aims to restore the parties to their precontractual positions. Money or goods which have changed hands must be returned. Like all equitable remedies, it is not available as of right. In particular, the court may refuse to award rescission in the following circumstances:

(a) *where the injured party has received some benefit under the contract or has in some way affirmed it*: a long delay in taking legal action is taken as evidence of affirmation (*Leaf* v *International Galleries* (1950));

(b) *where the parties cannot be restored to their original positions* because, for example, goods have been destroyed or they have been sold to a third party (*Lewis* v *Averay* (1971)).

DURESS AND UNDUE INFLUENCE

The general rule of law is that a contract will be valid only if the parties entered into it freely and voluntarily. At common law, where a party to a contract or his family is subjected to violence or threats of violence, the contract may be avoided on the grounds of duress.

Barton v *Armstrong* (1975)
Armstrong was the chairman and Barton the managing director of an Australian company. Armstrong threatened to have Barton killed if he did not sign an agreement to buy out Armstrong's interest in the company on very favourable terms. The Privy Council held that the agreement was signed under duress and could be avoided by Barton.

Traditionally, the common law doctrine of duress was limited to violence and threats of violence to the person. However, in recent years the courts have recognised economic duress as a factor which may invalidate consent and render a contract voidable.

North Ocean Shipping Co Ltd v *Hyundai Construction Co Ltd* (1978)
The defendant shipbuilders agreed to build a tanker for the claimant shipowners. The price was payable in US dollars in five instalments. After the first instalment had been paid, there was a sharp fall in the value of the US dollar and the defendants threatened to break the contract unless the claimants paid an extra 10 per cent on each of the remaining instalments. The claimants had already entered into a lucrative contract to charter the tanker on its completion and, anxious to take delivery, they reluctantly paid the increased instalments. Eight months later they brought an action to recover the excess over the original contract price. It was held that the contract was voidable on the grounds of economic duress, but that the claimants could not recover the excess because they had affirmed the contract by failing to protest before they did.

Atlas Express Ltd v *Kafco (Importers and Distributors) Ltd* (1989)
Atlas, a road carrier, entered into a contract with Kafco, a small company importing and distributing basketware, to deliver cartons of basketware which Kafco had sold to Woolworths. Atlas's manager had quoted a price of £1.10 per carton based on an assumption that each load would contain between 400 and 600 cartons. However, the first load contained only 200 cartons. Atlas's manager refused to carry any more cartons unless Kafco agreed to pay a minimum of £440 per load. Kafco was anxious about maintaining a good relationship with Woolworths but was unable easily to find another carrier. Accordingly, Kafco agreed to the new terms but later refused to pay. The High Court held that Kafco was not liable as Kafco's agreement to the new terms had been obtained by economic duress.

Equity recognises a more subtle form of pressure: undue influence. The relationship between the parties may be such that one occupies a position of dominance and influence over the other. There are several relationships, such as doctor and patient, solicitor and client, parent and child, where it is automatically assumed that undue influence has been at work. The contract will be set aside unless the dominant person can show that the complainant had independent advice. Where there is no special relationship between the parties, the claimant must prove that pressure was applied.

A number of cases have raised the question whether a presumption of undue influence is created by the relationship between a banker and his customer.

Lloyds Bank Ltd v Bundy (1974)

An elderly farmer, inexperienced in business matters, mortgaged his home and only asset to the bank to guarantee his son's business overdraft. The Court of Appeal set aside the guarantee and charge. The farmer had placed himself in the hands of the bank and had looked to the assistant bank manager for advice. It was clearly in the bank's interest that the farmer provided the guarantee. The court held that the presumption of undue influence applied. The bank had failed to rebut the presumption since the farmer had not been advised to seek independent advice.

The *Bundy* case is exceptional and normally the presumption does not apply to the banker/customer relationship.

National Westminster Bank plc v Morgan (1985)

Mrs Morgan agreed to the family home being mortgaged to secure an advance to her husband by the bank. They signed the mortgage after receiving assurances from the bank manager that the mortgage only covered the house loan and not her husband's business liability. Mr Morgan died. His only liability to the bank was in respect of the house loan. Mrs Morgan appealed against a possession order obtained by the bank, on the ground that the mortgage transaction should be set aside because of undue influence on the part of the bank. The House of Lords held that Mrs Morgan's action should fail. Although Mrs Morgan had not had the benefit of independent advice, the bank manager had not taken advantage of her and the transaction was not to her disadvantage.

The legal considerations involved in giving guarantees to secure business loans are discussed in detail in Chapter 4.

LEGALITY

The principle of freedom of contract is subject to a basic rule that the courts will not uphold an agreement which is illegal or contrary to public policy. Where the contract involves some kind of moral wrongdoing, it will be illegal. If, however, the conduct is neither immoral nor blameworthy, but simply undesirable, the contract will be void. A court may object to an agreement either because of a rule of common law or because it is contrary to statute.

Contracts illegal at common law

The following agreements come into this category:

(a) *Contracts to commit crimes or civil wrongs*, e.g. a contract to assassinate someone or to defraud the Inland Revenue.

(b) *Contracts involving sexual immorality*, e.g. an agreement to pay an allowance to a mistress or any contract with an immoral purpose.

Pearce v Brooks (1866)

Pearce let a coach out on hire to a prostitute (Brooks) knowing that it would be used by her to ply her trade. The coach was returned in a damaged state. Pearce was unable to recover the hire charges or for the damage, as the court refused to help him to enforce a contract for an immoral purpose.

(c) *Contracts tending to promote corruption in public life*, e.g. a contract to bribe an official or to procure a title.

(d) *Contracts of trading with an enemy in wartime*.

(e) *Contracts directed against the welfare of a friendly foreign state*, e.g. a partnership intending to import whisky into America during Prohibition (*Foster v Driscoll* (1929)).

(f) *Contracts prejudicial to the administration of justice*, e.g. a contract not to prosecute a person for an offence concerning the public.

Consequences of illegality

A contract which is illegal from the start will be void and unenforceable. Money or property transferred under the contract is not usually recoverable. This general rule is subject to three exceptions:

1 a party can recover money or property if he can establish his case without relying on the illegal contract, e.g. by suing in tort;
2 if the parties are not equally at fault, the less guilty party may be allowed to recover;
3 a party may recover if he repents before the contract has been substantially performed.

Some contracts are quite innocent at the outset, but become illegal because of the intention of one of the parties, e.g. a landlord lets out a flat, unaware of the tenant's intention to install his mistress in it. In this situation, one of the parties is innocent. The guilty party cannot sue on the contract or succeed in any way against the innocent party. The innocent party will protect his rights if he repudiates the contract as soon as he is aware of the illegality.

Contracts void at common law

There are three types of contract in this category:

1 **Contracts to oust the jurisdiction of the courts.** A clause which seeks to prevent the courts trying an issue is void. This rule does not affect 'binding in honour only' clauses, by which the parties agree not to create a contract.

2 **Contracts prejudicial to the status of marriage.** This includes a contract to restrain a person from marrying at all or except for one person. Contracts not to marry a person of a particular religious faith or nationality may be upheld if they are reasonable.

A contract which provides for a possible future separation of husband and wife will be void, but if the marriage is breaking up, they may make a contract to provide for their immediate separation. Contracts to introduce men and women with a view to their subsequent marriage are void. These are known as marriage-brokage contracts.

3 **Contracts in restraint of trade.** These are contracts which restrict the future liberty of a person to carry on his business, trade or profession in any way he chooses. A contract in restraint of trade is contrary to public policy and void unless it is shown to be reasonable as between the parties and from the point of view of the community. A restraint will be reasonable if it is designed to protect legitimate interests, such as trade secrets or business connections. A restraint which is excessive as regards its area, time of operation or the trades it forbids will be void.

There are four main types of restraint which we will consider.

(a) *A term in a contract of employment which restricts an employee's freedom of conduct either during the period of employment or after the employment has terminated.* Such a restraint will only be reasonable if it protects the employer's interests and is not excessive. The only matters in which an employer has a legitimate interest is the protection of trade secrets and his customer connections. The following case involves an employer seeking to protect his trade secrets.

Forster & Sons Ltd v Suggett (1918)
The plaintiffs were manufacturers of glass and glass bottles. They had trained their works manager in the use of certain secret processes, including the correct mixture of gas and air in the furnaces. The works manager had agreed that for a period of five years after his employment with the plaintiffs ended he would not carry on in the UK, or be interested in, glass bottle manufacture or any other business connected with glass-making as carried on by the plaintiffs. It was held that the restraint was enforceable. Secret processes are a legitimate object of protection and in this case the restraint was reasonable.

A distinction must be drawn between protecting trade secrets, which is a protectable interest, and preventing an employee from making use of knowledge and skills which he has acquired in the course of his employment, which is not protectable.

Herbert Morris Ltd v Saxelby (1916)
A seven-year restraint on an engineer employed by a leading UK manufacturer of hoisting machinery was declared void. Although the engineer had access to confidential information, such as drawings, charts and company systems, all that he could take away with him was a very general knowledge of the company's methods and systems. The House of Lords did not regard such knowledge as a trade secret.

In the *Forster* case, the employee was bound by an **express** term in his contract. An express term was not really needed as there is an implied duty on the part of employees not to reveal their employers' trade secrets or other highly confidential information. The implied duty will not cover all commercially sensitive information.

Faccenda Chicken Ltd v Fowler (1986)

The defendant, Fowler, had been employed as the claimant company's sales manager until he resigned to set up a rival business selling chickens from refrigerated vans. Several of Faccenda's employees joined Fowler in his new business. Their contracts of employment with Faccenda did not include an express term restricting their activities if they left their jobs with Faccenda. Faccenda argued that Fowler and his colleagues had broken an implied term of the contract by making use of confidential sales information. The Court of Appeal confirmed the existence of an implied duty of confidentiality but held that the information which Faccenda was trying to protect was not confidential.

An alternative form of protection for an employer is to insert a so-called 'garden leave' clause in an employee's contract of employment (*Evening Standard Co Ltd* v *Henderson* (1987)). Such a clause typically requires the employee to give a long period of notice, e.g. one year. During the notice period, the employee can be barred from the workplace to stop him from acquiring any further information, and he can also be prevented from working for a new employer until his notice period expires. Although he will continue to be paid, he is left with nothing to do but look after his garden.

An employer is also entitled to protect his customer connections by preventing employees from enticing his customers away from him. A restraint of this kind will only be valid if the nature of the employment is such that the employee has personal contact with customers and some influence over them. Restraints have been upheld in the case of a solicitor's clerk (*Fitch* v *Dewes* (1921)), a milk roundsman (*Home Counties Dairies* v *Skilton* (1970)) and an estate agent's clerk (*Scorer* v *Seymour Jones* (1966)). However, an agreement by a manager of a bookmakers not to engage in a similar business to his employer within a 12-mile

radius on the termination of his employment was not upheld as the manager did not have face-to-face contact with his customers (*S W Strange Ltd* v *Mann* (1965)).

Once it is established that the restraint only protects a legitimate interest, the next step is to show that it is reasonable in the circumstances. The restraint must not be excessive as regards its area and time of operation. The two factors are complementary: the wider the area of the restraint, the shorter the duration which might be regarded as reasonable, and vice versa. There are no precise limits, each case is decided on its merits. In *Fitch* v *Dewes* (1921) an agreement by a solicitor's clerk never to practise within seven miles of Tamworth Town Hall was held to be reasonable, whereas in *Commercial Plastics Ltd* v *Vincent* (1964) one of the grounds for finding a one-year restraint to be unreasonable in the context of the plastics industry was that it was unlimited in its area of operation.

If a restraint is upheld by the courts, it can be enforced by an injunction (see later).

(b) *A 'solus' agreement by which a trader agrees to restrict his orders from one supplier.* Although such an agreement is subject to the doctrine of restraint of trade, it may be enforceable if it is reasonable and not contrary to the public interest. A number of cases have arisen from the operation of 'solus' agreements in the petrol industry.

Esso Petroleum Ltd v Harper's Garage (Stourport) Ltd (1967)

Harper's owned two garages. It entered into a 'solus' agreement with Esso by which it agreed to buy all its motor fuel from Esso, to keep the garages open all reasonable hours and not to sell the garages without ensuring that the purchaser entered into a similar agreement with Esso. In return, Esso allowed a rebate on all fuels bought. The agreement was to last for four-and-a-half years in respect of one garage and 21 years for the other. The latter garage was mortgaged to Esso for a loan of £7 000 repayable over 21 years and not earlier. The House of Lords held that the agreements were in restraint of trade and, therefore, void, unless they could be justified as reasonable. The agreement which lasted for four-and-a-half years was reasonable, but the other, which lasted 21 years, was not.

Although the length of the restraint was the deciding factor in the *Harper's* case, a long restraint may be reasonable in certain situations.

Alec Lobb (Garages) Ltd v Total Oil (GB) Ltd (1985)

The Court of Appeal upheld a 21-year restraint tied to a loan agreement as reasonable in the circumstances. The loan was part of a rescue package which greatly benefited the garage. There were also opportunities for the garage to break the arrangement after 7 and 14 years. Taking these facts into account, the restraint was not unreasonable.

(c) *A contract for the sale of a business by which the seller agrees not to compete with the buyer.* This kind of restraint is more likely to be upheld by the courts than a restraint on an employee because there is a greater likelihood of the parties bargaining as equals. Nevertheless, the parties must be careful to ensure that the restraint is no wider than is necessary to provide protection for the purchaser.

British Reinforced Concrete Engineering Co Ltd v Schelff (1921)

The claimants carried on a large business manufacturing and selling 'BRC' road reinforcements. The defendant had a small business selling 'Loop' road reinforcements. The defendant sold his business to the plaintiffs and agreed not to compete with them in the manufacture or sale of road reinforcements. It was held that the restraint was void as it covered a wider area of business than the defendant had transferred to the claimants.

(d) *Contracts between traders and businessmen to regulate prices or output.* This branch of the law is now largely covered by legislation and will be considered later.

Consequences

A clause which is in restraint of trade is void and unenforceable. It may be possible, however, to separate out the void parts of the contract. The lawful main part can then be enforced by the court. Any money paid or property transferred is recoverable.

Contracts illegal by statute

Some statutes expressly prohibit a certain type of contract. For example, under Chapter 1 of the Competition Act 1998 agreements by two or more

persons to fix the price at which goods may be resold are unlawful. The provision outlaws the practice of 'blacklisting' retailers who sell goods below a minimum resale price fixed by suppliers. Not all statutes are quite so specific. Some contracts may incidentally infringe the provisions of an Act of Parliament because, for example, one of the parties is trading without a licence, or statutory requirements have not been observed. It seems that the contract will be illegal if it was Parliament's intention in the passing of the Act to preserve public order or protect the public.

Cope v Rowlands (1836)

A court refused to enforce a contract on behalf of an unlicensed broker because the purpose of the licensing requirements was to protect the public.

The contract will be valid if it appears that the statutory provision was imposed for an administrative purpose.

Smith v Mawhood (1894)

A tobacconist was able to sue on a contract for the sale of tobacco even though he did not have a licence as required by statute. The sole aim of the statute was to raise revenue, not to prohibit contracts made by unlicensed tobacconists

Consequences

The effects of the illegality on the contract are the same as for contracts which are illegal at common law.

Contracts void by statute

Two of the more important examples of these are gaming and wagering contracts and anti-competitive agreements.

1 Gaming and wagering contracts. **Gaming** is defined by the Betting, Gaming and Lotteries Act 1963 as 'the playing of a game of chance for winning in money or money's worth'. All the players must have an equal chance of winning. **Wagering** is where two opposing parties stake something on the result of a future uncertain event or the facts of a past or present event. The parties must not have a special interest in the event and it must be possible for one to win and the other to lose.

The Gaming Act 1845 provides that all contracts by way of 'gaming or wagering shall be null and void'. The contract cannot be enforced in the courts and any money or property transferred cannot be recovered.

2 Anti-competitive agreements. Statutory control of anti-competitive agreements in the UK is set out in the Competition Act 1998 and the Fair Trading Act 1973. The Competition Act introduces a new regime for dealing with anti-competitive practices based on European Community competition law contained in Arts 81 and 82 of the EC Treaty. The new competition law framework – which replaces the Restrictive Trade Practices Act 1976 and 1977, the Restrictive Trade Practices Court Act 1976, the Resale Prices Act 1976 and the anti-competitive practices provisions of the Competition Act 1980 – is discussed in more detail below.

COMPETITION POLICY

Competition is an essential requirement of a free-market economy. It encourages efficiency among producers and suppliers by providing consumers with a choice of goods and services at the best possible price. Paradoxically, however, unregulated competition in a free market leads inevitably to monopoly and other undesirable practices. A company which is aggressively competitive will seek to win as large a share of the market as is possible and in so doing reduce the competition it faces. If the company is too successful, it may in time completely eliminate any competition. Another problem which may arise is that companies may find it more profitable to cooperate with each other than to compete. Companies within a particular industry may form a cartel to fix minimum prices for their products or restrict production, denying consumers the benefits of a competitive market. Thus, it is necessary to regulate the competitive process in order to maintain a healthy free market which serves the interests of consumers. Statutory regulation of competition in the UK is relatively recent. Before the enactment of the Monopolies and Trade Practices Act 1948, the only control over anti-competitive practices was the common law doctrine of restraint of trade, but

this was of limited application. Statutory intervention was confined initially to the establishing of an investigatory system but tough powers to ban anti-competitive practices soon followed. Competition law in the UK developed in a piecemeal fashion after 1948 in response to changing needs and circumstances. By 1997 the law had become a complex mixture of UK and EC provisions with responsibility for the enforcement spread between a number of different agencies. In 1997 the government announced its intention of reforming UK competition law. The Competition Act 1998 received the Royal Assent on 9 November and came into force on 1 March 2000. An outline of the new legal framework is set out below.

European Community competition law

Under Arts 81 and 82 of the Treaty of Rome all agreements between businesses which operate to prevent or restrict competition in the EC are void. Article 81 bans practices which distort competition between members of the EC. These include price fixing, restrictions in production and market sharing. The European Commission may grant exemptions in relation to individual agreements and block exemptions for certain categories of agreement. Article 82 prohibits the abuse of a monopolistic position by an organisation within the EC. Practices which might be considered abuses include imposing unfair buying or selling prices. Responsibility for enforcing these provisions rests with the European Commission.

Publishers' Association v Commission of the European Communities (1992)

This European Court of Justice case involved the operation of the Net Book Agreement under which publishers enforced resale price maintenance in respect of books. The agreement had been approved by the Restrictive Practices Court under UK legislation (*Re Net Book Agreement* (1962)). However, in 1988 the European Commission found that the Agreement infringed Art 81 in respect of books sold from the UK to other EC states. The Commission turned down an application for exemption. The Publishers' Association applied to the European Court for an annulment of the Commission's decision. The European Court upheld the Commission's view that the Agreement infringed Art 81.

Comment. The European Court's judgment did not affect the operation of the Net Book Agreement within the UK. The Commission's challenge was confined to how it operated in other EC states. However, the Net Book Agreement only lasted for a few years after this judgment. The agreement collapsed in practice in 1995, and in March 1997 the Restrictive Practices Court discharged the orders which upheld the agreement.

The European Commission also has the power to control mergers with a Community dimension under an EC Merger Control Regulation which came into force in 1990. A merger will come within the terms of the EC Regulation if both:

(a) the aggregate worldwide turnover exceeds 5 billion ECU; and

(b) at least two of the parties have a community turnover in excess of 250 million ECU unless each of the undertakings makes more than two-thirds of its turnover in the same member state.

Mergers falling within the threshold must be notified to the Commission within a week of the conclusion of the agreement to acquire control. The Commission must decide within a month of notification whether to launch a full investigation, which must be completed within a further four months. If the Commission concludes that the merger will significantly impede effective competition in the whole or part of the EC, it must be blocked.

UK competition law

Competition Act 1998

The Competition Act introduces two prohibitions which are largely based on the prohibitions operating at European level under Arts 81 and 82.

Chapter I prohibition. The first prohibition, the Chapter I prohibition, is based on Art 81. It prohibits agreements which have the object or effect of preventing, restricting or distorting competition in the UK. The anti-competitive nature of the agreement will be judged according to its effects or intended effects on competition. The Act sets out illustrative examples of agreements to which the prohibition applies:

- agreeing to fix purchase or selling prices or other trading conditions;
- agreeing to limit or control production, markets, technical development or investment;
- agreeing to share markets or supply sources;
- agreeing to apply different trading conditions to equivalent transactions, thereby placing some parties at a competitive disadvantage;
- agreeing to make contracts subject to unrelated conditions.

The agreement must have an 'appreciable effect' on competition. An agreement is unlikely to be considered as having an appreciable effect where the combined market share of the parties does not exceed 25 per cent. However, agreements to fix prices, impose minimum resale prices or share markets will be seen as capable of having an appreciable effect even where the market share falls below 25 per cent.

Certain types of agreement are excluded from the Chapter I prohibition, such as where there are overriding considerations of national policy. Some agreements are exempt from the prohibition. There are three types of exemption:

1 Individual exemption. The parties to an individual agreement may apply to the Director General of Fair Trading for exemption for their agreement, if it can be shown that the agreement contributes to improving production or distribution, or to promoting technical or economic progress and allows consumers a fair share of the resulting benefit. Any restrictions in the agreement must be indispensable to achieving these aims and the agreement must not eliminate competition.

2 Block exemptions. These exemptions apply automatically to certain types of agreement which meet the same exemption criteria as for individual exemption.

3 Parallel exemptions. These exemptions automatically apply where an agreement is covered by an EC individual or block exemption under Art 81(3) of the EC Treaty, or would be covered by an EC block exemption if the agreement had an effect on trade between member states of the EU. In certain circumstances, the Director General may impose conditions on the exemption or vary or cancel the exemption.

Chapter II prohibition. The second prohibition, the Chapter II prohibition, is based on Art 82. It prohibits the abuse by an undertaking of a dominant position in the UK or part of the UK, where this affects trade within the UK. The Act contains an illustrative list of the kinds of conduct which may be deemed an abuse:

- imposing unfair purchase or selling prices;
- limiting production, markets or technical developments to the prejudice of consumers;
- applying different trading conditions to equivalent transactions, thereby placing certain parties at a competitive disadvantage;
- attaching unrelated supplementary conditions to contracts.

There are two tests for determining whether the Chapter II prohibition applies:

- whether an undertaking is dominant; and
- if it is dominant, whether it is abusing its dominant position.

An undertaking will be regarded as dominant if it can behave 'to an appreciable extent independently of its competitors and customers and ultimately of consumers' when making decisions. The Act does not set any market share thresholds for a presumption of dominance but guidance from EC case law is relevant. The European Court of Justice has stated that dominance can be presumed if an undertaking has a market share persistently above 50 per cent. The Director General takes the view that an undertaking is unlikely to be considered dominant if its market share is less than 40 per cent. Nevertheless, an undertaking with a lower market share may be considered dominant if, for example, the structure of the market enables it to act independently of its competitors. The Director General will consider the number and size of existing competitors as well as the potential for new competitors to enter the market.

The Chapter II prohibition is subject to similar exclusions to the Chapter I prohibition. There are, however, no exemptions from Chapter II.

Enforcement. Responsibility for enforcing the new legislation rests primarily with the Director General. He has the power to grant exemptions, investigate suspected breaches, make decisions enforceable by a court order and publish advice and information. The utility regulators enjoy equivalent powers within their own areas of responsibility.

If the Director General has reasonable grounds for suspecting an infringement of the Act, he may exercise the following powers:

- order the production of any relevant documents or information (he may take copies of any documents produced and require an explanation of the contents);
- enter premises without a warrant in order to obtain documents, take copies of them, obtain an explanation of the documents or obtain information held on a computer to be produced in a readable form (two working days' notice must be given to the occupier of the premises unless, for example, the undertaking is already under investigation);
- enter premises without notice on the authority of a High Court warrant, to search for documentary evidence.

Failure to cooperate with an investigation may amount to a criminal offence, punishable by a fine or imprisonment.

If the Director General concludes that infringement of either prohibition has occurred, he may give a direction to either party to bring the infringement to an end. This may include directions to modify or terminate the agreement or modify or cease the offending conduct. If a party fails to comply with a direction, the Director General can seek a court order to secure compliance. Any breach of a court order will be dealt with as a contempt of court.

Consequences of breach. The Director General has the power to impose civil fines of up to 10 per cent of an undertaking's turnover for infringement of either Chapter I or Chapter II prohibitions. Small businesses enjoy limited immunity from financial penalties in respect of small agreements (Chapter I prohibition) and conduct of minor significance (Chapter II prohibition).

An agreement which infringes the Chapter I prohibition is void and unenforceable. Third parties who believe that they have suffered loss as a result of an unlawful agreement or conduct may have a claim for damages in the courts under the terms of s 60, which requires the UK authorities to deal with cases in a way which is consistent with EC law.

Competition Commission. The Competition Act 1998 establishes the Competition Commission (CC), which replaces the Monopolies and Mergers Commission. The CC is an independent administrative tribunal whose chairman and members are appointed by the Secretary of State. The CC carries out two functions:

1 it hears appeals against decisions made by the Director General in enforcing the prohibitions;
2 it investigates specific markets or the conduct of companies or mergers, decides what is in the public interest and reports to the Secretary of State with any recommendations for action. It has no power to initiate its own inquiries. Examples of recent investigations include the supply of groceries by supermarkets and the supply of new cars.

Fair Trading Act 1973

This Act gives the Office of Fair Trading, led by the Director General of Fair Trading, wide powers to deal with monopolies and mergers.

1 **Monopolies.** It is the duty of the Director General to monitor the activities of companies and the workings of specific markets, and to evaluate allegations of monopoly abuse. If there is prima facie evidence of a monopoly situation, he may refer the case to the Competition Commission or obtain assurances from companies that they will alter their business practices. Under the Act a monopoly situation exists in the following circumstances:

(a) where one company supplies or purchases 25 per cent or more of all the goods or services of a particular type in the UK (scale monopoly) or in a part of the UK (local monopoly); or
(b) where a group of companies acting together controls 15 per cent of the market (complex monopoly).

The reference may be broad, asking the CC to undertake a general investigation of a market, or narrow, concentrating on a specific issue, such as the pricing policy in a particular market.

Following its investigation, the CC submits a report to the Secretary of State for Trade and Industry with recommendations for action. Acting on the advice of the Director General, the Secretary of State decides on appropriate action which may include making orders to remedy the situation or asking the Director General to obtain undertakings from those concerned.

2 **Mergers.** The Director General is also required to keep an eve on business activity to identify mergers which have taken place or are about to take place. A merger is liable to investigation in the following circumstances:

(a) where the gross assets of the company to be taken over are worth £70 million or more; or
(b) where, as a result of the merger, 15 per cent of the market for particular goods or services will be under the control of the merging enterprise.

If the Director General has reasonable grounds to believe that the merger would be contrary to the public interest, he can advise the Secretary of State to refer the case to the CC for a more detailed examination of the public interest. If the merger involves newspapers with a combined circulation of more than 500,000 copies, the permission of the Secretary of State must be obtained before the merger can proceed, and he is under a general duty to make a reference to the CC. If the CC concludes that the merger does not operate against the public interest, the merger will be allowed to proceed. If the CC concludes that the merger is contrary to the public interest, it will advise the Secretary of State accordingly and recommend ways in which the situation can be rectified. The Secretary of State is not obliged to accept the CC's recommendation. However, if he decides to act, he may use his powers to impose conditions on the merger or order divestment of shares. More usually, the Director General is asked to secure undertakings from the companies involved.

DISCHARGE OF CONTRACTS

The contract may come to an end and the parties be discharged from their contractual obligations in four ways: by performance, agreement, frustration and breach.

Performance

The general rule is that the parties must carry out precisely what they agreed under their contract. If one of the parties does something less than or different from that which he agreed to do, he is not discharged from the contract and, moreover, cannot sue on the contract.

Cutter v Powell (1795)

Cutter agreed to serve on a ship sailing from Jamaica to Liverpool. He was to be paid 30 guineas on arrival at Liverpool. The ship sailed on 2 August, arriving in Liverpool on 9 October, but Cutter died at sea on 20 September. It was held that his widow could not recover anything for the work he had done before he died. Cutter was obliged to complete the voyage before he was entitled to payment

Comment. This old case is often presented as classic illustration of the law's insistence on complete performance as a prerequisite of the right to sue in respect of an entire contract. Although the point being made is still valid, the case itself would not be decided in the same way today. Cutter's widow would now be able to argue that her husband's untimely death had frustrated the contract and that she should recover in respect of the valuable benefit her husband conferred on his employer before his death under s 1(3) of the Law Reform (Frustrated Contracts) Act 1943.

Bolton v Mahadeva (1972)

Bolton installed a central heating system in Mahadeva's house for an agreed price of £560. The work was carried out defectively and it was estimated that it would cost £179 to put matters right. The Court of Appeal held that since Bolton had not performed his side of the contract, he could recover nothing for the work he had done.

In each of these cases, one party has profited from the failure of the other to provide complete performance. A strict application of the rule about precise performance would frequently lead to injustice. It is not surprising, therefore, that certain exceptions to the rule have developed.

1 **Doctrine of substantial performance.** If the court decides that the claimant has substantially carried out the terms of the contract, he may recover for the work he has done. The defendant can counterclaim for any defects in performance.

Hoenig v Isaacs (1952)

The claimant agreed to decorate the defendant's flat and fit a bookcase and wardrobe for £750. On completion of the work, the defendant paid £400 but he complained about faulty workmanship and refused to pay the balance of £350. The Court of Appeal held that the contract had been substantially performed. The claimant was entitled to the outstanding £350, less the cost of remedying the defects, which was estimated at £55 18s 2d.

2 **Acceptance of partial performance.** If one of the parties only partially carries out his side of the contract, but the other party, exercising a genuine choice, accepts the benefit of the partial performance, the court will infer a promise to pay for the benefit received.

3 **Performance prevented by the promisee.** A person who is prevented from carrying out his side of the bargain by the other party can bring an action to recover for the work he has done.

Planche v Colburn (1831)

The claimant agreed to write a book on 'Costume and Ancient Armour', on completion of which he was to receive £100. After he had done the necessary research and written part of the book, the publishers abandoned the project. He recovered 50 guineas for the work he had done. The claimant's claim was based on quasi-contract. He could not sue on the contract because the obligation to pay him did not arise until he had completed and delivered the work to the publishers, which he had not done. He was able to sue on a *quantum meruit* for the work he had done.

4 **Divisible contracts.** Some contracts are said to be 'entire'. This means that a party is not entitled to payment until he has completely performed his part of the contract, e.g. *Cutter v Powell* (1795). Other contracts may be divisible, i.e. the obligations can be split up into stages or parts. Payment can be claimed for each completed stage. A contract to build a house usually provides for payment to be made in three stages: after the foundations have been laid, when the roof goes on, and on completion of the house.

Agreement

The parties may have agreed in their original contract that it should end automatically with the happening of some event or after a fixed period of time. The agreement may have included a term allowing either party to terminate the contract by giving notice. A contract of employment, for example, can be brought to an end by either the employer or employee giving reasonable notice to the other. The Employment Rights Act 1996 lays down statutory minimum periods of notice. Employers must also consider the rules about unfair dismissal and redundancy. A contract may be discharged by the execution of a separate agreement. The new agreement will only discharge the old contract if it possesses all the characteristics of a valid contract; in particular, consideration must be present. When neither party has yet performed his side of the contract, there is no difficulty. Both sides, by waiving their rights, are providing something of value which constitutes consideration. The situation is different where one side has already completely performed his obligations and the other party wishes to be released. The person seeking release must either provide fresh consideration or the agreement must be drawn up in the form of a deed.

Frustration

An agreement which is impossible of performance from the outset will be void for mistake, as in *Couturier v Hastie* (1856). But what is the legal position where initially it is perfectly possible to carry out the contract, and then a change in circumstances occurs making it impossible to carry out the agreement?

Until the last century, the rule was that the parties were under an absolute duty to perform their contractual obligations. A person was not excused simply because outside events had made performance impossible.

Paradine v *Jane* (1647)
During the course of the English Civil War a tenant was evicted from certain property by Prince Rupert and his army. In an action by the landlord to recover three years' arrears of rent, it was held that the tenant was not relieved from the obligation to pay rent simply because he had been unable to enjoy the property.

Starting with the case of *Taylor* v *Caldwell* (1863), the courts recognised an exception to the rule about absolute contracts under the doctrine of

frustration: if further performance of the contract is prevented because of events beyond the control of the parties, the contract is terminated and the parties discharged from their obligations. The doctrine will apply in the circumstances described below.

1 Physical impossibility. This is where something or someone necessary to carry out the contract ceases to be available.

Taylor v *Caldwell* (1863)
The claimant had hired the Surrey Gardens and Music Hall for a series of concerts. However, after making the agreement and before the date of the first performance, the hall was destroyed by fire. It was held that the contract was discharged and the parties were released from their obligations.

If the presence of a particular person is necessary for the execution of the contract, the death of that person will clearly discharge the contract. Frustration may also apply if a party is unavailable because of illness, internment or imprisonment.

Hare v *Murphy Bros* (1974)
Hare was sentenced to 12 months' imprisonment for unlawful wounding and was, therefore, unavailable to carry out his responsibilities as a foreman. It was held that this frustrated his contract of employment.

Comment. An employee who loses his job as a result of long-term illness or, as in Hare's case, a substantial term of imprisonment, may find that his contract of employment has been frustrated. The significance of such a finding is that there will not have been a 'dismissal' according to the statutory provisions relating to unfair dismissal (and redundancy). If there has been no 'dismissal', the employee cannot bring a claim for unfair dismissal (or redundancy) against his employer.

2 Supervening illegality. A subsequent change in the law or in circumstances may make performance of the contract illegal. An export contract will be discharged if war breaks out with the country of destination.

Denny, Mott & Dickson Ltd v *James B Fraser & Co Ltd* (1944)
The House of Lords refused to enforce an option to purchase a timber yard which was part of a contract involving the sale of timber because subsequent government regulations had made performance of the main part of the contract, trading in timber, illegal.

3 Foundation of the contract destroyed. The parties may have made their contract on the basis of some forthcoming event. If the event fails to take place and, as a result, the main purpose of the contract cannot be achieved, the doctrine of frustration will apply.

Krell v Henry (1903)

Henry hired a room overlooking the route of Edward VII's coronation procession. The procession was cancelled owing to the King's serious illness. Although it would have been possible to come and sit in the room, the main purpose of the contract, to view the procession, had been destroyed. The Court of Appeal held that the contract had been frustrated.

A contract will only be frustrated if the change in circumstances has had a substantial effect on the main purpose of the contract.

Herne Bay Steam Boat Company v Hutton (1903)

The claimant agreed to hire a steamboat, the 'Cynthia', to the defendant for two days so that the defendant could take paying passengers to see the naval review at Spithead on the occasion of Edward VII's coronation. An official announcement was made cancelling the review, but the fleet still gathered and the 'Cynthia' could have been used for a cruise around the fleet. The defendant did not make use of the boat and the claimant used her for ordinary sailings. The claimant sued for £200, which was the outstanding balance on the contract to hire the boat. A Court of Appeal held that the contract was not discharged through frustration. The happening of the naval review was not the foundation of the contract. The claimant was entitled, therefore, to recover the £200 he was owed under the contract.

The fact that the contract has become more difficult and more expensive to carry out will not excuse the parties.

Tsakiroglou & Co Ltd v Noblee and Thorl GmbH (1962)

In October 1956 sellers agreed to deliver ground nuts from Port Sudan to buyers in Hamburg, shipment to take place during November/December 1956. On 2 November the Suez Canal was closed to traffic. The sellers failed to deliver and, when sued for breach of contract, argued that the contract had been frustrated. Clearly, it had not become impossible to carry out the contract: shipment could have been made via the Cape of Good Hope – a longer and much more expensive operation. The House of Lords held that this was not sufficient to discharge the contract for frustration.

Davis Contractors Ltd v Fareham UDC (1956)

The claimant contractors agreed to build 78 houses in eight months for the defendant council. Owing to post-war shortages of skilled labour and building materials, it took the contractors 22 months to complete the houses at an additional cost of £17,651. The claimants argued that the contract was frustrated because of the long delay caused by circumstances beyond their control and they should be able to recover the full cost incurred on a *quantum meruit* basis. The House of Lords held that the contract was not discharged by frustration. The contractors could have foreseen the possibility of shortages and taken it into account when tendering for the work.

The doctrine of frustration will not apply in the following situations:

(a) where the parties have foreseen the likelihood of such an event occurring and have made express provision for it in the contract;

(b) where one of the parties is responsible for the frustrating event. This is known as 'self-induced frustration'.

Maritime National Fish Ltd v Ocean Trawlers Ltd (1938)

The appellants chartered a trawler from the respondents which needed to be fitted with an otter trawl. It was illegal to operate with an otter trawl unless a licence had been obtained. The appellants applied for five licences to cover four trawlers of their own and the trawler on charter; however, they were granted only three licences. They decided to nominate their own trawlers for licences rather than the chartered trawler. The Judicial Committee of the Privy Council held that the contract was not frustrated as the appellants had decided quite deliberately not to nominate the respondents' trawler and were, therefore, responsible for the frustrating event.

The consequences of frustration

At common law, a frustrating event has the effect of bringing the contract to an immediate end. The rights and liabilities of the parties are frozen at the moment of frustration. The rule was that money payable before frustration remained payable and money paid before frustration could not be recovered. Any money which did not become payable until after frustration ceased to be payable. The harsh consequences of this rule were modified by the House of Lords in the *Fibrosa* case (1943) and wider changes were introduced under the Law Reform (Frustrated Contracts) Act 1943. The Act made two important changes:

1 money payable before frustration ceases to be payable and money paid before frustration can be recovered (the court may in its discretion allow the payee to recover or retain all or part of the sums to cover any expenses incurred);
2 a party who has carried out acts of part performance can recover compensation for any valuable benefit (other than a payment of money) conferred on the other party.

The Act does not apply to (a) contracts for the carriage of goods by sea, (b) insurance contracts, or (c) contracts for the sale of specific goods, which are covered by s 7 of the Sale of Goods Act 1979. The parties may exclude the effect of the Act by express agreement.

Breach

A breach of contract may occur in a number of ways. It may be an anticipatory or an actual breach.

Anticipatory breach

This is where a party states in advance that he does not intend to carry out his side of the contract or puts himself in a position whereby he will be unable to perform. The injured party may sue immediately for breach of contract or, alternatively, wait for the time for performance to arrive to see whether the other party is prepared to carry out the contract.

Hochster v De la Tour (1853)

The claimant was engaged by the defendant in April 1852 to act as a courier for travel in Europe from 1 June 1852. On 11 May the defendant wrote to the claimant to inform him that his services were no longer required. The claimant started an action for breach of contract on 22 May. Although the date for performance had not yet arrived, it was held that the defendant's letter constituted an actionable breach of contract.

It can be dangerous to wait for the time for performance. The injured party may lose the right to sue for breach of contract if in the meantime the contract is discharged for frustration or illegality.

Avery v Bowden (1855)

The defendant chartered the claimant's ship, the Lebanon, and agreed to load her with a cargo at Odessa within 45 days. During this period, the defendant told the claimant on a number of occasions to sail the ship away as it would not be possible to provide a cargo. The claimant kept the ship at Odessa hoping that the defendant would carry out his side of the contract. Before the 45 days had expired, the Crimean War broke out. Odessa became an enemy port and it would have been illegal to carry out the contract. Assuming that the defendant's repeated statements amounted to an anticipatory breach, the claimant could have accepted the breach and sued at once. However, by choosing to keep the contract alive he lost his right to sue because of the illegality.

Actual breach

One party may fail completely to perform his side of the bargain or he may fail to carry out one or some of his obligations. Not every breach of contract has the effect of discharging the parties from their contractual obligations. The terms of a contract may be divided into those terms which are important (**conditions**) and the less important terms (**warranties**). The distinction will be considered in more detail in Chapter 9. A breach of condition does not automatically terminate the contract. The injured party has a choice: he may wish to be discharged from the contract or he may prefer to carry on with the contract and claim damages for the breach. A breach of warranty only entitles the injured party to sue for damages.

REMEDIES

So far we have looked at the essential elements of a valid contract, the factors which may affect the validity of an agreement and the way in which a contract may come to an end. We now turn to the remedies available to the injured party when a term of the contract has been broken. Every breach of contract will give the injured party the common law right to recover damages (financial compensation). Other remedies, such as specific performance and injunction, may be granted at the discretion of the court as part of its equitable jurisdiction.

Damages

In the business world it is quite common for the parties to agree in advance the damages that will be payable in the event of a breach of contract. These are known as liquidated damages. If there is no prior agreement as to the sum to be paid, the amount of damages is said to be unliquidated.

Liquidated damages

It makes commercial common sense for the parties to establish at the outset of their relationship the financial consequences of failing to live up to their bargain. Provided the parties have made a genuine attempt to estimate the likely loss, the courts will accept the relevant figure as the damages payable. In practice, knowing the likely outcome of any legal action, the party at fault will simply pay up without argument. An example of liquidated damages are the charges imposed for cancelling a holiday (see Fig 7.2).

Of course, there is a temptation for a party with stronger bargaining power to try to impose a penalty clause, which is really designed as a threat to secure performance. The distinction between liquidated damages and penalty clauses is illustrated by the following cases.

Dunlop Pneumatic Tyre Co Ltd v New Garage & Motor Co Ltd (1915)

Dunlop supplied tyres to New Garage under an agreement by which, in return for a trade discount, New Garage agreed to pay £5 by way of 'liquidated damages' for every item sold below list prices. The House of Lords held that since the sum was not extravagant, it was a genuine attempt by the parties to estimate the damage which price undercutting would cause Dunlop. The £5 was liquidated damages.

Sunkist Tours – Cancellation charges	
Cancellation notified	*Charges*
Over 6 weeks prior to departure	Loss of deposit
Within 4 to 6 weeks of departure	30% of holiday cost
Within 2 to 4 weeks of departure	45% of holiday cost
Within 1 day to 2 weeks of departure	60% of holiday cost
On or after the day of departure	100% of holiday cost

Fig 7.2 An example of a cancellation charges notice

Ford Motor Co v Armstrong (1915)

Armstrong, a retailer, agreed to pay £250 for each Ford car sold below the manufacturer's list price. The Court of Appeal held that the clause was void as a penalty.

If the court holds that the sum is liquidated damages, it will be enforced irrespective of whether the actual loss is greater or smaller.

Cellulose Acetate Silk Co Ltd v Widnes Foundry Ltd (1933)

Widnes Foundry agreed to pay £20 for every week of delay in completing a plant for the Silk Co. The work was completed 30 weeks late. The Silk Co claimed that its actual losses amounted to nearly £6,000. It was held that Widnes Foundry was only liable to pay £20 a week (i.e. £600) as agreed.

Unliquidated damages

The aim of unliquidated damages is to put the injured party in the position he would have been in if the contract had been carried out properly. Damages are designed to compensate for loss. If no loss has been suffered, the court will only award nominal damages: a small sum to mark the fact that there had been a breach of contract. The courts observe the following guidelines when awarding damages:

1 The damage can include sums for financial loss, damage to property, personal injury and distress, disappointment and upset caused to the claimant.

Jarvis v Swans Tours (1973)

Jarvis, a solicitor, paid £63.45 for a two-week winter sports holiday in Switzerland. The Swans Tours brochure promised a 'house party' atmosphere at the hotel, a bar which would be open several evenings a week and a host who spoke English. The holiday was a considerable disappointment: in the second week, he was the only guest in the hotel and no one else could speak English. The bar was only open one evening and the skiing was disappointing. The Court of Appeal awarded him £125 to compensate for 'the loss of entertainment and enjoyment which he was promised'.

Exemplary or punitive damages designed to punish the party in breach are not normally awarded in contract.

2 The injured party cannot necessarily recover damages for every kind of loss which he has suffered. The breach might have caused a chain reaction of

events to occur. Clearly, there is a point beyond which the damage becomes too remote from the original breach. The rules relating to remoteness of damage were laid down in *Hadley* v *Baxendale* (1854). The injured party may recover damages for:

(a) loss which has resulted naturally and in the ordinary course of events from the defendant's breach; and

(b) the loss which, although not a natural consequence of the defendant's breach, was in the minds of the parties when the contract was made.

The practical application of these rules can be seen in the following cases.

Victoria Laundry (Windsor) Ltd v Newman Industries Ltd (1949)

The claimant company of launderers and dyers wished to expand its business and, for this purpose, had ordered a new boiler from the defendants. The boiler was damaged during the course of its removal and, as a result, there was a five-month delay in delivery. The claimant claimed:

(a) damages of £16 per week for the loss of profits it would have made on the planned expansion of the laundry business; and

(b) damages of £262 a week for loss of profits it would have made on extremely lucrative dyeing contracts.

The Court of Appeal held that the claimant was entitled to recover for the normal loss of profits on both cleaning and dyeing contracts, but it could not recover for the especially profitable dyeing contracts of which the defendants were ignorant.

Simpson v London and North Western Rail Co (1876)

Simpson entrusted samples of his products to the defendants for delivery to Newcastle, for exhibition at an agricultural show. The goods were marked 'must be at Newcastle on Monday certain'. They failed to arrive in time. The defendants were held liable for Simpson's prospective loss of profit arising from his inability to exhibit at Newcastle. They had agreed to carry the goods knowing of the special instructions of the customer.

3 Provided the loss is not too remote, the next matter to consider is how much is payable by way of damages. As we have already seen, the object is to put the injured party in the same position as if the contract had been performed. This is some-

times described as providing compensation for loss of expectation. Expectation losses may include loss of profit which would have been made but for the breach or the cost of achieving agreed performance. In some situations the claimant may prefer to recover the losses he has incurred in reliance on the contract. Reliance loss includes wasted expenditure. It seems that the claimant may claim for reliance losses rather than expectation losses if he so chooses.

Anglia Television Ltd v Reed (1971)

The claimants engaged the defendant, a well-known American actor, to play the lead in a film they were making for television. At the last moment the defendant repudiated the contract and, as the claimants were unable to find a suitable replacement, the film was abandoned. The claimants did not attempt to claim for loss of profits as it was not possible to say whether the film would have been a success. However, they were successful in recovering their wasted expenditure (on employing a director, scriptwriter and other actors, researching locations and so on), even though some of the expenses had been incurred before the defendant entered into the contract. Lord Denning explained the decision as follows: 'it is plain that, when Mr Reed entered into this contract, he must have known perfectly well that much expenditure had already been incurred on director's fees and the like. He must have contemplated – or at any rate, it is reasonably to be imputed to him – that if he broke his contract, all that expenditure would be wasted, whether or not it was incurred before or after the contract.'

Comment. This unanimous decision of the Court of Appeal has been criticised for allowing recovery of pre-contractual expenditure which has not been incurred in reliance on the defendant's promise.

If the claimant has not suffered a loss as a result of the breach, the court will only award nominal damages.

C & P Haulage v Middleton (1983)

C & P had granted Mr Middleton a six-month renewable licence to occupy a garage which he used to carry on his business. Mr Middleton spent some money equipping the premises, but the terms of his agreement prevented him from removing such equipment at the end of the licence. The parties quarrelled and, as a result, Mr Middleton was unlawfully evicted from the garage ten weeks before the end of a six-month period. Fortunately, Mr Middleton's local council allowed him to use his own garage for more than ten weeks, which meant that he did not have to pay rent. He sued C & P for the cost of equipping the premises. The Court of Appeal held that he was entitled to nominal damages only. The cost of equipping the garage would have been lost even if the contract had been carried out as agreed. It is not the function of the courts to put the injured party in a better financial position than if the contract had been properly performed.

Where the breach of contract consists of defective performance of a building contract, the courts have sometimes based the award of damages on the difference between the value of the building contracted for and the defective building, and sometimes on the cost of curing the defect.

Ruxley Electronics and Construction Ltd v *Forsyth* (1995)

The claimant company agreed to build a swimming pool for Mr Forsyth. It was a term of the contract that the pool should be 7ft 6in at the deep end, to allow for safe diving. When the pool was built, however, it had a maximum depth of 6ft 9in and was only 6ft under the diving board. The trial judge held that even though the pool was not as deep as specified in the contract, it was still safe for diving. There was no evidence that the value of the pool had decreased because of the shortfall in depth. The only way of curing the defect would be to demolish the pool and build a new one at a cost of £21,560. The judge doubted whether Mr Forsyth would build a new pool as it would not be reasonable to do so. The judge awarded £2,500 for loss of amenity. The Court of Appeal reversed the decision of the trial judge and awarded Mr Forsyth the full cost of achieving a cure, i.e. £21,560. The House of Lords reversed the decision of the Court of Appeal and reinstated the trial judge's original decision. Their lordships took the view that if the cost of cure was unreasonable, the measure of damages should be the difference in value. Although the pool was probably no less valuable, Mr Forsyth was entitled to some compensation for his loss of satisfaction.

Breaches of contract for the sale of goods are subject to the rules laid down in the Sale of Goods Act 1979. They will be considered in more detail in Chapter 10.

4 Once a breach of contract has occurred, the innocent party is under a duty to mitigate (minimise) his loss. He cannot stand back and allow the loss to get worse. A seller whose goods have been rejected, for example, must attempt to get the best possible price for them elsewhere. The claimant will not be able to recover for that part of the loss which has resulted from his failure to mitigate.

Brace v *Calder* (1895)

The claimant was dismissed by his employers but offered immediate re-engagement on the same terms and conditions as before. He refused the offer and instead sued to recover the salary he would have received for the remaining 19 months of his two-year contract. It was held that the claimant should have mitigated the loss by accepting the employer's reasonable offer of re-employment. He was entitled to nominal damages only.

The duty to mitigate any loss does not arise until there has been a breach of contract which the injured party has accepted as a breach.

White and Carter (Councils) Ltd v *McGregor* (1961)

The claimants were advertising agents who supplied local authorities with litter bins on which they displayed advertisements. The defendant entered into a contract with the claimants to advertise his garage in this way for a three-year period. Later the same day, however, the defendant cancelled the contract. The claimants refused to accept the cancellation and proceeded to carry out the contract by preparing advertising plates and attaching them to litter bins. The claimants sued for the full amount due under the contract. The House of Lords upheld their claim. The claimants were under no duty to mitigate their loss because they had not accepted the defendant's breach.

Comment. Although the reasoning in this case is logical, the result, as Lord Keith put it, is 'startling'. However, a limitation to the principle was suggested by Lord Reid when he said that the rule would not apply if the injured party has no legitimate interest in performing the contract rather than claiming damages. This approach has been accepted in subsequent cases *(Clea Shipping Corpn* v *Bulk Oil International Ltd (The Alaskan Trader) (No 2)* (1984).

Debt recovery

So far we have considered the basis on which **damages** can be recovered for a **breach of contract.** It is worth noting at this point that where one party performs his part of the contract, e.g. by delivering goods, and the other party refuses to pay, the claim is for payment of the **debt** rather than an action for damages.

Late payment of bills has been a persistent problem for UK businesses, often causing serious cash flow difficulties, particularly for small businesses. It is, of course, possible to include a clause in a supply contract providing for the payment of interest if payment is not made by the due date. Alternatively, debts can be pursued through the courts and the courts can award interest. Neither course of action is appropriate for small businesses. The relatively weak bargaining position of small businesses means that they are, in practice, unable to insist on default clauses, while pursuing a debt through the courts can be a costly and lengthy process, which a small business can ill afford.

The Late Payment of Commercial Debts (Interest) Act 1998 introduces a statutory right for businesses to claim interest on the late payment of commercial debts. The right is being introduced in three stages:

- *stage 1* (from 1 November 1998) – small businesses have a statutory right to claim interest from large businesses and the public sector;
- *stage 2* (from 1 November 2000) – the statutory right is extended to allow small businesses to claim interest from other small businesses;
- *stage 3* (from 1 November 2002) – all businesses and the public sector can claim interest from all businesses and the public sector.

'Small' businesses are defined as businesses having no more than 50 employees or their part-time equivalent. A 'large' business is a business with more than 50 full-time employees or their part-time equivalent.

Businesses are encouraged to agree their own contractual terms providing for contractual interest to be payable if bills are paid late. However, the Act prevents abuse of contractual interest, by requiring any contractual remedy to be 'substantial'. A remedy for late payment will be 'substantial' if it is enough to compensate the supplier for the cost of late payment and it deters late payment and it is fair and reasonable, in all the circumstances, to allow the contractual remedy to replace the statutory right. In deciding whether a contractual remedy is reasonable, the courts will consider all the circumstances, including the rate of interest applying to late payments and the length of credit periods. If the credit period is found to be excessive, the court can strike it down and replace it with the 30-day statutory default period.

If the parties do not agree to contractual interest for late payment, the Act will apply. Payment will be classed as late if it is made after the expiry of:

- the credit period agreed by the parties;
- the credit period determined by trade custom or practice or a course of dealings between the parties;
- the statutory default credit period of 30 days from delivery of the invoice or the goods or the service.

The rate of statutory interest is set by the Secretary of State and is currently the UK base rate (as announced by the Monetary Policy Committee of the Bank of England) plus 8 per cent.

The EC has adopted a Directive on Late Payment of Commercial Debts (Directive 2000/35/EC) which must be implemented by member states by 8 August 2002. The Directive will ensure a common approach to the problem of late payment across the EU.

Equitable remedies

The normal remedy for a breach of contract is an award of damages at common law. There are some situations, however, where damages would be neither adequate nor appropriate. Equity developed other forms of relief to ensure that justice is done. The more important of these equitable remedies are specific performance and injunction.

Specific performance

A decree of specific performance is an order of the court requiring the party in breach to carry out his contractual obligations. Failure to comply with the directions of the court lays the defendant open to the imposition of penalties for contempt of court. Like all equitable remedies, the grant of specific performance is discretionary. It may be withheld in the following circumstances:

1 **Damages adequate.** An order for specific performance will not be made if damages would be an adequate remedy. Most breaches of contract can be remedied by an award of monetary compensation. If it is a contract for the sale of a unique item, however, no sum of money can compensate the disappointed buyer for his lost

opportunity, and specific performance will be granted. Each piece of land is regarded as being unique and thus the remedy is available for contracts for the sale of land.

2 Mutuality. Equity requires mutuality as regards its remedies. This means that both parties must potentially be able to seek an order of specific performance. An adult cannot obtain such an order against a minor, so a minor will not be awarded specific performance either.

3 Supervision. An order will not be made unless the court can adequately supervise its enforcement. It is for this reason that specific performance will not be awarded to enforce building contracts, because the court cannot supervise on the day-to-day basis which would be necessary. Similar principles apply to employment contracts..

Ryan v *Mutual Tontine Westminster Chambers Association* (1893)

The landlord of a flat agreed to provide a resident porter who would undertake certain duties for residents. A porter was appointed but he had another job as a chef in a nearby club, which meant he was absent from the building for several hours each day. While he was away, his duties were performed by various non-resident cleaners and boys. It was held that the only remedy for the breach of contract was an action in damages. Specific performance would not be granted.

Comment. In a more recent similar case, the court had no difficulty in awarding specific performance of a contract to provide a resident porter. It was held that damages would not be an adequate remedy. It was relatively easy to define what was required under the contract and it did not involve constant supervision (*Posner* v *Scott-Lewis* (1986)).

4 Discretion. The court may refuse specific performance where it is felt that it would not be just and equitable to grant it.

Injunction

This is an order of the court requiring the party at fault not to break the contract. Its main use is to enforce the negative promises that can occasionally be found in employment contracts. The employee may agree, for example, not to work in a similar capacity for a rival employer during the period of his contract.

Warner Bros v *Nelson* (1936)

The film actress, Bette Davis, had agreed not to work as an actress for anyone else during the period of her contract with Warner Bros. In breach of this agreement, she left the USA and entered into a contract with a third party in the UK. The court held that Warner Bros were entitled to an injunction to prevent the star from breaking the negative provision in the contract.

It should be noted that an injunction cannot be used as a back-door method of enforcing a contract of employment for which specific performance is not available. Warner Bros could prevent Miss Davis from working as an actress for anyone else. They could not have obtained a degree of specific performance to force her to return to their studio.

Claims for restitution: quasi-contract

The law of restitution may provide a claimant with a remedy in situations where the defendant has obtained an unjust benefit. The requirement to repay money does not arise because of a breach of a legal duty, such as a breach of contract or a tort, but because the defendant has been unjustly enriched. The liability is said to be quasi-contractual – *as if* from a contract – although in reality there is no liability in contract.

An action for restitution may arise in the circumstances summarised below.

Claims on a *quantum meruit*

Instead of claiming a precise sum, the claimant may be able to sue on a *quantum meruit* for payment for work he has actually done. A *quantum meruit* claim can arise either contractually or quasi-contractually in the following situations:

(a) *Contractually*: where the contract is for the supply of goods and services but the parties have not fixed a sum to be paid. The common law position is supported now by statutory provisions. Section 8 of the Sale of Goods Act 1979 provides that if the price of goods cannot be fixed by the contract or in a way agreed under the contract or by trade custom, the buyer must pay a reasonable price. There is similar obligation to pay a reasonable sum for services under s 15 of the Supply of Goods and Services Act 1982 (see also Chapter 10).

(b) *Quasi-contractually*:

- where the defendant has abandoned or refused to perform his part of the contract, as was the case in *Planche* v *Colburn* (1831);
- where work has been performed by the claimant and accepted by the defendant under a void contract. In *Craven-Ellis* v *Canons Ltd* (1936) a managing director of a company was able to recover a reasonable sum by way of remuneration for work he had done until it was discovered that his appointment was invalid under the company's articles;
- where one party confers a benefit on the other with the intention on both sides that the benefit is to be paid for even though a contract is not finally concluded (*British Steel Corporation* v *Cleveland Bridge & Engineering Co Ltd* (1984)).

Total failure of consideration

If the claimant has paid money to the defendant in respect of a valid contract, and the defendant completely fails to honour his part of the bargain, the claimant has a choice of remedy. He can bring a claim for breach of contract and claim damages for breach or he can terminate the contract and sue in quasi-contract to recover the money he has paid over on the basis that there has been a total failure of consideration. *Rowland* v *Divall* (1923), which will be considered in detail in Chapter 10, is an example of claim based on a total failure of consideration.

Money paid under a mistake

A claimant may recover money which has been paid over under a **mistake of fact**. A mistake of fact would include, for example, errors in a restaurant bill because the waiter had made a mistake when adding up all the items, or at the supermarket checkout when a cashier inadvertently scans an item twice. In *Admiralty Comrs* v *National Provincial and Union Bank Ltd* (1922), money paid into a bank account of a customer on the basis that he was alive, was held to be recoverable under a mistake of fact, when he turned out to be dead.

Until recently it was settled law that moneys paid under a **mistake of law** could not be recovered. However, this rule has now been overturned by the House of Lords in the following case.

Kleinwort Benson Ltd v Lincoln City Council (1998)
The case involved the use of 'interest rate swap' transactions by local authorities. Following a case brought by an auditor appointed by the Audit Commission, such contracts were held to be *ultra vires* for local authorities and, therefore, void. Kleinwort Benson (KB) claimed restitution of the money it had paid to four local authorities under these transactions. KB claimed that the money had been paid under a mistake so as to avoid the six-year time limit laid down in the Limitation Act 1980. The House of Lords held that the 'mistake of law rule' under which money was not recoverable in restitution because it had been paid under a mistake of law should no longer form part of English law.

Comment. This case is an interesting example of judicial law-making. The 'mistake of law rule' had been the subject of much criticism over the years and had been referred to the Law Commission. The Law Commission concluded that the rule should be changed by legislation. Their Lordships decided to press ahead with the reform themselves, rather wait for Parliament to legislate, even though considerable difficulties have been created because of the retrospective effect of the judgment. These problems could have been avoided if the change had been made by legislation.

LIMITATION OF ACTIONS

The right to sue does not last indefinitely. The Limitation Act 1980 imposes time limits within which an action for breach of contract must be brought. They are:

1. an action on a simple contract must be brought within six years of the date when the cause of action accrued;
2. an action on a contract made in the form of a deed will be statute barred after 12 years from the date when the cause of action accrued.

These time limits may be extended as follows:

(a) where fraud or mistake is alleged, time does not start to run until 'the claimant has discovered the fraud, concealment or mistake or could with reasonable diligence have discovered it';

(b) if the claimant is under a disability, such as minority or mental incapacity, the time limits do not start to operate until the disability is removed, e.g. in the case of a minor on reaching 18;

(c) where the claim is for a debt or a liquidated sum, and the defendant acknowledges the claim or makes part-payment, time will run from the date of acknowledgement or part-payment.

The rules about limitation of actions do not apply to the equitable remedies. Nevertheless, the equitable maxim of 'delay defeats equity' will apply to defeat a plaintiff who waits too long before taking legal action.

QUESTIONS/ACTIVITIES

1 Make a list of all the agreements you made (a) today, and (b) yesterday. Identify which agreements are contracts and explain why they are legally binding.

2 Are these statements true or false?
   (a) Most of the law of contract can be found in Acts of Parliament.
   (b) All contracts must be in writing.
   (c) Conveyances of land must be in the form of a specialty contract.
   (d) The absence of an essential element will always render a contract void.

3 Analyse the following transactions in terms of offer and acceptance:
   (a) filling a job vacancy;
   (b) parking a car in a multi-storey car park;
   (c) taking a bus ride;
   (d) buying a cup of coffee from an automatic vending machine;
   (e) buying a packet of soap powder from a supermarket;
   (f) buying an antique dresser at an auction;
   (g) acquiring shares in a privatisation issue;
   (h) buying a book via the Internet.

4 On 13 September, Fiona, a newly qualified dentist, receives the following note from her uncle:

10 Park Street
LONDON
WI A54

Dear Fiona
We talked some time ago about your buying some of my dental equipment when I retire from my London practice at the end of this month. I am prepared to let you have everything for £15,000. Let me know fairly quickly if you're interested because I've already had a very good offer from one of my colleagues.
Your affectionate uncle
Arnold

Fiona is keen to take advantage of her uncle's offer but is unsure whether she can raise such a large amount of money by the end of September. She phones her uncle to find out whether she can have until after Christmas to pay. Her uncle is away at a conference and so Fiona leaves a message with his secretary. Two weeks pass by and, as Fiona has not heard from her uncle, she arranges a loan with her bank. On 28 September she writes to her uncle accepting his offer and enclosing a cheque for £15,000. On September 30, her uncle phones to say that he has already sold the equipment to someone else. Advise Fiona.

5 Lynx Cars Ltd, the manufacturers of a revolutionary fuel-efficient small car, enter into a five-year dealership agreement with Roadstar Ltd, a northern-based firm of car dealers, in November 2000. A clause in the agreement states: 'This agreement is not intended to be legally binding but the parties honourably pledge that they will carry out its terms.' Roadstar Ltd place an initial order for 2,000 cars to be delivered by the end of 2001, which is accepted by the manufacturers. One month after the successful launch of the car at the Motor Show, Lynx Cars Ltd write to Roadstar Ltd informing them that, owing to production difficulties, they estimate that they will be able to deliver only 200 cars by the end of 2001. They further state that they will be withdrawing from the dealership agreement from the end of 2001 so that they can concentrate their resources on their south of England car dealers. Advise Roadstar Ltd.

6 Mrs Harris, the owner of three rented houses in Extown, asks her next-door neighbour, Ted, to collect rent from the tenants for her while she is abroad on business. Ted collects the rents and when Mrs Harris returns she says to him, 'I'll give you £50 for your work.' Can Ted enforce the promise?

7 John, a plumber, installs a new bathroom for Mr and Mrs Bolton for an agreed price of £500. Five weeks after sending the bill John still has not received payment. He rings the Boltons and speaks to Mrs Bolton. She says that she is unhappy about the quality of John's work, which she claims is only worth £350 at most. She also tells John that her

husband has just lost his job and they can only afford to pay £100. John reluctantly agrees to accept a cheque for this amount 'in full settlement'. Three months later John hears that Mr Bolton is back in employment and he wonders whether he can recover the outstanding money.

8 Jeremy, a prosperous City trader, decides to pay for his parents, Bill and Irene, to go on holiday to celebrate their silver wedding anniversary. Jeremy enters into a contract with Sunset Cruises, to provide his parents with a deluxe cabin for a two-week cruise round the Caribbean. Bill and Irene are very disappointed with their holiday. As a result of a booking error by Sunset Cruises, they are not allocated a deluxe cabin. The ship's engines suffer a mechanical failure on the third day and, as a result, the ship does not visit all the islands on its itinerary. Bill and Irene wish to take action against Sunset Cruises. Advise them. How would your advice differ if Jeremy took action on behalf of his parents?

9 What formalities, if any, must be completed for the following contracts?
   (a) a guarantee for a bank overdraft;
   (b) the sale of a second-hand car;
   (c) a contract of employment;
   (d) the lease of a house for 21 years;
   (e) a promise to pay £50 a year for the next five years to a charity.

10 Kathy, aged 17, decides to leave home because she does not get on with her parents. Over the next three weeks she enters into the following agreements:
   (a) She borrows £500 from her older brother to tide her over until she can find a job.
   (b) She takes a two-year lease on a bed-sit, paying three months' rent in advance.
   (c) By pretending to be 21, she orders a £700 suite of furniture from Palatial Pads Ltd on 12 months' interest-free credit.
   (d) She sets up a home catering business and immediately agrees to cater for 100 people attending a 21st birthday party for a price of £300. She insists on £100 deposit. As the day for the party approaches, she finds that she has taken on too much work for one person, so she rings her customers on the afternoon of the party to say that she will not be able to do the catering after all. Discuss the legal effects of these transactions.

11 Arthur, the manager of Lookout Cars Ltd, asks his young assistant, Terry, to look after the business while he is away on holiday. It is an eventful week for Terry.
   (a) Early Monday morning Terry sells a second-hand Escort to Doris. The car had been advertised in the local press as follows:

   93 (N) Ford Escort 45,000 miles. Blue £6,995

   Doris returns on Wednesday to tell Terry that the Escort's clock has been turned back and that it has actually done 90,000 miles.
   (b) On Tuesday, Terry finalises a part-exchange deal with Mr Walker. Unknown to either of them, Mrs Walker was involved, earlier in the day, in a serious car crash while driving the old car. The car is a 'write-off'.
   (c) On Wednesday, a man calls into the showrooms introducing himself, falsely, as James Dean MP. He agrees to buy a new Orion car, but when he pulls out a cheque book, Terry says that he is reluctant to accept a cheque. The man then produces a pass to the House of Commons as proof of his identity. Terry accepts the cheque and the man drives off in the car. Terry has just learned from the bank that the cheque has been dishonoured. The man sold the car to Pete, a university student.
   (d) On Thursday, Daisy, Lookout Ltd's secretary, puts a number of letters in front of Terry for his signature. Terry is busy talking to the workshop manager at the time and signs his name without reading each one. He has now discovered that one of the letters was an undertaking to act as a guarantor for a £5,000 loan to Daisy by the Midshires Bank plc.
   Explain to Terry the legal position in each situation.

12 George is the owner of a confectioner's shop in Chorley, which is world famous for its unique Chorley Chocolate Bar. The secret recipe for the chocolate bar has been handed down four generations of George's family. George himself is a bachelor and, with no one to carry on the business, he decides to retire and sell the shop. After much careful vetting, George agrees to sell the shop, including the goodwill and the secret recipe, to Maria. As part of the contract George agrees that:
   (a) he will not engage in any form of sweet-making in the whole of the United Kingdom for the next 20 years; and

(b) he will not reveal the secret formula for the chocolate bar to anyone else.

Maria bought the business with the aid of a 20-year mortgage from the Castletown Cocoa Co Ltd. Maria has further agreed to obtain all her supplies of cocoa from this company for the next 20 years. After three very successful years in Chorley, Maria hears that George is supplying Chorley Chocolate Bars to shops near to his retirement home in Bournemouth. About the same time, Maria is approached by Cocoa Suppliers Ltd which offers to supply all her cocoa needs at cheaper prices than she is currently paying Castletown Cocoa Co Ltd. Advise Maria.

13 Kevin is the owner of a small Hull-based firm, which specialises in office removals. He operates with two vans and three employees. He contracts to remove two partners in a firm of accountants, who are moving from their main office in Hull to establish a branch office in Scunthorpe. To minimise the disruption to office routine, the move is to take place on a Sunday. What is the legal position in the following situations?

(a) The Humber bridge is closed because of high winds (the only alternative route is a much longer and more expensive journey via Goole).

(b) As a conservation measure, the government imposes regulations banning business traffic from the roads on Sundays.

(c) Kevin takes on a house removal for the same day. One of the vans fails its MOT on the Friday and Kevin decides to use the only one available for the house removal.

(d) Kevin and his three employees are taken ill with influenza and are not well enough to carry out the move.

(e) Kevin completes the removal except for one filing cabinet which he did not have room for. He refuses to make a special journey for it because 'it would cost too much in petrol'.

14 Wholesome Foods Ltd decided to build an extension to its Newtown bakery to cope with increased demand for its wholemeal bread. The contract is awarded to Bettabuilders Co Ltd, which agrees to complete the work by 1 May. On the strength of the planned increased capacity at the bakery, Wholesome Foods Ltd concludes an extremely profitable contract with the Newtown Council to supply all the bread to local schools from 4 May. Owing to extreme bad weather in February and March, Bettabuilders Co Ltd completes the extension ten weeks late. Wholesome Foods Ltd estimats its losses as:

- £100 a week for the profits it would have made on the expected general increase in bread sales: and
- £400 a week for the profits it would have made on the schools contract.

(a) What damages will Wholesome Foods Ltd recover?

(b) How would your answer differ if Bettabuilders Co Ltd had agreed to pay £50 for every week of delay in completing the extension?

15 Wreckless Eric, a rock concert promoter, pulls off one of the sensations of the rock world by getting the American rock star, Tex Toucan, to come to Britain to give a six-concert tour to coincide with the release of his latest album. Tex agrees to give his exclusive services to Eric and promises that he 'will not sing, perform as a musician or act as an entertainer' for anyone else during the period of his stay. After completing the first sell-out concert in Dagenham, Tex is approached by Crispin Green, a rival promoter, who persuades Tex to break his contract with Eric and appear instead at alternative venues arranged by Crispin. Eric, who has made a considerable investment in this tour, wants to know what remedies are available to him.

Chapter 8

TYPES OF BUSINESS CONTRACT

In this chapter we move away from studying basic principles of general application to all contracts to look at specific kinds of contracts in common use in the business world. The fundamentals of the law of contract are still largely governed by the common law. Over the past 100 years, however, business transactions have increasingly become subject to statutory provisions. Parliament's original aim was to translate established common law rules into a format which would be more accessible and understandable to businessmen. As the years passed so the legislators' motives changed. Parliamentary interest in commercial law over the last century has been prompted mainly by the need to regulate and control unfair business practices.

It is important that you can distinguish between different kinds of business transactions because different legal principles apply to each. The rights and duties of the parties will be determined by the nature of their contract and the legal rules which govern that particular kind of agreement. For example, contracts for the sale of goods are covered by the Sale of Goods Act 1979, as amended by the Sale and Supply of Goods Act 1994 and the Sale of Goods (Amendment) Acts 1994 and 1995, while contracts for the sale of land are governed by the Law of Property Act 1925, as amended by the Law of Property (Miscellaneous Provisions) Act 1989. This chapter is designed to provide you with a brief guide to the different kinds of business contracts and the source of any legal rules which regulate them. The most important contracts will be considered in more detail in later chapters.

CONTRACTS FOR THE SUPPLY OF GOODS

Sale of goods

The most common form of transaction in the business world is a contract for the sale of goods. Whenever you buy goods, whether from a supermarket, market stall, doorstep salesman or by mail order, you have entered into a contract for the sale of goods. As we have already mentioned, the rights and duties of the parties to this type of contract are set out in the Sale of Goods Act 1979 (as amended). The Act applies to all contracts for the sale of goods, from buying a sandwich at lunchtime to a multi-million pound deal to supply new aircraft to an airline company. A contract for the sale of goods is defined in s 2(1) of the Sale of Goods Act 1979 as:

> A contract by which the seller transfers or agrees to transfer the property in goods to the buyer for a money consideration called the price.

This definition is extremely important because only those contracts which fall within it will be covered by the provisions of the 1979 Act. A closer look at the definition will help you distinguish a contract for the sale of goods from other similar kinds of contracts in which goods change hands.

Section 2(1) covers two possibilities: an actual sale and an agreement to sell at some future time. The essence of the transaction is the transfer of property in goods from the seller to the buyer. ('Property' in this context means ownership of the goods.) Goods include all tangible items of personal property such as food, clothes and furniture: land and money are excluded from the definition. The consideration for the goods must be money, although a part-exchange deal in which goods are exchanged for other goods plus money will be covered by the Act because some money has changed hands.

The law relating to sale of goods contracts will be examined in more detail in Chapter 10.

Exchange or barter

No money changes hands in this type of contract. Instead there is a straight exchange of goods between the parties. The absence of money from the consideration means that the Sale of Goods Act 1979 does not apply to these contracts. Previously the obligations of the parties were governed by the common law, but now the Supply of Goods and Services Act 1982 (as amended by the Sale and Supply of Goods Act 1994) imposes certain statutory duties on the supplier of goods under a contract of exchange.

Work and materials

Another way in which you can acquire goods is in consequence of a contract whose main purpose is the provision of services. If you take your car to be serviced by a garage, the main substance of the contract is the skill and labour of the mechanic in checking the car. The supply of such items as brake fluid and the renewal of spark plugs is an ancillary part of the contract.

The distinction between a contract of sale and a contract of work and materials is often a fine one.

Robinson v Graves (1935)

Robinson, an artist, was commissioned to paint a portrait for 250 guineas. The Court of Appeal held that this was a contract for Robinson's skill as an artist and not a contract for the sale of goods, i.e. the finished portrait.

However, a contract to buy a painting from an art gallery would be a sale of goods contract. Contracts for work and materials are now subject to the Supply of Goods and Services Act 1982 (as amended by the Sale and Supply of Goods Act 1994). The provisions of this Act will be discussed in Chapter 10.

Supply of goods on credit

There are a bewildering number of ways in which goods can be acquired and then paid for over a period of time. Hire-purchase, 'interest-free' credit, credit cards and bank loans are all readily available, enticing us to buy more than we can probably afford. Consumer credit – credit granted to an individual, sole trader or partnership not exceeding £25,000 – is strictly regulated by the Consumer Credit Act 1974. This Act is examined in detail in Chapter 13.

The more important forms of consumer credit agreement are described below.

1 **Hire-purchase (HP).** This is one of the best known ways of buying goods on credit. HP is essentially an agreement for the hire of goods, at the end of which the hirer may exercise an option to purchase them from the owner. The hirer obtains the immediate use and enjoyment of the goods, but he does not become the owner unless and until all the instalments are paid. There is a subtle distinction between HP and a contract for the sale of goods. You will remember that the definition of a sale of goods includes agreements to transfer the ownership in goods at some time in the future. An HP agreement, however, does not bind the hirer to buy. He may choose to pay for the hire of the goods and then decline to purchase them.

2 **Conditional sale.** A conditional sale is very similar to HP. The customer obtains immediate possession of the goods in return for the payment of regular instalments. The transfer of ownership is delayed until some specified condition is fulfilled. The difference between the two agreements is that the buyer under a conditional sale agreement is committed to buy from the outset. Thus, a conditional sale is really a type of sale of goods contract.

3 **Credit sale.** This is another way of buying goods and paying for them later. Unlike HP and conditional sale agreements, ownership of goods passes to the buyer at the start of the agreement.

CONTRACTS OF BAILMENT

A contract of bailment arises when the owner of goods (the bailor) entrusts possession of them into the care of another (the bailee). Examples of bailment include placing important documents in safe custody at a bank, taking clothes to be dry-cleaned and hiring a TV set.

The bailee's main duties are:

1 to take reasonable care of the goods whilst they are in his possession; and
2 to return them to the bailor, at the end of an agreed period or when requested.

Hiring is a particular example of a contract of bailment.

Hire

Under a hire agreement, the owner of goods allows someone else (the hirer) to make use of them in return for regular rental payments. The hirer obtains possession of the goods but ownership never passes to him and at the end of the agreement the goods must be returned to the owner. Most people are familiar with hire contracts in the context of TV and video rentals. A typical rental agreement can be seen in Fig 8.1. Consumer hire agreements are covered by the provisions of the Consumer Credit Act 1974. Businesses also take advantage of hire as a method of obtaining the use of equipment which they require. (Hire in this context is usually referred to as 'leasing', the owner being known as the 'lessor' and the hirer as the 'lessee'.) The leasing agreement often includes an undertaking by the lessor to service the equipment regularly and effect repairs when necessary. Equipment leasing has allowed businesses to take advantage of the opportunities created by the rapidly changing new technology in the field of computing and word processing. Goods supplied under hire contracts are subject to Part I of the Supply of Goods and Services Act 1982 (as amended by the Sale and Supply of Goods Act 1994). (See Chapter 10.)

EMPLOYMENT CONTRACTS

There are two ways in which a person's services may be acquired. He may be engaged either as an employee under a contract of service or as an independent contractor under a contract for services.

1 **Contract of service.** This type of contract creates the relationship of employer and employee between the parties. An employee provides his labour for his employer in return for wages. The employer exercises control over the way in which an employee carries out his work.

2 **Contract for services.** A self-employed person is engaged under a contract for services. He is an independent contractor, agreeing to do work or provide services as and when he wishes. He enjoys considerable independence from the person who employs him. Thus, a chauffeur has a contract of service, whereas a taxi driver transports his fares under a contract for services.

The distinction between employees and independent contractors is important for the following reasons:

1 an employer is vicariously liable only for the torts of employees, not for those committed by independent contractors;

2 only employees are entitled to claim the benefit of various employment rights contained principally in the Employment Rights Act 1996. These include protections in respect of unfair dismissal, redundancy, maternity pay and leave, minimum periods of notice and so on. A self-employed person cannot claim any of these rights. The law relating to the contract of employment will be examined in more detail in Chapter 16.

CONTRACTS OF AGENCY

An agent is someone who is employed by a principal to make contracts on his behalf with third parties. An employee who makes contracts on behalf of his employer is acting as an agent. A shop assistant, for example, is in this category. Alternatively, an agent may be an independent contractor who is engaged for his specialist skills and knowledge. A person who wishes to sell his

RA
(d)

Hire Agreement *regulated by the Consumer Credit Act 1974*   Agreement No. _____

No right of cancellation – minimum hire period not more than 17 months   **Original**

This agreement sets out the terms on which we (the owners) agree to let on hire the goods described below to you (the hirer) for the rental payments and on the terms set out below and overleaf.

The Owners _____
Name and Address

_____

The Hirer _____
Full names please

Address _____

_____

Particulars of Goods and Period of Hire	Rentals (including VAT)	£	p
Description _____	**A. Advance Rental** (rent for the		
_____	first _____ months of the hiring)		
Maker's Name _____	**B. Rentals (for the remainder of the hiring)**		
Model No. _____	For each of the next _____ months		
Serial No. _____	For each of the next _____ months		
Accessories _____	For each of the next _____ months		
Minimum Hire Period _____ months commencing on the date of this agreement	For each month thereafter		

First monthly rental payable on _____ 20 _____
Subsequent rentals on the same day of each succeeding month.
We may at our discretion vary the rentals payable after the minimum hire period by one month's notice in writing.
We may vary the rentals if the VAT rate alters.
See Clause 4 overleaf for further details.

Maintenance of the Goods	
Maintenance by the Owner	YES/NO

IMPORTANT – YOU SHOULD READ THIS CAREFULLY

YOUR RIGHTS

The Consumer Credit Act 1974 covers this agreement and lays down certain requirements for your protection which must be satisfied when the agreement is made. If they are not, we cannot enforce the agreement against you without a court order.

If you would like to know more about the protection and remedies provided under the Act, you should contact either your local Trading Standards Department or your nearest Citizens' Advice Bureau.

Witness: Signature _____

Name _____
Block letters please

Address _____

_____

Signature of (or on behalf of) Owners

_____

Date of Owners' Signature (Date of Agreement)

_____

DECLARATION BY HIRER

By signing this agreement you are declaring that all the information you have given us is correct and that you realise that we rely on that information when deciding whether to enter into this agreement.

You acknowledge that before granting credit we may search the files of one or more credit reference agencies which will keep a record of our enquiry. We may also disclose details of the account and your conduct of it to that agency (or agencies). Information thus held is used only to help make credit decisions affecting you or members of your household or occasionally for fraud prevention or tracing customers.

This is a Hire Agreement regulated by the Consumer Credit Act 1974. Sign it only if you want to be legally bound by its terms.

Signature(s)
of Hirer(s) _____

Under this agreement the goods do not become your property and you must not sell them.

Copyright © Consumer Credit Trade Association (original size A4)

Fig 8.1 A typical hire agreement form

RA
(d)
Original

TERMS OF THE AGREEMENT

1 Ownership of the goods

This is a hire agreement. The goods will remain our property at all times and can never become yours. You must not sell or dispose of them.

2 Period of hire

You agree to hire the goods until the end of the minimum hire period stated overleaf or until the expiry of notice under Clause 11, whichever is the later.

3 Payment

Before signing this agreement you must have paid the advance rental shown. By signing this agreement you agree to pay the rentals set out overleaf by their specified dates to us at the address stated overleaf or to any person or address notified by us in writing. Punctual payment is essential. If you pay by post you do so at your own risk.

4 Variation of rentals

We have the right to vary the rentals payable after the end of the minimum hire period by giving you one month's notice in writing expiring at or after the end of that period.
We may vary the rentals at any time to take account of a change in the rate of VAT.

5 Failure to pay on time

We have the right to charge interest at the rate of 10% per annum on all overdue amounts. This interest will be calculated on a daily basis from the date the amount falls due until it is received.

6 Place where goods are kept

You must keep the goods safely at your address stated overleaf and may not move them elsewhere without first obtaining our written consent.

7 Care of the goods

You must use the goods in a careful and proper manner and (apart from any arrangements for maintenance under Clause 9) keep them in good working order, and replace batteries in remote control units, at your own expense. However you may not interfere with the internal working parts of the goods or attempt to clean tape heads, which only our representative may do.

8 Insurance against loss or damage

You are responsible for all loss or damage to the goods (except fair wear and tear) even if caused by acts or events outside your control. You must therefore insure the goods against loss or damage.

9 Maintenance

Where the agreement shows that we are to maintain the goods, you must notify us when the goods require maintenance or adjustment. We or our authorised representative will then carry this out.

If at any time we decide that it is no longer practicable to keep the goods in working order or, in the case of a radio or television set, if the transmission is unsatisfactory, we may either:

(a) replace the goods by other goods as similar as possible to those replaced or

(b) end this agreement by giving you seven days' notice in writing.

If we end this agreement under paragraph (b) you must let us collect the goods. You will not be liable for rentals falling due after such termination and will be entitled to recover any rental paid in advance in respect of the period after termination. This clause will not affect your statutory rights.

10 Licences

You must keep the goods properly licensed and produce the licence or payment receipt to us at our request.

11 Right to end the agreement

You or we may end this agreement by giving one month's notice in writing expiring at or after the end of the minimum hire period. You must then return the goods or make them available for collection by us.

12 Our further right to end the agreement

We may end this agreement and take back the goods, after giving you written notice, if at any time:

(a) you fail to pay any amount within 14 days of its due date or commit any other breach of your obligations;

(b) you have an interim or bankruptcy order made against you or you petition for your own bankruptcy, or are served with a creditor's demand under the Insolvency Act 1986 or the Bankruptcy (Scotland) Act 1985, or make a formal composition or scheme with your creditors, or call a meeting of them;

(c) execution is levied or attempted against any of your assets or income or, in Scotland, your assets are poinded or your wages arrested;

(d) the landlord of the premises where the goods are kept threatens or takes any step to distrain on the goods or, in Scotland, exercises his right of hypothec over the goods;

(e) you have given false information in connection with your entry into this agreement;

(f) the goods are destroyed or the insurers treat a claim under the policy for the goods on a total loss basis.

13 Your liability if we end the agreement

If we end this agreement you must pay us all rentals up to the date when this agreement comes to an end.

If we end this agreement under Clause 12 before the expiry of the minimum hire period you must also pay us a sum equal to the rentals for the period remaining to the end of the minimum hire period less any rentals obtained by us during this period by re-letting the goods and any other deduction which we may consider reasonable.

14 Expenses

You must repay on demand our expenses and legal costs for:

(a) finding your address if you change address without first informing us or finding the goods if they are not at the address given by you;

(b) taking steps, including court action, to recover the goods or to obtain payment for them.

15 TV transmissions

If the goods comprise a television set we undertake only that it will receive those transmissions which are received when it is installed.

16 General provisions

(a) The word 'goods' includes any replacements, renewals or additions made to them by us or by you with our prior written consent.

(b) No relaxation or indulgence which we may grant to you shall affect our strict rights under this agreement.

(c) Where two or more of you are named as the hirer, you jointly and severally accept the obligations under this agreement. This means that each of you can be held fully responsible under this agreement.

(d) We may transfer our rights under this agreement.

17 When this agreement takes effect

This agreement will only take effect if and when it is signed by us or our authorised representative.

Fig 8.1 (continued)

shares will usually employ the services of a stockbroker to arrange the sale for him. Travel agents, estate agents, auctioneers, insurance brokers are all examples of agents. An agent may fall into one or more of the following categories:

1 A **general agent** has the power to act for his principal in relation to particular kinds of transaction, e.g. an estate agent.

2 A **special agent** is limited to acting for the principal in respect of one specific transaction.

3 A **mercantile agent** or factor is defined under s 1(1) of the Factors Act 1889 as an 'agent having in the customary course of his business as such agent authority either to sell goods or to consign goods for the purpose of sale, or to buy goods, or to raise money on the security of goods'.

4 A *del credere* agent is an agent who, in return for extra commission, guarantees that if the third party he has introduced fails to pay for goods received, the agent will indemnify the principal.

Formation of agency

An agency is usually created by agreement between the principal and agent, but in some situations an agency can be created without such an agreement. The main ways in which an agency can be formed are as follows:

1 **Express appointment.** This is the main way in which an agency is created. A principal will expressly appoint an agent either to carry out a particular job or to undertake a range of transactions. The relationship between the principal and agent will usually be contractual.

2 **By implication.** This form of agency usually arises where there is a pre-existing agency relationship and it is assumed by a third party that the principal has given the agent authority to act as an agent in matters not covered by the express appointment. This implied or ostensible authority may arise from the position held by the agent. For example, a company secretary has implied authority to enter into contracts on behalf of a company which are related to the day-to-day operation of the business (see the *Panorama* case which was discussed in Chapter 6).

3 **By ratification.** This arises where a principal retrospectively adopts a contract made on his behalf by an agent. Ratification will only be effective if strict conditions are met:

- the agent must have disclosed that he was acting for a principal;
- the principal must have been in existence when the agent entered into the contract, e.g. if the principal is a company, the certificate of incorporation must have been issued;
- the principal must have had the capacity to enter into the contract not only when the contract was made but also at the time of ratification;
- the principal must ratify the whole contract;
- ratification must take place within a reasonable time.

4 **By necessity.** This type of agency arises where a person takes urgent action on behalf of another in the event of an emergency. There will normally be some kind of pre-existing contractual relationship between the parties, e.g. a contract to transport perishable goods. The person who purports to act as an agent of necessity must show that he acted in the best interests of the 'principal', his actions were reasonably necessary in the circumstances, and that it was impossible to contact the 'principal' to obtain instructions.

5 **By estoppel.** This arises where a principal represents that a person is acting as his agent. The principal will be prevented (estopped) from later denying that the person had authority to act as his agent (see *Freeman & Lockyer* v *Buckhurst Park Properties* (1964), discussed in Chapter 6).

The rights of the parties

Even the most straightforward agency creates complicated legal rights between three parties: the principal, the agent and a third party. The rights of the third party depend largely on whether the third party is aware that he is dealing with an agent. If the agent discloses that he is an agent, he will drop out of the picture and the third party can only sue and be sued by the principal. As we have already seen in Chapter 7, the common law rules relating to privity of contract do not apply in agency situations. If the agent does not reveal that he is an agent, either the agent or the principal can sue on the contract. When the third party discovers the agency, he can choose whether to sue the agent or the now-revealed principal. Once he has made his choice of whom to sue, the election is binding and he cannot change his mind if, for example, the person he has chosen to sue cannot or will not pay.

Sometimes an agent will act without authority or he may exceed his actual or implied authority. The principal will only be bound by the agent's actions if the agent is acting within the scope of his apparent (ostensible) authority or through necessity or the principal ratifies the contract. If none of the situations apply, the agent will be liable to the third party for breach of warranty of authority.

The duties of the principal and agent

The agent owes a number of duties to his principal. These include:

- a duty to carry out the wishes of the principal in accordance with the agency agreement;
- to exercise reasonable care and skill;
- to carry out his duties personally unless there is express or implied authority for him to delegate his duties;
- to account for all money and property received on behalf of the principal and to keep proper accounts;
- not to take bribes or make a secret profit;
- to avoid a conflict of interest.

The agent has the following rights against the principal:

- to be paid the agreed amount or, if no fee is agreed, a reasonable amount;
- to be indemnified for any expenses incurred in performing his duties;
- to exercise a lien over the principal's goods and to stop them in transit where payment is outstanding.

Termination of agency

The agency may come to an end either by the actions of the parties or by operation of the law.

1 **Termination by the parties.** The principal and agent may terminate their relationship by mutual agreement or the agency contract may allow either party to terminate by giving notice. Even if the contract does not provide for termination by notice, either party can end the contract unilaterally by giving reasonable notice.

2 **Termination by operation of the law.** The relationship will come to an end automatically with the death or insanity of either party or by the bankruptcy of the principal. The agency can also come to an end because of frustration or illegality.

CONTRACTS CONCERNING LAND

Every businessman must consider where he will locate his operations. A sole trader, such as a painter and decorator, may find that he can work successfully from home. In many cases, however, the nature of the business or the size of the operation will mean that separate premises have to be found. One of the decisions that must be taken is whether to buy or rent.

Transactions relating to land are governed primarily by the Law of Property Act 1925. This subject will be examined in detail in Chapter 15.

Mortgages

A mortgage is a method of borrowing money on the security of some property. The borrower (mortgagor) transfers an interest in the property to the lender (mortgagee): the lender may realise this interest if the loan is not repaid. Any kind of property (land, goods, insurance policies) may be the subject of a mortgage but, in practice, most mortgage advances are secured on land.

CONTRACTS FOR FINANCIAL SERVICES

Banking contracts

Banks provide a wide range of financial services to the commercial customer from current accounts, loan and overdraft facilities, to specialist services for those involved in foreign trade. The relationship between a bank and its customers is contractual. The rights and duties of the parties to this contract have been developed over many years from the practice of merchants. Some aspects of banking law are contained in statutes, such as the Bills of Exchange Act 1882 and the Cheques Act 1957.

Insurance contracts

A prudent businessman will always assess the risks that might befall his business: he may fall ill, his premises might be destroyed by fire, or his stock stolen. These risks may be minimised by insurance. A contract of insurance is an agreement whereby an insurance company undertakes to compensate a person, called the insured, if the risk insured against does in fact occur. The insured will be required to complete a proposal form. The contract is formed when the insurer accepts the proposal. Insurance contracts are contracts of utmost good faith (*uberrimae fidei*). This means that the insured must voluntarily disclose all relevant information which may affect the insurer's decision to insure or the premium that will be charged. Failure to do so, however innocent, will allow the insurer to avoid the contract.

The financial services industry is subject to a system of regulation under the Financial Services Act 1986 and the Financial Services and Markets Act 2000.

STANDARD FORM CONTRACTS

Whatever the nature of a contract, the law is based on the assumption that the terms of an individual contract are the result of bargaining between equals. It has long been the case, however, that businesses contract on the basis of standard terms contained in a pre-printed document known as a standard form contract. The terms are not usually open to negotiation: the customer must either accept them in their entirety as part and parcel of the deal or take his business elsewhere.

The use of standard form contracts has several clear advantages for business:

1 If the terms of the contract are contained in a written document, the parties will be quite clear about what they have agreed to and this is likely to minimise the possibility of disputes at a later stage.

2 It would be very time-consuming to negotiate individual terms with every customer, especially where a fairly standard service is offered to a large number of people. For example, train services would soon come to a standstill if every intending passenger had to negotiate an individual contract before setting out on a journey.

3 Once an organisation has adopted standard terms of business, the formation of a contract becomes a relatively routine matter which can be delegated to junior staff.

4 Businesspeople are constantly seeking ways to minimise their potential risks. A standard form contract can be used to 'dictate' terms which will he favourable to the businessman. He may include, for example, limitation or exclusion clauses which seek to limit or exempt him completely from liabilities which might otherwise be his responsibility.

The use of standard form contracts may be convenient and economical for the businessman, but it puts his customers at a considerable disadvantage.

The drawbacks are as follows:

1 Standard terms of business are often expressed in language which is virtually unintelligible to most people. A consumer may find himself bound by a contract even though he did not properly understand what had been 'agreed'. In some cases, the document may be so awe-inspiring that it is not read at all.

2 The concept of freedom of contract, on which the law of contract is founded, would seem to suggest that if the terms contained in a standard form contract are unacceptable, the customer can simply shop around for a better deal. This may well happen in a competitive market where the parties possess equal bargaining powers, but, in practice, the parties rarely contract as equals. Consumers, in particular, have found themselves in a weak bargaining position, victims of very one-sided contracts. In recent years, Parliament has stepped in to redress the balance in such measures as the Unfair Contract Terms Act 1977. We will return to this subject in the next chapter.

An example of a standard form contract appears in Fig 8.2.

Road Haulage Association Limited
CONDITIONS OF CARRIAGE 1998 - Effective 1 September 1998

PLEASE NOTE THAT THE CUSTOMER WILL NOT IN ALL CIRCUMSTANCES BE ENTITLED TO COMPENSATION, OR TO FULL COMPENSATION, FOR ANY LOSS AND IS THEREFORE RECOMMENDED TO SEEK PROFESSIONAL ADVICE AS TO APPROPRIATE INSURANCE COVER TO BE MAINTAINED WHILE CONSIGNMENTS ARE IN TRANSIT.

Company stamp or details

RHA membership number

(hereinafter referred to as *"the Carrier")* is not a common carrier and accepts goods for carriage only upon that condition and the Conditions set out below. No servant or agent of the Carrier is permitted to alter or vary these Conditions in any way unless expressly authorised in writing to do so by a Director, Principal, Partner or other authorised person. If any legislation is compulsorily applicable to the Contract and any part of these Conditions is incompatible with such legislation, such part shall, as regards the Contract, be overridden to that extent and no further.

1. Definitions

In these Conditions:

"Customer" means the person or company who contracts for the services of the Carrier including any other carrier who gives a Consignment to the Carrier for carriage.

"Contract" means the contract of carriage between the Customer and the Carrier.

"Consignee" means the person or company to whom the Carrier contracts to deliver the Consignment.

"Consignment" means goods, whether a single item or in bulk or contained in one parcel, package or container, as the case may be, or any number of separate items, parcels, packages or containers sent at one time in one load by or for the Customer from one address to one address.

"Dangerous Goods" means goods named individually in the Approved Carriage List issued from time to time by the Health and Safety Commission, explosives, radioactive material, and any other goods presenting a similar hazard.

2. Parties and Sub-Contracting

(1) The Customer warrants that he is either the owner of the Consignment or is authorised by such owner to accept these Conditions on such owner's behalf.

(2) The Carrier and any other carrier employed by the Carrier may employ the services of any other carrier for the purpose of fulfilling the Contract in whole or in part and the name of every other such carrier shall be provided to the Customer upon request.

(3) The Carrier contracts for itself and as agent of and trustee for its servants and agents and all other carriers referred to in (2) above and such other carriers' servants and agents and every reference in these Conditions to "the Carrier" shall be deemed to include every other such carrier, servant and agent with the intention that they shall have the benefit of the Contract and collectively and together with the Carrier be under no greater liability to the Customer or any other party than is the Carrier hereunder.

(4) Notwithstanding Condition 2(3) the carriage of any Consignment by rail, sea, inland waterway or air is arranged by the Carrier as agent of the Customer and shall be subject to the Conditions of the rail, shipping, inland waterway or air carrier contracted to carry the Consignment. The Carrier shall be under no liability whatever to whomsoever and howsoever arising in respect of such carriage: Provided that where the Consignment is carried partly by road and partly by such other means of transport any loss, damage or delay shall be deemed to have occurred while the Consignment was being carried by road unless the contrary is proved by the Carrier.

3. Dangerous Goods

Dangerous Goods must be disclosed by the Customer and if the Carrier agrees to accept them for carriage they must be classified, packed and labelled in accordance with the statutory regulations for the carriage by road of the substance declared. Transport Emergency Cards (Tremcards) or information in writing in the manner required by the relevant statutory provisions must be provided by the Customer in respect of each substance and must accompany the Consignment.

4. Loading and Unloading

(1) Unless the Carrier has agreed in writing to the contrary with the Customer:

(a) The Carrier shall not be under any obligation to provide any plant, power or labour, other than that carried by the vehicle, required for loading or unloading the Consignment.

(b) The Customer warrants that any special appliances required for loading or unloading the Consignment which are not carried by the vehicle will be provided by the Customer or on the Customer's behalf.

(c) The Carrier shall be under no liability whatever to the Customer for any damage whatever, however caused, if the Carrier is instructed to load or unload any Consignment requiring special appliances which, in breach of the warranty in (b) above, have not been provided by the Customer or on the Customer's behalf.

(d) The Carrier shall not be required to provide service beyond the usual place of collection or delivery but if any such service is given by the Carrier it shall be at the sole risk of the Customer.

(2) The Customer shall indemnify the Carrier against all claims and demands whatever which could not have been made if such instructions as are referred to in (1)(c) of this Condition and such service as is referred to in (1)(d) of this Condition had not been given.

5. Signed Receipts

The Carrier shall, if so required, sign a document prepared by the sender acknowledging the receipt of the Consignment but no such document shall be evidence of the condition or of the correctness of the declared nature, quantity, or weight of the Consignment at the time it is received by the Carrier and the burden of proving the condition of the Consignment on receipt by the Carrier and that the Consignment was of the nature, quantity or weight declared in the relevant document shall rest with the Customer.

6. Transit

(1) Transit shall commence when the Carrier takes possession of the Consignment whether at the point of collection or at the Carrier's premises.

(2) Transit shall (unless otherwise previously determined) end when the Consignment is tendered at the usual place of delivery at the Consignee's address within the customary cartage hours of the district: Provided that;

(a) if no safe and adequate access or no adequate unloading facilities there exist then transit shall be deemed to end at the expiry of one clear day after notice in writing (or by telephone if so previously agreed in writing) of the arrival of the Consignment at the Carrier's premises has been sent to the Consignee; and

(b) when for any other reason whatever a Consignment cannot be delivered or when a Consignment is held by the Carrier 'to await order' or 'to be kept till called for' or upon any like instructions and such instructions are not given or the Consignment is not called for and removed within a reasonable time, then transit shall be deemed to end.

7. Undelivered or Unclaimed Consignments

Where the Carrier is unable for any reason to deliver a Consignment to the Consignee or as he may order, or where by virtue of the proviso to Condition 6(2) hereof transit is deemed to be at an end, the Carrier may sell the Consignment, and payment or tender of the proceeds after deduction of all proper charges and expenses in relation thereto and of all outstanding charges in relation to the carriage and storage of the Consignment shall (without prejudice to any claim or right which the Customer may have against the Carrier otherwise arising under these Conditions) discharge the Carrier from all liability in respect of such Consignment, its carriage and storage: Provided that:

(1) the Carrier shall do what is reasonable to obtain the value of the Consignment; and

(2) the power of sale shall not be exercised where the name and address of the sender or of the Consignee is known unless the Carrier shall have done what is reasonable in the circumstances to give notice to the sender or, if the name and address of the sender is not known, to the Consignee that the Consignment will be sold unless within the time specified in such notice, being a reasonable time in the circumstances from the giving of such notice, the Consignment is taken away or instructions are given for its disposal.

8. Carrier's Charges

(1) The Carrier's charges shall be payable by the Customer without prejudice to the Carrier's rights against the Consignee or any other person: Provided that when any Consignment is consigned 'carriage forward' the Customer shall not be required to pay such charges unless the Consignee fails to pay after a reasonable demand has been made by the Carrier for payment thereof.

(2) Charges shall be payable when due without reduction or deferment on account of any claim, counterclaim or set-off. The Carrier shall be entitled to interest at 8 per cent above the Bank of England Base Rate prevailing at the date of the Carrier's invoice or account, calculated on a daily basis on all amounts overdue to the Carrier.

Fig 8.2 A standard form contract

9. Liability for Loss and Damage

(1) The Customer shall be deemed to have elected to accept the terms set out in (2) of this Condition unless, before the transit commences, the Customer has agreed in writing that the Carrier shall not be liable for any loss or mis-delivery of or damage to or in connection with the Consignment however or whenever caused and whether or not caused or contributed to directly or indirectly by any act, omission, neglect, default or other wrongdoing on the part of the Carrier, its servants, agents or sub-contractors.

(2) Subject to these Conditions the Carrier shall be liable for:

  (a) physical loss, mis-delivery of or damage to living creatures, bullion, money, securities, stamps, precious metals or precious stones comprising the Consignment only if:

    (i) the Carrier has specifically agreed in writing to carry any such items; and

    (ii) the Customer has agreed in writing to reimburse the Carrier in respect of all additional costs which result from the carriage of the said items; and

    (iii) the loss, mis-delivery or damage is occasioned during transit and is proved to be due to the negligence of the Carrier, its servants, agents or sub-contractors;

  (b) physical loss, mis-delivery of or damage to any other goods comprising the Consignment unless the same has arisen from, and the Carrier has used reasonable care to minimise the effects of:

    (i) Act of God;

    (ii) any consequences of war, invasion, act of foreign enemy, hostilities (whether war or not), civil war, rebellion, insurrection, terrorist act, military or usurped power or confiscation, requisition, or destruction or damage by or under the order of any government or public or local authority;

    (iii) seizure or forfeiture under legal process;

    (iv) error, act, omission, mis-statement or misrepresentation by the Customer or other owner of the Consignment or by servants or agents of either of them;

    (v) inherent liability to wastage in bulk or weight, faulty design, latent defect or inherent defect, vice or natural deterioration of the Consignment;

    (vi) insufficient or improper packing;

    (vii) insufficient or improper labelling or addressing;

    (viii) riot, civil commotion, strike, lockout, general or partial stoppage or restraint of labour from whatever cause;

    (ix) Consignee not taking or accepting delivery within a reasonable time after the Consignment has been tendered.

(3) The Carrier shall not in any circumstances be liable for loss or damage arising after transit is deemed to have ended within the meaning of Condition 6(2) hereof, whether or not caused or contributed to directly or indirectly by any act, omission, neglect, default or other wrongdoing on the part of the Carrier, its servants, agents or sub-contractors.

10. Fraud

The Carrier shall not in any circumstances be liable in respect of a Consignment where there has been fraud on the part of the Customer or the owner, or the servants or agents of either, in respect of that Consignment, unless the fraud has been contributed to by the complicity of the Carrier or of any servant of the Carrier acting in the course of his employment.

11. Limitation of Liability

(1) Except as otherwise provided in these Conditions, the liability of the Carrier in respect of claims for physical loss, mis-delivery of or damage to goods comprising the Consignment, howsoever arising, shall in all circumstances be limited to the lesser of

  (a) the value of the goods actually lost, mis-delivered or damaged; or

  (b) the cost of repairing any damage or of reconditioning the goods; or

  (c) a sum calculated at the rate of £1,300 Sterling per tonne on the gross weight of the goods actually lost, mis-delivered or damaged;

and the value of the goods actually lost, mis-delivered or damaged shall be taken to be their invoice value if they have been sold and shall otherwise be taken to be the replacement cost thereof to the owner at the commencement of transit, and in all cases shall be taken to include any Customs and Excise duties or taxes payable in respect of those goods: Provided that:

  (i) in the case of loss, mis-delivery of or damage to a part of the Consignment the weight to be taken into consideration in determining the amount to which the Carrier's liability is limited shall be only the gross weight of that part regardless of whether the loss, mis-delivery or damage affects the value of other parts of the Consignment;

  (ii) nothing in this Condition shall limit the liability of the Carrier to less than the sum of £10;

  (iii) the Carrier shall be entitled to proof of the weight and value of the whole of the Consignment and of any part thereof lost, mis-delivered or damaged;

  (iv) the Customer shall be entitled to give to the Carrier written notice to be delivered at least 7 days prior to commencement of transit requiring that the £1,300 per tonne limit in 11 (1)(c) above be increased, but not so as to exceed the value of the Consignment, and in the event of such notice being given the Customer shall be required to agree with the Carrier an increase in the carriage charges in consideration of the increased limit, but if no such agreement can be reached the aforementioned £1,300 per tonne limit shall continue to apply.

(2) The liability of the Carrier in respect of claims for any other loss whatsoever (including indirect or consequential loss or damage and loss of market), and howsoever arising in connection with the Consignment, shall not exceed the amount of the carriage charges in respect of the Consignment or the amount of the claimant's proved loss, whichever is the lesser, unless;

  (a) at the time of entering into the Contract with the Carrier the Customer declares to the Carrier a special interest in delivery in the event of physical loss mis-delivery or damage or of an agreed time limit being exceeded and agrees to pay a surcharge calculated on the amount of that interest, and

  (b) at least 7 days prior to the commencement of transit the Customer has delivered to the Carrier written confirmation of the special interest, agreed time limit and amount of the interest.

12. Indemnity to the Carrier

The Customer shall indemnify the Carrier against:

(1) all liabilities and costs incurred by the Carrier (including but not limited to claims, demands, proceedings, fines, penalties, damages, expenses and loss of or damage to the carrying vehicle and to other goods carried) by reason of any error, omission, mis-statement or misrepresentation by the Customer or other owner of the Consignment or by any servant or agent of either of them, insufficient or improper packing, labelling or addressing of the Consignment or fraud as in Condition 10;

(2) all claims and demands whatsoever (including for the avoidance of doubt claims alleging negligence), by whomsoever made and howsoever arising (including but not limited to claims caused by or arising out of the carriage of Dangerous Goods and claims made upon the Carrier by HM Customs and Excise in respect of dutiable goods consigned in bond) in excess of the liability of the Carrier under these Conditions in respect of any loss or damage whatsoever to, or in connection with, the Consignment whether or not caused or contributed to directly or indirectly by any act, omission, neglect, default or other wrongdoing on the part of the Carrier, its servants, agents or sub-contractors.

13. Time Limits for Claims

(1) The Carrier shall not be liable for:

  (a) damage to the whole or any part of the Consignment, or physical loss, mis-delivery or non-delivery of part of the Consignment unless advised thereof in writing within seven days, and the claim is made in writing within fourteen days, after the termination of transit;

  (b) any other loss unless advised thereof in writing within twenty-eight days, and the claim is made in writing within forty-two days, after the commencement of transit.

Provided that if the Customer proves that,

  (i) it was not reasonably possible for the Customer to advise the Carrier or make a claim in writing within the time limit applicable, and

  (ii) such advice or claim was given or made within a reasonable time,

the Carrier shall not have the benefit of the exclusion of liability afforded by this Condition.

(2) The Carrier shall in any event be discharged from all liability whatsoever and howsoever arising in respect of the Consignment unless suit is brought within one year of the date when transit commenced.

(3) In the computation of time where any period provided by these Conditions is seven days or less, Saturdays, Sundays and all statutory public holidays shall be excluded.

14. Lien

(1) The Carrier shall have a general lien against the Customer, where the Customer is the owner of the Consignment, for any monies whatever due from the Customer to the Carrier. If such a lien is not satisfied within a reasonable time, the Carrier may, at its absolute discretion sell the Consignment, or part thereof, as agent for the Customer and apply the proceeds towards the monies due and the expenses of the retention, insurance and sale of the Consignment and shall, upon accounting to the Customer for any balance remaining, be discharged from all liability whatever in respect of the Consignment.

(2) Where the Customer is not the owner of the Consignment, the Carrier shall have a particular lien against the said owner, allowing the Carrier to retain possession, but not to dispose of, the Consignment against monies due from the Customer in respect of the Consignment.

15. Unreasonable Detention

The Customer shall be liable to pay demurrage for unreasonable detention of any vehicle, trailer, container or other equipment but the rights of the Carrier against any other person in respect thereof shall remain unaffected.

16. Law and Jurisdiction

The Contract shall be governed by English law and United Kingdom courts alone shall have jurisdiction in any dispute between the Carrier and the Customer.

© Road Haulage Association Limited 1998
  Registered under the provisions of the Restrictive Trade Practices Act 1976

> **THESE CONDITIONS MAY ONLY BE USED BY MEMBERS OF THE ROAD HAULAGE ASSOCIATION**

Fig 8.2 *(continued)*

Road Haulage Association Limited
CONDITIONS OF CARRIAGE 1998
Explanatory Notes

STATUS OF THE CONDITIONS

The RHA Conditions of Carriage 1998 result from a review of the RHA Conditions of Carriage 1991. They take effect from 1st September 1998 and include amendments reflecting changes in Law and Members' use of the RHA Conditions of Carriage 1991. The opportunity has also been taken to bring other Specialist Group Conditions into line with the new RHA Conditions of Carriage and these will be introduced as self-standing Conditions of Carriage for Specialist Trades.

The 1998 Conditions have been registered with the Office of Fair Trading as an update of the 1991 Conditions. The use of the Conditions by Members is not compulsory but Members are recommended to use them as they are designed to enable a contractual balance to be struck between the interests of Members as carriers and those of their customers. It is recommended that Members seek professional advice before making or agreeing any variation in the Conditions to meet special circumstances.

The Conditions are the copyright of the RHA and may not be used by non-members. It is most important that Members should arrange to have the printed forms stamped with their details in the box provided at the top and with their Membership number in the space provided as this will deter the use of the form by non-members.

TO USE THE CONDITIONS

A Member who intends to trade under these Conditions, or any of the Specialist Group Conditions, should take the following action:

1. Refer the Conditions to his insurers or brokers and secure any necessary adjustments to existing insurance covers.

2. Inform existing customers in writing, by Recorded Delivery, of the intention to trade subject to the new Conditions saying for example: 'Please note that as from the ... day of ... 1998 goods will be accepted for carriage only subject to the RHA Conditions of Carriage 1998 a copy of which is attached'. If it is intended to use the Specialist Group Conditions reference should instead be made to the relevant specialist conditions.

3. Inform existing sub-contractors in writing, by Recorded Delivery, that as from the ... day of ... 1998 goods will be accepted for carriage and sub-contracted only subject to the RHA Conditions of Carriage 1998. If it is intended to use the Specialist Group Conditions reference should instead be made to the relevant Specialist Conditions. You should confirm that any previously agreed amendment in the financial limit per tonne continues to apply.

4. Retain Recorded Delivery receipts or, if the above letters are not sent by Recorded Delivery, maintain a permanent record of customers and sub-contractors and the dates on which letters were dispatched.

5. Print (or overprint) at the foot of all letter heads, quotation forms, fax forms, confirmation forms and notes, Consignment Notes and invoices etc: 'Goods are accepted for carriage (and sub-contracted) only subject to the RHA Conditions of Carriage 1998 a copy of which is available on request'. If it is intended to use the Specialist Group Conditions, reference should instead be made to the relevant Specialist Conditions. If present letter heads etc refer to the 'current RHA Conditions of Carriage' this will probably suffice provided that all existing customers and sub-contractors have been informed in accordance with 2-4 above that you are now operating under the 1998 Conditions.

6. Maintain a stock of the printed Conditions for issue to customers or sub-contractors as and when requested.

7. Specifically mention that the Conditions will apply during any telephone call in which the terms of the Contract are first agreed verbally, and confirm this immediately afterwards to the customer by fax, e-mail, letter, note or memo. Clear, simple, contemporary, dated and timed documents provide better proof than later conflicting oral evidence of recollections of conversations.

EFFECT OF THE CONDITIONS

The intention in revising the RHA Conditions is to retain their distinctive style and layout. The order of Clauses found in the 1998 Conditions will also be used in Specialist Group Conditions which will make them more user friendly. The principal amendments are set out below:

PREAMBLE: It now includes a notice to the customer making it clear that the carrier does not 'insure' the goods. This should help prevent later allegations by customers that they did not know that the liability of the carrier was limited under the Conditions and that the carrier insured its liabilities under the Conditions but did not cover the goods themselves on an 'All Risks' basis. The preamble also clarifies who can agree variations to the Conditions and that the Conditions will not override Statute such as CMR, where applicable.

CONDITION 1: The Definitions have been up-dated taking account of changes in Law since 1991 but are not substantively altered.

CONDITION 2: There are no substantive changes.

CONDITION 3: There are no substantive changes.

CONDITION 4: There are no substantive changes.

CONDITION 5: The wording has been amended in order better to protect the carrier against 'hollow pallet syndrome' type claims where the 'missing' goods were never loaded in the first place.

CONDITION 6: There are no substantive changes.

CONDITION 7: There are no substantive changes.

CONDITION 8: The 'volumetric' or 'size' based method of calculation of charges has been dropped. This was originally introduced with containerisation in the 1967 Conditions to enable carriers to charge other than on a tonnage basis. Charging techniques have become considerably more sophisticated since then and carriers now maintain a variety of different charging methods with individual customers. This aspect of charging is more appropriately left to individual negotiation than dealt with in the Conditions. Also, as the result of a recent Court decision the existence of the 'volumetric' Clause opened up the possibility of some substantially larger claims by customers, whether or not charges had been calculated or quoted on a volumetric basis. The opportunity has been taken to remove this distortion in the interpretation of the Conditions by deleting all reference to the basis of charging in Condition 8.

CONDITION 9: This is little altered but additional exceptions from liability in the case of a terrorist act or faulty design are introduced to deal with some commonly occurring problems which are outside the control of the carrier and for which the carrier should not be liable. Reference is now made to 'living creatures' rather than 'livestock' in Condition 9(2)(a) to include non-commercial consignments such as pigeons.

CONDITION 10: There are no substantive changes.

CONDITION 11: Clause 11(1) has been up-dated stylistically to reflect the fact that most goods are carried under the standard limit and not under specially uplifted compensation limits. 11(1)(b) also now refers specifically to repair costs. A modified version of the previous Clause 18 from the 1991 Conditions has been incorporated into the main text of Condition 11(1) to bring those details concerning calculation of compensation into a more appropriate place in the Conditions. Other relevant elements for calculating compensation have been brought together as a set of provisos to Clause 11(1) with clarification of the way in which compensation is calculated in the event of partial losses being given in proviso (i).

In the light of the Court case mentioned in relation to Clause 8, the volumetric calculation is also deleted for the purposes of defining compensation payable under Clause 11. Carriers can continue to charge on whatever basis they agree with their customers, but liability will be calculated solely on the basis of gross weight, as is done under CMR and all other commonly encountered Trading Conditions. Some existing customers may wish to discuss revised arrangements for the carriage of particularly light bulky goods. It will be open to customer and carrier, after discussion with respective insurers, to agree an uplift in the tonnage financial limitation under Clause 11(1)(c). In this way an agreed and appropriate level of compensation will apply, rather than the arbitrary formula which applied with the 'volumetric' calculation. The opportunity has also been taken to abandon the obscure proviso for 'proportional loss', which could in practice create quite arbitrary limits of liability quite different from those for loss of the whole consignment.

Note that, under general Law, a contract of carriage need only be completed within a reasonable time unless the contract makes time of the essence of the contract by, for example, stipulating a specific delivery time or date, in which case failure to deliver on time could result in a claim. As in previous RHA Conditions, the 1998 Conditions provide for this situation in Clause 11(2) and limit the amount of compensation recoverable where a carrier is in breach of contract to a maximum of the haulage charges paid by the customer, unless special uplifts in liability have been agreed in writing, in advance of the transit commencing.

CONDITION 12: The former Clause 13 becomes Clause 12, as it used to be in the 1982 Conditions. The indemnities to which the carrier is entitled from the customer remain broadly the same but the former 1982 and 1991 sub-clauses (2), (3) and (4) have now been combined in one sub-clause.

CONDITION 13: The provisions on time limits have been simplified to make them clearer and the notice provision for damage or partial loss brought in line with some other commonly encountered Trading Conditions, with 7 and not 3 days being available for notification of loss by the customer. A time period of one year is introduced within which legal proceedings must be brought against the carrier. This should prevent Writs appearing unexpectedly several years after events and when the carrier no longer has any recollection of those events.

CONDITION 14: There are no substantive changes.

CONDITION 15: This now refers specifically to the right to demurrage and the right extends to any equipment of the carrier which is detained. Carriers must establish their own scales for demurrage based on operating costs as Restrictive Trade Practices Law prevents the RHA from making specific recommendations.

CONDITION 16: A new Clause states that English Law applies to the contract and proceedings should be brought only in the United Kingdom. Carriers and their customers can of course vary the Clause to apply whatever Law and Jurisdiction they wish, for example, Scots Law.

Fig 8.2 *(continued)*

QUESTIONS/ACTIVITIES

1 For each of the examples given below identify:
   (a) the different kinds of contracts described, and
   (b) any statutes which apply to them.
   (i)   Fixit Ltd agrees to install gas central heating in Jim Frost's bungalow for a price of £1,200. £400 is to be paid in advance, with the balance due on completion of the work.
   (ii) James buys a new Ford Sierra from Smiths Motors by trading in his A-reg Capri, topped up by £5,000 in cash.
   (iii) Kelly, Murphy & Co, Solicitors, enter into a two-year agreement with Copytech Ltd for the use of a photocopier. Copytech Ltd agrees to keep the equipment 'in good repair'.
   (v)   Newtown Industrials plc employ Lorna Doone as a Sales Representative for the south-western region.
   (vi) Bill Archer orders 500 kg of fertiliser for use on his farm from Greener Fields Ltd. Payment is to be made within one month of delivery.
   (vii) Kate buys a bottle of lemonade from her corner shop for 60p, plus 5p on the bottle.
   (viii) Jack and Jill, up and coming young fashion designers, buy shop premises in Bath, with the aid of a loan secured on the property from their bank, West Country Bank plc.

2 When Eddy gets into financial difficulties, he agrees to sell his farm to Agri-Enterprises Ltd. Eddy is installed as farm manager and the farm continues to trade under its old name, Hill Top Farms. It is agreed that Eddy can enter into contracts on behalf of the company in respect of the day-to-day running of the farm, but that if he needs to purchase farm machinery in excess of £2,000, he must obtain the prior approval of Agri-Enterprises Ltd. During the harvest, the farm's combine harvester breaks down and cannot be repaired. Eddy is unable to hire a replacement at such short notice and so he agrees to buy a new combine harvester from Farm Machines Ltd at a cost of £20,000. Eddy has dealt with Farm Machines Ltd on many occasions in the past. Agri-Enterprises Ltd is now refusing to pay for the harvester. Advise Farm Machines Ltd.

3 You are a partner in a newly formed firm of removers, Lift and Shift. Consider the arguments for and against drawing up a standard form of contract for your business. What terms might you include in such a document?

Chapter 9

THE TERMS OF BUSINESS CONTRACTS

As we have already seen, a contract comprises a set of promises which the law will enforce. The obligations undertaken by the parties are known as the terms of the contract. If a dispute arises, the terms will become the object of intense scrutiny as the parties seek to justify their positions. The first task for any court is to establish exactly what was agreed by the parties. This may appear to be a relatively simple matter where the details of the agreement have been enshrined in a written contract, but even then problems can arise. The parties may have failed to express their intentions clearly; they may have omitted to mention a particular matter which later assumes great importance; or the written document may contradict what was said during the course of oral negotiations. Where the contract is made wholly by word of mouth, the job of ascertaining the contents of the contract becomes even more difficult.

The terms of a contract are essentially a matter of express agreement between the parties. It should be noted, however, that additional terms can be implied into an agreement, even against the wishes of the parties, and certain terms which have been clearly stated, such as exclusion clauses, can be rendered completely ineffective by operation of the law.

In this chapter we examine the basic requirement of certainty of terms for the creation of a contract, how the contents of a contract are determined and the relative importance that may be attached to the duties and obligations undertaken by the parties. Finally, we will consider the effect of clauses which purport to exclude or limit the liability of one of the parties.

CERTAINTY OF TERMS

The terms of an agreement may be so vague and indefinite that in reality there is no contract in existence at all.

Scammell v Ouston (1941)

Ouston agreed to buy a new motor van from Scammell. When placing the order for a particular type of van, Ouston wrote: 'This order is given on the understanding that the balance of the purchase price can be had on hire-purchase terms over a period of two years.' Scammell accepted the order but no discussions subsequently took place about the details of the hire-purchase arrangement. Scammell later refused to deliver the van and Ouston sued for damages for non-delivery. Scammell defended the case by arguing that a contract had never been concluded. The House of Lords held that the phrase 'hire-purchase terms' was so vague and indefinite that there was no contract at all. The decision might have been different if there had been usual or standard hire-purchase terms to which the court could refer to ascertain the intention of the parties. The parties needed to complete the agreement by reaching a consensus about unresolved matters such as rates of interest and frequency of payments.

Bushwall Properties Ltd v Vortex Properties Ltd (1976)

The parties concluded an agreement for the sale of $51\frac{1}{2}$ acres of land at £500,000 to be paid in three instalments. The first payment of £250,000 was to be followed in 12 months by a second payment of £125,000 with the balance to be paid after a further 12 months, and 'on the occasion of each completion a proportionate part of the land' should be released to the buyers. The Court of Appeal held that as the parties had failed to provide a mechanism for allocating the 'proportionate part of the land', the entire agreement failed for uncertainty.

The presence of a vague term will not prove fatal in every case. Various devices exist for ascertaining the meaning of terms.

1 The contract itself may provide the machinery whereby any disputes about the operation of the agreement can be resolved.

Foley v Classique Coaches Ltd (1934)

Foley sold part of his land to a coach company for use as a coach station, on condition that the company would buy all their petrol from him 'at a price to be agreed between the parties'. It was also agreed that any dispute arising from the contract should be submitted to arbitration. The parties failed to agree a price and the company refused to buy petrol from Foley. The agreement to buy petrol was held to be binding despite the failure to agree a price because the parties had agreed a method by which the price could be ascertained, i.e. by arbitration.

2 A court can ascertain the terms of a contract by reference to a trade custom or a course of previous dealings between the parties.

Hillas & Co Ltd v *Arcos Ltd* (1932)

The parties concluded a contract for the sale of a certain quantity of softwood timber 'of fair specification' over the 1930 season. The agreement also contained an option to buy further quantities in 1931, but no details were given as to the kind or size of the timber or the date of shipment. The 1930 agreement was carried out without difficulty but when the buyers tried to exercise the option for 1931, the sellers refused to supply the wood, claiming that they had only agreed to negotiate a further contract for 1931. The House of Lords held that the sellers were bound to carry out the 1931 option. The terms of the contract could be ascertained by reference to the previous course of dealings between the parties.

3 A meaningless term which is subsidiary to the main agreement can be ignored and the rest of the contract enforced.

Nicolene Ltd v *Simmonds* (1953)

The claimants placed an order with the defendant for the supply of 3,000 tons of steel reinforcing bars. The defendant wrote to the claimants to accept the order adding that 'we are in agreement that the usual conditions of acceptance apply'. There were no usual conditions of acceptance, so the words were meaningless. The Court of Appeal held that as the rest of the contract made sense, the meaningless clause could be ignored.

PUFFS, REPRESENTATIONS AND TERMS

The first step in determining the terms of a contract is to establish what the parties said or wrote. That is not to say that all statements made during the course of negotiations will automatically be incorporated in the resulting contract. The statement may be a trader's puff, a representation or a term, and if it turns out to be untrue, the claimant's remedy will depend on how the statement is classified. The differences are as follows:

1 Trader's puff. If a car is described as 'totally immaculate and 'incredible value' this is nothing more than typical advertising exaggeration. We are not expected to take such sales talk seriously and, consequently, there is no civil remedy if the statement turns out to be untrue.

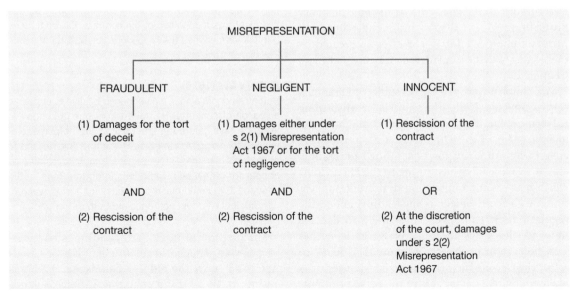

Fig 9.1 Remedies for misrepresentation

2 Representation. This is a statement of fact made by one party which induces the other to enter into the contract. As we have already seen in Chapter 7, the remedy for a misrepresentation is determined by the type of misrepresentation. You can refresh your memory by referring to Fig 9.1.

3 Term. Breach of a term of the contract entitles the injured party to claim damages and, if he has been deprived of substantially what he bargained for, he will also be able to repudiate the contract. The distinction between a mere representation and a statement which becomes a term of the contract used to be very important. Before 1967 damages were not available for a misrepresentation unless it was made fraudulently, and the only remedy, rescission, could be easily lost. The injured party, therefore, would be keen to establish that the statement had been incorporated into the contract, so that he could claim damages for a breach of a contractual term. This generated a considerable body of complex case law. The Misrepresentation Act 1967, however, opened the way for an award of damages for non-fraudulent misrepresentation and, as a result, the distinction between terms and representations has become much less important.

It should be noted that the civil remedies in respect of false statements are complemented by criminal sanctions for breaches of the Trade Descriptions Acts 1968, Part III of the Consumer Protection Act 1987 and the Property Misdescription Act 1991. The offences created by these Acts will be considered in more detail in Chapter 12.

Misleading advertising is also subject to administrative controls. Under the Control of Misleading Advertisements Regulations 1988 (which implemented an EC Directive on misleading advertising), the Director General of Fair Trading may refer misleading advertising to the High Court which may grant an injunction to prevent publication. An advertisement is misleading under the regulations if it deceives or is likely to deceive those to whom it is addressed or whom it reaches and, because of its deceptive nature, it is likely to affect their economic behaviour, or it injures or is likely to injure a competitor of the person promoting the advertisement.

TYPES OF CONTRACTUAL TERMS

The terms of a contract delineate the obligations of the parties and these may vary greatly in importance. Traditionally terms have been divided into two categories: conditions and warranties.

1 Conditions. A condition is a major term which is vital to the main purpose of the contract. A breach of condition will entitle the injured party to repudiate the contract and claim damages. The breach does not automatically end the contract and the injured party may choose to go on with the relationship, despite the breach, and recover damages instead.

2 Warranties. A warranty is a less important term: it does not go to the root of the contract. A breach of warranty will only give the injured party the right to claim damages; he cannot repudiate the contract.

The difference between a condition and warranty is illustrated by the following cases.

Poussard v *Spiers* (1876)
Madame Poussard was engaged to appear in an operetta from the start of its London run. Owing to illness, she was not available until a week after the show had opened and the producers were forced to engage a substitute. They now refused Madame Poussard's offer to take up her part. It was held that the obligation to perform from the first night was a condition of the contract. Failure to carry out this term entitled the producers to repudiate Madame Poussard's contract.

Bettini v *Gye* (1876)
Bettini, an opera singer, was engaged by Gye to appear in a season of concerts. He undertook to be in London at least six days before the first concert for the purpose of rehearsals. He arrived three days late and Gye refused to accept his services. It was held that the promise to appear for rehearsals was a less important term of the contract. Gye could claim compensation for a breach of warranty but he could not repudiate Bettini's contract.

The division of terms into conditions and warranties was included in the original Sale of Goods Act 1893 (now the Sale of Goods Act 1979, as amended). In s 11(3) a condition is described as a stipulation 'the breach of which may give rise to a right to treat the contract as repudiated', while a warranty is a stipulation 'the breach of which may give rise to a claim for damages but not a right to reject the goods and treat the contract as repudiated'. In recent years, the courts have recognised that it may be impossible to classify a term neatly in advance as either a condition or a warranty. Some undertakings may occupy an intermediate position, in that the term can be assessed only in the light of the consequences of a breach. If a breach of the term results in severe loss and damage, the injured party will be entitled to repudiate the contract; where the breach only involves minor loss, the injured party's remedies will be restricted to damages. These intermediate terms have become known as innominate terms.

Cehave NV v Bremer Handelsgesellschaft mbH (The Hansa Nord) (1975)
A clause in a contract for the sale of citrus pulp pellets stipulated that shipment was 'to be made in good condition'. Part of one consignment arrived in Rotterdam in a damaged condition and the buyers rejected the whole cargo. The defects were not particularly serious because some time later the buyers bought the very same cargo at a considerably reduced price, which they then proceeded to use for their original purpose. The Court of Appeal held that the clause in question was an intermediate term. The breach was not so serious that it entitled the buyers to reject the whole cargo. It could be dealt with by an award of damages.

EXPRESS AND IMPLIED TERMS

Another way in which the contents of a contract can be classified is according to whether the terms are express or implied.

Express terms

Express terms are the details of a contract which have been specifically agreed between the parties. They may be contained wholly in a written document or ascertained entirely from what the parties said to each other. In some cases, the terms may be partly written and partly verbal.

Harling v *Eddy* (1951)
A heifer was put up for sale by auction at Ashford Cattle Market. The sale was subject to the auctioneer's printed conditions of sale which stated that the auctioneer did not guarantee the condition of the animals sold. The appearance of this particular heifer was so poor when she entered the auction ring that no one was prepared to make a bid for her. The auctioneer then stated that there was nothing wrong with her and he would guarantee her in every respect. The heifer was sold to the claimant but was dead from tuberculosis within three months. The claimant successfully sued the auctioneer for damages. The Court of Appeal held that the auctioneer was bound by his oral guarantee despite the contents of the written conditions of sale.

Types of express terms

The most common types of express terms, which are often a particular feature of standard form contracts, are exemption clauses, liquidated damage clauses and price variation clauses.

Exemption clause – generally

This term is used to describe an express term in a contract or a statement in a notice or sign which seeks to exclude or limit the responsibilities that might otherwise belong to a party.

Example 1 (sales brochure)
'We reserve the right to change component type, manufacturers, sources of supply and technical specifications at any time. Dimensions, weights and colours contained in this brochure are approximate. Products and prices may be altered without notice at any time.'

Example 2 (car park ticket)
'Entry to or use of this car park is subject to the current terms and conditions of the company. These conditions contain limited exemption clauses affecting all persons who enter or use the car park. Entry to and use of this car park is at your own risk.'

The legal effect of exemption clauses will be examined in detail later in this chapter.

Liquidated damages clause

This is a term in a contract which lays down the amount of damages that will be payable in the event of a breach of contract. Cancellation charges are an example of a liquidated damages clause.

Price variation clause

Calculating a contract price in a period of inflation can be a very hit-and-miss operation. A contractor may find himself bound by a fixed price which has failed to take sufficient account of increases in the cost of raw materials, wages or overheads, such as business rates. One solution to this problem is to insert a term in a contract which allows a variation in the contract price under certain circumstances.

Example 1 (holiday brochure)

'Our prices are based on known costs and projections at 1 March 2001 and we do not expect to make any changes. However, we reserve the right to increase prices at any time until 30 days before departure to allow for variations in: (a) exchange rates, (b) transportation costs, and (c) increases in tax rates imposed in any country including dues, taxes or fees chargeable for services such as landing taxes or embarkation or disembarkation fees at ports and airports. Even in these cases we will absorb an amount equivalent to 2 per cent of the price. Any increase will be calculated by reference to the total cost of the variation, to be divided by our best estimate of the number of passengers likely to be affected, so as to arrive at an increase for each passenger. If this means paying more than 10 per cent on the price, you will be entitled to cancel with a full refund of money paid. Should you decide to cancel because of this, you must exercise your right to do so within 14 days from the issue date printed on the invoice.'

Example 2 (building contract)

'Unless otherwise stated the contract price is based on the cost of labour, materials and all necessary services at the date of the quotation and increases or decreases in any such costs shall be a net addition to or deduction from the contract price.'

Implied terms

In general, the contents of a contract are determined by agreement between the parties. Nevertheless, there are various circumstances in which additional terms may be implied into the agreement.

1 **By custom.** A contract must always be examined in the light of its surrounding commercial context. The terms of a contract may have been negotiated against the background of the customs of a particular locality or trade. The parties automatically assume that their contract will be subject to such customs and so do not deal specifically with the matter in their contract.

Hutton v Warren (1836)

The tenant of a farm was given six months' notice to quit. His landlord insisted that he continue to cultivate the land during the notice period in keeping with custom. The tenant successfully argued that the same custom entitled him to a fair allowance for the seeds and labour he used on the land.

2 **By the common law.** The courts will be prepared to imply a term into a contract in order to give effect to the obvious intentions of the parties. Sometimes the point at issue has been overlooked or the parties have failed to express their intention clearly. In these circumstances, the court will supply a term in the interests of 'business efficacy' so that the contract makes commercial common sense.

The Moorcock (1889)

The owner of a wharf agreed to provide mooring facilities for *The Moorcock*. The ship was damaged when it hit a ridge of rock at low tide. The court implied an undertaking on the part of the wharf owner that it was a reasonably safe place to moor the ship. The wharf owner had broken his implied undertaking and was, therefore, liable in damages to the ship owner

Certain standard terms have been implied by the common law in a number of business contracts. The courts will imply a term into a lease of a furnished house that it will be reasonably fit for habitation at the start of the tenancy. A contract of employment is subject to a number of implied terms. An employer is under a common law duty to provide a safe system of work for his employees, while an employee is under common law duties to obey legitimate orders and show good faith towards his employer.

By implying a term into the contract, the court is imposing reasonable obligations, which the parties would have no doubt included in their agreement if they had troubled to think about the matter. These implied terms may be excluded by express agreement between the parties.

3 **By statute.** A term may be implied into a contract by Act of Parliament. In many cases, these implied terms began life among the customs of merchants, were recognised by the courts and then included in the statute which codified the common law rules. The best example of this process is provided by the law relating to the sale of goods. The original Sale of Goods Act 1893 was a codification of the common law rules which had been developed by the courts during the 19th

century. The present Sale of Goods Act 1979 re-enacts the 1893 Act, incorporating the changes made in the intervening years. The Sale and Supply of Goods Act 1994 and the Sale of Goods (Amendment) Acts 1994 and 1995 make a number of changes to the 1979 Act.

Some terms are implied into a contract for the sale of goods under the Sale of Goods Act 1979. The best known are contained in ss 12–15.

(a) *Section 12 (title)*. There is an implied condition in every contract for the sale of goods that the seller has the right to sell the goods and that he will transfer good title to the buyer. The seller will break this term, for example, if it transpires that the goods were stolen.

(b) *Section 13 (description)*. Where there is a sale of goods by description there is an implied condition that the goods will correspond with the description. A shirt described as 100 per cent cotton, for example, should not contain man-made fibres.

(c) *Section 14 (quality and suitability)*. Although this section preserves the well-established principle of *caveat emptor* (let the buyer beware), it does impose two duties on a seller who sells in the course of a business. First, there is an implied condition that the goods are of satisfactory quality. This means that if you buy a washing machine, it should actually work when you get it home. Second, where the buyer expressly or impliedly makes known any particular purpose for which the goods are required, there is an implied condition that the goods will be fit for that purpose. If you ask the salesman to recommend a heavy-duty carpet which would be suitable for a lounge, it should not be threadbare after a couple of months.

(d) *Section 15 (sample)*. In sales by sample, there is an implied condition that the bulk will correspond with the sample. This means that if you have curtains made up for you, the quality of the material should match the sample that you examined in the shop.

Similar terms are implied into contracts for the supply of goods by way of hire-purchase. hire, barter, and under work and materials contracts. Warranties relating to title and quality are implied on the redemption of trading stamps for goods. The sources of these implied terms are summarised in Fig 9.2.

		Goods supplied by way of:				
		Sale of goods	*Hire-purchase*	*Barter, work and materials*	*Hire*	*Redemption of trading stamps*
		Sale of Goods Act 1979	Supply of Goods (Implied Terms) Act 1973*	Supply of Goods and Services Act 1982	Supply of Goods and Services Act 1982	Trading Stamps Act 1964**
Implied Terms	Title	s 12	s 8	s 2	s 7	s 4
	Description	s 13	s 9	s 3	s 8	–
	Quality and suitability***	s 14	s 10	s 4	s 9	s 4
	Sample	s 15	s 11	s 5	s 10	–

* As amended by the Consumer Credit Act 1974
** As amended by the Supply of Goods (Implied Terms) Act 1973
*** The implied term as to quality has been amended by the Sale and Supply of Goods Act 1994

Fig 9.2 The sources of statutory implied terms in contracts for the supply of goods

EXEMPTION CLAUSES – THE LAW

Exemption clauses are a common feature of business contracts. They are express terms which seek to exclude or limit the liability that might belong to one party in the event of a breach of contract. Such clauses are perfectly fair where they are the result of free negotiations between equals, but, all too often, they are imposed on a weaker party by a stronger party. This abuse of freedom of contract was most commonly practised against consumers. The courts attempted to deal with the problem, but the common law ultimately proved unequal to the ingenuity of those who sought the protection of the exemption. Over the years, Parliament stepped in to control the use of unfair exemption clauses in particular kinds of contracts and now the overwhelming majority of these clauses are covered by the provisions of the Unfair Contract Terms Act 1977, as supplemented by the Unfair Terms in Consumer Contracts Regulations 1999. Statutory control of exemption clauses has been grafted on to the pre-existing common law rules. It is still necessary, therefore, to examine the attitude of the courts to these clauses. After we have done this, we will consider how Parliament has dealt with the problem.

Judicial control

The judges based their attack on exemption clauses on two main fronts: incorporation and interpretation.

Incorporation

The person wishing to rely on the exclusion clause must show that it formed part of the contract. In this connection note the following rules.

1 **Signed documents.** Where the exemption clause is contained in a document which has been signed, it will automatically form part of the contract. The signer is presumed to have read and understood the significance of all the terms contained in the document.

L'Estrange v *Graucob* (1934)
Miss L'Estrange bought an automatic cigarette vending machine for use in her café. She signed a 'sales agreement' which provided that 'Any express or implied condition, statement or warranty statutory or otherwise, not stated herein is hereby excluded.' She did not read this document and was completely unaware of the sweeping exclusion clause hidden in the small print. The machine did not work properly but it was held that she was still bound to pay for it because by signing the agreement she had effectively signed her rights away.

This general rule will not apply where the signer can plead *non est factum* (see Chapter 7) or if the other party has misrepresented the terms of the agreement.

Curtis v *Chemical Cleaning and Dyeing Co* (1951)
Mrs Curtis took a wedding dress to be cleaned by the defendants. She signed a piece of paper headed 'Receipt', after being told by the assistant that it exempted the cleaners from liability for damage to beads and sequins. The 'Receipt', however, contained a clause excluding liability 'for any damage howsoever arising'. When the dress was returned it was badly stained. It was held that the cleaners could not escape liability for damage to the material of the dress by relying on the exemption clause because its scope had been misrepresented by the defendant's assistant.

2 **Unsigned documents.** The exemption clause may be contained in an unsigned document such as a ticket or a notice. The clause will only form part of the contract if two conditions are met. First, the document must be regarded by a reasonable man as contractual in nature and, as such, likely to contain exemption clauses.

Chapelton v *Barry Urban District Council* (1940)
Mr Chapelton hired two deck chairs for three hours from the defendant council. He received two tickets which he put into his pocket unread. Each ticket contained a clause exempting the defendant from liability for 'any accident or damage arising from the hire of the chair'. Mr Chapelton was injured when the chair he sat on collapsed. He successfully sued the council. The Court of Appeal held that a reasonable man would assume that the ticket was a mere receipt and not a contractual document which might contain conditions. The defendant had not succeeded in incorporating the exemption into its contract with Mr Chapelton.

Notice of the exemption clause must have been given before the contract was made or at the time the contract was made. Attempts to give notice after the contract has been concluded will be ineffective.

Olley v *Marlborough Court Ltd* (1949)

Mr and Mrs Olley booked in for a week's stay at the defendants' hotel. There was a notice in the bedroom which stated that 'the proprietors will not hold themselves responsible for articles lost or stolen unless handed to the manageress for safe custody'. A stranger gained access to the Olleys' room and stole Mrs Olley's furs. The Court of Appeal held that the defendants were liable. The Olleys saw the notice only after the contract had been concluded at the reception desk. The exclusion clause could not protect the defendants because it had not been incorporated into the contract with the Olleys.

Thornton v *Shoe Lane Parking Ltd* (1971)

Mr Thornton decided to park his car in the defendant's car park. There was a notice at the entrance which stated: 'All cars parked at owner's risk'. As Mr Thornton drove into the car park, a light changed from red to green and he took a ticket from an automatic machine. He noticed that there was some writing on the ticket but he did not read it. The ticket stated that it was 'issued subject to the conditions of issue as displayed on the premises'. The conditions which were displayed inside the car park purported to exempt the defendant for not only damage to vehicles but also injury to customers. When Mr Thornton returned to the car park to collect his car, he was involved in an accident and he suffered personal injury partly as a result of the defendant's negligence. The Court of Appeal held that the defendant could not rely on the exemption clause displayed inside the car park because it had been introduced after the contract was formed. The contract was concluded when the lights changed from red to green and the machine dispensed a ticket. It is important to note that Mr Thornton was using the car park for the first time. If he had visited the car park before, the defendant may have been able to argue that the notice inside the car park had been incorporated into the contract by a previous source of dealings (see later).

The person seeking to rely on the exemption clause must show that reasonable steps have been taken to give notice of the clause to the other contracting party. What amounts to reasonably sufficient notice will vary according to the nature of the clause. As Denning LJ commented in *Spurling* v *Bradshaw* (1956) (see later):

> The more unreasonable a clause is the greater the notice which must he given of it. Some

clauses would need to be printed in red ink with a red hand pointing to it before the notice could he held to he sufficient.

The 'red hand rule' was applied by the Court of Appeal in the following case.

Interfoto Picture Library v *Stiletto Visual Programmes Ltd* (1988)

Stiletto, an advertising agency, ordered 47 photographic transparencies from Interfoto, which operated a photo library. The transparencies were accompanied by a delivery note which contained a number of conditions. Condition 2 provided that a holding fee of £5 per day was payable in respect of each transparency retained after 14 days. Stiletto did not return the transparencies on time and Interfoto sued for the holding fee payable under Condition 2, which amounted to £3,785. The Court of Appeal held that Condition 2 had not been incorporated into the contract. Interfoto had not taken reasonable steps to bring such an unusual, unreasonable and onerous term to Stiletto's attention. Interfoto was awarded £3.50 per transparency per week on a *quantum meruit* basis.

3 **Previous course of dealings.** An exclusion clause may be binding even though it has not been included in the contract in question, if a previous course of dealings between the parties on the basis of such terms can be established. This principle has been accepted more readily in commercial contracts than in consumer transactions.

J Spurling v *Bradshaw* (1956)

The defendant delivered eight barrels of orange juice to the claimants who were warehousemen. A few days later the defendant received a document from the claimants which acknowledged receipt of the barrels. It also contained a clause exempting the claimants from liability for loss or damage 'occasioned by the negligence, wrongful act or default' caused by themselves, their employees or agents. When the defendant collected the barrels, some were empty and some contained dirty water. He refused to pay the storage charges and was sued by the claimants. Although the defendants did not receive the document containing the exclusion clause until after the conclusion of the contract, the clause had been incorporated into the contract as a result of a regular course of dealings between the parties over the years. The defendant had received similar documents on previous occasions and he was now bound by the terms contained in them.

Hollier v Rambler Motors (AMC) Ltd (1972)

Mr Hollier entered into an oral contract with the defendant garage to have his car repaired. While the car was in the garage, it was damaged in a fire caused by the defendant's negligence. Mr Hollier had had his car repaired by the defendant on three or four occasions in the previous five years. In the past he had been asked to sign a form which stated: 'The company is not responsible for damage caused by fire to customers' cars on the premises', but he did not sign such a form on this occasion. The defendant argued that the exemption clause had been incorporated into the oral contract by a previous course of dealings. The Court of Appeal rejected this argument and held that the defendant was liable. Three or four transactions over five years did not constitute a regular course of dealings.

4 Privity of contract. According to the doctrine of privity of contract, a person who is not a party to a contract can neither benefit from the contract nor be made liable under it. So while a duly incorporated exemption clause may protect a party to a contract, it will not protect his servants or agents. They are strangers to the contract and so cannot take advantage of an exclusion or limitation clause.

Scruttons Ltd v Midland Silicones Ltd (1962)

A shipping company (the carrier) agreed to ship a drum of chemicals belonging to the claimants from New York to London. The contract of carriage limited the liability of the carrier for damage to $500 (£179) per package. The drum was damaged by the negligence of the defendants, a firm of stevedores, who had been engaged by the carriers to unload the ship. The claimants sued the defendants in tort for the full extent of the damage, which amounted to £593. The defendants claimed the protection of the limitation clause. The House of Lords held in favour of the claimants. The defendants were not parties to the contract of carriage and so they could not take advantage of the limitation clause.

Comment. During the course of his speech in the House of Lords, Lord Reid suggested a way in which the benefit of an exemption could be made available to a third party, such as the firm of stevedores in this case. He said that four conditions must be fulfilled: (1) a contract of carriage must specifically state that the stevedore is intended to be protected by the exemption clause; (2) the carrier must make it clear that he is contracting both on his own behalf and as agent for the stevedores; (3) the carrier has authority from the stevedore to act in this way; and (4) there is some consideration moving from the stevedores.

Legal draftsmen duly took notice of the formula and it received the approval of the Privy Council in *New Zealand Shipping Co Ltd v A M Satterthwaite & Co Ltd (The Eurymedon)* (1974).

This common law position is now subject to the provisions of the Contracts (Rights of Third Parties) Act 1999, which was discussed in detail in Chapter 7. The Act allows contracting parties to confer third-party rights in relation to exclusion clauses in contracts such as those dealt with in the *Satterthwaite* case. (You should note, however, the effect of s 7(2) of the 1999 Act in relation to s 2(2) of the Unfair Contract Terms Act 1977, which is discussed later.)

Interpretation

Where a clause is duly incorporated into a contract, the courts will proceed to examine the words used to see if the clause covers the breach and loss which has actually occurred. The main rules of interpretation used by the courts are as follows:

1 Strict interpretation. An exemption clause will be effective only if it expressly covers the kind of liability which has in fact arisen. A clause, for example, which excludes liability for a breach of warranty will not provide protection against liability for a breach of condition.

Baldry v Marshall (1925)

The claimant asked the defendants, who were motor dealers, to supply a car that would be suitable for touring purposes. The defendants recommended a Bugatti, which the claimant bought. The written contract excluded the defendant's liability for any 'guarantee or warranty, statutory or otherwise'. The car turned out to be unsuitable for the claimant's purposes, so he rejected it and sued to recover what he had paid. The Court of Appeal held that the requirement that the car be suitable for touring was a condition. Since the clause did not exclude liability for breach of a condition, the claimant was not bound by it.

Andrews Bros Ltd v Singer & Co Ltd (1934)

The claimants agreed to buy some new Singer cars from the defendants. A clause in the contract provided that 'all conditions, warranties and liabilities implied by common law, statute or otherwise are excluded'. One of the cars supplied was not new and the claimants were seeking damages for breach of contract. The defendants argued that they were protected by the exclusion clause. The Court of Appeal held that the promise to supply new cars was an express term of the contract. As the exclusion clause only covered implied terms, the defendant could not rely on the exclusion.

2 *Contra proferentem*. If there is any ambiguity or doubt as to the meaning of an exemption clause the court will construe it *contra proferentem*, i.e. against the party who inserted it in the contract. Very clear words must be used before a party will be held exempt from liability in negligence.

White v *John Warwick & Co Ltd* (1953)

The claimant hired a tradesman's cycle from the defendants. The written hire agreement stated: 'Nothing in this agreement shall render the owners liable for any personal injury'. While the claimant was riding the cycle, the saddle tilted forward and he was injured. The defendants might have been liable in tort (for negligence) as well as in contract. The Court of Appeal held that the ambiguous wording of the exclusion clause would effectively protect the defendants from their strict contractual liability, but it would not exempt them from liability in negligence.

3 Repugnancy. Under this rule, a court can strike out an exemption clause which is inconsistent with or repugnant to the main purpose of the contract.

J Evans & Sons (Portsmouth) Ltd v *Andrea Merzario Ltd* (1976)

The claimants had imported machines from Italy for many years and for this purpose they used the services of the defendant forwarding agents. When the defendants changed over to containers, the claimants were orally promised by the defendants that their goods would continue to be stowed below deck. On one occasion, the claimants' container was stored on deck and it was lost when it slid overboard. The Court of Appeal held that the defendants could not rely on an exemption clause contained in the standard conditions of the forwarding trade, on which the parties had contracted, because it was repugnant to the oral promise that had been given.

The doctrine of fundamental breach

The doctrine of fundamental breach was developed particularly by Lord Denning MR in the Court of Appeal as an additional weapon in the judiciary's fight against exclusion clauses which

had been properly incorporated into a contract. According to the doctrine, no exemption clause, however clear and unambiguous, could, as a matter of law, protect a party from liability for a serious or fundamental breach of contract. This line of argument was rejected by the House of Lords in the *Suisse* case (1966) but was then revived by the Court of Appeal. The House of Lords re-established its authority and finally demolished the doctrine in *Photo Production Ltd* v *Securicor Transport Ltd* (1980).

Photo Production Ltd v *Securicor Transport Ltd* (1980)

The defendant security company agreed to provide a visiting patrol service at nights and weekends for the claimants' factory. One night, the defendant's patrolman lit a fire inside the factory. The fire got out of control and the factory and its contents, worth a total of £615,000, were completely destroyed. The defendant relied on an exclusion clause in its contract which stated that it would not be responsible 'for any injurious act or default by any employee … unless such act or default could have been foreseen and avoided by the exercise of due diligence' by the defendant. The claimants did not allege that the defendant had been negligent in employing the man who lit the fire. The House of Lords held that the defendant was protected by the exemption clause. Although a breach of contract with serious consequences had taken place, the exclusion clause, as a matter of construction, was clear and unambiguous and it covered even the 'fundamental' breach that had taken place.

The contract in the *Photo Production* case was entered into before 1 February 1978 and so the House of Lords could not apply the provisions of the Unfair Contract Terms Act 1977. Nevertheless, their Lordships' decision was greatly influenced by the principles contained in the Act. In the words of Lord Wilberforce,

> After this Act, in commercial matters generally, when the parties are not of unequal bargaining power, and when risks are normally borne by insurance, there is everything to be said for leaving the parties free to apportion the risks as they think fit and for respecting their decision.

In this case the parties had contracted as equals and were clearly in the best position to decide how to allocate the risk of the factory being damaged or destroyed.

Statutory control

At first, Parliament intervened on a piecemeal basis to control the use of exemption clauses in specific types of contract. Section 43(7) of the Transport Act 1962 (repealed in 1977), for example, declared that any clause which purports to exclude or limit the liability of the British Railways Board in respect of injury or death to a passenger 'shall be void and of no effect'. Other examples of statutory control of exemption clauses include the Occupiers' Liability Act 1957, the Carriage of Goods by Sea Act 1971 and the Defective Premises Act 1972. Parliamentary interest in exemption clauses culminated in the enactment of the Unfair Contract Terms Act 1977, which lays down rules of general application to most contracts. The 1977 Act is now supplemented by the Unfair Terms in Consumer Contracts Regulations 1999.

UNFAIR CONTRACT TERMS ACT 1977

Preliminary matters

1 The Act came into force on 1 February 1978. It does not apply to contracts made before that date.

2 The title of the Act is misleading in two respects. First, it affects the law of tort as well as contract law because it covers non-contractual notices and signs. Second, it does not deal with all unfair terms in contracts, only unfair exemption clauses.

3 Most of the provisions of the Act apply only to 'business liability', i.e. liability for things done in the course of business or from the occupation of premises used for business purposes. A business includes a profession, the activities of government departments and those of a local or public authority.

4 The Act does not apply to international supply contracts, and ss 2–4 do not apply to certain contracts listed in Sch 1, which include:

(a) contracts of insurance;

(b) contracts in relation to land.

5 The Act affords the greatest protection to consumers: under s 12 (1) a person 'deals as a consumer' if:

(a) he neither makes the contract in the course of a business nor holds himself out as doing so; and

(b) the other party does make the contract in the course of a business; and

(c) where it involves a contract for the supply of goods, they are of a type ordinarily supplied for private use or consumption.

The possibilities are summarised in Fig 9.3.

The courts have interpreted s 12 so as to confine the impact of the more limited protection afforded to non-consumer transactions only to those business contracts which form an integral part of the business.

R & B Customs Brokers Co Ltd v United Dominions Trust Ltd (1988)

The claimant company, which was in the business of freight forwarding and shipping agency, bought a second-hand car for the use of a director. The sale was arranged through the defendant finance company under a conditional sale agreement which contained exclusion clauses. The car was defective. The Court of Appeal held that the car was not fit for the purpose as required by s 14(3) of the Sale of Goods Act 1979 and that, as the claimant company was dealing as a consumer, this implied term could not be excluded by virtue of s 6 of the Unfair Contract Terms Act 1977. The court decided that there was not a sufficient degree of regularity to make the transaction an integral part of the company's business and, therefore, a contract made in the course of a business.

The parties	Types of transaction
Business person/private person	Consumer transaction*
Business person/ business person	Non-consumer transaction
Private person/private person	Non-consumer transaction
* If goods are supplied, they must be of a type ordinarily supplied for private use or consumption for the contract to be classed as a consumer transaction.	

Fig 9.3 Consumer and non-consumer transactions under the Unfair Contract Terms Act 1977

6 Exemption clauses are regulated by the Act in two ways. They are either rendered void and completely ineffective or they are made subject to a test of reasonableness. Although the application of the 'reasonableness test' is a matter for the court to decide in the light of all the circumstances of a particular case, the Act lays down some guiding principles for the judges.

(a) Reasonableness must be judged in the case of a contractual term in the light of circumstances at the time when the contract was made and, in the case of a non-contractual notice or sign, when the liability arose.

(b) It is up to the person who claims that a term or notice is reasonable to show that it is.

(c) Where the clause seeks to limit liability rather than exclude it completely, the court must have regard to two factors: the resources available to meet the liability and the extent to which insurance cover was available.

(d) Where the exemption clause appears in any kind of contract under which goods are supplied its reasonableness may be judged according to the criteria contained in Sch 2, which are as follows:

(i) *The bargaining strengths of the parties relative to each other and the availability of alternative supplies.* A monopoly supplier, for example, will find it difficult to justify a wide exclusion clause.

(ii) *Whether the customer received an inducement to agree to the term.* The supplier may have offered the customer a choice: a lower price, but subject to an exemption clause, or a higher price without the exemption. Where a real choice is available, the supplier will probably be able to show that the exemption clause was reasonable.

(iii) *Whether the customer knew or ought reasonably to have known of the existence and extent of the term.* If the customer goes into the contract with his eyes wide open, he may have to accept the exemption clause.

(iv) *Where the term excludes or restricts any relevant liability if some condition is not complied with, whether it was reasonable at the time of the contract to expect that compliance with that condition would be practicable.* A supplier, for example, may limit his liability to

defects which are brought to his attention within a certain time, e.g. three days. The court will consider whether compliance with such a time limit is practicable.

(v) *Whether the goods were manufactured, processed or adapted to the special order of the customer.* An exemption clause may well be reasonable if the customer has insisted on the supplier complying with detailed specifications.

The reasonableness of exemption clauses in contracts other than for the sale or supply of goods must be judged without the benefit of these criteria. The leading case on unreasonableness is a decision of the House of Lords in which the reasonableness test contained in the sale of goods legislation which preceded s 6 of the Unfair Contract Terms Act 1977 was considered.

George Mitchell (Chesterhall) Ltd v Finney Lock Seeds Ltd (1983)

The defendant seed merchants supplied the claimant farmers with 30 lb of Dutch winter cabbage seed for a price of £192. The claimants planted the seed on 63 acres but the seed was defective and the crop was a total failure. When the claimants claimed compensation for loss of the crop (over £60,000), the defendants sought to rely on a clause in the contract which purported to limit their liability to replacing the seed or refunding the purchase price. The House of Lords held that the defendants could not rely on the clause since it did not satisfy the reasonableness test. The House referred to the following factors as indicating that the clause was unreasonable: (a) the defendants had made *ex gratia* payments in similar cases in the past; (b) the breach had occurred as a result of the defendants' negligence; and (c) the defendants could have insured against the risk of crop failure without significantly increasing the price of the seed. In an attempt to discourage appeals on the question of reasonableness, Lord Bridge indicated that the decision of the trial judge should be treated with the utmost respect and should not be interfered with on appeal unless it was plainly and obviously wrong.

The following case provides a more recent example of the reasonableness test.

St Albans City and District Council v International Computers Ltd (1996)

The defendant company supplied the claimant local authority with a computer software system for administering the collection of the Community Charge. The software was defective with the result that the local authority collected far less than it expected. The supply contract contained a clause limiting the liability for the defendant company to £100,000. The trial judge held that the limitation clause was not reasonable. The parties did not enjoy equal bargaining power; the defendant was a multinational company with large resources. The company was insured for £50 million and was, therefore, clearly better able to bear the loss than the local authority's Community Charge payers. The defendant appealed. Although the discussions in the Court of Appeal focused on the amount of damages recoverable, the Court also considered whether the contract had been made on the company's written standard terms of business (see below). Although some negotiations had taken place between the parties, the company's conditions were accepted with a few changes. The contract, therefore, had been made on the company's written standard terms of business.

Exemption of liability for negligence (s 2)

Under s 2(1) no one acting in the course of a business can exclude or restrict his liability in negligence for death or personal injury by means of a term in a contract or by way of a notice. Liability for negligence for any other kind of loss or damage can be excluded if the term or notice satisfies the 'reasonableness test' (s 2(2)).

Phillips Products Ltd v *Hyland* (1987)

The claimant company hired an excavator and driver from the defendant plant hire company. A term in the standard form hire contract provided that the hirer was responsible for all claims arising in connection with the operation of the plant by the driver. The driver negligently drove the excavator into the claimant's building, causing damage. The trial judge held that the term was covered by s 2(2) of the Unfair Contract Terms Act 1977 and was, therefore, subject to the reasonableness test. The exclusion of liability was unreasonable because the hire was for a short period, arranged at short notice and on the defendant's standard terms. The claimant had little experience of such hiring agreements and virtually no opportunity to arrange insurance cover. Moreover, the claimant did not have the power to select the driver or to control the way in which he did his job. As the defendant was unable to satisfy the judge that the term was fair and reasonable, the exclusion of liability was invalid. The defendant was held liable for the damage caused to the claimant's building. The Court of Appeal dismissed the defendant's appeal.

Section 2(2) will not apply where the negligence consists of a breach of an obligation arising from a contract and the person seeking to enforce the obligation is a third party (s 7(2) of the Contracts (Rights of Third Parties) Act 1999). The effect of this provision is best explained by the following example.

Alan enters into a contract with Brian, a builder, to build a detached double garage for his mother, Cynthia. The contract contains an exemption clause which seeks to exclude Brian's liability for negligent construction work. Brian carries out the work defectively and, as a result, the roof of the garage collapses. If Alan and Cynthia were in the garage at the time and were injured, the exemption clause would be void under s 2(1) of the Unfair Contract Terms Act 1977, and both Alan and Cynthia would be able to bring a claim against Brian: in Alan's case as party to the contract, and in Cynthia's case under the provisions of s 1 of the Contracts (Rights of Third Parties) Act 1999. If, however, the roof collapse only caused damage to Alan and Cynthia's cars, the position would be different. Alan would be able to sue Brian as a party to the contract unless Brian were able to show that the exemption clause was reasonable under s 2(2) of the Unfair Contract Terms Act 1977. If Cynthia sues Brian as a third party to the contract, the effect of s 7(2) of the Contracts (Rights of Third Parties) Act 1999 is that Brian will be able to rely on the exemption clause no matter how unreasonable.

Exemption of liability for breach of contract (s 3)

Section 3 applies to two types of contract made in the course of a business:

(a) where the other party deals as a consumer; and

(b) where the businessman contracts on his own written standard terms of business.

In both cases, the businessman cannot exclude or limit his liability for breach of contract, non-performance of the contract or different performance of the contract unless the exemption clause satisfies the requirement of reasonableness.

Unreasonable indemnity clauses (s 4)

An indemnity clause is a term in a contract between two parties (A and B) in which B agrees to indemnify A for any liability that A may be under. A may incur liability in respect of a third party (C), in which case B must compensate A for any claim which is made by C against A. A builder, for example, may get the owner of a house to agree to indemnify him for any injury or damage that his work on the house might cause to third parties. So if the builder negligently demolishes a wall and injures a next-door neighbour, the builder can call on the house owner to make good any award of damages. In some cases, B is required to indemnify A in respect of a liability that A may be under to B himself. Such an indemnity clause has the same effect as an exclusion clause.

Under s 4, indemnity clauses in contracts where one of the parties deals as a consumer are unenforceable unless they satisfy the requirement of reasonableness.

Guarantees of consumer goods (s 5)

At one time, it was common practice for guarantees given with goods to contain a clause exempting the manufacturer from liability in negligence if the product proved defective. Under s 5 a manufacturer or distributor cannot exclude or restrict his liability in negligence for loss arising from defects in goods ordinarily supplied for private use or consumption by means of a term or notice contained in a guarantee. (Manufacturers' guarantees will be examined in Chapter 10.)

Exemption of implied terms in contracts of sale and hire-purchase (s 6)

The original Sale of Goods Act 1893 gave the parties complete freedom to exclude the implied terms contained in ss 12–15. Retailers often used the opportunity to deprive consumers of their rights by getting customers to sign an order form, which included an exemption clause hidden in the small print, or by displaying suitably worded notices at the point of sale. The Molony Committee on Consumer Protection, which reported in 1962, identified the ease with which the implied terms could be excluded as a major defect in the Act, and in 1969 the Law Commission made firm proposals for reform. The changes were effected by the Supply of Goods (Implied Terms) Act 1973 and incorporated into the revised Sale of Goods Act 1979. The implied obligations as to the title contained in s 12 of the Sale of Goods Act 1979 (sale of goods) and s 8 of the Supply of Goods (Implied Terms) Act 1973 (hire-purchase) cannot be excluded or restricted by any contract term. The implied terms as to description, quality, etc. contained in ss 13–15 of the Sale of Goods Act 1979 (sale of goods) and ss 9–11 of the Supply of Goods (Implied Terms) Act 1973 (hire-purchase) cannot be excluded or restricted by any contract term against a person dealing as a consumer. Where the person is not dealing as a consumer, the exemption clause is subject to the 'reasonableness test'.

Exemption of implied terms in other contracts for the supply of goods (s 7)

Terms as to title, description. satisfactory quality, fitness for purpose and sample are now included in contracts for the supply of goods by way of hire, exchange or work and materials contracts by virtue of the Supply of Goods and Services Act 1982. The implied obligation as to title contained in s 2 of the 1982 Act (contracts of exchange or work and materials) cannot be excluded or restricted. Exclusion clauses relating to title in contracts of hire, contained in s 7, are subject to the reasonableness test. The other implied terms cannot be excluded or restricted at all in consumer contracts but in other transactions the exemption is subject to the reasonableness test. The complicated provisions of the Unfair Contract Terms Act 1977 in relation to the exclusion of statutory implied terms are summarised in Fig 9.4.

		Exemption clauses in contracts for the supply of goods by way of:			
		Sale, HP, exchange and work + materials		Hire	
		Consumer transaction	*Non-consumer transaction*	*Consumer transaction*	*Non-consumer transaction*
Implied Terms	Title	Void	Void	Subject to reasonableness test	Subject to reasonableness test
	Description	Void	Subject to reasonableness test	Void	Subject to reasonableness test
	Quality and suitability	Void	Subject to reasonableness test	Void	Subject to reasonableness test
	Sample	Void	Subject to reasonableness test	Void	Subject to reasonableness test

Fig 9.4 Exemption of statutory implied terms in contracts for the supply of goods

Exemption of liability for misrepresentation (s 8)

Section 3 of the Misrepresentation Act 1967, as amended by s 8 of the Unfair Contract Terms Act 1977, provides that any clause which excludes or restricts liability for misrepresentation is ineffective unless it satisfies the requirement of reasonableness.

Cases decided under the Unfair Contract Terms Act 1977

Lally and Weller v *George Bird* (1980)
The defendant agreed to undertake a house removal for the claimants for £100.80. The contract contained exemption clauses which limited the defendant's liability for losses or breakages to £10 per article and excluded all liability unless claims were made within three days. It was held that these clauses were unreasonable.

Waldron-Kelly v *British Railways Board* (1981)
The claimant placed a suitcase in the care of BR at Stockport railway station for delivery to Haverford West

railway station. BR's General Conditions of Carriage limited its liability for non-delivery to an amount assessed by reference to the weight of the goods. The suitcase disappeared and the claimant claimed £320.32 as the full value of the suitcase. BR sought to rely on its Conditions which limited BR's liability to £27. It was held that BR could not rely on the exemption clause because it did not satisfy the requirement of reasonableness. The claimant was awarded £320.32.

Woodman v *Photo Trade Processing Ltd* (1981)
Mr Woodman deposited a reel of film containing pictures of a friend's wedding with the defendants for processing. Unfortunately most of the pictures were lost and when sued the defendants relied on the following exclusion clause: 'All photographic materials are accepted on the basis that their value does not exceed the cost of the material itself. Responsibility is limited to the replacement of the films. No liability will be accepted consequential or otherwise, however caused.' The county court judge held that the clause was unreasonable for the following reasons: (a) the clause was in standard use throughout the trade and so Mr Woodman had no real alternative but to have his film processed on these terms; and (b) the code of practice for the photographic industry envisaged the

possibility of processors offering a two-tier service, either a lower price but with full exclusion of liability or a higher price with the processor accepting fuller liability. Mr Woodman was not offered such a choice. He was awarded £75 in compensation.

Comment. The *Woodman* case indicates that failure to provide customers with an alternative is likely to lead to any exemption clause being declared unreasonable. However, it is not enough merely to inform customers that an alternative exists: sufficient detail must be provided for customers to be able to exercise a genuine choice. In *Warren* v *Truprint Ltd* (1986), another county court case involving lost film, the defendant film processors had made the following addition to their limitation clause: '. . . we will undertake further liability at a supplementary charge. Written details on request'. The judge held that this did not pass the reasonableness test since the defendants had failed to 'plainly and clearly set out the alternative' and the cost to the customer.

UNFAIR TERMS IN CONSUMER CONTRACTS REGULATIONS 1999

The statutory restrictions on the use of exemption clauses contained in the Unfair Contract Terms Act 1977 have been supplemented by the Unfair Terms in Consumer Contracts Regulations 1999. The regulations implement a 1993 EC Directive on Unfair Terms in Consumer Contracts. The 1999 regulations replace, with amendment, the 1994 regulations of the same name which came into force on 1 July 1995.

Although there is a certain amount of overlap between the 1977 Act and the regulations as well as points of similarity (i.e. the test of reasonableness in the Act and the tests of fairness in the regulations), there are some important differences, as illustrated in Fig 9.5.

The above regulations apply, with certain exceptions, to unfair terms in contracts between a business seller or supplier and a consumer (reg 4(1)). A consumer is defined as a natural person who is acting for purposes outside his trade, business or profession. A business includes a trade or profession, any government department and local and public authorities. The regulations do not cover terms in non-consumer contracts such as:

Unfair Contract Terms Act 1977	Unfair Terms in Consumer Contracts Regulations 1999
Mainly exemption clauses	All unfair terms
Business and consumer contracts	Only consumer contracts
Negotiated and non-negotiated contracts	Only non-negotiated contracts
Exemptions in contracts and notices	Only terms in consumer contracts
Exemptions are either automatically void or rendered void if unreasonable	Unfair terms are rendered voidable
Individual right of civil action	Individual right of civil action and administrative control by the Director-General of Fair Trading and other qualifying bodies, who may seek an injunction to prevent the continued general use of an unfair term

Fig 9.5 A comparison of the Unfair Contract Terms Act 1977 and the Unfair Terms in Consumer Contracts Regulations 1999

(a) employment contracts;
(b) agreements dealing with succession rights;
(c) family law rights;
(d) the incorporation or organisation of companies or partnerships.

Also excluded are terms which have been incorporated to comply with or reflect statutory or regulatory provisions of the UK or the provisions or principles of international conventions to which either the UK or the EC is party.

Terms in consumer contracts, which have not been individually negotiated, will be regarded as unfair if, contrary to the requirement of good faith, they cause a significant imbalance in the parties' rights and obligations under the contract, to the detriment of the consumer (reg 5(1)). A term will always be regarded as not having been individually negotiated where it has been drafted in advance and the consumer has not been able to influence the substance of the term. The burden of proof is placed on the trader to show that the term has been individually negotiated.

Schedule 2 of the regulations sets out an indicative, non-exhaustive list of terms which may be regarded as unfair. It should not be assumed that terms covered by the list are automatically unfair; they may be unfair in some circumstances but fair in different circumstances. It is also the case that certain terms not covered by the list may be regarded as unfair. There are 17 examples set out in Sch 2, including the following terms:

- excluding or limiting the legal liability of a seller or supplier for the death of or personal injury to a consumer arising from an act or omission of the seller or supplier, e.g. *'products are used at customers' own risk'*;
- allowing the seller or supplier to keep sums paid by the consumer in case the consumer decides to cancel without providing for the consumer to receive compensation of an equivalent amount if the seller or supplier cancels, e.g. *'no refunds of deposits if orders are cancelled'*;
- enabling the seller or supplier to unilaterally change the terms of a contract without a valid reason which is set out in the contract, e.g. *'products supplied may vary in specification from those ordered'*;
- providing that the price of goods can be varied without giving the consumer the right to cancel if the price is too high, e.g. *'the price of goods may be increased where there is an increase in costs prior to delivery'*;
- restricting the consumer's right to take legal action, for example by requiring disputes to be resolved by arbitration, or by restricting the evidence available or by changing the usual burden of proof, e.g. *'all disputes concerning this agreement will be resolved by arbitration'*.

'Core terms' which define the main subject matter of the contract or concern the adequacy of the price of the goods or services are not subject to an assessment of fairness provided they are in plain and intelligible language. Any written term of a consumer contract must be 'expressed in plain intelligible language'. Where there is any doubt about the meaning of a term, the interpretation which is most favourable to the consumer must prevail.

Two different types of remedy are available under the regulations. First, unfair terms are deemed voidable as against the consumer, although the contract itself will still be binding if it can continue in existence without the unfair term. Second, the Director General of Fair Trading is under a duty to receive and consider complaints that a contract term drawn up for general use is unfair. Having considered such a complaint and any undertakings given about the continued use of such unfair terms, the Director General may apply for an injunction from the High Court to prevent the continued use of the particular unfair term and any similar terms by any party to the proceedings. The 1999 Regulations provide for the first time that certain qualifying bodies (e.g. statutory regulators, such as the Rail Regulator and the Director General of Gas Supply, trading standards departments and the Consumers' Association) can also apply for an injunction to prevent the continued use of an unfair term.

The following case provides an interesting example of the application of the regulations.

Director General of Fair Trading v First National Bank plc (2000)

The Director General of Fair Trading applied to the High Court for an injunction to restrain the defendant bank from using a term in its standard form loan agreement. The term in question provided for the accrual of interest on any judgments obtained by the bank under the loan agreement. The Director General was concerned that customers who agreed to judgment on terms involving payment of the balance by instalments would find themselves faced with further payments of interest once the balance had been cleared. The Director General argued that the term was unfair in that 'contrary to the requirement of good faith, [it caused] a significant imbalance in the parties' rights and obligations ... to the detriment of the consumer'. The bank argued that the provision concerning interest on judgments was a 'core term' as it related to the adequacy of the price or remuneration, and so was not subject to the requirement of fairness. The Court of Appeal held that the term in question could not be classed as a 'core term' as it did not define the main subject matter of the contract, nor did it relate to the adequacy of the remuneration as it only applied where a consumer was in default. The court took the view that the term was unfair. It did not satisfy the requirement of good faith and caused a significant imbalance in the rights and obligations of the parties. At the time of writing, First National Bank obtained leave to appeal to the House of Lords.

REFORM

The UK government has indicated its intention to consolidate the provisions of the Unfair Contract Terms Act 1977 and the Unfair Terms in Consumer Contracts Regulations 1999 to create a unified code of regulation. Meanwhile, the European Commission is undertaking a review of the EC Directive on Unfair Terms in Consumer Contracts.

The main areas under review are:

- the scope of the Directive, in particular the possible removal of the exclusions in relation to individually negotiated terms and terms which reflect mandatory statutory or regulatory provisions and the partial exclusion of 'core terms';
- the list of terms which may be regarded as unfair set out in Sch 2 of the 1999 regulations, in particular whether the list should be expanded and the examples specified in more detail;
- the principle of transparency, i.e. the requirement that terms should be drafted in plain and intelligible language, and whether consumers should have an express right to become effectively acquainted with the terms of a contract before it is concluded, with increased protection for consumers in the event of infringement;
- the effectiveness of the current sanctions, including possible reinforcement of the existing civil remedy of non-enforceability of the term by providing, for example, that consumers should be entitled to compensation for any direct loss suffered arising from the use of the unfair term;
- strengthening the procedures for eliminating unfair terms, including the possible introduction of an administrative system for prohibiting unfair terms, e.g. by empowering the Director General of Fair Trading to ban unfair terms, with appeals to the courts against his decision; introducing a special procedure whereby an injunction against one organisation in respect of an unfair term can be extended to all other organisations involved in the same kind of business.

It is unlikely that there would be any change in UK legislation, arising from the EC review, until 2004/5.

FAIR TRADING ACT 1973

Parliament chose to focus the fight against exemption clauses by changing the civil law. The most offensive exemptions from liability, though void, were not illegal. Retailers continued to display notices such as 'No Refunds', and to include exclusion clauses in sales agreements. In many cases, the consumer was 'conned' into believing that he had been deprived of his rights. The Fair Trading Act 1973, however, opened the way for such unfair consumer trade practices to be made illegal. The Consumer Transactions (Restrictions on Statements) Order 1976 (as amended) makes it a criminal offence for a trader to continue to use exclusion clauses rendered void by ss 6 and 7 of the Unfair Contract Terms Act 1977. This outlaws the use of 'No money refunded' notices.

QUESTIONS/ACTIVITIES

1 (a) Explain what is meant by the following saying: 'The terms of a contract must be certain or capable of being made certain.'

(b) Consider the legal position in each of the situations given below:

(i) Sally, an actress, accepts an offer to play Ophelia in a new London production of *Hamlet* 'at a West End salary to be mutually agreed'. Sally and the producers cannot agree on an appropriate salary.

(ii) Gary agrees to buy a motorcycle from Speedy Garages Ltd 'on usual HP terms'.

Gary has now learnt that he will be required to pay a 50 per cent deposit. He has not saved up enough money.

(iii) After lengthy negotiations for the sale of a flat, Anne, the purchaser, writes to the vendors, 'I accept your offer to sell 12A Sea Terrace, Sandy Bar, for £38,000, subject to the usual conditions of acceptance appropriate to this kind of sale.' Anne has been offered a job 100 miles away and now wishes to withdraw from the purchase.

(iv) Mercurial Property Co Ltd grant a five-year lease on shop premises to Frosted Foods Ltd at a rent of £3,000 a year. It is agreed that Frosted Foods Ltd will be able to extend the lease by a further three years 'at such rent as may be agreed between the parties', and that any dispute should be referred to arbitration. The parties have failed to agree the rent for the extension of the lease.

2 Paul is looking for a second-hand car when he sees an advertisement in his local evening paper which reads:

SLICK CAR SALES LTD

Hundreds of used car bargains. Lowest prices you've ever seen.

Definitely the lowest prices in Britain
All cars purchased this month will include Road Fund Tax, Radio, Stereo and a full tank of petrol

---

Paul visits the showrooms of Slick Cars and selects a car priced £3,995 which the salesman tells him is a 1994 Mondeo which has done 30,000 miles and has had only one owner. Paul signs a sales agreement which describes the car as '1994 Ford Mondeo. Cayman Blue. Registration Number L931 AJU'.

(a) From the facts given above, identify an example of each of the following: trader's puff, a representation, a condition and a warranty.

(b) What remedies will be available to Paul if any of the statements you identified in your answer to (a) turns out to be false.

(c) Identify three terms which will be implied into the contract.

3 While on holiday at the seaside, Jim agrees to take his family to 'Fun Park'. He pays £1 to park his car on a car park run by the Strand Council. A notice at the entrance of the car park, which has been partly obscured by overgrown shrubs, states: 'Cars parked entirely at owner's risk'. Jim pays £7 for a family admission ticket to 'Fun Park', which is managed by Leisure Ltd. The back of the ticket contains the following clause: 'The company does not accept liability for death or personal injury to visitors, howsoever caused.' Jim and his wife are watching their children on the 'waltzer' when a metal bar flies off, injuring Jim and his wife. After receiving hospital treatment, Jim returns to his car to discover that it has been damaged by a Strand Council refuse van. Advise Jim and his wife.

4 Angela buys an 'Onion' personal computer from Future Computers Ltd. She signs a sales note in the shop which states: 'Any express or implied condition, statement or warranty, statutory or otherwise is hereby excluded'. After a week's satisfactory use, the 'Onion' refuses to work. What is the legal position if:

(a) Angela bought the 'Onion' for her own personal use?

(b) Angela bought the 'Onion' to help in her work as an accountant?

Chapter 10

CONTRACTS FOR THE SUPPLY OF GOODS AND SERVICES

In this chapter we explore the legal rules which regulate contracts for the supply of goods and services. The rights and responsibilities of the parties are determined primarily by agreement. However, Parliament has intervened increasingly in this area of law to provide a statutory framework for such transactions. For example, contracts for the sale of goods are covered by the Sale of Goods Act 1979, as amended by the Sale and Supply of Goods Act 1994 and the Sale of Goods (Amendment) Acts 1994 and 1995, while contracts for the supply of goods and services are governed by the Supply of Goods and Services Act 1982, as amended by the Sale and Supply of Goods Act 1994. Both pieces of legislation will be examined in detail. The chapter concludes by considering the effectiveness of the law of contract as a means of providing redress in respect of defective goods and services, and the responsibility in contract of a manufacturer for his products.

SALE OF GOODS

The law relating to contracts for the sale of goods is contained in the Sale of Goods Act 1979. This Act replaced the original Sale of Goods Act 1893 and included all the amendments that had been made in the intervening years. The 1979 Act has been amended by three Acts: the Sale and Supply of Goods Act 1994, and the Sale of Goods (Amendment) Acts 1994 and 1995. The Sale of Goods Act 1979 provides a framework for the relationship between the buyer and seller and covers such matters as the rights and duties of the parties and their remedies in the event of a breach.

It would be wrong to think that the Act governs every aspect of a sale of goods contract. Many of the general principles of contract law which we studied in Chapter 7 still apply. A valid contract for the sale of goods, just like any other contract, must possess all the essential elements. The rules relating to the requirements of offer and acceptance, intention, consideration, etc. are largely untouched by the Act. The other important thing to remember is that the Act, in general, does not stop the parties from making their own tailor-made agreement. In many situations, the rules contained in the Act only apply where the parties have failed to make express arrangements as to their obligations. We will now look at some of the more important provisions of the Sale of Goods Act 1979. Section references are to the 1979 Act, unless otherwise indicated.

DEFINITION

A contract of sale of goods is defined by s 2(1) as: 'a contract by which the seller transfers or agrees to transfer the property in goods to the buyer for a money consideration called the price'.

You should refer back to Chapter 8 for a detailed explanation of the key elements of this definition. The provisions of the Act only apply to those transactions which fall within the definition.

FORMATION

It is not necessary to observe complex formalities to create a contract for the sale of goods; it may be in writing or by word of mouth, or partly in writing and partly by word of mouth, or even implied from the conduct of the parties. Capacity to enter into a binding sale of goods contract is governed by the general law of contract, which we have already considered in Chapter 7.

THE IMPLIED TERMS

The parties are generally free to agree between themselves the details of their contract. However, the Act also automatically includes a number of conditions and warranties in every contract for the sale of goods. These are known as the implied terms and they can be found in ss 12–15.

Title (s 12)

There is an implied condition on the part of the seller that in the case of a sale he has a right to sell the goods, and in the case of an agreement to sell he will have the right to sell when the property is to pass (s 12(1)). If the seller cannot pass good title (rights of ownership) to the buyer, he will be liable for breach of a condition.

Rowland v Divall (1923)

Rowland bought a car from Divall for £334 and used it for four months. It later transpired that Divall had bought the car from someone who had stolen it, and it had to be returned to the true owner. Rowland sued Divall to recover the full purchase price that he had paid. The Court of Appeal held that Divall was in breach of s 12. Rowland had paid £334 to become the owner of the car. Since he had not received what he had contracted for, there was a total failure of consideration entitling him to a full refund.

Section 12(2) implies two warranties into sale of goods contracts:

1 that the goods are free from any charges or encumbrances (third-party rights) not made known to the buyer before the contract; and
2 that the buyer will enjoy quiet possession of the goods.

Microbeads v Vinhurst Road Markings Ltd (1975)

The buyers purchased road marking machines from the sellers. Shortly after the sale, another company obtained a patent in respect of the machines and this company was seeking to enforce the patent against the buyers. The sellers brought an action against the buyers for the purchase price, and the buyers wished to include in their defence a breach of s 12(2). The Court of Appeal held that the buyers' quiet possession of the machines had been disturbed and, therefore, it would be appropriate to raise a breach of s 12(2) as a defence to an action for the price when the case came to full trial.

Section 12(3)–(5) provides for a situation where the seller is unsure about his title to goods. He can sell them on the basis that he is transferring only such rights of ownership as he may have. If he does, this there is no implied condition that he has the right to sell the goods, but the sale is subject to implied warranties relating to freedom from third-party rights and quiet possession.

Description (s 13)

Where there is a contract for the sale of goods by description, there is an implied condition that the goods will correspond with the description (s 13(1)). If the buyer does not see the goods before he buys them (e.g. from a mail order catalogue), there has clearly been a sale by description. Even where the buyer has seen the goods and, perhaps, selected them himself, it may still be a sale by description, if he has relied to some extent on a description.

Beale v Taylor (1967)

The defendant advertised a car for sale as a 1961 Triumph Herald. The claimant inspected the car before he bought it. He later discovered that the vehicle consisted of a rear half of a 1961 Herald, which had been welded to the front half of an earlier model. The Court of Appeal held that the claimant was entitled to damages for breach of s 13, even though he had seen and inspected the car. He had relied to some extent on the description contained in the advertisement.

If the buyer has forgotten about the description by the time he buys the goods or does not believe what he has been told and checks the details for himself, he may lose the protection of s 13 because he has not relied on the description.

Harlingdon & Leinster Enterprises Ltd v Christopher Hull Fine Art Ltd (1990)

The defendant sold a painting to the claimant which turned out to be a fake. The defendant believed that the painting was by Munter, an artist of the German Expressionist School, because he had seen it attributed to Munter in an auction catalogue. He described the painting as a Munter during negotiations with the claimant, although he made it clear that he knew nothing about Munter's work and lacked expertise in German Expressionist painting. The claimant, who was also lacking in relevant expertise, inspected the painting and decided that it was authentic. He agreed to buy it. The painting was described in the defendant's invoice as a Munter. When the claimant discovered that the painting was a fake, he sued under s 13(1) to recover the purchase price. The Court of Appeal held that the defendant had made it clear that his attribution could not be relied upon and that the claimant should have exercised his own judgment. A contract will not be a sale by description merely because the seller has issued some statement about the goods. The buyer must show that the description influenced the decision to buy. Since the claimant was unable to show this, his action failed.

Comment. The claimant also argued that the painting was not of merchantable quality under s 14 of the Sale of Goods Act 1979 (see later). The court held that the misattribution did not detract from the quality of the painting so as to make it unmerchantable. In the words of Nourse LJ: 'It could still have been hung on a wall somewhere and been enjoyed for what it was ...'

The description of the goods may cover such matters as size, quantity, weight, ingredients, origin or even how they are to be packed. The slightest departure from the specifications will entitle the buyer to reject the goods for breach of a condition of the contract.

Re Moore & Co and Landauer & Co (1921)

The claimants agreed to supply 3,000 tins of Australian canned fruit, packed in cases containing 30 tins each. When the goods were delivered, it was discovered that about half of the consignment was packed in cases containing 24 tins. Although the correct quantity had been delivered, the defendants decided to reject the whole consignment. It was held that this was a sale by description under s 13 and since the goods did not correspond with that description, the defendants were entitled to repudiate the contract.

Comment. This decision seems to be at odds with a well-established principle that the law does not concern itself with trifling matters. Lord Wilberforce in *Reardon Smith Line v Yngvar Hanson-Tangen* (1976) cast doubt on the correctness of the *Moore and Landauer* decision and suggested that it should be re-examined by the House of Lords.

A seller may ensure that the transaction is not a sale by description by including such phrases as 'Bought as seen' or 'Sold as seen' in the contract (*Cavendish-Woodhouse Ltd v Manley* (1984)).

Quality and suitability (s 14)

Section 14 of the original 1893 Sale of Goods Act incorporated two implied terms into every sale of goods contract by a trader: that the goods were of merchantable quality, and that they were fit for a particular purpose. The implied term relating to quality attracted sustained criticism over the years. The failure to define what was meant by 'merchantable quality' in the original 1893 Act was remedied in 1973 with the introduction of a statutory definition. Goods were of merchantable quality, according to the new definition, if they were 'as fit for the purpose(s) for which goods of that kind are commonly bought as it is reasonable to expect having regard to any description applied to them, the price (if relevant) and all other relevant circumstances'. However, the inclusion of a statutory definition of 'merchantable quality' did not completely remove the uncertainty about the scope of the implied term. A report by the Law Commission highlighted a number of criticisms of the implied term of merchantable quality. The Sale and Supply of Goods Act 1994, which came into force on 3 January 1995, implemented the recommendations of the Law Commission contained in its Report on the Sale and Supply of Goods (1987). The new definition of quality applies to all contracts for the sale and supply of goods, including all agreements for the transfer of property in goods such as barter, work and materials, hire-purchase, hire and the exchange of goods for trading stamps.

Caveat emptor

Section 14 starts by stating that there is no implied condition or warranty as to quality or fitness for a particular purpose, except as provided by ss 14 and 15. This preserves the principle of *caveat emptor*: let the buyer beware. Both of the conditions implied by s 14 apply 'where the seller sells goods in the course of a business'. In a recent case the Court of Appeal confirmed that the implied terms in s 14 apply to every sale by a business, even though the goods sold may not be part of the 'stock in trade'.

Stevenson v Rogers (1999)

A fisherman sold his only fishing boat in order to replace it. The purchaser claimed that the boat was not of merchantable (satisfactory) quality. At first instance the High Court decided that the contract of sale did not contain an implied term as to merchantable quality because the sale was not 'in the course of business'. The High Court arrived at this conclusion by reference to the interpretation of 'in the course of a business' in the context of the Unfair Contract Terms Act 1977 in *R & B Customs Brokers Co Ltd* v *United Dominion Trust Ltd* (1988) (see Chapter 9) and cases decided under the Trade Descriptions Act 1968 (see *Havering LBC* v *Stevenson* (1970) and *Davies* v *Sumner* (1984) in Chapter 12). In these earlier cases, some degree of 'regularity' had been required for the transaction to be 'in the course of a business'. Only those sales which were integral to the business (i.e. stock in trade) would come within the scope of business sales. The Court of Appeal held that the sale of the fishing boat was in the course of a business for the purposes of s 14 and that the implied term as to merchantable quality did apply. The court was greatly influenced by the fact that the wording of s 14 of the Sale of Goods Act had been deliberately changed in 1973 so as to broaden the scope of its protection by covering all sales by traders, even those which may be incidental to the main business. The earlier authorities in relation to the Unfair Contract Terms Act 1977 (*R & B Customs Brokers*) and the Trade Descriptions Act 1968 (*Havering LBC* and *Davies*) were distinguished.

Section 14 implies two conditions into every sale by a trader: that the goods are of satisfactory quality and that they are fit for a particular purpose. The requirement of s 14, that the sale must be 'in the course of a business', means that the implied terms of quality and fitness cannot apply to sales by private individuals. So, if you buy something privately and it is defective or unsuitable, you cannot complain under s 14.

Satisfactory quality

Section 14(2), as amended by the Sale and Supply of Goods Act 1994, provides that where a seller sells goods in the course of a business there is an implied condition that the goods supplied are of satisfactory quality, except to the extent of defects which are brought specifically to the buyer's attention before the contract is made or ought to have been noticed by the buyer if he has examined the goods. Goods are of satisfactory quality according to s 14(2A) 'if they meet the standard that a reasonable person would regard as satisfactory, taking into account any description of the goods, the price (if relevant) and all other relevant circumstances'. Section 14(2B) explains that the quality of goods includes their state and condition and the following non-exhaustive aspects of quality:

(a) fitness for all purposes for which goods of the kind in question are commonly supplied;
(b) appearance and finish;
(c) freedom from minor defects;
(d) safety; and
(e) durability.

It is likely to be some time before any cases are reported on the new definition of quality. The following explanation of the new implied term as to quality, of necessity, is illustrated by cases decided according to the old definition of 'merchantable quality'. The requirement that goods must be of satisfactory quality means that a brand new washing machine should wash your clothes properly; new shoes should not fall apart on their first outing; and a meat pie bought for your lunch should not make you ill. Section 14(2) does not impose absolute standards of quality with which all goods must comply. However, the goods must be satisfactory to a reasonable person. A reasonable person is unlikely, for example, to find the quality of new goods satisfactory if they have minor or cosmetic defects.

Rogers v *Parish (Scarborough) Ltd* (1987)

The claimants bought a new Range Rover for £16,000. After a few weeks of unsatisfactory use, the vehicle was returned to the dealers and the claimants accepted another Range Rover as a substitute. Unfortunately, the second vehicle proved no better than the first. Six months after delivery, the engine was misfiring at all road speeds and excessive noise was coming from the gearbox. There were also substantial defects in the bodywork. The claimants notified the dealers that they were rejecting the vehicle. The Court of Appeal held that the suppliers were in breach of the implied term as to quality. The Court held that the definition of merchantability involved considering not only if the car was capable of getting from A to B safely, but also the buyer's reasonable expectations of being able to do so with the appropriate degree of comfort, ease of handling and reliability, and with appropriate pride in the vehicle's appearance. The Court found that the buyers' reasonable expectations of a £16,000 new Range Rover had not been met in this case. The claimants had not received value for money.

Comment. In an earlier case, *Millars of Falkirk Ltd* v *Turpie* (1976), the Inner House of the Scottish Court of Session held that a car with a slight oil leak in the power-assisted steering (which could be repaired for about £25) was of merchantable quality. Factors relevant to the decision were: (i) the minor nature of the defect, (ii) the ease with which the defect could be cured, (iii) the willingness of the dealers to effect a repair, (iv) the obvious nature of the defect, (v) the absence of serious risk, and (vi) many new cars have minor defects on delivery. This case raised doubts whether a car which could be driven safely but with minor repairable defects could be said to be unmerchantable. The *Rogers* case resolved some of those doubts by deciding that merchantable quality should not be tested by usability alone. The Law Commission cited the decision in the *Rogers* case with approval. The Commissioners also took the view that the car in the *Millars* case would fail the new test of quality proposed in their report.

Shine v *General Guarantee Corp Ltd* (1988)

Mr Shine purchased an enthusiast's car. When he inquired subsequently whether there was a manufacturer's rust warranty, he discovered that the car had been written off after having been submerged in water for 24 hours. Mr Shine terminated the agreement. The Court of Appeal held that the car was unmerchantable. Mr Shine thought he was buying a second-hand enthusiast's car in good condition for a fair price when in fact he was buying, in the words of Bush J, 'one which no member of the public would touch with a barge pole unless they could get it at a substantially reduced price to reflect the risk they were taking'.

If you buy goods second-hand or very cheaply, you cannot reasonably expect the highest standards of quality.

Bartlett v *Sidney Marcus Ltd* (1965)

The claimant bought a second-hand car from the defendants who were car dealers. The claimant was warned that the clutch was defective and he agreed to a reduction in the price of the car to take account of this. The defect turned out to be more serious and, therefore, more costly to repair than he expected. He claimed that the defendants were in breach of the implied term as to quality. The Court of Appeal held that in the circumstances the car was of merchantable quality. As Lord Denning MR pointed out, 'A buyer should realise that when he buys a second-hand car defects may appear sooner or later.'

There had been some doubt under the old standard of merchantable quality whether goods commonly used for a number of purposes had to be fit for all such purposes. In *M/S Aswan Engineering Establishment Co* v *Lupdine Ltd* (1987) the Court of Appeal held that the definition of merchantable quality required goods to be suitable for one or more (but not all) purposes for which they were commonly bought. The Law Commission recommended that goods of a particular description and price should be fit for all common purposes. This recommendation is given effect by s 14(2B), which requires goods to be fit for 'all the purposes for which goods of the kind in question are commonly supplied'. A buyer is not obliged to examine goods before he buys them and, if he chooses not to do so, he will still be entitled to full protection under s 14(2). The buyer can lose his right to complain in two situations: first, where the seller specifically points out that the goods are faulty; second, where he decides to check the goods, but fails to spot an obvious defect (s 14(2C)).

Fitness for a particular purpose

Section 14(3) provides that where the seller sells goods in the course of a business and the buyer, expressly or by implication, makes known to the seller any particular purpose for which the goods are being bought, there is an implied condition that the goods supplied are reasonably fit for that purpose, except where it can be shown that the buyer has not relied – or that it would be unreasonable for him to rely – on the seller's skill and judgment. If the buyer specifies the particular purpose for which he requires the goods (e.g. shoes suitable for running in a marathon), the goods must be suitable for the stated purpose. Where the buyer purchases goods with only one normal purpose, he makes his purpose known by implication. Food must be fit for eating and clothes fit for wearing.

Grant v *Australian Knitting Mills Ltd* (1936)

Dr Grant bought a pair of woollen underpants from a shop. The manufacturers neglected to remove properly a chemical which was used in the manufacturing process. Dr Grant developed a skin rash which turned into dermatitis. It was held that the underpants were not of merchantable quality or reasonably fit for the purpose. Although Dr Grant had not specifically stated the purpose for which he required the underpants, it was clear by implication that he intended to wear them.

If the buyer has any special requirements, these must be made known to the seller.

Griffiths v Peter Conway Ltd (1939)

The claimant purchased a Harris tweed coat from the defendants. After wearing the coat for a short period of time, she contracted dermatitis. She failed in her claim for damages under s 14(3). It was shown that the coat would not have affected someone with a normal skin. The claimant had not made known to the defendants the fact that she had an abnormally sensitive skin.

In order to be successful under s 14(3), the buyer must show that he relied on the seller's skill and judgment. Reliance will normally be assumed from the fact that the buyer has taken his custom to that particular shop. However, if a buyer asks for an item under its brand name or lays down detailed specifications as to what he wants, he will find it difficult to show that he has relied on the seller's skill and judgment.

Sample (s 15)

Section 15 provides that in a contract of sale by sample there is an implied condition:

(a) that the bulk will correspond with the sample in quality;

(b) that the buyer will have a reasonable opportunity of comparing the bulk with the sample;

(c) that the goods will be free from any defect making their quality unsatisfactory which would not be apparent on reasonable examination of the sample.

This section, like s 13, applies to both business and private sales. The application of s 15 can be illustrated by the following case.

Godley v Perry (1960)

The claimant, a six-year-old boy, bought a plastic toy catapult for 6d from a newsagent's shop run by Perry, the first defendant. The catapult broke while in use and the claimant lost an eye. He sued Perry for breach of the implied conditions in s 14(2) and (3). Perry had bought the catapults by sample from a wholesaler. He had tested the sample catapult by pulling back the elastic, but no defect had been revealed. Perry now brought the wholesaler into the action claiming a breach of the conditions in s 15. The wholesaler had bought his supply of catapults by sample from another wholesaler, who had obtained the catapults from Hong Kong. The first wholesaler brought the second wholesaler into the action alleging a similar breach of s 15.

It was held that (1) the claimant could recover damages from the first defendant for breach of s 14: the catapult was not of merchantable quality or fit for the purpose for which it had been bought; and (2) the first defendant could recover damages from the first wholesaler, who in turn could recover damages from the second wholesaler, in both cases because there had been a breach of s 15, which was implied in the relevant contract.

TRANSFER OF PROPERTY IN THE GOODS

The essence of a contract for the sale of goods is the transfer of property (ownership) in goods from the seller to the buyer. It is important to ascertain exactly when the property in goods passes from the seller to the buyer for the following reasons:

1 If the goods are accidentally destroyed, it is necessary to know who bears the loss. Section 20 provides that risk normally passes with ownership.

2 If either the seller or the buyer becomes bankrupt or, in the case of a company, goes into liquidation, it is necessary to discover who owns the goods.

3 The remedy of an unpaid seller against a buyer will depend on whether ownership has been transferred. If property has passed to the buyer, he can be sued for the price of the goods. If property has not passed to the buyer, the seller can only sue for non-acceptance. (Remedies under the Sale of Goods Act 1979 will be discussed later in this chapter.)

The rules relating to the transfer of ownership depend on whether the goods are classified as specific goods or unascertained goods. Specific goods are 'goods identified and agreed on at the time a contract of sale is made'. This includes contracts such as purchasing groceries from a supermarket or buying a sheepskin coat from a market trader. Unascertained goods are those goods which are not identified and agreed on when the contract is made. An order for 10 cwt of coal to be delivered in three days' time involves unascertained goods, because it is impossible to identify which specific lumps of coal lying in the coal merchant's yard will make up the order. As soon as the 10 cwt of coal is set aside to fulfil this order, the goods are said to be ascertained.

Specific goods

Section 17 provides that the property in specific goods passes when the parties intend it to pass, and to ascertain the intention of the parties, 'regard shall be had to the terms of the contract, the conduct of the parties and the circumstances of the case'. If the parties do not indicate, expressly or impliedly, when they want ownership to pass, s 18 sets out various rules to ascertain their presumed intention.

> Rule 1 – where there is an unconditional contract for the sale of specific goods in a deliverable state, the property in the goods passes to the buyer when the contract is made, and it is immaterial whether the time of payment or the time of delivery, or both, be postponed.'

This means that a buyer can become the owner of goods even though he has not paid for them yet and they are still in the seller's possession.

Tarling v *Baxter* (1827)
A haystack was sold, but before the buyer had taken it away it was burned down. It was held that the buyer was still liable to pay the price because he became the owner of the haystack when the contract was made. It was immaterial that he had not yet taken delivery of the goods.

> Rule 2 – where there is a contract for the sale of specific goods and the seller is bound to do something to the goods for the purpose of putting them into a deliverable state, the property does not pass until the thing is done and the buyer has notice that it has been done.

Where the seller agrees to alter the goods in some way for the buyer, ownership will pass when the alterations are completed and the buyer has been informed.

> Rule 3 – where there is a contract for the sale of specific goods in a deliverable state but the seller is bound to weigh, measure, test or do some other act or thing with reference to the goods for the purpose of ascertaining the price, the property does not pass until the act or thing is done and the buyer has notice that it has been done.

If, for example, you agree to buy a particular bag of potatoes, at a price of 10p a pound, you will not become the owner of the potatoes until the seller has weighed the bag and informed you of the price payable. If, however, it is agreed that the buyer will do the weighing, measuring or testing, ownership of the goods will pass in accordance with Rule 1, i.e. when the contract is made.

> Rule 4 – when goods are delivered to the buyer on approval or on sale or return ... the property in the goods passes to the buyer:
>
> (a) when he signifies his approval or acceptance to the seller or does any other act adopting the transaction;
>
> (b) if he does not signify his approval or acceptance to the seller but retains the goods without giving notice of rejection, then, if a time has been fixed for the return of the goods, on the expiration of that time, and, if no time has been fixed, on the expiration of a reasonable time.

Property in goods delivered on approval will pass under part (a) of this rule either when the buyer informs the seller that he wishes to buy them or he 'adopts' the transaction, for example by re-selling the goods. Part (b) of the rule is illustrated by the following case.

Elphick v *Barnes* (1880)
The seller handed a horse over to a prospective buyer on approval for eight days. Unfortunately, the horse died on the third day. It was held that ownership of the horse had not passed to the buyer and, therefore, the seller would have to bear the loss.

Unascertained goods

In a sale of unascertained goods, the property passes to the buyer only when the goods have been ascertained (s 16). If the parties then fail to mention when they intend ownership to pass, s 18 Rule 5 will apply.

> Rule 5 – (1) where there is a contract for the sale of unascertained or future goods by description, and goods of that description and in a deliverable state are unconditionally appropriated to the contract, either by the seller with the assent of the buyer or by the buyer with the assent of the seller, the property in the goods then passes to the buyer; and the assent may be express or implied and may be given either before or after the appropriation is made.

Goods are unconditionally appropriated to the contract when they are separated from the bulk and earmarked for a particular buyer. Delivery to a carrier will amount to an 'appropriation' if the buyer's goods can be clearly identified.

Healy v *Howlett & Sons* (1917)

The claimant agreed to sell 20 boxes of mackerel to the defendant. He despatched 190 boxes of mackerel by rail for delivery to various customers, but the boxes were not labelled for particular customers. Employees of the railway company were entrusted with the task of allocating the correct number of boxes to each destination. The train was delayed and the fish deteriorated before 20 boxes could be set aside for the defendant. It was held that the property in the goods had not passed to the buyer because the defendant's boxes had not been appropriated to the contract.

The Sale of Goods (Amendment) Act 1995, which came into force on 19 September 1995, contains two provisions in respect to the transfer of property in unascertained goods. The first provision, which becomes s 18 Rule 5(3), gives statutory effect to the principle of 'ascertainment by exhaustion'. This is a situation where goods are successively drawn from a bulk until all that remains are the goods which fulfil the contract in question. For example, if restaurant A buys ten bottles of whisky from a bulk of 200 bottles stored in a distillery and the distiller sells 190 bottles to other customers, the remaining ten bottles belong to restaurant A. The property in the goods passes to the buyer when the bulk is so reduced as to match the buyer's contract. The buyer need not have made any payment but the goods must be in a deliverable state.

The second provision introduces a new concept of co-ownership of a bulk. Section 16 must now be considered subject to a new s 20A. Section 20A deals with the following type of situation: a buyer agrees to buy 500 tonnes of coal out of a cargo of coal in the holds of the ship *Icebreaker*. In the past, if 500 tonnes were not ascertained for a particular buyer, property in the goods did not pass to the buyer. If the seller became insolvent, the buyer would have no claim on the goods, even though he may have made some payment for them. He could usually only make a claim as an unsecured creditor in the insolvency proceedings. Under the new pro-visions, if the buyer has made whole or partial pre-payment, he will become a co-owner with any other buyers who might have a claim on the goods. The legal consequences of co-ownership are modified in a new s 20(B) to allow trading in the bulk goods in the normal way.

Reserving a right of disposal

The seller's overriding concern is to ensure that he receives payment in full for his goods. Clearly, this presents no problem to a retailer: he can insist on payment in cash or near cash (i.e. by a cheque guaranteed with a cheque card, or by a recognised credit card) before he releases the goods. In the business world, however, sellers are expected to do business on credit terms. If ownership of the goods passes to the buyer before he pays for them and he subsequently becomes bankrupt or, in the case of a company, goes into liquidation, the seller will be treated as an ordinary trade creditor. As such, the seller is unlikely to recover what he is owed. He can protect himself from these considerable risks, by stating that the property in the goods shall not pass to the buyer until the contract price has been paid. Section 19 provides that where the seller has reserved the right of disposal of the goods until some condition is fulfilled, ownership of the goods will not pass to the buyer until that condition is met. The inclusion of such a reservation of title clause in the contract of sale will enable a seller to retrieve his goods and resell them if the buyer becomes bankrupt or goes into receivership or liquidation before paying for them.

The position becomes much more complicated in the following situations:

1 where the buyer has resold the goods; and
2 where the buyer has mixed them with other goods during a manufacturing process and then sold the manufactured product.

Clearly, the seller cannot simply reclaim 'his' goods. However, he may be able to protect himself in relation to point 1 by including a carefully worded clause in the contract, allowing him to trace the goods and claim the proceeds of sale. These terms are known as *Romalpa* clauses, after the name of the case in which they achieved prominence.

Aluminium Industrie Vaassan BV v Romalpa Aluminium Ltd (1976)

AIV, a Dutch company, sold aluminium foil to RA, an English company. A clause in the contract provided that (1) ownership of the foil would not pass to RA until it was paid for; (2) if the foil became mixed with other items during a manufacturing process, AIV would become the owner of the finished product and property would not pass until RA had paid for the foil; (3) unmixed foil and finished products should be stored separately; (4) RA was authorised to sell the finished product on condition that AIV was entitled to the proceeds of the sale. RA became insolvent and a receiver was appointed. The Court of Appeal held that AIV was entitled to recover a quantity of unmixed foil and the proceeds of resale of some unmixed foil.

The seller in the *Romalpa* case confined its claim to unmixed goods and so the Court of Appeal did not give a decision as to the position in relation to mixed goods. Later cases suggest that a *Romalpa* clause will be effective in respect of mixed goods only if it is registered with the Registrar of Companies as a charge over the assets of the buying company. The effect on retention clauses of the appointment of an administrator to an insolvent company was examined in Chapter 6.

Transfer of risk

The general rule is that risk of accidental loss or destruction passes with ownership. Thus, s 20 provides that, unless otherwise agreed, the goods remain at the seller's risk until the property in them is transferred to the buyer, but when the property in them is transferred to the buyer, the goods are at the buyer's risk whether delivery has been made or not. Suppose you buy a painting from an art gallery during an exhibition and it is agreed that you will take delivery at the end of the exhibition. If the gallery is destroyed by fire before the end of the exhibition, you must bear the risk of loss.

Where delivery has been delayed through the fault of either the seller or buyer, the goods are at the risk of the party at fault in respect of any loss which might not have occurred but for the fault (s 20(2)).

Demby, Hamilton & Co Ltd v Barden (1949)

The buyer neglected to take delivery of consignments of apple juice which the seller had prepared and stored in casks. As a result of the delay, the juice went off and had

to be thrown away. The seller sued for the price of the goods sold and delivered. The buyer was liable. Under s 20(2) the goods were at the buyer's risk because he was responsible for the delay.

SALE BY A PERSON WHO IS NOT THE OWNER

As a general rule, a buyer cannot acquire ownership from someone who himself has neither ownership nor the owner's authority to sell. This rule, which is known as the *nemo dat* rule from the phrase *nemo dat quod non habet* – no one can give what he has not got – is embodied in s 21: 'Where goods are sold by a person who is not their owner, and who does not sell them under the authority or with the consent of the owner, the buyer acquires no better title to the goods than the seller had ...'

In these circumstances, the buyer will be required to return the goods to their true owner. The buyer's only remedy is to sue the person who sold him the item for breach of s 12. In most of these cases, however, the seller is a rogue who disappears before the buyer can take action against him. The unsuspecting buyer is left to bear the full brunt of the rogue's misdeeds. It is not surprising, therefore, that exceptions to the *nemo dat* rule have developed. The exceptions are outlined below.

Estoppel (s 21)

If the true owner by his conduct allows the innocent buyer to believe that the seller has the right to sell the goods, ownership of the goods will pass to the buyer because the true owner will be prevented (estopped) from denying that the seller had the right to sell.

Eastern Distributors Ltd v Goldring (1957)

Murphy was the owner of a van. He wanted to buy a car from Coker, a dealer, but he could not raise enough money for a deposit. Murphy and Coker then devised a scheme to generate the necessary finance. Coker would pretend that he owned the van: he would then sell the van and the car to a finance company, which would let both vehicles out on HP to Murphy. The proceeds of the sale of the van would raise sufficient money to finance the required HP deposits. Unfortunately, the finance company accepted the proposal for the van but turned the car down. Unknown to Murphy, Coker proceeded to sell the van to the finance company. It was held that the finance company had become the owner of the van, because the original owner (Murphy) by his conduct had allowed the buyer (the finance company) to believe that the seller (Coker) had a right to sell the goods.

Section 21 (1) applies where goods are 'sold' by a person who is not their owner; it has no application to an agreement to sell.

Shaw v Commissioner of the Police of the Metropolis (1987)

The claimant agreed to buy a Porsche from a rogue. The rogue had obtained the car from its owner by saying that he wanted to show it to a prospective buyer. The rogue also acquired a document from the owner stating that he had bought the car, but this was untrue. The rogue left the car with the claimant and disappeared before being paid. The claimant argued that he had acquired good title under s 21(1) since the document signed by the owner raised an estoppel against him. The Court of Appeal held that the original owner was entitled to recover his car. Section 21(1) did not apply where the buyer had only agreed to buy.

Agency (s 21(2))

The law of agency applies to contracts for the sale of goods. An agent who sells his principal's goods in accordance with the principal's instructions passes a good title to the buyer because he is selling the goods with the authority and consent of the owner. The buyer may even acquire a good title to the goods where the agent has exceeded his actual authority, if the agent was acting within the scope of his apparent or ostensible authority and the buyer was unaware of the agent's lack of authority.

Section 21(2) expressly preserves the rules contained in the Factors Act 1889 which enables the apparent owner of goods to dispose of them as if he were their true owner. A factor is an independent mercantile agent who buys and sells goods on behalf of other people, but does so in his own name. A factor can pass good title to a buyer if the following conditions are met:

1 the goods being sold were in the possession of the factor with the consent of the true owner;
2 the factor, in selling the goods, was acting in the ordinary course of business; and
3 the buyer was unaware of any lack of authority on the part of the factor.

Sale under a common law or statutory power (s 21(2))

Certain persons have the power under common law or statute to sell goods that belong to another. A pawnbroker, for example, has the right to sell goods which have been pledged with him, where the loan has not been repaid. The purchaser will acquire a good title to the goods.

Sale by a person with a voidable title (s 23)

A person may obtain possession of goods under a contract which is void (e.g. for mistake). A void contract is, in fact, no contract at all. A purchaser in these circumstances does not acquire title to the goods and, therefore, cannot pass good title on to anyone else. The original owner will be able to maintain an action in the tort of conversion to recover the goods or their value from a third party who bought them in good faith. This is what happened in *Cundy* v *Lindsay* (1878). A person may also acquire goods under a contract which is voidable (e.g. for misrepresentation). In this case, the contract is valid unless and until it is avoided. Section 23 provides that where goods are resold before the contract has been avoided, the buyer acquires a good title to them provided he buys them in good faith and without notice of the seller's defect of title (see *Lewis* v *Averay* (1972)). If the original owner acts quickly to rescind the contract and then the goods are resold, the seller may be prevented from passing a good title to a purchaser (but see *Newtons of Wembley Ltd* v *Williams* (1964)).

Sale by a seller in possession of the goods (s 24)

Where a seller sells goods but remains in possession of them, or any documents of title relating to them, any resale to a second buyer who actually takes physical delivery of the goods or the documents of title will pass a good title to the second buyer. The disappointed first buyer may sue the seller for non-delivery of the goods. The remedies of a buyer will be considered later in this chapter.

Resale by a buyer in possession of the goods with the consent of the seller (s 25)

Section 25 provides:

> where a person who has bought or agreed to buy goods obtains possession of the goods with the consent of the seller, any resale to a person who takes the goods in good faith and without notice of the rights of the original seller, has the same effect as if the person making the delivery or transfer were a mercantile agent in possession of the goods ... with the consent of the owner.

This exception to the *nemo dat* rule can be illustrated by the following case.

Newtons of Wembley Ltd v Williams (1964)

The claimants sold a car to a rogue, who paid for it by a cheque which was later dishonoured. The claimants took immediate steps to rescind their contract with the rogue (by informing the police). Some time later, the rogue resold the car in Warren Street in London, a well-established street market in used cars. The buyer then sold the car to the defendant. The Court of Appeal held that the defendant acquired a good title to the car. When the rogue sold the car in Warren Street, he was a buyer in possession with the owner's consent, and he acted in the same way as a mercantile agent (or dealer) would have done. He passed a good title to the purchaser, who in turn passed title to the defendant.

Section 25 does not operate so as to make good a defective title, i.e. where the goods are stolen.

National Employers Mutual Insurance Association Ltd v Jones (1987)

Thieves stole H's car. H recovered under her car insurance policy. The thieves sold the car to L, who sold it to T, who sold it to A (a dealer), who sold it to M (a dealer), who finally sold it to Jones. The insurer sought to recover the car from Jones. The Court of Appeal held that Jones had not acquired a good title to the car by virtue of s 25. If a person buys a car from a thief and then resells it, he is not a seller within the terms of the section because the transaction with the thief was not a contract of sale. A resale to a third party in these circumstances cannot cure a defective title.

Sale of motor vehicles on hire-purchase (Hire Purchase Act 1964, Part III)

If a vehicle which is subject to a hire-purchase (HP) agreement is sold by the hirer to a private person who buys in good faith and without notice of the HP agreement, the buyer acquires a good title to the vehicle, even as against the owner. Motor dealers and finance companies cannot claim the benefit of this provision, so they will not acquire good title to a vehicle which is already subject to an HP agreement. The majority of finance companies are members of Hire Purchase Information Ltd (HPI). This organisation maintains a register where finance companies can register their HP agreements. When a car dealer is offered a car for sale, he can check with HPI to see if it is already subject to an HP agreement.

REFORM OF THE LAW RELATING TO TRANSFER OF TITLE CONTAINED IN SS 21–26 OF THE SALE OF GOODS ACT 1979

The rules relating to transfer of title contained in ss 2l–26 have been the subject of considerable scrutiny over the years. In 1966 the Law Reform Committee made a number of recommendations for reform aimed at simplifying the rules in favour of the innocent purchaser. The Committee also recommended that the decision in *Rowland* v *Divall* (1923) should be modified so that the purchaser's right of recovery should take into account any benefit he may have had from the goods while in his possession. A further recommendation was that a purchaser of goods by normal retail sale or at a public auction should acquire good title to the goods irrespective of the seller's title. The Law Reform Committee's proposals were not implemented.

The issue was considered again in 1989 by Professor A L Diamond in his review of security interests in property (A *Review of Security Interests in Property* (DTI) 1989). He considered that innocent purchasers were inadequately protected by the law. He recommended strengthening the rights of the innocent purchaser by providing that where the owner of goods has entrusted those goods to, or acquiesced in their possession by, another person, then an innocent purchaser of those goods should acquire good title. In 1994 the government initiated consultations on whether reform of the law was required. Views were sought on the following proposals:

(a) simplification of the law and increased protection for innocent purchasers based on Professor Diamond's recommendations;

(b) abolition of the rule of market overt (see below);

(c) extension of the principle in Part III, Hire Purchase Act 1964 to all goods subject to HP or conditional sale agreements and goods held on lease or covered by a bill of sale.

While the consultations were taking place, a private member's Bill to abolish the rule of market overt was enacted with government support.

Repeal of s 22 (sale in market overt)

The principle of *nemo dat* used not to apply to sales in market overt. The rule of market overt was established in the Middle Ages. It provided that if a purchaser bought goods according to the usages of the market in good faith and without notice of any defect in the title of the seller, he acquired good title. The term 'market overt' applied to every shop in the City of London and every public market legally constituted by Royal Charter, statute or custom. The common law rules of market overt were included in the statutory exceptions to *nemo dat* by s 22 of the Sale of Goods Act 1979. The rule of market overt led to some curious decisions. For example, in *Reid* v *Commissioner of Police of the Metropolis* (1973) title to a pair of stolen Adam candelabra depended on whether the purchase from a stall at the New Caledonian Market in Southwark had taken place before or after sunrise. (The rules of market overt only applied to sales which took place between sunrise and sunset.) The innocent purchaser did not acquire good title because the sale took place early in the morning before the sun had risen. Although the government was in the process of seeking views about the rule of sale in market overt, it allowed the rule to be abolished by the Sale of Goods (Amendment) Act 1994. The Act came into force on 3 January 1995. From that date, the purchaser of goods in market overt obtains no better title to them than the seller had.

PERFORMANCE OF THE CONTRACT

It is the duty of the seller to deliver the goods and the buyer's duty to accept and pay for them. The parties are free to make their own arrangements about the time and place of delivery and payment. The Act sets out the obligations of the seller and buyer when they have not dealt with these matters specifically in their agreement. Section 28 provides: 'Unless otherwise agreed, delivery of the goods and payment of the price are concurrent conditions...' This means that the seller can hold on to the goods until the buyer has paid for them.

Delivery

Delivery in the context of the Act means the voluntary transfer of possession from one person to another. The delivery may consist of:

1 physically handing over the goods;
2 handing over the means of control of the goods, e.g. the keys to the premises where they are stored;
3 transferring documents of title; or
4 where the goods are in the possession of a third party, an acknowledgement by the third party that he is holding the goods on behalf of the buyer.

Place of delivery

In the absence of any agreement to the contrary, the place of delivery is the seller's place of business; it is up to the buyer to come and collect the goods (s 29(1)). If, however, the seller agrees to send the goods and engages a carrier for this purpose, s 31 provides that delivery to the carrier is deemed to be delivery to the buyer. The seller must make the best possible contract with the carrier on behalf of the buyer to ensure the safe arrival of the goods.

Time of delivery

The parties may have fixed a delivery date. Failure to make delivery by that date is a breach of condition, which entitles the buyer to repudiate the contract and sue for non-delivery (see below). Where the seller agrees to send the goods and no time for sending them has been agreed, he must despatch them within a reasonable time (s 29(3)). A demand for delivery by the buyer or an offer of delivery by the seller will not be valid unless made at a reasonable hour (s 29(3)). What is reasonable is a question of fact. If the seller is ready and willing to deliver the goods and he requests the buyer to take delivery, but the buyer does not comply with the request within a reasonable time, the buyer will be liable for any resulting loss and a reasonable charge for the care and custody of the goods (s 37).

Delivery of the wrong quantity (s 30)

If the seller delivers a smaller quantity than ordered, the buyer may reject the consignment, but if he decides to accept the goods, he must pay for them at the contract rate. If the seller sends a larger quantity than agreed, the buyer has the following choices:

1 he may accept the goods he ordered and reject the rest;
2 he may reject the lot;
3 he may accept the whole consignment, paying for the extra goods at the contract rate.

If the seller delivered the wrong quantity, the buyer used to be entitled under s 30 to reject the whole consignment no matter how slight the excess or shortfall. The buyer's rights were only qualified by the application of the legal maxim *de minimis non curat lex* – the law does not concern itself with trifling matters. Thus, in *Shipton, Anderson & Co Ltd v Weil Bros & Co Ltd* (1912) an excess of 55 lb in relation to a contract for 4,950 tons of wheat was held to be such a microscopic deviation from the contract specifications that it did not entitle the buyers to reject the whole consignment. The Law Commission considered the buyer's right to reject when the wrong quantity is delivered in its Report on the Sale and Supply of Goods (1987). It recommended that in non-consumer contracts the buyer should not be entitled to reject where the shortfall or excess delivered is so slight that rejection would be unreasonable. This recommendation is given effect by the Sale and Supply of Goods Act 1994. Section 30(2A) of the Sale of Goods Act 1979 now provides that a commercial buyer may not reject goods for delivery of the wrong quantity where the seller can show that the excess or shortfall is so slight that it would be unreasonable for the buyer to reject the goods.

Delivery by instalments

Unless otherwise agreed, the buyer is not bound to accept delivery by instalments (s 31 (1)). The parties may, of course, agree that the goods are to be delivered in stated instalments. A breach of contract may occur in respect of one or more instalments (e.g. the seller may deliver goods which are unsatisfactory or the buyer may refuse to take delivery of an instalment). Clearly, the injured party will be able to sue for damages, but the question then arises whether he is also entitled to repudiate the contract. The answer depends on whether the contract is indivisible or severable. A contract is usually treated as being severable if each instalment is to be separately paid for.

1 **Indivisible contracts (ss 11(4) and 35(A).** The general rule used to be that if the buyer accepted some of the goods he was deemed to have accepted all of them and had no right to reject part of the goods. In practice, this meant that where delivery was by instalments a buyer could repudiate the whole contract where the breach was in respect of the first instalment, but where the breach occurred in the second and subsequent instalments his rights were limited to an action for damages. The only exception to this rule was where the seller delivered unwanted goods of a different description to those in the contract. In this case the buyer could accept the contract goods and reject the unwanted goods or reject all the goods (s 30(4)). This right of partial rejection did not apply where part of the goods were defective.

The Law Commission in its Report on the Sale and Supply of Goods (1987) recommended that there should be a right of partial rejection where the goods are not in conformity with the contract. This recommendation is implemented by the Sale and Supply of Goods Act 1994. A new s 35A of the Sale of Goods Act 1979, which also applies to instalment contracts, provides that where a buyer has accepted some of the goods, he will not lose his right to reject the goods because of his acceptance where there is a breach in respect of some or all of the goods. Section 30(4) is repealed.

2 Severable contracts (s 31(2)). Whether a breach in relation to one or more instalments will entitle the injured party to repudiate the whole contract depends 'on the terms of the contract and the circumstances of the case'. If the contract is silent on the matter, the courts apply two main tests:

(a) the size of the breach in relation to the whole contract; and
(b) the likelihood that the breach will be repeated.

Maple Flock Co Ltd v *Universal Furniture Products (Wembley) Ltd* (1934)

The sellers agreed to deliver 100 tons of flock by instalments. The first 15 instalments were satisfactory but the 16th was not up to the required standard. The buyers then took delivery of four more satisfactory loads before refusing further deliveries. The court held that the buyers were not entitled to repudiate the contract. The defective flock constituted a small proportion of the total quantity delivered and there was little likelihood of the breach being repeated.

Acceptance

The buyer is bound to accept the goods which the seller delivers in accordance with the contract. If the goods do not meet the requirements of the contract, the buyer will have a claim against the seller. The remedies for breach of a condition depend on whether the goods have been 'accepted'. If the goods have not been accepted, the buyer is entitled to reject the goods and claim his money back. He may also bring a claim for damages. However, if the goods have been accepted, the buyer loses his right to reject the goods, although he can still claim damages. What constituted 'acceptance' was set out in ss 34 and 35(1). Under these sections there were three ways in which a buyer could accept the goods:

1 he could expressly tell the seller that he had accepted the goods; or
2 he could do something to the goods which was inconsistent with the seller's ownership; or
3 he could retain the goods for a reasonable time without telling the seller that he had rejected them.

A buyer was not deemed to have accepted the goods until he had had a reasonable opportunity to examine them to check that they were in accordance with the terms of the contract. The Law Commission's Report on the Sale and Supply of Goods (1987) identified a number of problems relating to the rules on acceptance:

1 the rules of acceptance only applied to contracts of sale and not to other contracts for the supply of goods;
2 the right to reject could be easily lost before defects become apparent (see *Bernstein* v *Pamsons Motors (Golders Green) Ltd* (1987);
3 buyers have lost the right to reject the goods before they have had a chance to examine them because they have signed an 'acceptance note';
4 it was unclear whether a buyer would lose his right to reject if he asked the seller to repair defective goods;
5 it was unclear what amounted to an act inconsistent with the seller's ownership for the purpose of acceptance.

The Law Commission made a number of recommendations in relation to rules on acceptance, which have been implemented by the Sale and Supply of Goods Act 1994. An amended s 35 retains the three ways of accepting the goods (set out above), but adds the following qualifications:

1 a consumer cannot lose his right to reject the goods by agreement unless he has had a reasonable opportunity to examine them (s 35(3)), i.e. a consumer cannot be deprived of his right to examine the goods by means of an acceptance note;
2 a material factor in deciding whether goods have been accepted after the lapse of a reasonable time is whether the buyer has been given a reasonable opportunity to examine the goods (s 35(5));
3 a buyer is not deemed to have accepted the goods because he has asked for or agreed to a repair or where the goods have been sold or given to a third party (s 35(6));
4 where a buyer accepts goods which are part of a larger commercial unit, he is deemed to have accepted all the goods which make up the commercial unit, e.g. if you buy a pair of shoes and accept one shoe, you will be deemed to have accepted the pair.

Payment

The price is such a fundamental part of the transaction that it will normally be fixed by the contract. However, it may be ascertained by the course of dealing between the parties or the contract may provide a mechanism for fixing the price, such as by arbitration. The parties may make their own agreement as to the time of payment. The seller may insist on payment in advance of delivery or he may be prepared to extend a period of credit. In the absence of such express agreement, payment is due when the goods are delivered.

REMEDIES

Seller's remedies

Two sets of remedies are open to the seller. He can pursue personal remedies against the buyer himself and real remedies against the goods.

Personal remedies

The seller can sue the buyer for the contract price or for damages for non-acceptance.

1 Action for the price (s 49). The seller can bring an action for the contract price in two situations: where the property in the goods has passed to the buyer or where the buyer has failed to pay by a specified date, irrespective of whether ownership has passed to the buyer.

2 Damages for non-acceptance (s 50). If the property in the goods has not passed and the buyer will not accept the goods, the seller can sue for non-acceptance. The measure of damages is the estimated loss directly and naturally resulting in the ordinary course of events from the buyer's breach of contract (s 50(2)). If the buyer wrongfully refuses to accept and pay for the goods, the seller is expected to mitigate his loss and sell them elsewhere for the best possible price. Section 50(3) provides guidance as to the measure of damages where there is an available market for the goods. If the market price is less than the contract price, the seller can recover the difference by way of damages. Where the market price is the same or even higher than the contract price, the seller will be entitled to nominal damages only. (The market price is calculated at the time when the goods ought to have been accepted.)

The following cases illustrate how s 50 is applied by the courts.

W L Thompson Ltd v *Robinson (Gunmakers) Ltd* (1955)
The defendants ordered a new Vanguard car from the claimant car dealers, but then refused to accept it. The defendants argued that they were only liable to pay nominal damages, since the contract price and the market price were the same. It was held that there was no 'available market' for Vanguard cars because supply exceeded demand and, therefore, s 50(3) did not apply The dealers had sold one car less and under s 50(2) they were entitled to their loss of profit on the sale.

Charter v *Sullivan* (1957)
A buyer refused to accept a new Hillman Minx car that he had ordered from a dealer. In contrast to the previous case, the demand for Hillman Minx cars exceeded supply and the dealer would have had no difficulty in finding another buyer. It was held that the dealer was entitled to nominal damages only. The buyer's breach would not have affected the total number of cars sold over a period of time.

Real remedies

The unpaid seller has three possible remedies in respect of the goods, even though the property in the goods has passed to the buyer. They are lien, stoppage in transit and resale.

1 Lien (ss 41–43). A lien is the right to retain possession of goods (but not to resell them) until the contract price has been paid. It is available in any of the following circumstances:

(a) where the goods have been sold without any mention of credit;
(b) where the goods have been sold on credit but the period of credit has expired;
(c) where the buyer becomes insolvent.

The seller will lose his right of lien if the price is paid or tendered or the buyer obtains possession of the goods. The seller cannot exercise this right to retain the goods if he has handed the goods to a carrier for transportation to the buyer without reserving the right of disposal of the goods or where he has given up the right.

2 Stoppage in transit (ss 44–46). This is the right of the seller to stop goods in transit to the buyer, regain possession of them and retain them until payment has been received. The seller can exercise his right to stoppage in transit in only one situation – where the buyer has become insolvent.

3 Right of resale (ss 47 and 48). The rights of lien and stoppage in transit by themselves do not give the seller any right to resell the goods. He is allowed, however, to resell the goods in the following circumstances:

(a) where the goods are of a perishable nature;
(b) where the seller gives notice to the buyer of his intention to resell and the buyer does not pay or tender the price within a reasonable time;
(c) where the seller expressly reserves the right of resale in the event of the buyer defaulting.

The seller can exercise the right of resale and also recover damages for any loss sustained by the buyer's breach of contract. The original contract of sale is rescinded and the new buyer acquires a good title to the goods as against the original buyer.

Buyer's remedies

Various remedies are available to the buyer where the seller is in breach of contract.

Rejection of the goods (ss 11 and 15A)

The buyer is entitled to repudiate the contract and reject the goods where the seller is in breach of a condition of the contract. Most of the implied terms contained in ss 12–15 are designated conditions, so if the goods do not correspond with their description or are not of satisfactory quality or fit for a particular purpose, the buyer is entitled to reject them. The right to reject is lost as soon as the goods have been accepted under the rules set out in s 35. The rules relating to acceptance have already been considered. If the buyer is deemed to have accepted the goods, he must treat the breach of condition as a breach of warranty, thus limiting his remedy to a claim for damages. As the following case illustrates, the right to reject can be lost after a relatively short period of use.

Bernstein v Pamsons Motors (Golders Green) Ltd (1987)

Mr Bernstein bought a new Nissan car from Pamsons at a price of just under £8,000. After three weeks of use (and 140 miles on the clock) the engine seized up. Mr Bernstein immediately informed Pamsons that he was rejecting the car since he did not regard it as being of merchantable quality. The car was then repaired under the manufacturer's warranty, but Mr Bernstein refused to take it back. Rougier J, in the High Court, held that Pamsons was in breach of the implied condition under s 14(2), but Mr Bernstein was deemed to have accepted the car under s 35 and thereby had lost his right to treat the contract as repudiated and reject the car.

Comment. (i) The judge in this case felt Mr Bernstein had had a reasonable time in which to examine and try out the car, and so had lost his right to reject. It is unfortunate that the Court of Appeal did not get an opportunity to consider whether the length of time which acted as a bar to rejection was reasonable. Pamsons gave Mr Bernstein his money back when it heard he was going to appeal. (ii) The Law Commission in its Report on the Sale and Supply of Goods (1987) explored the possibility of laying down fixed periods during which the buyer would retain his right to reject. The suggestion was rejected on the ground that a single time limit would be inappropriate to the very different kinds of goods covered by the Act, while different time limits for different types of goods would require very complex legislation. The Law Commission felt that the 'reasonable time' provision in s 35 provided the appropriate flexibility and, in practice, gave rise to few disputes.

If the goods have not been accepted, the buyer has a right to reject for any breach of the implied promises as to title, description, quality and suitability set out in ss 12–15, no matter how slight the breach. This is because the Act classifies these promises as 'conditions'. (Any breach of a condition entitles the injured party to terminate the contract and claim damages.) However, not all breaches of the implied terms in ss 13–15 will be so serious as to justify the buyer's right to reject. It would seem unfair to the seller that a buyer should be able to reject goods for a very slight breach. There is also the danger that where a buyer is trying to reject goods because of a very minor breach, the court may conclude that the claim is so unreasonable that there was really no breach at all.

The Law Commission considered the issue in its Report on the Sale and Supply of Goods (1987). It concluded that a distinction should be drawn between consumers and commercial buyers in relation to remedies. It recommended that a consumer's right to reject for breach of the implied terms in ss 13–15 should be retained but that a non-consumer buyer should be prevented from rejecting goods where the breach is so slight that it would be unreasonable to reject. This recommendation is implemented by the Sale and Supply of Goods Act 1994, which introduces a new s 15A to the 1979 Act. Section 15A provides that where a seller can show that the breach of ss 13–15 is so slight that it would be unreasonable for a non-consumer buyer to reject, the breach is to be treated as a breach of warranty and not as a breach of condition. The modification of the buyer's rights does not apply where the contract indicates a contrary intention.

An action for damages

1 **Non-delivery (s 51).** The buyer can sue for non-delivery when the seller wrongfully neglects or refuses to deliver the goods. The measure of damages is the estimated loss directly and naturally resulting in the ordinary course of events from the seller's breach of contract. Where there is an available market for the goods, the measure of damages is usually the difference between the contract price and the higher price of obtaining similar goods elsewhere. If the buyer has paid in advance and the goods are not delivered, he can recover the amount paid (s 54) because there has been a total failure of consideration.

2 **Breach of warranty (s 53).** The buyer can sue for damages under s 53 in the following circumstances:

(a) where the seller is in breach of a warranty;
(b) where the seller is in breach of a condition, but the buyer has chosen to carry on with the contract and claim damages instead;
(c) where the seller is in breach of a condition, but the buyer has lost the right to reject the goods (because he has accepted them).

The measure of damages is the estimated loss directly and naturally resulting from the breach. This is usually the difference in value between the goods actually delivered and goods fulfilling the warranty.

Specific performance (s 52)

The buyer may sue for specific performance, but only in cases where the goods are specific or ascertained and where monetary damages would not be an adequate remedy. A court is unlikely to make such an order if similar goods are available elsewhere.

EU DIRECTIVE ON THE SALE OF CONSUMER GOODS AND ASSOCIATED GUARANTEES

In 1999 the EC adopted a Directive on the sale of consumer goods and associated guarantees, which must be implemented by member states by 1 January 2002. The Directive will introduce some significant changes to UK legislation on the sale of consumer goods. The main changes are:

- **reversed burden of proof for the first six months**: where a business seller delivers consumer goods which do not conform with the contract of sale because, e.g., they do not match the description or their quality of performance is unsatisfactory, it is presumed that any lack of conformity which appears within six months existed at the time of delivery. The effect of this provision is to reverse the normal burden of proof for a period of six months from delivery;
- **a hierarchy of remedies**: where there is a lack of conformity, the consumer is entitled to a repair or replacement free of charge within a reasonable period and without major inconvenience to the consumer. If repair or replacement is impossible or disproportionate, or if the seller has not remedied the shortcoming within a reasonable time or without major inconvenience, the consumer will be entitled either to a reduction in the price or rescission of the contract (unless the shortcoming is minor);
- **legally binding guarantees**: the requirements of the Directive in relation to consumer guarantees is outlined later in this chapter.

The government has indicated that it does not intend to reduce current consumer protection provisions in areas where the Directive falls short of existing levels of protection.

SUPPLY OF GOODS AND SERVICES

The provisions of the Sale of Goods Act 1979, including the protection afforded the buyer by the implied terms contained in ss 12–15, apply only to contracts where goods are sold for a money consideration. The sale of goods legislation did not cover other methods of obtaining goods (e.g. by HP, hire, barter or contracts for work and materials), although the need for protection was just as great, nor did it have anything to say about the provision of services.

Implied terms as to title, description, quality, fitness for purpose and correspondence with sample, similar to those in the Sale of Goods Act, were put on a statutory basis first in respect of goods supplied on HP and later in relation to goods acquired using trading stamps. In 1979, the Law Commission recommended that the protection of statutory implied terms should be extended to all contracts for the supply of goods. This was achieved by the Supply of Goods and Services Act 1982. The Act also places on a statutory footing certain terms which had hitherto been implied by the common law in contracts for services.

The Supply of Goods and Services Act 1982 is divided into two main parts: Part I deals with implied terms in contracts for the supply of goods, while Part II covers implied terms in contracts for services. Section references are to the 1982 Act, as amended by the Sale and Supply of Goods Act 1994, unless otherwise indicated. We will now examine the provisions of the Act in more detail.

IMPLIED TERMS IN CONTRACTS FOR THE SUPPLY OF GOODS (PART I)

Part I of the Act was based on the recommendations of the Law Commission contained in its Report on Implied Terms in Contracts for the Supply of Goods (Law Com No 95), published in 1979. The provisions of Part I, which came into force in January 1983, consist of two sets of implied terms. The first set applies to contracts for the transfer of property in goods, the second set to contracts of hire.

Contracts for the transfer of property in goods

The first set of terms, detailed in ss 2–5 (see below), are implied into contracts for work and materials and

barter, under which a person acquires ownership of goods. The terms, which were previously implied into these contracts by the common law, follow the pattern established by ss 12–15 of the Sale of Goods Act 1979, in relation to contracts for the sale of goods.

Section 2 contains an implied condition that the transferor has the right to transfer the property in the goods, and implied warranties that the goods are free from undisclosed third-party rights and that the buyer will enjoy quiet possession of the goods. Where there is a contract for the transfer of goods by description, under s 3 there is an implied condition that the goods will correspond to the description. Section 4 provides that where goods are transferred in the course of a business, there are implied conditions that the goods are of satisfactory quality, and reasonably fit for the purpose. According to s 5, where there is a transfer of goods by reference to a sample, there is an implied condition that the bulk will correspond with the sample.

These implied terms apply in exactly the same way as the terms implied by ss 12–15 of the Sale of Goods Act 1979. Similarly, attempts to exclude the obligations contained in ss 2–5 of the 1982 Act are subject to control on the 'Sale of Goods' model. The implied terms as to title (s 2) cannot be excluded or restricted by any contract term. Sections 3–5 cannot be excluded or restricted where the transferee is dealing as a consumer; if the transferee is not dealing as the consumer, the exemption is subject to the reasonableness test, as laid down in the Unfair Contract Terms Act 1977.

Contracts for the hire of goods

The second set of implied terms in Part I can be found in ss 7–10. They apply to contracts under which 'one person bails or agrees to bail goods to another by way of hire' (s 6). This includes both consumer and commercial hire agreements, but HP agreements are expressly excluded. The terms implied in hire contracts by ss 7–10 match, as far as is possible, the implied terms in contracts for the sale of goods. Section 7 provides that there is an implied condition that the bailor has a right to transfer possession of the goods to the bailee and that the bailee will enjoy quiet possession of the goods during the period of hire. By s 8, where there is a contract for the hire of goods by description, there is an implied condition that the goods will correspond with the description. Section 9 provides that where goods are hired in the course of a business, there are implied conditions that the goods are of satisfactory quality and reasonably fit for the purpose. Section 10 covers implied conditions in relation to contracts for the hire of goods by reference to a sample.

The implied terms contained in s 7 (right to transfer and quiet possession) can be excluded or restricted if the exemption satisfies the reasonableness test. The implied terms as to description, quality and sample cannot be excluded or restricted as against a person dealing as a consumer; in a non-consumer transaction, these implied terms can be excluded subject to the requirement of reasonableness.

IMPLIED TERMS IN CONTRACTS FOR THE SUPPLY OF SERVICES (PART II)

Recent years have witnessed a dramatic growth in the service industry, which has been matched by a corresponding increase in customer dissatisfaction. The National Consumer Council (NCC) highlighted the problems in its report, *Services Please*, published in 1981. Part II of the Supply of Goods and Services Act 1982, which deals with contracts for services, is based largely on the recommendations put forward by the NCC. Part II of the Act came into force on 4 July 1983. A contract for the supply of services is one 'under which a person ("the supplier") agrees to carry out a service' (s 12). This covers agreements where the supplier simply provides a service and nothing more, such as dry-cleaning or hairdressing. It also includes contracts where the provision of a service also involves the transfer of goods (e.g. installing central heating or repairing a car). The Act does not apply to contracts of service (employment) or apprenticeship. The terms implied into a contract for services by this part of the Act are as follows.

Care and skill (s 13)

Section 13 provides that where the supplier is acting in the course of a business there is an implied term that the supplier will carry out the service with reasonable care and skill. So, if you take your raincoat to be dry-cleaned and it is returned with a large tear in the fabric, clearly the cleaning process will not have been carried out with reasonable care and skill. The duty to exercise reasonable care and skill was considered in the following case.

Wilson v Best Travel Ltd (1993)

The claimant sustained serious injuries when he tripped and fell through glass patio doors at the Greek hotel he was staying in while on a package holiday organised by the defendant tour operator. The doors had been fitted with 5mm glass which complied with Greek, but not British, safety standards. The claimant sought damages against the defendant, arguing that the defendant was in breach of the duty of care which arose from s 13 of the Supply of Goods and Services Act 1982. It was held that the defendant tour operator was not liable: its liability was to check that local safety standards had been complied with, provided that the absence of a safety feature was not such that a reasonable holidaymaker would decline to take a holiday at the hotel. A tour operator might be in breach of duty if, for example, it used a hotel where there were no fire precautions at all. In this case, the doors met Greek safety standards and the absence of thicker safety glass in doors was unlikely to cause the claimant to decline the holiday.

Time for performance (s 14)

Under s 14, where the supplier is acting in the course of a business and the time for performance cannot be determined from the contract or ascertained by a course of dealing between the parties, there is an implied term that the supplier will carry out the service within a reasonable time. What is a reasonable time is a matter of fact. If you take your car into a garage for minor repairs, it is reasonable to allow a few days and, if spare parts have to be ordered, possibly a couple of weeks for the repairs to be completed. If the car is still in the garage six months later, the repairer will be in breach of s 14.

Consideration (s 15)

Section 15 provides that where the consideration cannot be determined from the contract or by a course of dealing between the parties, there is an implied term that the customer will pay a reasonable charge for the service. If you call a plumber out to mend a burst pipe and no reference is made to his charges, he is entitled to a reasonable amount for his services on completion of the job.

You should note the following points about Part II of the Act:

1 Sections 13–15 imply 'terms' into contracts for services. This means that the remedy available to the injured party will depend on the circumstances of the breach. If the breach goes to the root of the contract, it will be treated as a breach of a condition and the customer can repudiate the contract and claim damages – where the breach is slight, it will be regarded as a breach of a warranty and the customer can recover damages only.

2 The Secretary of State has the power to exempt certain contracts for services from one or more of the sections in Part II. An order has been made, for example, excluding s 13 from applying to:

(a) the services of an advocate in a court or tribunal, e.g. a solicitor appearing in a magistrates' court; and
(b) the services of a company director.

3 Under s 16 the rights, duties and liabilities imposed by ss 13–15 may be excluded or limited subject to the provisions of the Unfair Contract Terms Act 1977. The implied term contained in s 13 (care and skill) is, therefore, subject to s 2 of the 1977 Act, while the implied terms in ss 14 and 15 (time for performance and consideration) seem to be covered by s 3 of the 1977 Act.

MANUFACTURER'S LIABILITY IN CONTRACT

Generally

So far in this chapter we have examined the rights and responsibilities of the parties to a contract, concentrating especially on the duties of a supplier of goods and services. We now turn our attention to the person who produces the goods. What exactly are the responsibilities of a manufacturer who puts defective products into circulation? A striking feature of modern life is the constant bombardment we receive from expensive advertising or promotions conducted by manufacturers who are trying to persuade us to buy their products. It is hardly surprising, therefore, that if anything goes wrong with the product, the majority of people think that the manufacturer is responsible in law to put matters right. Certainly, most retailers do little to dispel this belief. It is true that if the manufacturer supplies goods directly to the customer, the customer is entitled to sue him on the contract for breach of the terms which are implied now in all contracts for the supply of goods. Very often, however, goods are not sold straight to the customer, but are distributed through a wholesaler, who sells them to a retailer, who in turn supplies them to the ultimate consumer. If the goods are faulty, the consumer's rights lie against the retailer, not against the person who created the problem in the first place.

The primary responsibility for compensating the consumer in respect of defective products is placed by the law of contract on the person who sold or supplied the goods; he is liable irrespective of whether he was at fault. Thus, the law imposes what is known as 'strict liability' on retailers in respect of faulty goods. A good example of this principle is the case of *Godley* v *Perry* (1960), which was discussed earlier in this chapter. The action involved a young boy who lost an eye when his toy catapult broke. The boy had purchased the catapult three days earlier from a newsagent's shop. The newsagent had taken reasonable care to ensure that the catapults he sold were safe. Nevertheless, under the Sale of Goods Act, he was held strictly liable for injuries caused to the boy.

The law of contract provides the main avenue for redress in respect of faulty goods. However, a contractual solution to the problem of defective goods has its limitations.

1 The traditional doctrine of privity of contract meant that the rights and duties created by a contract were confined to the parties. Only the purchaser could take action in contract in respect of a defective product. For example, if in *Godley* v *Perry* the boy had received the catapult as a Christmas present from his parents, he would not have been able to sue the newsagent for compensation for his injuries under the Sale of Goods Act because of the absence of a contract between himself and the newsagent.

However, under s 1 of the Contracts (Rights of Third Parties) Act 1999, a third party may have the right to enforce a term in the contract, such as the implied term contained in s 14 of the Sale of Goods Act 1979, where either the contract contains an express term to this effect or a term of the contract purports to confer a benefit on the third party. So, if a doting aunt buys a wedding present for her nephew and delivery is to be made to the nephew's house, it can be argued that the contract purports to confer a benefit on the nephew, and he will be able to sue if the present is defective.

2 The common law doctrine of privity also means that the consumer's rights in contract are restricted to an action against the person who sold or supplied him with the goods. Such 'rights' may prove illusory. The retailer may not have the means to pay compensation or he may have ceased trading because of insolvency.

3 The retailer is required to bear the brunt of claims for compensation from aggrieved customers, even though he may be completely blameless. Of course, the retailer can sue his immediate supplier in contract for breach of the implied terms in the Sale of Goods Act 1979. The supplier can sue the next person in the chain of contracts which ultimately ends with the manufacturer. This chain of responsibility is illustrated in Fig 10.1.

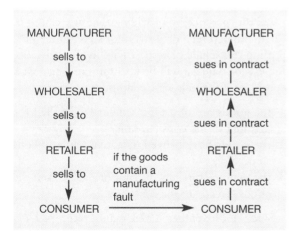

Fig 10.1 The chain of responsibility in contract for a defective product

Thus, the manufacturer is required, albeit in a roundabout way, to accept responsibility for his defective products. However, the chain of responsibility may be broken where, for example, there are reasonable exemption clauses in the contract between the retailer and the wholesaler. If this is the case, the manufacturer will escape liability and the innocent retailer must absorb the cost of compensation. There is a case for a consumer, irrespective of whether he purchased the defective item, being able to take direct action against the manufacturer, but there are limited circumstances in which the manufacturer can be sued. These are:

1 under a collateral contract between the manufacturer and the consumer;
2 in tort;
3 under Part I of the Consumer Protection Act 1987.

Collateral contract

A manufacturer would soon go out of business if he directed all his energies to producing his goods as cheaply as possible. He must develop a marketing strategy to ensure that potential customers know about his products and are encouraged to buy them. This can be achieved, for example, by an advertising campaign, special promotions, personal visits by sales reps, or the inclusion of a 'guarantee' or 'warranty' with the goods. Such activities may result in the manufacturer being directly liable in contract to the consumer, even though the consumer buys the goods from the retailer. In this situation there is clearly a contract of sale between the consumer and the retailer to which the manufacturer is not a party, but there may also be another contract between the consumer and the manufacturer. The second less obvious contract is known as a collateral contract: it is, in effect, an implied contract between the manufacturer and the consumer. A collateral contract may arise in two situations:

(a) from advertising and sales talk; and
(b) under a manufacturer's guarantee or warranty.

Advertising and sales talk

The classic example of a manufacturer being held to account for extravagant claims in an advertising campaign is the case of *Carlill* v *Carbolic Smoke*

Ball Co (1893). You will recall that the company promised in an advertisement to pay £100 to anyone who contracted 'flu after using the smoke ball three times daily for two weeks. Mrs Carlill saw this advertisement, bought a smoke ball from a chemist and used it as directed but still caught 'flu. Even though Mrs Carlill had not bought the smoke ball directly from the company, there was a contract between them. The essential requirements of offer and acceptance and consideration were all present. The company had made Mrs Carlill an offer in its advertisement, which she had accepted by purchasing the smoke ball. The company's promise was supported by consideration from Mrs Carlill because she had bought the smoke ball from a retail chemist.

The same principle applies where the manufacturer's salesman calls on the consumer and makes promises about the performance of a product. If the consumer acts on the sales talk by obtaining the product from his supplier and not directly from the manufacturer, the consumer will be able to hold the manufacturer to his promises under a collateral contract.

Shanklin Pier Ltd v *Detel Products Ltd* (1951)

Shanklin Pier Ltd engaged a firm of painting contractors to paint its pier at Shanklin on the Isle of Wight, specifying that they should use a paint called DMU, which was manufactured by Detel products Ltd. A director of Detel Products had called previously on the managing director of the pier company and recommended DMU for the job, saying that it would last seven to ten years. In fact, the paint only lasted three months. The pier company could not sue the manufacturer for breach of a condition implied under the Sale of Goods Act (that the paint would be reasonably fit for the stated purpose) because it had not bought the paint itself. Nor could it sue the painters, who, after all, had only followed the instructions they were given. So the pier company sued Detel Products Ltd for breach of its promise that the paint would last seven to ten years.

It was held that, in addition to the contract for the sale of the paint (between the manufacturer and the painters) and the contract to paint the pier (between the painters and the pier owner), there was also a collateral contract between the pier company and the manufacturer. The bargain was that the manufacturer guaranteed the suitability of DMU and in return the pier company specified in its contract with the painters that DMU paint should be used.

Manufacturer's guarantees and warranties

Sometimes the manufacturer's confidence in his product is expressed formally in the shape of a written guarantee or warranty which accompanies the goods. A manufacturer's guarantee has become an expected standard feature of the sale of 'consumer durables'. The guarantee usually consists of an undertaking by the manufacturer to repair or replace faulty goods within a certain period of time.

The question arises of whether a manufacturer is bound to honour the promises contained in his guarantee. In other words, can the guarantee form the basis of a contract between the consumer and the manufacturer? Unfortunately, the legal position is far from clear. If the consumer can show that he knew about the guarantee before he bought the goods, he should be able to establish the existence of a collateral contract with the manufacturer by applying the reasoning employed in the *Carlill* case. The liability of the manufacturer of defective goods which are under guarantee can be established in another way. The guarantee often takes the form of a postcard, which the consumer must complete and send off to the manufacturer within a certain period of time. The inconvenience that this entails may be sufficient consideration to support the manufacturer's promise. In the past, guarantees often contained an exemption clause, which deprived the consumer of the rights he might otherwise have had against the manufacturer. Section 5 of the Unfair Contract Terms Act 1977 now prevents this practice by providing that any clause in the manufacturer's or distributor's guarantee purporting to exclude or restrict liability in negligence for loss or damage will be unenforceable against a consumer if the following conditions are met:

1 the goods are of a type ordinarily supplied for private use and consumption;
2 the goods have proved defective while in consumer use;
3 the manufacturer or distributor did not sell the goods directly to the consumer.

Since 1 November 1978 manufacturers have been required to include a statement in their guarantees to the effect that the consumer's statutory rights are unaffected by the terms of the guarantee. Failure to make such a statement is a criminal offence by virtue of orders made under the Fair Trading Act 1973.

REFORM AND GUARANTEES

The problems relating to guarantees were highlighted in an Office of Fair Trading (OFT) Report (Consumer Guarantees) published in 1984:

1 the consumer may buy an extended guarantee, which may become worthless if the guarantor goes out of business;
2 delays in dealing with complaints or authorising repair;
3 consumers have expectations of 'peace of mind', which often disappear when they come to enforce the guarantee;
4 the guarantee may not be transferable to a subsequent purchaser.

Over the years proposals for reform have been made variously by the OFT, the National Consumer Council and the DTI. A private members' Consumer Guarantees Bill was introduced in 1990, but was lost because of a lack of parliamentary time and government opposition.

The European Directive on the Sale of Consumer Goods and Associated Guarantees, adopted on 7 July 1999, introduces the notion of a legally enforceable guarantee. Member states will be required to amend domestic legislation in line with the Directive by 1 January 2002. The Directive provides that any commercial guarantee offered by a seller or producer will be legally binding and must place the beneficiary in a more advantageous position than available under any rules relating to the sale of goods.

The guarantee must:

- be in writing;
- be available for consultation before purchase;
- specify the duration and territorial scope;
- give the name and address of the guarantor.

QUESTIONS/ACTIVITIES

1 Sandra, who runs a flourishing florist's shop, decides to replace the van which she uses for making deliveries. She attends a long-established street market in used cars, where she sees a van with a notice in the front window which reads: 'For Sale. 1999 Bedford van'. After a thorough inspection and a test drive, she enters into a contract to buy the van from Mark. What is her legal position in the following circumstances?
   (a) Sandra discovers that the vehicle is made up of two Bedford vans. The front half of a 1996 model has been welded to the rear half of a 1999 model and, as a result, the van is in a dangerous condition.
   (b) During the test drive, Sandra noticed that the clutch was defective. Mark said that he was prepared to do the repairs himself or he would drop the price by £75. Sandra agreed to the reduction in price, but her local garage has now told her that it will cost £150 to put the defect right.
   (c) She has now been informed by the police that the van was stolen six months previously and that it must be returned to its true owner.

2 Greenacres, a firm of estate agents, decides to give its image a face-lift by refurbishing its reception area. Greenacres places the contract with a local company, Office Style Ltd, which agrees to supply the following items:
   (a) six easy chairs and matching coffee table selected from Office Style's existing stock by Greenacres' senior partner;
   (b) a new carpet which has to be ordered direct from the manufacturer;
   (c) a set of free-standing display units, already in stock, which Office Style agrees to adapt to hold the particulars of houses for sale.
   The night before the refitting is due to take place, Office Style's warehouse, containing all the items for the Greenacres job, is completely destroyed by fire. Advise Greenacres.

3 Luigi owns an Italian restaurant. He has experienced a few problems with recent deliveries from his suppliers and he seeks your advice.
   (a) He orders 500 tins of Italian tomatoes. The supplier delivers 400 tins of Italian tomatoes and 100 tins of Greek tomatoes.

(b) He orders 10 lb of parmesan cheese, but the supplier delivers only 2 lb.

(c) He orders 50 lb of spaghetti. The supplier delivers 100 lb.

(d) He has a regular order with a local baker for 100 bread rolls to be delivered by 11 am every day. On one occasion the rolls do not arrive until 2 pm.

4 Jim agrees to supply 300 turkeys to a London butcher's shop during a three-week period prior to Christmas. What are Jim's remedies in each of the following situations?

(a) The butcher rings up at the end of November to cancel the order, because he has found a cheaper supplier.

(b) While the second consignment of 100 turkeys is being transported by rail to London, Jim hears from a neighbouring farmer that the butcher is having difficulty paying his debts.

5 Fred recently obtained a 24-inch remote control colour TV set. What are Fred's rights and the source of these rights in the following circumstances?

(a) Just as he is sitting down to watch 'Match of the Day' there is a flash and a puff of smoke from the back of the TV and the screen goes blank. Fred bought the set new from a local department store. He paid for it in cash.

(b) Fred obtained the TV from his brother-in-law, Tom, by swapping his music centre. Fred was assured by Tom that it was a colour TV, but so far he has only got a black-and-white picture.

(c) Fred is an American football enthusiast. He told the salesman at TV World Ltd, a local electrical shop, that he wanted a TV that would receive Channel 4 broadcasts because of his interest in American football. Fred, who is buying the TV on HP, has now discovered that he cannot get Channel 4 with this particular model.

(d) The remote control unit refuses to work. Fred acquired the TV on hire from a local TV rental firm.

6 Mr and Mrs Carter decide to install double-glazing in their house. They get three firms to provide 'estimates' for the job, the cheapest (£400) being submitted by Kozee Ltd, which they ask to do the work. The Carters sign a contract, but the document does not mention the price payable for the work or how long it will take to complete. The workmen start the job in July, but the work proceeds in fits and starts and is finished finally in December. The Carters are very unhappy with the workmanship; the house is still very draughty and there has been no noticeable saving in their fuel bills. They have now received a bill from Kozee Ltd for £900 and they seek your advice.

Chapter 11

BUSINESS TORTS

In the last chapter we examined the scope of a businessman's liability in contract for the goods and services he provides. In this chapter we will consider how the activities of business organisations may give rise to liability in tort.

TORTIOUS LIABILITY

A tort is a civil wrong. Unlike the obligations voluntarily accepted by the parties to a contract, a tort consists of the breach of a duty imposed by the law. The law of tort seeks to provide a legal remedy for the victims of certain forms of harmful conduct. Tort duties are owed to a wide range of persons and are not dependent on the existence of a contractual relationship. Although this area of law is often referred to as the law of tort, in reality a number of distinct areas of tortious liability have been developed to protect people from the many forms of wrongful conduct which may occur in modern society. Examples of the kinds of harmful conduct which the law provides protection against include:

- interference with a person's ownership or possession of land or personal property, e.g. the torts of trespass to land and trespass to goods;
- injury to business or personal reputations, e.g. tort of defamation;
- interference with a person's use and enjoyment of land, e.g. tort of nuisance;
- damage to land, e.g. tort of negligence, rule in *Rylands* v *Fletcher*;
- personal injury and death, e.g. torts of negligence and trespass to the person;
- damage to commercial interests e.g. torts of deceit, passing-off, inducement of breach of contract, conspiracy.

Each tort is governed by its own special rules covering such matters as the basis of liability, defences and remedies. General principles relating to these issues are set out below.

BASIS OF TORTIOUS LIABILITY

Liability in tort is essentially 'fault-based'. This means that a claimant must prove that the defendant acted intentionally or negligently and was, therefore, blameworthy. The defendant's reasons or motive for committing a wrongful act are generally not relevant to liability in tort. However, the presence of malice is relevant to some torts; malice is an essential ingredient of some torts, e.g. conspiracy requires proof of an intention to injure the claimant rather than to promote the defendant's legitimate interests; proof of malice can defeat certain defences to defamation, e.g. qualified privilege will not protect a defendant who acted maliciously; malice may make an otherwise reasonable act unreasonable so as to establish liability, e.g. in the tort of nuisance.

There are two situations where tortious liability may be imposed despite the defendant not being at fault.

1 Torts of strict liability. These are torts where the claimant can recover compensation for loss or damage without having to prove fault or intention on the part of the defendant. Part I of the Consumer Protection Act 1987, for example, provides that a manufacturer is strictly liable for injuries caused by his defective products. The rule in *Rylands* v *Fletcher*, breach of statutory duty and conversion are further examples of torts imposing strict liability.

2 Vicarious liability. In certain situations one person may be held liable for the torts of another. This type of liability is known as vicarious liability. An employer, for example, is vicariously liable for the torts of his employees committed during the course of their employment. Vicarious liability may also arise between partners and between a principal and agent. There are various justifications for the principles of vicarious liability:

- liability is incurred by the person best able financially to meet any award of damages (usually because the risk is covered by insurance);
- the claimant is given an additional defendant to sue, who is more likely to be able to satisfy any judgment;
- harm may be prevented by imposing liability on the person in control of the activity;
- the claimant is provided with a defendant in cases where it is impossible to establish precisely who was responsible within a particular organisation for the wrongful conduct.

The vicarious liability of an employer for the acts of his employees will be studied in more detail in Chapter 16.

PROOF OF DAMAGE

The law in tort is concerned with providing a remedy for certain forms of wrongful conduct. In most torts, the claimant must prove that he has suffered some damage, e.g. personal injury or damage to his property, in order to establish liability. However, the fact that the claimant has suffered damage is not sufficient on its own to establish liability. The claimant must also prove that the damage was caused by the defendant's infringement of a right vested in the claimant which is recognised by the law. For example, the construction of an out-of-town shopping centre may result in a loss of trade for town centre shops, but since the law does not provide a right to protection from competition, affected shopkeepers will not have a remedy, no matter how severe their losses.

Although proof of damage is an essential component in most torts, some rights are regarded as so important that the law will provide a remedy even though the claimant has not suffered any damage. These torts are said to be 'actionable *per se*' (actionable in itself) and the most important examples are libel and trespass. Nominal damages can be recovered in respect of these torts even though no loss has occurred.

CAUSATION

Liability of tort is dependent on making a connection between the defendant's wrongful conduct and the damage suffered by the claimant. If the damage was caused by some other factor, the defendant will escape liability. The factual cause of the damage is established by applying the 'but for' test, i.e. would the damage have occurred 'but for' the defendant's tortious conduct? An example of the application of this test in the context of a claim in negligence is given below.

Barnett v Chelsea & Kensington Hospital Management Committee (1968)

Mr Barnett, a nightwatchman, attended the defendant's hospital in the early hours of the morning complaining of vomiting. The casualty doctor failed to examine him but instead sent a message that Mr Barnett should see his own GP in the morning if he was still unwell. Mr Barnett died five hours later from arsenic poisoning. The court held that, although the hospital doctor was negligent in failing to examine Mr Barnett, the failure to take reasonable care was not the cause of his death. The evidence was that, even if Mr Barnett had been examined, correctly diagnosed and treated, he would have died anyway.

Even if a claimant can establish a causal connection between the defendant's tortious conduct and the damage he has suffered using the 'but for' test, he cannot necessarily recover his loss. The damage may be too remote a consequence of the defendant's actions and, therefore, not the cause in law. The test for remoteness in tort derives from the decision of the Privy Council in a case known as the *Wagon Mound (No 1)* (1961).

Overseas Tankship (UK) Ltd v Morts Dock and Engineering Co Ltd (The Wagon Mound) (1961)

The defendants were the charterers of a ship called the *Wagon Mound*. As a result of the carelessness of the defendant's servants, a quantity of furnace oil was spilled in Sydney harbour. The oil was carried towards the claimant's wharf where welding operations were being carried out. After receiving expert advice that the oil would not ignite on water, welding continued. However, a few days later the oil ignited when hot metal fell on a piece of cotton waste floating in the oil. The resulting fire caused extensive damage to the claimant's wharf. The Judicial Committee of the Privy Council held that reasonable forseeabilty was the proper test of remoteness of damage in tort. The court would have awarded damages for oil damage to slipways had this been claimed since such damage was a reasonably foreseeable consequence of the defendant's negligence. However, it was not reasonably foreseeable that the oil would ignite in the circumstances which occurred and, therefore, damage caused by the fire was not recoverable.

Damage may be too remote if the chain of causation is broken by a new unforeseen act of a third person. Such an event is referred to as a ***novus actus interveniens*** – a new act intervening – and its effect is to relieve the defendant of the liability for the claimant's loss.

Cobb v Great Western Railway (1894)

The defendant railway had allowed a railway carriage to become overcrowded. The claimant was jostled and robbed of £89. The claimant sued the defendant to recover his loss. The court held the loss was too remote as the actions of the thief were a *novus actus interveniens*, which broke the chain of causation.

DEFENCES

There are several defences which are available generally to a defendant facing an action in tort. They are consent, contributory negligence, statutory or common law justification, necessity and illegality. Special defences which apply to particular torts will be considered in the context of the tort concerned.

Consent

Consent – or assumption of risk, as it is sometimes known – is a complete defence to an action in tort. Consent may arise either from an express agreement to run the risk of injury or may be implied from the claimant's conduct. An example of express agreement is where a patient signs a consent form before an operation. If this formality were not carried out, the surgeon could be sued for trespass to the person (battery). Implied consent is often referred to as ***volenti non fit injuria*** (no harm is done to one who is willing). Participants in a boxing match, for example, are deemed to have consented to the intentional infliction of harm which would otherwise amount to a trespass. The defence of consent was of greater importance in the 19th century when it was used by employers to defeat claims by their employees for injuries suffered during the course of employment caused by the employer's negligence. However, the significance of the defence in employment cases diminished greatly as a result of the decision of the House of Lords in *Smith* v *Baker & Sons* (1891). Their Lordships held that an employee who continued working despite knowing that he ran the risk of injury from stones falling from an overhead crane was not *volenti*. Consent cannot be inferred from knowledge of the risk: it must also be shown that the claimant freely and voluntarily accepted the risk. So, to establish the defence today, the defendant must prove that the claimant not only had full knowledge of the risk but also freely consented to run the risk.

Morris v Murray (1990)

The claimant and defendant had engaged in a prolonged drinking session before taking a flight in a light aircraft piloted by the defendant. The plane crashed, the defendant pilot was killed and the claimant was seriously injured. The Court of Appeal held that the claimant's action against the deceased pilot's estate was barred by *volenti*.

Conduct which might give rise to the defence of consent is also likely to involve contributory negligence (see further below). These days the courts are more likely to make a finding of contributory negligence which has the effect of apportioning fault between the parties, rather than consent which is a complete defence. The defence of consent is not normally available in what are known as 'rescue cases'. These are situations where a claimant is injured while attempting to rescue someone or something from a dangerous situation caused by the defendant's negligence. Provided that the claimant's actions are reasonable in the circumstances, the defences of consent and contributory negligence will not apply.

Haynes v Harwood (1935)

The claimant policeman was injured trying to stop runaway horses pulling a van along a crowded street. The defendant had left the horses and van alone and a boy had caused them to bolt. It was held that the claimant could recover damages for his injuries. The defences of *volenti* and contributory negligence (below) did not apply.

Contributory negligence

Before 1945 contributory negligence was a complete defence to liability in tort. However, the Law Reform (Contributory Negligence) Act 1945 modified this harsh rule by providing for apportionment of blame between the claimant and defendant. Section 1 (1) provides as follows:

Where any person suffers damage as the result partly of his own fault and partly of the fault of any other person or persons, a claim in respect of that damage shall not be defeated by reason of the fault of the person suffering the damage, but the damages recoverable in respect thereof shall be reduced to such an extent as the court thinks just and equitable having regard to the claimant's share in the responsibility for the damage.

The effect of the provision is that any award of damages may be reduced to the extent that the claimant was to blame for the injury or loss. For example, if the court assesses the claimant's loss as £100,000, but finds that he was 25 per cent to blame for what happened, his damages will be reduced by 25 per cent and he will receive £75,000 damages. Failure to wear a seat belt is contributory negligence and can result in a 25 per cent deduction if wearing the belt would have prevented the injury, and a 15 per cent deduction if the belt would have reduced the injury (*Froom* v *Butcher* (1975)).

Contributory negligence does not just apply to actions based in the tort of negligence. Section 4 of the 1945 Act defined 'fault' very broadly so as to include most forms of liability in tort. The only major torts for which the defence is not available are deceit and conversion.

Statutory or common law justification

A person may have a good defence to an action in tort if he can show that his acts are covered by statutory authority. The Police and Criminal Evidence Act 1984, for example, sets out police powers of arrest, entry and search. If these powers are exercised lawfully, the Act will provide a good defence to an action in tort. There may also be justification at common law for tortious acts. Self-defence and chastisement of a child by a parent are both defences to the tort of trespass to the person, provided that the force used is reasonable.

Necessity

If a person commits a tort but only in order to prevent a greater harm from occurring, he may be able to raise the defence of necessity. The defendant must be able to show that there is an imminent threat of danger to person or property and that his actions were a reasonable response to the circumstances. Necessity was successfully raised by prison officers who forcibly fed a suffragette who was on hunger strike (*Leigh* v *Gladstone* (1909)) and by an oil company facing an action for nuisance in respect of a discharge of oil from one of its ships into an estuary (*Esso Petroleum Co Ltd* v *Southport Corporation* (1955)).

Illegality

It is a general principle of law that a person will not be able to maintain a cause of action if he has to rely on conduct which is illegal or contrary to public policy. This principle is expressed in the Latin phrase of *ex turpi causa non oritur actio*. The following case is an example of how the defence of illegality applies in the law of tort.

Thackwell v *Barclays Bank* (1986)

Thackwell brought an action against the bank for conversion of a cheque to which he claimed to be entitled. The cheque represented the proceeds of fraud against a finance company in which Thackwell had been a party. The court held that Thackwell's claim was barred by illegality. It was contrary to public policy to allow him to enjoy the proceeds of his fraud.

REMEDIES

The remedies which are generally available in respect of tortious conduct are damages and an injunction. Damages consist of a payment of money by the defendant to the claimant. Tort damages are intended to be compensatory, i.e. the aim is to put the injured party in the position he would have been had he not sustained the wrong. In some situations the courts will award non-compensatory damages. Nominal damages, for example, will be awarded in respect of torts which are actionable *per se*, e.g. trespass to land, where the claimant cannot show that he has suffered any loss. Exemplary damages, which are designed to punish the defendant, are available only in certain special cases, e.g. where there is arbitrary, unconstitutional or oppressive action by government servants such as false imprisonment by the police.

An injunction is a discretionary order of the court requiring the person to cease committing a tort. There are different kinds of injunction. An interim injunction is a temporary order which can be granted pending a full trial of the action. A *quia timet* injunction may be ordered before any damage is done as a preventative measure. A prohibitory injunction will stop the defendant committing a tort, while a mandatory injunction requires the defendant to take positive steps to stop a tort being committed. If the defendant fails to obey the injunction, he will be in contempt of court and may be dealt with by way of fine or imprisonment.

LIMITATION OF ACTIONS

The right to bring legal action does not last indefinitely. The time limits within which action must be brought are covered by the Limitation Act 1980 and are as follows:

1 An action in tort must normally be brought within six years of the date when the cause of action accrued (s 2). The period of limitation normally runs from the date when the tort was committed or when the damage occurred.

2 An action in negligence, nuisance or breach of statutory duty for damages for personal injury must be brought within three years (s 11). The period of limitation runs from the date when the cause of the action accrued (i.e. the date of injury) or the date of the claimant's knowledge that the injury was significant and that it was attributable in whole or in part to the acts or omissions which are alleged to constitute the negligence, nuisance or breach of duty. These time limits may be extended as follows:

(a) where fraud, concealment or mistake is alleged, time does not run until the claimant has discovered the fraud, concealment or mistake or could with reasonable diligence have discovered it;

(b) if the claimant is under a disability, such as minority or mental capacity, the time limits do not start to operate until the disability is removed, i.e. in the case of a minor, on reaching the age of 18.

The Defamation Act 1996 reduced the limitation period for actions in defamation and malicious falsehood from three years to one year. The court can exercise its discretion to allow a later claim if this is reasonable.

SPECIFIC TORTS RELEVANT TO BUSINESS

Negligence

The tort of negligence is concerned with certain kinds of careless conduct which cause damage or loss to others. The foundations of the modern law of negligence were laid down in one of the best known cases in English law – *Donoghue v Stevenson* (1932).

Donoghue v Stevenson (1932)

Mrs Donoghue and a friend visited a café in Paisley run by Mr Minchella. The friend bought a bottle of ginger beer for Mrs Donoghue. Mr Minchella opened the bottle, which was made of dark opaque glass, and poured some of the ginger beer into a tumbler. Unsuspecting, Mrs Donoghue drank the contents, but when her friend refilled the tumbler, the remains of a decomposing snail floated out. Mrs Donoghue suffered shock and severe gastro-enteritis as a result. She could not sue Mr Minchella for compensation for her injuries because she had not bought the ginger beer herself. So she brought an action against the manufacturer of the ginger beer, Stevenson, arguing that he had been negligent. The House of Lords held that, provided Mrs Donoghue could prove her allegations, she would be entitled to succeed. We shall never know whether there was, in fact, a snail in the bottle because the case was settled out of court for £100.

In order to establish negligence a claimant must prove that:

1 the defendant owed him a legal duty of care;
2 the defendant was in breach of this duty; and
3 the claimant suffered injury or loss as a result of the breach.

All three elements are essential to a successful negligence claim. We shall consider each of the requirements in turn.

Duty of care

It is important to know in what circumstances one person will owe a duty of care to another. In *Donoghue* v *Stevenson* (1932), Lord Atkin formulated a general test for determining the existence of a duty of care which could be applied to most situations. His statement of general principle, which was to become known as the 'neighbour' principle, is as follows:

> You must take reasonable care to avoid acts or omissions which you can reasonably foresee would be likely to injure your neighbour. Who, then, in law, is my neighbour? The answer seems to be – persons who are so closely and directly affected by my act that I ought reasonably to have them in contemplation as being so affected when I am directing my mind to the acts or omissions which are called in question.

Lord Atkin's statement of the requirements for duty of care to exist involved two main elements: reasonable foresight and proximity. A duty of care would be imposed if the damage was reasonably foreseeable and the relationship between the parties was sufficiently close (proximate).

The flexible nature of the 'neighbour' principle enabled the courts to recognise the existence of a duty of care in a variety of fact situations unless there were policy reasons for excluding it. This approach culminated in Lord Wilberforce's now discredited two-stage test for establishing the existence of a duty of care which he propounded in *Anns* v *Merton London Borough Council* (1977). Stage one required courts to apply the neighbour principle by asking whether there was sufficient proximity between the parties that the harm suffered by the claimant was reasonably foreseeable. Stage two involved the courts in considering whether the duty should be restricted or limited for reasons of economic, social or public policy.

In recent years the courts have sought to place limits on the expansion of the duty of care to new situations by adopting a so-called 'incremental' approach. The three-stage approach to establishing a duty of care recommended in *Caparo Industries plc* v *Dickman* (1990) requires consideration of the following questions:

- Was the harm suffered reasonably foreseeable?
- Was there a relationship of proximity between the parties?
- Is it fair, just and reasonable in all the circumstances to impose a duty of care?

An example of the application of this approach is provided by the following case.

John Munroe (Acrylics) Ltd v London Fire Brigade & Civil Defence Authority and Others (1997)

Four fire engines were called out to a fire on wasteland. When they arrived, it appeared that the fire had been extinguished and, as there were no signs of fire, they left. Unfortunately, some of the debris was still smouldering. It later set alight and destroyed the claimant's premises, which were adjacent to the wasteland. The Court of Appeal held that a fire brigade is not under a duty to answer a call nor is it under a duty to take care when it is at the scene of a fire. There was not a sufficient proximity between a fire brigade and the owners of property for a duty of care to be imposed. It was not fair, just or reasonable to impose a personal duty of care to individual occupiers in addition to the statutory duty which was designed to benefit the public in general.

Comment. Although the courts have been reluctant to find that the emergency services, such as the fire brigade and coastguard, owe a duty of care to members of the public, in *Kent* v *Griffiths and Others* (1999) the Court of Appeal took the view that the ambulance service may owe a duty of care to individuals to provide a prompt service and to provide appropriate treatment during the journey to hospital.

Breach of duty

After establishing the existence of a duty of care, the claimant must show that this duty has been broken by the defendant. The test for deciding whether there has been a breach of duty is whether the defendant has failed to do what a reasonable person would have done or has done what a reasonable person would not have done. Whether the defendant's conduct amounts to a breach of duty depends on all the circumstances of the case. The court will consider a range of factors including:

- the likelihood that damage or injury will be incurred;
- the seriousness of any damage or injury;
- the cost and ease of taking precautions;
- the social need for the activity.

It is normally the responsibility of the claimant to show that the defendant did not act reasonably, i.e. the burden of proof lies with the claimant. If the claimant is unable to present appropriate evidence, his case will fail. However, there are some situations where the only or most likely explanation of an accident is that the defendant was negligent. If this is the case, the claimant may claim *res ipsa loquitur* – the facts speak for themselves. This has the effect of placing the burden of proof on the defendant who must show either how the accident occurred or that he has not been negligent. Two conditions must be satisfied for *res ipsa* to come into play:

(a) the event which caused the accident must have been within the defendant's control; and

(b) the accident must be of such a nature that it would not have occurred if proper care had been taken by the defendant.

Cassidy v *Ministry of Health* (1951)

The claimant went into hospital for treatment with two stiff fingers. When he left hospital he had four stiff fingers and a useless hand. The Court of Appeal held that the defendant hospital was liable for the injuries. *Res ipsa loquitur* could be applied to assist the claimant in establishing his case. Lord Denning took the view that the claimant was entitled to say: 'I went into hospital to be cured of two stiff fingers. I have come out with four stiff fingers and my hand is useless. That should not have happened if due care had been used. Explain it, if you can.'

Damage

Finally, the claimant must show he has suffered some damage, that it has been caused by the defendant's breach of duty and is not too remote a consequence of it. The kinds of damage which will give rise to an action in negligence are: death, personal injury, nervous shock, damage to property and, in limited circumstances, financial loss.

Defences

The defendant may raise a number of defences to an action in negligence. Consent, for example, is a complete defence and negates any liability. Contributory negligence is a partial defence and has the effect of reducing any award of damages.

We will now examine in more detail the potential business liability by considering the extent of liability in tort for defective goods and services.

DEFECTIVE GOODS

There are three circumstances when the person responsible for putting defective goods into circulation will incur liability in tort for his products. These are:

1 in the tort of negligence;

2 strict liability under Part I of the Consumer Protection Act 1987; and

3 for breach of statutory duty under Part II of the Consumer Protection Act 1987.

Negligence

A manufacturer may be liable to a consumer for loss and damage caused by his defective product under the tort of negligence.

A consumer must establish first of all that the manufacturer owed him a duty of care. In *Donoghue* v *Stevenson* the House of Lords established the principle that a manufacturer owes a duty of care to all persons who are likely to come into contact with his goods:

> ... [A] manufacturer of products which he sells in such a form as to show that he intends them to reach the ultimate consumer in the form in which they left him with no reasonable possibility of intermediate examination and with the knowledge that the absence of reasonable care in the preparation or putting up of the products will result in an injury to the consumer's life or property, owes a duty to the consumer to take that reasonable care.

There is no limit to the type of goods covered by the principle established in *Donoghue*: cases have involved goods as diverse as cars (*Herschtal* v *Stewart & Arden Ltd* (1940)), underpants (*Grant* v *Australian Knitting Mills* (1936)) and hair dyes (*Holmes* v *Ashford* (1950)). Since 1932, the pool of potential defendants has been extended from manufacturers to cover anyone who does some work on the goods, for example a repairer. The word 'consumer' has been given a wide interpretation to cover anyone who is likely to be injured by the lack of care.

Stennet v Hancock and Peters (1939)

Mrs Stennet was walking along a pavement when she was struck and injured by a piece of wheel which had come off a passing lorry. She received damages from the owner of the garage where the wheel had been negligently repaired shortly before the accident.

Probably the most difficult problem for a consumer to overcome is to establish a breach of the duty of care. This means that the consumer must be able to prove that the manufacturer failed to act reasonably in all the circumstances. In determining whether the defendant has acted reasonably the courts engage in a cost-benefit analysis in which they consider a number of factors. These include the likelihood and seriousness of injury or harm, the cost and ease of instituting precautions to eliminate or reduce the risk and the social need for the product. The following case is a good illustration of how the courts decide whether a manufacturer has exercised reasonable care.

Walton v British Leyland (UK) Ltd (1978)

The claimants were injured in a collision caused by a wheel coming off the Austin Allegro car they were travelling in at 60 mph on the M1. Although the accident happened in 1976, the manufacturer of the car, Leyland, had been aware since 1973 that there was a problem with wheels coming adrift on the Allegro. Leyland considered recalling all cars affected by the fault and even made an estimate of what it would cost (£300,000 in 1974). However, Leyland decided not to follow this course of action for commercial reasons. Instead it issued a product bulletin to all service managers of its accredited dealers advising them of a change in the method of adjusting the rear hub bearings. The court held that the failure to recall all Allegro cars was a breach of Leyland's duty to care for the safety of those put at risk by the fault, i.e. occupants of the Allegro and other road users.

Liability in negligence is fault-based and the onus of proving that the manufacturer was at fault is upon the consumer. This can be a very difficult task as usually the consumer has no means of knowing exactly what went wrong in the manufacturing

process. Sometimes, however, the only reasonable explanation for the defect is that someone acted negligently; buns do not usually have stones in the middle of them. In this kind of situation the consumer may be able to plead *res ipsa loquitur*, the facts speak for themselves. This has the effect of reversing the normal burden of proof; the manufacturer is presumed to have acted negligently unless he can prove that he took all reasonable care.

Steer v Durable Rubber Manufacturing Co Ltd (1958)

A girl aged six was scalded when her three-month-old hot water bottle burst. She could not prove exactly how the defect occurred, but she did establish that hot water bottles are expected to last three years. The Court of Appeal held that in the circumstances it was up to the manufacturer to show that it had not been negligent. Since the manufacturer could not do this, it was liable.

Finally, the consumer must be able to prove that he has suffered loss or damage as a result of the manufacturer's breach of duty. If the damage is caused by some other factor, the manufacturer will not be liable.

Evans v Triplex Safety Glass Co Ltd (1936)

The manufacturer of a car windscreen was not liable in negligence when the windscreen shattered causing injury and shock to the occupants of the car because there was a number of possible causes of the accident. The claimants were unable to prove that the disintegration of the windscreen had been caused by the glass manufacturer's failure to take reasonable care.

Even if the consumer can establish a causal link between the breach of duty and the damage, he cannot necessarily recover damages for all the consequences of the manufacturer's negligence. A manufacturer is only liable for loss and damage which is reasonably foreseeable. It is well established that a consumer can recover damages if the defective product causes personal injury or damage to property. However, the position is far from clear where the defect does not result in physical injury or damage to other property. Until fairly recently it was a settled point of law that a consumer could not recover damages for pure economic loss, unless:

(a) it was caused by a negligent misstatement (see *Hedley Byrne & Co Ltd v Heller and Partners Ltd*); or

(b) it was consequent upon foreseeable physical injury or damage to property.

So, if a product simply ceased to work because of a manufacturing defect, the consumer could not sue the manufacturer in negligence for the cost of repair or replacement. The decision of the House of Lords in the *Junior Books* case suggested that in limited circumstances it may be possible to recover damages for economic or financial loss.

Junior Books Ltd v Veitchi Co Ltd (1982)

Junior Books entered into a contract with a building firm for the construction of a new factory. Under this contract, the architects acting for Junior Books were entitled to nominate which subcontractor was to be employed by the building firm to lay the flooring. The architects nominated Veitchi. The floor proved defective and Junior Books brought an action in negligence against Veitchi. Even though there was no suggestion that the floor was dangerous, Junior Books claimed damages for the cost of re-laying the floor and the consequential financial loss that this would involve (i.e. the factory would have to be closed down to enable the floor to be replaced). The House of Lords held that Junior Books Ltd was entitled to recover damages from Veitchi. The relationship between the parties was so close that it gave rise to a duty to avoid careless work which would inevitably cause financial loss.

This decision raised expectations of a significant extension of the general principle laid down by Lord Atkin in *Donoghue v Stevenson* by imposing liability for pure economic loss. However, their Lordships stressed that their decision was based on the very close proximity between the parties which fell just short of a direct contractual relationship. A manufacturer does not normally have such a close relationship with the consumers of his products. Subsequent cases have demonstrated the limited application of *Junior Books*.

Muirhead v Industrial Tank Specialities Ltd (1985)

Muirhead, a wholesale fish merchant, wished to expand his lobster trade by buying lobsters cheaply in the summer, storing them in a tank and reselling them at Christmas when the prices are high. The scheme required sea water to be pumped continuously through the tank to oxygenate the water and thereby keep the lobsters alive. The tank and pumps were installed by ITS. The pumps were supplied to ITS by ITT. They were powered by electric motors made by a French company and supplied through its English subsidiary of Leroy Somer Electric Motors Ltd. Within a few days of installation, the pumps started to cut out and on one occasion Muirhead lost his entire stock of lobsters. The cause of the problem was that the motors were unsuitable for the English voltage system. Muirhead obtained judgment against ITS, but since it had gone into liquidation, the judgment was not satisfied. Muirhead, therefore, brought an action in negligence against ITT and Leroy Somer claiming compensation for the cost of the pumps, the cost of electrical engineers called out to deal with the pumps, the loss of lobsters and the loss of profit on intended sales of the lobsters. The Court of Appeal held that a manufacturer could be liable in negligence for economic loss suffered by a consumer if there was a very close relationship between the parties and the consumer had placed reliance on the manufacturer rather than on the retailer as was the case in *Junior Books*. However, there was no evidence in this case of such a close relationship or reliance. Therefore, Muirhead could not recover his economic loss, i.e. the loss of profit on the intended sales of lobsters (£127,375), although he could recover for loss of his lobster stock (£11,000) as this amounted to reasonably foreseeable physical damage.

Even if the consumer manages to overcome all the difficulties involved in proving negligence, the manufacturer may still be able to defeat the claim or secure a reduction in damages by showing that the accident was caused wholly or partly by the consumer's own negligence. The defence of contributory negligence may apply where, for example, the consumer has ignored operating instructions or continued to use a product knowing that it was defective. As we saw earlier, under the Law Reform (Contributory Negligence) Act 1945, contributory negligence on the part of the consumer has the effect of reducing the damages awarded to the extent that the claimant was to blame for the accident. For example, if a court assesses the claimant's damages at £10,000, but finds that he was 50 per cent to blame for what happened, his damages will be reduced by 50 per cent and he will receive £5,000.

Part I of the Consumer Protection Act 1987

The difficulties of bringing an action and establishing liability in negligence against a manufacturer led to a growing interest in the subject of 'product liability'. This American term is used to describe a system of strict liability for manufacturers in respect of injury or loss caused by their defective products.

The question of product liability was considered by no less than four bodies in the 1970s: the Law Commission, the Council of Europe, the Royal Commission on Civil Liability (chaired by Lord Pearson) and the EC. In every single case, the recommendations of these bodies involved imposing strict liability on the manufacturer of defective products. In 1985 the EC Council of Ministers adopted a directive on product liability and, consequently, the British government was committed to implementing changes to UK law within three years. Part I of the Consumer Protection Act 1987 (CPA) implements the EC Directive.

Liability under Part I of the CPA

Part I of the CPA, which came into force on 1 March 1988, introduces a regime of strict liability for personal injury and damage to property caused by defective products. This means that a producer will be liable for harm caused by his products unless he can establish one of the defences provided by the CPA. It is no longer necessary for a claimant to prove negligence. Nevertheless, to establish liability under the CPA the claimant must prove that:

1 he has suffered damage;
2 the product was defective; and
3 the damage was caused by the defective product.

A 'producer' is defined in s 1(2) as:

(a) the manufacturer of a product;
(b) in the case of a substance which has been won or abstracted, the person who won or abstracted it, e.g. a mining company producing iron ore; and
(c) in the case of a product neither manufactured nor won or abstracted, but essential characteristics of which are attributable to an industrial or other process having been carried out, the person who carried out that process, e.g. the producer of canned vegetables.

Section 2 identifies those who are liable for injury or damage arising from a defective product. They are:

1 the producer of the product (as defined in s 1(2));
2 any person who by putting his name on the product or using a trade mark or other distinguishing mark in relation to the product has held himself out to be the producer of the product, e.g. 'ownbranders' who market goods under their own label, even though manufactured by someone else;
3 any person who imports the product into the EC in the course of a business; and
4 where the producer cannot be identified within a reasonable time, any person who supplied the product, e.g. retailers or wholesalers who cannot identify the manufacturer of the product.

The net of strict liability under the CPA is cast fairly widely over the chain of supply with the objective of ensuring that an injured consumer will have someone in the EC against whom he can bring an action. However, there are some groups of people involved in the supply of products who are not specifically caught in the net. They include designers, retailers, repairers and installers. (These people will be liable, however, if they also fall into one of the categories of persons liable set out in points 1–4 above, i.e. a designer may be liable as a producer.)

'Product' is defined by s 1(2) as any goods or electricity. The definition covers not just finished goods but also components and raw materials. Game and agricultural produce which had not undergone an industrial process were specifically excluded from the scope of the CPA, as originally enacted. The CPA did not define what was meant by an industrial process, and this had given rise to some uncertainty. It was not clear, for example, whether spraying crops amounted to an industrial process. In 1999 the EC adopted an amending Directive extending the scope of product liability to primary agricultural products and game. The UK implemented the amendment with effect from 4 December 2000.

Defect (s 3)

Section 3(1) provides that there is a defect in a product if the safety of the product is not such as persons are generally entitled to expect. Section 3(2) specifies a number of factors which should be taken into account when deciding what persons are entitled to expect. They include:

(a) the manner and purposes for which the product has been marketed;
(b) the use of any mark, instruction or warning;
(c) what might reasonably be expected to be done with the product; and
(d) the time when the product was supplied by the producer to another.

In a recent case the High Court held that the defendant, National Blood Authority (NBA), was liable to the recipients of blood infected with the Hepatitis C virus as a result of blood transfusions which took place after March 1988. Hepatitis C was identified in 1988 but the NBA did not introduce screening tests until September 1991. Blood and blood products contaminated with the virus were 'defective products' under Art. 6 of the Product Liability Directive and s 3 of the CPA, and the NBA, as a producer of the product, was liable to the recipients of the infected blood (*A & Others* v *National Blood Authority & Others* (2001)).

Damage (s 5)

The damage for which compensation is recoverable under the CPA is defined as death, personal injury or damage to any property (including land). The right of recovery in respect of property damage is restricted. There is no liability for damage to the product itself or to any product in which it was comprised. No claim can be brought for property damage if the amount claimed is less than £275. Furthermore, a claim for damage to property can only be made in respect of property ordinarily intended for private use, occupation or consumption and intended by the claimant mainly for his own private use, occupation or consumption.

Defences (s 4)

The following defences are available to an action under the CPA:

1 *The defect is attributable to compliance with UK legislation or EC obligations.* The defence does not extend to compliance with, for example, British standards.

2 *The person proceeded against did not at any time supply the product to another,* e.g. where the product is an experimental prototype which is stolen by a rival.

3 *The product was not supplied in the course of a business or for profit,* e.g. a home-made product given as a Christmas present.

4 *The defect did not exist in the product at the relevant time.*

5 *The state of scientific and technical knowledge at the relevant time was not such that a producer of products of the same description as the product in question might be expected to have discovered the defect if it had existed in his products while they were under his control.* This is the controversial 'development risks' defence. Under the EC Directive the adoption of such a defence was optional. The British government justified inclusion of the defence on the ground that to impose liability would stifle innovation and make British industry less competitive. Opponents of the defence argue that it seriously weakens the principle of strict liability, so that the victims of another Thalidomide-type disaster would still have great difficulty establishing liability. Doubts about whether the defence, as it is worded in the CPA, complied with the requirements of the EC Directive were resolved in 1997 when the European Court of Justice dismissed an application by the European Commission that the UK had failed to properly implement the provisions of the Directive in relation to this defence (*Commission of the European Communities* v *UK* (1997).

6 *In the case of a component or raw material, it was comprised in another product and the defect is wholly attributable to the design of the other product or to compliance with instructions given by the producer of the other product.*

In addition to the defences provided by s 4, the person proceeded against can raise contributory negligence on the part of the injured party with a view to reducing any award of damages (s 6(4)).

Exclusion or limitation of liability (s 7)

Section 7 provides that liability under the CPA cannot be limited or excluded by any contract term, notice or any other provision.

Limitation of actions (Sch 1)

Schedule 1 of the CPA adds a new s 11A to the Limitation Act 1980. Actions in respect of personal injury and loss or damage to property must be brought within three years from the date of the cause of action accruing or the date of the claimant having knowledge of the cause of action or of any previous owner having such knowledge. The three-year limit may be extended in the case of legal disability, fraud, concealment or mistake. All claims are subject to a maximum limitation period of ten years from the date of supply. A person injured nine years after a product was supplied must bring an action before the expiration of ten years and cannot claim three years from the date of injury. The ten-year time limit operates as an absolute bar to proceedings.

Breach of statutory duty

The legal framework of protection for the public from the hazards of unsafe goods is contained in the General Product Safety Regulations 1994 and Part II of the CPA (see Chapter 12). This aim is achieved in the following ways:

1 creation of a **criminal offence** of supplying consumer goods which fail to comply with the general safety requirement;

2 empowering the Secretary of State to make **safety regulations** in respect of specific types of goods (failure to comply with the regulations is a criminal offence);

3 enabling the Secretary of State to take action in respect of unsafe goods already on the market by issuing **prohibition notices, notices to warn** and **suspension notices** (it is a criminal offence to contravene these instructions);

4 providing a **civil remedy** for an individual consumer who has suffered loss or damage as a result of a trader's failure to comply with safety regulations. For example, a child who is injured by a toy which contravenes the safety regulations will be able to sue the manufacturer for **breach of statutory duty**. There are two advantages to this kind of action: the child can claim compensation even if he received the toy as a gift, and he does not have to prove that the manufacturer acted negligently.

The criminal liability imposed by the General Product Safety Regulations 1994 will be examined in more detail in the next chapter.

DEFECTIVE SERVICES – GENERALLY

The law of negligence has an important application to the provision of services. It opens up a remedy to those who are strangers to the contract for services but nevertheless have suffered a loss as a result of the contractor's negligence. Thus, the principle established in *Donoghue* v *Stevenson* (1932) applies not just to manufacturers but also to repairers who carry out their work carelessly. If a person is contracted to maintain and repair a lift, for example, he owes a legal duty, quite separate from his contractual obligations, to those using the lift to exercise reasonable care in his work.

Liability for physical injury or damage caused by a negligent act is well established. But what is the position of a person whose job involves giving professional advice? Clearly, he owes a duty to the person who has engaged his services, but does it extend to others who may have acted on his statements? In the last 30 years or so, the courts have developed the *Donoghue* v *Stevenson* principle to encompass negligent statements which cause financial loss. Professional groups, such as solicitors, accountants, bankers and surveyors, have felt the full impact of the change in judicial attitudes in this area of negligence liability. In this section, we will consider the fast developing area of law referred to as professional negligence. Prior to 1963, it was generally accepted that in the absence of fraud, liability for making careless statements which caused financial loss depended on the existence of a contractual or fiduciary relationship between the parties. If the statement was made fraudulently, the injured party could recover damages for the tort of deceit. This view of the limited scope of a professional person's liability for careless statements is illustrated by the following case.

Candler v *Crane, Christmas & Co* (1951)

The defendants, a firm of accountants, prepared a company's balance sheet and accounts, knowing that they were going to be used by the managing director to persuade the claimant, Candler, to invest money in the company. Relying on the accounts, the claimant invested £2,000, which he lost when the company was wound up a year later. The claimant sued the defendants in negligence, alleging that the accounts had been prepared carelessly and did not accurately represent the true state of the company's affairs. The Court of Appeal held (Denning LJ dissenting) that the defendants were not liable to the claimant because, in the absence of any contractual or fiduciary relationship, they did not owe him a duty of care. In a powerful dissenting judgment, Denning

LJ argued that the defendants did owe the claimant a duty of care. In his opinion, 'Accountants owe a duty of care not only to their own clients but also to all those whom they know will rely on their accounts in the transactions for which those accounts are prepared.' The duty of care arose from the close relationship between the parties and it followed, therefore, that no duty would be owed to complete strangers. Denning LJ had to wait 12 years for his arguments to be accepted.

The new judicial approach to negligent statements was heralded in a case involving bankers' references.

Hedley Byrne & Co Ltd v *Heller and Partners Ltd* (1963)

Hedley Byrne was a firm of advertising agents and Easipower Ltd was one of its clients. Before placing advertising contracts on behalf of Easipower in circumstances which involved giving credit, Hedley Byrne instituted enquiries about Easipower's creditworthiness. Hedley Byrne asked its own bank, the National Provincial Bank Ltd, to obtain a reference from Easipower's bankers, Heller and Partners. Heller's reference, which was headed 'without responsibility on the part of the bank or its officials', stated that Easipower was 'a respectably constituted company considered good for its ordinary business engagements'. Relying on this satisfactory reply, Hedley Byrne executed advertising contracts for Easipower, but lost £17,000 when Easipower went into liquidation. Hedley Byrne sued Heller for the amount of the financial loss suffered as a result of the negligent preparation of the banker's reference. The House of Lords held that Heller and Partners were protected by the disclaimer of liability. Their Lordships then considered (*obiter dicta*) what the legal position would have been if the disclaimer had not been used. They all agreed that there could be liability for negligent misstatement causing financial loss, even in the absence of a contractual or fiduciary relationship (the decision in *Candler* v *Crane, Christmas & Co* was disapproved and the dissenting judgment of Denning LJ approved).

Comment. The disclaimer which so successfully protected Heller from liability would now be subject to the test of reasonableness set out in s 2(2) of the Unfair Contract Terms Act 1977. It is unlikely that such a disclaimer could be justified as reasonable.

In the *Hedley Byrne* case, their Lordships recognised a new type of liability: they indicated that damages could be received for careless statements. However, they were careful to avoid unleashing a Pandora's box of litigation. They ruled that the existence of a duty of care in respect of negligent misstatements was dependent on a 'special relationship' between the parties. Lord Morris described the relationship in the following terms:

> If someone possessed of a special skill undertakes, quite irrespective of contract, to apply that skill for the assistance of another person who relies on such skill, a duty of care will arise. Furthermore, if, in a sphere in which a person is so placed that others could reasonably rely on his judgement or his skill, or on his ability to make careful inquiry, a person takes it on himself to give information or advice to, or allows his information or advice to be passed on to, another person who, as he knows or should know, will place reliance on it, then a duty of care will arise.

Their Lordships made it clear that a duty of care in respect of a negligent statement would only be owed to persons who the maker of the statement knows will rely on it and the use to which it will be put (knowledge test). The duty of care would not extend to those who the maker of the statement might foresee would rely on the statement (foresight test). Although the *Hedley Byrne* case involved a banker, it is clear that the rule applies equally to the advice given by other professionals. We shall examine how the *Hedley Byrne* rule has been developed in relation to three particular professional groups: lawyers, accountants and valuers.

LAWYERS

The liability of a legal adviser used to depend on the nature of the work he was engaged on. The decision of the House of Lords in *Rondel* v *Worsley* (1967) established that a barrister owed no duty of care to clients for whom he acted as advocate. In *Saif Ali* v *Sydney Mitchell & Co* (1978) the House extended the immunity from legal action to protect solicitors acting as advocates, but limited it so as only to protect pre-trial work closely associated with the conduct of a trial. When it came to work outside of court, however, both branches of the legal profession could be held accountable in the tort of negligence. However, in

Arthur Hall and Co v *Simons* (2000) the House of Lords decided that the immunity from liability for the negligent conduct of a case in court, as set out in *Rondel* v *Worsley* and explained in *Saif Ali* v *Sydney Mitchell & Co*, could no longer be justified. The immunity has now been removed in respect of both civil and criminal proceedings.

The duties owed by a solicitor to third parties are illustrated by the following cases.

Ross v Caunters (1979)

Mrs Ross was an intended beneficiary under a will drawn up on the testator's behalf by Caunters, a firm of solicitors. Caunters failed to advise the testator that attestation by a beneficiary or a beneficiary's spouse invalidates the gift. Mr Ross witnessed the will, and when the testator died the legacy to Mrs Ross was declared invalid. The court held that a solicitor owes a duty of care not just to his client, in this case the testator, but also to third parties, such as Mrs Ross, who were intended to be benefited by his work. Mrs Ross succeeded in her action.

White v Jones (1995)

A father quarrelled with his two daughters and cut them out of his will. A few months later the father changed his mind and instructed his solicitor to change his will and to give each of the daughters £9,000. The father died two months later before the solicitor had completed the changes to the will. The daughters did not receive the intended legacy because of their solicitor's delay in carrying out their father's instructions. The daughters succeeded in their action against the solicitor, even though they had not relied on the solicitor's skill. Lord Goff in the House of Lords took the view that a duty of care should be owed to beneficiaries under a will for reasons of 'practical justice'. 'If such a duty is not recognised, the only persons who might have a valid claim (i.e. the testator and his estate) have suffered no loss, and the only person who has suffered a loss (i.e. the disappointed beneficiary) has no claim.'

ACCOUNTANTS AND AUDITORS

The extent of an accountant's liability to non-clients was the subject of Lord Denning's influential judgment in *Candler* v *Crane, Christmas & Co* (1951). He expressed the opinion that a duty of care was owed only to third parties of whom they had knowledge; it did not extend to strangers. This view is echoed in the 'special relationship' restriction on liability laid down in the *Hedley Byrne* case. But in a subsequent case involving accountants, Woolf J broadened the scope of liability to include persons of whom the accountants had no prior knowledge.

JEB Fasteners Ltd v Marks, Bloom & Co (1983)

The defendants, a firm of accountants, prepared the accounts of a client company called JEB Fasteners. The audit report inflated the value of the company's stock and, as a result, a misleading picture of the company's financial health was given. The accounts were shown to the claimants who later took over the company. The claimants sued the defendants to recover the money they had spent in keeping the ailing company afloat. Woolf J found that the claimants had taken over the company in order to secure the services of its directors. They would have bought the company even if they had been aware of its true financial position. The defendants were not liable because their negligence was not the cause of the claimants' loss.

Comment. This case is significant because the judge accepted that an accountant could owe a duty of care to a person of whom he had no actual knowledge but where it was reasonably foreseeable that such a person would see the accounts and rely on them. The Court of Appeal upheld Woolf J's decision that the defendants were not liable because of the lack of a causal connection between the defendants' alleged carelessness and the claimants' loss. It was, therefore, unnecessary to consider Woolf J's views on the scope of an accountant's liability when auditing company accounts.

More recently, the courts have retreated from the foresight test advocated by Woolf J in *JEB Fasteners* and reaffirmed the requirement of knowledge of the user of the statement and the purpose to which it will be put to establish liability.

Caparo Industries plc v Dickman (1990)

Caparo, which already held shares in Fidelity plc, acquired more shares in the company and later made a takeover bid on the strength of accounts prepared by the defendant auditors. Caparo alleged that the accounts were inaccurate in that they showed a pre-tax profit of £1.3 million when there had been a loss of £400,000. Caparo claimed that if they had known the true situation, they would not have made a bid at the price they did, and may not have made a bid at all. They argued that they were owed a duty of care as new investors and as existing shareholders, who in reliance on the accounts had bought more shares. The House of Lords held that no duty was owed by auditors to members of the public in general who might invest in a company in reliance on published accounts. Although it was foreseeable that the accounts might be used by members of the public contemplating investing in the company, foreseeability alone was not sufficient to create liability. If it were otherwise, auditors might face almost unlimited liability. The purpose of preparing audited accounts under the Companies Act 1985 is to provide shareholders with certain information so that they can exercise their rights in respect of the company, i.e. voting at company meetings. The auditors did not owe a duty of care to individual shareholders, such as Caparo (which used the information for a quite different purpose), but to shareholders as a body. The auditors were, therefore, not liable.

Comment. This judgment confirms that liability for a negligent statement causing economic loss is based on knowledge of the persons relying on the statement and the likely purpose to which it will be put. If during a contested takeover bid the directors and financial advisers of a victim company make express statements to an identifiable bidder intending them to be relied upon, there will be sufficient proximity to establish a duty of care (*Morgan Crucible Co plc* v *Hill Samuel Bank Ltd* (1991)).

The law relating to the duty of care owed by professionals, such as accountants and auditors, is still being developed. The following cases are examples of how the extent of liability is being tested.

Coulthard v Neville Russell (1997)

A firm of accountants sought to have a statement of claim in negligence against them struck out. It was alleged that they had failed to advise the directors of a company that a transaction that they intended to carry out might be in breach of the financial assistance provisions of the Companies Act 1985. The Court of Appeal refused to strike out the claim as there was an arguable case. The courts may be prepared to extend liability to omissions as well as positive statements.

Yorkshire Enterprise Ltd v Robson Rhodes (1998)

The claimants, who were providers of venture capital, invested £250,000 in a shopfitting company, which 18 months later went into liquidation. The claimants, having lost most of their investment, brought an action for damages against the shopfitters' auditors, claiming that they had relied on negligent misstatements contained in the audited accounts and in letters sent to the claimants. The main problem with the accounts was that the provi-

sion for bad debts was inadequate with the result that the shopfitting company appeared to be profitable when, in fact, it was not. The High Court held that the defendant auditors were liable. They were aware of the claimants as potential investors and the use to which the accounts would be put. The claimants were not contributory negligent in relying on the information contained in the accounts and subsequent letters, without instituting their own enquiries. They were entitled to take the information they received at face value.

VALUERS AND SURVEYORS

The scope of liability for negligent statements by valuers and surveyors was considered in the following cases.

Yianni v Edwin Evans & Sons (1981)

The claimants agreed to buy a house for £15,000 with the aid of a £12,000 mortgage from the Halifax Building Society. The building society instructed the defendants, a firm of surveyors and valuers, to value the house for them. Although the claimants had to pay for the valuation, the contract was actually between the building society and the valuers. The building society made it clear that it did not accept responsibility for the valuers' report and that prospective purchasers were advised to have an independent survey carried out. The defendants' valuation report indicated that the house was satisfactory security for a £12,000 mortgage. After the claimants had purchased the property, they discovered structural defects which would cost £18,000 to put right. The claimants successfully sued the defendants in negligence. Despite the standard building society warning, only 10–15 per cent of purchasers have independent surveys carried out. It was reasonable, therefore, that the defendants should have the claimants in contemplation as persons who were likely to rely on their valuation. The relationship between the parties gave rise to a duty of care. Accordingly, the valuers were held liable.

Smith v Eric S Bush and Harris v Wyre Forest District Council (1989)

In a twin appeal, the House of Lords had to consider the scope of valuers' and surveyors' liability for negligence and the effectiveness of any disclaimer of liability. The facts of the two cases were similar. The details of the Harris case are as follows. The claimants, Mr and Mrs Harris, were a young couple buying their first house. They applied to the council for a mortgage. They filled in an application and paid £22 for a valuation to be carried out.

The application form contained a disclaimer which stated that the valuation was confidential and intended solely for the benefit of the council and no responsibility was accepted for the value and condition of the house. Applicants were advised to obtain their own survey. The council instructed its own in-house surveyor to inspect the property. He valued the house at the asking price and recommended a mortgage, subject to minor conditions. When the claimants tried to sell the house three years later, they discovered that it was subject to settlement and, as a result, the property was unsaleable. The House of Lords found in favour of the claimants and awarded them £12,000. Their Lordships held that a valuer owes a duty to purchasers to exercise reasonable care in carrying out a valuation. Furthermore, the disclaimer contained in the application form was ineffective under the Unfair Contract Terms Act 1977 since it did not satisfy the requirement of reasonableness. It was not fair and reasonable for valuers to impose on purchasers the risk of loss arising as a result of their incompetence or carelessness for the following reasons:

1 the parties were not of equal bargaining strength (the disclaimer was imposed on the claimants and they had no real power to object):

2 it was not reasonably practicable for the claimants to have obtained their own survey report (they were first-time buyers who could not easily afford to pay twice for the same service);

3 the task undertaken by the surveyor was not particularly difficult and it was not unreasonable to expect a valuer to take responsibility for the fairly elementary degree of skill and care involved; and

4 surveyors will carry insurance. If they are denied the opportunity of excluding their liability insurance premiums will rise and the increased costs passed on to house purchasers in higher fees. It was fairer that the risk be distributed among all house purchasers by a modest increase in fees rather than the whole risk falling on one unlucky purchaser.

OTHER TORTS RELEVANT TO BUSINESS

Trespass

The tort of trespass is one of the oldest torts. It takes three forms: trespass to the person, trespass to land and trespass to goods. Trespass to the person comprises three separate actions: battery, assault and false imprisonment. Battery is a direct and intentional application of force against the person. The slightest touch can amount to a battery. Assault involves putting a person in fear of a battery. Examples include swinging a punch, even if it doesn't connect, or pointing a gun at somebody. False imprisonment consists of unlawfully restraining a person from going wherever he wants, e.g. unlawful detention by a store detective who mistakenly believes that a customer has been shoplifting. Trespass to land can be defined as unlawful interference with the possession of someone's land. Straying off a footpath is an example of trespass to land. Trespass to goods is the wrongful interference with a person's possession of goods. This tort may be committed by destroying another's goods, stealing or simply moving them from one place to another.

Conversion

The tort of conversion involves doing some act in relation to another's goods which is inconsistent with the other's right to the goods. The wrongful act must constitute a challenge to, or a denial of, the claimant's title to the goods. Examples of conversion include stealing goods and reselling them, wrongfully refusing to return goods or destroying them. Conversion is one aspect of the tort of trespass to goods: both are examples of wrongful interference with goods which is now subject to legislation in the shape of the Torts (Interference with Goods) Act 1977.

Nuisance

There are two kinds of nuisance: public and private. Public nuisance (an act or omission which causes discomfort or inconvenience to a class of Her Majesty's subjects) is essentially a crime. However, individuals who have been particularly affected by the nuisance may bring an action in tort. Polluting a river could amount to a public nuisance. Private nuisance consists of unreasonable interference with a person's use or enjoyment of land. The following requirements must be present to establish liability for a private nuisance:

(a) an indirect interference with the use of enjoyment of land, e.g. by smoke, smells, noise;

(b) either physical damage to land or interference with the land causing loss of enjoyment or discomfort; and

(c) interference which is unreasonable.

In order to determine the question of unreasonableness, the court will consider both the conduct of the defendant and the effect of that conduct on the claimant. Factors which may be considered include:

- *The character of the locality in which the interference occurs.* In the words of Thesinger LJ in *Sturges* v *Bridgman* (1879): 'What would be a nuisance in Belgrave Square would not necessarily be so in Bermondsey.'
- *The duration of the interference.* A single occurrence will not normally amount to a nuisance; a certain degree of continuity is required. However, if the interference is of only a short duration, it is less likely to constitute a nuisance.
- *Malice on the part of the defendant.* Although malice is not an essential ingredient of nuisance, it may be relevant to ascertaining whether the defendant's conduct was reasonable.

A person who is in occupation of land may sue in nuisance the creator of the nuisance, the occupier of the land from which the nuisance came or, in limited circumstances, the landlord of the person in occupation. The following defences are available to the defendant:

(a) consent to the nuisance, but consent will not be implied because the claimant came to the nuisance;

(b) prescription, e.g. carrying out the acts complained of for 20 years;

(c) statutory authority.

A successful claimant is entitled to compensation for damage caused by the nuisance, e.g. physical damage to land or loss in value of the property. It is also usual for a claimant to seek an injunction to prevent any continuance of the nuisance. The following case provides an illustration of how the law of nuisance tries to reconcile conflicting interests over the use of land.

Kennaway v *Thompson* (1980)

In 1972 the claimant had a house built on land next to a lake which she knew was used for power-boat racing and waterskiing. Not long after the claimant moved into her house, the club became an international centre for power-boat racing and, as a result, there was an increase in the number of days on which racing took place and larger and

much noisier boats took part. The claimant sought damages for the nuisance and an injunction. The trial judge found that the interference with the claimant's enjoyment of her land had gone beyond what was reasonable and awarded damages. However, he refused to grant an injunction on the ground that it was in the public interest to allow the club to continue to provide sports facilities. The Court of Appeal allowed the claimant's appeal against the refusal to grant an injunction. An injunction was granted restricting the number of occasions on which the club could hold noisy power-boat race meetings.

Bringing a civil action in the tort of nuisance is a cumbersome and very expensive way of protecting people's enjoyment of their property from pollutants such as noise. The law of statutory nuisance contained in the Environmental Protection Act 1990 and the Noise and Statutory Nuisance Act 1993 provides an alternative avenue for redress in respect of activities which are either prejudicial to health or a nuisance, e.g. smoke, fumes, dust, smells and noise. Local authority environmental health officers have the power to serve abatement notices requiring the person responsible for a statutory nuisance to abate, prohibit or restrict its occurrence or recurrence. Failure to comply with such a notice is a criminal offence and could lead to a fine, in the case of an offence on industrial, trade or business premises, not exceeding £20,000. It should be noted that the Environmental Protection Act 1990 also enables a private individual who is aggrieved by a statutory nuisance to initiate proceedings in a magistrates' court to obtain a court order to abate the nuisance.

Rule in *Rylands* v *Fletcher*

The rule in *Rylands* v *Fletcher* is an example of a tort of strict liability. The rule derives from the case of *Rylands* v *Fletcher*, which was decided by the House of Lords in 1868.

Rylands v *Fletcher* (1868)

A mill owner engaged competent contractors to construct a reservoir on his land to provide water for his mill. In the course of their work, the contractors came across disused mine shafts which appeared to be blocked by earth. These old mine workings, in fact, communicated with a neighbour's coal mine. So, when the reservoir was filled up, the water escaped and flooded the coal mine. The House of Lords held that the mill owner was liable for the damage caused to his neighbour's mine, even though he had not been negligent. Blackburn J, who heard the case in the Court of Exchequer Chamber, stated the rule in the following terms: '... the person who for his own purposes brings on his land and collects and keeps there anything likely to do mischief if it escapes, must keep it at his peril, and if he does not do so, is *prima facie* answerable for all the damage which is a natural consequence of its escape.' Lord Cairns added in the House of Lords that the defendant must be making a non-natural use of his land.

The rule has been applied to the escape of such things as fire, electricity, gas and vibrations. The rule was more recently considered by the House of Lords in the following case.

Cambridge Water Co Ltd v *Eastern Counties Leather plc* (1994)

The defendants used a solvent in their tanning business. The solvent escaped from containers and seeped into the ground beneath the works. The solvent eventually percolated into the water supply, polluting the claimant's borehole. The claimants were forced to abandon the borehole and develop new water supplies. Their claim for compensation under the rule in *Rylands* v *Fletcher* failed in the House of Lords on the ground that the defendants could not reasonably have foreseen that the spillage of solvent over time would contaminate the water supply. Their Lordships held that foreseeability was an essential requirement of liability under the rule in *Rylands* v *Fletcher*. Although this requirement limits the availability of a claim under the rule of *Rylands* v *Fletcher*, Lord Goff possibly expanded the scope of the rule when he stated that the storage of chemicals was a classic example of a non-natural use of land.

Defamation

Defamation is the publication of a false statement which damages a person's reputation and tends to lower him in the estimation of right-thinking members of society or tends to make them shun or avoid that person. It takes two forms: libel and slander. **Libel** is defamation in a permanent form, such as writing, pictures, a film or a play. **Slander** is defamation in a transitory form, for example speech or gestures. Examples of defamation include a bank mistakenly 'bouncing' a customer's cheque for lack of funds, when there is plenty of money in the account, or an employer writing a damaging character reference for an employee. An important difference between libel and slander is that in the case of libel the claimant does not have to prove that he suffered damage, i.e. libel is actionable *per se*. In contrast, most slanders are only actionable on proof of damage. The exceptional situations where slander is actionable *per se* are an imputation that the claimant is guilty of a criminal offence for which he could be sent to prison; an imputation of unchastity made against any woman or girl; an imputation that the claimant has an infectious or contagious disease so that people would avoid him; and any words that suggest that the claimant is unfit to carry on his trade, business or profession. In order to establish a case in defamation, the claimant must establish the following requirements in relation to the statement:

(a) it must be false;
(b) the statement must be defamatory in the sense that it lowers the claimant's reputation;
(c) it must refer to the claimant;
(d) it must be published, i.e. it must be communicated to someone other than the claimant.

The law tries to strike a balance between the right of an individual to protect his reputation and society's interest in freedom of speech by providing a number of defences to an action in defamation.

1 Justification or truth. A person cannot complain about a true statement, since the effect is to reduce an inflated reputation to its proper level.

2 Fair comment on a matter of public interest. Those who place themselves in the public eye must expect honest criticism of what they do. The defence is not available where the defendant acted out of malice or spite.

3 Privilege. Statements made on some occasions, for example in Parliament or in court, are absolutely privileged and the person whose reputation has been injured is deprived of legal redress. Some statements attract qualified privilege – for example job references. This means that the defence is only available to the extent that the defendant acted honestly and without malice.

4 Unintentional defamation under the Defamation Act 1996. The publisher of an innocent defamation may escape liability by making an offer of amends (the publication of a correction and apology), with damages assessed by a judge.

A successful claimant may be awarded damages or granted an injunction. Defamation is one of the few areas of the civil law where juries are still commonly used. There has been considerable criticism in recent years of high awards made by juries in defamation cases, especially when compared with awards in personal injury cases. Under the Courts and Legal Services Act 1990, the Court of Appeal may now substitute its own award for that of a jury award which it deems inadequate or excessive. The Defamation Act 1996 provides for a new summary procedure for defamation cases, with judges assessing the damages rather than a jury.

An injunction may be granted, in addition to an award of damages, to prevent either initial or further publication of the defamatory material.

Injurious or malicious falsehood is a separate tort which is related to defamation. It consists of maliciously making a false statement about a person or his property, which is calculated to cause damage, and damage is suffered as a result (see further, Chapter 15).

Economic torts

The term 'economic torts' is often used to describe a number of torts which seek to protect business interests. Some of these torts are considered in outline below.

Inducement of breach of contract

This tort consists of one person (A) inducing another (B) to break his contract with a third person (C). C can sue B for breach of contract, but he can also sue A in tort.

Lumley v *Gye* (1853)
Gye persuaded a singer to break her exclusive contract to sing at Lumley's theatre and to sing for him instead. It was held that Lumley was entitled to sue Gye in tort for inducing a breach of the singer's contract.

A modern example of the tort is where trade union officials instruct their members to take industrial action. If the union officials act within limits contained in recent legislation, e.g. holding a secret postal ballot of its members, any liability in tort will be covered by a statutory immunity.

Conspiracy

This tort consists of an agreement between two or more persons to do an act which is intended to injure another person and does result in damage. There are two forms of tortious conspiracy: conspiracy where the means used are lawful, and agreements where the means used are unlawful.

1 **Conspiracy using lawful means.** It is not necessary to show that the conspirators used lawful means; the tort encompasses conduct which would be perfectly lawful if committed by an individual acting alone. However, the claimant must be able to prove that the conspirators intended to injure him. If the conspirators intended to further or protect their own interests, there can be no liability.

Crofter Hand Woven Harris Tweed Co Ltd v *Veitch* (1942)
The defendants, officials of the Transport and General Workers Union, imposed a ban on cheap imports of yarn on to the island of Lewis by the claimant company and any subsequent export of Harris tweed made from the yarn. The union's instructions were carried out by docker members of the union without any breach of contract on their part, so the claimant company sued instead for conspiracy. The House of Lords held that, as the union's action was intended to protect the legitimate interests of its members rather than to inflict injury on the claimants, the union officials were not liable in conspiracy.

2 **Conspiracy using unlawful means.** If the conspirators intentionally injure a person and use means which are unlawful, i.e. a tort or a crime, they will not escape liability by showing that their purpose was to protect their own interests (*Lonrho plc* v *Fayed* (1991).

Deceit

This tort, which is also known as fraud, consists of knowingly or recklessly making a false statement to another person who acts on it to his detriment.

Passing-off

This tort protects a trader whose competitors pass off their goods as the trader's. Examples of passing-off include using another's trade name and imitating another's goods, for example by using similar wrappings or containers. Passing-off will be considered in more detail in Chapter 15.

QUESTIONS/ACTIVITIES

1 In what circumstances does the law impose liability on a person who is not at fault? How can liability without fault be justified?

2 'Death, injury and loss from manufacture is a commonplace in our society, but compensation for it is pure roulette...', *Sunday Times*, 27 June 1976.
  Discuss with reference to the law as it stands at present. How did implementation of the Consumer Protection Act 1987 improve the rights of consumers in respect of faulty goods?

3 Percy Brown's grandchildren club together to buy him a 'fully guaranteed' Warmglo Deluxe electric blanket for his 80th birthday. As the winter evenings draw in, Percy decides that he would be warmer in bed with his new electric blanket than in his draughty sitting room. He establishes a routine – he puts the blanket on for 30 minutes before he goes to bed and, despite warnings in the operating instructions, he keeps the blanket switched on at the highest setting, while he reads in bed. One particularly cold January night, the electric blanket catches fire (as a result of faulty wiring), just as Percy is about to go to sleep. He suffers slight burns to his leg, but the fire causes extensive damage to his bed. Advise Percy.

4 Steven, an accountant, returning from his office, calls into a pub for a relaxing drink. He bumps into Paul, an old school friend, whom he has not seen for many years. During the course of the conversation over a number of pints, it emerges that Paul has recently inherited a substantial sum of money and is interested in investing in local businesses. Steven mentions that one of his clients, Precarious Ltd, is seeking financial backing and would make an attractive investment. By chance, he has a copy of the company's accounts in his briefcase which he gives to Paul. Relying on these accounts, Paul invests £10,000 in Precarious Ltd, but loses everything when Precarious goes into liquidation six months later. In fact, the accounts had been prepared negligently and did not reflect the parlous state of the company's affairs. Advise Paul.

5 Devise practical steps that might be taken by a person wishing to avoid liability for professional negligence.

6 Mr and Mrs Sharp decide to buy a holiday cottage at Cliffville-on-Sea. They approach the Beach Building Society for a mortgage. The building society instructs ABC Valuers and Surveyors to carry out a mortgage valuation. ABC send their staff valuer, Sandy, to carry out the survey. Despite evidence of subsidence, Sandy's valuation report is favourable. The report clearly states that it has been prepared for mortgage purposes only and is not a structural survey. Mr and Mrs Sharp, who are sent a copy of the report, decide to proceed with the purchase without undertaking their own survey, having secured the required loan. Shortly after completing the purchase, they discover that the cottage requires underpinning. Advise Mr and Mrs Sharp of any causes of action that may be available to them.

7 Ian and John, employees of Oldtown Council, carelessly erect a temporary grandstand overlooking the finishing line at the council-owned sports arena. The grandstand collapses during an athletics event, fatally injuring several spectators. Discuss the civil liability of Ian and John and their employer for the accident.

8 Dilip lives in a quiet residential area. Next door, Kwickbuild Ltd is carrying out extensive building work to a dilapidated old house. The builders, who are working from dawn to dusk, seven days a week, use a crane which passes over Dilip's house. Dilip and his family are annoyed by the dust, dirt and noise caused by the building work. Advise Dilip as to his legal position and any legal remedies he may have.

Chapter 12

CRIMINAL LIABILITY IN BUSINESS

In this chapter we will examine how the activities of those in business may be affected by the criminal law.

CRIMINAL LAW AND THE SUPPLIER OF GOODS AND SERVICES

So far in this book we have examined the civil liability of a businessman for his activities in contract and tort. The civil law is concerned with the rights and obligations which arise between individuals, with enforcement of the law the responsibility of the person who has been wronged. So, if a consumer alleges that a supplier is in breach of contract or has acted negligently, it is up to the individual consumer to bring an action in the civil courts for redress. In reality, consumers are reluctant to embark on litigation to enforce their rights, especially where small sums of money are involved. If consumers' rights can be ignored with relative impunity, suppliers may be tempted to drop their standards in pursuit of increased profit margins. The result will be that not only are consumers denied protection at a practical level which the civil law in theory purports to afford them, but honest traders seeking to maintain high standards of quality and care are placed at a competitive disadvantage.

Since the earliest times, the criminal law has been used to protect consumers and restrain dishonest and unfair trading practices. This approach has clear advantages. The maintenance of high standards in business and protection of the public are not dependent on isolated individual action. Instead, since crimes are regarded as offences against the community as a whole, responsibility for enforcement is entrusted to public officials who bring proceedings against rogue traders at public expense. Traders who ignore the rules run the substantial risk of prosecution and criminal conviction, especially as most of the crimes against consumers are strict lia-

bility offences which do not require proof of fault. This is a powerful incentive to compliance. Suppliers today are subject to extensive criminal controls over their activities. In this chapter we shall concentrate on some of the more significant provisions of the criminal law as they affect the supplier of goods and services, namely in relation to:

1 misdescriptions of goods and services;
2 misleading price indications about goods and services;
3 safety of consumer goods;
4 safety and quality of food.

Other areas of business activity relating to the supply of goods and services which are subject to the criminal law are also noted.

MISDESCRIPTION OF GOODS AND SERVICES

The Trade Descriptions Act 1968 (TDA) prohibits the use of certain false trade descriptions by a person acting in the course of a trade or business. The main offences created by the TDA are:

1 applying a false trade description to any goods or supplying goods to which a false trade description is applied (s 1);
2 knowingly or recklessly making a false statement in respect of the provision of services, accommodation or facilities (s 14).

We will now examine the offences in more detail.

False trade description of goods (s 1)

Section 1(1) provides that any person who in the course of a trade or business applies a false trade description to goods or supplies or offers to supply any goods to which a false trade description is applied is guilty of an offence. The following points should be noted about the offences created by s 1(1):

1 Strict liability. The offences set out in s 1(1) are strict liability offences, i.e. proof of *mens rea* is not required. Nevertheless, s 24 provides the defendant with defences if he has taken 'reasonable precautions' and exercised 'due diligence'. In practice, therefore, most convictions under these provisions are likely to involve blameworthy conduct.

2 In the course of trade or business. An offence can only be committed by a person acting in the course of a trade or business. It follows that a private person cannot commit an offence under this section, although it should be noted that he may be caught by the 'by-pass provision' contained in s 23 (see later). Section 1 is intended to apply where the supply of goods in question constitutes the main activity of the business. The position is less clear, however, where the supply of such goods is peripheral to the principal business. In *Havering LBC v Stevenson* (1970), the Divisional Court of the Queen's Bench held that the purchase and sale of cars used in a car hire business formed an integral part of the business and was therefore covered by s 1. In contrast, the House of Lords held in *Davies v Sumner* (1984) that the sale of a car which had been used by the defendant in his business as a self-employed courier was not 'in the course of a trade or business' since the transaction lacked the degree of regularity which was present in the *Havering* case.

Until recently there was some doubt whether 'trade or business' covered the activities of the professions. The Court of Appeal has now clarified that the professions fall within the scope of the legislation.

Roberts v Leonard (1995)

The defendants were vets who had been appointed to carry out inspections of calves being exported to Europe. They certified that 557 calves were fit for export, although they had only examined less than half of the group. The defendants were charged with applying a false trade description to the calves which had not been examined. The Court of Appeal dismissed the argument that professionals did not act in the course of a business. As Simon Brown LJ stated: 'There is no sufficient reason to exclude professional men from the scope of the legislation nor for their being any better placed than others in its application.'

3 False trade description. Section 2(1) defines a trade description as 'an indication, direct or indirect, and by whatever means given' of any matters listed which are as follows:

(a) quantity, size or gauge, e.g. a size 12 dress;
(b) method of manufacture, production, processing or reconditioning, e.g. hand-made crafts;
(c) composition, e.g. 100 per cent cotton;
(d) fitness for purpose, strength, performance, behaviour or accuracy, e.g. a waterproof watch;
(e) any physical characteristics not included in the preceding paragraphs. e.g. all cars fitted with a sunroof;
(f) testing by any person and results thereof, e.g. *Which?* magazine 'Best Buy';
(g) approval by any person or conformity with a type approved by any person, e.g. BEAB approved;
(h) place or date of manufacture, production, processing or reconditioning, e.g. made in Britain;
(i) person by whom manufactured, produced, processed or reconditioned, e.g. Chanel perfume;
(j) other history including previous ownership or use, e.g. one owner, 15,000 miles.

False or misleading indications as to price are covered by Part III of the Consumer Protection Act 1987 and are dealt with later in this chapter.

A trade description is false if it is false or misleading to a material degree (s 3). Descriptions which, though not false, are misleading will be caught, e.g. describing a car as having had one owner when, in fact, it was owned by a leasing company that had leased it to five successive hirers (*R v Inner London justices, ex parte Wandsworth LBC* (1983)). The description must be false or misleading to a material degree. This is an enactment of the *de minimis* rule, which means that the law will not concern itself in trifling discrepancies.

R v Ford Motor Co Ltd (1974)

Ford supplied a car, described as 'new', to a dealer, who in turn sold it to a customer. The car had sustained minor damage before delivery to the dealer and had been repaired at a cost of £50. The Court of Appeal held that the description was not false as the repairs had made the car as good as new.

4 Applying a false trade description (s 1(1)(a)). The first of the offences under s 1 is committed when a person 'applies a false trade description to any goods'. The ways in which a description may be applied to goods are set out in ss 4 and 5. They include labels, packaging, oral statements and advertisements. The courts have given a wider meaning to 'applies' so that it covers both positive acts and omissions, for example where the customer requests goods of a particular description and the supplier without comment supplies goods which do not match the description.

5 Supplying and offering to supply goods to which a false trade description is applied (s l(l)(b)). The second of the offences under s 1 is usually committed by a retailer who sells goods to which a description has already been applied by someone else higher up in the distribution chain, e.g. a manufacturer or importer. However, an offence can also be committed under s 1(1), where goods taken in for repair are subsequently returned to the owner but the agreed work has not been carried out properly (*Formula One Autocentres Ltd* v *Birmingham City Council* (1998)).

Although the provisions are designed to protect the consumer by imposing strict obligations on retailers, a retailer may be able to avoid conviction by pleading a defence under s 24(3) (see below). To avoid the problem that the display of goods in a shop window or on a supermarket shelf is not an offer to sell in the contractual sense, s 6 provides that 'a person exposing goods for supply or having goods in his possession for supply shall be deemed to offer to supply them'.

6 Disclaimers. The question arises as to whether a trader can protect himself from prosecution for an offence under s 1(1)(b) by using a disclaimer. Most of the cases on disclaimers have involved false odometer readings in cars. The guidelines as to the effectiveness of any disclaimer were laid down by Lord Widgery in the leading case of *Norman* v *Bennett* (1974) as follows:

> To be effective a disclaimer must be as bold, precise and compelling as the trade description itself and must effectively be brought to the attention of any person to whom the goods may be supplied, in other words the disclaimer must equal the trade

description in the extent to which it is likely to get home to anyone interested in receiving the goods.

In practical terms, a disclaimer is more likely to be effective if it is printed boldly in a written document which is given to the buyer at or before the time of delivery. Oral disclaimers, notices on the walls of business premises and disclaimers hidden in small print in contractual documents have all been held to be ineffective.

A disclaimer will not serve to protect a trader from the consequences of his own wrongdoing. So, if a second-hand car dealer himself turns back the odometers on the cars he sells and is charged under s 1(1)(a) with the active offence of applying a false trade description, he cannot escape liability by using a disclaimer (*R* v *Southwood* (1987)). A Court of Appeal case indicates that a disclaimer may protect a trader from a conviction under s 1 (1)(a) in certain circumstances.

R v *Bull* (1996)

The defendant car dealer displayed a car for sale which had previously changed hands many times. The odometer gave a reading of 47,000 miles, but as the dealer was unable to verify the mileage, he placed a sticker on the odometer which stated that the mileage should not be regarded as accurate. The mileage was copied on to a sales invoice. It was later discovered that the mileage indicated was false. The dealer was charged under s 1(1)(a) with applying a false trade description to goods, which was committed by copying the mileage on to the sales invoice. The dealer successfully argued that the disclaimer contained in the sticker over the odometer meant that the trade description was not false as a reasonable purchaser would realise that the mileage might not be accurate.

False statements as to services (s 14)

Section 14(1) provides that it is an offence for any person in the course of any trade or business to make a statement which he knows to be false or recklessly to make a statement which is false in respect of the following matters:

(a) the provision of any services, accommodation or facilities;

(b) the nature of any services, etc.;

(c) the time at which, manner in which or persons by whom such services, etc. are provided;

(d) the examination, approval or evaluation by any person of any such services, etc.;

(e) the location or amenities of any accommodation so provided.

The following points should be noted about the offence contained in s 14:

1 Requirement of *mens rea*. Unlike the offences under s 1, the offence of making a false statement about services is not a strict liability offence. The *mens rea* requirements contained in s 14(l)(a) and (b) will be considered separately.

Under s 14(1)(a) the prosecution must show that the defendant made the statement knowing it to be false. Establishing knowledge of the falsity of the statement is always difficult, but the decision of the House of Lords in *Wings Ltd* v *Ellis* (1984) indicates that the offence may be more properly described as one of 'semi-strict liability'.

Wings Ltd v *Ellis* (1984)

Wings Ltd published a brochure in May 1981 in which it falsely described a hotel in Sri Lanka as having air-conditioned bedrooms. When it realised the mistake a month later, it took steps to correct the description. Nevertheless, in January 1982 a Mr Wade read an original copy of the brochure and booked a holiday at the hotel on the strength of the description. The House of Lords held that Wings had committed an offence under s 14(1)(a). Although Wings was unaware that the description was false when the brochure was published and, therefore, lacked the necessary *mens rea* at the time the statement was made, Wings did know that the description was incorrect when it was read by Mr Wade in January 1982, and this was sufficient for a conviction. It should be noted that Wings did not attempt to advance a defence under s 24 (see below).

Under s 14(1)(b) the prosecution must prove that the defendant made the statement recklessly. A reckless statement is defined in s 14(2)(b) as one 'made regardless of whether it is true or false whether or not the person making it had reasons for believing that it might be false'. It seems that dishonesty is not a requirement for conviction.

MFI Warehouses v *Nattrass* (1973)

MFI advertised louvre doors for sale by mail order on 14 days' free approval with a 25p carriage charge on each door. The advertisement also offered sliding door gear 'carriage free'. MFI intended that the door gear should only be sold with the doors and that no extra carriage charge should be made in respect of the inclusion of the door gear. A purchaser placed a separate order for door gear and was asked to pay carriage. The chairman of MFI had studied the advertisement, but he failed to appreciate that it might be interpreted as indicating a willingness to supply the door gear separately. The company was convicted of recklessly making a false statement as to the provision of facilities contrary to s 14(1)(b).

2 In the course of any trade or business. The offence set out in s 14 cannot be committed by a private individual.

3 Statements. Section 14 applies to statements about existing facts, but does not cover statements which are really promises about the future.

Beckett v *Cohen* (1972)

A builder agreed to construct a garage within ten days but failed to do so. The Divisional Court of the Queen's Bench Division held that an offence had not been committed because the promise related to the future and was therefore not capable of being true or false when made.

Some promises about the future may involve a statement of existing fact.

British Airways Board v *Taylor* (1976)

The House of Lords held that the confirmation of a reservation on an overbooked flight amounted to a false statement since it was the airline's intention not to honour the reservation if too many people turned up for the flight. The defendants escaped conviction because the confirmation had been sent by their precedessor BOAC.

Section 14 will not apply to statements of opinion, but there are some situations where a purported opinion will be deemed to be a statement of fact.

R v *Bevelectric Ltd* (1993)

The defendant company operated a washing machine repair service. Customers who complained that their washing machine motor was not working were advised that the motor needed replacing even if it could be repaired. The Court of Appeal held that the statements that the motor needed replacing were statements of fact not opinion because it could be implied that a genuine assessment of the need for a repair had been carried out.

4 Services, accommodation and facilities. The TDA does not define these terms. The job of interpretation has been left to the courts. In *Newell* v *Hicks* (1984) Robert Goff LJ defined 'services' as 'doing something for somebody', referring to dry-cleaning and repairing a car as examples, and a 'facility' as 'providing somebody with the wherewithal to do something for himself', giving a car park and a swimming pool as examples. 'Accommodation' has come to mean short-term accommodation, for example in hotels.

Defences

A number of defences are available to a person accused of an offence under the TDA. Section 24(1) provides a general defence which applies to all offences, while s 24(3) is a special defence which may be raised only in relation to the offence of supplying or offering to supply contained in s 1 (1)(b). Section 25 affords a special defence in respect of advertisements.

General defence (s 24(1))

The defendant must establish:

(a) that the commission of the offence was due to a mistake or to reliance on information supplied to him or the act or default of another person, an accident or some other cause beyond his control; and

(b) that he took all reasonable precautions and exercised all due diligence to avoid the commission of such an offence by himself or any person under his control.

The causes set out in (a) are alternative. The defendant must prove one of them and the requirements in (b). The cause most frequently relied upon is that the commission of the offence was due to the act or default of another person, e.g. where a previous owner of a car has tampered with the odometer. An employer may rely on the act or default of an employee. In the case of a company, only the board of directors, managing director and any other officer who has authority to act independently of the board are deemed to be 'employers'. The operation of the defence in the context of a company is illustrated by the following case.

Tesco Supermarkets Ltd v *Nattrass* (1971)

Tesco advertised a 'flash offer' of money off a particular brand of washing powder. The store had run out of the specially marked 'flash packs' and a shop assistant, unknown to the store manager, filled the shelves with ordinary full-price packets. A customer was charged the full price for a packet. The House of Lords held that the company would have committed an offence under s 11(2) (now repealed by Part III of the Consumer Protection Act 1987) had it not been able to establish a defence under s 24(1). The company was able to prove that the supermarket manager was 'another person' and that the company had exercised all reasonable precautions and due diligence by establishing procedures to ensure employees complied with the TDA.

Special defences (ss 24(3) and 25)

Section 24(3) provides a defence to the offence of supplying or offering to supply goods under s 1(1)(b) where the defendant can prove that he did not know and could not with reasonable diligence have ascertained that the goods did not conform to the description or that the description had been applied to the goods.

Naish v *Gore* (1971)

The defendant dealer bought a car from a person with whom he had done business for many years. He then resold the car before he had received the log book. The car showed a false odometer reading. The defendant successfully pleaded the defences in s 24(1) (the act or default of another person) and s 24(3) (he did not know of the false trade description).

Section 25 provides a special defence in relation to the 'innocent' publication of an advertisement which contravenes the TDA by a publisher or advertising agency.

By-pass provision

The 'by-pass provision' contained in s 23 allows the prosecution to take action against the person who is really responsible for the false trade description. For example, a manufacturer who has applied a false trade description to his goods may be prosecuted under s 23 in respect of an offence committed by a retailer under s 1(1)(b), whether or not the retailer is prosecuted. (The manufacturer could be prosecuted directly for an offence under s 1(1)(a) in this example.) The real value of s 23 is that it enables the prosecution of a person, such as a private seller, who could not otherwise be charged under the TDA.

Olgeirsson v Kitching (1986)

The defendant, a private individual, sold his car to a dealer, John Roe, representing that the car had done some 38,000 miles. The defendant knew that the true mileage was in excess of 74,000. Roe sold the car to another dealer who discovered that the mileage was incorrect and informed Roe to this effect. Roe complained to the local trading standards department, who brought this prosecution against the defendant. The defendant could not have been prosecuted directly under s 1 because he was not acting in the course of trade or business but he was convicted under s 23.

Enforcement and penalties

The TDA is enforced by local authority trading standards officers who have powers to enter premises and inspect books and other business documents. The penalties for contravening the TDA are a maximum fine of £5,000 in the magistrates' court and a prison sentence not exceeding two years and/or an unlimited fine in respect of a Crown Court conviction. The TDA makes no provision for civil action for breach of statutory duty. However, aggrieved consumers may claim compensation under the Powers of Criminal Courts (Sentencing) Act 2000 where a conviction is secured.

REFORM OF THE TRADE DESCRIPTIONS ACT 1968

In 1999, in the White Paper 'Modern Markets: Confident Consumers' the government indicated that it intended to amend the TDA so as to treat misdescriptions of services in the same way as misdescriptions of goods. The government's proposals were set out in greater detail in a DTI consultation document published in 2000. The changes proposed are as follows:

- The supplier of services should be subject to the same liability as the supplier of goods. The offence set out in s 14 should be amended to become one of strict liability.

- The supplier of services should be liable for promises about the future supply of services. The liability would apply if it can be shown that at the time of making the statement the supplier had no intention of providing the service in the form described or at all; or if the statement is accurate when made, but has subsequently been rendered inaccurate, the supplier fails to take reasonable steps to inform the customer of the true position as soon as is reasonably practicable.

- The scope of s 14 should be extended from 'services, accommodation and facilities' to explicitly include, e.g. the standing, capabilities or qualifications of the service provider, and the duration and location of the service.

- The Act should clarify that 'statements' about services, accommodation and facilities include pictorial representations.

- A new offence is proposed of making a false or misleading statement about the condition of goods, the physical state of real property or the availability of spares, etc., made as an inducement to enter into a transaction or with a view to influencing the terms of any transaction. The offence will not be one of strict liability; prosecutors will need to establish that the supplier knew the statement was false when he made it or that it was made recklessly. This new offence is designed to deal with, for example, rogue builders who deliberately exaggerate the amount of work needed on a leaking roof.

MISLEADING PRICE INDICATIONS

Controls over false and misleading statements as to prices are now contained in Part III of the Consumer Protection Act 1987 (CPA). Previously misleading price indications had been prohibited by s 11 of the TDA which was flawed in that it only applied to goods and not services, and the complex Price Marking (Bargain Offers) Order 1979, which applied to both goods and services. Part III of the CPA creates a new general offence of giving a misleading price indication, which is supported by a code of practice to give practical guidance to traders. The main features of the provisions are as follows.

Giving a misleading price indication

Section 20(1) of the CPA provides that a person shall be guilty of an offence if, in the course of any business of his, he gives (by any means whatever) to any consumers an indication which is misleading as to the price at which any goods, services, accommodation or facilities are available (whether generally or from particular persons). Liability is imposed in respect of statements which are misleading when they are given but also for statements which subsequently become misleading because circumstances have changed, unless the trader has taken reasonable steps to prevent consumers relying on the indication (s 20(3)). Note the following features of the offence created by s 20.

1 Consumers. Section 20(6) defines 'consumers' as anyone who might want the goods, services, accommodation or facilities other than for business purposes. The legislation is selective in the protection it provides. It only extends to private individuals.

2 Price. The definition of 'price' in s 20(6) covers the total amount payable, as well as any method of determining the total amount.

Toyota (GB) Ltd v North Yorkshire County Council (1998) Toyota ran an advertisement for one of its cars, which indicated in bold headlines that the car was for sale at a price of £11,665. At the foot of the advertisement, in very small print, was a statement about additional delivery charges being payable. Toyota's conviction under s 20 was upheld by the Divisional Court. The delivery charges should have been incorporated into the advertised purchase price or made conspicuous in the headline price.

3 Misleading. Section 21 sets out a list of circumstances in which the prices or the methods of determining the price will be considered misleading. They are suggestions that:

(a) the price is less than it in fact is (or the method is not what in fact it is), e.g. shelf price £1.99, but being charged £2.99 at the checkout;

(b) the price (or method) does not depend on facts or circumstances when in reality it does, e.g. an advertised offer of a free toaster with every washing machine sold, but the offer is only available on purchases above £400;

(c) the price (or method) includes other things, but in fact it does not, e.g. inclusive price given for fitted kitchen, but additional charges made for installing the kitchen;

(d) the price (or method) might be expected to be altered (whether or not at a particular time or for a particular period) but this will not happen, e.g. 'introductory offer' price which the retailer has no intention of increasing;

(e) the facts or circumstances by which consumers might reasonably be expected to judge the validity of any comparison made or implied by the indication are not what in fact they are. For this purpose a comparison is one made between the price (or method) and any past, present or future price (or method), e.g. bookcase £45 (self-assembly), £99 (ready assembled), but the retailer does not stock the ready-assembled bookcase.

It should be noted that the list in s 21 is not exhaustive and other circumstances not detailed could be held to be misleading.

4 Services or facilities. A list of items included in the definition is provided in s 22(1) as follows:

(a) credit, banking or insurance services;
(b) the purchase or sale of foreign currency;
(c) the supply of electricity;
(d) off-street car parking;
(e) holiday caravan parks.

Services and facilities specifically excluded are those services provided by an employee for his employer, by an authorised or appointed representative under the Financial Services Act 1986 and facilities for a residential caravan site.

5 Accommodation. Part III of the CPA applies to short-term accommodation, such as hotels and holiday flats, and new freehold homes for sale, and homes on lease for more than 21 years. Homes for rent are not covered. Fees charged by estate agents are also covered.

6 In the course of any business of his. An offence can only be committed under s 20 by a person acting in the course of a business of his. This wording limits the scope of the offence to the owners of a business; employees cannot be made liable for misleading price indications, even when acting in the course of their employment.

Warwickshire County Council v *Johnson* (1992)

Mr Johnson was the manager of the Stratford-upon-Avon branch of Dixons. Acting with the authority of Dixons, he placed a notice outside the shop which stated: 'We will beat any TV, HiFi and Video price by £20 on the spot'. While the notice was on display, a customer saw a TV set for sale elsewhere for £159.95. The customer took Mr Johnson to see the TV and then asked to buy an identical set from Dixons for £139.95. Mr Johnson refused to sell him the TV, despite having stock available. The customer complained to the local trading standards department, which decided to prosecute Mr Johnson under s 20(1) of the CPA. The House of Lords held that the notice was a misleading price indication as Mr Johnson had refused to honour its terms. However, the offence set out in s 20(1) can be committed only by a person who is the owner of the business or has a controlling interest in it. Since Mr Johnson was only an employee, he could not be guilty of an offence.

Regulations

Section 26 empowers the Secretary of State to make regulations about price indications. Contravention of the regulations constitutes a criminal offence. Two regulations have been made under the provisions: the Price Indications (Method of Payment) Regulations 1991 are designed to ensure customers are made aware of any differences in price depending on the method of payment, e.g. extra charges if paying by credit card. The Price Indications (Bureaux de Change) Regulations 1992 require *bureaux de change* to provide clear and prominent information in relation to selling, buying and commission rates, and differences in rates for traveller's cheques and notes.

Codes of practice

The Secretary of State may approve codes of practice, which are designed either to give practical guidance on the requirements of s 20 or to promote desirable practices in relation to the giving of price indications. Contravention of a code of practice does not of itself constitute a criminal offence or give rise to any civil liability. However, the fact that a trader has adhered to or ignored the recommendations of a code of practice can be taken into account in any court proceedings. Thus, if a trader shows that he has complied with a code, it will tend to show that he has not committed an offence. Similarly, if the trader has flouted the advice in a code, it may tend to show that he is guilty. The first Code of Practice on Price Indications was published in November 1988.

Defences

The defences available to an accused person under Part III are contained in s 24. They are:

1 compliance with any regulations made under s 26;
2 the price indication was published in a book, newspaper, magazine, film, radio or TV broadcast, but not in the form of an advertisement;
3 the innocent publication of an advertisement by a publisher or advertising agency;
4 in the case of an offence under s 20(1), that:

   (a) the indication did not relate to the availability from him of any goods, services, etc.;
   (b) the price had been recommended to every supplier of the goods and services;
   (c) the price was misleading only because the supplier did not follow the recommendation;
   (d) it was reasonable for the recommender of the price to assume that his recommendation was being followed;

5 in the case of a charge under s 20(1) only, that the defendant took all reasonable steps and exercised due diligence to avoid committing the offence (s 39).

Enforcement and penalties

Enforcement is the responsibility of the local trading standards department. Its officers have the power to require the production of records, seize goods and business records and obtain information. It is an offence to obstruct a trading standards officer or to fail to give assistance or information which he requires. A person convicted under s 20 is liable to a fine.

PRODUCT SAFETY

The legal framework for dealing with the problem of unsafe general products is contained in the General Product Safety Regulations 1994 and Part

II of the Consumer Protection Act 1987. It should be noted that food is also covered by the Food Safety Act 1990.

The General Product Safety Regulations 1994

The regulations implement the provisions of the EC Directive on General Product Safety, adopted by the Council of Ministers in 1992. They impose new requirements concerning the safety of products intended for consumers or likely to be used by consumers where such products are placed on the market by producers or supplied by distributors. The regulations came into force on 3 October 1994.

1 Scope of the regulations. The regulations apply to products intended or likely to be used for consumer use which have been supplied in the course of a commercial activity. A consumer is a person who is not acting in the course of a commercial activity. A commercial activity is defined as any business or trade. The regulations apply whether the products are new, used or reconditioned. Products used exclusively in the context of a commercial activity, even if for or by a consumer, are not subject to the regulations.

The regulations do not apply to the following types of products (reg 3):

(a) second-hand products which are antiques;
(b) products supplied for repair or reconditioning before use, but the supplier must inform the customer to that effect;
(c) products that are subject to specific provisions of EC law covering all aspects of their safety;
(d) products that are subject to specific provisions of EC law which cover an aspect of safety (reg 4).

The general safety requirement in respect of goods contained in s 10 of the Consumer Protection Act 1987 is disapplied.

2 General safety requirement. Regulation 7 provides that a producer may not place a product on the market unless it is a safe product. It is an offence to fail to comply with the general safety requirement (reg 12). It is also an offence for a producer or distributor to offer or agree to place (or supply) a dangerous product or expose or possess such a product for placing on the market (or for supply) (reg 13).

3 Safe product. Regulation 2 sets out what is meant by a 'safe product'. A product will be safe if, under normal or reasonably foreseeable conditions of use (including duration), there is no risk or the risk has been reduced to a minimum. Any risk must be compatible with the product's use, considered acceptable and consistent with a high level of health and safety protection. In this respect, account should be taken of the following matters:

(a) the characteristics of the product, including its composition, packaging instructions for assembly and maintenance;
(b) the effect on other products, if it is likely to be used with other products;
(c) the presentation of the product, the labelling, any instructions for use and disposal and any other instructions or information provided by the producer;
(d) the categories of consumer at serious risk in using the product, particularly children.

The fact that higher levels of safety can be achieved or that there are less risky products available will not of itself render a product unsafe.

Products which comply with UK legal requirements concerning health and safety are presumed to be safe products (reg 10). If no specific rules exist, the safety of a product will be assessed according to:

(a) voluntary UK standards which give effect to a European standard; or
(b) EC technical specifications; or
(c) if neither of the above exist, UK standards, or industry codes of practice relating to health and safety or the state of the art or technology, and the consumer's reasonable expectations in relation to safety.

4 Producer. A 'producer' is defined in reg 2 as:

(a) a manufacturer established in the EC;
(b) where the manufacturer is not established in the EC, his representative or the importer of the product;
(c) other professionals in the supply chain, but only to the extent that their activities might affect the safety of the product.

5 Information requirements. A producer is required under reg 8 to provide consumers with information so that they can assess inherent risks and take precautions. The duty only arises where the risks are not immediately obvious without adequate warnings. A producer must also adopt measures to keep himself informed of any risks which his products may present. This may include:

(a) marking the products (or product batches) so they can be identified;
(b) sample testing of marketed products;
(c) investigating complaints;
(d) keeping distributors informed of monitoring arrangements.

The producer must also take appropriate action to avoid risk which may include withdrawing the product from the market.

6 Duty of distributors. A distributor must act with due care to help producers comply with the general safety requirement. In particular, a distributor will commit an offence if he supplies dangerous products (reg 9(a)). He must also, within the limits of his activities, participate in monitoring the safety of products, including passing on information about product risks and cooperating in action to avoid the risks (reg 9(b)).

7 Defence of due diligence. It is a defence for a person accused of an offence under the regulations to show that he took all reasonable steps and exercised all due diligence to avoid committing the offence (reg 14). The defence cannot be relied on in the following situations:

(a) where the defendant has failed to serve a notice at least seven days before the hearing that his defence involves an allegation that the commission of the offence was due to either the act or default of another or reliance on information given by another;

(b) where it was unreasonable for the defendant to have relied on information supplied another (the court will have regard to the steps which were taken – or might reasonably have been taken – to verify the information

and whether the defendant had any reason to disbelieve the information);

(c) where the defendant is a distributor who has contravened reg 9(b).

8 By-pass provision. Regulation 15 provides a by-pass provision to enable the prosecution of the person, in the course of a commercial activity of his, whose act or default causes another to commit an offence.

9 Enforcement and penalties. The regulations are enforced by weights and measures authorities in Great Britain, except in relation to food, in which case enforcement is the responsibility of food authorities (reg 11). The power to issue prohibition notices, notices to warn and suspension notices contained in Part II of the Consumer Protection Act 1987 (see below) are extended to these regulations (reg 11). The penalties for offences under the regulations are a maximum prison sentence of three months and/or a fine not exceeding £5,000 on conviction in the magistrates' court (reg 17).

Part II of the Consumer Protection Act 1987

Until the General Product Safety Regulations were introduced in 1994, the legal framework for dealing with the problem of unsafe goods was contained in Part II of the Consumer Protection Act 1987. At the heart of the legislation was a general statutory offence, contained in s 10, of supplying consumer goods which fail to comply with the general safety requirement. The General Product Safety Regulations 1994 disapply the general safety requirement set out in s 10 of the Consumer Protection Act. The effect of the 1994 regulations is to make s 10 virtually redundant. Section 10 will only apply to cases which fall outside the scope of the 1994 regulations. Since such cases are likely to be very rare, we will not examine the detailed provisions of s 10 in this book.

Although the General Product Safety Regulations 1994 disapply s 10 of the Consumer Protection Act 1987 in respect of the duty to comply with the general safety requirement, the remaining provisions of

Part II of the Consumer Protection Act 1987 concerning the power to make safety regulations and issue various notices continue to apply.

Safety regulations

Section 11 empowers the Secretary of State to make safety regulations in respect of s 10(3) and for other purposes, such as ensuring that appropriate information is provided with goods or that goods which are unsafe in the hands of certain people are not made available to these persons. Section 11(2) sets out a list of matters which may be dealt with by such safety regulations. They include:

1 composition, contents, design, construction, finish or packaging of goods;
2 approvals of the goods;
3 requirements as to testing or inspection;
4 warnings, instructions or other information about the goods;
5 prohibitions on the supply of such goods or composition or raw materials;
6 requiring information to be given to officials.

Section 12 sets out a number of offences relating to contravention of the safety regulations including:

1 contravening a prohibition on the supply of goods in breach of the regulations;
2 failing to comply with tests or procedures required by the regulations;
3 failing to provide information as required by the regulations.

Notices

Unsafe goods can be dealt with by means of various notices. The Secretary of State can issue two kinds of notice: a **prohibition notice** requiring a trader to cease supplying a unsafe goods, and a **notice to warn** requiring a manufacturer or distributor to warn the public about the dangers of a product in circulation. Any enforcement authority such as the local authority trading standards department may issue a **suspension notice**, which requires a trader to cease supplying goods suspected of breaching any safety provisions for a period of six months. It is a criminal offence to contravene these notices.

Enforcement and penalties

The provisions of Part II of the CPA are enforced by trading standards officers. In addition to the power to obtain a suspension notice already mentioned, they may apply for a court order for the forfeiture of any goods which contravene any safety provision.

The penalties for offences are a maximum fine of £5,000 and six months' imprisonment on conviction in the magistrates' court.

SAFETY AND QUALITY OF FOOD

Food has been the subject of protective legislation since the Middle Ages. Modern food law is contained in the Food Safety Act 1990 (FSA). The scope of the FSA is not confined to food safety; it also covers matters such as composition, labelling and advertising.

As there is a substantial volume of complex subsidiary legislation in this area, we will consider the subject of the safety and quality of food in outline only.

Food Safety Act 1990

Before we consider the main offences created by the FSA, it is necessary to establish what is meant by the word 'food'. Section 1(1) makes it clear that 'food' includes drink (which includes bottled water, but not water covered by the Water Act 1989), substances of no nutritional value, chewing gum and ingredients used in the preparation of the foregoing (s 1(1)). Anything supplied to a customer which purports to be food will be treated as such. For example, if a customer in a restaurant orders lemonade but by mistake is supplied with caustic soda, the owner of the restaurant cannot argue that caustic soda is not 'food' because he purported to supply lemonade, which is within the definition of food (*Meah* v *Roberts* (1978)). Live animals, feeding stuffs for animals, controlled drugs and medicine are all excluded from the definition of 'food' (s 1 (2)).

The main offences under the Food Safety Act

Rendering food injurious to health (s 7)

It is an offence under s 7(1) for a person to render food injurious to health with the intent that it shall be sold for human consumption. An injury to health is defined as 'any impairment, whether permanent or temporary' (s 7(3)). In deciding whether food is injurious to health, regard should be had to 'the probable effect of the food on the health of the person consuming it' (s 7(2)(a)) and 'the probable cumulative effect of similarly constituted food on the health of a person consuming it in ordinary quantities' (s 7(2)(b)).

Something must have been done to the food to render it injurious to health. To be guilty of an offence under s 7, the defendant must have done some positive act, which has resulted in the food becoming injurious to health. Such acts include:

(a) adding an article to the food (s 7(1)(a));
(b) using an article or substance as an ingredient in the preparation of food (s 7(l)(b)) (preparation includes any form of processing and treatment, such as subjecting food to heat or cold);
(c) abstracting any constituent from the food (s 7(1)(c));
(d) subjecting the food to any other process or treatment (s 7(l)(d)) (processing and treatment may cover the early stages in the production of food, e.g. crop spraying).

Defects in food arising from inaction (i.e. natural growth of mould) and failure to remove natural features of food, e.g. naturally occurring toxins in red kidney beans, are not covered by s 7.

Selling food not complying with food safety requirements (s 8)

It is an offence to sell, offer for sale, expose or advertise for sale or have in one's possession for the purposes of sale or preparation for sale any food intended for human consumption, which fails to comply with food safety requirements (s 8(1)(a)). It is also an offence to deposit with or consign to another any food intended for human consumption which fails to comply with food safety requirements.

Food will fail to comply with food safety requirements in the following circumstances:

(a) *It has been rendered injurious to health under s 7(1)* (s 8(2)(a).

(b) *It is unfit for human consumption* (s 8(2)(b). Unfit for human consumption means that the food is 'putrid, diseased or unwholesome'. Some food may be **unsuitable** for human consumption because, for example, it contains harmless penicillin mould, but that does not make it **unfit** for human consumption.

(c) *It is contaminated within the meaning of the Act* (s 8(2)(c)). Contaminated food includes food which is mouldy, rancid, stale or suffering from minor infestation. It could also be contaminated with extraneous material, such as pesticide or unauthorised additives. The food must be contaminated to the extent that it must be unreasonable to use the food for human consumption in that state, i.e. it may be possible to treat the food so that it would be fit for human consumption.

No offence is committed unless the food is intended for human consumption. Two presumptions will be made:

(a) it is presumed that food commonly used for human consumption is intended for human consumption where it is sold, offered for sale, exposed or kept for sale unless the person charged can prove the contrary (s 3 (2));

(b) where food is found on premises used for preparation, storage or sale of food, it is presumed, unless the contrary is proved, that it is intended for human consumption (s 3(3)).

Selling food not of the nature, substance or quality demanded (s 14)

Section 14 provides that it is an offence for a person to sell to the purchaser's prejudice any food which is not of the nature or substance or quality demanded by the purchaser (s 14(1)). Again, the food must be intended for human consumption (s 14(2)).

Note the following features of the offence created by s 14:

1 Sale. An offence will be committed only where there is a sale. Sale is defined broadly to include all supplies of food in the course of a business (s 2(1)), giving food away as a prize at a place of public entertainment (s 2(2)(a)) or as part of a promotional exercise (s 2(2)(b)).

2 Nature or substance or quality. Section 14 is worded in such a way as to create three separate offences; the characteristics listed are alternatives. So far as 'nature' is concerned, an offence will be committed if the customer does not get what he asked for, e.g. where the customer asks for butter but is supplied with margarine. With respect to 'substance', an offence will be committed if the food contains unwanted additives or where the food fails to comply with a statutory standard, e.g. a fish cake which contained less fish than required by regulations. So far as 'quality' is concerned, an offence will be committed if the food fails to comply with the standard of quality demanded. The standard of quality expected will depend on factors such as price paid or any description which has been applied, e.g. extra lean mince should not contain an excessive amount of fat.

3 Sale to the purchaser's prejudice. The seller must have supplied food which is inferior to that which could be reasonably expected. It is not necessary to show actual damage. A seller may avoid liability by use of a very clear notice: a consumer who knows exactly what he's getting cannot claim to have been prejudiced.

Falsely describing or presenting food (s 15)

Section 15 creates an offence of giving with any food sold or displaying with any food exposed for sale or in possession for the purposes of sale, a label whether or not attached to or printed on the wrapper or container which (a) falsely describes the food, or (b) is likely to mislead as to the nature, substance or quality of the food. It is also an offence to publish or be a party to the publication of an advertisement which is false or calculated to mislead. Section 15 is supplemented by regulations as to the labelling and description of food.

Defences

A number of defences are available to a person charged with an offence under the FSA.

1 The defendant has taken all reasonable precautions and has exercised due diligence to avoid the commission of an offence by himself or a person under his control (s 21).
2 The innocent publication of an advertisement which contravenes the FSA by a publisher or advertising agency (s 22).

By-pass provisions

Under s 20 where the commission by any person of the relevant offence is due to the act or default of some other person, that other person shall be guilty of the offence. This provision is similar to the by-pass provisions of the TDA.

Enforcement and penalties

Enforcement authorities enjoy powers of inspection and seizure, the powers to apply to the court for an improvement notice, prohibition order or an emergency order to deal with suspected offenders. Enforcement has been assisted by the requirement since 1 May 1992 that all food premises register with local environmental health departments. Failure to comply is an offence.

The penalties for contravening the FSA are a prison sentence not exceeding two years and/or an unlimited fine in respect of a Crown Court conviction, and on summary conviction in the magistrates' court a prison sentence not exceeding six months and/or a £20,000 fine in respect of ss 7, 8 and 14 offences and the statutory fine of £5,000 in respect of other offences.

Food Standards Agency

Concerns about the quality of our food in recent times (BSE, salmonella, e-coli, etc.) led to the establishment of the Food Standards Agency by the Foods Standards Act 1999. The Food Standards Agency became operational on 3 April 2000. The main objective of the Agency is to protect public health in relation to food, and also to protect the wider food standards interests of consumers, such as labelling.

The Agency's functions are to:

- provide advice and information to the public and to the government on food safety from farm to fork, nutrition and diet;
- protect consumers through effective enforcement and monitoring;
- support consumer choice through promoting accurate and meaningful labelling.

The Ministry of Agriculture Fisheries and Food (MAFF) will no longer exercise responsibility for food safety and standards.

OTHER CRIMINAL LIABILITY FOR THE SUPPLY OF GOODS AND SERVICES

The range of criminal controls over the supply of goods and services is extensive and not confined solely to the provisions examined in this chapter. Other examples include:

1 Weights and Measures Act 1985 under which it is an offence to sell short weight, measure or number;

2 Consumer Transactions (Restriction on Statements) Order 1976 which makes it a criminal offence to display any notice containing a term rendered void by s 6 of the Unfair Contract Terms Act 1977 (see Chapter 9);

3 Consumer Credit Act 1974 which makes it an offence to carry on a consumer credit business without a licence (this Act is the subject of the next chapter);

4 Property Misdescription Act 1991 which makes it a criminal offence to make a false or misleading statement about property matters in the course of an estate agency or property development business;

5 Package Travel, Package Holidays and Package Tours Regulations 1992 which makes it an offence for an organiser or retailer of package holidays to make a brochure available to a possible consumer unless the brochure indicates in a legible, comprehensible and accurate manner the price and includes specified information about the package. It is also an offence under the regulations for an organiser or retailer to fail to provide the consumer with information before the contract is concluded about passport and visa requirements, health formalities, arrangements for security of money paid over and repatriation in the event of insolvency. It is also an offence to fail to provide the consumer in good time before the start of the journey with written information about the journey and the name, address and telephone number of a representative of the organiser on whose assistance a consumer in difficulty can call. Other aspects of the regulations will be considered in Chapter 14.

CRIMINAL LIABILITY – GENERALLY

A crime is an offence against the state. The consequences of a criminal conviction are not confined to the punishment inflicted by the court. For example, if a person is convicted of theft, his name will probably appear in the local papers causing shame and embarrassment, and he may even lose his job. The sanctions are so severe that the criminal law normally requires an element of moral fault on the part of the offender. Thus, the prosecution must establish two essential requirements: *actus reus* (prohibited act) and *mens rea* (guilty mind). For most criminal offences, both elements must be present to create criminal liability. If you pick up someone's umbrella thinking that it is your own, you cannot be guilty of theft because of the absence of a guilty mind.

As we have seen, there are, however, some statutory offences where Parliament has dispensed with the requirement of *mens rea*. Performance of the wrongful act alone makes the offender liable. These are known as **crimes of strict liability**. Selling food for human consumption which fails to comply with food safety requirements contrary to the Food Safety Act 1990 is an example of an offence of strict liability. The prosecutor is not required to show that the seller knew that the food did not comply with food safety requirements. He will secure a conviction by establishing that the food was unsafe and that it was sold. The seller may be able to defend himself by showing that he has taken all reasonable precautions and exercised due diligence to avoid commission of the offence.

OTHER CRIMES RELEVANT TO BUSINESS

Of the considerable number of criminal offences, students of business law may find it useful to have a knowledge of the following areas.

Theft

The Theft Act 1968 applies and s 1(1) of that Act provides: 'A person is guilty of theft if he dishonestly appropriates property belonging to another with the intention of permanently depriving the other of it.'

Actus reus

The prohibited act in theft is an act of appropriation of property in a situation where that property belongs to another. Appropriation occurs when a person other than the owner assumes the rights of that owner over the property (s 3(1)). The most usual form of assumption of rights is when the property is taken away but destruction of property is also included since this is in infringement of the owner's rights. In addition a later assumption of rights, as where property is kept after it should have been returned, can also amount to theft. Some sort of conduct is required so that a mere intention to own is not enough.

Partial assumption of rights. It is not necessary to assume all of the rights of the owner; it is enough if one or more of those rights is assumed, as the following cases show.

R v Morris (1984)

Morris took some items from the shelves of a supermarket and replaced the correct labels with others showing a lower price. He went through the checkout paying the lower price.

Anderton v Burnside (1984)

The defendant took a label off a joint of meat and put it on a more expensive piece of meat. This was discovered before he reached the checkout.

Comment. In both cases the House of Lords held that theft had been committed. The defendants had assumed rights in the owner's labels and this was adverse interference. Furthermore, since the offence was committed when the appropriation took place, it was irrelevant that Burnside had not left the store. There is no appropriation after a contract of sale has been made because the property in the goods will normally have passed to the buyer and the goods will not 'belong to another'.

In addition, a person who buys property in good faith only to find out later that they were stolen but does nothing is not guilty of theft (s 3(2)).

Authorised appropriation. If the appropriation is authorised, then theft is not committed as the following case illustrates.

Eddy v Niman (1981)

The defendant went to a supermarket with every intention of stealing. Accordingly, he put some goods in a basket but then decided not to go ahead with the theft and left the store. It was held that he had not appropriated the goods for the purpose of theft because he was only doing what the supermarket had by implication authorised him to do, i.e. put goods in the basket prior to going to the checkout.

However, in this connection the decision of the House of Lords in *R v Hinks* (2000) should be noted. There the defendant persuaded a man of limited intelligence to withdraw and give to her the sum of £60,000 from his savings over a period of eight months. The House of Lords agreed that she could be successfully charged with theft. There was an appropriation although the transfer was in the nature of a gift. Thus, a gift can amount to an appropriation if the jury decides, as here, that the recipient acted dishonestly in accepting it.

A further development occurred in *R v Gomez* (1993) where the House of Lords decided that a person could be guilty of theft by dishonestly appropriating goods belonging to another if the owner of the goods was induced by fraud, deception or a false representation to consent to or authorise the taking of the goods.

R v Gomez (1993)

Gomez, in order to assist a friend to dispose of stolen cheques which were undated and bore no payee's name, persuaded his boss, the manager of an electrical goods shop, to accept them for a quantity of goods which the manager authorised for delivery to the friend. The friend and Gomez were charged with theft. Gomez appealed on the issue of appropriation, their Lordships finding him guilty because there had been an appropriation.

Comment. The House of Lords followed one of its earlier cases, *Lawrence* v *Metropolitan Police Commissioner* (1972), where a tourist gave his wallet full of unfamiliar English money to a taxi driver so that the latter could take his fare. The driver 'appropriated' much more than was due and his act was regarded as an appropriation for the purposes of theft, even though the wallet and its contents had been handed over freely.

The line of cases cited above shows the ability of the court to distinguish cases on the facts, which is particularly common in the criminal law where the liberty of the subject is at stake. The degree of dishonesty in *Eddy* is clearly much less than in the other two cases.

Property. There must be a theft of property. Section 4 defines property as including real and personal property, money and intangible property, e.g. a credit balance in a bank account or a software program. In general terms and in spite of the inclusion in the definition of real property, a person cannot steal land or anything forming part of land, i.e. fixtures rather than fittings (see further, Chapter 15). However, things which can be severed from the land can be stolen so that a farmer who without authorisation grazes his cattle on another's land steals the grass which has been severed from the land. Wild plants, flowers and mushrooms can only be stolen if for commercial gain. Thus, picking mushrooms to sell in a local market would be theft if the owner of the land had not given permission. Wild animals cannot be stolen unless kept in captivity.

Belonging to another. Although the definition of theft states that the property must belong to another, a person can steal his own property from someone with an interest in it short of ownership as the following case illustrates.

R v Turner (1971)

The defendant left his car at a garage for repair. After the repairs were completed he removed the car from where it was parked with the intention of not paying for the repairs. The court held he was guilty of theft. For the purposes of the 1968 Act, the car belonged to the repairer when it was taken since the garage had control of it.

Property received on behalf of another. Section 5(3) provides: 'Where a person receives property from or on account of another and is under an obligation to the other to retain and deal with that property or its proceeds in a particular way the property or proceeds shall be regarded (as against him) as belonging to the other.' Examples under s 5 (3) most commonly involve receiving money from others to retain and use in a certain way, e.g. travel agents taking deposits for holidays, solicitors holding funds for mortgages or managers of pension funds collecting pension contributions. However, it is essential that a particular obligation be imposed and this obligation must have been known to the accused. The following cases provide contrasting examples.

Davidge v Bunnett (1984)

The defendant had been given money by her flatmates through the medium of cheques in order that the proceeds would be used to pay gas bills. She spent the proceeds on other things and was found guilty of theft. A specific obligation had been imposed on her as to the use of the money.

R v Hall (1973)

The defendant was a travel agent who had received money from clients and did not arrange trips and could not repay the money. He was not guilty of theft since the money was handed over as part of a contractual obligation and not specifically for use in a particular way.

Comment. The decision seems to be rather a technical one. Perhaps the court should have construed a constructive trust in the agent to use the money for holiday purposes. However, although the law often construes such a trust in order to allow recovery of property at civil law, it has never been prepared to do so for the purposes of criminal liability.

Receiving property under a mistake. Section 5(4) provides:

> Where a person gets property by another's mistake and is under an obligation to make restoration (in whole or in part) of the property or its proceeds or of the value thereof then as to the extent of that obligation the property or proceeds shall be regarded (as against him) as belonging to the person entitled to restoration ...

The provision only applies where the ownership of the property has passed to the defendant so that it will not apply in a contractual mistake as to identity where the contract is void and no ownership passes (see further, Chapter 7). An illustration is provided by the following case.

A-G's Reference (No 1 of 1983) (1985)

A woman police constable was paid a sum of £74.74 by crediting her bank account. It was said to be a payment for overtime which she had not, in fact, worked. She realised she had been overpaid but did nothing. The Court of Appeal decided that there had been an appropriation and that the necessary ingredients for theft were present.

The obligation to make restoration is a legal one so that where a betting shop paid out winnings against the wrong horse, there was no recovery of it by the bookmaker in civil law, and the recipient was not under an obligation to return it in terms of the Theft Act 1968 and had committed no offence by retaining it (see *R v Gilks* (1972) and Chapter 7).

Mens rea

The *mens rea* of theft has two branches:

- dishonesty; and
- an intention permanently to deprive another of his property.

Dishonesty. Section 2(1) sets out situations in which as a matter of law an individual is not dishonest. They are:

- where the defendant believes he has a legal right to deprive the owner of the property;
- where the defendant believes that the victim would have consented if he had known of the circumstances;
- where the defendant finds property when the owner cannot be found by taking reasonable steps.

Examples are to be found in *R v Wootton* (1990) where the defendant took some of his employer's pottery in lieu of wages due. Further, in *R v Flynn* (1970) a cinema manager took £6 as an advance on his wages in the belief that his employer would have consented. It should be noted that as regards finding, there may be an appropriation for the purposes of theft if the finder does not initially know who the owner is but later finds out and does nothing. In cases not falling within s 2(1) it is necessary to prove dishonesty. The test for deciding dishonesty was laid down in *R v Ghosh* (1982). The defendant was a surgeon who claimed fees from a hospital for operations he had not carried out. Although the case was concerned with obtaining money by deception, the Court of Appeal laid down a test for dishonesty which applies also to cases of theft. The test has two branches as follows:

- The jury to apply the ordinary standards of reasonable and honest people, and if the behaviour of the defendant was dishonest by those standards, he may be guilty. If not, he is not guilty.
- However, even if the defendant is dishonest by the above ordinary and decent standards, he will still not be guilty unless *he* realised that ordinary people would regard him as dishonest. The test is, therefore, subjective.

However, in the usual case of theft the judge may consider that there is no evidence to show that the defendant believed that he was not dishonest and where this is so the judge need not give a direction to the jury in terms of *Ghosh*. The test is a difficult one to explain to a jury and can lead to inconsistent decisions according to the make-up of the jury and the part of the country in which it sits. As an example, we may take a trial for theft of some committed anti-vivisectionists who have stolen animals from a laboratory. Apply the test and see what you think. What do your fellow students think? Fred regularly robs the rich to give to the poor. How do you find on Fred's trial for theft?

Intention permanently to deprive. This is the second branch of the *mens rea* of theft. Its main purpose is to prevent most unauthorised borrowings from being theft. An intention to return the property sooner or later is not an intention permanently to deprive. However, if there is an intention permanently to deprive at the time of taking, giving the property back will not change the fact of theft and the charge of theft will be made out (see *R v McHugh* (1993)). The concept is dealt with by s 6(1); it does not often apply. In addition, s 6(2) applies and covers an even smaller number of cases. It applies where A being in possession of B's property pawns it. Despite A's intention to retrieve the property and return it, he is regarded as having treated it as his own for the purposes of theft.

Intention may be **conditional** as where A puts his hand into B's pocket intending to deprive him permanently of any money he may find there. However, there is no money so the crime of theft is not committed. In such a case a charge of attempted theft is appropriate.

Fraud and malpractice

Here we consider some common types of fraud and malpractice. The subject is a difficult one to grasp because the criminal fraternity is always developing new variations of existing crimes. However, a knowledge of the following should satisfy examination requirements.

Computer fraud

In a typical case the fraudster will get access to a computer which controls the movement of money. An instruction will be given for money to be transferred to the fraudster's account which may often be outside the UK.

However, the House of Lords has ruled that the Data Protection Act 1984 is not breached if information on a computer screen is merely viewed and not used.

R v *Brown* (1996)

The defendant, who was at the relevant time a serving police officer, checked details of car registration numbers held on the police national computer on behalf of a debt collector friend. He was charged under the Data Protection Act 1984. Section 5(2)(b) states that it is an offence for a registered data user knowingly or recklessly to hold personal data to 'use' any such data for any purpose other than the one described in the relevant entry in the register. The House of Lords ruled that the defendant was not guilty. The term 'use' could not apply merely to accessing information and reading it. Since there was no evidence that the defendant had made any use of the information, as by passing it on to his friend, he had not broken the law.

Comment. Lord Griffith, one of the two judges dissenting, felt that the majority judgment left a serious gap in the protection the 1984 Act offered. He felt that the integrity and security of data were not now fully protected, as was the intention behind the Act. In particular, it might not be an offence to interfere in some way with data after processing it, short of using or applying it. He said: 'I cannot believe that in the Data Protection Act it was intended that wrongful interference with the data by those with access to it should not be an offence.' He went on to say this could be the result if the word 'use' was given the limited meaning adopted in this case. Subject to judicial interpretation of s 1 of the Data Protection Act 1998, Brown may now have been guilty.

Discounting or factoring frauds

Typically the fraudsters will say they are running a business and approach a merchant bank or other source of finance for a loan on the strength of orders received. To substantiate the fact that orders have been received, false documentation is used and the fraudsters pocket the money obtained.

Franchise frauds

In this case the fraudsters induce investors to buy franchises, often with equipment or plant, in, for example, the fast food business. They hold out prospects of large profits from the investment. Once the payment for the franchise has been made, the investor finds that it is worthless and the equipment promised does not arrive.

Insurance fraud

The fraud here consists of submitting false claims as to loss. In addition, a fraudulent insurance broker can defraud clients and/or insurance companies by, e.g., overcharging or submitting false applications for insurance on which commission is payable.

Investment frauds

There is wide scope for frauds on investors. High returns on money invested are promised by the fraudsters. The original investors may even be paid 'dividends' from money received from later investors so that the fraud is promoted and its life prolonged.

Long-firm fraud

Here the fraudsters will set up in business as wholesalers and place orders with suppliers. They pay promptly to show their creditworthiness. Further and larger orders are then placed. The goods are received and are sold quickly, for whatever they will fetch, and the fraudsters disappear.

Public sector fraud

This consists largely of bribes and other favours given by the fraudsters to public servants in order to corrupt them. In return, the fraudsters may, for example, get acceptance of an uncompetitive tender for work or have shoddy work overlooked.

Revenue and Customs and Excise frauds

These consist largely of falsifying relevant returns to the relevant departments. In a not untypical case the managing director of a private company defrauded the Revenue of £363,000 by filling in false tax returns, failing to deduct tax for employees and using the company's funds for personal expenses. The money was eventually repaid but he received a sentence of one year's imprisonment and a fine of £40,000, together with disqualification from company management for two years (see further Chapter 6). He was also required to pay costs of £20,000.

Stationery frauds

In this case the fraudster gets in touch with the stationery buyer of a large company and takes orders. At first deliveries are made as requested. After a while, large amounts of stationery are sent which have not been ordered and the company is pressed for payment. The success of this fraud depends upon the recipient company having lax systems and upon intimidating the buyer. Skilful pressure exerted on the buyer may well result in his accepting and paying for grossly excessive amounts of stationery.

Stock Exchange frauds

This may consist of influencing the price of shares to the fraudster's advantage. Suppose that A plc is making a bid to take over B plc by a share-for-share exchange plus some cash. If the directors of A lend the company's money to selected individuals to buy A's shares, this will create a false market in the shares and increase the price so that A need not find any or so much cash in the takeover. The shareholders of B take shares in A at the false price and discover later that a false market had been created and the value of the shares in A falls. The creation of a false market is an offence under the Financial Services and Markets Act 2000 and the loans described above would infringe the Companies Act 1985 as being unlawful assistance to buy A's shares.

Insider dealing

Persons may indulge in what is called insider dealing or trading, e.g. buying or selling shares on the basis of inside knowledge not available to others about matters likely to influence of the price of the shares.

Part V of the Criminal Justice Act 1993 applies and Sch 2 of that Act sets out the securities covered by its provisions. It is not necessary at this level to list all these, but obviously shares issued by companies are covered and examination questions will normally be set on the basis of dealings in shares of companies. However, the 1993 Act also covers gilts, which are interest-bearing securities as distinct from shares which pay a dividend, and where insider dealing could consist of dealing in such securities with inside information as to changes in interest rates either up or down.

The securities must also be listed on a regulated market such as the Stock Exchange, but dealing in differences is covered too. Those who deal in differences do not buy shares or even take an option on them. The deal consists of a forecast of the price of a particular security at a given future time, and those who enter into such deals with inside information which helps them to predict the price will commit an offence.

The Act does not apply to unlisted securities or face-to-face transactions as may be the case in the sale and purchase of private company shares.

Meaning of dealing

A person deals in securities if he acquires or disposes of the securities himself, whether for himself or as the agent of some other person, or procures an acquisition or a disposal of the securities by someone else. Therefore, A could acquire shares for himself, or acquire shares as a broker for his client or dispose of them in the same contexts. Alternatively, A may simply advise B to purchase or dispose of shares and still be potentially liable if he has inside information. B may also be liable in this situation if he is what is called a tippee (see below).

What is inside information?

Basically this is information which relates to the securities themselves or to the state of the company which issued them. It must be specific and precise so that general information about a company, e.g. that it was desirous of moving into the field of supermarkets, would not be enough. In addition, the information must not have been made public and must be the sort of information which, if it had been made public, would be likely to have had a significant effect on the price of those securities, e.g. falling or rising profits or decisions to pay a higher dividend than expected, or a lower one or no dividend at all.

Insiders

In order to be guilty of the offence of insider dealing, the individual concerned must be an insider.

A person has information as an insider if:

- the information which he has is and he knows it is 'insider information';
- he has the information and he knows that he has it from an 'inside source'.

A person is in possession of information from an 'inside source' if:

- he has the information through being a director, employee or shareholder of a company or by having access to it by reason of his employment, e.g. as auditor; *or*
- the source of the information is a person within the above categories.

So, A is a director of Boxo plc. He has inside information that Boxo's profits when announced in ten days' time will be up (or down). He buys (or sells) Boxo shares himself and is potentially liable. He advises his friend Fred to buy (or sell) Boxo shares but does not tell him why. A is potentially liable but Fred is not – he does not have the inside information. If A tells Fred about the future profit announcement and then Fred deals, Fred is potentially liable, as is A. If Fred advises his son to buy (or sell) Boxo shares but does not tell him why, A and Fred are potentially liable but Fred's son is not. If Fred gives his son the inside information and the son deals, then A and Fred and Fred's son are potentially liable.

Disclosure in the course of employment

Sometimes it is necessary for a person to pass on inside information as part of his employment, as may be the case with an audit manager who passes on inside information to a senior partner of the firm who is in charge of the audit. If the senior partner deals, he will be potentially liable, but the audit manager will not since the 1993 Act exempts such persons.

Necessity for intent

Since insider dealing is a crime, it requires, as most but not all crimes do, an intention to see a dealing take place to secure a profit or prevent a loss. It is unlikely that an examiner would go deeply into what is essentially the field of the criminal lawyer, but consider this example: A's son was at college and broke. He asked his father for a loan and his father said, 'Look son, you're not getting any more money from me – pity you cannot buy some shares in Boxo plc of which I am a director. Next month's profit announcement will be way up on last year's. You could make a killing.' If for some reason A's son was able to scrape up sufficient funds to buy shares in Boxo plc, it is unlikely that his father would be liable because he had no idea that his son would be in a position to buy the shares.

Penalty for insider dealing

The contract to buy or sell the shares is unaffected. The sanctions are criminal, the maximum sentence being seven years' imprisonment and/or a fine of unlimited amount. In order to be found guilty the offence must in general terms be committed while the person concerned was in the UK or the trading market was.

Exemptions

Schedule 2 to the Criminal Justice Act 1993 sets out, in particular, an exemption for persons operating as dealers, so that, for example, those engaged in dealing for clients on the Stock Exchange are exempt because they would find it difficult to operate deals in shares if they had to stop dealing in them when in possession of what might be inside information about some of them. It should be noted, however, that the exemption covers only the offence of dealing. They are not exempt from the offence of encouraging another to deal.

Market abuse – the civil powers of the Financial Services Authority (FSA)

Under the Financial Services and Markets Act 2000 market abuse is behaviour in relation to investments traded on recognised UK investment exchanges, e.g. the London Stock Exchange, which satisfies at least one of the following tests:

- *the misleading impression test*, being behaviour likely to give those participating in the market a mistaken impression as to supply, demand price or value;
- *the distortion test*, being behaviour likely to distort the market;
- *the privileged information test*, being behaviour based on information which is not available to participants in the market who would regard that information as relevant when deciding whether or not to trade.

Proof of market abuse is on a balance of probabilities (the civil standard). However, under guidance from the Treasury, those dealt with for market abuse, such as insider dealing, will get additional protection given for criminal trials, and there is to be some support for legal costs. Thus, the FSA will not be allowed to use evidence which it has compelled someone to give as part of an investigation of market abuse. In other words, there is to be a rule against self-incrimination. The accusation that the FSA might act as 'prosecutor', judge and jury has been addressed. The investigation and disciplinary roles of the FSA will be kept separate and cases will be heard by an independent tribunal. The Criminal Justice Act 1993 which privides a **criminal regime** will remain in force.

The 'true and fair' aspect of the definition was regarded as too vague, so the government has now amended the relevant section and replaced it with a requirement that for behaviour to be abusive it must be regarded by a 'regular user' of the market as a failure on the part of the person concerned to observe the standards which the regular user would reasonably expect of a person 'in his ... position in relation to the market'. A 'regular user' is defined as a reasonable person who regularly deals on the market concerned in relevant investments. Other changes introduced into the Act are:

- Before deciding whether or not to take action for market abuse, the FSA must have regard to the extent to which the person involved took care to avoid engaging in abuse or actually believed that his behaviour was not abusive. There is, however, no 'safe harbour' provision for those who take reasonable steps to avoid engaging in market abuse. It is a matter for the FSA.
- A person will not be found to have engaged in abuse if he has complied with rules made by the FSA as where, for example, he acts in accordance with the FSA's rules regarding the stabilisation of investments.
- In determining the amount of any penalty to be imposed for market abuse, the FSA must take into account whether the behaviour has had an adverse effect on the market and how serious the effect has been, together with the extent to which the behaviour was deliberate or reckless and whether the person who is to be penalised is an individual as distinct from, e.g., a corporate organisation.
- As regards the possibility that the FSA would not accept conduct that was within the City Code as a defence to market abuse, the Act now allows the FSA to offer a safe harbour status in market abuse enforcement where there has been compliance with the Code, though the FSA is still required to keep itself informed about the way the Takeover Panel interprets and administers the Code.

The FSA has given some examples of what could constitute market abuse under the Code of Market Conduct that it has published. These include:

- persons using Internet bulletin boards to post misleading information; and
- financial journalists using inside knowledge to trade in shares.

It appears that the FSA will be able to identify persons hiding behind aliases on the bulletin boards. As we have seen, because the FSA operates under civil regime, it will only have to prove 'on a balance of probabilities' that a market user behaved in a way that amounted to market abuse.

Arson

Arson is a form of criminal damage which is covered by the Criminal Damage Act 1971. The offence of criminal damage becomes arson when the damage is caused by fire.

Under s 1(1) of the Act:

> A person who without lawful excuse destroys or damages any property belonging to another intending to destroy or damage any such property or being reckless as to whether any such property would be destroyed or damaged shall be guilty of an offence.

Section 1(3) provides that 'an offence committed under this section by destroying or damaging property by fire shall be charged as arson'.

Property is defined as tangible property. The essence of criminal damage is damage to a physical thing.

The damage must be more than nominal but need not involve total destruction. The *actus reus* is, therefore, destroying or damaging property belonging to another; the *mens rea* is intention or **recklessness**. Thus, it is not necessary for the defendant to realise the risk of damage by fire if the ordinary prudent person would. The following case provides an illustration.

Elliott v C (1983)

C, who was a 14-year-old schoolgirl, spent one entire night awake and wandering around. She entered a toolshed and there poured white spirit on to a carpet and set light to it, destroying the shed. The magistrates found that she did not appreciate just how flammable the spirit was and having regard to her extreme tiredness she did not give any real thought to the risk of fire. She was accordingly acquitted. On appeal, however, she was convicted. The correct test was whether a reasonable prudent person would realise the danger of fire in the circumstances, even though the particular accused did not.

Lawful excuse – a defence

Section 5(2) of the Act contains the defence of lawful excuse. The defence is available:

- where the defendant honestly believed that he had the consent of the relevant person or would have had if that person had known of the circumstances;
- where he acted to protect property including his own which he believed was in need of immediate protection and he believed the means used were reasonable.

R v Denton (1982)

The defendant set fire to a cotton mill at the request of his employer, the latter intending to make a fraudulent claim on his insurance policy. He was not guilty because he believed that the person who was entitled to consent had done so. A more appropriate charge would have been conspiracy to defraud.

Where life is endangered

Section 1(2) of the Act contains the offence of destroying or damaging property with intention or recklessness as to endangering life. The offence is triable only on indictment and carries a maximum penalty of life imprisonment, and the defence of lawful excuse in s 5(2) does not apply.

QUESTIONS/ACTIVITIES

1 How, if at all, would you justify the use of the criminal law to control unfair trading practices? What are the advantages and disadvantages of imposing strict liability for criminal offences in the field of consumer protection?

2 David is the author of a guide to British cafés and snack bars. During the course of a year he travels considerable distances in his car pursuing his researches and consequently he changes his car regularly every 12 months. After three months' use David's current car develops a fault with the odometer which necessiates its replacement. When David trades the car in at the end of the year, he forgets tell Newtown Motor Co Ltd that the car has done 10,000 more miles than appears on the odometer. Newtown Motor Co Ltd sells the car to June, who discovers a few weeks later that the mileage displayed on the odometer is incorrect. She reports the matter to the local trading standards department.

(a) Discuss the criminal liability of David and Newtown Motor Co Ltd.

(b) What defences may be available to David and Newtown Motor Co Ltd if they are prosecuted?

(c) What advice would you give Newtown Motor Co Ltd to help it avoid prosecution in the future?

3 Basil and Sybil run a small hotel on the south coast. At the end of another disappointing summer season they place the following advert in several north of England newspapers: 'Small, friendly family hotel on South Coast, jacuzzi and swimming pool available. Winter Weekend Breaks; Dinner, Bed and Breakfast £30 per person per night.'

Stan books a room for a Saturday night in February. The weekend proves to be a great disappointment. The jacuzzi and sauna are still under construction and the swimming pool referred to is the municipal pool located half a mile away from the hotel. Stan is charged £40 for his night's stay. When he complains, he is informed by Basil that the advertised rate only applies to stays of more than two nights where two people share a room. On his return home, Stan complains to the local trading standards department.

Discuss the criminal liability of Basil and Sybil, bearing in mind any defences that may be available to them.

4 Skaters Ltd, a manufacturer of skateboards, supplies several hundred skateboards to retailers throughout the country in preparation for the Christmas market. It soon becomes apparent that the design of the skateboard is defective. Several children are injured attempting to execute 180-degree turns when the back pair of wheels shear off from their mountings on the skateboard. Despite these problems, Skaters Ltd continues to supply the skateboard to retailers and takes no steps to warn the public.

What action may be taken to protect the public from the potential dangers of the skateboard?

5 Margaret visits her local butcher, Chops Ltd, and buys 1 kg of Chops Ltd's own sausages, a pork pie bought in by Chops Ltd from a local pie manufacturer and 500 g of extra-lean minced beef, which is 25 per cent more expensive than ordinary minced beef. When Margaret and her family eat the food over the next few days they discover a piece of glass in one of the sausages, penicillin mould growing on the crust of the pork pie, and that there appears to be an excessive amount of fat in the minced beef.

(a) Discuss the criminal liability of Chops Ltd and the local pie manufacturer.

(b) What defences may be available to Chops Ltd and the pie manufacturer if they are prosecuted?

(c) Advise Margaret about any civil action she may be able to bring against Chops Ltd and/or the pie manufacturer.

6 John found a diamond ring at the local disco. He put it in his pocket thinking he might find the owner but then forgot about it. He was told two days later that the ring belonged to Jane. He rang her to say he had it, but because at the moment she was going off on a business trip, she asked him to keep it for her, saying she would be back in a week. John was short of cash and he pawned the ring hoping to redeem the pledge before Jane returned. Discuss John's possible liability under the Theft Act.

7 'A survey of price movements shows clearly that there is a tendency for the price of shares in bid-for companies to rise sharply before the announcement of takeover bids, which is evidence of "inside buying".'

On the assumption that the above statement is true, what measures have been introduced by government to alleviate the situation?

Chapter 13

CREDIT

At some time or another everyone makes use of credit. It may be a mortgage from a building society to buy your own home, or hire-purchase arranged by a car dealer to help you afford the latest model. When the monthly finances do not work out right, you will probably run up an overdraft at the bank. Even if it is just paying the milkman at the end of the week, you have made use of credit. People in business also rely on credit. A loan may be needed to translate a good idea into a marketable product. Established companies often have to look outside their own resources to finance expansion. Most businesses give and expect to receive a period of time in which to pay their trade bills.

Credit consists of either buying something and being given time to pay for it or borrowing money and paying it back later. The person giving the credit (the creditor) is providing service, which the borrower (the debtor) is usually required to pay for, the price being a certain rate of interest.

Credit is not a new idea. Moneylenders have been around for centuries. However, the 20th century witnessed a dramatic increase in the use of credit, particularly to finance private-home purchase and consumer spending on such items as cars, electrical goods and furniture. Despite the cautionary proverb, 'Neither a borrower nor a lender be', credit has several clear advantages. Most people lack the self-discipline to save up for expensive items. Credit allows them to enjoy the benefit of goods and services sooner than they otherwise would. In a period of inflation there is even the prospect of getting them more cheaply. But the easy availability of credit can bring dangers to both sides. The problems facing the consumer are neatly summarised in a comment attributed to a county court judge: being persuaded by a man you don't know to sign an agreement you haven't read

to buy furniture you don't need with money you haven't got. Since creditors face the risk that they may not be repaid, they channel their energies into finding effective ways of securing their financial interests. Occasionally this has led to the imposition of unreasonably severe terms on borrowers. At first, it was left to the judges to intervene to redress the balance; thus, from medieval times equity and the Court of Chancery came to the aid of mortgagors of land. With the passing of time, Parliament felt it necessary to impose piecemeal controls on credit agreements.

In the 1960s, concern about the inadequacies of our credit laws led the Labour government to set up a Committee on Consumer Credit under the chairmanship of Lord Crowther. The Committee reported in 1971 and some of its recommendations were enacted by the Consumer Credit Act 1974. The process of implementing the major overhaul of our credit laws has been a gradual one. The provisions of the Act were brought into force by means of statutory instrument supplemented by ministerial regulation. The outstanding sections came into force on 19 May 1985 – 11 years after the Act was passed by Parliament.

This chapter will examine the various types of credit available and how they are regulated by the law, particularly the Consumer Credit Act 1974.

TYPES OF CREDIT

Hire-purchase

Hire-purchase (HP) is probably the best known method of buying on the 'never-never'. From the legal point of view, it is something of an 'odd man out' since the customer pays regular amounts for the hire of goods, only becoming the owner if he exercises an option to buy. HP developed in the latter half of the 19th century. The traders of that time were looking for a form of credit to boost their sales which combined security for the creditor with a minimum of legal regulation. The chattel mortgage might have been a possibility, but the Bills of Sale Acts 1878 and 1882 provided for strict controls on mortgages of goods. Other ideas were tried and finally the right formula was found and judicially approved in *Helby* v *Matthews* (1895).

Helby v *Matthews* (1895)
Helby, a dealer, agreed to let a piano on HP to Brewster in return for 36 instalments of 10s/6d per month. The agreement stated that Brewster would become the owner of the piano on payment of the final instalment. However, he could end the agreement at any time and return the piano to Helby, his only liability being to pay any arrears of rent. Four months after the start of the agreement, Brewster pledged the piano with a pawnbroker (Matthews). The House of Lords held that Helby was entitled to recover the piano from the pawnbroker. Brewster was merely the hirer of the piano and, as such, he could not pass title to the pawnbroker under s 9 of the Factors Act 1889.

Comment. This is an application of the *nemo dat* rule, which we examined in Chapter 10.

The popularity of HP was guaranteed after this case. The advantages of this form of credit to traders were twofold: if the hirer failed to pay an instalment the owner could repossess the goods and if the goods fell into the hands of an innocent third party, the owner could recover them.

A modern HP agreement usually requires the customer to pay an initial deposit followed by equal weekly/monthly instalments for the hire of the goods. At the end of the agreement, the hirer may exercise an option to buy for a relatively small sum. A specimen HP agreement is reproduced in Fig 13.1. The owner may be the supplier of the goods but today it is more likely to be a specialist finance company introduced by the supplier. If this is the case, the HP arrangements will involve two transactions, as explained in Fig 13.2.

Conditional sale

Like HP, conditional sale gives the customer immediate possession of the goods, payment is by regular instalments and ownership only passes to the buyer when all the payments have been made. The important difference is that with HP the hirer may choose whether he wishes to buy the goods, while under a conditional sale agreement the customer is under an obligation to buy. The transfer of ownership is delayed until the buyer meets the condition specified in the agreement (usually payment of the final instalment).

Conditional sale has never been popular in this country and today its use is mainly confined to the purchase of industrial plant and equipment. It was one of the formulas considered by Victorian traders prior to the case of *Helby* v *Matthews* (1895). However, the decision of the Court of Appeal in *Lee* v *Butler* (1893) showed that since the customer had agreed to buy the goods he could pass good title to a third party under the Factors Act 1889, leaving the creditor without the security he required. Conditional sale was treated as a contract for the sale of goods, although in reality it has more in common with HP. The Hire Purchase Act 1964 (followed by the Consumer Credit Act 1974) resolved this difficulty by equating conditional sale with HP for most purposes.

Credit sale

This is a contract for the sale of goods whereby ownership and possession of the goods pass immediately to the buyer, but he is given time to pay. Since the purchaser becomes the owner of the goods straight away, he can resell them before the end of the agreement, provided that he pays off what he owes, and if he defaults on his repayments, the seller cannot repossess the goods. This is in marked contrast to the position under a HP agreement. A specimen credit sale agreement is reproduced in Fig 13.3. This form of credit is used, for example, in purchases from mail order catalogues.

Bank loans

There are various ways of borrowing from a bank.

1 **Overdraft.** An overdraft may arise in one of two ways: either the customer makes an arrangement with the bank to overdraw his current account up to an agreed amount or, without prior agreement,

HPA (h)
Hire-Purchase Agreement *regulated by the Consumer Credit Act 1974*　　Original
No right of cancellation

Agreement No. _____

This Hire-Purchase Agreement sets out below and overleaf the terms on which we (the owners) agree to let and you (the customer) agree to hire the goods described below:

The Owners _____
Name and address

_____

The Customer _____
Full names please

Address _____

_____

Financial Details and Payments

	Particulars of Goods	Cash Price incl. VAT £ p
Qty.	Description	
	Identification Nos:	

Total Cash Price (incl. VAT) £

Less: Pt. Ex. £_____

Cash £_____ Deposit (a) £

= Amount of Credit £

Hire Purchase Charge £

Documentation Fee* £

Option to Purchase Fee* £

= Total Charge for Credit £

APR _____ %

Balance Payable (b) £

Payable by:
A first payment (including documentation fee) of:† £

_____ payments each of: £

A final payment (incl. option fee) of:† £

Each payment payable the same day of each succeeding

month, commencing _____

Total Amount Payable (a) + (b) £

*Must include VAT if together more than £10 in total. Omit if not needed.

†Delete if not needed.

Signature of (or on behalf of) Owners

_____

Date of Owners' Signature (Date of Agreement)

TERMINATION: YOUR RIGHTS
You have a right to end this agreement. If you wish to do so, you should write to the person authorised to receive your payments. We will then be entitled to the return of the goods and to half the total amount payable under this agreement, that is £ _____.[1] If you have already paid at least this amount plus any overdue instalments, you will not have to pay any more, provided you have taken reasonable care of the goods.

1 Insert one half of the total amount payable.

REPOSSESSION: YOUR RIGHTS
If you fail to keep to your side of this agreement but you have paid at least one third of the total amount payable under this agreement, that is £ _____, we may not take back the goods against your wishes unless we get a court order. (In Scotland, we may need to get a court order at any time.) If we do take them without your consent or a court order, you have the right to get back all the money you have paid under the agreement.

2 Insert one third of the total amount payable.

DECLARATION BY CUSTOMER
By signing this agreement you declare that:

★ You have carefully examined the goods and your attention has been drawn to Clause 1 overleaf.

★ The information given by you before entering into this agreement is correct. You realise that we will rely on that information in deciding whether to enter into this agreement.

★ You acknowledge that before granting credit we may search the files of one or more credit reference agencies which will keep a record of our enquiry. We may also disclose details of the account and your conduct of it to that agency (or agencies). Information thus held is used only to help make credit decisions affecting you or members of your household or occasionally for fraud prevention or tracing debtors.

This is a Hire-Purchase Agreement regulated by the Consumer Credit Act 1974. Sign it only if you want to be legally bound by its terms.

Signature(s) of Customer(s) _____

The goods will not become your property until you have made all the payments. You must not sell them before then.

Witness: Signature _____

Name _____
Block letters please

Address _____

Fig 13.1 A typical hire-purchase agreement form

HPA
(h)
Original

TERMS OF THE AGREEMENT

1 Payment

Before signing this agreement you must have paid the deposit shown overleaf. By signing this agreement you agree to pay the Balance Payable by making the payments set out overleaf, by their specified dates, to us at the address stated overleaf or to any person or address notified by us in writing. Punctual payment is essential. If you pay by post you do so at your own risk.

2 Failure to pay on time

We have the right to charge interest at the annual percentage rate shown overleaf (less that part attributable to any documentation or option to purchase fee) on all overdue amounts. This interest will be calculated on a daily basis from the date the amount falls due until it is received and will run after as well as before any judgment.

3 Ownership of the goods

You will become the owner of the goods only after we have received all amounts payable for them under this agreement, including under Clauses 1, 2 and 11, and you exercise the option to purchase by paying any option to purchase fee shown overleaf or, if none is shown, by notifying us of your decision to retain the goods. Until then the goods remain our property and your rights are solely those of a hirer.

4 Selling or disposing of the goods

You must keep the goods safely at your address and you may not sell or dispose of them or transfer your rights under this agreement. You may only part with the goods to have them repaired. You may not use the goods as security for any of your obligations.

5 Repair of the goods

You must keep the goods in good condition and repair at your own expense. You are responsible for all loss of or damage to them (except fair wear and tear) even if caused by acts or events outside your control. You must not allow a repairer or any other person to obtain a lien on or a right to retain the goods.

6 Change of address

You must immediately notify us in writing of any change of your address.

7 Inspection

You must allow us or our representative to inspect and test the goods at all reasonable times.

8 Insurance of the goods

You must keep the goods insured under a fully comprehensive policy of insurance at your own expense. You must notify us of any loss of or damage to the goods and hold any monies payable under the policy in trust for us. You irrevocably authorise us to collect the monies from the insurers. If a claim is made against the insurers we may at our absolute discretion conduct any negotiations and effect any settlement of the claim with the insurers. You agree to abide by such settlement and to pay us any shortfall under the agreement. Where the goods are for use in a business the insurance must include liability insurance to a reasonable limit of liability or to a limit of liability that we specify.

9 Your right to end the agreement

You have the right to end this agreement as set out in the notice 'Termination: Your Rights' overleaf. You must then at your own expense return the goods to us.

10 Our right to end the agreement

We may end this agreement, after giving you written notice, if:
(a) you fail to keep any of your obligations under clauses 1, 4, 5, 7 or 8, the complete and punctual performance of which is the essence of this agreement;
(b) a meeting is called of your creditors or any arrangement, composition or trust deed is made or proposed with or for the benefit of them;
(c) a petition is presented for the making of a bankruptcy order against you or you are deemed unable to pay your debts or you become apparently insolvent within the meaning of the Insolvency Act 1986 or the Bankruptcy (Scotland) Act 1985 respectively;

(d) you cease to carry on business or, being a partnership, it is dissolved or proceedings for its dissolution are commenced;
(e) execution or, in Scotland, any poinding or arrestment (otherwise than on the dependence of an action) is levied or attempted against any of your assets or income;
(f) the landlord of the premises where the equipment is kept threatens or takes any step to distrain on or, in Scotland, exercise any right of hypothec over the goods or any of your other goods;
(g) you have given false information in connection with your entry into this agreement;
(h) the goods are destroyed or the insurers treat a claim under the above policy on a total loss basis.

If we end this agreement then, subject to your rights as set out in the notice 'Repossession: Your Rights' overleaf, we may retake the goods. You will also then have to pay to us:
(1) all overdue payments and
(2) the rest of the Total Amount Payable under the agreement less:
   (a) a rebate for early payment required by law; and
   (b) the net proceeds of sale of the goods (if any) after deduction of the costs of recovery, insurance, storage and sale.

11 Expenses

You must repay on demand our expenses and legal costs for:
(a) finding your address if you change address without first informing us or finding the goods if they are not at the address given by you;
(b) taking steps, including court action, to recover the goods or to obtain payment for them.

12 Exclusion

(a) If you are dealing as consumer (as defined in the Unfair Contract Terms Act 1977) nothing in this agreement will affect your rights under the Supply of Goods (Implied Terms) Act 1973.
(b) In all other cases:
   (i) you rely on your own skill and judgement as to the quality of the goods and their fitness for their intended purpose;
   (ii) we will not be responsible for their quality, their fitness for any purpose or their correspondence with any description or specification.

13 General provisions

(a) The word 'goods' includes replacements, renewals and additions which we or you may make to them with our consent.
(b) No relaxation or indulgence which we may extend to you shall affect our strict rights under this agreement.
(c) Where two or more persons are named as the customer, you jointly and severally accept the obligations under this agreement. This means that each of you can be held fully responsible under this agreement.
(d) We may transfer our rights under this agreement.

14 When this agreement takes effect

This agreement will only take effect if and when it is signed by us or our authorised representative.

IMPORTANT – YOU SHOULD READ THIS CAREFULLY
YOUR RIGHTS

The Consumer Credit Act 1974 covers this agreement and lays down certain requirements for your protection which must be satisfied when the agreement is made. If they are not, we cannot enforce the agreement against you without a court order. The Act also gives you a number of rights. You have a right to settle this agreement at any time by giving notice in writing and paying off all amounts payable under the agreement which may be reduced by a rebate.

If you would like to know more about the protection and remedies provided under the Act, you should contact either your local Trading Standards Department or your nearest Citizens' Advice Bureau.

Fig 13.1 *(continued)*

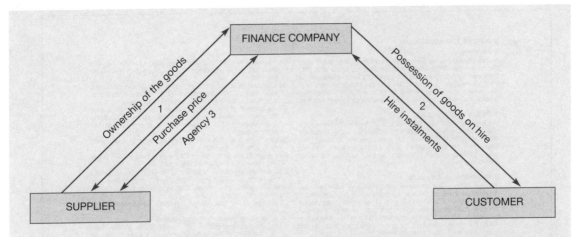

Notes

(1) Contract for the sale of goods between the supplier and the finance company covered by the Sale of Goods Act 1979.

(2) HP contract between the finance company and the customer. The agreement will be regulated by the Consumer Credit Act 1974, if the amount of the credit does not exceed £25,000 for agreements made after 1 May 1998 and the customer is not a company. If the Act does not cover the agreement, the common law applies.

(3) If the HP agreement is a regulated agreement under the Consumer Credit Act 1974, the dealer is regarded as an agent of the finance company. The finance company is equally responsible with the supplier for any misrepresentation or breach of contract.

Fig 13.2 A typical hire-purchase arrangement

he simply writes cheques for an amount greater than in his account. A variable rate of interest is charged on the amount drawn by the customer, calculated on a daily basis, and bank charges usually become payable. Security may be needed for large sums. The bank can insist on repayment in full at any time. An overdraft is usually the cheapest way of borrowing from a bank.

2 **Ordinary loan.** This type of loan is extended to bank customers and for a particular purpose – to buy a car, for example. A specific sum of money is borrowed for an agreed period of time. A separate loan account is opened by the bank into which the instalments are paid, usually by means of a standing order from the customer's current account. Variable interest is charged and security may be required.

3 **Personal loan.** The loan is available to anyone, customer and non-customer alike, usually for a particular purpose. The period of the loan and interest are fixed when the credit is arranged. Again, security may be asked for. It is usually a more expensive way of borrowing than either the overdraft or ordinary loan.

4 **Budget account.** A budget account is used to help spread the payment of bills over the year. The customer calculates his annual outgoings on such items as gas, electricity and Council Tax. The bank adds to this its service charge for operating the account. The total is divided by 12 and a standing order for this amount is placed to the credit of the budget account. The bills can then be paid with confidence as and when they arrive.

Credit cards

A credit card allows the holder to pay (usually up to a limit) for goods and services or to obtain a cash advance by producing a plastic personalised card. There are three main kinds of credit card.

1 **Bank credit cards (e.g. Access, Visa).** Although these cards are linked to particular banks, an application may be made to any bank for its card. The holder is given a personal credit limit and he can use the card to buy goods and services or obtain a cash advance wherever the card is accepted, up to this limit. Traders involved in the scheme send details of purchases to the credit card company and are then

CSC
(c) **Credit Agreement** *regulated by the Consumer Credit Act 1974*   Original
With right of cancellation

Agreement No. _____

This credit sale agreement sets out below and overleaf the terms on which you (the customer) agree to purchase from us (the supplier) the goods or services described below.

The Supplier _____
Name and address

_____

The Customer _____
Full names please

Address _____

_____

Particulars of Goods or Services		Cash Price incl. VAT	
Qty.	Description	£	p
	Total Cash Price (incl. VAT)		

Financial Details and Payments	£	p	
Total Cash Price			
Less Deposit: Cash £_____ Pt. Ex. £_____			(a)
= Amount of credit			
Add: Charges			
= Balance Payable			(b)
Total Amount Payable (a)+(b)			
A.P.R.		_____	%
Number of monthly payments			
Commence			
Subsequent payments on same day of each succeeding month			
Amount of each payment			
Amount of final payment (if different)			

DECLARATION BY CUSTOMER
By signing this agreement you are declaring that:
★ All the information you have given us before entering into this agreement is correct
★ You realise that we rely on this information when deciding whether to enter into this agreement.

Witness: Signature _____

Name _____
Block letters please
Address _____

Signature of (or on behalf of) the Supplier

_____

Date of the Supplier's Signature (Date of Agreement)

Before granting credit we may search the files of a credit reference agency which will keep a record of that search. We may also disclose details about your conduct of the account to that agency. Information thus held is used only to help make credit decisions or occasionally for fraud prevention or tracing debtors.

This is a Credit Agreement regulated by the Consumer Credit Act 1974. Sign it only if you want to be legally bound by its terms.

Signature(s)
of Customer(s) _____

Date(s) of Signature(s) _____

✂ ─────────────────────────────

CANCELLATION FORM
(Complete and return this form ONLY IF YOU WISH TO CANCEL THE AGREEMENT).

To: _____ [1]

_____

I/We* hereby give notice that I/we* wish to cancel

agreement _____ [2]

Signed _____

Date _____

Name _____

Address _____

YOUR RIGHT TO CANCEL
Once you have signed this agreement, you will have for a short time a right to cancel it. Exact details of how and when you can do this will be sent to you by post by us.

Notes for cancellation form:
[1] Sellers to insert name and address.
[2] Sellers to insert reference number, code or other identification details.
*Delete inapplicable word.

Copyright © Consumer Credit Trade Association (original size A4)

Fig 13.3 A typical credit agreement form

CSC
(c)
Original

TERMS OF THE AGREEMENT

1 Payment

Before signing this agreement you must have paid the deposit shown overleaf. By signing this agreement you agree to pay the Balance Payable by making the payments set out overleaf, by their specified dates, to us at the address stated overleaf or to any person or address notified by us in writing. Punctual payment is essential. If you pay by post you do so at your own risk.

2 Failure to pay on time

We have the right to charge interest at the annual percentage rate shown overleaf on any amount payable under this agreement and not received by us by the date on which the final payment falls due. This interest will be calculated on a daily basis from that date until it is received.

We may also charge you for any legal costs or other expenses incurred by us in obtaining payment by you of any sum overdue.

3 Right to demand earlier payment

If any amount is overdue for more than fourteen days we have the right, by sending you a notice of default, to require you to bring your payments up to date within seven days after service of the notice. If you do not do so, the whole of the balance remaining unpaid on the agreement shall then become due and payable immediately.

4 Earlier payment by you

If you pay off the balance on this agreement before the date on which the final payment falls due you will usually be entitled to a rebate of part of the charges.

5 General provisions

(a) No relaxation or indulgence which we may extend to you shall affect our strict rights under this agreement.
(b) We may transfer our rights under this agreement.
(c) You must inform us in writing within seven days of any change of your address. If you fail to do so you must repay our reasonable costs in finding your new address.
(d) Where two or more of you are named as the customer you jointly and severally accept the obligations under this agreement. This means that each of you can be held fully responsible under the agreement.

6 When this agreement takes effect

This agreement will only take effect if and when it is signed by us or our authorised representative.

IMPORTANT — YOU SHOULD READ THIS CAREFULLY
YOUR RIGHTS

The Consumer Credit Act 1974 covers this agreement and lays down certain requirements for your protection which must be satisfied when the agreement is made. If they are not, we cannot enforce the agreement against you without a court order.

The Act also gives you a number of rights. You have a right to settle this agreement at any time by giving notice in writing and paying off all amounts payable under the agreement which may be reduced by a rebate.

If you would like to know more about the protection and remedies provided under the Act, you should contact either your local Trading Standards Department or your nearest Citizens' Advice Bureau.

Fig 13.3 *(continued)*

reimbursed after a charge of between 1 per cent and 4 per cent has been deducted. At the end of each month, the holder receives an account of his spending and details of the minimum amount that must be paid that month (£5 or 5 per cent, whichever is the greater). If the holder pays the account in full by the stipulated date, he is not charged interest on the credit obtained. (This does not apply to cash advances, for which a service charge is made.) Alternatively, part-payment may be sent, in which case interest is charged. Most banks now charge an annual fee for use of their credit cards.

2 Charge cards (e.g. American Express, Diners Club). These cards work in much the same way as bank credit cards, allowing the holder to pay for goods and services at home and abroad by producing his card. The main differences are:

(a) the card holder pays an initial joining fee plus an annual membership fee;

(b) there is no pre-set credit limit; and

(c) the companies insist that the account is paid in full each month.

3 Retailers' credit cards (e.g. Marks & Spencer Chargecard). Many chain stores, supermarkets and garages issue their own credit cards to regular customers for use in their own establishments. The period of credit is usually a few weeks between making the purchases and the presentation of the account.

The relationship between suppliers, credit or charge card-issuers and card-holders was examined by the Court of Appeal in *Re Charge Card Services Ltd* (1988). A company operating a charge card service had gone into liquidation and the question arose whether unpaid suppliers could recover payment direct from card-holders. The court held that when a card-holder uses his card to acquire goods and services, this operates as an unconditional discharge of his obligation to the supplier. An unpaid supplier can, therefore, only take action against the card-issuer to recover what he is owed.

Shop budget account

This form of credit is operated by many large stores. The customer decides how much he can afford to pay each month. He is then allowed a spending limit of, for example, 12 times the £15 agreed. This allows the customer to spend up to £180 but never more than this. As regular repayments are made, he can make more purchases if he does not exceed the £180 limit. This is known as 'revolving credit' or 'running account credit'. Interest is usually charged on the amount owing at the end of a specified period (usually a month).

Trading checks and vouchers

The check trader issues a check or voucher for a specified amount to his customer. The checks can be spent in any shop which has already agreed to accept them. The shop receives payment from the check trader, less a discount. The customer repays the check trader by small regular instalments including interest. Check trading is more common in the north of England. It is a fairly expensive way to borrow.

Credit unions

These are a form of self-help organisation which are particularly popular in North America and are now catching on in this country. Credit unions are formed by people with something in common; they may belong to the same club or work together. They agree to make regular savings to form a pool of money. If any of the members need money unexpectedly, they can borrow from the pool. They are governed by the Credit Unions Act 1979.

Insurance policy loan

This is a loan obtained from an insurance company based on the security of an insurance policy with a 'cash-in' value.

Finance company personal loan

Big stores, car dealers, gas and electricity companies often arrange these loans to finance large purchases. They are also advertised in local newspapers.

Moneylenders

Moneylenders are often used by people who get credit from more traditional sources. They are usually prepared to lend without security and, as a result, their interest charges can be very high.

Pawnbroking

This is one of the oldest ways of lending money. A pawnbroker will advance money for a short period of time, and in return will take possession of goods (for example, jewellery) as security. If the loan and interest are repaid, the goods are returned to the borrower; if the pawn is not redeemed, the goods may be sold by the pawnbroker.

Mortgage

Building societies, banks and local authorities are willing to lend money to help people buy their own homes. The mortgage is the interest taken by the lender in the property which acts as security for the loan.

CONSUMER CREDIT ACT 1974

Background to the Act

The Crowther Committee, which had been set up in 1965 to investigate consumer credit, found that our credit laws were in a mess. The rules having developed in a piecemeal way were to be found in a large number of statutes and in the common law. Different rules had been created for different kinds of credit, and in some areas the consumer was inadequately protected.

The Committee recommended the passing of two pieces of legislation. The government rejected the need for a Lending and Security Act, which would have set up, amongst other things, a security register. However, it accepted the argument for a Consumer Sale and Loan Act to extend and improve the protective rules, which already existed in relation to HP. This proposal became the Consumer Credit Act 1974. It replaces most of the earlier credit legislation with the exception of the Bills of Sale Acts 1878 and 1882 and the Hire Purchase Act 1964, Part III.

For the rest of this chapter, section references are to the 1974 Act unless otherwise indicated.

Terminology

The Act introduced a new set of terms, the most important of which are explained below.

1 Debtor-creditor-supplier agreement (DCSA) (s 12) and debtor-creditor agreement (DCA) (s 13). A DCSA arises where there is a connection between the creditor and the transaction for which the finance is being provided. The creditor and supplier of the goods or services for which the credit is being made available may be the same person. Where they are different people, it will be a DCSA if there is an arrangement between the supplier and credit. Examples include HP, credit cards and trading checks. If there is no connection between the creditor and any supplier, it will be a DCA. An overdraft from a bank to be spent as the customer wishes is an example.

2 Restricted-use credit agreement and unrestricted-use credit agreement (s 11). If the debtor is free to use the credit as he or she pleases, e.g. overdraft, it will be an unrestricted-use credit agreement. Where the credit is tied to a particular transaction, it will be restricted-use credit. Examples include HP, credit sale, shop's budget account, check trading and the use of credit cards to obtain goods and services.

3 Fixed-sum credit and running-account credit (s 10). Fixed-sum credit is where the agreement is made for a specific sum of credit (e.g. HP, bank loan). Running-account credit is sometimes referred to as revolving credit. It is where the debtor can receive cash, goods or services from time to time to an amount which does not exceed his credit limit (e.g. overdraft, shop's budget account).

4 Credit tokens (s 14). The definition of a credit token covers credit cards, trading checks and vouchers, but not cheque guarantee cards.

5 APR. The Act promotes its primary objective of 'truth in lending' by creating a standard measure of the true cost of borrowing, which is the annual percentage rate of charge (APR). This allows the consumer to make a fair comparison between different credit deals. The first step in calculating the APR is to work out the total charge for credit. The figure includes all the costs involved in borrowing the money such as interest charges and all other costs associated with the credit transaction, e.g. arrangement fees or insurance. The total is then expressed as an annual percentage rate (APR), calculated according to complex regulations made under s 20. The current regulations, which came into effect on 14 April 2000, set out a statutory formula for calculating the APR. The method of calculating APR is very technical and involves the use of complex concepts and mathematical methods. The Office of Fair Trading publishes a booklet, *Credit Charges and*

APR, which explains how the APR is calculated, with illustrative examples of calculations based on typical credit agreements.

AGREEMENTS COVERED BY THE ACT

Most of the Act only applies to 'regulated agreements'. Some agreements are 'partially regulated' while other agreements are said to be 'exempt'.

Regulated agreements

Two types of agreement are regulated by the Act – consumer credit agreements and consumer hire agreements.

1 Regulated consumer credit agreement. This is a personal credit agreement by which the creditor provides the debtor with credit not exceeding £25,000 for agreements made after 1 May 1998 (s 8). It is personal credit if the borrower is an individual or partnership, but not a company. Credit is defined in s 9 as a 'cash loan or any other form of financial accommodation'. This covers HP, conditional sale, credit sale, loans, overdrafts, credit cards, shop budget accounts and trading checks.

   The monetary limit refers to the credit given. It does not include any deposit or interest charges. The total price paid, therefore, may exceed the limit but the agreement could still be regulated, as explained in the example below.

Example
Cash price of the goods = £27,000 paid for by:

£2,500	deposit
£24,500	credit
£750	interest

Total credit price = £27,750

Although the debtor pays a total of £27,750, the credit obtained is only £24,500, and so the agreement will be regulated.

2 Regulated consumer hire agreement. This is an agreement under which goods are hired, leased, rented or bailed to an individual, which is capable of lasting more than three months and does not require the hirer to pay more than £25,000 in rentals, for agreements made after 1 May 1998 (s 15).

   A recent House of Lords case provides an interesting illustration of how the framework of regulation applies in practice.

Dimond v Lovell (2000)

The case arose out of a car accident in which Mr Lovell drove into the back of Mrs Dimond's car. While Mrs Dimond's car was being repaired, she hired a replacement car from 1st Automotive Ltd. 1st Automotive specialises in hiring cars to drivers whose cars have been damaged by the negligence of other drivers and are off the road being repaired. 1st Automotive does not ask drivers, like Mrs Dimond, to pay anything until the claim for damages against the negligent driver is settled. Mr Lovell's insurer, the Co-operative Insurance Society (CIS), paid Mrs Dimond's repair bills promptly, but it refused to pay 1st Automotive's hire charges, which amounted to £346.63. The CIS put forward two defences. The first was that the agreement between Mrs Dimond and 1st Automotive was a regulated consumer credit agreement but it was unenforceable because it did not comply with the requirements of the Consumer Credit Act. If it was unenforceable, Mrs Dimond did not owe 1st Automotive £346.63 and, therefore, she could not recover that amount from Mr Lovell as she had not suffered any loss. The second line of defence was that Mrs Dimond had not mitigated her loss. The 'spot rate' for car hire was considerably lower than 1st Automotive's charges. The House of Lords held that the agreement entered into by Mrs Dimond with 1st Automotive was a regulated consumer credit agreement. The agreement was unenforceable because it did not contain all the terms 'prescribed' in regulations made under the Consumer Credit Act 1974. Lord Hoffman noted that 1st Automotive could obtain exemption from the 1974 Act by including a clause in its agreement requiring that the hire charges be paid within 12 months. (For details of 'exempt agreements' see below.) Their Lordships also considered what the position would have been if the agreement had been exempt and, as a result, enforceable. They took the view that although Mrs Dimond acted reasonably in engaging the services of 1st Automotive, it did not mean she was entitled to recover the full amount of the charges. She had obtained additional services (e.g. not having to pay over the cost of the hire car, relief from the trouble and anxiety of pursuing a claim against Mr Lovell). These additional services are not recoverable in English law. Mrs Dimond's claim would, therefore, have been limited to the 'spot rate' for hire cars.

Comment. In the Court of Appeal, the Vice-Chancellor found that the 1st Automotive agreement was a **personal credit** agreement, a **consumer credit** agreement, an agreement for a **fixed-sum credit** facility, a **restricted-use credit** agreement and a **debtor-creditor-supplier** agreement. It would also have been a **consumer hire** agreement if it had been capable of lasting for more than three months.

Partially regulated agreements

Two kinds of agreements are only partially regulated by the Act.

1 Small agreement. A small agreement is either a regulated consumer credit agreement (other than an HP or conditional sale agreement) where the credit does not exceed £50, or a regulated consumer hire agreement which does not require the hirer to pay more than £50 in rentals (s 17).

2 Non-commercial agreement. This is a consumer credit agreement or consumer hire agreement which is not made by the creditor or owner in the course of a business carried on by him (s 189(1)).

Exempt agreement (s 16)

1 Exempt consumer credit agreements. The exemptions are as follows:

(a) *mortgage lending* – loans secured by land mortgages made by building societies, local authorities and other bodies to finance the buying or developing of land;
(b) *low-cost credit* – e.g. DCAs where the APR does not exceed the highest of the London and Scottish clearing banks' base rates plus 1 per cent, or 13 per cent, whichever is higher;
(c) *finance of foreign trade* – credit agreements made in connection with the export of goods and services outside of the UK or their import into this country;
(d) *normal trade credit* – the exemption covers two situations: first, where traders advance credit to sell goods and services and require the bill to be paid in one instalment (e.g. the milk and paper bill). Second, a DCSA for fixed-sum credit where the number of payments does not exceed four, within a year of the start of the agreement or, where it is for running-account credit, the credit is payable in one amount (e.g. American Express and Diners' Club cards). The agreement will not qualify for exemption if it is an HP or conditional sale or secured by an article taken in pawn;
(e) *land transaction lending* – DCSAs to finance the purchase of land or buildings repayable in four instalments or less;
(f) *certain insurance policy loans* – the exemption is confined to loans made by building societies and other bodies whose lending is already exempt (see (a) above) to cover the payment of insurance premiums related to the mortgage, i.e. mortgage protection insurance premiums.

2 Exempt consumer hire agreements. The only exempt consumer hire agreements are those for the hire of meters or metering equipment for electricity, gas and water, where the owner is an organisation authorised by statute to supply electricity, water or gas.

General provisions with wider application

Some parts of the Act apply to otherwise exempt agreements. For example, the safeguards on extortionate credit affect all credit irrespective of the amount, and from 1 September 1985 the regulations concerning advertisements and quotations only apply to all institutions engaged in house mortgage lending.

LICENSING OF CREDIT AND HIRE BUSINESSES

The Act set up a comprehensive licensing system to control the activities of those in the credit and hire business. There are six categories of business activity which need a licence:

1 consumer credit business, e.g. banks, moneylenders, finance companies;
2 consumer hire business, e.g. TV and car rental companies;
3 credit brokerage, e.g. car dealers, estate agents;
4 debt adjusters and debt counselling, e.g. CABs, accountants;
5 debt collecting;
6 credit reference agencies.

The applicants must show that they are fit persons to be in this kind of business. Anyone who carries on any of the activities listed above without a licence commits a criminal offence. Moreover, an agreement made by an unlicensed trader is enforceable only at the discretion of the Director General of Fair Trading.

SEEKING BUSINESS

The Act controls three ways of attracting business: advertising, giving quotations and canvassing.

Advertising (ss 43–47)

The Act requires the Secretary of State to make regulations about the form and content of advertisements to ensure that they convey a fair and reasonably comprehensive indication of the nature of the credit and hire facilities offered and their true cost. The aim is to promote 'truth in lending' and so encourage consumers to shop around for the best credit bargain.

The Consumer Credit (Advertisements) Regulations 1989 apply to advertisements published on or after 1 February 1990. They permit three types of advertising: simple, intermediate and full (see Fig.13.4). Advertisers can choose under which rules they wish to advertise.

A criminal offence is committed if the advertisement fails to comply with the regulations or contains false or misleading information. It is also an offence to advertise goods or services on credit where the advertiser does not hold himself out as prepared to sell for cash.

Quotations (s 52)

Traders used to be under an obligation to give a written quotation if one was requested. The relevant regulations were revoked in 1997. However, the Consumer Credit (Content of Quotations) and the Consumer Credit (Advertisements) (Amendment) Regulations 1999, which came into force on 28 February 2000, require the inclusion of certain prescribed information where a quotation is provided by the trader. Quotations must include a statement, if applicable, that the security is or may be required and the warning 'Your home is at risk if you do not keep up repayments on a mortgage or other loan secured on it'.

Canvassing (ss 48–51)

It is an offence to canvass a DCA off trade premises. This outlaws the practice of stopping people in the street or calling uninvited at their houses to persuade them to take a loan. Traders need a special licence to canvass off trade premises credit agreements linked to the supply of goods and services or the hire of goods. It is an offence to send

---

LOANSTAR LTD
Finance Company

12 High Street, Barchester BC9 7XY
Telephone 0123–765–4321

(a) Simple advertisement

CASH LOANS
£200 – £5,000
17.2% APR (variable)

LONESTAR LTD
Finance Company
Phone 0123-765-4321

All loans subject to status.
Written details on request.

(b) Intermediate advertisement

FAST LOANS
£1,000 – £200,000
FOR ANY PURPOSE

Typical example

Borrow £2,000 and pay back 24 monthly instalments of £99.32. Total amount repayable £2,383.68. APR (variable) 18.8%

Written quotations on request.

Loans secured against property.
Warning: Your home is at risk if you do not keep up repayments on a mortgage or other loan secured on it.

LONESTAR LTD
12 High Street
Barchester
BC9 7XY
0123–765–4321

(c) Full advertisement

Fig 13.4 Types of credit advertising

any documents to a minor inviting him to borrow money, obtain goods or services on credit, or to apply for information or advice on borrowing. It is also an offence to give or send a person a credit token if he has not asked for it. This rule does not apply to the renewal of credit cards.

SIGNING CREDIT OR HIRE AGREEMENTS

Creditors or owners must observe certain formalities if they wish to enforce any agreement. These rules do not apply to non-commercial agreements. Small DCSAs for restricted-use credit are only subject to the rules about pre-contractual disclosure (see **1** below).

1 Before signing (s 55). The prospective debtor or hirer must be given full details of the agreement he is about to sign.

2 The agreement (s 61). The agreement must:

(a) be readily legible;
(b) contain all the terms of the agreement (other than implied terms);
(c) comply with the regulations as to its form and content;
(d) in the case of a cancellable agreement, contain details of debtor's right to cancel;
(e) be signed personally by the debtor and by or on behalf of the creditor.

3 Copies (ss 62 and 63). The debtor must receive either one or two copies of the agreement depending on the circumstances. He must always receive a copy at the time of signing. However, the agreement is not normally completed at this time as it is usually sent way for acceptance by the creditor or owner. If this is the case, the debtor must receive a second copy within seven days of the agreement being concluded. If it is a cancellable agreement, the second copy must be sent by post.

Failure to comply with the requirements as to formalities renders the agreement improperly executed. This means that it can be enforced against the debtor only by order of court (s 127). However, the Court of Appeal has recently held that the provisions of s 127(3), which prevent a court from making an enforcement order in certain circumstances, are incompatible with Art 6 of the European Convention on Human Rights in that the section excludes all judicial remedies and disproportionately affects the rights of the lender (*Wilson v First Country Trust* (2001)).

CANCELLATION

Sections 67–74 provide a limited right for debtors or hirers to change their mind and withdraw from an agreement they have signed. This cooling-off period applies to regulated agreements signed off trade premises where there has been some personal contact between the debtor or hirer and the salesman.

The debtor or hirer may serve notice of cancellation at any time between signing the agreement and five clear days after receiving the second copy of the agreement. If this right is exercised, the parties are returned to the position they were in before the agreement was signed. Any money received must be repaid, and if the debtor or hirer has acquired goods, they must be made available for return.

CREDIT REFERENCE AGENCIES

These organisations collect information about people's creditworthiness. It is normal practice for traders in the credit business to use the services of such an agency to vet the suitability of applicants for credit. Sections 157–159 give consumers the right to obtain the name and address of any agency used and for a £2 fee a copy of any files held. If the information is wrong, the consumer can add a correction to the file.

LIABILITY OF THE SUPPLIER AND CREDITOR

A supplier of goods and services will be liable for any false statements he makes which persuade a customer to enter into an agreement. In addition, certain terms are implied into contracts for the supply of goods and services. If the supplier does not live up to his obligations, he may be sued by the customer for breach of contract.

If credit is involved, the situation may be complicated by the fact that the creditor and supplier are not the same person. For example, a credit card may have been used to buy goods. The Act contains two provisions which have the effect of making the credit grantor equally liable for any misrepresentations or breach of contract by the supplier.

1 Section 56. In the case of regulated agreements, the dealer is deemed to be acting as the creditor's agent. The creditor is, therefore, responsible for the negotiations conducted on his behalf by the supplier including, for example, any misrepresentations.

2 **Section 75.** This makes the creditor equally responsible with the supplier for any misrepresentation or breach of contract. However, the section only applies if the agreement meets the following conditions:

(a) it is a regulated credit agreement;
(b) the cash price of the item is between £100 and £30,000;
(c) the credit is granted under an agreement between the creditor and supplier.

Equal liability does not apply to non-commercial agreements or where the customer has arranged his own credit, such as a bank overdraft or a cash advance from a credit card company.

The scope of the equal liability provisions

The precise effect of s 75, particularly in relation to transactions paid for by credit card, has been the subject of ongoing discussions between the Director General of Fair Trading and the credit card companies. The problem areas are as follows:

- Section 75 came into effect on 1 July 1977 and applies to regulated agreements made on or after that date. It is unclear whether s 75 applies to card-holders who first obtained their cards before 1 July 1977. Following discussions with the Director General of Fair Trading, Barclaycard and Access voluntarily agreed to accept liability to card-holders who first obtained their cards before 1977. However, this voluntary liability is limited to the amount of the transaction charged to the credit card account.
- It is unclear whether the equal liability provisions apply to second card-holders or just to the account holder.
- The credit card companies have argued that card-holders should be required to exhaust all remedies against the supplier of the goods and services before taking action against the credit card company. In particular, it has been argued that where a holiday tour operator goes into liquidation, holidaymakers who have paid by credit card should have recourse to the special fund set up by tour operators to deal with this situation. The Director General rejected the idea

that card-holders should look first to the supplier, but he did propose that liability be limited to the amount of the transaction.

- There is some doubt about whether card-holders who book a package tour with a tour operator through a travel agent can claim the protection of s 75. Although the Office of Fair Trading takes the view that s 75 does apply if the travel agent is acting as the agent of the tour operator, card-holders are advised to pay the tour operator directly to avoid potential problems.
- It has been argued that the liability of a credit card company ceases once the credit has been repaid. If this were the case, card-holders who paid their credit card bills in full each month would enjoy greatly reduced protection.
- It has been argued that the equal liability provisions do not apply to overseas transactions by UK card-holders. However, in *Jarrett* v *Barclays Bank plc* (1996), the Court of Appeal held that English courts had jurisdiction over a transaction in which a Barclaycard had been used to pay for a timeshare in a Portuguese property.

Loss or misuse of credit tokens

Section 66 and 84 set out the extent of a debtor's liability if his credit token (i.e. credit card) is misused. Under s 66 the debtor is not liable at all for another person's use of the credit token unless the debtor has previously accepted the credit token or the use by the other person constituted an acceptance by him. The debtor accepts the credit token when (a) he signs it; (b) he signs a receipt for it; or (c) it is first used, either by the debtor himself or a person authorised to use it.

Section 84 deals with the debtor's liability for misuse which occurs after acceptance. The debtor should give notice as soon as possible to the creditor (card issuer) that the credit token has been lost, stolen or liable to misuse because he will not be liable for any loss arising after notice has been received by the creditor. Notice can be given orally but the agreement can provide that it will not be effective unless written confirmation is received within seven days. The extent of any liability for misuse in the period before notice takes effect depends on the circumstances. If the person who misuses the token obtained possession of it with the debtor's consent, the debtor is liable without limit. If the debtor did not consent (i.e. the token was lost or stolen), the debtor's liability is limited to £50 or the credit limit if lower.

The Consumer Protection (Distance Selling) Regulations 2000 introduce increased protection for consumers who use credit cards in connection with 'distance selling' contracts, such as purchases made via the Internet or by mail order. If a credit card is used fraudulently in connection with the distance contract, the consumer is entitled to cancel the payment, or if the payment has already been made the consumer will be entitled to a re-credit or to have all sums returned by the card issuer. The regulations also amend the Consumer Credit Act 1974, so as to remove the potential liability of a card-holder for the first £50 of any loss arising from misuse in connection with a distance contract.

Extortionate terms (ss 137–140)

Sections 137–140 introduce sweeping new powers for the courts to re-open extortionate credit bargains so as to do justice between the parties. The provisions apply to all credit, irrespective of the amount involved. They allow an individual debtor or surety (a person who has given security for credit) to bring the credit bargain to the attention of the court either in a specific action or during the course of proceedings relating to the agreement. A credit bargain is extortionate if it requires the debtor or his relatives to make payments which are grossly exorbitant or which otherwise contravene the ordinary principles of fair dealing.

The Act is not precise about what should be regarded as an extortionate rate of interest. Instead, it mentions general factors which should be taken into account by the court such as:

1 prevailing interest rates;
2 the age, experience, business capacity and state of health of the debtor;
3 the degree of financial pressure put on the debtor and the nature of that pressure;
4 the degree of risk accepted by the creditor;
5 the creditor's relationship with the debtor;
6 whether the cash price quoted for the goods was true or 'colourable', i.e. inflated to make the credit charges appear more reasonable.

In *Barcabe* v *Edwards* (1983) the court held that a loan with an APR of 319 per cent was, prima facie, extortionate. It re-opened the agreement and substituted a flat rate of interest of 40 per cent which is equivalent to an APR of 92 per cent! In *A Ketley Ltd* v *Scott* (1981), a bridging loan with an estimated APR of 57.35 per cent was held not to be extortionate. The court took into account the high degree of risk taken by the creditors and the business experience of the debtor.

If the court finds that the credit bargain is extortionate, it may:

1 direct a state of account between the two parties to be taken to establish, for example, how much money has been paid by the debtor and the amount still outstanding;
2 set aside any obligation under the agreement;
3 require the creditor to repay all or part of any sum paid under the agreement;
4 direct the return of any property provided as security; or
5 alter the terms of the credit agreement.

TERMINATION AND DEFAULT

Both debtor and creditor may have reasons why they want their relationship to end. The debtor could have come into some money and wish to pay off his debt. Alternatively, he may have lost his job and no longer be able to afford the repayments. The creditor will want to take action against people who have not lived up to the agreements they have made.

Early settlement (ss 94–97)

The debtor under a regulated consumer credit agreement is entitled to pay off what he owes at any time on giving notice to the creditor of his intention to do this. This may entitle him to a rebate of interest.

Termination (ss 98–101)

1 By the debtor. The debtor under a regulated HP or conditional sale agreement may give notice to terminate the agreement at any time before the final instalment is due. He must return the goods and pay off any arrears. In addition, he must pay the smaller of the following:

(a) a minimum amount specified in the agreement;
(b) half of the total purchase price;
(c) an amount ordered by the court to compensate the creditor for his loss.

If the debtor has failed to take reasonable care of the goods, he must pay damages to the creditor.

2 By the creditor. Usually the creditor will wish to terminate the agreement because the debtor has broken the agreement in some way (this is dealt with below). However, it should be noted that some agreements allow the creditor to terminate where there has been no default by the debtor. The agreement may specify that it can be terminated at any time or if, for example, the creditor becomes unemployed or is convicted of a crime of dishonesty. If it is an agreement for a specified period, which has time to run, the creditor must give seven days' notice of his intention. The debtor may apply to the court for a 'time order'.

Default (ss 87–89)

If the debtor has committed a breach of the agreement, the creditor must serve a 'default notice' before he takes any of the following actions:

1 to terminate the agreement;
2 to demand earlier payment;
3 to recover the possession of any goods or land;
4 to regard rights conferred on the debtor by agreement as terminated, restricted or deferred;
5 to enforce any security.

The default notice must explain to the debtor the nature of his alleged breach, what he must do to put it right and by when or, if the breach cannot be remedied, what must be paid by way of compensation.

Woodchester Lease Management Services Ltd v Swain & Co (1998)

The defendants, a firm of solicitors, had entered into an agreement with the claimants for the hire of a photocopier. Payments were made regularly by the defendants for more than two years when they suddenly stopped. The claimants sent a default notice to the defendants, but a mistake was made in calculating the amount which should be paid to remedy the default, with the result that the amount was overstated by more than £240. The Court of Appeal held that the default notice must specify accurately the sum of money to be paid to remedy the default. Although a court might be prepared to overlook a minor discrepancy, the overstatement in this case was substantial. The notice was, therefore, invalid.

The time allowed for the debtor to remedy the breach must be at least seven days from the service of the default notice. It must contain certain information about the consequences of failing to comply with the notice.

If the debtor carries out the requirements of the notice, the breach is treated as if it had never happened. Where the notice is not heeded, the creditor may pursue any remedies contained in the agreement, subject to the provisions of the Act. At this point the debtor may seek the help of the court by applying for a time order.

Time orders (ss 129–130)

A debtor may apply to the court for a time order where he has been served with either a default or a non-default notice or in the course of an action by the creditor to enforce a regulated agreement. The court can allow the debtor time to remedy a breach or, where the breach consists of non-payment, time in which to pay the arrears. In the case of an HP or conditional sale agreement, the court may re-arrange the pattern of future instalments.

Repossession of the goods (ss 90–92)

One of the attractions of HP to Victorian traders was that if the hirer defaulted at any stage, the owner could recover the goods. Many HP agreements even gave creditors the right to enter the hirer's home for this purpose.

Debtors under regulated HP and conditional sale agreements now enjoy protection against the so-called 'snatch back':

1 a creditor must obtain a court order before be enters any premises to repossess goods; and

2 if the debtor has paid at least one-third of the total price and he has not terminated the agreement, the goods are protected. The creditor cannot recover possession of protected goods unless he obtains a court order. If a creditor ignores this requirement, he faces severe penalties. The agreement terminates immediately; the debtor is released from all liabilities under the agreement and, in addition, can recover money already paid.

Capital Finance Co Ltd v *Bray* (1964)

Bray had paid over a third of the HP price of a car when he fell into arrears. A representative of the finance company took the car back without either Bray's consent or a court order. The company realised its mistake and returned the car to Bray. When the repayments were still not forthcoming, the company sued for possession of the car. This was granted by the court, which further held that Bray was entitled to recover everything that he had previously paid to the finance company.

REFORM OF THE CONSUMER CREDIT ACT

In its 1998 Consumer White Paper, 'Modern Markets, Confident Consumers', the government made the following commitments:

1 **APR** – to implement changes to the way the APR is calculated in accordance with the requirements of the EC APR Directive and to ensure that the APR reflects the total charge for credit over the full period of the loan. The new regulations are now in force.

2 **Extortionate credit** – to review the rules on extortionate credit. The DTI is proposing that the courts should have the power to re-open credit agreements on their own initiative rather than, as is the case at present, only at the request of the debtor or a surety.

3 **Consumer credit licensing** – to review the operation of the licensing system. In a discussion paper published in 2000, the DTI set out a number of possibilities for change including:

- dispensing with the renewals process;
- excluding certain kinds of credit activity from the licensing provisions;
- replacing the licensing system with a compulsory registration system;
- reducing the number of licence categories from six to one;
- increasing or even abolishing the monetary limits for regulated agreements;
- reforming the powers of the Director General of Fair Trading to deal with unfit licence holders.

4 **Consumer Credit Directive** – to participate in the EC review of the Consumer Credit Directive.

QUESTIONS/ACTIVITIES

1 What kinds of credit are likely to be used by:
   (a) a typical family,
   (b) a sole trader,
   (c) a limited company?

2 What forms of credit would be available for the following purchases:
   (a) furniture,
   (b) clothes,
   (c) a car,
   (d) a house?
   What kinds of institutions would provide the credit?

3 What are the current rates of interest for the following types of credit:
   (a) bank personal loan,
   (b) shop budget account,
   (c) building society mortgage,
   (d) bank credit card,
   (e) finance company personal loan,
   (f) overdraft,
   (9) HP?

4 What are the points of similarity between HP and credit sale? What are the differences?

5 Using the terminology of the Consumer Credit Act 1974 contained in List A below, describe the credit transactions in List B below.

List A:

(a) DCSA,

(b) DCA,

(c) restricted-use credit,

(d) unrestricted-use credit,

(e) fixed-sum credit,

(f) running account credit,

(g) credit token agreement,

(h) regulated consumer credit agreement,

(i) regulated consumer hire agreement,

(j) small agreement,

(k) non-commercial agreement,

(l) exempt agreement.

List B:

(a) Arthur buys a suite of furniture from Matchstick Furniture plc, paying 12 monthly instalments of £50 each. Ownership of the furniture passes to Arthur immediately.

(b) The Portland Bank plc allows Beryl to overdraw her current account up to a limit of £1,000.

(c) Colin sees a new car that he wishes to buy in the showrooms of Rattle Cars Co Ltd. The company introduces him to Shady Finance Co Ltd, which agrees to let Colin have the car on HP. Colin pays a deposit of £1,500 and 24 monthly instalments of £20 each.

(d) Doris uses her credit card (on which she has a personal limit of £800) to buy a camera from Snapshot Ltd.

(e) Evan has the *Financial Times* delivered to his home every day. He pays the bill at the end of each month.

(f) Freda buys and obtains possession of a coat and dress from Bondsman Mail Order Co Ltd for £90. She pays this in 20 instalments of £4.50 each.

6 Gerald buys a new video. After two weeks' use the machine starts to mangle tapes. What are his rights, and against whom, if the purchase was financed in the following ways:

(a) cash payment direct to the retailers, Viewscene Ltd;

(b) bank credit card;

(c) HP arranged by Viewscene Ltd with Eazimoney Finance Co Ltd;

(d) bank overdraft?

7 Harold agrees to take a car on HP from Tite Finance Co Ltd for a total HP price of £3,250, made up of a deposit of £850 plus 24 monthly payments of £100.

(a) The company receives a letter from Harold terminating the agreement because he has lost his job. What will Harold have to pay if he terminates in the following situations:

(i) after he has paid three instalments but before the fourth is due;

(ii) after he has paid four instalments and the fifth and sixth are still owing;

(iii) after he has paid 12 instalments and before the 13th is due, but the car was badly damaged in an accident.

(b) Harold does not terminate the agreement but fails to pay any instalments after the seventh instalment. What action can Tite Finance Co Ltd take?

Chapter 14

CONSUMER PROTECTION

So far in Part 3 of this book we have examined the law governing the supply of goods and services. We have investigated the nature and extent of any civil or criminal liability which can arise from business activities, mainly from the perspective of businesses providing the goods or services. In this chapter, we turn our attention to the **consumer** of the product or service. We will consider the nature and scope of the law of consumer protection, the rights of consumers and the role of various organisations which protect and represent consumers. First, we will explore the questions of who is a consumer and why consumers need protecting.

WHO IS A CONSUMER?

At the outset it is important to establish who is intended to be benefited by the law of consumer protection. Dictionary definitions of the word 'consumer' are either so broad that they cover anyone who consumes goods or services, including even those who are acting in a commercial capacity, or so narrow that they only cover purchasers, rather than all users, or just goods, rather than both goods and services.

A 'consumer transaction' generally has three essential elements: an individual who purchases or uses goods and services for his own private purposes; a supplier who is acting in a business capacity; and goods or services which must be intended for private use or consumption. Despite this consensus, Parliament and the courts have had considerable difficulty in deciding precisely who is worthy of special protection, as an examination of each of the elements will show.

1 Individual purchaser or user acting in a private capacity. The net of protection has often been cast so widely that even businesses have benefited from protective measures. Although the provisions of the Consumer Credit Act 1974 only apply where the debtor is an individual, the definition of an 'individual' is so broad that it encompasses borrowing by sole traders and partnerships. The Unfair Contract Terms Act 1977 also purports to extend the greatest protection in respect of exclusion clauses to those who 'deal as a consumer' (s 12(1)). However, the courts have interpreted the requirements of s 12(1) so generously that even occasional purchases by a company, provided they are not an integral part of the business, may be classed as consumer transactions (*R & B Customs Brokers Ltd* v *United Dominions Trust Ltd* (1988), see Chapter 9).

2 Supplier acting in the course of a business. The requirement that the supplier must be acting in a business capacity has not always been consistently applied. The implied terms in s 14 of the Sale of Goods Act 1979 apply to all sales by a business, not just to those which form a regular part of the business (see *Stevenson* v *Rogers* (1999) in Chapter 10). In contrast, the offence of applying a false trade description contained in s 1 (l)(a) of the Trade Descriptions Act 1968 can only be committed by a person acting in the course of a trade or business where the goods supplied form an integral part of the business (*Davies* v *Sumner* (1984)), see further Chapter 12. The more exacting requirements developed by the courts in relation to trade description can be justified because the Trade Descriptions Act 1968 imposes criminal penalties, while the Sale of Goods Act 1979 merely establishes civil liability.

3 Goods and services intended for private use or consumption. Section 12 of the Unfair Contract Terms Act 1977, for example, stipulates that a person only deals as a consumer where there is a contract for the supply of goods if the goods are of a type ordinarily supplied for private use or con-

sumption. There are problems with such an approach. Is a person dealing as a consumer if the goods are used for both business and private purposes? What is the position in relation to goods which are ordinarily supplied for business purposes but then put to private use, or vice versa?

Consumers do not have to have a contract with the business supplier in order to attract protection. Many consumers will have purchased the goods and services and have a contractual relationship with the supplier, but there are also other consumers who make use of goods and services without having entered into a contract. In recent years, there has been growing recognition of the need to protect non-contractual consumers.

WHY DO CONSUMERS NEED PROTECTION?

The idea that consumers need protecting has been around since the Middle Ages, yet most of the consumer protection measures which exist today have been developed over the past 30 or so years. The earliest forms of consumer protection were designed to discourage fraudulent trading practices and to protect the consumer from danger. The main justification for intervening on behalf of consumers today is that the nature of modern markets is such that consumers can no longer make prudent shopping decisions. Enormous changes in the way we acquire goods and services have taken place since the Second World War. Consumers now have access to a much wider range of more technologically complex goods. Whereas in the past retailers were expected to use their skill and judgement to select good quality products, today's retailer often has limited technical knowledge of the product he sells. There has been a move towards large-scale retail businesses, e.g. supermarkets and, more recently, the development of large out-of-town shopping complexes. At the same time, advertising and marketing techniques have become much more sophisticated. Today's consumers enjoy far greater spending power than their grandparents did; disposable incomes are higher and credit is more easily available. Expensive and highly complex goods can be purchased relatively easily, but there is less time for consumers to spend on

shopping. Changes in working patterns and, in particular, the increased participation of women in the labour market mean that shopping often has to be fitted around work. The overall effect of these changes has been to increase the power of suppliers at the expense of consumers. The underlying aim of most modern consumer protection law is to redress the balance of power.

CONSUMER PROTECTION INSTITUTIONS

A large number of organisations have a role in protecting consumers.

European institutions

The UK became a member of the European Community (EC) in 1973 and since that time has been subject to a new source of law emanating from the Council and Commission in the form of regulations, directives and decisions. The UK is also bound by the decisions of the European Court of Justice. The Treaty of Rome, which established the European Economic Community in 1957, provides that the main aim of the EC is the establishment of a common market. Although the original Treaty of Rome did not contain a specific provision in relation to consumer protection, it was recognised that the creation of a genuine common market would entail harmonisation of the consumer protection laws of member states. A Consumer Protection Programme was approved in 1972 and a Consumers' Consultative Committee was set up by the Commission in the following year. A second Consumer Protection Programme followed in 1981. Unfortunately, progress was very slow because of the requirement that any directives must be adopted unanimously by all member states. The Single European Act, which took effect in 1987, amended the relevant treaty Article (Art 94, previously Art 100) to allow proposals in relation to consumer protection to be adopted by qualified majority voting. The 1991 Maastricht Treaty makes a specific reference to the role of the EC in contributing to 'the attainment of a high level of consumer protection'. EC Directives on consumer protection already adopted include:

- Directive on Liability for Defective Products, implemented in the UK as Part I of the Consumer Protection Act 1987 (see Chapter 11);
- Directive on Misleading Advertisements, implemented by the Control of Misleading Advertisements Regulations 1988 (see Chapter 9);
- Directive on Doorstep Selling, implemented by the Consumer Protection (Cancellation of Contracts Away From Business Premises) Regulations 1987;
- Directive on Package Travel, Package Holidays and Package Tours, implemented by the Package Travel, Package Holidays and Package Tour Regulations 1992 (discussed later in this chapter);
- Directive on General Product Safety, implemented by the General Product Safety Regulations 1994 (see Chapter 12);
- Directive on Unfair Terms in Consumer Contracts, implemented by the Unfair Terms in Consumer Contracts Regulations 1999 (see Chapter 9);
- Directive on Timeshare, implemented by the Timeshare Regulations 1997;
- Directive on Distance Selling, implemented by the Consumer Protection (Distance Selling) Regulations 2000.

Directives awaiting implementation in the UK include:

- Directive on injunctions for the protection of consumers' interests (to be implemented by January 2001);
- Directive on sale of consumer goods and associated guarantees (to be implemented by January 2002).

The Commission is currently working towards implementing its fourth three-year action plan (1999–2001) in respect of consumer policy. The plan includes the following elements:

(a) creating a more powerful voice for consumers throughout the EU through:
- more effective consumer associations;
- better dialogue between consumers and business;
- establishing *Euroguichets*, which provide advice and information to consumers in all member states;
- providing better information and education for consumers;

(b) promoting a high level of health and safety for EU consumers through:
- science-based policy making;
- better analysis of risks to consumer health and safety;
- safer products and services;
- reinforcing consumer confidence in food;
- better enforcement, monitoring and response to emergencies;
- greater international consensus;

(c) ensuring full respect for the economic interests of EU consumers through:
- an up to date regulatory framework;
- a single currency for consumers;
- a consumer-friendly internal market in financial services;
- better enforcement and monitoring of existing legislation;
- unlocking the potential of the information society for the benefit of consumers;
- better integration of consumers' economic interests in other EU policies.

The interests of UK consumers in relation to EC policy are represented by the Consumers in the European Community Group.

Central government institutions

Department of Trade and Industry (DTI)

The DTI is responsible for developing policy and promoting legislation in the fields of trading standards, fair trading, weights and measures, consumer credit and consumer safety. It also has functions in relation to competition policy, i.e. monopolies, mergers and restrictive practices. In addition, the DTI has responsibility for a number of agencies, e.g. Office of Fair Trading, Monopolies and Mergers Commission, British Hallmarking Council, Hearing Aid Council, National Consumer Council, OFWAT, OFTEL, OFGEM, and it sponsors the British Standards Institute.

In 1998 the DTI published a White Paper on consumer matters: 'Modern Markets: Confident Consumers'. The government's new agenda for consumers includes the following key aims:

- to promote open and competitive markets;
- to provide people with the skills, knowledge and information they need to become knowledgeable and demanding consumers;
- to encourage responsible businesses to adopt good practice;
- to reduce the burden of unnecessary regulation;
- to protect the public from rogue traders and unsafe goods.

The Home Office

The Home Office is responsible for supervision of the control of explosives, firearms, dangerous drugs, poisons and liquor licensing. It legislates in relation to shops and advises on fire hazards in consumer products.

The Department of Health

The Department of Health and the Ministry of Agriculture, Fisheries and Food were both partly responsible for matters of food hygiene and safety and used to share responsibility for the enforcement of the Food Safety Act 1990 and the Medicines Act 1968. Food issues are now the responsibility of the Food Standards Agency. The Department of Health offers medical advice on contamination of consumer goods and is involved in the control of drugs.

The Ministry of Agriculture, Fisheries and Food (MAFF)

The aim of MAFF is 'to ensure that consumers benefit from competitively priced food, produced to high standards of safety, environmental care and animal welfare and from a sustainable, efficient food chain'. One of MAFF's objectives is the protection of public health in relation to farm produce and to animal diseases transmissible to humans.

The Office of Fair Trading (OFT)

The OFT was established in 1973 under the terms of the Fair Trading Act 1973. The OFT, which is headed by a Director General of Fair Trading, has two main roles: consumer protection and promoting competition. Its consumer protection functions comprise:

(a) *Developing policies to protect consumers.* This involves keeping under review commercial activities in the UK which relate to the supply of goods and services to consumers and making appropriate recommendations to the DTI, either if asked by the DTI or on its own initiative;

(b) *Taking action under Part III of the Fair Trading Act 1973 against individual traders who have persisted in a course of conduct which is unfair to consumers* (discussed in more detail later in this chapter);

(c) *Educating consumers by providing information in the form of information leaflets;*

(d) *Encouraging voluntary regulation by trade associations through the medium of codes of practice for their members* (discussed in more detail later in this chapter);

(e) *Controlling consumer credit by licensing traders who carry on consumer credit and consumer hire businesses, and enforcing the Consumer Credit Act by criminal proceedings* (see Chapter 13).

In May 2000 the Government published proposals for structural reform of the OFT. It is proposed that the current arrangement, whereby the statutory powers of the OFT are vested in the Director General of Fair Trading, should be replaced by a statutory authority, with a chairman as head of a board. The effect would be to de-personalise decision-making and broaden the base of expertise informing strategy formulation.

Food Standards Agency (FSA)

The FSA, which was established by the Food Standards Act 1999, became operational in April 2000. The main objective of the FSA is to protect the interests of consumers in relation to food. The FSA has responsibility for the development of food policy and for providing advice, information and assistance in relation to food safety, and other consumer interests in relation to food, to public authorities.

Local government

Local authorities have two main roles in respect of consumer protection: enforcement of regulatory statutes and the provision of consumer advice and information.

1 **Enforcement.** Local government has the day-today responsibility for enforcing many of the statutory consumer protection measures. Most local authorities have consumer protection or trading standards departments which have responsibility for enforcing the provisions of the Trade Descriptions Act 1968, the Consumer Credit Act 1974, the Weights and Measures Act 1985, the Food Safety Act 1990 and various orders made under consumer protection legislation. Local authorities also have responsibility for testing equipment used by traders and sampling products put on the market by manufacturers and retailers.

2 **Consumer advice.** Many local authorities have set up consumer advice centres to provide pre-shopping advice and to give advice on complaints. Sometimes they will take up individual complaints.

Government-sponsored bodies

Consumer Protection Advisory Committee

The Committee was established under the Fair Trading Act 1973 to consider references on the question of whether a consumer trade practice adversely affects the economic interests of UK consumers. Membership of the Committee has been suspended since 1982.

National Consumer Council (NCC)

The NCC was set up in 1975 to represent consumer interests in dealings with the government, local authorities, the Office of Fair Trading and trade bodies. It also advises on consumer-protection policy through the publication of reports and making representations to relevant bodies. It is sponsored by the government.

Public services and privatised industries

Newly privatised, large-scale suppliers of goods and services, such as British Gas, BT, the water and electricity supply companies, have found themselves in a position of having a monopoly or near-monopoly of supply. It has, therefore, been thought necessary to regulate their operations by appointing statutory 'regulators', and, in some cases, formalising consumer representation in the industry (see Fig 14.1). The duties of the regulators may include promoting competition and protecting the consumer in relation to pricing and terms of supply.

In 1991 the government launched its Citizens' Charter initiative for public services. The aim of the initiative is to raise standards in public services such as health, education and the courts, by producing charters which set out what kind of services consumers are entitled to expect and how they can complain if things go wrong.

Voluntary organisations

Consumers' Association

The Consumers' Association was established in 1957. The inspiration for its creation came from the USA. It has five main aims:

Industry	Regulator	Office	Consumer representation
Telecommunications	Director General of Telecommunications	OFTEL	Advisory committees on telecommunications
Gas and electricity	Chairman of Gas and Electricity Markets Authority	OFGEM	Gas and Electricity Consumer Council
Water	Director General of Water Services	OFWAT	National Customer Council and local customer service committees
Rail transport	Rail Regulator	ORR	Rail Passengers Council

Fig 14.1 Regulation of privatised industries

(a) to encourage people to spend their money wisely;

(b) to reduce the inequality between the shopper and the manufacturer or supplier;

(c) to improve the quality of British goods, creating more discriminating purchasers;

(d) to tackle the growing complaints about unsatisfactory goods;

(e) to combat the power of advertising by providing information so the consumer can choose goods on more rational grounds.

The main aim of the Consumers' Association is to provide information to the consumer about products and services by testing them thoroughly and giving the subscriber an independent appraisal through the medium of its magazine *Which?* In addition, the Consumers' Association seeks to influence consumer protection policy by lobbying Parliament or by representation on other bodies in the UK and Europe.

Citizens' Advice Bureaux (CABs)

These were first established in 1939 by the National Council of Social Service. They deal with a wide range of problems: employment rights, social security, landlord and tenant disputes, etc. Approximately 20 per cent of the enquiries they deal with are consumer problems. They are funded by central government and local authorities.

National Federation of Consumer Groups (NFCG)

The NFCG co-ordinates the activities of the growing number of local consumer groups. The NFCG is funded by grants from the Consumers' Association and the DTI.

British Standards Institute (BSI)

The BSI was established in 1929. It sets standards, dimensions and specifications for manufactured goods. A 'British Standard' is a document which stipulates the specifications, requirements for testing or measurements with which a product must comply in order to be suited for its intended purpose and work efficiently. Compliance with such a standard is a matter of choice on the part of the producer. However, in some cases compliance is compulsory, e.g. crash helmets. A producer may apply to the BSI for certification of his products, in which case he may display a BSI kitemark on the product.

Other organisations

Trade associations

An important aspect of consumer protection is the extent to which laws are supplemented by codes of practice drawn up by trade associations in consultation with the Office of Fair Trading (discussed in more detail later in this chapter).

Advertising Standards Authority (ASA)

The ASA was established in 1962 to provide independent supervision of the advertising industry's system of self-regulation through a monitoring programme and investigation of complaints. The main instrument of control is the British Code of Advertising Practice (BCAP) which was published in 1961. It is kept under continuous review and amendment by the Committee of Advertising Practice (CAP). The code applies to all advertisements in newspapers, magazines, posters, brochures and leaflets for the public, cinema, commercial and viewdata services. The ASA and CAP also administer the British Code of Sales Promotion Practice. Separate systems operate in relation to broadcasting and cable operations.

Professional bodies

The Law Society, for example, operates a compensation fund for the victims of dishonest or insolvent solicitors and requires compulsory insurance against negligence.

Ombudsmen

The financial sector has appointed a number of 'ombudsmen' to deal with complaints, e.g. insurance, building societies, pensions, banking. The powers of these ombudsmen vary from scheme to scheme, but, as a minimum, they provide a channel for complaints and, at best, they can require an organisation to pay compensation.

DIFFERENT APPROACHES TO CONSUMER PROTECTION

The law on consumer protection has been developed on a piecemeal basis over many years and has a variety of sources: EC regulations and directives, statutes, ministerial regulations and case law. Over the years different approaches have been taken, causing problems of overlap and complexity. The four main approaches are: providing civil remedies, imposing criminal liability, administrative controls, and business self-regulation.

Providing civil remedies

An individual consumer may be able to bring a civil action against a trader for a breach of contract or for liability in tort, e.g. negligence. The liability of a supplier of goods and services for breach of contract was examined in Chapter 10, and his liability in tort was considered in Chapter 11.

Imposing criminal liability

Certain types of trading activities are deemed to he so harmful that the law imposes criminal sanctions on the offending trader. Some of the more important criminal offences in relation to traders were explored in Chapter 12.

Administrative controls

An alternative to using the civil or criminal law as a means of consumer protection is to place responsibility for the regulation of traders in the hands of an administrative body which is given powers to deal with unfair trade practices. The advantages of administrative controls compared to legal controls are as follows:

(a) Individual consumers are often ignorant of their rights or reluctant to enforce them in the courts. The creation of administrative controls allows action to be taken on behalf of all consumers.
(b) Depending on the powers vested in the administrative agency, it may be able to act more quickly than Parliament to deal with new forms of unfair trading.

(c) The administrative agency may be able to achieve the desired effect by persuasion rather than using the threat of legal action, and it may be able to use its influence to raise standards above the minimum acceptable by encouraging self-regulation.
(d) Dishonest traders may not be deterred by the threat of legal action. Some forms of control, such as licensing, may stop undesirable traders from operating in the market.

The Director General of Fair Trading enjoys a number of administrative powers which are designed to ensure fair trading practices. The main forms of administrative control are to be found in the Fair Trading Act 1973 and the Consumer Credit Act 1974.

Administrative controls under the Fair Trading Act 1973

Outlawing undesirable trade practices (Part II)

If trading practices come to light which adversely affect the economic interests of consumers, the Director General has the power under Part II of the 1973 Act to refer such matters to the Consumer Protection Advisory Committee (CPAC), which may recommend to the Secretary of State that the law should be changed to restrict the undesirable trading practice.

A 'consumer trade practice' is defined as any practice carried on in connection with the supply of goods and services to consumers and which relates to one of the six matters specified in s 13, namely:

(a) the terms or conditions of supply;
(b) the manner in which those terms are communicated;
(c) promotion;
(d) methods of salesmanship;
(e) packaging;
(f) methods of demanding or securing payments.

The CPAC reports to the Secretary of State, who may give effect to any proposals by means of an order made by statutory instrument. The order will take effect after approval by a resolution of both Houses of Parliament. Orders are enforced by criminal sanction only. Penalties, defences and enforcement are similar to those under the Trade Descriptions Act 1968. Four references were made to the CPAC between 1974 and 1977.

1 The purported exclusion of inalienable rights of consumers and the failure to explain their existence. This reference covered three practices:

(a) the continuing use by traders of void exemption clauses;

(b) written statements given by suppliers of goods which purport to set out the rights of the parties but fail to advise consumers of their inalienable rights;

(c) written statements which relate to consumers' rights against third parties.

The CPAC found that all three practices fell within the Act and adversely affected the economic interests of consumers. The Director-General's proposals, as modified by the CPAC, were implemented by the Consumer Transactions (Restrictions on Statements) Order 1976 (see also Chapter 9). Article 3 of the regulations makes it an offence to display at any place where consumer transactions are effected a notice containing a term invalidated by s 6 of the Unfair Contract Terms Act 1977. It is also an offence under Art 4 to supply goods, their container or a document to a consumer with a statement about his rights against the supplier with regard to defects, fitness for purpose or correspondence with description unless there is in close proximity to the statement another clear and conspicuous statement to the effect that the statutory rights of the consumer are not affected. Article 5 is similar to Art 4 except that it applies, although there is no direct consumer transaction between the business supplier and the consumer, where the supplier intended or reasonably expected his goods to become the subject of a subsequent consumer transaction.

2 Prepayment in mail order transactions and in shops. This reference concerned the practice whereby suppliers require prepayment in full or a deposit when goods are ordered without specifying a delivery period or specifying a delivery date which is not met. The Director General proposed that mail order catalogues and adverts should state a delivery period by prescribed wording and if the goods were not supplied on time the supplier would have to send a refund within seven days of receiving a request. The CPAC modified the proposals and the Secretary of State refused to make traders criminally liable for failure to return money on time. The result was the Mail Order Transactions (Information) Order 1976, which merely requires the name and address of the business to be given where an advertisement, circular or catalogue invites orders for goods by post where payment is to be made before the goods are dispatched.

3 Seeking to sell goods without revealing that they are being sold in the course of a business. This reference concerned the practice of traders disguising themselves as private persons. The Director General's proposals were accepted by the CPAC and put into effect by the Business Advertisements (Disclosure) Order 1977. The order requires business sellers of goods to make it clear in their advertisements directed at consumers that they are traders. The fact can be made apparent by the content of the advertisement, its format or size.

4 VAT exclusive prices. This reference concerned two practices. The first is the practice of advertising, displaying or quoting to consumers as the price of goods or services an amount which excludes a sum to be added on for VAT. The second practice is that of advertising recommended retail prices which take no account of the VAT amount which the retailer is likely to add when selling to a consumer.

The CPAC agreed with the Director General that the first practice (but not the second) adversely affected the economic interests of consumers and his proposal that only VAT inclusive charges should be shown. However, no order was forthcoming.

No references have been made since 1977, and in 1982 the CPAC was stood down. However, the government has indicated its intention of reviving the existing provisions in Part II with some amendment. In particular, it is proposed that the CPAC should be abolished and its investigatory and reporting role transferred to the OFT.

Unfair traders (Part III)

The Director General has the power under Part III of the Fair Trading Act 1973 to ask a trader who has persistently committed criminal offences, or who has been in breach of civil obligations to the detriment of the consumer, to give a written assurance that he will not persist in his course of conduct. If the trader refuses to give such an assurance or having given it fails to comply with it, he may be taken before a court (the Restrictive Trade Practices Court or the county court). The court may make an order forbidding the trader to continue with the undesirable course of conduct. If the trader still persists with the practice(s), he may be dealt with by the court for contempt by means of a fine or imprisonment.

Assurances may be obtained not only from a company but also from its directors or officers in their personal capacity. This assurance will then follow the individual into whatever business he is operating.

Reform of Part III of the Fair Trading Act

In September 1997 the Director General made a number of proposals to the government to strengthen the powers available to deal with rogue traders under Part III. The Director General identified the following weaknesses in the existing legislation:

- slowness of response: the procedures contained in Part III are very time-consuming and in some cases ineffective in dealing with dishonest and unscrupulous traders;
- persistence: a considerable length of time may be required to accumulate sufficient evidence to satisfy a court that a trader has persisted in an unfair course of conduct as specified by Part III;
- unfair and unlawful conduct: the requirement that the trader's unfair conduct must involve a breach of the civil or criminal law fails to take into account new practices which although not unlawful may be unfair.

The government's proposals for amending Part III include:

- a power for a court to grant an injunction against a trader who has engaged in a course of conduct consisting of breaches of legal obligations which are unfair and detrimental to the interests of consumers;

- local trading standards authorities as well as the OFT to be able to apply for a 'course of conduct' injunction;
- the current requirement of persistence to be replaced by a requirement of showing that the trader has engaged in a course of unfair conduct;
- conduct to be regarded as unfair if the trader contravenes one or more enactments which are enforceable by criminal proceedings or consists of conduct in breach of contract or non-contractual duties enforceable by civil proceedings;
- the injunction would require the trader to desist from the unfair conduct;
- introduction of a banning order, to prevent a trader from carrying on business with consumers for up to 15 years;
- an enforcement authority to be able to apply for a banning order where a trader has breached an injunction, or committed an offence involving fraud, or other dishonesty or violence; or has engaged in conduct which is detrimental to consumers with such frequency or over such a period of time or a wide geographical area as to demonstrate that the trader is not a fit person to engage in business with consumers.

Administrative controls in relation to misleading advertising

The Control of Misleading Advertisements Regulations 1988 implement the 1984 EC Directive on Misleading Advertising. The Director General may refer misleading advertising to the High Court which may grant an injunction to prevent publication. An advertisement is misleading under the regulations if it deceives or is likely to deceive those to whom it is addressed or reaches, and, because of its deceptive nature, it is likely to affect their economic behaviour or injures or is likely to injure a competitor of the person promoting the advertisement.

The Control of Misleading Advertisements (Amendment) Regulations 2000 implements the requirements of a 1997 Directive amending the Misleading Advertising Directive, so as to include comparative advertising.

Licensing of traders under the Consumer Credit Act 1974

The Director General of Fair Trading is responsible for administering the system of licensing for consumer credit and hire businesses (see further, Chapter 13). Undesirable traders may be refused a licence or have their licences withdrawn.

Business self-regulation

The Director General of Fair Trading is under a statutory duty to encourage relevant trade associations to prepare and disseminate to their members codes of practice for guidance in safeguarding and promoting the interests of consumers in the UK. The aim of such codes is to enable a particular industry to try to regulate the practices of its members. The advantages of voluntary codes of practice are as follows:

(a) codes can deal with matters which it would be difficult to deal with by means of legislation, e.g. availability of spare parts;

(b) codes may be able to go further than the existing law or improve upon legal remedies, e.g. the Code of Practice for the Motor Industry provides that copies of information provided by previous owners of a car concerning its history should be passed on to the new owner;

(c) any change in trading practices can be dealt with quickly by the association, whereas changing the law to deal with an undesirable trade practice may take a long time;

(d) codes encourage an industry to put its own house in order; complaints may be dealt with within the spirit of the code rather than according to the letter of the law; and the code may even explain legal requirements to its members;

(e) codes are developed for a particular trade or industry and can, therefore, deal with the problems which are specific to the industry;

(f) disputes can be dealt with in a less formal way, e.g. by conciliation;

(g) most codes provide for arbitration in the event of a dispute; arbitration may be preferable to bringing a case through the courts.

Although codes of practice have a number of advantages, there are some significant drawbacks to self-regulation. They are:

(a) not all traders are members of the trade associations and subject to its rules and code of practice;

(b) members of the public are often not aware of the existence of codes of practice and their rights under them;

(c) the sanctions which a trade association can impose against a member for failing to comply with the code are often very weak;

(d) codes are drawn up by a trade or industry and may not adequately address the interests of consumers.

A summary of the different approaches to consumer protection is set out in Figure 14.2.

In the next part of this chapter we will examine how the law is applied to protect consumers by considering a consumer transaction which gives rise to a large number of complaints: the package holiday.

CONSUMER PROTECTION CASE STUDY – PACKAGE HOLIDAYS

Over the past 30 years there has been an enormous growth in the package holiday market. As the volume of trade has increased, the real cost of taking a package holiday has fallen. A package holiday to popular European destinations such as Spain, Greece and Turkey is now well within the financial resources of most people. Intense price competition between the main tour operators has led to UK holidaymakers enjoying the lowest prices in Europe, but at the expense of standards. There is a high level of dissatisfaction with package holidays. An Association of British Travel Agents (ABTA) survey revealed 17,450 complaints received in 1995 about holidays, an increase of nearly 17 per cent compared to the previous year. A report by the OFT published in 1988 found that 40 per cent of holidaymakers had some problem with their package holiday and 20 per cent made a formal complaint to the travel agent or tour operator. Before we examine the law regulating package holidays, we need to establish why package holidays give rise to so many complaints.

Civil law	Criminal law	Administrative controls	Business self-regulation
Aims To remedy a wrong suffered by an individual consumer	To protect all consumers by punishing traders who fail to meet minimum standards To protect honest traders from unfair competition by unscrupulous traders	To ban dishonest traders To persuade traders to improve upon minimum legal standards To promote competition between traders by regulation of anti-competitive practices	To encourage traders to observe high standards To tailor standards to particular industries To allow traders to police themselves
False/misleading statements **Advertisements** No civil liability for inaccurate 'trader's puff' unless specific promise made as in *Carlill's* case Directors/experts are liable for false/misleading descriptions in company prospectuses (Financial Services and Markets Act 2000) Package holiday providers are liable for misleading descriptions of package holidays (Package Travel etc. Regulations 1992)	Offence to apply false/misleading description to goods and services in advertisements (Trade Descriptions Act 1968) Offence to give misleading price indication in an advertisement (Part III, Consumer Protection Act 1987) Offence to fail to disclose specified information to package holiday customers (Package Travel etc. Regulations 1992) Offence for estate agents to give false/misleading statements about property (Property Misdescriptions Act 1991)	Director General of Fair Trading may apply for an injunction to stop publication of misleading advertisements (Control of Misleading Advertisements Regulations 1988) Statutory order to ban undesirable trade practices (Part II, Fair Trading Act 1973) Action by Director General of Fair Trading to deal with unfair trading conduct (Part III, Fair Trading Act 1973)	The British Code of Advertising Practice requires advertisements to be legal, decent, honest and truthful. Breaches of the Code are publicised and offenders warned. Independent Television Commission has powers to deal with misleading TV advertising Trade association codes of practice
Representations Civil liability for misrepresentation. Rescission of the contract and/or damages (i) at common law (tort of deceit or tort of negligence) (ii) under the Misrepresentation Act 1967	Offences under Trade Descriptions Act 1967 and Part III, Consumer Protection Act 1987, Property Misdescriptions Act 1991 (see above) Deception offences under the Theft Act 1968 Offence to apply false descriptions to food (Food Safety Act 1990)	Parts II and III, Fair Trading Act 1973 (see above)	Trade association codes of practice
Terms Damages for breach of express or implied terms of contract and repudiation of the contract for breach of condition or serious breach of innominate term	Offences under Trade Descriptions Act 1968 and Part III, Consumer Protection Act 1987 (see above)	Parts II and III, Fair Trading Act 1973 (see above)	Trade association codes of practice
Unsolicited goods/services No contractual obligation to pay for unsolicited goods. They are treated as unconditional gift (Consumer Protection (Distance Selling) Regulations 2000)	Offence to demand payment for or threaten proceedings in respect of unsolicited goods and services (Unsolicited Goods and Services Act 1971 and Consumer Protection (Distance Selling) Regulations 2000)	Part III, Fair Trading Act 1973 (see above)	Trade association codes of practice

Fig 14.2 Consumer protection – a summary

Civil law	Criminal law	Administrative controls	Business self-regulation
Cancellation rights Credit agreements signed away from business premises are cancellable (Consumer Credit Act 1974)		Parts II and III, Fair Trading Act 1973 (see above)	Trade association codes of practice
Non-credit agreements involving payments over £35 signed away from business premises are cancellable (Consumer Protection (Cancellation of Contracts Concluded Away from Business Premises) Regulations 1987)		Licence required to carry on consumer credit business (Consumer Credit Act 1974)	
Timeshare agreements made in the UK are cancellable (Timeshare Act 1992)	Offence not to inform timeshare customer of cancellation rights (Timeshare Act 1992)		Timeshare Council Code of Practice
Distance contracts are cancellable (Consumer Protection (Distance Selling) Regulations 2000			
Defective goods Strict liability for breach of implied contractual terms as to quality and suitability (Trading Stamps Act 1964, Supply of Goods (Implied Terms) Act 1973, Sale of Goods Act 1979, Supply of Goods and Services Act 1982)	Offence to supply unsafe consumer goods (General Product Safety Regulations 1994) Various offences related to the sale of food (Food Safety Act 1990)	Secretary of State can issue prohibition notices and notices to warn; trading standards officers can issue suspension notices and apply for forfeiture orders in respect of unsafe goods (Part II, Consumer Protection Act 1987)	Trade association codes of practice
Fault-based liability in the tort of negligence		Food authorities can apply for improvement notices, prohibition orders or emergency orders to deal with unsafe food. Food premises must be registered (Food Safety Act 1990)	
Strict liability for breach of statutory duty under Part II, Consumer Protection Act 1987			
Strict liability under Part I, Consumer Protection Act 1987		Part III, Fair Trading Act 1973 (see above)	
Defective services Liability for breach of implied contractual terms as to use of reasonable care and skill, time of performance and consideration (Supply of Goods and Services Act 1982)	Offences under the Trade Descriptions Act 1968, Package Travel etc. Regulations 1992 (see above)	Parts II and III, Fair Trading Act 1973 (see above). Licence required to carry on consumer credit business (Consumer Credit Act 1974)	Trade association codes of practice Professional bodies' codes of practice
Fault-based liability in the tort of negligence			Citizens' Charter standards for public services
Liability for breach of implied contractual terms in package holidays (Package Travel etc. Regulations 1992)		Bonding requirement for package travel organisers and retailers (Package Travel etc. Regulations 1992)	
Exclusion of liability Exclusion clauses may be ineffective under the common law or rendered void by statute (Unfair Contract Terms Act 1977, Unfair Terms in Consumer Contracts Regulations 1999)	Offence to display 'no refunds' notices (Consumer Transactions (Restriction on Statements) Order 1976)	Parts II and III, Fair Trading Act 1973 (see above). The Director General of Fair Trading and other qualifying bodies can challenge unfair contract terms (Unfair Terms in Consumer Contracts Regulations 1999)	Trade association codes of practice

Fig 14.2 *(continued)*

The problems with package holidays

1 A package holiday involves a complex set of legal relationships between the travel agent, tour operator, hotelier, carrier and local suppliers of services. In most cases, the tour operator does not own the airlines or hotels but contracts with independent suppliers to make up the package. Although the contract is usually made in this country, most of the components of the package are delivered abroad. The consumer may be unsure who, exactly, is responsible if something goes wrong and which country's law applies.

2 The holiday is often arranged by one individual on behalf of himself and his family or a group of friends. The rights of holidaymakers who did not personally make a booking may not be clear.

3 Holiday selections are made on the basis of advertising, descriptions in a brochure and advice by travel agents. Customers need adequate and accurate information to make an appropriate choice, but brochures are usually prepared a long time in advance of the holidays to which they relate.

4 The holiday may be disrupted by events beyond the control of the tour operator: flights may be delayed by bad weather or industrial action by airport staff, or independent hoteliers may have overbooked their hotels. To what extent should the operator be held responsible for the holidaymakers' loss of enjoyment when such things happen?

5 Competitive pricing policies have led to low profit margins and the need to reduce financial risk to a minimum by restricting consumers' rights through the use of standard terms and conditions.

Legal controls over package holidays

Before 1993 there were few legal rules designed specifically to control the package holiday industry. By and large, general consumer protection measures were used.

1 Civil law remedies. Individual holidaymakers could bring actions in contract or tort against the tour operator if the holiday failed to live up to expectations (see, e.g., *Jarvis* v *Swan Tours* (1973)). Although the travel agent acts on behalf of the tour operator, he may incur liability to the consumer in tort if, for example, he makes untrue statements about a holiday. Consumers' civil remedies were enhanced by general consumer protection legislation, such as:

(a) the Misrepresentation Act 1967, which provided a remedy for a negligent misrepresentation;

(b) the Consumer Credit Act 1974, which by s 75 imposed equal liability on credit card companies;

(c) the Unfair Contract Terms Act 1977, which controlled the use of unfair exemption clauses;

(d) the Supply of Goods and Services Act 1982, which provided that the supplier of services should exercise reasonable care and skill.

2 Criminal penalties. Travel agents and tour operators were vulnerable to prosecution under legislation to deal with false and misleading descriptions of services and prices contained in s 14 of the Trade Descriptions Act 1968 and Part III of the Consumer Protection Act I 987.

3 Administrative controls. One of the consequences of cut-throat price competition in the travel industry has been a high rate of company failures because of insolvency. The problem for the consumer is that he may find himself stranded abroad. Administrative controls have, therefore, tended to concentrate on putting in place arrangements to safeguard holidaymakers in the event of the tour operator becoming insolvent. The Civil Aviation Authority, for example, required anyone organising inclusive holidays involving air travel to obtain an Air Travel Organiser's Licence (ATOL). Such operators were required to satisfy financial requirements and to provide a **bond** to cover liabilities, which may arise from insolvency. An Air Travel Reserve Fund was set up as an additional precaution.

4 Business self-regulation. The Association of British Travel Agents (ABTA) was set up in 1951 and, despite its name, represents the interests of both travel agents and tour operators. All ABTA members are bound by the codes of practice: the Tour Operator's Code of Conduct and the Travel Agent's Code of Conduct.

The fragmented nature of the controls over the package holiday industry, the high level of consumer dissatisfaction and the obvious European dimension to the industry made this form of consumer transaction a natural target for EC legislation. The EC Directive on Package Travel, Package Holidays and Package Tours was adopted by the EC Council in 1990. Member states were required to implement the measure by 31 December 1992. The Directive was given effect in the UK by the Package Travel, Package Holidays and Package Tour Regulations 1992, which came into force on 23 December 1992.

The Package Travel, Package Holidays and Package Tour Regulations 1992

The main provisions of the regulations as they affect consumers are as follows:

1 Package. The regulations do not apply to travel or accommodation, which are separately arranged. The regulations only apply to 'packages' which are sold or offered for sale in the UK. The definition of a 'package' requires the existence of the following elements:

(a) a pre-arranged combination of at least two or more specified components which are:
(i) transport; (ii) accommodation; (iii) other tourist services not ancillary to transport or accommodation, but which account for a significant proportion of the package.
(b) the combination is sold or offered for sale at an inclusive price;
(c) the service covers a period of 24 hours or more or includes overnight accommodation.

2 The parties. The regulations use the terms 'organiser' and 'retailer' to describe the tour operator and travel agent respectively. The 'consumer' is given a broad definition so as to include not only the person who makes the contract for the package but also anyone else on whose behalf he has contracted, i.e. members of a family or someone to whom the contracting person has transferred the package.

3 Misleading information. Regulation 4 provides that a consumer is entitled to be compensated by the organiser or retailer for any loss arising from misleading information about the package, its price or any other conditions applying to the contract.

4 Provision of information. The regulations set out what information must be given to consumers in brochures and before the package starts:

(a) *Brochures.* Regulation 5 provides that brochures must contain certain specified information, e.g. the destination, the means of transport, the type of accommodation, its location, main features and category, inclusive meals and the itinerary. It is an offence for an organiser to make available a brochure which does not comply with the requirements. It is also an offence for a retailer to make a brochure available to a possible consumer which he knows or has reasonable cause to believe does not comply with the requirements. The penalties are a maximum fine of £5,000 in the magistrates' court or an unlimited fine in respect of a Crown Court conviction.

Inspirations East Ltd v Dudley MBC (1997)

Inspirations, an organiser of package holidays, included a statement in its 'Inspirations Cyprus' brochure that a certain hotel in Limassol was very suitable for people who use a wheelchair. A customer booked a holiday at the hotel but discovered on arrival that there was no access to the swimming pool for people in wheelchairs. Inspirations' conviction was upheld. The magistrates were entitled to find that the indication that the hotel was suitable for the disabled was a misdescription about a main feature of the package in breach of reg 5.

Regulation 6 provides that particulars in the brochure have the status of implied warranties, unless the parties agree otherwise. If the brochure contains an express statement that particulars are subject to change and any changes are clearly communicated to the consumer before the contract is concluded, then no liability for breach of warranty will arise.

(b) *Before the package starts.* Regulation 7 requires the organiser and retailer to provide the consumer information about matters such as passport and visa requirements, health formalities and arrangements for security of money paid and arrangements for repatriation. Regulation 8 requires the organiser and retailer to provide the consumer in good time before the journey starts with information about transport arrangements and local representatives. Both regulations create criminal offences with maximum penalties of £5,000 on conviction in the magistrates' court and an unlimited fine in the Crown Court.

5 Content of the contract. It is an implied condition of the contract that the organiser or retailer supplies a written copy of the terms of the contract to the consumer before the contract is made and that the contract contains specified elements, e.g. travel destination(s), travel dates, accommodation, the itinerary, inclusive meals and excursions, the price and payment schedule and time limits for complaints (reg 9).

6 Transfer of bookings. If the consumer is prevented from going ahead with the package, he has the right under reg 10 to transfer the package to a third party if he gives reasonable notice. However, a transfer may involve extra costs and the transferor and transferee are jointly and severally liable for the price of the package.

7 Surcharges. Price variation clauses will be void under reg 11 unless they comply with the following requirements:

(a) the clauses provide for both upward and downward revision; and

(b) the contract states precisely how the revised price is to be calculated; and

(c) the variation is solely due to changes in the cost of transportation; or dues, taxes or fees for services, such as landing taxes; or exchange rates.

A price increase cannot be made within 30 days of departure or where the increase is less than 2 per cent of the price.

8 Alteration of the terms. Regulation 12 incorporates an implied term into every contract that the organiser will inform the consumer of a significant alteration of any of the essential terms of the contract, e.g. price, so the consumer can decide whether to cancel, or accept the alteration. If the consumer decides to cancel, he is entitled to a substitute package of the same or superior quality, or a lower quality package with an adjustment of price, or a full refund (reg 13).

9 Significant proportion of services not provided. Regulation 14 provides that there is an implied term that where after a departure a significant proportion of the services contracted for are not provided, the organiser must make suitable alternative arrangements for the consumer to continue the package, at no extra cost. If there is a difference in the services supplied under the alternative arrangements, the consumer must be compensated. If it is impossible to make alternative arrangements or the consumer reasonably refuses to accept the alternative offered, the consumer must be provided with equivalent transport back to the departure point or another place agreed by the consumer.

10 Liability for proper performance of the contract. Under reg 15 the organiser and retailer are liable to the consumer for the proper performance of the contract, irrespective of whether the obligations are to be performed by the organiser or retailer of by other suppliers. Liability will not arise where the failures in performance are attributable:

(a) to the consumer himself; or

(b) to a third party unconnected with the services contracted for; or

(c) to unusual or unforeseeable circumstances beyond the control of the organiser or retailer (known as *force majeure*).

Where (b) and (c) occur, the organiser and retailer must give prompt assistance to any consumer in difficulty. The contract can include a reasonable term, which limits the amount of compensation payable for non-performance or improper performance of the contract. However, liability for death or personal injury cannot be excluded. If the consumer complains, the organiser or retailer or his local representative must take prompt action to find a solution. For their part, consumers are under an obligation to make their complaints known to the supplier of the service at the place where the service is supplied. If, for example, the consumer is unhappy with the standard of his hotel room, he must make his complaint known to the hotel management.

11 Protection against insolvency. The regulations provide that the organiser and retailer must provide evidence of security for the refund of money

paid over and for the repatriation of a consumer in the event of insolvency. The protection against insolvency is further strengthened by compulsory bonding arrangements.

12 Offences and enforcement. As we have seen already, the regulations create a number of new offences. It is a defence for a defendant to show that he took all reasonable steps and exercised due diligence to avoid committing a crime (reg 24). The regulations are enforced by local trading standards departments.

ENFORCING CONSUMER RIGHTS

There has been a considerable improvement in consumers' rights over the past 30 years, which is set to continue as the EC pursues its aim of a high level of protection for consumers. However, creating more and better rights will count for little if consumers do not have a cheap and simple way of enforcing those rights. There are currently three main ways in which a consumer may obtain redress: compensation orders, conciliation or arbitration under a code of practice, and arbitration under the county court small claims procedure.

Compensation orders

If a trader is convicted of a criminal offence, e.g. under the Trade Descriptions Act 1968, the court may make a compensation order requiring the trader to pay compensation for 'any personal injury, loss or damage' resulting from the offence under the Powers of Criminal Courts (Sentencing) Act 2000. Magistrates' courts are limited to £5,000 in respect of each offence for which the trader is convicted. There is no limit to the amount of compensation which can be awarded by the Crown Court. Compensation orders are beneficial to the consumer in the following situations:

(a) where the amount of loss suffered by the consumer is so small that it is not worth bringing a civil action to try and recover it;
(b) where the consumer has no remedy in civil law, e.g. there is no civil remedy for misleading advertising but an offence under the Trade Descriptions Act 1968 may have been committed.

Conciliation or arbitration under a code of practice

The trader may be a member of a trade association which operates a conciliation or arbitration scheme to deal with complaints against members. The aim of conciliation is to get the parties to resolve their differences in an informal way. If conciliation does not result in agreement, the consumer is still free to take the matter to arbitration or to the courts. Arbitration consists of an independent person hearing both sides of the dispute and then making a decision which is binding on the parties. Arbitration is usually very informal and is often done in writing. It is usually inexpensive but in some cases can be more expensive than going to court. One of the problems with some arbitration schemes was that an agreement to refer the dispute to arbitration precluded the consumer from bringing an action in the ordinary courts. The Consumer Arbitration Agreements Act 1988 was designed to deal with this problem by providing that a consumer was not bound by a clause in a contract which said that any dispute must be referred to arbitration where the amount claimed fell within the small claims limit for county court arbitrations (see below). It has now been decided that consumer arbitration agreements should be dealt with as potentially unfair terms in a consumer contract and therefore subject to the protections contained in the Unfair Terms in Consumer Contracts Regulations 1999. The Arbitration Act 1996 repealed the Consumer Arbitration Agreements Act 1988 and extended the application of the 1994 regulations to consumer arbitration agreements. A term which constitutes an arbitration agreement is unfair if it relates to a claim for a pecuniary remedy which does not exceed an amount specified by an order made under the Act.

The small claims track

Since 1973 the county court has operated a special scheme for 'small claims'. If a claim for £5,000 or less (or £1,000 or less in the case of a personal injury claim) is defended the case will be allocated to the small claims track. Small claims cases are usually heard by a district judge but complex cases can be referred to a circuit judge. The judge can adopt any procedure he considers fair. The court

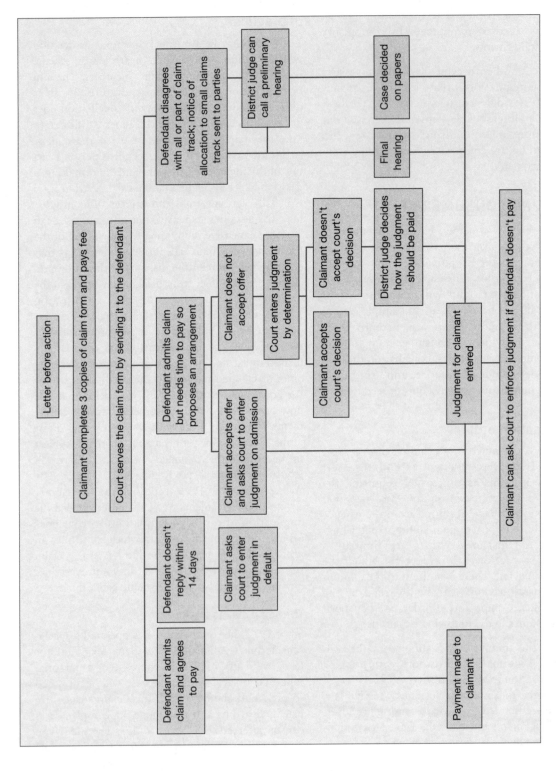

Fig 14.3 Small claims track

has the power to use an external arbitrator if the parties agree. The procedure for bringing a claim is relatively straightforward so that it should not be necessary to have legal assistance. There are a number of leaflets available from the county court which provide a step-by-step guide to making a small claim. The parties are discouraged from using lawyers by the 'no-costs' rule which means that each side must pay its own legal costs whatever the outcome. The only exception is where one of the parties has incurred unnecessary cost because of the unreasonable behaviour of the other, e.g. failing to turn up to a hearing. The procedure for bringing a small claim in the county court is summarised in Fig 14.3.

Although the small claims procedure is a more user-friendly method of obtaining redress for consumer problems than normal civil court procedure, it is not particularly well-used by consumers. It is often used by businesses to recover money owing by consumers! The reluctance to use the procedure suggests that consumers are generally unaware of the small claims system or daunted by the prospect of taking DIY legal action. Even where a consumer pursues a claim and obtains a judgement it may be more difficult to then enforce it and get payment. A further problem is that an appeal can only be made against the judge's decision on very limited grounds. Moreover, if a consumer appeals and is unsuccessful he may have to pay costs.

QUESTIONS/ACTIVITIES

1 How would you define a consumer for the purposes of framing protective legislation?

2 What justification could you give for providing special protection for consumers?

3 What contribution has the EC made to the law of consumer protection?

4 If you had a consumer problem, where could you go to obtain advice and assistance?

5 What powers does the Director-General of Fair Trading have to protect consumers?

6 How have the Package Travel etc. Regulations 1992 improved the rights of consumers in relation to package holidays?

7 What matters should you consider before deciding to sue a trader?

8 What are the advantages and disadvantages of arbitration as a mechanism for resolving consumer complaints?

9 Your friends have just returned from a holiday in Spain complaining bitterly about a catalogue of disasters which occurred, namely:
   ● 24 hours before departure your friends received a telephone call from the tour operator to say that the hotel was overbooked and it would be necessary to transfer surplus holidaymakers to another hotel in a different, less attractive resort;
   ● the flight to Spain was delayed by 18 hours because of industrial action by British air traffic controllers;
   ● the hotel to which your friends were transferred had a lower star rating than the hotel originally booked; it is further away from the sea and there is no swimming pool:
   ● the free excursions advertised in the brochure were not available.
   One of your friends paid by credit card. The others paid by cheque. Using a copy of a current package holiday brochure as a guide, advise your friends of any rights they may have against the tour operator.

Part 4

BUSINESS RESOURCES

Chapter 15

BUSINESS PROPERTY

GENERALLY

English law divides property into real property and personal property. The assets of a business are usually made up of both sorts of property.

The distinction between the two sorts of property is mainly that real property cannot be moved but personal property can.

However, this is not the only test because some things which can be moved are regarded as real property and called fixtures, while other moveables are regarded as fittings which do not become part of the real property to which they are attached. A diagram showing the broad classification of property in English law appears at Fig 15.1.

FIXTURES AND FITTINGS

As we have seen, fixtures become part of the land itself; fittings do not. If a piece of personal property is securely attached to the ground it is probably a fixture, but a second test needs to be applied in order to finally decide. If the piece of personal property was put on the land so that it could be better enjoyed for itself, it is not a fixture. However, if it was put on the land so that the land can be better enjoyed, then it is a fixture.

Leigh v Taylor (1902)

A person put some valuable tapestries on the wall of his house, the house being real property. He used tacks to fit them on a framework of wood and canvas which he then nailed to the wall. Upon his death the court had to decide whether the tapestries were real or personal property and it was decided that they were still personal property. They had been fixed to the wall so that they could be better enjoyed for themselves.

Comment. A contrast is provided by *D'Eyncourt* v *Gregory* (1866) where certain statues, vases and stone garden furniture standing on their own weight were decided to be real property because they formed part of the design of a landscaped garden. They were there for the better enjoyment of the land.

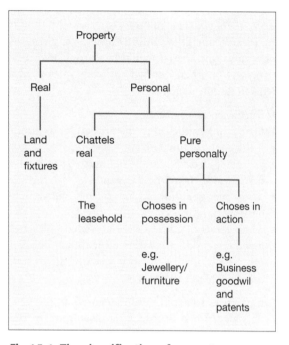

Fig 15.1 The classification of property

The importance of the idea of fixtures and fittings is that if you buy land and buildings, say as a business asset, then in the absence of a special provision in the conveyance to the contrary, the conveyance will pass the fixtures to the buyer and they cannot be removed by the seller. They are also regarded as included in the price. Fittings are not and can be removed by the seller in the absence of an agreement to the contrary.

The distinction is also important to lenders on mortgages since if they take possession of a property because of the borrower's default, the mortgage will give the lender a charge over fixtures but not fittings in the premises. The matter came before the High Court in *TSB Bank plc* v *Botham* (1995) when the lending bank, which had taken possession of the borrower's flat, claimed that certain items were fixtures and as a result were subject to its mortgage and could be sold to the new flat buyer.

The judge said that whether a chattel had become a fixture depended first on the object and purpose for which it had been fixed. If the object and purpose was to make a permanent and substantial improvement to the land or buildings, the chattel would be regarded as a fixture. If it was attached so that it could be better enjoyed for itself, it would be a fitting, on the lines of the tapestry in *Leigh*. The judges also thought that if significant damage would be done to the premises on removal the chattel would be more likely to be a fixture. He then applied the principles to the items in dispute as follows:

- fitted carpets – fixtures;
- light fittings attached to the property – fixtures;
- mock coal gas fire piped in – fixture;
- curtains, blinds and pelmets specifically designed for the particular windows – fixtures;
- towel rails, soap fittings, tap fittings and shower heads – all fixtures;
- white goods fitted into standard-sized holes and piped or wired in and aligned with and abutted on to each other so as to be part of the overall fitted kitchen – all fixtures.

In practice, to avoid misunderstanding, the Law Society's National Protocol 'Transaction' for the sale of residential property requires a seller to complete a fixtures form detailing those fixtures that are included in the sale and those which are excluded. It is equally sensible and usual in sales of commercial property to follow a similar course in order to avoid disputes.

THE LEASE

A lease of land, e.g. office premises, is obviously an interest in land (or realty) but for historical reasons it is regarded as personal property and not real property.

This distinction has lost much of its importance in law, though still today if a person, T, were to leave by his will 'all my personal property to P and all my real property to R', P would get any leases which T had when he died.

PURE PERSONALTY AND CHATTELS REAL

The word personalty is another name for personal property. The word chattel is also used to describe personal property.

Although leaseholds are regarded as personalty, they are over land and result in a person having use of land, and so they are referred to as chattels real to distinguish them from pure personalty, such as a watch or a fountain pen.

PURE PERSONALTY – CHOSES IN POSSESSION AND CHOSES IN ACTION

Things such as jewellery and furniture which are tangible objects and have not only a money value but can also be enjoyed by the person who owns them **in a physical way** through the senses are called choses (or things) in possession.

Things which cannot be enjoyed by the person who owns them in a physical way, but which nevertheless are worth money, are called choses (or things) in action. Examples are patents, copyrights, trade marks, shares and cheques and the goodwill of a business. The value lies not in the thing itself but the legal right to money which it represents and the right to bring an action at law to enforce or protect that right should this become necessary.

Thus, if you have a fire in your business premises, you will no doubt value your fire extinguisher (a chose in possession), but you will find your insurance policy (a chose in action) to be of greater value!

EASEMENTS AND PROFITS

We have already dealt with a property right called a lease. This is a right to use another person's land for a period of time in return for the payment of rent. It is, however, also possible to have ownership of other rights over someone else's property.

Easements

A may have what is called an **easement** over B's land. This might be **a right of way** so that, for example, A could get goods and services into his business premises by bringing them across land belonging to another business.

An easement may also be a **right to light** which would prevent the owner of a neighbouring business from building on his own land but so close to A's premises that A was unable to use them without constant artificial light. A could stop such a building from being put up by asking the court for an injunction to protect his right of light.

An easement may also be a **right to support** from other buildings. Where a house or business premises are attached to other property, as with a semi-detached house, one property needs the support of the other.

Thus, if B decides to pull down his semi-detached premises which will leave A's premises in danger of collapsing, A can, once again, ask the court for an injunction to prevent B from doing this.

The case of *Batchelor* v *Marlow* (2000) is also of interest in a modern context. In that case it was decided that the right to park cars on another's property could exist as an easement.

The deeds of the various properties will usually reveal what easements exist between the land-owners, as will entries relevant to the property in the Land Registry. However, a legal easement is an overriding interest that binds the land, *whether mentioned in the deeds or register or not*. It is important to make stringent enquiries of the seller because the existence of easements over land can be a nuisance and affect its value.

It is important to note that **an easement** is a **private** right (a public right of way is a different matter with which we shall not deal!), enjoyed by owners or occupiers of **land** over **neighbouring** land. You cannot by owning land in Essex have an easement over land in Yorkshire.

Finally, it is not uncommon in business for a purchaser to take out indemnity insurance if vital easements, e.g. of access, are later successfully challenged or easements are established that might prove a nuisance to the business.

Profits

Sometimes the right which exists over someone else's land is to take something from the land. It may, for example, be a right to fish or cut wood.

These rights can be purchased over any land. Unlike an easement, they are **not** restricted to rights over neighbouring land. You can, therefore, buy fishing rights over a river in Surrey even though you live in Lancashire and do not own any land at all in Surrey.

SECURITIES

A person may raise a loan on the security of his property, whether real (say, his house) or personal (say, his shareholding in a company), and the lender has certain rights over the property so used as a security if the loan is not repaid.

The use of mortgages on their own assets, such as the family home, by sole traders, partners and directors of companies together with the use of personal guarantees of business debt and fixed and floating charges over the assets of a company were considered in Chapter 4 as part of the topic of raising finance.

A LICENCE

Legislation giving business tenants (but not licensees) security of occupation has encouraged property owners to attempt to create licences rather than leases. A licence can be ended on reasonable notice; the rights of a business tenant may under the Landlord and Tenant Act 1954, Part II, survive the end of the period of the lease. In particular, the tenant is able to apply to the court for a new lease and the landlord can only oppose the application on one of the grounds set out in the Act, e.g. poor state of repair of the premises owing to a breach of the tenant's repair obligations in the lease.

If the agreement is to be a licence, the main test must be satisfied, which is that a licence will exist if the tenant does not have *exclusive possession* of the premises. Thus, in *Dresden Estates Ltd* v *Collinson* (1987) the landlord's right to relocate the licensee of an industrial unit to different premises deprived the licensee of exclusive possession and confirmed the agreement as a licence and not a lease.

Those in business should therefore ensure, through legal advice, that their tenancy agreement is indeed a lease covered by the 1954 Act.

ACCESS TO LAND

Access to Neighbouring Land Act 1992

The Access to Neighbouring Land Act 1992 deals with a situation in which a person who owns a building which is badly in need of repair cannot carry out necessary work on that building without entering on to his neighbour's property, and he cannot do this without committing a trespass because the neighbour will not consent to access. Under the Act the owner of the building can apply to the court for what is called an 'access order', under which he may enter the neighbouring property and carry out the necessary work on his own property. The applicant for an access order must show that the work is reasonably necessary to preserve the whole or part of his land including buildings, and that the work cannot be done at all, or that it would be substantially more difficult to do it, if entry to neighbouring land was not granted. The order will be made against the person who could otherwise sue for trespass, and so if the neighbouring property is let it will be made against the tenant.

The order may restrict entry to a specified area and provide for compensation to be made to the neighbouring owner if this is appropriate. It may also require the person given access to make a payment to the neighbouring owner, reflecting the financial benefit which the person given access has received. This does not apply where the property subject to the access order is residential land.

Countryside and Rights of Way Act 2000

This act also provides for access to land by non-owners. The main provisions are as follows:

- a right of access on foot for open air recreation to mountain, moor, heath, down and registered common land (or open country);
- land over 600 metres above sea level is automatically covered;
- open land will be shown on maps that will be available to the public (there is an appeal to the Secretary of State where land is included by mistake);
- there are exceptions for land that is cultivated, land covered by buildings, parks and gardens, mineral workings, railway land and golf courses, aerodromes, race courses and development land where planning permission has been granted, though it is unclear whether development must have been implemented;
- landowners must not erect false or misleading signs likely to deter people from using their statutory right of access, though signs indicating boundaries are acceptable so long as they do not deter walkers by giving them false information;
- landowners may need to provide for new access to open country where public rights of way do not exist or are insufficient;
- open country access may be closed for up to 28 days each year, but not over bank holidays or weekends.

RESTRICTIVE COVENANTS

These covenants control the way in which a person uses his land. There is **public** control of the use of land through Town and Country Planning Acts (see further, Chapter 4) and there are also building regulations to cover the way in which buildings are constructed. As well as **public** control, however, there is also **private** control by means of restrictive covenants. If these are put into a lease of land the landlord can enforce them against the tenant because they are parties to the contract; in other words, there is a privity of estate or contract between them.

However, it is often desirable that covenants (or agreements) restricting the use of land should be enforceable between those who own freehold properties. For example, when estates of private houses are built, it is desirable in order to preserve the residential nature of the estate that covenants, e.g. to use the premises for residential purposes only, should be complied with by the purchasers of the individual houses and also by those who buy from them and so on, and that these covenants should be enforceable by the house owners as between themselves.

The covenants are taken by the common seller of the property, e.g. the builder or developer (whoever owns the land), and then they can be enforced by the purchasers of the houses as between themselves. The builder or developer will not normally be able to enforce them because he will not usually own any land on the estate, having sold it all off for housing plots.

These covenants can be enforced between subsequent owners of the houses as an exception to the rule of privity of contract (see also Chapter 7). They are, however, void unless registered as a land charge at the Land Registry in London.

When a person buys a house a solicitor acting in the matter will get a search of the Land Register done and will find the restrictive covenants which exist over the property. If he does not find any, because they are not registered, then they are void.

As far as business premises are concerned, these covenants can be a nuisance, in that they may restrict the development of the business. A person who wishes to get rid of a covenant is able to pursue an application to the Lands Tribunal, which deals with certain disputes over land, for modification or discharge.

However, the expense and delay which are unfortunately typical of so many legal procedures apply to Lands Tribunal applications so that developers of land who are faced with the possible enforcement of a covenant making development more expensive may insure against that possible loss. A Lands Tribunal application may be considered for a major development where insurance is expensive and not an economic option. It can also be used to sound out the strength and identity of possible objectors.

The method of enforcement is by a claim for damages or an injunction. The right to an injunction may be lost by delay and/or acquiescence (see further Chapter 7 on the remedy of injunction). Thus, it was held in *Gafford v Graham* (1998) that a landowner enjoying the benefit of a restrictive covenant over adjoining land who, with full knowledge of his rights, failed to seek relief to restrain the unlawful erection of an indoor riding school in breach of covenant could have damages only when he eventually brought a claim. Delay and acquiescence, which is assumed from delay, had barred his claim to injunctive relief.

LEGAL ESTATES IN LAND

There are only two legal estates in land – the fee simple absolute in possession (usually called a freehold) and the term of years absolute (usually called a leasehold).

The word 'estate' is used because in theory at least the Queen owns all our land and we can only hold an estate, as it is called, from her; in other words, part of what she owns. However, the Queen has now no right to take back these estates from their owners.

The freehold

If we have an estate from the Queen, we want to know how long it will last. The fee simple absolute in possession (or freehold) lasts indefinitely and the word 'fee' means that the land can be inherited, as where it is left by the owner to another person by a will. 'Simple' means that it can be passed on to anyone. The word 'absolute' means that it must not be what is called a modified fee, such as a life interest, which can only be an equitable interest behind a trust (see below).

There must also be possession of the land, though the freehold owner need not be living on the property; it is enough if he receives rent for it, as where he has let it on a lease to a tenant and is himself a landlord.

So, if freehold land is sold or left by will to X, the freehold will belong to X and he can pass it on to another.

If, however, land is left 'to X for life and after his death to Y', X does not take a legal estate of freehold, nor does Y. Y's interest is absolute but not yet in possession until X dies. X's interest is in possession but is not absolute because it is only for his life.

The above interests are equitable interests and can only be held on a trust. The trustees would have the freehold and when X died they would transfer the freehold to Y who would then be the absolute owner and the trust would come to an end.

The leasehold

A term of years absolute, usually called a lease, is an estate which lasts for a fixed time. It is usually given by a freehold owner to a tenant. It will normally be for a fixed period, e.g. 21 years.

A lease for a fixed term comes to an end when the term finishes, though in the case of business leases there may be statutory protection, in terms, e.g., of security of tenure under the Landlord and Tenant Act 1954, Part II, which was considered earlier in this chapter.

Reform– commonhold

The Lord Chancellor's Department has consulted on a draft Commonhold Bill. The following are the main features of a proposed new legal interest in a new type of freehold:

1 A commonhold is a freehold development which consists of two or more separate properties or units which are managed together. Collective management is necessary where the units form different parts of the same building or where they share services and facilities such as lifts, entrance halls and stairs, refuse areas, gardens and driveways so that collective management is necessary for these common parts. It should be noted that commonhold development will be available for commercial developments, such as offices and business parks.

2 Commonhold should not be confused with leasehold enfranchisement under which flat owners in blocks of flats collectively buy out the freehold owner of the property and so obtain control of the freehold of the block but not their individual flats in the sense that they are still tenants for a period of years however long. The commonhold will, like a freehold, have no term of years but be 'for ever', as it were. Implementation of commonhold will necessitate the passing of detailed legislation, much of it highly technical, but a start has been made.

3 A commonhold will be the first form of non-terminable interest in land that does not necessarily cover a property whose foundations are on the ground. A second storey flat may in the developed future be held on commonhold. This is why a commonhold is sometimes referred to as a 'flying freehold'.

THE RIGHTS AND DUTIES OF AN OCCUPIER OF LAND

The main right of an occupier of land is to seek an injunction against persons who trespass on his land or, alternatively, sue the trespasser for damages. These matters were considered in Chapter 11. However, in addition to the general rules which apply to trespass to land, there are aspects specific to occupiers of land which are considered below. In addition, the question of the liability of occupiers of land and premises to persons suffering injury arising from that occupation may be regarded as an aspect of negligence (which has also been considered in general terms in Chapter 11). However, specific aspects of liability applying to occupiers and arising from legislation are covered in the material which follows.

Duties to those who are not on the premises

We must look separately at liability to persons on the road (or highway), if any, which is next to the premises. We must also consider liability to persons on premises which are next to the property.

1 **Liability to persons on the highway.** The occupier has a duty not to injure persons on the highway by allowing a harmful situation to develop on his land.

Holling v Yorkshire Traction Co Ltd (1948)

Steam and smoke from the Traction Company's factory went across a road next to it and made it difficult to see. As a result, two vehicles collided and this caused the death of Holling. The court said that the Traction Company was liable. It was negligent of the company not to post a man at each end of the affected area to warn of the danger.

2 **Liability to persons on adjoining premises.** An occupier has a duty not to injure persons on adjoining premises by allowing a harmful situation to develop on the land.

Taylor v Liverpool Corporation (1939)

The claimant was the daughter of the tenant of some flats owned by the Corporation. She was injured when a chimney stack from adjoining premises, also owned by the Corporation, fell into a yard. The Corporation had been negligent in that it had not maintained the chimney properly. The Corporation was liable in negligence and the claimant won her case.

Duties to persons on the premises

Under the Occupiers' Liability Act 1957 an occupier of premises must take reasonable care to see that a visitor to his premises will be reasonably safe in using the premises for the purposes for which he is invited or permitted by the occupier to be on them.

Visitors – generally

The above duty is owed to all lawful visitors. These are individuals who enter the premises with the **express** permission of the occupier, as where A (an occupier) invites B (a plumber) to enter his home to repair a leaking pipe.

However, permission to enter premises is also **implied** by the law. So, for example, persons who enter premises to read, for example, gas and/or electricity meters are there by the implied permission of the occupier, as would also be a policeman with a search warrant, though in the last case it is unlikely that the occupier would expressly invite him on to the premises! The term 'visitor' does not apply to trespassers.

Children

The 1957 Act provides that persons who occupy premises must take into account the fact that children may be less careful than adults and therefore the duty of care owed to children is higher.

An example of this is that things which constitute a trap or are especially alluring to children must be given special attention by an occupier, because he may be liable for any damage which such things cause, even if the child involved is a trespasser.

Glasgow Corporation v Taylor (1922)

A boy aged seven years died after he had eaten some poisonous berries which he picked from a tree in a park owned by the Corporation.

There was a notice in the park but the court decided that this was not adequate as a means of communicating the danger to young children. Also, the berries were within easy reach and were attractive to children. The Corporation was liable.

Visitors who are experts

The 1957 Act provides that persons who enter premises as part of their job, e.g. plumbers and electricians, ought to have a better appreciation of the risks which may arise while they are doing their work.

Roles v Nathan (1963)

N employed two chimney sweeps to clean out the flues of a heating system fuelled by coke. Although N warned the sweeps against it, they blocked off a ventilation hole while the coke fire was still alight. They were later killed by the escape of carbon monoxide fumes. This action, which was brought by the dependants of the sweeps, failed. The court decided that an occupier is entitled to assume that a chimney sweep will guard against such dangers.

Warnings

The 1957 Act states that if the occupier gives a warning of the danger, it will free him from liability, but only if the warning makes the visitor safe.

It would not be enough, for example, for a cinema to give warning of a dangerous roof over what was the only approach to the ticket office. However, if customers in a shop are told not to go to the far end of it because builders have opened up a dangerous hole, the shopkeeper might well have no duty to a customer who defied his instruction and fell down the hole.

Exclusion of liability

The 1957 Act provides that an occupier may 'restrict or exclude his duty by agreement or otherwise'. However, because of the Unfair Contract Terms Act 1977 (see Chapter 9) there can be no exclusion of liability for death or personal injury on business premises. In regard to other loss, e.g. damage to the goods of a visitor, liability can be excluded only if it is reasonable to do so.

Faulty work of outside contractors

The 1957 Act allows an occupier to escape liability if the damage results from the faulty work of an outside contractor (called also an independent contractor) whose expertise is necessary to get the job done, provided the occupier behaved reasonably in the selection of the contractor.

Cook v Broderip (1968)

The owner of a flat, Major Broderip, employed an apparently competent electrical contractor to fix a new socket. Mrs Cook, who was a cleaner, received an electric shock from the socket while she was working in the flat. This was because the contractor had failed to test it properly. The court decided that Major Broderip was not liable to Mrs Cook but the contractor was.

Trespassers

The position of trespassers is covered by the Occupiers' Liability Act 1984. The Act deals with the duty of an occupier to persons other than his visitors and this includes trespassers and persons entering land without the consent of the owner, but in the exercise of a private right of way or public access. In these cases the occupier owes a duty, if he is aware of the danger which exists, or has reasonable grounds to believe that it exists.

He must also know, or have reasonable grounds to believe, that the non-visitor concerned is in the vicinity of the danger – whether he has lawful authority to be in that vicinity or not.

Furthermore, the risk must be one which in all the circumstances of the case it is reasonable to expect the occupier to offer the non-visitor protection against. It was held, for example, in *Proffit* v *British Railways Board* (1984) that British Rail (as it then was) had no general duty to erect or maintain fences sufficient to keep trespassers out. The case applies to Railtrack, which is the successor to British Rail.

The duty is to take such care as is reasonable in all the circumstances of the case to see that the non-visitor does not suffer injury because of the danger concerned. The duty may be discharged by giving a warning of the danger or taking steps to discourage persons from incurring risk. Thus, the defence of assumption of risk is preserved.

A case in point is *Ratcliff* v *McConnell* (1999) where the claimant sued for tetraplegic injuries sustained by diving into the shallow end of a college swimming pool when the pool was closed for the winter. He had climbed over a locked gate in the early hours of the morning. There were warning notices and notices prohibiting use. The claimant, who was an adult, did not recover any damages against the college (represented by the defendant who was a governor). He willingly accepted the risk, said the Court of Appeal.

INTELLECTUAL PROPERTY AND ITS PROTECTION

Generally

Intellectual property is a term used to refer to a product or a process which is marketable and profitable because it is unique.

This uniqueness is protected by **patent law**, which gives protection to technological inventions. The law relating to **registered designs** protects articles which are mass produced but distinguished from others by a registered design which appears upon them. The law of **copyright** protects, e.g. rights in literary, artistic, and musical works. The law of **trade marks** and **service marks** protects the use of a particular mark if it is used in trade.

The law also protects those in business from competitors who maliciously disparage their products or who pass off their own products as those of another business. There is also some protection in regard to the commercial use, e.g. by employees without permission, of confidential information.

The current main legislation is to be found in the Patents Act 1977, the Copyright, Designs and Patents Act 1988 and the Trade Marks Act 1994.

Patents

Application

An application for a patent can be made by or on behalf of the inventor of a new process or device and the grant of a patent will be made to the inventor himself or to any person who is entitled to it, as where the inventor has sold the idea before patenting it.

What can be patented?

It should not be assumed that every bright idea can be the subject of a patent. When application is made for a patent certain essential criteria must be met. It must be shown that the applicant has an invention; the invention must not be excluded (see below); it must be new and not something that would be obvious to lots of people. The 1977 and 1988 Acts do not define an invention, but do require that it be made or used in industry. However, a product, article, material apparatus or process will generally come within the term 'invention' and the method of its operation or manufacture should be patentable. Thus, a toothbrush with an integral toothpaste tube, and the method of making a particular type of chocolate bar, should be patentable, as was the bagless vacuum cleaner invented by Dyson. As a matter of interest, the High Court has ruled that a bagless cleaner subsequently made by Hoover was an infringement of Dyson's patent for its bagless cyclonic vacuum cleaner (see *Dyson Appliances Ltd* v *Hoover Ltd* (2000)).

Exclusions

Under the Patents Act 1977 certain items cannot be protected by a patent. Among these are discoveries, so that if you had been the first person to discover gravity (actually it was Newton), you could not have patented the principle of gravity. However, the inventor of a pendulum clock which utilised gravity could seek to protect the device.

Computer programs (software) are generally protected by copyright, but exceptionally, if a program was invented which enabled the computer to work faster, patent protection would be available for the programmed computer and the method of operating it.

Registration

An application for a patent can be made by or on behalf of the inventor of a new process or device, and the grant of a patent will be made to the inventor himself or to any person who is entitled to it, as where the inventor has sold the idea before patenting it. Application is made to the Patent Office in London or in Newport, Gwent, South Wales. The Patent Office is part of the Department of Trade and Industry and it deals with the granting of patents, registered trade marks and registered designs.

The Comptroller-General maintains at the Patent Office a register of patents and the date of entry gives priority over later inventions. A patent lasts for 20 years but must in effect be renewed annu-ally by payment of a fee to the Patent Office. These fees are payable on the anniversary of the filing date and increase with the age of the patent. A patent cannot be extended beyond 20 years.

Using patents

It should be noted that a patent does not necessarily give the patent holder a right **to use** his invention. For example, a patented drug may have to be withdrawn from the market if it does not comply with government regulations. The right given by a patent is the right of the holder **to control** his invention, in the sense of having a total monopoly in the market or allowing others to market the invention subject to conditions imposed upon them by the patent holder.

Infringement

A UK patent will, in general, be infringed by making, using or selling something in the UK which is subject to the patent without the owner's consent. However, a UK patent applies only within the UK so that a German competitor could legally make the invention in Germany, unless of course there was also a German patent. The German goods could also quite legally be exported to any other country where there was no patent, though not of course to the UK.

Infringement of a patent is a matter for the civil rather than the criminal law and actions for an injunction, damages, or an account of profits, are brought in the Patents Court which is part of the Chancery Division of the High Court. However, the 1988 Act sets up the Patents County Court (see Chapter 3) where the cost of actions against infringement are lower.

The matter of infringement of patented goods by repair was raised in *United Wire Ltd* v *Screen Repair Services (Sotland) Ltd* (2000) where the Court of Appeal decide that, while in the normal way a repair would not amount to an infringement of the patent, much would depend on the extent of the repair. If, for example, it amounted to manufacture of a large part of the product, it might do so. In this instance repairs to filtering screens used in the oil industry were sufficiently extensive to infringe the patent in the screens held by United Wire.

Employees' inventions

Under the Patents Act 1977 an invention of an employee belongs to the employer if the employee arrives at it during his normal employment or during a specific job outside his normal duties. Other inventions, e.g. those made during the employee's spare time, belong to the employee.

Under the 1977 Act, where the invention turns out to be of outstanding benefit to the employer the employee may be awarded compensation by the Comptroller-General or the court so as to ensure that the employee gets a fair share of the benefit. The court will come in where the Comptroller-General will not deal with the matter because it is felt that the issues in a particular case would be better dealt with by the court. Terms of a contract of service which cut down an employee's rights in inventions where these exist are unenforceable.

Designs

What is meant by a design?

A design refers only to the features of shape, pattern or ornament applied to an article by an industrial process which appeals to, and is judged solely by, looking at the article, e.g. the shape of a Coca-Cola bottle.

For example, a firm making a special design of fabric for use in curtains or chair covers might register the design.

It is now possible to register the Coca-Cola bottle as a trade mark under the Trade Marks Act 1994 (see further later in this chapter).

Registration

Designs may be registered at the Patent Office (Designs Registry) under the Registered Designs Act 1949 (as amended by the 1988 Act), and there is an appeal to the Registered Designs Appeal Tribunal if the Registrar refuses to register a particular design. Registration gives the owner of the design protection for five years and this can be extended for four further periods of five years on payment of four further fees every five years, making 25 years in all. The Register of Designs can be inspected on payment of a fee.

Infringement

The registered or unregistered design right owner's remedies for infringement are to sue the person responsible for damages and/or an injunction, or an account of profits made from the wrongful use of the design or an order for the delivery up of the infringing copies.

Unregistered design right

The Copyright Act 1956 gave protection against the reproduction of articles from drawings of them. The provisions were primarily intended to give protection against unauthorised use of drawings of cartoon characters, as by making dolls from them. Also, while the protection offered to an article under a registered design was limited to 15 years (now 25 years, see above) the copyright protection lasted for 50 years (now 70 years).

The law of copyright was therefore increasingly used to protect articles in effect by copyright law, by protecting a drawing from which they were made. This approach was used, in particular, by motor manufacturers to protect their exclusive production of spare parts for their vehicles.

The 1988 Act abolishes copyright protection for drawings but gives instead a new design right which is automatically acquired and does not require registration. It lasts for ten years from the end of the year when the article is first marketed or 15 years after it was first designed, whichever period is the first to expire. During the last five years of its life anyone will be able to get a licence to make the article by paying a royalty to the owner at a rate to be determined by the Patent Office in the absence of agreement.

The Act excludes from the new right items which 'must fit' or 'must match', e.g. an exhaust system which 'must fit' a particular car or a body panel which 'must match' a particular car body. The exclusions are therefore those features of a design which are made to ensure that it fits or matches with another part. These exclusions will, in the main, deny protection to car manufacturers in regard to spare parts for their vehicles and prevent what many regarded as the use of intellectual property law to sustain a restrictive practice.

Nevertheless, other aspects of a design are covered. Suppose, for example, that the open end of a replacement bag for a 'Hover' vacuum cleaner needs to be of a particular shape to fit the end of the hose of the 'Hover'. Anyone can copy this part of the 'Hover' bag but it would be an infringement of the 'Hover' bag design to copy other aspects of its shape which were not essential to the fitting of the 'Hover' bag.

The shape of the 'Hover' bag should now also be registrable as a trade mark under the Trade Marks Act 1994.

Infringement

The owner's remedies for infringement are to apply to the court for damages, an injunction and for delivery-up of infringing materials.

Copyright

The 1988 Act does not require the owner of a copyright to register it or to follow any formalities in respect of it. The protection is given by the Act to every original literary, dramatic, musical and artistic work which was previously unpublished. Copyright does not protect ideas. Anyone is entitled to incorporate those ideas in a new work provided that substantially the same words and examples are not used.

Ownership and duration

The author of the work is the owner of the copyright. However, it may be a term of the contract between, say, a newspaper company and its journalists that the entire copyright in the journalist's work is to belong to the newspaper company.

Under the Act, protection of copyright existed in a work during the lifetime of the author of it and until the end of the period of 50 years from the end of the calendar year in which the author of the work died. The copyright then came to an end.

The relevant rules are now contained in a statutory instrument (SI 1995/3297) entitled the Duration of Copyright and Rights in Performance Regulations 1995, passed in order to harmonise UK law with that of the EU. The regulations increase the basic term of copyright in literary, dramatic, musical and artistic works. This raises the former provision of the present life of the author plus 50 years after his death to life plus 70 years. Copyright in film now lasts for 70 years from the last to die of the principal director, the authors of the screenplay and dialogue, and the composer of any music specifically for the film. The regulations came into force on 1 January 1996 and apply to existing works. Copyrights that were due to expire on 31 December 1995 are continued in force and will be extended.

Infringement – generally

The person infringing the copyright will usually have copied from the work and an action can be brought for an injunction and/or damages or for an account of profits made from the wrongful use of the copyright work.

It was held in *Redrow Homes Ltd* v *Bett Brothers plc* (1997) that a claimant owner who asks the court to order the wrongful user of a copyright to hand over the profits made from the wrongful use cannot have, in addition, an award of damages. The case involved the infringement of copyright in drawings containing the designs of houses. The decision will presumably have application in other areas of intellectual property where there is an alternative remedy of damages and an account of profits.

Infringement – press cuttings

Many companies institute a press-cuttings service for circulation among staff to alert them and inform them as to developments in relevant areas of business.

A property right subsists in the typographical arrangement of published editions (s 1 of the Copyright, Designs and Patents Act 1988). The term 'published edition', so far as a newspaper is concerned, means the whole newspaper, and questions as to the infringement of this property right by copying parts of a newspaper must focus on whether the infringement related to a *substantial part* of the whole newspaper (s 16(2) and (3)(a)).

In this connection, the Court of Appeal has ruled that Marks and Spencer plc did not infringe the copyright in a newspaper's typographical arrangement when it photocopied an article for its internal press-cuttings service (see *Newspaper Licensing Agency* v *Marks and Spencer plc* (2000), below).

The Newspaper Licensing Agency (NLA) is a company formed to protect the intellectual property rights of national and provincial newspapers relating to press-cuttings. It operates a collective licensing scheme for making copies of press cuttings. Marks and Spencer plc (the defendant) needs no introduction. Its involvement in these proceedings arose from its use of a press-cuttings agency (duly licensed by the NLA) to make copies of cuttings from newspapers; the defendant copied certain articles for circulation within the company.

Newspaper Licensing Agency v *Marks and Spencer plc* (2000)

The NLA sued the defendant for breach of copyright and Lightman J held in the High Court that the distribution of copies of such cuttings to 70 persons within the defendant company infringed copyright. The defendant appealed to the Court of Appeal, wherein Peter Gibson LJ (with whom Mance LJ agreed, Chadwick LJ dissenting) said that the first issue was to determine what was meant by the 'typographical arrangement of published editions' in s 1. One possible interpretation of this phrase was the typographical arrangement of each article published in a newspaper, but he preferred the view that the phrase referred to the typographical arrangement of the whole newspaper. The latter view was supported by an Australian decision, *Nationwide New Pty Ltd* v *Copyright Agency Ltd* (1996).

He turned next to the question of whether the defendant's copying of some articles constituted a copying of a substantial part of the copyright work. Although the court had been shown samples of cuttings and of the complete pages from which they had been extracted, the issue of whether substantial parts had been copied could be determined by judicial knowledge of the form of newspapers. The compiler of the cuttings had re-arranged the format of the original article and accordingly the articles appeared in a different image from that in which they had appeared in the newspaper. Nevertheless, there was a facsimile copy of each part of any article which was cut up and pasted. Each such part was a seperate part of the image on the page, and the 'substantiality' of each part had to be considered.

However, the court had not been shown any cutting which could properly be regarded as a 'substantial part' of the published edition from which it had been taken. That was decisive in the appeal, and was supported by the *Nationwide* case. The court had heard argument whether the copying constituted fair dealing in reporting current events in accordance with s 30(2). Peter Gibson LJ felt that, if what the defendant had done had been a prima facie breach of copyright, s 30(2) would have

afforded no defence, but a decision on the point was not necessary in view of the decision which the court had reached.

Comment. The test laid down by the Court of Appeal is not without its problems. It means, for example, that in a publication consisting of, say, technical articles in the form of a compilation, copyright would only be infringed if the copying of a substantial part of the compilation occurred. Individual authors could protect the copyright but only if the copyright had been reserved to them. The NLA has been granted leave to appeal to the House of Lords.

Exceptions

There are no statutory defences to copyright infringement. However, there are common law defences, the principal being known as 'non-derogation from grant'. This defence was developed from the decision of the House of Lords in *British Leyland* v *Armstrong Patents Co* (1986). In this case the House of Lords refused to allow British Leyland (as it was then) to enforce its copyright in drawings relating to replacement exhaust pipes so as to prevent car owners from obtaining replacement exhausts from independent makers. The House of Lords said this would derogate from British Leyland's implied grant of rights to buyers of British Leyland cars, allowing them to repair their cars by the most economical method during the normal working life of the vehicle.

However, in *Canon Kabushiki* v *Green Cartridge Co (Hong Kong) Ltd* (1997) the Privy Council approved a decision of the court of trial granting an injunction to the claimants, thus prohibiting the defendants from infringing copyright in the claimants' drawings of replacement toner cartridges for photocopiers and laser printers.

The Privy Council said that the cost of a replacement exhaust was relatively small in relation to the capital and running costs of a car. In contrast, the cost of replacement cartridges for a laser printer substantially exceeded the cost of the printer itself. There was also competition for the claimants, as suppliers of replacement cartridges, from those who refilled exhausted toner cartridges. It could not, therefore, be said that the claimants were unfairly using their intellectual property rights to abuse their monopoly in replacement toner supplies.

Moral rights

Under the 1988 Act authors are given certain moral rights in their work which exist quite independently of copyright. They provide protection alongside a copyright and would be especially useful and necessary to an author who had sold the copyright to someone else.

The right of paternity

This is a right to be identified as the author of a literary, dramatic, musical or artistic work. In general terms this right operates whenever the work is performed in public, or issued to the public or commercially exploited. It includes the right to be identified as the author of a work from which any adaptation is made. The right extends to copies of the piece and to signs on buildings such as theatres, where the sign can be seen by people entering or approaching the building. This right of paternity must be specifically claimed by the author.

The *exceptions* to the right of paternity are quite extensive and include what are called fair dealing exceptions that also apply to copyright. These include the use of extracts of works for the purpose of reporting current events, incidental inclusion in a broadcast or cable television programme and extracts for use in examination papers. If the author consents to the publication of the work in collective works, such as encyclopedias and/or dictionaries, he or she forgoes the right to be credited in the work.

The right of integrity

Under this right the author may object to changes in his or her work by way of additions, deletions, alterations or adaption which amount to a distortion or mutilation of the work, or in some way harm the author's honour or reputation. Film directors are included in the expression 'authors' for this purpose.

As regards *exceptions*, an author may not exercise the right of integrity in translations of the underlying literary or dramatic work. So, authors may have to put up with poor translations of their work with no remedy.

False attribution

This gives the author a right against false attribution which mirrors the right of paternity referred to above. Under the paternity right an author is entitled to be recognised as the creator of the work. The right of attribution gives a person such as an author the right to prevent a work which he has *not produced* being attributed to him, or a film falsely attributed to him as a director.

Private or domestic commissions

There are special rights given to those who commission photographs or films for their own private or domestic purposes. Where there is copyright in the resulting work, the person who commissioned it has the right not to have the work issued, exhibited or shown to the public, or broadcast or included in a cable programme service.

Infringement

An author whose moral rights have been infringed is entitled to an injunction and damages. These moral rights continue for the same length of time as copyright, i.e. the life of the author plus 70 years except for false attribution which continues for only 20 years after the person's death. Moral rights can be left by will or separately from any copyright and the beneficiary would then be able to enforce them in the same way as the original author. So a son or daughter made the beneficiary of an author/parent's moral rights could protect those rights after the death of the parent, even though the parent had sold the copyright during his lifetime.

Semiconductor product topographies

This is a new form of intellectual property protection introduced into the UK by statutory instrument under an EC Directive. It protects integrated circuit layout designs found in computers, and in home equipment such as hi-fi, compact disc players and food processors, in a similar way to literary copyright.

Computer software

The 1988 Act continues the previous position under which computer software is protected in the same way as that of literary copyright.

Copyright and the Internet

Advances in technology have resulted in the 1988 Act being applied in novel fact situations. Thus, in

Shetland Times Ltd v *Jonathan Wills* (1997) the court decided that it would be appropriate to issue an injunction to prevent the defendants placing their newspaper headlines on the claimant's Website.

Trade marks

Types of trade marks

There are two types of trade marks:

(a) common law or unregistered trade marks; and
(b) registered trade marks.

A common law trade mark is any mark which has been so widely used on or in connection with a certain class of goods that it can be shown that the public recognised goods with such a mark as coming from the owner of the mark. The remedy to restrict improper use is a passing-off action. In this category would come 'Persil' and 'Polaroid', which are household names in regard to the products concerned.

Registered trade marks

The law of registered trade marks in the UK was reformed by the Trade Marks Act 1994 which came into force on 31 October 1994. The impetus for the Act was the implementation of the EC Trade Marks Directive (89/104) which harmonised the law of trade marks throughout the EC. The distinction between trade marks on goods and on services, e.g. the black horse of Lloyds Bank, has gone. These are now under the same law. Also abolished was the system of registration as a Part A mark or a Part B mark. The main provisions which affect UK law appear below.

Definition

Section 1 of the Act states that a trade mark is any sign capable of being represented graphically which is capable of distinguishing goods or services of one undertaking from those of others. It can include words (including personal names), designs, letters, numerals or the shape of goods or their packaging. It is also expected to include sounds, smells and colours. The first application for registration of a smell was the scent of roses impregnated into Sumitomo tyres.

Although personal names are allowed, they must comply with s 3 which allows the refusal of registration where the so-called mark is not distinctive. Thus, if Mr Brown trades in a business name of Brown & Co, this cannot be registered as a mark since it is not distinctive. In this connection it is of interest to note that the Court of Appeal held in *Elvis Presley Enterprises Inc* v *Sid Shaw Elvisly Yours* (1999) that the name Elvis Presley was too well known to have the inherent distinctiveness which is required for a registered trade mark for goods such as perfumes, soaps and other toiletries. The Trade Mark Registrar had therefore been in error when he registered the name in favour of Elvis Presley Enterprises Inc. The court decided in favour of a London businessman, Sid Shaw, who had been trading in Elvis products since 1979 and could continue to do so.

Mr Shaw also complained that the Elvis Presley Enterprises registration was an infringement of his own registration of the expression 'Elvisly Yours' as a trade mark, which is, of course, registrable since it is not merely a name. The court quoted from the judgment in *Du Boulay* v *Du Boulay* (1896) where it was said: '. . . in this country we do not recognise the absolute right of a person to a particular name to the extent of entitling him to prevent the assumption of that name by a stranger . . . [this] is a grievance for which our law affords no redress.' It would therefore be impossible, in the UK at least, to copyright as a trade mark the name 'Diana', though 'Diana Queen of Hearts' should be acceptable as should 'Diana Princess of Wales'.

However, if, say, a geographical location is added then it may be that a business name can be registered as a trade mark, e.g. Mr Ahmed trading as 'Ahmed's Barbican Tandoori'. This is an important change and since such geographical marks are registrable under the 1994 Act registration, where possible, should give better protection to a business name than the tort of passing-off (see later in this chapter). All that needs to be established once the mark has been registered is whether the marks are confusingly similar and they are in respect of goods or services covered by the registration. The case for infringement is then established. Passing-off is a much more difficult matter to prove. Deception is the essence of an action for passing-off. In the absence of any patent or trade mark infringement it is only unlawful for a trader to copy and market a rival's product if the rival can show that purchasers are being or will be deceived into buying the copy instead of the real thing *(Hodgkinson & Corby* v *Wards Mobility Services* (1994)).

Since the shape of goods is now covered, the decision of the House of Lords in *Coca-Cola Trade Marks* (1986) in which their Lordships held that the shape of a Coca-Cola bottle could not be registered as a trade mark under previous legislation, is now reversed. The change has produced a major revival of interest in trade marks as a cheap and effective way of protecting brands. In fact, Coca-Cola became the first company to register a three-dimensional shape as a trade mark in 1995.

In this regard, the Trade Marks Registry has granted trade mark status to Heinz for the shade of turquoise used on its tins of baked beans.

Procedure for registration

Any person who claims to be the proprietor of a registrable trade mark and who wishes to register it must apply to the Registrar of Trade Marks giving a statement of the goods or services and a representation of the mark. The Registrar may accept the mark absolutely or approve registration subject to conditions or refuse to register the mark. The applicant is entitled to be heard before refusal. Where registration is acceptable, the Registrar must advertise the application in the *Trade Marks Journal*. Persons aggrieved by the application may then object to the Registrar giving grounds for their objection. The period for objection is three months from the advertisement with no provision for extension. If no application is made within that period or is made but fails, the mark will be registered and will be valid for ten years from the date of application renewable every ten years. Even after registration, application can be made to the Registrar or the court to rectify any error or omission in the Register, but not in respect of matters affecting the validity of the registration.

Collective and certification marks

The Act allows the registration of collective marks, e.g. the Wool Mark on clothing, and certification marks such as the mark of the British Standards Institute (the kitemark).

Enforcement

The effect of a registered trade mark is to give rights of exclusive use to the owner. The general remedy is an injunction to prevent wrongful use. In this connection, use of a mark in a different business is no defence. Thus, in *Discovery Communications Inc* v *Discovery FM Ltd* (2000) the court granted an injunction to prevent the use of the claimants' registered mark 'Discovery Channel' by the defendants who were trading under 'Discovery 102'. The fact that the claimants were engaged in cable and satellite television, whereas the defendants were in radio, was no defence.

Section 92 of the Trade Marks Act 1994 contains the criminal offence of unauthorised use of trade mark materials and goods. The maximum penalty is an unlimited fine and/or imprisonment for up to ten years. The section is used by trading standards in regard to the control of counterfeit goods. This produces the rather bizarre result of prosecutions being brought by trading standards to protect the consumer, but incidentally to protect the interests of enormously wealthy organisations, e.g. Microsoft, *at the UK taxpayers' expense*. The cost of these prosecutions awarded out of public funds may in some cases exceed £100,000!

The Community Trade Mark

The Community Trade Mark (CTM) is a single trade mark right which extends throughout the EU. The system is available to any country which is a member of the EU or person who is domiciled in a country in the EU or has a commercial establishment in the EU.

A CTM may consist of any distinctive sign capable of being represented graphically.

Applications are filed at any National Trade Marks Registry such as the UK Registry in London or directly at the CTM office in Alicante, Spain. The CTM office is known as the Office for Harmonisation in the Internal Market.

Enforcement

A CTM is enforced by what is called 'an infringement action' in a national court. It is possible to ask for a pan-European injunction covering the whole community and damages.

Advantages and disadvantages of the CTM system

A main advantage is that a single application allows a trade mark to be registered throughout the EU at less cost and administrative effort than individual applications to each country, making enforcement easier.

However, since CTM gives rights to so many countries it is likely that large numbers of conflicts will arise so that it will be difficult to select a CTM which will not be opposed at registration stage. The registry is required to publish applications and oppositions must be lodged with the Registrar within three months.

Trade marks and comparative advertising

The law on comparative advertising (which is advertising by reference to a competitor's name or product) has been relaxed by the provisions of the Trade Marks Act 1994. It appears from the following case that the court felt that in considering the new provisions for the first time the main object of those provisions was to allow comparative advertising and that they should not be read in such a way as to effectively prohibit it.

Barclays Bank plc v *RBS Advanta* (1996)
RBS wished to promote its new credit card. It published a leaflet listing 15 ways in which its card was superior to others and in a brochure it included a comparative table listing six other credit cards including Barclaycard and Standard Visa, setting out their annual fees, annualised rates of interest on purchases and on cash advances, and their monthly interest rates. Barclays Bank, the owner of Barclaycard, claimed that in setting down details RBS had not been comparing like with like and had implied that its own card was superior on all 15 points. The bank asked for an injunction to prevent RBS from referring to its mark (Barclaycard) in literature promoting the RBS card.

Section 10(6) of the 1994 Act was at the root of the case. It provides as follows: 'Nothing in the preceding provisions of this section shall be construed as preventing the use of a registered trade mark by any person for the purpose of identifying goods or services as those of the proprietor or a licensee. But any such use otherwise than in accordance with honest practices in industrial or commercial matters shall be treated as infringing the registered trade mark if the use without due cause takes unfair advantage of, or is detrimental to, the distinctive nature or repute of the trade mark.' The court decided that the literature conveyed the honest belief of RBS that its card, taken as a whole, offered customers a better deal, and refused the application by Barclays for an injunction.

Internet domain names

The Trade Mark Registry has issued guidelines on the treatment of Internet domain names. Signs including *http://, www., .co, .gov, .org* do not have any distinctive character as trade marks for goods and services sold via the Internet. Instead, trade mark examiners and hearing officers will look at the rest of the domain name. If it has a distinctive element, it will be considered for acceptance as a trade mark in the electronic information services class or in the software class.

Domain names containing the words 'web' and 'net' tacked on to descriptive or non-distinctive words will probably not be registrable as they are considered generic terms for discussing the Internet.

Injurious falsehood

In our present context a person is liable for injurious (or malicious) falsehood if he makes a statement about the goods of another which is malicious and is intended to cause and does cause damage to the business of the other person.

Injurious falsehood is an aspect of defamation and where the false statement is made about another's goods it is sometimes called 'slander of goods'.

De Beers Abrasive Products Ltd v *International General Electric Company of New York Ltd* (1975)
De Beers made a diamond abrasive known as and marketed under the trade mark 'Debdust'. It was used for cutting concrete. International made and marketed a competing product under the trade name 'MBS-70'.

International stated in a trade pamphlet that laboratory experiments had shown that MBS-70 was superior to Debdust. De Beers alleged that the contents of the pamphlet were false and misleading. The court said that the pamphlet would amount to an actionable slander of goods if De Beers could prove the allegations and show malice on the part of International.

Passing-off

Any person, company or other organisation which carries on or proposes to carry on business under a name calculated to deceive the public by confusion with the name of an existing concern, commits the civil wrong of passing-off and will be restrained by injunction from doing so. Other examples more important in our context of passing-off are the use of similar wrappings, identification marks, and descriptions. Thus, in *Bollinger* v *Costa Brava Wine Co Ltd* (1959) the champagne producers of France objected to the use of the name 'Spanish Champagne' to describe a sparkling wine which was made in Spain and they were granted an injunction to prevent the use of that term. The remedies other than an injunction are an action for damages or for an account of profits made from wrongful use of the wrapping, mark or description.

The use of the passing-off rules in the context of branded products is illustrated by the following case.

United Biscuits (UK) Ltd v Asda Stores Ltd (1997)

This case concerned two chocolate sandwich biscuits: Penguin, which is the brand leader owned by United Biscuits, and Puffin, a biscuit manufactured by Asda and retailed at a price 25 per cent lower than Penguin. The High Court ruled that Puffin's packaging and get-up was in a material sense deceptively similar to that of Penguin, so that Asda was guilty of passing-off its own cheaper brand as though it was connected with the Penguin brand. The court drew attention, in particular, to the names of the two products and to the seabird pictured on them both. The court granted United Biscuits an injunction preventing further sales of Puffin, but suspended the operation of the injunction for 35 days to allow Asda, among other things, to dispose of five weeks' stock of biscuits by selling them. However, the case failed on the use of the word 'Penguin'. Evidence showed that, as regards the two names, 'Penguin' and 'Puffin' taken alone did not cause significant confusion to consumers. Asda could therefore continue to use the 'Puffin' brand name.

The advantage of registration as a trade mark where possible has already been considered, as has the protection of Internet domain names (see *Pitman Training Ltd* v *Nominet UK* (1997)).

The High Court has also ruled that the fact that a company may find it harder to achieve brand recognition when another company is actively promoting a similar brand is not enough in itself to allow the aggrieved company to claim an injunction, particularly if there is no serious confusion. Thus, in *HFC Bank plc* v *Midland Bank plc* (2000) Midland Bank rebranded its business and associated businesses as HSBC. HFC Bank tried for an injunction to restrain the use of the HSBC brand name and failed. The High Court judge did not feel there was a serious likelihood of confusion and felt that the matter could in any case be solved by proper marketing. Interesting, therefore, the judge was putting forward a commercial rather than a legal solution.

However, the High Court held in *Pfizer Ltd* v *Eurofood Link (UK) Ltd* (1999) that giving the name 'Viagrene' to a beverage that was to be marketed as an aphrodisiac was a passing-off of the name 'Viagra', the anti-impotence drug, as well as an infringement of UK and Community trade marks.

Confidentiality

Certain activities by employees are regarded by the law as breaches of the duty of faithful service which an employee owes to his employer. Breaches of this duty of fidelity will sometimes be prevented by the court, so that a person who retains secret processes in his memory can be restrained from using them to his employer's disadvantage **without any contract in restraint of trade.**

An employer who copies names and addresses of his employer's customers for use after leaving his employment can be restrained from using the lists **without any express restrictions in his contract.**

Robb v Green (1895)

The claimant was a dealer in live game and eggs. The major part of his business consisted of procuring the eggs and the hatching, rearing and sale of gamebirds. His customers were numerous and for the most part were country gentlemen and their gamekeepers. The claimant kept a list of these customers in his order book. The defendant, who was for three years the claimant's manager, copied these names and addresses, and after leaving the claimant's employment set up in a similar business on his own and sent circulars, both to the claimant's customers and to their gamekeepers, inviting them to do business with him. The claimant asked for damages and an injunction and the Court of Appeal decided that although there was no express term in the defendant's contract to restrain him from such activities, it was an implied term of the contract of service that the defendant would observe good faith towards his employer during the existence of the confidential relationship between them. The defendant's conduct was a breach of that duty of good faith in respect of which his employer was entitled to damages and an injunction.

Comment. In connection with the duty of fidelity, it should be noted that it does not matter who initiates the infidelity; although in most cases the employee approaches the customer, the rule still applies even where the customers approach the employee.

Although cases such as *Robb* can still be relied upon on their own facts, where the employer relies on the implied term of good faith to protect trade secrets or business connections that have simply been learned as part of doing the job, the implied-term theory is much less secure, and today a commercial lawyer would recommend an express contractual term setting out clearly what it is intended to protect. The complexity of some modern products is such that the court needs guidelines through the contractual term as to what is to be protected. Thus, in *Pocton Industries Ltd* v *Michael Ikem Horton* (2000) the Court of Appeal ruled that although an electro-plating apparatus was a trade secret, it was not protectable under an implied duty of good faith and non-disclosure. There was no contractual provision regarding which part of the employee's knowledge was to be regarded as confidential and the plating process was only part of a number of pieces of information that the employee could not help but acquire from his duties. The implied term was too vague: more specific guidance was needed.

DATA PROTECTION

One of the most important resources a business makes use of is information. Increasingly the information collected is stored on computer and processed automatically. Some organisations, however, still keep a substantial amount of information in the form of paper records which are processed manually. The collection and processing of all forms of information about people is now subject to the provisions of the Data Protection Act 1998 (DPA). The DPA replaces the Data Protection Act 1984, which was limited in its scope to data processed automatically, i.e. by computer.

We will examine the main provisions of the DPA and consider its implications for business. But first, why has it been necessary to legislate on data protection?

Background to the 1984 Act

There are two main reasons why the government decided in 1984 to take action to regulate the use of computers to process personal information: first, concern had been growing since the 1960s that the widespread use of increasingly sophisticated computers posed a considerable threat to the right to privacy. Computers not only had the ability to process large quantities of information at high speed, but could also transfer data quickly from one system to another, and combine information from different systems in ways which had not been possible before. Existing laws were inadequate to deal with this new threat to our civil liberties.

The second and main reason why the government introduced legislation was to avoid commercial isolation. In 1981 the UK had become a signatory to the Council of Europe Convention on Data Protection. The Convention permits ratifying countries to prohibit the transfer of personal data to countries without comparable data protection legislation. Failure to introduce such legislation in this country would have led some British businesses with international interests to face a boycott.

The government's response to these developments was the enactment of the Data Protection Act 1984, which became fully operational from 11 November 1987.

The background to the 1998 Act

We have noted how the 1984 Act was enacted to implement the Council of Europe Convention 'for the protection of individuals with regard to automatic processing of personal data'. Both the Convention and the 1984 Act were limited in scope to data which is processed automatically, i.e. by computer. In October 1995, the EC adopted a Data Protection Directive, which had to be implemented by member states by October 1998. Although the 1984 Act met many of the requirements of the Directive, there were some important differences which necessitated changes in the UK legislation. The DPA 1998, which came into force on 1 March 2000, introduces a new framework for the protection of data.

The 1998 Act itself

The DPA establishes a legal framework to regulate the storage and processing of personal information. Most persons who process, or have processed for them, personal information are affected by the legislation. At the centre of the scheme of regulation is the Data Protection Commissioner (previously known as the Data Protection Registrar). The Commissioner is responsible for maintaining a public register of those involved in processing personal information, promoting good practice by data controllers and observance of the requirements of the DPA, and disseminating information about the DPA.

The DPA gives rights to individuals, including the right to obtain details of information held about them and a right to obtain compensation for damage suffered as the result of any contravention of the requirements of the DPA by a data controller. The DPA does not establish blanket regulation of all personal data: there are exemptions from some or all of its provisions.

Terminology

The terms used in the DPA are described below.

Data. This refers to:

(a) information which can be processed automatically, i.e. by computer; or
(b) information which is recorded as part of a 'relevant filing system', that is a set of information in which the records are structured either by reference to individuals or by criteria relating to individuals; or
(c) information which does not fall within (a) and (b) above but which forms part of an 'accessible record', e.g. school pupil, housing, social services and health records.

The definition of data in the 1998 Act broadens the scope of regulation and protection to include not only information held on computers but also some manual information, i.e. paper records. It is important to note that not all manual information is covered by the DPA; only manual information which falls within the definition of 'data' set out above is subject to regulation. It should also be noted that transitional arrangements will exempt manual information kept in a relevant filing system before 24 October 1998 from full compliance with the DPA until 2007. However, individuals will have the right to gain access to information held in paper records from 24 October 2001 irrespective of the date from which the information was held.

Personal data. These are items of information about a living individual who can be identified. 'Personal data' includes factual information about the person, expressions of opinion about him and any indications of the intentions of the data controller in respect of that individual.

Data controller. This is a person who (either alone or jointly or in common with other persons) determines the purposes for which and the manner in which any personal data are, or are to be, processed.

Data processor. This refers to a person (other than an employee of the data controller) who processes personal data on behalf of the data controller.

Data subject. A data subject is an individual who is the subject of personal data. Information about corporate bodies is not covered.

Processing. In relation to information or data, this means obtaining, recording or holding the information or data or carrying out any operation on the data including:

(a) organisation, adaptation or alteration of the data;
(b) retrieval, consultation or use of the data;
(c) disclosure of the data;
(d) alignment, combination, blocking, erasure or destruction of the data.

The data protection principles

As under the 1984 Act, the DPA sets out eight data protection principles, which must be complied with by data controllers, subject to any exemption. The principles are as follows:

1 Personal data shall be processed fairly and lawfully, and, in particular, shall not be processed unless –

(a) at least one of the conditions in Sch 2 is met, and

(b) in the case of sensitive personal data, at least one of the conditions in Sch 3 is also met.

At least one of the following Sch 2 conditions for processing must be met:

- the data subject has given his consent to processing;
- the processing is necessary in relation to a contract to which the data subject is party;
- the processing is necessary to comply with a legal obligation to which the data controller is subject;
- the processing is necessary to protect the vital interests of the data subject (i.e. matters of life or death);
- the processing is necessary for the administration of justice, for the exercise of any statutory functions, or any functions of the Crown, ministers or government departments or other public functions carried out in the public interest;
- the processing is necessary for the legitimate interests of the data controller, except where the processing is unwarranted because of the prejudice to the rights, freedoms and legitimate interests of the data subject.

The DPA introduces special rules prohibiting the processing of sensitive personal data revealing, for example, racial or ethnic origin, political opinions, religious or philosophical beliefs, trade union membership, criminal proceedings or convictions and data concerning health or sexual life.

At least one of the Sch 3 conditions relating to processing sensitive data must be satisfied, in addition to one of the conditions applying to all personal data. The conditions include:

- the data subject has given his explicit consent;
- the processing is necessary for the purposes of fulfilling legal obligations in relation to employment;
- the processing is necessary to protect the vital interests of the data subject or another person and the data subject cannot give consent or the data controller cannot reasonably be expected to gain consent, or the data subject has unreasonably withheld consent and the processing is necessary to protect the vital interests of another person;

- the processing is carried out by not for profit organisations which exist for political, philosophical, religious and trade union purposes, subject to certain requirements;
- the personal data has been deliberately made public by the data subject;
- the processing is necessary in connection with legal proceedings, obtaining legal advice, or establishing, exercising or defending legal rights;
- the processing is necessary for medical purposes;
- the processing relates to racial or ethnic origins and the processing is necessary for equal opportunities monitoring.

As well as fulfilling one of the conditions for processing personal data, data controllers must also ensure that the processing is carried out fairly in accordance with the fair processing code. The code requires that data is obtained fairly (i.e. the provider of data must not be misled or deceived) and that certain information is provided to the data subject.

2 Personal data shall be obtained only for one or more specified and lawful purposes, and shall not be further processed in any manner incompatible with that purpose or those purposes. There are two methods by which a data controller can specify the purposes for which the data is obtained. First, by giving notice to the data subject in accordance with the fair processing code, and secondly by notifying the Data Protection Commissioner under the notification procedures.

3 Personal data shall be adequate, relevant and not excessive in relation to the purpose or purposes for which they are processed. Data users must be selective about the data held; it must relate directly to the purposes for which it is obtained.

4 Personal data shall be accurate and, where necessary, kept up to date. Data controllers should take steps to check the accuracy of information. Data subjects have the right to compensation for damage caused by inaccurate data. Files should be reviewed from time to time to update the information.

5 Personal data processed for any purpose or purposes shall not be kept for longer than is necessary for that purpose or purposes. Once the specific purpose for which the data was collected has been achieved, the data should be destroyed.

6 Personal data shall be processed in accordance with the rights of data subjects under this Act. A data controller will contravene this principle if he fails to supply information following a subject access request or fails to comply with certain other notices under the DPA.

7 Appropriate technical and organisational measures shall be taken against unauthorised or unlawful processing of personal data and against accidental loss or destruction of, or damage to, personal data. Data controllers and data processors must take steps to secure the personal data they hold. The level of security will depend on the nature of the personal data and the damage likely to be caused by a breach of the principle and the measures necessary to ensure security.

8 Personal data shall not be transferred to a country or territory outside the European Economic Area, unless that country or territory ensures an adequate level of protection for the rights and freedoms of data subjects in relation to the processing of personal data. This principle will not apply in certain circumstances, for example where the data subject consents to the transfer or the transfer is necessary for reasons of public interest or in connection with legal proceedings.

Notification

The 1984 Act established a Data Protection Register, which was open to public inspection. The DPA introduces a new simpler notification system. A data controller will be required to provide the following information:

(a) the data controller's name and address;
(b) the name and address of any representative;
(c) a description of the personal data being processed and the category of data subject to which they relate;
(d) a description of the purpose(s) for which the data is being processed;
(e) a description of any recipients of the data;
(f) a name or description of countries outside the European Economic Area to which the data may be transferred;
(g) a statement that the personal data is exempt and notification does not extend to that data;

(h) a general description of security measures to protect the data (this information will not appear on the register).

The notification requirements do not apply to manual data contained within a relevant filing system or data within non-automated accessible records.

The period of notification lasts for one year and the fee (in 2001) is £35.

It is an offence to process personal data without notification, unless it can be shown that a person exercised all due diligence to comply with the requirements. Offences are triable either by magistrates or in the Crown Court. If convicted, the offender is liable to a fine of £5,000 in the magistrates' court or an unlimited fine in the Crown Court.

Business organisations should decide who will take responsibility for ensuring that the organisation complies with the requirements of the DPA. The duties of such a data protection officer must be defined and lines of responsibility established. The data protection officer should ensure that the notification requirements are complied with and the entry in the register kept up to date. This includes devising a system to monitor any changes taking place so that they can be recorded on the register.

Data Protection Commissioner

In addition to maintaining the Register, the Commissioner is charged with promoting good practice by data controllers and in particular promoting observance of the data protection principles. The Commissioner is under a duty to make an assessment of whether processing of personal data is being carried out in compliance with the DPA, if so requested.

The Commissioner has the power to issue the following notices:

1 *an enforcement notice* requires a data controller to observe the data protection principles;

2 *an information notice* requires a data controller to provide information relating to a request for assessment or to compliance with the data protection principles within a specified time;

3 *a special information notice* may be served to ascertain whether personal data are being processed only for special purposes or with a view

to the publication of any journalistic, literary or artistic material not previously published by the data controller.

There is a right of appeal against the issue of any notice to The Information Tribunal.

The Commissioner can apply to a circuit judge for a warrant to enter and search premises if there are reasonable grounds for suspecting that an offence has been committed or that the data protection principles are being contravened.

Rights of data subjects

The DPA gives a number of rights to data subjects in respect of the personal data held about them. The corresponding duties of data controllers may give rise to claims for compensation. Business organisations should consider the possibility of obtaining insurance cover against such risks. The rights are as follows:

1 Access to personal data. A data subject is entitled to be informed of whether a data controller holds any data about him and to be supplied with a copy of such data in an intelligible form. The data controller may insist on receiving a written request, checking the data subject's identity and the payment of a fee (subject to a maximum fee of £10 in 2001). The information must be available within 40 days. Obviously, business organisations must establish a clear procedure for dealing with requests for access to data.

2 Right to prevent processing likely to cause damage or distress. A data subject can ask a data controller to stop, or not to begin, processing personal data relating to him where it is causing or is likely to cause substantial unwarranted damage or substantial distress to him or to another person. There are situations where this right is not available (e.g. where the data subject has previously consented) and data controllers do not always have to comply with the request.

3 The right to prevent processing for direct marketing. A data subject can ask a data controller to stop, or not to begin, processing data relating to him for the purposes of direct marketing. If the data controller does not comply with such notice, the data subject can apply for a court order to that effect.

4 Rights in relation to automatic decision-taking. An individual can ask a data controller to ensure that no decision which significantly affects him is based solely on the processing of his personal data by automatic means. Examples of the purposes for which automatic decision-taking might be used include establishing creditworthiness or reliability. There are some exemptions to these rights.

5 Right to compensation. The data subject can claim compensation from a data controller for damage or damage **and** distress caused by a breach of the DPA, where the data controller is unable to show that he has taken such care as is reasonable to ensure compliance. Damages for distress alone can only be claimed where the breach of the DPA relates to processing personal data for special purposes.

6 The right of rectification, blocking, erasure and destruction. Individuals can apply to the court for an order requiring a data controller to rectify, block, erase or destroy personal data which are inaccurate or contain expressions of opinion based on inaccurate data.

7 The right to request an assessment. Any individual may ask the Commissioner to assess whether the processing of personal data is being carried out in compliance with the DPA. Depending on the outcome of the Commissioner's assessment, this may lead to enforcement action.

Exemptions

The nature and extent of each exemption is a complex matter and the guidance produced by the Data Protection Commissioner should be consulted.

Exemptions are referred to as either 'primary' exemptions, meaning that they are more likely to be claimed or more wide ranging in scope, or 'miscellaneous' exemptions. 'Primary' exemptions include personal data related to:

- safeguarding national security;
- prevention and detection of crime;
- assessment and collection of taxation;
- health, education and social work;
- regulatory activity of certain bodies;
- special purposes covering journalism, artistic and literary purposes;

- historical or statistical research;
- information made available to the public by statute;
- disclosures required by law or in connection with any legal proceedings;
- domestic purposes, i.e. household matters.

The 'miscellaneous' exemptions include:

- confidential references given in connection with, for example, employment;
- information which would prejudice the combat effectiveness of the armed forces;
- processing personal data in connection with judicial appointments and honours;
- processing personal data in connection with assessing suitability for crown employment and Crown or ministerial appointments;
- personal data used by businesses in connection with management forecasting and planning;
- personal data consisting of the intentions of the data controller in relation to any negotiations with the data subject;
- personal data processed in connection with a corporate finance service, where there may be concerns in relation to price sensitivity;
- personal data recorded by candidates in examinations;
- in the case of examination marks, a candidate's right of access can be delayed for up to five months or 40 days from the announcement of the results;
- personal data subject to professional legal privilege;
- self-incrimination by complying with a subject access request.

Offences under the DPA

The DPA creates a number of criminal offences. These include processing personal data without complying with the notification requirements, unlawfully obtaining or disclosing personal data without the consent of the data controller and unlawfully selling personal data.

COMPUTER MISUSE

The Computer Misuse Act 1990, which came into force on 29 August 1990, creates three criminal offences to deal with the misuse of computers. The offences are as follows:

1 **Unauthorised access to computer material.** It is an offence knowingly to cause a computer to perform any function with intent to secure unauthorised access to programs or data held in a computer. This basic offence is designed to criminalise the activities of both outside 'hackers' who obtain access to computers using the public telecommunications system and insiders who knowingly exceed the limits of their authority. The offence is triable summarily and is punishable by a maximum of six months' imprisonment or a fine of £5,000.

2 **Unauthorised access with intent to commit or facilitate commission of further offences.** It is an offence triable either by magistrates or in the Crown Court to commit the basic unauthorised access offence with intent to commit or facilitate the commission of any serious offence for which the sentence is fixed by law or where the maximum sentence could be five years or more. These serious crimes would include theft and blackmail. This offence would cover a 'hacker' who obtains unauthorised access to a computer in order to hijack funds in the course of an electronic funds transfer. The maximum penalty for this offence if convicted on indictment is five years' imprisonment or an unlimited fine.

3 **Unauthorised modification of computer material.** It is an offence intentionally to cause the unauthorised modification of the contents of any computer with intent to impair a computer's operation, or to prevent or hinder access to any program or data held in any computer, or impair the operation of any such program or the reliability of any such data. This offence is designed to cover interference with computer programs and data such as the deletion or alteration of material or the introduction of computer viruses. The offence is triable either by magistrates or in the Crown Court where the maximum penalty is five years' imprisonment or an unlimited fine.

The Act also takes into account the international dimension of computer crime by giving UK courts wide jurisdiction to hear cases, provided that there is some connection between the offender's activities and the UK, and by making provision for extradition for these offences.

QUESTIONS/ACTIVITIES

1 Explain the difference between real property and personal property. What kinds of personal property are there?

2 John wants to buy a house. He tells you that he has seen some advertised as 'freehold' and some as 'leasehold'.

    Write a note explaining these terms stating how he would be affected as a buyer in each case.

3 Explain what is meant by an easement. How does an easement differ from a profit? Give two examples of each.

4 Anton is the owner of the Napoli restaurant. He engaged Edgar, a builder who was made redundant by Bodge Builders Ltd but has recently started up his own business, to renovate the restaurant.

    On Monday, the day before Anton re-opened the restaurant to the public, he invited the mayor and his wife, Mr and Mrs Snooks, to take a meal at the restaurant.

    During the meal a large piece of plaster fell from the false ceiling which Edgar had installed. It fell on the mayor's table, injuring both him and Mrs Snooks.

    Several pieces of plaster hit and injured a local press photographer, Archie, who had got into the restaurant uninvited through a side door. Archie was hiding behind a rubber plant in the hope of getting some exclusive pictures of the new restaurant.

    Advise Mr and Mrs Snooks and Archie.

5 If you had registered a patent and a design, for how long would registration protect you, and what remedies would you have if someone infringed your rights?

6 Jane's father has died. He left her by his will the copyright in a very successful novel which he wrote five years before his death. For how long will the publishers pay royalties to Jane?

7 Distinguish a trade mark from a service mark. How are trade and service marks protected?

8 Bob and Jane run a newsagents' shop. They have just acquired a computer to help them run the business more efficiently. They anticipate that they will use the computer for the following purposes: stock control, calculating the wages of their paper-boys and girls and customer records. Will Bob and Jane need to register under the DPA? If they are required to register, what will their obligations be under the DPA?

Chapter 16

EMPLOYING LABOUR

In this chapter we are concerned with employment law. This is based upon and deals with the relationship of employer and employee. Employment law is made up of common law and, more and more these days, of statute law passed by Parliament.

EMPLOYER AND EMPLOYEE

Generally

It is important to know how this relationship comes into being and to distinguish it from the relationship between a person who buys the services of someone who is self-employed (often called an independent contractor).

Usually it is not difficult to decide whether A is employed by B so that the relationship of employee and employer exists between them. If A is an employee, he or she will have been **selected** by B; A will usually work **full-time** for B under a degree of **supervision** for a **wage or salary**. Of course, A may still be an employee though working **part time**.

Also, if A is an employee, B will deduct **income tax** from A's pay (if it exceeds A's allowances) under PAYE (pay as you earn) arrangements. B will also make **social security contributions** for A and will often provide a **pension scheme** which A can join. In addition, although a contract of employment (or service) need not be in writing, if A is an employee, then B must, under the Employment Rights Act 1996, give A within two months after the beginning of the employment **written particulars** of the major terms of the contract.

The control test

In earlier times the above tests would not all have been available, particularly the deduction of income tax which, after some earlier experiments beginning in 1799, was finally brought in for good in 1842. Social security legislation and the modern deductions from pay, together with contributions from the employer, have only come in on the present scale since the Second World War.

In times past, therefore, a person, whether employed or self-employed, would simply receive money from the employer and it was less easy to distinguish one from the other.

There was, even so, a need to do so, because an employer was liable to pay damages to those injured by his employee if those injuries took place during the course of the employee's work. This is called an employer's vicarious liability and it is dealt with in greater detail later in this chapter.

A person was not vicariously liable for injury caused to others by a self-employed (or independent) contractor who was doing work for him. Obviously, then it was necessary to find a test to decide whether A was, or was not, an employee of B.

The earliest test was called 'the control test'. Since it is not normally necessary to use this test today in order to decide whether A is the employee of B because we have much more evidence of the relationship now, why should we bother with it?

The answer is that it is sometimes necessary to decide whether B, who is truly employed by A, has been temporarily transferred to another person, C, so that C (the temporary employer) and not A (the general employer) is liable vicariously for the injuries caused to a person or persons by B.

Mersey Docks and Harbour Board v Coggins & Griffiths (Liverpool) Ltd (1946)
The Board owned and hired out mobile cranes driven by skilled operators who were employees of the Board. Coggins & Griffiths, who were stevedores, hired one of the Board's cranes and an operator, Mr Newell, to unload a ship.

In the course of unloading the ship, a person was injured because of Mr Newell's negligence and the court had to decide whether the Board or Coggins & Griffiths were vicariously liable along with Mr Newell for the latter's negligence. The matter was one of control because the Board was quite clearly the general employer. Actually, the answers given by Mr Newell to questions put to him by counsel in court were highly important. At one point he said: 'I take no orders from anybody.' Since he was not truly employed by Coggins & Griffiths **and** since he did not, so he said, take orders from them, there was no way in which he could be regarded as under their control. Therefore, his true employer, the Board, was vicariously liable for Mr Newell's negligence.

Comment. It is **presumed** in these cases that the general employer continues to be liable and it is up to him to satisfy the court that control has passed to a temporary employer. This is a very difficult thing to do and the temporary employer will not be liable very often, though it is a possibility.

In spite of the fact that a majority shareholder and/or a director of a company are not, strictly speaking, under the control of the company which, of course, they in large measure control, it seems from the decision of the Court of Appeal in *Secretary of State for Trade and Industry* v *Bottrill* (1999) and of the Employment Appeal Tribunal in *Connolly* v *Sellers Arenascene Ltd* (2000) that majority shareholders and directors will be regarded as employees of the company where there is a written contract of employment and all the usual hallmarks of employment are present. Certainly, the almost blanket ban introduced by earlier cases such as *Buchan* v *Secretary of State for Employment* (1997) has been considerably eroded. The cases have generally arisen where the company has gone into an insolvency procedure and cannot pay wages and salaries. In such an event **employees** may make a claim for outstanding remuneration on the state through what is now the Department of Trade and Industry. Recent case law gives employed controlling shareholders and directors a better chance of doing that. Fee-paid directors could not claim.

In any case, controlling shareholders and directors would seem to satisfy the organisation test set out below and come in as employees under that.

The organisation test

Later on a test called the 'organisation or integration' test was brought in because the control test was not really suitable for employees who were highly skilled.

There was a possibility that even though there was a lot of general evidence of employment, such as PAYE deductions from pay, an employer would not be vicariously liable for the acts of a highly skilled employee, such as a doctor, or, really, anyone qualified and experienced and acting in a professional field, if that employer could convince the court in his defence that he did not have the necessary control of the skilled person.

This has not been possible because of the organisation test put forward by Lord Denning in *Stevenson, Jordan & Harrison Ltd* v *Macdonald & Evans Ltd* (1952). He decided in that case, in effect, that an employee is a person who is integrated with others in the workplace or business, even though the employer does not have a detailed control of what he does.

INDEPENDENT CONTRACTORS – SELF-EMPLOYMENT

The main feature here is the absence of control or meaningful supervision which can be exercised by those who buy the services of an independent contractor by means of what is called a **contract for services**.

Particular cases examined

In the majority of cases there is no difficulty in deciding whether a person is employed or self-employed. For example, factory employees, office clerical staff and agricultural workers are clearly employees. Garage proprietors, house-builders and dry cleaners are contractors independent of the members of the public who use them.

As we have seen, a particularly compelling example comes from a comparison between a chauffeur and a person who owns and drives his own taxi. The chauffeur is an employee; the taxi-driver is an independent contractor. Suppose, then, that Fred is employed as my chauffeur: I would have enough control over him to ask him to drive more slowly in a built-up area. In the case of the taxi-driver, I would not have (or even feel I had) the necessary control to insist on a change of speed.

Contract of service or for services – why distinguish?

First of all, because of the existence of **vicarious liability**, an employer is liable, for example, for damage caused to another by his employee's negligent acts while that employee is acting in the course of his employment, that is, doing his job, but not otherwise.

Second, the **rights and remedies provided by employment legislation**, such as the Employment Rights Act 1996, are available to an employee, but not all of them are available (but see below) to the self-employed. We shall be looking at these rights and remedies more closely later in this chapter.

Rights of non-employees

Certain statutory rights are given to persons who are not employees in any sense of the word. Rights in respect of racial and sex discrimination are enjoyed by job applicants, contract workers and partners. Job applicants also have the right not to be refused a job on the grounds of trade union membership or because they do not belong to a union.

An employer may also be liable for sex discrimination **after** employment has ceased. The Employment Appeals Tribunal (EAT) has ruled that the Sex Discrimination Act 1975 covers acts of discrimination, e.g. by failure to give a reference, even though the relevant acts took place after the claimant ceased to be employed (see *Coote* v *Granada Hospitality Ltd* (1999).

A contract worker is one who is employed by a third party, such as an agency, and whose services are supplied under a contract with that third party. A claim against an employer could be made, for example, by a temporary secretary who is turned away or treated in a hostile manner on grounds of colour or who is subjected to sexual harassment.

The same would be true of a salesman without a contract of service who was paid by commission only, who was not given work because of his race (see *Hill Samuel Services Group Ltd* v *Nwauzu* (1994).

As regards disability discrimination, the right not to be discriminated against covers employees and applicants for employment including contract workers, apprentices and self-employed people who contract personally to do any work (Disability Discrimination Act 1995, s 68(1)). However, while the Act covers partnerships in their capacity as employers, it does not prohibit, for reasons of disability, discrimination against the partners or prospective partners themselves. This contrasts with sex and race discrimination which covers discrimination against partners or prospective partners, albeit only for firms consisting of six or more partners in the case of discrimination on racial grounds.

In this connection, it is worth noting s 23 of the Employment Relations Act 1999, which gives the government power to extend employee status and rights to all workers other than the genuinely self-employed and so ensure that none are excluded merely because of technicalities relating to their working arrangements, which are often designed by less scrupulous employers to produce a virtually rightless and bogus self-employment.

THE CONTRACT OF EMPLOYMENT

Generally

The ordinary principles of the law of contract apply. So, in a contract of employment there must be an offer and an acceptance, which is in effect the agreement. There must also be an intention to create legal relations, consideration, and capacity, together with proper consent by the parties, that is, no mistake, misrepresentation, duress or un-due influence. In addition, the contract must not be illegal.

However, since we have already looked at these general principles of the law of contract, it is only necessary to highlight certain matters which are of importance in the context of employment law.

Fraud and illegality

The general rule is that the courts and employment tribunals will not do anything to enforce either party's rights under a contract which is illegal. The general rule does not apply, however, if the party seeking to enforce the contract was not aware of the illegality or, possibly, if his or her involvement is minimal compared to that of the other party.

If any employer and employee agree that the latter be treated as non-existent for tax and national insurance purposes, with all payments being unrecorded cash payments, neither party will be able to enforce the contract. The employee would have rights, however, if the employer deducted tax and national insurance contributions (NICs) and, without the employee's knowledge, failed to account for the payments or submit any records.

Legitimate tax avoidance schemes do not render a contract of employment illegal. Thus, in *Lightfoot* v *D & J Sporting Ltd* (1996), L was employed as a head gamekeeper and was assisted by his wife who initially received no remuneration from his employer. Later the employer entered into an agreement to pay one-third of L's income to his wife to save some liability on L's tax and NICs. This did not make the arrangement illegal and the husband and wife could claim unfair dismissal when they were later dismissed.

A party to a contract may also be unable to enforce the contract if it has been entered into as a result of that party's fraud. Suppose, therefore, that an accountancy firm employs a person purporting to be a qualified accountant. In fact, he has failed his examinations. Even if he carries out his work in an exemplary fashion, the employer will be entitled to terminate his employment forthwith when his fraud is discovered.

Written particulars

A contract of employment does not require any written formalities and can be made orally. However, certain written particulars of it are required to be given to the employee by the Employment Rights Act 1996. These particulars must be given to all employees within two months of starting work but not if the job is to last for less than one month. In addition, the statement of particulars need not be given if the employee has entered into a written contract with the employer containing all the relevant terms.

Furthermore, it was held in *Carmichael* v *National Power plc* (2000) that casual workers operating under 'zero hours' contracts are not entitled to written particulars. In these contracts there are no fixed requirements to attend for work. Those involved may attend if called upon to do so. In this case the claimants were, when at work, engaged in showing visitors round a nuclear power station.

Contents – generally

The statement must contain the following information:

1 **The names of the employer and the employee.** A letter of engagement will usually be sent to the employee at his address. This will identify him and the letter-heading will identify the employer.

2 **The date when the employment began.** This is important if it becomes necessary to decide what period of notice is to be given. The 1996 Act provides for certain minimum periods of notice to be given by employers. For example, they must give one week's notice after one month's continuous service, two weeks' after two years' service, and so on up to 12 weeks' after 12 years' service. The date when the job began obviously settles this point.

In addition, the length of the employment affects the period necessary to make certain claims. For example, redundancy claims require two years' continuous service **since the age of 18**. Unfair dismissal requires two years of continuous service with some exceptions which will be noted, e.g. maternity dismissals, usually with a particular employer (but see below), regardless of the age at which the service began, unless the dismissal is automatically unfair, as where it was because the employee was (or proposed to become) a member of a trade union.

3 **Whether the employment counts as a period of continuous employment with a previous employment, and the date of commencement of the previous employment where this is so.** This is important because the rights of an employee to complain of unfair dismissal or to claim a redundancy payment, depend upon whether that employee has served the necessary period of continuous employment. This may be with one

employer, but if it is with more than one employer, it must be possible to regard the employments with the various employers as continuous. Situations of continuous employment, despite a change of employer, taken from the Employment Rights Act 1996, are:

(a) *A transfer between associated employers.* For example, if A is employed by B Ltd and is transferred to work for C Ltd, and B Ltd and C Ltd are subsidiaries of X plc, then A's employment with B Ltd and C Ltd is regarded as continuous;

(b) *A sale of the business in which the employee was employed to another person.* (See also below.)

There are provisions which relate to the situation in (b) above and protect employees from a break in continuous employment on a change of employer. The Transfer of Undertakings (Protection of Employment) Regulations 1981 (TUPE) apply. The main provisions of the regulations in regard to business transfers are that employees who are employed by the old employer before the transfer automatically become the employees of the new employer. The new employer takes over the employment protection liabilities of the old employer, including, according to the decision of the EAT in *Kerry Foods* v *Creber* (2000), liability to pay a protective award. The earlier decision of *Angus Jowett & Co Ltd* v *National Union of Tailors and Garment Workers* (1985) should no longer apply, said the EAT. The *Jowett* case decided that the duty to pay a protective award remained with the transferor. A protective award is payable when an employer fails to consult with a recognised trade union or elected representatives of the workforce, as the case may be, when he is intending to make the workforce or some part of it redundant. So, if A gives notice of future redundancy to his employees without proper consultation with their union or elected representatives of the workforce, as the case may be, and they are still working for him when he sells the business to B, then B and not A is liable to pay the protective award.

The 1981 regulations provide that an employee has to be employed by the company being transferred 'immediately before' the transfer if the purchaser of the company is to take over employment protection duties in respect of the employee.

Administrative receivers (see Chapter 6) who took over insolvent companies on behalf of secured creditors such as banks, used this when selling off the company. Purchasers would commonly insist, as a condition of buying the company, that all employees be dismissed before the transfer. The administrative receiver concerned would therefore see that the employees were dismissed, sometimes only one hour before the contract of purchase was signed. In cases brought by employees for unfair dismissal or a redundancy payment the courts had ruled that they were not transferred and must pursue their claims against the insolvent transferor company with little prospect of success since the purchase money would normally be taken by secured creditors to pay off debts owed to them.

However, in *Litster* v *Forth Dry Dock and Engineering Co Ltd* (1989) the House of Lords held that an employee dismissed shortly before the transfer of the business for a reason connected with the transfer, e.g. purchaser insistence, was to be regarded as being employed 'immediately before' the transfer so that employment protection liabilities were transferred to the purchaser. This is a fairer interpretation of the regulations but it will make it more difficult to sell off insolvent companies. It appears also to have encouraged sackings at the beginning of an insolvency; in other words, an earlier loss of a job than might previously have been the case.

The 1981 regulations excluded transfers of undertakings not in the nature of a 'commercial venture'. This seemed to exclude the contracting out of services by government, local authorities and the NHS so that employees' contracts were not transferred to the new provider of the service. This greatly assisted the privatisation of public services since the attraction and profitability of these privatisation schemes often depends as much on the private contractor being able to change the terms of employment – sometimes for the worse – as it does on the alleged efficiency of the new private sector management. Under the ERA 1996 the 'commercial venture' requirement is abolished and will assist in terms that the regulations as amended will now cover public sector outsourcing of services.

However, another problem continues to raise its head. The regulations apply only if there is the transfer of an 'economic entity' which initially was felt to exclude the transfer of employees such as cleaners without any business assets. Much public sector outsourcing is like this. However, two recent cases have made it clear that a business which consists only of the provision of labour without a transfer of other assets is capable of being a transfer of an 'economic entity' within the meaning of the 1981 regulations and the European 'Business Transfers' Directive. The cases are *Rask v IISS Kantineservice* (1993) (European Court) and *Dines v Initial Health Care Services and Pall Mall Services Group* (1993) (Court of Appeal).

However, the European Commission proposals for a revised version of the transfer rules puts greater emphasis on the need for the transfer of a 'business' as distinct from an 'activity' of any business, so the above rulings of the ECJ and the Court of Appeal may not survive the revised rules (which are not yet in force). Under the Commission's proposals there will also be a more flexible approach in insolvency situations possibly enabling the transfer provisions to be modified where the transfer of the undertaking is part of a rescue package which is being inhibited because the terms and conditions of contracts of employment cannot be changed by the buyer of the business from the insolvency practitioner.

The materials set out above apply only to first-generation contractors, i.e. an outsourcing of services to the first private contractor. If the first-generation contractor is replaced by another (or second-generation) contractor, the position may be different. In the *Süzen* case (1997) the ECJ stated that there will not be a transfer of economic activity merely because the incoming contractor is carrying out a similar economic activity as the outgoing contractor. There must be a transfer of significant tangible and intangible assets *or* the new employer must take over a major part of the workforce. The decision had impact in the UK in *Betts v Brintel Helicopters* (1997) where the Court of Appeal adopted the reasoning in *Süzen* and held that there was no transfer when Shell changed the supplier of its helicopter transport contract from Brintel to KLM. The results of this case are that

first-generation contractors may find themselves faced with redundancy costs which they would previously have expected to pass on to the new and second-generation contractor, although he might have taken an indemnity against them from the outgoing contractor as part of the deal.

The insistence on the requirement in *Süzen* that employees be transferred or a significant number of tangible and intangible assets was downplayed in *ECM (Delivery Services) Ltd v Cox* (1998) where the EAT (affirmed by the Court of Appeal) held that an incoming contractor taking over from the original contractor could not avoid the application of TUPE merely by refusing to take on *any* of the outgoing contractor's employees. By so refusing, the incoming contractor was held to have unfairly dismissed them.

The decisions of the Court of Appeal in *Betts* and *ECM* were reviewed by the EAT in *UNISON v RCO Support Services Ltd* (2000). The case involved the transfer of cleaning services from one contractor to another. Some staff were transferred but no assets were taken over. Those who were not offered work claimed unfair dismissal against the transferee company. This involved a consideration of the application of TUPE. The EAT decided to follow *ECM* giving little by way of reasons other than the fact that *ECM* was the more recent case.

The EAT's approach to TUPE is a matter of some concern in that it is causing confusion for those organisations involved in the outsourcing of services. The ruling of the ECJ in *Süzen*, where it was decided that the transfer of an 'entity', as TUPE requires, cannot be reduced to a mere transfer of an 'activity', e.g. office cleaning, binds UK courts and tribunals, and the decision of the Court of Appeal to get round it in the *ECM* case does not, in the view of some lawyers, stand up to legal analysis. Contractors are, therefore, uncertain as to the applicability of TUPE. In particular, the incoming contractor cannot properly evaluate the potential risks of the venture for which he will normally take indemnities from the outgoing contractor.

The ERA 1996 provides that an employee who does not wish to transfer may tell the old or new employer this and his contract terminates. He is not to be regarded as unfairly dismissed or redundant. If he wants notice, he should transfer and give notice to the new employer who may make a payment in lieu.

(c) It was held in *Allen* v *Amalgamated Construction Co Ltd* (2000) that rights of transfer of employees can apply between companies in the same group that have the same ownership, management and premises and that are engaged on the same work. The ruling follows the well-established concept of the separate legal personality of companies. The business application of the above case is that the provisions of TUPE should always be taken into account when considering group reconstructions.

(d) *A change in the partners where a person is employed by a partnership.* A general partnership is not a separate person at law as a company is. Employees of a general partnership are employed by the partners as people. So, if A works for a partnership of C and D, and D retires and is replaced by E, then A's employers have changed but his employment with C and D and C and E is regarded as continuous. Therefore, if C and E unfairly dismiss A, he can make up his two years' continuous service to be able to claim by adding together his service with C and D and C and E in order to make a claim against C and E.

The legal context shown above would not apply to a limited liability partnership, which is a legal person, so that change of partners would not operate to change the employer.

(e) *A succession of contracts between the same parties is regarded as continuous.* So, if A works for B as a clerk and is then promoted to a manager under a new contract, the two contract periods can be added together to make a period of continuous employment.

Contents – terms of the employment

The written particulars then go on to set out the terms of the employment. The terms which must be given are:

1 the scale or rate of pay and the method of calculating pay where the employee is paid by commission or bonus (the employer must here have regard to the national minimum wage – see later in this chapter);

2 when the payment is made – that is weekly or monthly, and the day or date of payment;

3 hours to be worked, e.g. 'The normal working hours are . . .' Compulsory overtime, if any, should be recorded to avoid disputes with employees who may sometimes not want to work it;

4 holiday entitlement and provisions relating to holiday pay if the employee leaves in a particular year without taking holiday (if holiday entitlement is set out clearly, it can help to avoid disputes regarding a requirement to work in what is a normal holiday period in the area or during the school holidays);

The terms and conditions to be specified at 3 and 4 above must, of course, be considered in the light of the Working Time Regulations 1998 (see later in this chapter).

5 sick pay and injury arrangements;

6 whether or not there is a pension scheme;

7 the length of notice which the employee must give and the length of notice the employee is entitled to receive (we have already said that there are minimum periods of notice required to end contracts of employment and full details of these appear later in this chapter; the contract can, of course, provide for a longer period of notice but not a shorter one);

8 the job title, which is important in dealing with redundancy cases where to justify that a dismissal is because of redundancy and is not an unfair dismissal, the employer may show that there has been a reduction in 'work of a particular type' (the job title indicates what type of work the employee does; in equal pay claims also, it may show that a man or woman is employed on 'like work').

Under changes made by the ERA, the employer can give a brief job description instead of a job title.

9 The ERA also adds the following items to the required particulars:

- the duration of temporary contracts;
- work location or locations;
- collective agreements affecting the job;
- where the job requires work outside the UK for

more than one month the period of such work, the currency in which the employee will be paid and any other pay or benefits provided by reason of working outside the UK. Employees who begin work outside the UK within two months of starting must have the statement before leaving the UK.

Particulars can be given in instalments, provided all are given within two months, but there must be a 'principal statement' in one document giving the following information:
- the identities of the parties;
- the date when the employment began;
- where the employment counts as a period of continuous employment with a previous one, a statement that this is so and the date when it began;
- the amount and frequency of pay, e.g. weekly or monthly;
- the hours of work;
- holiday entitlement;
- job title (or description);
- work location.

Certain particulars can be given by reference to a document, e.g. a collective agreement with a trade union or a staff handbook, but any such document must be readily accessible to the employee. These particulars are pension arrangements, sickness provisions, notice entitlement and details of disciplinary matters and grievance procedures.

Contents – disciplinary rules and grievances

Disciplinary procedures deal, for example, with the number of warnings, oral or written, which will be given before suspension or dismissal. **Grievance procedures** relate to complaints in regard to any aspect of the employment with which the employee is not satisfied. The employee should be told who to complain to and any right of appeal, as it were, beyond that to, say, a more senior manager. This procedure is to be available if the employee is not satisfied with the **disciplinary decision** or for some **other grievance**.

Employers who along with associated employers (as in a group of companies where there are subsidiaries) have fewer than 20 employees are exempt from the need to provide disciplinary procedures but must give the name of a person to

whom a grievance complaint can be made. Presumably if the number of employees grows to 20 or more the employer must set up disciplinary procedures and notify employees of them but there is nothing *specific* about this in the Act, though it is clearly *implied*.

The Employment Relations Act 1999 now gives employees the right to be accompanied by a trade union representative or fellow employee at disciplinary hearings. Details are given later in this chapter.

Changes in the particulars

Changes must be given to the employee in writing as soon as possible and in any case not later than one month after the change. They may be given by reference to a document which is readily accessible provided a similar document was used to give the original information.

Terms of employment – collective agreements

If the terms of the employment can be changed by a collective agreement with a trade union, the particulars should say so because if this is the case, the terms of the job can be changed **without** the employees' consent. The results of the employer's negotiations with the unions are incorporated into the contracts of the employees and become binding as between employer and employee even though the agreement between the employer and the trade union is, as is usual, binding in honour only (*Marley* v *Forward Trust Group Ltd* (1986)). In other cases, the terms of the employment cannot be changed unless the employee has agreed and if the employer introduces a variation in the contract as by, say, lowering pay, then the employer is in breach of the contract.

It was held in *Rigby* v *Ferodo Ltd* (1986) that an employer cannot impose a pay cut on employees without breaking their contracts of employment.

Employees who have had a pay cut imposed on them may take proceedings in the ordinary courts for breach of contract or make an application to an industrial tribunal under the ERA 1996 for money wrongfully deducted from pay (see further later in this chapter).

Alternatively, they can regard themselves as constructively dismissed and make a claim to an employment tribunal on that basis.

A valid reduction in pay can be achieved by negotiating a new contract with employees and under the original contract if this allows the employer to vary its terms without the employees' consent.

Failure to comply with the obligation to give written particulars

The 1996 Act provides that if an employer fails to give written particulars at the start of the employment, or fails to notify changes in the terms of the contract, the employee can go to an employment tribunal. If a statement is given but the employee thinks it is not complete, either the employee or the employer can go to an employment tribunal to see which of them is right. No period of service is required by the employee. Reference to a tribunal can be made while in employment or at any time up to three months after the employment ends.

The tribunal may make a declaration that the employee has a right to a statement and also say what should be in it. However, following the decision in *Eagland* v *British Telecommunications plc* (1992) this must be done on the basis of evidence as to what the parties have agreed, either expressly or impliedly by conduct, as where the employer has referred in conversation to the fact that the job has a certain title. The tribunal cannot invent terms and, in the absence of any evidence as to what was agreed expressly or impliedly, no term on the subject can be inserted. The statement as approved by the tribunal is then assumed in law to have been given by the employer to the employee and forms the basis of the contract of employment. Failure to give written particulars does not make the contract of employment unenforceable by the parties. However, written particulars are a right of the employee, not a mere entitlement. Therefore, they must be given whether the employee asks for them or not (*Coales* v *John Wood (Solicitors)* (1986)).

Even so, an employee has a right to request a statement if he has never had one or it is out of date. Dismissal for asserting this right is unfair regardless of service and hours worked, under s 104 of the ERA.

Health and safety

The Health and Safety at Work Act 1974 states that an employer must prepare, and revise when necessary, a statement of his policy in regard to the health and safety at work of his employees and arrangements for carrying out the policy. This must be contained in a separate document but it is often given out with the written particulars which we are now looking at. Employers with fewer than five employees are not required to give this statement.

Exemptions from the written particulars requirements

There are some situations under the 1996 Act where an employer does not have to give the written particulars. Those which may be found in the average business are:

1 Employees with fully written contracts containing all the necessary terms need not be given also the written particulars.

2 It is not necessary to give an employee written particulars if he is employed for a specific job, e.g. to clear a backlog of office work, which is not expected to last more than one month. If it does last for more than one month, the worker is entitled to written particulars.

A sample statement in terms of an actual employment appears in Fig 16.1.

Legal status of the statutory particulars

In this connection the decision of the EAT in *Lovett* v *Wigan Metropolitan Borough Council* (2000) is worth noting. The claimant in this case was told at his interview and in a subsequent letter of appointment that his promotion would depend on his 'gaining the appropriate qualifications and experience'. When he received his written particulars there was a document attached that added another requirement, i.e. 'the needs of the department'. The EAT held that the terms of the document also applied since they amplified and explained the letter of appointment. The EAT was applying *Robertson and Jackson* v *British Gas Corporation* (1983), where the Court of Appeal ruled that the statutory statement of particulars is neither the contract itself nor conclusive evidence of it.

To   *Ms Jane Doe,*
     350, Elton Road,
     Manchester M62 10AS

The following particulars are given to you pursuant to the Employment Rights Act 1996

1.   The parties are as follows:

Name and address of Employer: *Michael Snooks Ltd.*
                                      520 London Square
                                      Manchester M42 145A

Name and address of employee: *Jane Doe*
                                        350, Elton Road
                                      Manchester M62 10AS

2.   The date when your employment began was: *5 February 2001*

Your employment with John Bloggs Ltd from whom Michael Snooks Ltd purchased the business and which began on 7 February 2000 counts as part of your period of continuous employment with Michael Snooks Ltd. No employment with a previous employer counts as part of your period of continuous employment.

3.   The following are the particulars of the terms of your employment

    as at   *9 March 2001*

    (a) You are employed at   *520 London Square, Manchester M62 145A*

         as   *a Secretary in the Educational Department*

    (b) The rate of your remuneration is *£400* per *week*

    (c) Your remuneration is paid at weekly intervals

    (d) Your normal working hours are from *9.30 am* to *5.00 pm*   Mondays to Fridays inclusive

    (e) (i)   You are entitled to *four weeks* holiday with pay after *one* completed year of service and to *five weeks* holiday with pay every year after *two* completed years of service.

         These holidays are to be taken at a time convenient to the employer between *1 May* and *30 October* in each year. If an employee's employment terminates before all holiday accrued due has been taken, the employee is entitled to payment in lieu thereof on leaving the said employment. You are also entitled to the customary holidays with pay, i.e. New Year's Day, Good Friday, Easter Monday, May Day, Spring Bank Holiday, Late Summer Bank Holiday, Christmas Day and Boxing Day.

         (ii) Regulations as to payment while absent during sickness or injury are available for inspection during normal working hours *in the office of the Secretary/PA to the Personnel Manager*

         (iii) There is no pension scheme applicable to you.

                                                             (cont.)

Fig 16.1 Contract of employment

(f) The length of notice which you are obliged to give to end your contract of employment is _one week_ and the length of notice you are entitled to receive unless your conduct is such that you may be summarily dismissed is as follows:

  (i) One week if your period of continuous employment is less than two years.

  (ii) One week's notice for each year of continuous employment if your period of continuous employment is two years or more but less than twelve years: and

  (iii) Twelve weeks if your period of continuous employment is twelve years or more.

(g) There are no collective agreements which affect the terms and conditions of the employment

(h) There is no requirement for work outside the United Kingdom

(i) NOTE

  If you are not satisfied with any disciplinary decision relating to you or seek redress of any grievance relating to your employment you can apply in the first place to _the publisher, Educational Department_

  Details of the procedure available and to be followed in connection with your employment are _posted in the staff room_

  Dated _ninth_ day of _March 2001_

  Signed

  Sarah Snooks

  Company Secretary

Comment
The employee should be required to sign the employer's copy in the following way:

'I have received and read a copy of the above particulars which are correct in all respects.'

Signed _____

Date _____

Note: The employer is required to offer a stakeholder pension from 1 October 2001 if there are more than four employees.

Fig 16.1 Contract of employment

RIGHTS AND DUTIES OF THE PARTIES TO THE CONTRACT

The duties of an employer and an employee come from common law and Acts of Parliament. They will be dealt with under the headings which follow.

Duties of an employer

To provide remuneration

In business organisations the duty of the employer to pay his employees and the rate or amount of pay are decided as follows:

1 by the contract of employment; or
2 by the terms of what is called a collective agreement made between a trade union and the employer. The terms of this agreement, including the part on pay, are then assumed to be part of the individual contracts of employment of the members.

The pay which the worker is to get should nearly always be definite because it is included in the written particulars which we have just dealt with and also because the ERA requires itemised pay statements.

If there is no provision for payment in the contract – which is highly unlikely – then if the worker sued for payment, the court would fix a fair rate of pay for the job by taking evidence as to what rates of pay were usual in the type of work being done.

Unless the employment contract allows an employer to reduce an employee's pay during short-time working, or the employee agrees to the reduction, the employer must continue to pay full wages during a period of short-time working (*Miller* v *Hamworthy Engineering Ltd* (1986)). However, if an employee refuses to perform his contractual duties because he is taking industrial action his employer can, understandably, lawfully withhold wages for the relevant period (*Miles* v *Wakefield Metropolitan District Council* (1987)).

Where a worker returns to work after a strike but refuses to work normally, the employer is not bound to accept part performance and can terminate the contract. However, if he does not but decides to accept the part performance, he can withhold wages for the hours lost (see *British Telecommunications* v *Ticehurst* (1992)).

Cashless pay. As a general rule, wages can now be paid by cheque or credit transfer. However, employees who have been continuously employed since before the beginning of 1987 and who have always been paid in cash may have a contractual right to continue to be paid in that way. If an employer wishes to start paying such employees by cheque or by credit transfer, he should either obtain their consent or take the necessary steps to vary the contract.

National minimum wage (NMW)

The National Minimum Wage Act 1998 was brought into force by regulations over the period of 1998/9. The Act and connected regulations provide workers with a floor below which their wages will not fall, regardless of the size of the employer's business. Those who work part time have benefited most. Section references are to the 1998 Act.

Entitlement. Those entitled must be 'workers' who work or ordinarily work in the UK under a contract of employment and are over compulsory school leaving age (ss 1(2) and 54(3)). Casual workers are included as are agency workers (s 34) and home-workers (s 35).

There are a number of exclusions including au-pairs living and working as one of a family in their employer's home, and members of a family carrying out household duties or working in the family non-corporate business.

Owner-managed businesses. The 1998 Act applies to directors of owner-managed businesses. Thus, a person who works as a director of his company but takes no salary (or very little), relying on dividends as income, falls foul of the Act and must receive the minimum wage or adjust the hours worked to comply. The company must also pay employer's NIC. If the business is disincorporated, the former director would come under the exemption for the self-employed. Those who are starting up a business as a company and cannot initially pay themselves also fall foul of the Act though they could notionally pay themselves the minimum wage but remain as a creditor until the company can pay them. As an alternative. they could set up in partnership because partners are excluded from the minimum wage provisions, unless they are salaried employees as distinct from profit-sharing partners. A spouse employed in a family business is excluded from the provisions under the 'family business' exception but not if the employer is a family company.

A further solution for those directors who wish or have to work for less than the minimum wage is not to have a contract of employment, so that they are not employees. This appears to be accepted by the National Minimum Wage Office.

Level. The NMW is such single hourly rate as the Secretary of State may prescribe (ss 1(3) and 2). The NMW is now at the rate of £4.10 an hour before deductions. A minimum 'development rate' applies to 18–21-year-olds and for up to six months to those aged 22 or over starting a new job with a new employer under a scheme of accredited training such as a National Vocational Qualification.

The development rate introduced in April 1999 was – for 18 to 21-year-olds £3.00 an hour (rising to £3.20 an hour in June 2000) and £3.20 an hour for accredited trainees.

Increases in level. This will depend upon the advice of the Low Pay Commission (LPC) and the economic situation and is not automatic. The LPC is given a statutory framework by ss 5–8 and Sch 1. The NMW rates for adults rose to £4.10 on 1 October 2001. For 18–21-year-olds the rate rose to £3.20 on 1 June 2000 and the same rate, i.e. £3.20 an hour, continues for workers aged 22 and over for six months after starting a new job with a new employer if they are receiving accredited training.

Extensions. There is power to apply the Act to those who do not fit the current definition of a 'worker' (s 41). This could be used to deal with changes in working practices and to close loopholes which bad employers may exploit.

Calculation. The regulations set out the averaging period to be used in calculating whether a worker has been paid the NMW. It is set at a month (i.e. 'calendar month') except where workers are currently paid by reference to periods of shorter than one month, e.g. a week, a fortnight or four weeks. In the latter cases the pay reference period for NMW purposes will be the worker's existing pay period. In addition, the hourly rate for those who are paid an annual salary will be calculated on an average basis. Therefore, the lowest salary for a 35-hour week would be £4.10 x 35 x 52 = £7,462.

What counts as remuneration? The regulations deal with a number of instances of what does and does not count towards discharging an employer's obligation to pay the NMW. Examples of things which do not count are advances of wages, pensions, redundancy payments and benefits in kind with the exclusion of living accommodation.

Payments during absences from work such as sick pay, holiday pay, maternity pay and guarantee payments are not included and neither are service charges, tips, gratuities or cover charges *not paid through the payroll*. Thus, discretionary tips left for a worker by a customer and pocketed by the worker do not count nor would tips pooled under an employees' informal scheme and distributed, but where tips are pooled by the employer and paid through the payroll they do count as remuneration.

Enforcement. The Secretary of State appoints enforcement officers (s 13) and the Inland Revenue and Contributions Agency (combined in April 1999) is responsible for enforcement by checking employers' records to ensure compliance. Complaints by employees will be investigated and spot checks will be made on employers.

Penalties. Organisations that refuse to pay the NMW will face fines of twice the NMW, i.e. £8.20 a day for each employee (s 21). If defiance continues, the fine goes up to a maximum of £5,000 for each offence (s 31). Workers have the right to recover the difference between what they have been paid and the NMW before a tribunal as an unlawful deduction from wages (s 17). There is no limit of time on back claims.

Action by employees. A worker who is dismissed for asking for the NMW can claim unfair dismissal. In *Butt v Euro Fashion* (MCLR) Ltd (ET Case No 240341499) B was paid £2.60 per hour. He asked for £3.60 (the then rate) and was told to get another job if he wanted the NMW. He resigned and subsequently a tribunal held that he had been constructively dismissed and that the dismissal was unfair.

Records. The record-keeping obligations were eased following consultation and it is now merely provided that an employer has to keep records 'sufficient to establish that he is remunerating the worker at a rate at least equal to the national minimum wage'. The records may be in a format and with a content of the employer's choosing and must be capable of being produced as a single document when requested either by an employee or the Inland Revenue. The DTI has published guidance on the kinds of records that will be regarded as sufficient.

Employers are not required to keep detailed records of the pay and hours of workers earning less than £1,000 a month or £ 12,000 a year gross. Records can be kept on a computer, but the employer must be able to produce them in a single document which can be of any length on request.

Access to tax records. A government amendment made to the Employment Relations Act 1999 allows information obtained by a tax inspector to be supplied:

- by the Revenue to the DTI for any purpose relating to the National Minimum Wage Act 1998; and
- by the DTI with the authority of the Revenue to inspectors required to enforce the NMW or minimum agricultural wages.

Corporate offences. Where a relevant offence is committed by a company, its directors and other officers are jointly responsible with the company where they have consented to or connived at the offence or been neglectful in regard to it (s 32).

Contracting out. Section 29 makes void any agreement to exclude or limit the Act's provisions or prevent a complaint being made to a tribunal unless there has been conciliation by a conciliation officer or a valid compromise agreement.

Victimisation and unfair dismissal. Section 23 gives workers the right not to be subject to any detriment, e.g. failure to promote, because they have asserted rights under the 1998 Act. Under s 25 employees who are dismissed or selected for redundancy for similarly asserting rights will be regarded as unfairly dismissed.

Capability and the minimum wage. A Birmingham employment tribunal has ruled that a textile company was entitled to dismiss a worker who, though entitled to the minimum wage, did not in the employer's view have productivity to match.

Gurdev Kaur v Ambertex Clothing (2000)
Mrs Kaur, aged 54, was dismissed by Ambertex in July 1999, three months after the national minimum wage was introduced. It appeared that the company had been quite willing to employ Mrs Kaur during the previous two and half

years while she was being paid on a piecework arrangement for sewing buttons on shirts. She was then paid about £2 per hour based on the speed with which she worked.

All Ambertex's employees were paid the minimum wage of £3.60 an hour when the legislation was brought into force, but employees were told that payment of the wage required a set level of productivity. Mrs Kaur failed to meet the required level and was dismissed. She claimed damages for unfair dismissal because of the introduction of the minimum wage. The tribunal rejected that argument. The principal reason for dismissal was in effect 'incapability' (or underperformance) which can be an acceptable reason for dismissal under s 98(2)(a) of the Employment Rights Act 1996. The tribunal did, however, decide that Mrs Kaur had been unfairly dismissed by reason of the *procedure* adopted. She had only been given one, rather than two, written warnings. Her compensation due to underpayment in some weeks because of clerical errors was £412.95.

Comment. This does appear to have been a capability dismissal rather than a minimum wage dismissal which would have been unfair. It does not appear on its own facts to suggest that there is a loophole in the minimum wage law.

Low Pay Commission. The government has asked the Low Pay Commission,which was put on to a statutory footing when ss 5–8 of the National Minimum Wage Act 1998 came into force on 1 November 1998, to report on a number of matters. These include whether or not 21-year-olds should be covered by the NMW's adult rate. The Commission has also been asked to monitor and evaluate the impact of the NMW in terms of pay, employment and competitiveness in low-paying sectors and small businesses and the effect on pay differentials.

The DT1 has published the Commission's terms of reference for its third report to be made by July 2001. In addition to continuing its role of monitoring and evaluating the impact of the NMW, the Commission is to consider whether there is a case for increasing the NMW and to include earnings growth in its assessment as well as inflation and the effect on employment. The inclusion of earnings growth has led to a higher minimum wage in 2001.

To give holidays and holiday pay

The rights and duties of the parties here depend upon what the contract of employment says or what the terms of a collective agreement with the union are. Again, there should be no doubt about holidays and holiday pay because the 1996 Act states that this information is to be given to the employee in the written particulars.

The employer must also bear in mind the Working Time Regulations 1998, under which the employee is entitled to four weeks of paid holiday. These regulations, which are part of the health and safety provisions, are considered later in this chapter.

To provide sick pay

Entitlement to sick pay must be dealt with by the written particulars. An employer has **no general duty to provide sick pay from his own funds**. There is no implied term in the contract of service that an employee is entitled to sick pay (*Mears v Safecar Security* (1982)). There is a **statutory duty** under the 1996 Act to pay an employee who goes sick during the statutory period of notice and is not able to work out all or part of the notice.

Employers are required to provide what is called **statutory sick pay** (SSP) on behalf of the government to employees who are aged 16 or over but not over 65. The law is to be found, in the main, in the Social Security Contributions and Benefits Act 1992. The Social Security Administration Act 1992 deals with the administration of statutory sick pay and statutory maternity pay. It is not necessary in a book of this nature to go into details in regard to the statutory sick pay scheme but the main principles are that when an employee falls sick he or she gets a weekly amount from the employer and not from the Department of Social Security.

The Statutory Sick Pay Act 1994 removed (from 6 April 1994) an employer's right to recover sums paid by way of SSP from the total amount of employers' and employees' national insurance contributions due to the Collector of Taxes. However, this led to protests from employers, and the government intro-

duced regulations under which all employers recover SSP under the 'percentage threshold scheme'. Under this scheme the employer takes the figure of NIC (employers and employees) due in any given tax month. The employer then ascertains the SSP paid in the same month. If this is more than 13 per cent of the NIC figure, the employer recovers the excess.

A further change arising from the Act is that although employees over pensionable age are not entitled to SSP women employees between the ages of 60 and 65 are now entitled to SSP. This is because the virtual abolition of reimbursement brings SSP within the EC Equal Treatment Directive.

There is no other change to entitlement to SSP except that s 7 of the Social Security (Incapacity for Work) Act 1994 abolished the lower rate of SSP. There is now only one rate, this being currently £62.20 per week.

The provisions relating to SSP are notoriously difficult if taken in full detail, but in broad terms SSP is paid by an employer (or a series of employers) for up to 28 weeks of incapacity for work during a three-year period. The first three days of sickness are waiting days and no SSP is payable. However, as regards the second and subsequent periods of sickness, if the employee has not been back at work following the first period of sickness for eight weeks or more the periods are linked and there are no waiting days, SSP beginning on the first day of sickness in the second or subsequent period. We can illustrate what happens (see below).

In Norma's case, since she has not returned to work for the requisite period of more than eight weeks, her periods of incapacity are linked and no waiting days are applied to the second period of incapacity because it is not a new one. Both John and Norma have now exhausted their entitlement to SSP against their employer. An employer's liabil-

John's pattern of sickness

3 waiting days $\rightarrow$ 10 weeks of incapacity and SSP $\rightarrow$ 10 weeks at work $\rightarrow$ 3 waiting days $\rightarrow$ 18 weeks of incapacity and SSP

Norma's pattern of sickness

3 waiting days $\rightarrow$ 10 weeks of incapacity and SSP $\rightarrow$ 5 weeks at work $\rightarrow$ 8 weeks of incapacity and SSP $\rightarrow$ 4 weeks at work $\rightarrow$ 10 weeks of incapacity and SSP

ity to pay SSP ends when he has paid the employee SSP for 28 weeks during a three-year period commencing with the first incapacity. During the remainder of the three years John and Norma cannot have SSP but will be able to resume that right when a new period of three years begins three years after the first incapacity.

Employees who are still incapacitated after their entitlement has run out are entitled to state benefits. It is not possible to avoid the statutory sick pay provisions and any clause in a contract of employment which sets out to do this is void.

Exceptions

In addition to those who have reached pensionable age, a person who is employed for a fixed period of not more than three months is not eligible and in all cases the claimant must have earned the qualifying level, currently £72 a week.

Enforcement

If an employee is dissatisfied with an employer's decision in regard to entitlement to SSP or the employer has failed to make a decision, the employee can write to the Inland Revenue asking for a decision on entitlement. Employer and employee have a right of appeal to a commissioner. The Inland Revenue has power to pay SSP itself and should also pay SSP if the employer is liable but insolvent.

To provide pay during suspension

1 **On medical grounds.** Under the ERA an employee who has had at least one month's continuous service with his employer and who is suspended from work, for example under the Health and Safety at Work Act 1974, normally on the advice of an Employment Medical Adviser, not because he is ill but because he might become ill if he continues at work, since he is currently engaged on an industrial process which involves a potential hazard to his health – is entitled to be paid his normal wages while he is suspended for up to 26 weeks. This could occur, for example, where there was a leak of radioactivity at the workplace.

An employee may complain to an industrial tribunal under the ERA if his employer has not paid him what he is entitled to during a period of suspension and the tribunal may order the employer to pay the employee the money which he should have had.

2 **On disciplinary grounds.** Suppose an employee takes a day off without permission, in order to go to a football match. His employer decides to suspend him for a further day without pay: is this legal? Well, there is no implied right to suspend an employee for disciplinary reasons without pay. In practice, if the employer wants a power to suspend it must be made an express term of the contract which is agreed to by the employee and be in the written particulars of the job. If so, it will be justified and the employee will have to accept it.

It should be noted also that there is no implied contractual term allowing an employer to suspend or fine a worker for poor quality work. An express term is required.

3 **On maternity grounds.** The ERA provides for suspension on maternity grounds. Formerly, a pregnant woman could be fairly dismissed if because of her condition she could not do her work, e.g. because of health and safety regulations and either there was no suitable alternative work or she had refused it. The ERA substitutes suspension on the grounds of pregnancy, recent childbirth or breast feeding while the health hazard continues. The employee may complain to a tribunal if she is not offered available and suitable alternative work. Suspension continues even if such an offer is refused but pay ceases. For those who have not refused an offer, as where it was not possible for the employer to make one, pay continues during suspension but only to a maximum of 'a week's pay' (currently £240) or normal remuneration if her contract so provides. Those whose employer does not make the payment can claim compensation before a tribunal.

If an employer dismisses an employee who tries to assert his or her rights in these various suspension matters, the dismissal is automatically unfair whatever the employee's length of service. A claim to an employment tribunal must be made within three months of the employment ending.

Maternity provision

The law under this heading has been drastically changed by the Maternity and Parental Leave etc. Regulations 1999, made under the Employment Relations Act 1999. The following is a general introduction to the relevant law.

Antenatal care

A pregnant employee who has, on the advice of her doctor, midwife or health visitor, made an appointment to get antenatal care must have time off to keep it and she must also be paid. Except for the first appointment, the employer can ask for proof of the appointment in the form, for example, of an appointment, card. An employer who, acting unreasonably, does not give the employee these rights can be taken to a tribunal by the employee but this must normally be during the three months following the employer's refusal. Compensation may be given to the employee, both where the employer has failed to give time off and also where he has given time off but has failed to pay the employee. In either case the compensation will be the amount of pay to which she would have been entitled if time off with pay had been given as the law requires. All female employees are entitled to this time off and it does not make any difference how many hours they work each week; there is no service requirement.

Maternity leave

The provisions which are set out below came into force on 15 December 1999 by reason of the Maternity and Parental Leave Regulations 1999 (SI 1999/3312) and new provisions of the ERA 1996 inserted by the Employment Relations Act 1999.

The new Chapter I of the new Part VIII of the ERA sets out three different periods of maternity leave:

- *ordinary maternity leave* (OML), which is not less than 18 weeks (and replaces the former right to 14 weeks maternity leave) of which –
- not less than two weeks is *compulsory maternity leave* (CML), to be taken during the two weeks from the day on which childbirth occurs; and
- *additional maternity leave* (AML), which replaces the right to return to work within 29 weeks of giving birth.

It should be noted that the period of 18 weeks of OML will be extended for the compulsory period of two weeks after childbirth if necessary (or for any period where there is a relevant, e.g. health and safety, statutory provision prohibiting the woman from working).

Ordinary maternity leave

Generally. This is leave under new s 71 of the ERA 1996. It gives a general right to all employees regardless of their length of service to a minimum period of maternity leave that is extended from 14 weeks to 18 weeks in line with the period for which statutory maternity pay is payable.

Entitlement. This arises where the employee, at least 21 days before the leave is to start (or as soon as is reasonably practicable), notifies her employer:

- that she pregnant;
- of her expected week of childbirth by a certificate from her doctor or midwife if the employer so requests; and
- of the date she intends to start her OML. This must be in writing if the employer requests that the notice be in writing. It need not be given at the same time as the other notifications and cannot be before the beginning of the 11th week before her expected week of confinement (EWC).

If the woman's OML is automatically triggered by a pregnancy-related absence in the last six weeks before the EWC, e.g. a premature birth, she must notify her employer (in writing if he so requires) as soon as is reasonably practicable that she is absent due to pregnancy or childbirth. Failure to do this will result in the loss of OML.

EWC means the week beginning with midnight between Saturday and Sunday in which it is expected that childbirth will occur.

Length of OML. OML starts at the earliest of:

- the date notified to the employer; or
- the beginning of the sixth week before her EWC on which she is away from work wholly or partly because of pregnancy;
- the day she gives birth to a premature or still-born child after 24 weeks of pregnancy.

OML continues:

- for a period of 18 weeks after its commencement; or
- until the end of her CML if later; or
- until the end of any later period during which she is prohibited by law from working because she has recently given birth, e.g. a health and safety reason.

If the employee is dismissed after the start of her OML but before that period would otherwise have ended, the period ends when she is dismissed.

During OML – what are the rights? An employee taking OML:

- is entitled to the benefit of the terms and conditions of her employment that do not relate to remuneration. Thus, she is not entitled to the monetary element of her pay which is normally replaced by SMP or maternity allowance unless her contract of employment otherwise provides. She is, however, entitled to benefits in kind such as private medical or permanent health insurance if these prevail in the workforce whether they are contractual or not. She will also continue to accrue contractual and also statutory minimum paid holiday entitlement and other benefits depending on length of service during the OML;
- is bound by any obligations arising under the terms and conditions of her contract which are not inconsistent with her right to be off work during OML, e.g. the implied obligation of good faith to the employer in terms of, say, trade secrets.

If any changes are made to her terms and conditions of work or are proposed she should, as a matter of principle, be consulted and allowed to comment. This applies to changes favourable or otherwise.

OML – the right to return to work. An employee who has taken OML is entitled to return to her old job with seniority and pension as they would have been and on terms and conditions not less favourable than those which would have applied if she had not been absent. The Social Security Act 1989 provides in Sch 5 para 5 for pension rights to continue during any paid maternity leave on the basis of the employee's normal pay. There has been no implementation of the suggestion that women be allowed to return initially on a part-time basis.

An employee returning need not give notice of that fact unless she intends to return early. If so, she must give her employer 21 days' notice as a minimum. Any attempt to return early without notice as required means that the employer can postpone her return up to 21 days so as to ensure

his period of notice but not beyond the end of her OML. The employer may also notify the employee that she is not to return before the end of her OML and if she does regardless of that he is under no contractual obligation to pay her until the end of the OML period. This is to avoid a situation in which a temporary replacement has been employed until the end of OML and to avoid paying two persons where the employee on OML returns before the end of the notice period of the temporary employee.

If a woman is unable to return after her OML due to sickness, the normal sick-leave procedures at her workplace will apply.

Compulsory maternity leave

This is leave under the new s 72 of the ERA 1996. An employer of a woman who has taken OML is prohibited from allowing her to work during the two weeks from the day on which the childbirth occurs. An employer who contravenes this requirement will commit a criminal offence and be liable to a fine not exceeding £500. The woman is unlikely to want to return. The provision is to prevent the employer from pressurising her to do so.

Additional maternity leave

This is leave under the new s 73 of the ERA 1996. It is a right to leave for a period of 29 weeks from the beginning of the week of childbirth and not, as before, a right to return within that period. It is available to women who have been continuously employed for one year, and not two years as previously.

Entitlement to AML. The woman must have been continuously employed for at least one year by the beginning of the 11th week before her EWC. She does not have to notify her employer that she intends to take AML. This will be presumed unless she gives notice to return early.

Duration of AML. AML begins on the day after the last day of OML. It continues until the end of a period of 29 weeks beginning with the week she gives birth. If she is dismissed after AML begins and during AML, the AML period ends when she is dismissed.

AML – what are the rights? The new s 73(4) and (5) of the ERA 1996 apply. In essence, the woman is not entitled to be paid unless her contract requires this. She is entitled to notice of termination of her contract and must give notice if she wishes to terminate it. She is entitled to compensation in case of redundancy and to have access to disciplinary or grievance procedures. She is required not to disclose confidential information or to accept gifts or other benefits in a situation inimical to her employer. She must not participate in any other business. A particular contract of employment may give wider rights and duties.

AML – the right to return. The woman is entitled to return to her old job or another suitable job, unless during the AML she has been made redundant. The remuneration must not be less favourable and she must retain her seniority and pension rights. She must also receive the benefit of any salary increases awarded during her OML and AML. Pension rights will be suspended during AML and resume on return. This applies if she is not paid during AML. If her contract continues pay, then her pension rights will not be suspended but accrue on the basis of the pay she would have been receiving if she had been working normally. If pension rights are suspended, neither she nor her employer will make pension contributions and the period will not count as pensionable service as it will if her contract provides for pay and contributions are made.

Beyond this she must give at least 21 days' notice of return to work, but only if she returns to work early. She may not postpone her return to work by reason of illness, nor may the employer postpone it for sickness reasons. Instead the normal sickness procedures at her place of work will apply once AML is over. The employer is entitled to ask the woman not earlier than 21 days before the end of her OML to notify him of the date she gave birth and whether she intends to return to work at the end of her AML. The employee must give this information within 21 days of receiving the employer's request, provided that the employer's notice containing the request was in writing and accompanied by a written statement explaining how the employee could ascertain the date on which her AML would end

and informing her that failure to respond could lead e.g. to dismissal on her return, though the basic right to return is retained.

A woman who fails to respond to the employer's request will lose her protection against detriment or automatic unfair dismissal, although, depending on the circumstances, she may still have an ordinary unfair dismissal claim.

Redundancy during maternity leave

Although an employer may be excused from taking a woman back if her post has become redundant during maternity leave, there is the usual provision that she be offered suitable alternative employment if possible with the employer, his successor or an associated employer.

Unpaid parental leave

The new ss 76–78 of the ERA 1996 apply. These sections together with the regulations provide for collective agreements to be made with trade unions and workforce agreements to be made with employees in regard to parental leave. Nevertheless, employees retain their rights under what is called the statutory fallback scheme unless the collective or workforce scheme is more generous, in which case such schemes can replace the fallback scheme. This book considers only the fallback scheme as follows.

The fallback scheme. An employee who has been continuously employed for a period of not less than one year has a right to 13 weeks of parental leave in respect of each child born on or after 15 December 1999 and each child under 18 who is adopted by the employee on or after that date. Women who qualify for parental leave can take it immediately after taking maternity leave. A week means seven days' absence from work, even though the employee would not have been required to work on every one of the working days. Leave must be taken in one-week blocks (or the part-time equivalent) up to a maximum of four weeks' leave in respect of an individual child during a particular year calculated from the first time the employee became entitled to take parental leave. Leave may be taken in blocks of one day or multiples of one day where the child is disabled. The leave must be taken during the period of five years from the date of birth or adoption or until the child turns 18 years if disabled. As regards the adoption of older children, the leave period ends when they reach 18 even if five years from placement for adoption has not by then elapsed. Entitlement to leave after the child's fifth birthday occurs if the employer has previously postponed leave.

Notice

The employer must receive notice (not necessarily written notice) of 21 days specifying the dates on which leave is to begin and end. Where the leave is to be taken on birth, the notice must specify the EWC and the duration of leave to he taken and be given 21 days before the beginning of EWC. The same with adoption, except that notice must be given 21 days before the expected week of placement.

Evidence

The employer is entitled to require evidence of the employee's legal responsibility for the child as well as evidence of the child's age.

Postponement of leave

The employer may postpone a period of leave where he considers that the operation of the business would be affected in terms that it would be 'unduly disrupted'. He has only seven days to make his mind up about postponement which may be for a maximum period of six months. No postponement is allowed if leave is taken on the birth or adoption of a child.

The employment contract during leave

While on parental leave, employees remain bound by their obligation of good faith towards their employer and any express undertakings in the contract in regard to non-disclosure of confidential information and competition. The employer must continue to abide by the implied obligations of trust and confidence and offer the right to return to the same job but if that is not possible to another job which is suitable and appropriate in the circumstances. There is also protection in regard to salary, continuity of employment and pension rights on return.

Making a claim

The relevant provision is the new s 80 of the ERA 1996. It gives employees a right to complain to an employment tribunal within three months from the date when any of the rights under the parental leave arrangements are denied, in the sense that these have been unreasonably postponed or prevented. Any related dismissal is automatically unfair and there is no cap on the compensation that may be awarded.

Records

The regulations do not require the keeping of records, but it will be impossible for employers to avoid keeping them for accounting purposes to show that leave has been unpaid and that the rights are not being abused. Bearing in mind also that time off for domestic emergencies (also unpaid) exists (see below), employers must consider the need to set up systems and procedures to cope with the new rights and look at how they can run along with any existing contractual rights to paid parental leave that employees already have within a particular organisation.

Dependant leave

This is the new s 57A of the ERA 1996. It entitles every employee, regardless of length of service, to take a reasonable amount of time off work 'to take action that is necessary':

- to help when a dependant gives birth, falls ill or is assaulted;
- to make longer term arrangements for the care of a sick or injured dependant;
- as a result of a dependant's death;
- to cope when the arrangements for caring for a dependant break down unexpectedly; or
- to deal with an expected incident that involves a dependant child during school hours, or on a school trip or in other situations when the school has responsibility for the child.

Dependants. This means a husband or wife or a child or parent of the employee whether they live with him or not or any member of the employee's household who is not employed by him or her and is not a tenant, lodger or boarder.

Amount of time off. There is no set limit. In every case the right is limited to the amount of time that is reasonable in the circumstances. Employment tribunals will be the ultimate arbitrators if a claim is brought by an employee.

Payment for time off. The employer is under no obligation to pay the employee for time taken off.

Notification. The right only applies if the employee 'as soon as is reasonably practicable' tells the employer why he or she is absent and unless the employee is already back at work for how long the absence is likely to last.

Enforcing the right. The new s 57B of the ERA 1996 entitles an employee to complain to an employment tribunal that the employer has unreasonably refused to allow time off as required by s 57A. The period for application is three months from the employer's refusal, and compensation may be an uncapped award such as is just and equitable.

Victimisation and dismissal. There is protection in terms of a tribunal complaint for any victimisation, detriment or dismissal resulting from the exercise or purported exercise of the right in a proper way and dismissal is automatically unfair. Selection for redundancy for the same reason will be automatically an unfair dismissal.

Reform

There are proposals to change some of the material set out above relating to working parents. They appear in a government Green Paper entitled *Work and Parents: Competitiveness and Choice.* The proposals are:

1 *Employees' options*
- two weeks' paid paternity leave for fathers;
- period of paid maternity leave to be extended to six months;
- extension of unpaid maternity leave period to allow a woman to stay at home for a year;
- allowing an adoptive parent to take paid leave similar to maternity leave when adopting a child.

2 *Flexible working options*
- mothers who return early from maternity leave to be given the right to work reduced hours for the rest of that time;
- giving fathers the right to work reduced hours until the end of maternity leave;
- giving all employers the right to refuse a request to work reduced hours where it would harm the business.

3 *Options for businesses*
- small businesses would qualify for compensation for money paid out in maternity pay as indicated later in this chapter;
- encouraging small businesses to make use of their right to seek maternity payments in advance from the Inland Revenue to assist with cash flow problems.

It is also worth noting that an attempt was made in *R* v *Secretary of State for Trade and Industry, ex parte TUC* (2000) to challenge the back-dating provision for parental or paternity leave of 15 December 1999. It is contended that the cut-off period should not exist so that, e.g., a parent with a child aged, say, two years on 15 December 1999 would be able to take advantage of three years of leave. The suggestion is that the EC Parental Leave Directive has not been properly implemented here. In the above case the Court of Appeal referred the matter to the European Court and refused to make any interim order. The government has conceded and will extend entitlement in regard to all children under five on 15 December 1999.

Dismissal rights – sex discrimination

An employee can also argue that a pregnancy dismissal amounts to sex discrimination. The House of Lords in *Webb* v *EMO Air Cargo (UK) Ltd* (1995) accepted the validity of this approach, following the line taken by the ECJ in an earlier decision in the same case. This type of case was brought by women who did not have the required service for a straightforward dismissal claim on the grounds of pregnancy. Now, of course (as we have seen above), the ERA makes it automatically unfair to dismiss a woman on pregnancy grounds regardless of her service. Even so, a woman may choose the *Webb* approach because there is no cap on a compensatory award for sex discrimination, whereas the cap for unfair dismissal is currently £50,000, but some claims for sex discrimination have produced much higher awards. In addition, those who use or combine a claim for unfair dismissal with a claim for sex discrimination can use the discrimination questionnaire procedure that is not available where the claim is only for unfair dismissal. These questionnaires require the employer to answer certain questions, such as who took the decision to dismiss and when? Who was consulted and what were their views? and so on. These questionnaires are admissible in evidence at the tribunal. Furthermore, in some cases a woman may only be able to use the discrimination procedure because she has not followed the procedural requirements described above or is not employed so that the unfair dismissal provisions do not apply, though the discrimination rules do.

An example of the sex discrimination aspect of a maternity dismissal case appears in *Rees* v *Apollo Watch Repairs plc* (1996) where the EAT decided that a woman who was dismissed while on maternity leave after her employers found that the person appointed to replace her was more efficient suffered sex discrimination because if she had not been pregnant a replacement would not have been employed and a performance comparison followed by dismissal would not have taken place. The House of Lords' interpretation of UK law in *Webb* is available to both public and private-sector employees since it concerns 'pay' and is therefore within Art 119 (now Art 141) of the Treaty of Rome which is directly applicable in the UK and does not require further UK legislation. Normally employees in the private sector cannot rely directly on EC directives but must wait for the relevant member state to implement the directive. This is the result of the ruling of the ECJ in *Faccini Dori* v *Recreb* (1995). Employees of state organisations such as civil servants and local authority workers can rely directly on the provisions of directives as interpreted by the ECJ.

Redundancy during maternity leave

This mirrors the right of the longer-serving employees and now all employees, regardless of service, who become redundant during maternity leave must be offered any suitable available vacancy on terms not substantially less favourable than the original contract. The new contract must start immediately. Unfair dismissal can be claimed by those to whom no such offer is made where it is possible to make it.

Statutory maternity pay and maternity allowances

The arrangements are as follows:

- A woman who has been continuously employed in the same employment for 26 weeks by the beginning of the 15th week before the expected

week of childbirth will be entitled to SMP regardless of hours of work provided that her average earnings are at least £72 per week.
- The SMP rate for all qualifying women is 90 per cent of earnings for six weeks followed by pay at the rate of £62.20 a week for 12 weeks. If 90 per cent of earnings is less than £62.20 per week, then the woman will receive £62.20 for 18 weeks.

The employer will deduct tax and national insurance from the first six weeks of maternity pay. There may be other deductions, such as pension contributions.

- Women cannot receive SMP for any period during which they remain at work.
- A maternity allowance of £62.20 is paid for 18 weeks to claimants in employment who do not qualify for SMP but who have paid Class 1 national insurance contributions for at least 26 weeks in the 66 weeks before the baby is due. These contributions could have been made in different and not continuous employment as SMP requires.
- As will be seen from the above, women who are in employment when they claim receive a maternity allowance of £62.20. The allowance is the same for those who are self-employed or have recently become unemployed.
- A woman who works on beyond the beginning of the sixth week before the expected week of childbirth will not automatically lose any SMP.

The above provisions are subject to any improved benefits which a particular employee's contract may provide. It is also worth noting that in *Gillespie* v *Northern Health and Social Services Board* (1996) the ECJ decided that the principle of equal pay under Community law does not require that women should continue to receive full pay during maternity leave.

Statutory maternity pay – low earners

Section 53 of the Welfare Reform and Pensions Act 1999 makes changes in the maternity allowance provisions. They operate in regard to women expecting a child on or after 20 August 2000. The allowance is extended to employed pregnant women who earn less on average than the lower earnings limit for paying NICs (currently £72 a week) but at least £30 a week from all jobs they do, provided that they have been employed for at least 26 weeks in the 66-week period ending with the EWC. These women receive 90 per cent of their average earnings for up to 18 weeks.

Statutory maternity pay – remedies

If the employer does not make payments of SMP to which the employee thinks she is entitled, she may:

- require the employer to supply her within a reasonable time with a written statement of his position in the matter. This will indicate whether he feels there is no entitlement or a smaller entitlement;
- if the employee is dissatisfied with the employer's decision or if he fails to make one, application should be made to the Inland Revenue at the local Inland Revenue national insurance contribution office. The Inland Revenue will make a decision. The employee and the employer may appeal against this decision to the tax appeal commissioner. This procedure is also followed for appeals concerning statutory sick pay.

An employer who refuses to pay, after a final decision has been made that he should pay, commits a criminal offence. The Inland Revenue should normally pay SMP if the employer is liable but insolvent.

Reimbursement

Employers are reimbursed 92 per cent of the SMP they have paid out by deduction from their national insurance bill or, under special arrangements for small employers, 105 per cent (i.e. more than they have paid out) if their total NI liability in the previous tax year was no more than £20,000.

The government Green Paper, referred to above, proposes to double the NI liability amount to £40,000.

Maternity leave – pension rights

The government has implemented s 23 and Sch 5 of the Social Security Act 1989 requiring pension schemes to provide accrual of pension rights during any period of paid maternity absence, including any period during which the employer pays any contractual remuneration or statutory maternity pay. The same conditions extend to any period of parental and dependant leave during which the employer pays the contractual remuneration (which, of course, he is not required to do).

To make payments during lay-off – guarantee payments

1 Lay-off. To avoid difficulty the right of the employer to lay off employees without pay because of lack of work should be made an express term of the contract of employment. However, even if the employer has given himself that right in the contract he must still comply with the provisions of the ERA in the matter and cannot have clauses in the contract which are worse for the employee than the basic statutory rights which provide for guarantee payments.

2 Guarantee payments. The ERA provides that employees with four weeks or more of continuous service are entitled to a guarantee payment up to a maximum sum, which is currently £16.70 per day, if they are not provided with work on a normal working day, e.g. because of a threatened power cut (*Miller* v *Harry Thornton (Lollies) Ltd* (1978)). The precise formula is the average daily wage or £16.70, whichever is the smaller. This does not apply if the failure of the employer to provide work is because of industrial action by his employees or if the employee has been offered suitable alternative work but has refused it. In order to qualify for a guarantee payment, an employee must have been continuously employed for one month ending with the day before the workless day.

An employee can only receive a payment for five workless days during any period of three months. The effect of this is that in order to get payment for a day of lay-off the three months before that day of lay-off must be looked at to see whether the employee has already received the maximum five days' guarantee pay. If the lay-off was, for example, on 20 June and the worker had been paid for lay-offs on 5 June, 27 May, 21 May, 4 April, and 2 April, he would not be entitled to a payment, but he would for a lay-off on 3 July.

An employee can go to a tribunal if the employer fails to pay all or part of a guarantee payment which the employee should have had. The tribunal can order the employer to pay it. The employee must apply to a tribunal within three months of the workless day or within such longer period as the tribunal thinks reasonable if it is satisfied that it was not reasonable or practicable for the employee to present the claim in three months.

To pay during statutory time off

The ERA gives employees certain rights to time off work (see later in this chapter). In **two** cases the employee is also entitled to be paid during the time off. These situations are dealt with here as part of the law relating to the right to be paid. They are:

1 **Time off with pay for carrying out union duties.** Sections 168 to 173 of the Trade Union and Labour Relations (Consolidation) Act 1992 now apply and provide that officials, e.g. branch officers and shop stewards, of a recognised and independent trade union must be given paid time off in order to carry out their duties as union officials. These include negotiation with the employer and representing members in disciplinary matters but not, perhaps obviously, lobbying Parliament in regard to unwanted legislation as in *Luce* v *Bexley London Borough Council* (1990). Paid time off must also be given to union officials to take training in aspects of industrial relations **which are relevant to matters for which the union is recognised by the employer**. An independent trade union is a union which is not dominated or controlled by the employer and is not liable to interference by the employer as some staff associations are.

It will be noted therefore that, although trade union officials will be allowed paid time off for core union activities, such as collective bargaining with management, they will not be allowed paid time off for, for example, courses to improve general education and training such as courses on the general issues raised by mergers and takeovers of companies, in particular the pension rights of employees. However, voluntary arrangements between employers and employees may well ensure that such courses may continue in some organisations. The employee is entitled to be paid his normal hourly rate.

If there is a breach by the employer of this duty, the employee may complain to a tribunal which may declare the employee's rights in its order, so that the employer may carry them out, and may also award money compensation.

2 **Redundant employees.** An employee who has been continuously employed by his employer for at least two years and who is given notice of dismissal because of redundancy has a right before the period of his notice expires to reasonable time off during working hours so that he can look for another job or make arrangements for training for future employment.

Where the employee exercises the above rights, he must be paid the amounts to which he would have been entitled if working normally. If an employer is in breach of the above provisions, the employee can complain to a tribunal within three months but the tribunal's compensation is limited to two-fifths of a week's pay.

Other cases

There are other circumstances in which employees are entitled to paid time off. Some of these are set out below:

- pregnant employees who require time off for antenatal care;
- employee/pension fund trustees under the Pensions Act 1995 who are allowed paid time off so that they may perform their duties and undergo relevant training;
- where, in a redundancy situation, the employer is to consult with worker representatives instead of, or as well as, a trade union representative the elected worker representatives are entitled to reasonable time off with pay during normal working hours to carry out their duties as representatives and to seek election;
- similar provisions apply also to employee safety representatives;
- the Employment Rights Act 1996 (as amended by the Teaching and Higher Education Act 1998) gives employees aged 16 to 18 the right to take resasonable paid time off work in order to study or train for a designated qualification by a specified awarding body. These include a range of NVQ award. These rights are enforceable by way of complaint to an employment tribunal and dismissal for asserting these rights is automatically unfair, so that no minimum period of service is required.

In all cases the right is to 'reasonable' time off in all the circumstances of the case.

Itemised pay statements

Under the ERA itemised pay statements must be provided for employees regardless of service, and whether they ask for them or not. It is an absolute right, said the EAT in *Coales* v *John Woods and Co (Solicitors)* (1986). All workers are entitled to a statement, including part-timers.

Under the Act the employee must receive a statement at the time of or before receiving his pay, showing gross pay and take-home pay and the variable deductions, e.g. income tax, which make up the difference between the two figures. Details of how it is paid must also be given, e.g. is it contained in the pay packet or has it been credited to a bank account?

Fixed deductions, e.g. saving or repayment of a season ticket loan, need not be itemised every pay day. If the employer gives the employee a separate statement setting out the fixed deductions, this may simply be shown as a lump sum in the weekly/monthly pay statement. This fixed deduction statement must be updated in writing if it is changed and in any case it must be re-issued every 12 months.

If the employer does not comply with the pay statement requirements, the employee can complain to a tribunal which will make a declaration of the law that a statement should have been given and as to what it should have included. The employer must comply with this declaration. In addition, the tribunal may order the employer to give back to the employee any deductions which were made from the employee's pay and which were not notified to him during the 13 weeks before the date of the application by the employee to the tribunal.

It is worth noting that the section is penal, i.e. in the nature of a penalty, and so where, for example, an employer has deducted tax and paid it over to the Revenue but has not given the employee a written statement, he can be made to pay the employee the deductions made up to 13 weeks, *even though this means he has paid twice* (see *Cambiero* v *Aldo Zilli, etc.* (1998)).

If the particulars are complete but the employee wishes to question the accuracy of what has been deducted, then this is a contractual matter which can be dealt with by an employment tribunal:

- if the employment has ended; or
- if the employer's action amounts to an unlawful deduction from pay, as where the employee has not consented to a deduction for alleged shortages in cash received for sales.

Otherwise, the matter must be taken before a civil court, e.g. the county court.

Method of payment and deductions from pay

Under the ERA employees no longer have a right to be paid in cash. The Truck Acts 1831–1940, which used to give this right, are repealed. Payment may still, of course, be made in cash, but an employer can if he wishes pay the employee, for example, by cheque or by crediting the employee's bank account by credit transfer. It should be noted, however, that if a worker was paid in cash before 1987 when the repeal came into force the method of payment may only be changed if the worker agrees to a variation of the contract of service.

Deductions from pay are unlawful unless they are:

1 authorised by Act of Parliament, such as income tax and national insurance deductions; or

2 contained in a written contract of employment or the worker has previously signified in writing his agreement or consent to the making of them. In *Discount Tobacco and Confectionery Ltd* v *Williamson* (1993) the Employment Appeal Tribunal (EAT) held that deductions from an employee's pay in regard to stock shortages will be legal only if they relate to losses that occurred *after* the employee gave written consent. If not, the deductions are invalid and must be repaid to the employee. Deductions from the wages of workers in the retail trade, e.g. petrol station cashiers, for stock and cash shortages are limited to 10 per cent of the gross wages and deductions may be made only within the period of 12 months from the date when the employer knew or ought to have known of the shortage. Outstanding amounts may be recovered from a final pay packet when the employee leaves even though the deduction exceeds 10 per cent.

These provisions are enforceable by the employee against the employer in employment tribunals.

Low pay

Reference has already been made to the National Minimum Wage Act 1998 and to the functions of the Low Pay Commission.

Equal pay

The Equal Pay Act 1970 (EPA) (as amended by the Sex Discrimination Act 1975 (SDA) and the Equal Pay (Amendment) Regulations 1983) imply a term called an equality clause into contracts of service. This clause means that a man or a woman must be given contractual terms not less favourable than those given to an employee of the opposite sex, i.e. the comparator, when they are each employed:

1 on like work, in the same employment (but not necessarily in the same kind of job); or

2 on work rated as equivalent in the same employment, e.g. by a job evaluation scheme; or

3 on work which is in terms of demands made on the worker, under such headings as effort, skill and decision-making, of **equal value** to that of a worker in the same employment.

As regards the relationship between the EPA and the SDA, the EPA covers not only matters concerning wages and salaries, but also other terms in the contract of service, such as sick pay, holiday pay and unequal working hours. Other forms of sex discrimination in employment, such as discrimination in recruitment techniques, are covered by the SDA.

In addition, unlike the SDA, a woman must find an actual man with whom she can be compared. It is not enough to ask a tribunal to imply that her pay and conditions are worse than a man's would have been.

Application of the Equal Pay Act. The Act applies to all forms of full- and part-time work. There are no exemptions for small firms or in respect of people who have only recently taken up the employment, though the Act does not apply, for example, to those who do their work wholly outside Great Britain. There is no service requirement.

The Act applies to discrimination against men and women but in practice claims are normally made by women. We shall from now on consider the law on the basis of a claim by a woman.

Main provisions of the Equal Pay Act. These are as follows:

1 If a woman is engaged in the same or broadly similar work as a man and both work for the same or an associated employer (see below), the woman is entitled to the same rate of pay and other terms of employment as the man.

The comparison can be made with a previous holder of the same job. In *Macarthys* v *Smith* (1980) the Employment Appeal Tribunal decided that Mrs Smith, a stockroom manageress, was entitled to pay which was equal to that of a previous manager of the stockroom, a Mr McCullough. However, the EAT did say that tribunals must be cautious in making such comparisons unless the interval between the two employments is reasonably short and there have not been changes in economic circumstances.

In *Hallam Diocese Trustee* v *Connaughton* (1996) the EAT decided that an employment tribunal could hear a claim for equal pay under Art 119 of the Treaty of Rome where the applicant relied for arrears of pay on the salary of a man appointed *after* her resignation. A claim under the EPA requires employment *at the same time* but Art 119 is of direct application, as it was in the *Macarthys* case.

The term 'broadly similar work' means that although there may be some differences between the work of the man and the woman, these are not of sufficient practical importance to give rise to what the EPA calls a 'material difference'. Thus, in a case where women clean offices and toilets and men also clean offices but also urinals, the fact that the men clean urinals would be a difference but not a 'material difference', so that the women would be entitled to the same pay as the men. The following case illustrates a material difference.

Capper Pass v Lawton (1976)

A female cook who worked a 40-hour week preparing lunches for the directors of Capper was paid a lower rate than two male assistant chefs who worked a 45-hour week preparing some 350 meals a day in Capper's works canteen. The female cook claimed that by reason of the EPA (as amended) she should be paid at the same rate as the assistant chefs since she was employed on work of a broadly similar nature.

It was held by the EAT that if the work done by a female applicant was of a broadly similar nature to that done by a male colleague it should be regarded as being like work for the purposes of the EPA unless there were some practical differences of detail between the two types of job. In this case the EAT decided that the work done by the female cook was broadly similar to the work of the assistant chefs and that the differences of detail were not of practical importance in relation to the terms and conditions of employment. Therefore, the female cook was entitled to be paid at the same rate as her male colleagues.

Comment. An interesting contrast is provided by *Navy, Army and Airforce Institutes* v *Varley* (1977). Miss Varley worked as a Grade E clerical worker in the accounts office of NAAFI in Nottingham. NAAFI conceded that her work was like that of a Grade E male clerical worker employed in NAAFI's London office. However, the Grade E workers in Nottingham worked a 37-hour week, while the male Grade E clerical workers in the London office worked a $36\frac{1}{2}$-hour week. Miss Varley applied to an employment tribunal under the EPA for a declaration that she was less favourably treated as regards hours worked than the male clerical workers in London and that her contract term as to hours should be altered so as to reduce it to $36\frac{1}{2}$ hours a week. The employment tribunal granted that declaration but NAAFI appealed to the EAT which held that the variation in hours was genuinely due to a material difference other than the difference of sex. It was due to a real difference in that the male employees worked in London where there was a custom to work shorter hours. Accordingly, NAAFI's appeal was allowed and Miss Varley was held not to be entitled to the declaration. The judge said that the variation between her contract and the men's contracts was due really to the fact that she worked in Nottingham and they worked in London.

Another common example of a sensible material difference occurs where, for example, employee A is 21 and employee B is a long-serving employee of 50, and there is a system of service increments, then it is reasonable to pay B more than A though both are employed on like work. Obviously, however, it is not enough to say that because at the present time men are on average paid more than women this is a material difference justifying paying a woman less in a particular job. This was decided in *Clay Cross (Quarry Services) Ltd* v *Fletcher* (1979). It is also a material difference when the men work nights and the women do not (*Thomas* v *National Coal Board* (1987)).

2   If the job which the woman does has been given the same value as a man's job under a job evaluation scheme, then the woman is entitled to the same rate of pay and other terms of employment as a man. On the other hand, an employer will have a complete answer to a claim for equal pay if the jobs of the woman and the male comparator have been given different ratings under a job evaluation scheme, provided that the scheme has been carried out objectively and analytically, preferably by specialist consultants, and that the scheme itself is not directly or indirectly discriminatory, as where, for example, it overvalues traditional male skills and attributes, such as greater physical strength.

3   Equal value. If the job which a woman does is in terms of the demands made upon her, for instance under such headings as effort, skill and decision-making, of equal value to that of a man in the same employment, then the woman is entitled to the same pay and other contractual terms as the man, as she is if her work has been graded as of higher value (*Murphy* v *Bord Telecom Eireann* (1988)). It might be thought that in such a case she should be paid more but at least the law can ensure equal pay for her.

The point about the 'equal value' ground is that it is available even if the jobs are totally dissimilar, so that a woman secretary may name a male accounts clerk as a comparator.

A complaint may be made to a tribunal on the grounds of equal value even if the two jobs have been regarded as unequal in a job evaluation study. However, there must be reasonable grounds to show that the study was itself discriminatory on the grounds of sex.

When a complaint about equal value is made, the tribunal can (but is not obliged to) commission a report from an expert on the matter of value. The report of the expert goes to the tribunal and copies go to the parties. Although the report will obviously be extremely important in the decision which the tribunal makes, it is not in any way bound by it and can disregard it.

It was once thought that in claims for equal pay the tribunal must look not merely at pay, but also at fringe benefits.

In *Hayward* v *Cammell Laird Shipbuilders Ltd* (1986) a qualified canteen cook, Miss Julie Hayward, who had convinced a tribunal that she was of equal value with male painters, joiners and thermal heating engineers and therefore entitled to equal pay, was told by the Employment Appeal Tribunal that she could not isolate the term about pay. The EAT asked the Tribunal to look at the case again. Although Miss Hayward's pay was not equal, her employers claimed that she had better sickness benefit than the men and also paid meal breaks and extra holidays which they did not have. So it might be possible to say that she was, looked at overall, treated as well. However, Julie Hayward won her appeal in the House of Lords. It was held that her claim to equal pay for work of equal value was justified even though she had better fringe benefits. Her employers were not entitled to compare her total package but should instead consider her basic pay. The decision should ensure that miscellaneous benefits are not seen as 'pay' and will not be used to keep wages down in future.

It is also interesting to note that in *Pickstone* v *Freemans plc* (1986) the Employment Appeal Tribunal decided that a woman could not bring a claim that her work was of equal value to that done by a man employed by the same firm in a different job because men were employed in the same job as her own on the same rates of pay and terms.

On the facts of the case this meant that the woman could not claim that her work as a warehouse packer was of equal value to that of a checker warehouse operative merely because she worked on the same terms with other male warehouse packers. The decision was eventually overruled by the House of Lords which decided that a woman is not debarred from making a claim for parity of pay with a male comparator in a different job merely because a man is doing the same job as herself for the same pay. The decision effectively kills off the device of employing a 'token man' with the women employees as a way of defeating equal pay claims, as by employing one or two low-paid men in a predominantly female area of work.

Associated employers. Comparison of contracts of service for equality purposes is usually made with people who work at the same place. However, comparison can be made with people who work at different places so long as the employer is the same or is an associated employer. As regards an associated employer, this would be the case with a group of companies. Thus, if H plc has two subsidiaries, A Ltd and B Ltd, workers in A Ltd could compare themselves with workers in B Ltd, and workers in B Ltd with those in A Ltd, and workers in A Ltd and B Ltd could compare themselves with workers in H plc. Workers in H plc could, of course, compare themselves with workers in A Ltd and B Ltd.

Also important in these days, where outsourcing of public services is common, workers employed by a private contractor can compare themselves with other persons still employed by a local authority, as the House of Lords decided in *Ratcliffe* v *North Yorkshire County Council* (1995). This ruling may put off some private contractors who might have tendered for council services, intending to do the job more cheaply by cutting wages.

Reference to an employment tribunal. There is no qualifying service required for claims for equal pay. A complaint of unequal treatment under the EPA may be made to a tribunal at any time while the person who wants to complain is still doing the job or within six months after it came to an end. There is no power to extend the time.

The effect of a sucessful claim is twofold. For the future, the complainant has a contractual entitlement to the higher rate of pay or other contract term enjoyed by the comparator. The tribunal can also award compensation in respect of the disparity to date, but under the 1970 Act no back pay can be awarded for a period more than two years before the date of the employment tribunal application. There is no actual financial limit on the amount which can be awarded, so that if, say, the disparity in net pay were £10,000 per annum at the commencement of proceedings and the case were to be heard one year afterwards, the amount awarded could be as much as £30,000.

A challenge to the compensation limit failed in terms of the general period of two years but succeeded in the special circumstances of the case. In *Levez* v *T H Jennings (Harlow Pools) Ltd* (1999) the ECJ ruled that the two-year limitation on backdated compensation under the UK Equal Pay Act 1970 is not *as such* contary to the EC law. However, Community law does preclude its application in some situations, as in this case, where the employer misled the employee as to the pay of her comparators.

The ECJ remitted the case to a UK tribunal to decide whether the two-year rule was equivalent to similar domestic claims and whether the exercise of the UK rights was effective. In *Levez* v *T H Jennings (Harlow Pools) Ltd (No 2)* (1999) the EAT ruled that the two-year period in s 2(5) of the EPA 1970 did not satisfy the principles of equivalence and effectiveness. Equality clauses are implied into contracts of employment and in other cases of breach of contract in ordinary courts a six-year limit applies as also in the cases of sex discrimination damages and unlawful deductions from wages. Therefore, the two-year limit in s 2(5) must be ignored and a six-year limit established. The EAT did, however, reject a submission that there should be no limit.

Community law. It is important to note that any gaps or exceptions in UK legislation can be overcome by resort to Community law. Article 141 of the Treaty of Rome is relevant since it establishes the principle that men and women are entitled to equal pay for work of equal value.

As we have seen in *Macarthys* v *Smith* (1980), it was decided that where a man who leaves his employment is replaced by a woman who receives a lower rate of pay the woman cannot make a claim under UK legislation based on the former male employee's pay, but she can do so under Art 141 (and note also the decision in *Hallam Diocese Trustee* v *Connaughton* (1996).

An important consequence of the applicability of Art 141 is to be found in the field of pensions, redundancy and severance and termination payments. UK legislation contains exceptions for all these matters but Art 141 overrides this and follows from the decision of the European Court in *Barber* v *Guardian Royal Exchange Assurance Group* (1990). The effect of this decision is that pension, redundancy, severance and termination payments are treated as pay for the purposes of Art 141 and there must not be an inequality on the grounds of sex in relation to the payments made.

The Pensions Act 1995 now deals with the main provisions relating to equality in pensions law, and in broad terms provides equal treatment for men and women in regard to the terms and conditions on which they become members of the scheme and their rights once members.

Reform

The government has announced that the Equal Pay Act 1970 is to be strengthened to deal with the average gap of 19 per cent across the workforce in terms of pay differential between men and women. There will be a simpler system of tribunal procedure to speed up the hearing of claims and the employer will be required to complete a questionnaire from tribunals within a fixed period to prevent employers from prolonging the process. Where more than one woman is challenging the same employer, their cases will be heard at the same time.

Employer's duty to provide work

There is, *in general*, no duty at common law for an employer to provide work. If the employer still pays the agreed wages or salary, the employee cannot regard the employer as in breach of contract. The employee has no right to sue for damages for wrongful dismissal but must accept his pay. The main authority for this is *Collier* v *Sunday Referee* (1940) where Mr Justice Asquith said: 'If I pay my cook her wages she cannot complain if I take all my meals out.'

There are some exceptions at common law. For example, a salesman who is paid by commission must be allowed to work in order to earn that commission and if he is not his employer is in breach of contract and can be sued for damages. This is also the case with actors and actresses because they need to keep a public image which requires occasional public performances.

However, in the *William Hill Organisation Ltd* v *Tucker* (1998) the Court of Appeal decided that there could be a duty to provide work beyond the traditional bases for it, i.e. publicity-based careers and commission-based remuneration. The case would appear to extend the common law duty to provide work (in this case during a long six-month notice period) to all skilled workers who may need work to preserve and enhance their skills. If in such a situation an employer wishes to pay the employee but not allow him to work out the notice, there must be a specific provision in the contract to that effect. Otherwise, the employer may be in breach of contract which would allow the employee to leave at once so that the employer loses the advantage of delaying the employee's competition straightaway, which these long notice periods are designed to postpone.

Employee's property

An employer has in fact no duty to protect his employee's property.

Deyong v Shenburn (1946)

The claimant entered into a contract of employment with the defendant under which the claimant was to act the dame in a pantomime for three weeks. Rehearsals took place at a theatre and on the second day the claimant had stolen from his dressing room his overcoat as well as two shawls and a pair of shoes forming part of his theatrical equipment. In the county court the judge found that the defendant had been negligent in failing to provide a lock on the dressing room door and having no one at the stage door during the morning of the particular rehearsal day to prevent the entry of unauthorised persons. However, the county court judge decided that the defendant was under no duty to protect the clothing. The claimant appealed to the Court of Appeal which also decided that the defendant was not liable. The Court of Appeal accepted that if there was an accident at work caused by the employer's negligence, then in an action for personal injury the employee could also include damage to his clothing if there had been any. In addition, if in such an accident the employee's clothes were, say, torn off his back but he suffered no personal injury, then it would seem that he could be entitled to recover damages in respect of the loss of his clothes. However, outside of this an employer has no duty to protect the property of his employee.

Comment. This decision was also applied in the later case of *Edwards* v *West Herts Group Hospital Management Committee* (1957) where the claimant, a resident house physician at the defendants' hospital, had some articles of clothing and personal effects stolen from his bedroom at the hostel where he was required to live. He brought an action for breach of an implied duty under his contract of employment to protect his property. His action was dismissed in the county court and his appeal to the Court of Appeal was also dismissed on the basis that there was no such contractual duty in respect of property.

Employee's indemnity

An employer is bound to indemnify (that is, make good) any expenses, losses and liabilities incurred by an employee while carrying out his duties.

Re Famatina Development Corporation Ltd (1974)

A company employed a consulting engineer to make a report on its activities. The written report contained matters which the managing director alleged were a libel upon him and he brought an action against the engineer in respect of this on the basis of the publication of the report to the directors of the company, all of whom had received a copy. The managing director's action failed but the engineer incurred costs in defending the claim, not all of which he could recover and he now sought to recover them from the company.

The Court of Appeal decided that the comments made in the report were within the scope of the engineer's employment. His terms of engagement required him to report fully and frankly and in the circumstances he was entitled to the indemnity.

Comment. There is no duty to indemnify an employee against liability for his own negligence. Thus, if by negligence an employee injures a third party in the course of employment and the third party sues the employee, the employer is not required to indemnify the employee and indeed, if the employer is sued as vicariously liable (see later in this chapter) he has a right to an indemnity against the employee. This was decided in *Lister* v *Romford Ice and Cold Storage Ltd* (1957), though the action is unlikely to be brought because it upsets industrial relations.

Trade union matters – recognition

Employers were free to decide for themselves whether they wished to recognise trade unions regardless of the wishes of their employees, and irrespective of the level of union membership among their workers. Under the provisions of the Employment Relations Act 1999, which are in force, employers will have to recognise trade unions where a majority of those voting in a ballot and at least 40 per cent of those eligible to vote are in favour of recognition. Organisations employing fewer than 21 workers will be exempt. However, in those organisations where more than 50 per cent of the workers are members of the union, there will be automatic recognition on the grounds that there is a manifest demonstration that the employees wish to be represented by the union for the purposes of collective bargaining. The Employment Relations Act 1999 gives protection against dismissal for those campaigning on behalf of recognition and unions will be allowed reasonable access to the workforce to seek their support and to inform employees about ballots. Those who employ less than 21 workers are exempt.

The compulsory recognition provisions give trade unions the right to negotiate on matters relating to pay, hours of work and holidays. Union recognition also gives the union, through its representatives, the right to be consulted on redundancies and on a transfer of business and to accompany a worker at a grievance or disciplinary hearing. In addition, the employer must respond to requests for information about the business which the union needs for collective bargaining.

However, whether or not there is a recognised union, the Trade Union and Labour Relations (Consolidation) Act 1992 gives employees the right to belong or not to belong to a trade union and whether or not that or any other union is recognised by the employer, individuals are given some basic protection against being penalised because they are or are not or have been members of a trade union. These are set out below.

Trade union matters – employment protection

Under the Trade Union and Labour Relations (Consolidation) Act 1992 employers have a duty not to take action against employees, including dismissal and selection for redundancy, just because they are members of, or take part in at an appropriate time the activities of, a trade union which is independent of the employer. According to the decision in *Post Office* v *Union of Post Office Workers* (1974), this includes activities on the employer's premises. Under the provisions of s 152 of the 1992 Act dismissal for failure to join a trade union is always automatically unfair even if there is a closed shop situation within the industry concerned. This provision greatly weakens the maintenance by trade unions of closed shops.

If action is taken against employees, they may complain to a tribunal which can award money compensation or make an order saying what the trade union rights of the employee are so that the

employer can grant them in the future. If the employee has been dismissed, the unfair dismissal remedies apply.

In addition, s 137 of the 1992 Act gives job seekers a right not to be refused employment or the services of an employment agency on the grounds that they are or are not trade union members. Any individual who believes that he or she has been unlawfully refused employment or the services of an employment agency because of union or non-union membership can complain to a tribunal within three months of refusal. If the case is made out, the tribunal can award compensation. The matter is treated as a form of discrimination and an employment tribunal can award unlimited compensation.

The compensation will generally be paid by the employer or employment agency concerned but in cases where a trade union is joined as a party and the tribunal decides that the unlawful refusal resulted from pressure applied by the union where the employee refused to join the union it may order the union to pay some or all of the compensation. The tribunal can also recommend that the prospective employer or employment agency should take action to remedy the adverse effect of their unlawful action on the complainant.

In *Harrison* v *Kent County Council* (1995) it was held that an employer's refusal to employ an applicant because of his previous activities in another post could amount to an unlawful refusal of employment on grounds of union membership.

Time off work

Under the ERA 1996 employees have a right to time off work in certain circumstances. Sometimes they are also entitled to pay, as in the case of trade union officials and of redundant employees who are looking for work or wanting to arrange training for another job. These and other cases have already been looked at as part of the law relating to pay. However, there are two other cases in which employees are entitled to time off but the employer is not under a duty to pay wages or salary for it. These are as follows:

1 **Trade union activities.** An employee who is a member of an independent trade union *which the employer recognises* is entitled to *reasonable* time off for trade union activities. The employee is not

entitled to pay unless he is a trade union official and the time off is taken under provisions previously considered. The Advisory, Conciliation and Arbitration Service (ACAS), a statutory body set up by the Employment Protection Act 1975 to promote, for example, the improvement of industrial relations, has published a *Code of Practice 3* which gives guidance on the time off which an employer should allow.

2 **Public duties.** Employers also have a duty to allow employees who hold certain public positions and offices reasonable time off to carry out the duties which go along with them. Details are given in the ERA which covers such offices as magistrate, member of a local authority, member of an employment tribunal, and member of certain health and education authorities. There has more recently been an extension made by statutory instrument to cover members of boards of visitors and visiting committees for prisons, remand centres and young offender institutions.

Complaints in regard to failure to give time off under **1** and **2** above may be taken to an employment tribunal. In general the complaint must be made within three months of the date when the failure to give time off occurred. An employment tribunal may make an order declaring the rights of the employee so that these can be observed by the employer and may also award money compensation to be paid by the employer where there is injury to the employee, e.g. hurt feelings.

Testimonials and references

There is no law which requires an employer to give a reference or testimonial to an employee or to answer questions or enquiries which a prospective employer may ask him. This was decided in *Carroll* v *Bird* (1800). An exception occurs where a reference is required by a regulatory body, such as the Financial Services Authority as part of its duty to ensure that financial services are handled only by authorised and competent persons.

However, if an employer does give a reference or testimonial, either orally or in writing, which is false, he commits a criminal offence under the Servants' Characters Act 1792. The employer may also be liable in civil law to pay damages to certain persons as follows:

1 To a **subsequent employer**, who suffers loss because of a false statement **known** to the former employer to be untrue (*Foster* v *Charles* (1830)), or made **negligently** without reasonable grounds for believing the statement to be true, because it was decided in *Lawton* v *BOC Transhield Ltd* (1987) that an employer who gives another employer a reference concerning an employee owes a duty of care in negligence to the recipient employer. It should be noted that if words of disclaimer such as 'This reference is given in good faith. No responsibility is accepted for any errors or omissions which it contains or for any loss or damage resulting from reliance on it' are used they will have to satisfy the test of 'reasonableness' under the Unfair Contract Terms Act 1977. A court might think such a clause reasonable in regard to a reference given to an employee expressing a view upon his ability to do a type of job which he had not done before.

The Rehabilitation of Offenders Act 1974 is also relevant here. The provisions of the Act are an attempt to give effect to the principle that when a person convicted of crime has been successfully living it down and has avoided further crime, his efforts at rehabilitation should not be prejudiced by the unwarranted disclosure of the earlier conviction.

The Act therefore prevents any liability arising from failure by an employee to disclose what is called a spent conviction to a prospective employer. For example, the Act removes the need to disclose convictions **resulting in a fine** recorded more than five years before the date of the reference or testimonial.

Sentences of imprisonment for life or of imprisonment for a term exceeding 30 months are not capable of rehabilitation. The rehabilitation period for a prison sentence exceeding six months but not exceeding 30 months is ten years, and for a term not exceeding six months it is seven years or, as we have seen, if the sentence was a fine, it is five years.

If an employer does refer to a spent conviction in a testimonial or reference the employee may sue him for **libel** in the case of a written testimonial or reference, or **slander** where the testimonial or reference is spoken. The defence of justification, i.e. that the statement that there was a conviction is true, will be a defence for the employer only if he can show that he acted without malice.

While discussing the 1974 Act it is worth noting that it makes provision for questions by employers relating to a person's previous convictions to be treated as not applying to spent convictions.

The Act also provides that a spent conviction or any failure to disclose a spent conviction shall not be a proper ground for dismissing or excluding a person from any office, profession, or occupation, or employment, or for prejudicing him in any way in any occupation or employment.

However, the Rehabilitation of Offenders Act 1974 (Exceptions) (Amendment) Order 1986 (SI 1986/1249) allows those who employ persons who will have contact with those under 18 to ask, for example, questions designed to reveal even spent convictions, particularly any with a sexual connotation.

Certain employees are excluded from the 1974 Act and their convictions can be disclosed. Included in the exceptions are doctors, chartered and certified accountants, insurance company managers and building society officers (see s 189 of the Financial Services Act 1986).

2 To the former employee, for libel or slander if things have been stated in a testimonial or reference which damages the employee's reputation. However, the employer has the defence of qualified privilege, as it is called, so that he can speak his mind about the employee and so in order to get damages the employee would have to prove that the employer made the statement out of malice, as where there was evidence that the employer had a history of unreasonable bad treatment of the employee and knew that what he said or wrote was untrue. It is also possible, however, for the employee to sue the employer in negligence and there is then no defence of qualified privilege available to the employer, and the defence can be bypassed. The following case gives an illustration.

Spring v Guardian Assurance plc (1992)
Mr Spring failed to get three jobs for which he applied because of a bad reference given to him by the defendant employer. It stated that while he had been employed by the defendants as an insurance sales manager he had not managed the sales team fairly, and among other things had kept the best leads (i.e. client contacts) to himself. The person who prepared the reference on behalf of the company did so on the basis of internal memoranda though she was not malicious in any way. However, the judge found that there was a duty of care and that the plaintiff could base his case in negligence. There should have been a more rigorous check on the memoranda and it had been negligent not to do this. The statements made about Mr Spring were not in the view of the judge always justified and it was no defence to an action in negligence that the person preparing the reference may have honestly believed them.

This decision of the High Court was eventually affirmed by the House of Lords in 1994.

Given then that there is a claim in negligence for a breach of duty by the employer, what is the employer's duty of care? It was held in *Bartholomew* v *Hackney LBC* (1999) that the duty imposed upon the employer is to ensure that the reference is fair, just and reasonable and that the employer should take all reasonable care to ensure that there is no misstatement. This duty applies, said the court in *Bartholomew*, even if the factual statements in the reference are correct. The overall impression must be fair.

In this connection, the Employment Appeal Tribunal has ruled that an employer was in fundamental breach of contract justifying a successful claim of constructive dismissal by revealing to a prospective employer in a reference complaints about the applicant which had not been disclosed to her. This blocked her progress in the financial services sector.

TSB Bank plc v Harris (2000)
H was a savings and investment advisor with the TSB. She received a final written warning following an incident in which she forged a client's initials on a corrected form entry. A number of unconnected complaints were made against her. In accordance with standard practice in the industry, these complaints were investigated without her knowledge. She applied for another job and told her prospective employer about the forgery. However, TSB supplied a reference in which it stated that 17 complaints had been made against her, four of which had been valid, and eight of which were still to be investigated. H was not offered the job. She resigned and claimed unfair constructive dismissal. The Employment Appeal Tribunal held that she had been constructively dismissed and that the dismissal was unfair. The fact that H had had no opportunity to refute the complaints was capable of being a fundamental breach of the implied term of trust and confidence.

If TSB supplied a reference, it had to be fair and reasonable. The fact that the procedure for investigating complaints was the standard one in the financial services industry did not justify the misleading nature of the reference. Bald accuracy was not necessarily enough to make a reference reasonable. TSB could have ensured that H was not taken by surprise by the allegations being revealed for the first time in the arena of her application for another job. The fact that she had intended to leave in any case did not alter the fact that when she actually left she had no other job to go to.

Comment. If employers give references, they must ensure that they are not only truthful and accurate but also fair and reasonable. It is also worth noting that under the Data Protection Act 1998 an employee may be able to apply to the new employer for a copy of the reference.

3 **What constitutes a satisfactory reference?** If an employer offers a job 'subject to satisfactory references' which are then taken up, who decides whether or not the references are satisfactory? In *Wishart* v *National Association of Citizens' Advice Bureaux* (1990) the Court of Appeal said it was a matter for the potential employer. So, if the potential employer does not think the reference is satisfactory, it is not. **The test is a subjective one** but presumably the employer must be reasonable and not regard a perfectly good reference as unsatisfactory in order to get out of the contract made subject to the reference condition. It is better in any case not to make an offer of any kind until references are to hand.

4 **Defacing references.** Finally, an employee who maliciously defaces his own reference or testimonial commits a criminal offence under the Servants' Characters Act 1792.

References and discrimination

The Employment Appeal Tribunal has ruled that the Sex Discrimination Act 1975 covers acts of discrimination, such as failure to give a reference, even though the relevant acts took place after the claimant ceased to be employed.

Coote v *Granada Hospitality Ltd* (1999)

Belinda Coote complained of sex discrimination. The company settled the claim by agreeing compensation but requiring her to leave the company. At that time the company had made a decision that they would refuse to give her a reference. Some months later she became aware that the company was refusing to answer requests for references. She then made a claim against the company on the basis that she was being subjected to sex discrimination. The company contended that her claim could not succeed because the 1975 Act did not apply to acts or omissions after leaving employment.

The case was referred to the European Court of Justice which gave a ruling that the Equal Treatment Directive did cover discrimination which was post-employment. The case then came back to the EAT to resolve the issue.

The 1975 Act covers discrimination in recruitment and during employment but has no specific section dealing with post-employment discrimination. Section 6(2)(b), however, applies if the woman is subjected to 'any other detriment'.

The EAT ruled that the 1975 Act should be interpreted so as to be consistent with the equal treatment directive and s 6(2)(b) could be regarded as applying to a post-employment situation. 'Detriment' could cover any adverse treatment including failure to give a reference, and in any case the decision not to give her a reference was made in this case before she left employment. She was therefore doubly covered.

Comment. Although there is in general terms no obligation to give a reference, sex discrimination claims can now be brought by ex-employees in terms of the refusal to give a reference or of its contents if an astute ex-employee alleges that this constitutes a gender or marital detriment.

Non-contractual duties of the employer

Before leaving the contractual duties of the employer, it should be noted that he has other duties in regard to the health, safety and welfare of his employees. These are based mainly on the common law of tort and statutes such as the Health and Safety at Work Act 1974. These duties will be considered later.

It is, however, appropriate at this point to deal with legislation concerning the monitoring of workplace communications.

Employee surveillance

The Telecommunications (Lawful Business Practice) (Interception of Communications) Regulations 2000 came into force in October 2000. They provide employers with lawful no-consent access to their employees' use of e-mail and other communications in order to establish whether the use is related to business. In addition, the employer is enabled to record all communications without obtaining the consent of the employee for the following purposes: (1) to establish the existence of facts relevant to the business as by keeping records of transactions and other communications in situations where it is desirable to know the specific facts of the conversation; (2) to ascertain compliance with regulatory or self-regulatory practices or procedures applying to the business; (3) to demonstrate or ascertain standards that are or ought to be achieved by persons using the telecoms system, such as monitoring for quality control and/or staff training; (4) to prevent or detect crime; (5) to investigate and detect unauthorised use of the employer's telecoms systems; (6) to ensure the effective operation of the system as by monitoring for viruses or other matters that threaten the system.

Monitoring, but not recording, may also take place without consent in the following situations: (a) to determine whether or not the communications are relevant to the business as by checking e-mail accounts to access business communications in staff absence; and (b) in regard to communications that are to a confidential, anonymous counselling or support helpline.

Businesses that wish to rely on the above exceptions are required to make all reasonable efforts to tell those who use their telecoms system that their communications might be intercepted. This applies only to the employer's own staff.

Note. The regulations are a significant relaxation of the prohibitions contained in the Regulation of Investigatory Powers Act 2000 and are made under a provision in the Act that allows the Secretary of State to sidestep the general requirement of consent in the case of conduct where it is felt legitimate to dispense with consent. However, the situation is not without confusion. The Data Protection Commissioner has issued a draft Code of Practice on the Use of Personal Data in Employer/Employee Relationships that places greater restrictions on an employer's freedom to monitor. However, the code was drawn up before the regulations were made and it is understood to be the intention of the Data Protection Commissioner to take the regulations into account in the final draft. However, the TUC has threatened to challenge the regulations as being in breach of the right to privacy enshrined in the European Convention on Human Rights, as implemented by the Human Rights Act 1998. Until the position is clarified, employers should consider a clearly defined policy covering telecoms privacy and then make sure that all employees know of it and the sanctions or penalties for breaching it, making it clear that non-consensual monitoring is for legitimate business reasons and that the monitoring is in proportion to that end.

Duties of an employee

To use reasonable skill and care in the work

The **common law** provides that an employee who claims to have a particular skill or skills but shows himself to be incompetent may be dismissed without notice. His employer can also raise the matter of the incompetence of the employee if the employer is sued under **statute law**, i.e. the ERA for unfair dismissal.

The common law also requires unskilled employees to take reasonable care in carrying out the job. However, they may be dismissed only if there is a serious breach of this implied term of the contract.

To carry out lawful and reasonable instructions

The law implies a term into a contract of employment which requires the employee to obey the lawful and reasonable instructions of his employer. However, an employee is not bound to carry out illegal acts. In *Gregory* v *Ford* (1951) one of the decisions of the court was that an employee could not be required to drive a vehicle which was not insured so as to satisfy the law set out in what is now the Road Traffic Act 1988. If the employee does refuse, he is not in breach of his contract.

The duty to give faithful service (or the duty of fidelity)

This is an implied term of a contract of employment. Certain activities of employees are regarded by the law as breaches of the duty to give faithful service. Thus, as we have seen, an employee who while employed copies the names and addresses of his employer's customers for use after leaving the employment can be prevented from using the information (*Robb* v *Green* (1895)).

However, the implied term relating to fidelity does not apply once the contract of employment has come to an end. Therefore, a former employee cannot be prevented under this implied term from encouraging customers of his former employer to do business with him, though he can be prevented from using actual lists of customers which he made while still employed. If an employer (A) wants to stop an employee (B) from trying to win over his, A's, **customers**, then the contract of employment between A and B must contain an **express** clause in restraint of trade preventing this. Such a clause must, as we have seen, be reasonable in time and area (see also Chapter 7).

A former employee can, however, be prevented by the court from using his former employer's **trade secrets** or **confidential information** without a clause in the contract about restraint of trade.

However, as we have seen, the ruling of the Court of Appeal in *Pocton Industries Ltd* v *Michael Ikem Horton* (2000) stresses the importance to employers of putting **express terms** into their contracts of employment to control the use and disclosure of confidential information after the employment contract ends. The courts seem to prefer the contractual approach to the rather vague concept of the implied term. The contract can give more specific guidance to the court as to what is to be protected.

Confidential information

It is an implied term of a contract of service that the employee must not disclose **trade secrets**, e.g. a special way of making glass as in *Forster & Sons Ltd* v *Suggett* (1918), or **confidential information** acquired during employment. There is strictly no need for an express clause in the contract.

However, the use by an employee of knowledge of trade secrets and information cannot be prevented if it is just part of the total job experience. An employee cannot be prevented from using what he could not help but learn from doing the job.

Printers & Finishers v *Holloway (No 2)* (1964)

The claimants brought an action against Holloway, their former works manager, and others, including Vita-tex Ltd, into whose employment Holloway had subsequently entered. They claimed an injunction against Holloway and the other defendants, based, as regards Holloway, on an alleged breach of an implied term in his contract of service with the claimants that he should not disclose or make improper use of confidential information relating to the claimants' trade secrets. Holloway's contract did not contain an express covenant relating to non-disclosure of trade secrets.

The claimants were flock printers and had built up their own fund of 'know-how' in this field. The action against Vita-tex arose because Holloway had, on one occasion, taken a Mr James, who was an employee of Vita-tex Ltd, round the claimants' factory. Mr James' visit took place in the evening and followed a chance meeting between himself and Holloway. However, the plant was working and James did see a number of processes. It also appeared that Holloway had, during his employment, made copies of certain of the claimants' documentary material and had taken these copies away with him when he left their employment. The claimants wanted an injunction to prevent the use or disclosure of the material contained in the copies of documents made by Holloway.

The court held that the claimants were entitled to an injunction against Holloway so far as the documentary material was concerned, although there was no express term in his contract regarding non-disclosure of secrets.

However, the court would not grant an injunction restraining Holloway from putting at the disposal of Vita-tex Ltd his memory of particular features of the claimants' plant and processes. He was under no express contract not to do so and the court would not extend its jurisdiction to restrain breaches of confidence in this instance. Holloway's knowledge of the claimants' trade secrets was not readily separable from his general knowledge of flock printing.

An injunction was granted restraining Vita-tex Ltd from making use of the information acquired by Mr James on his visit.

It is worth noting that the above principles may not be applied where there is an *express* restraint of trade in the contract. In *SBJ Stevenson Ltd* v *Mandy* (1999) the High Court stated that whether information is confidential should be assessed by its *nature* and not by the way in which it has been *acquired*. It was unacceptable, said the court, that an employee who has entered into a restrictive covenant as to confidentiality and soliciting of customers should be allowed to use information learned as part of doing the job even if at the time he acquired it he had no intention to misuse it.

The High Court's approach appears to be right. If not, nearly all express confidentiality restraints would be unenforceable. The High Court in *Mandy* was dealing with the insurance broking industry, which is highly competitive.

Before leaving the topic of confidentiality, three further points should be noted.

(a) *Setting up a competing business.* If an employee leaves without giving the employer proper notice in order to set up a competing business or work for a competitor, the employer may be able to get an injunction to prevent the employee from acting in this way. The action is most useful where the employee has a contract requiring a long period of notice. Suppose that a senior manager in a business is employed under a contract which requires 12 months' notice and that the manager deals with the affairs of two important clients or customers. He or she resigns giving only one month's notice in order to set up in business and take the work of the two major clients or customers. There are no post-employment restraints of trade in the contract. In these circumstances it may be possible for the employer to get an injunction to prevent the setting up of the new business for 12 months. This principle was established in *Evening Standard Co Ltd* v *Henderson* (1987), though it is, of course, a relevant consideration in the employer's favour if he is prepared to pay the employee during the notice period even though he does not return to work.

The principle is sometimes referred to as 'garden leave' since the employee cannot go back to work and cannot work for another employer so he may prefer to tend his garden to pass the time!

It is necessary now to consider the 'garden leave' cases in the light of the Court of Appeal decision in *William Hill Organisation* v *Tucker* (1998) where the ruling was that if the court considered that the employee should be allowed to work out his notice even though he was not in the traditional categories, e.g. commission workers, then an injunction would not be granted unless there was an express term in the contract allowing the employer to pay but specifically to refuse to allow the employee to work.

(b) *Confidentiality in reverse.* It is also of interest to note that while it is normal for employers to bring claims against employees to prevent them from using confidential information obtained in the employment, confidentiality works both ways. Thus, in *Dalgleish* v *Lothian and Borders Police Board* (1991) the Lothian Council asked the Board for details of the names and addresses of its employees so that the Council could identify community charge defaulters. The court granted the employees an injunction to prevent this. The information was confidential between employer and employee. As more and more people become concerned about data protection, this case shines a welcome light on the employee's right of privacy and the employer's duty not to infringe it by wrongful disclosure.

(c) *Whistleblowing.* When discussing an employee's duty of confidentiality, mention should be made of the provisions of the Public Interest Disclosure Act 1998. The Act protects workers from being dismissed or penalised for disclosing information about the organisation in which they work that they reasonably believe exposes financial malpractice, miscarriages of justice, dangers to health and safety, and dangers to the environment. Disclosure may be made to an employer, but where the disclosure relates to the employer or there is danger of victimisation, it may be made, for example, to a regulator such as the Financial Services Authority for City frauds. Whistleblowers who are dismissed or otherwise victimised may complain to an employment tribunal.

A number of successful claims under the Public Interest Disclosure Act 1998 have been made (see e.g. *Fernandes* v *Netcom Consultants (UK) Ltd* (2000). Mr Fernandes, the claimant, is an accountant and was employed by Netcom Consultants, a telecoms consultancy, as finance officer. Netcom is a subsidiary of the US XSource Corporation. As part of his job, Mr Fernandes checked expenses claims, including those of his boss Steven Woodhouse. It appeared that Mr Woodhouse failed to provide receipts to back up his claims and Mr Fernandes reported this matter to the US parent company. Despite making requests for supporting documents, Mr Woodhouse 'fobbed him off' with explanations but did not produce receipts. Mr Fernandes sent a fax to an official of the US company making clear his concerns but was instructed to destroy his copy of the fax and told, 'You must look after your butt.' Later Mr Woodhouse's expenses rose steeply but were still not backed by receipts. The company's cash flow was causing concern and Mr Fernandes complained by letter to the US parent company. He was later sacked from his £70,000-a-year post after being told by XSource that he had lost the respect of the US parent for not acting sooner! Mr Woodhouse remained in employment, but after investigation was asked to resign. Mr Fernandes complained to an employment tribunal in Reading and was found to be protected by the 1998 Act and, therefore, automatically unfairly dismissed. The tribunal said that the US company had made a clear attempt to intimidate and pressurise Mr Fernandes to resign to keep the matter quiet. Mr Fernandes' award was £290,000.

Even in the absence of legislation, it may still be a breach of contract for an employer to dismiss an employee for making or attempting to make disclosures of fraud. An employment tribunal has made an award of damages for breach of contract to a salesman who attempted to alert his employer to an alleged fraud in the organisation. He reported the matter to his managing director and was dismissed. He could not claim unfair dismissal because he did not have the required service, but was awarded damages for breach of contract (see *Financial Times*, 10 September 1997, *re Richard Jordan* (Birmingham Employment Tribunal)).

The employment contract and shop workers

The Sunday Trading Act 1994, which came into force on 26 August 1994, repealed previous restrictions on Sunday trading. Recognising the impact of this on shop workers, Sch 4 to the Act provided them with new and important rights. These rights, which are now contained in the ERA (Part IV), are:

- not to be dismissed or made redundant for refusing to work on Sunday; and
- not to suffer a detriment for the same reason.

These rights extend to all shop workers in England and Wales if they are asked to do shop work on a Sunday. They are not available to Sunday-only workers.

The ERA defines a shop worker as an employee who is required or may be required by contract to work in or about a shop on a day when the shop is open to serve customers.

However, the worker need not actually serve customers and the provisions extend beyond sales assistants and check-out operators to clerical workers doing work related to the shop, managers and supervisors, cleaners, storepersons, shelf fillers, lift attendants and security staff. Even those employed by outside contractors (but not self-employed) could be covered as also could van drivers based at the store who deliver goods to customers.

A shop is defined as including any premises where any retail trade or business is carried on. This does not include the sale of meals, refreshments, or intoxicating liquor for consumption on the premises, e.g. public houses, cafés and restaurants, nor places preparing meals or refreshments to order for immediate consumption off the premises, e.g. take-aways.

The ERA defines two categories of shop workers:

- Protected shop workers, i.e. those employed as such when the Act came into force, and those taking up employment afterwards whose contracts do not require Sunday working.
- Opted-out shop workers, i.e. those who are employed after commencement of the Act under contracts which require them to work on Sundays but who opt out of this by giving three months' notice to the employer (see below).

Protected workers will have the rights immediately regardless as to whether they have previously agreed to a contract requiring them to work on a Sunday. No procedures are involved. They can simply decide they no longer wish to work on Sundays.

Protected workers are able to give up their right to refuse to work on Sundays but only if:

- the employer is given a written 'opting-in notice' which must be signed and dated and state expressly that they do not object to Sunday working or actually wish to work Sundays; and
- they then enter into an express agreement with the employer to work Sundays or on a particular Sunday.

Opted-out workers, i.e. those engaged after commencement of the Act or who have opted in to Sunday working, have the right to opt out. To do this they must give the employer a signed and dated written notice stating that they object to Sunday work. They then have to serve a three-month notice period. During this time they are still obliged to do Sunday work and if they refuse will lose statutory protection under the Schedule. However, they cannot be dismissed or made to suffer some other detriment merely because they have given an opting-out notice. After the period of three months has expired, the worker has a right not to do Sunday work.

The ERA provides that dismissal or redundancy of protected and opted-out workers will be regarded as unfair dismissal if the reason or principal reason was that the worker(s) concerned have refused or proposed to refuse to work on Sundays.

The ERA also gives protected and opted-out workers the right not to be subjected to any other detriment, e.g. non-payment of seniority bonuses, for refusing to work on a Sunday. Under the ERA the rights set out above apply regardless of age, length of service or hours of work.

Employer's explanatory statement

The ERA provides that employers are required to give every shop worker who enters into a contractual agreement to work on Sundays after the new Act comes into force a written explanatory statement setting out their right to opt out. If an employer does not issue such a statement within two months of the worker entering into such a contractual agreement, the opt-out period is reduced from three months to one.

The ERA gives a prescribed form of statement to be given to employees (see Fig 16.2).

Other important provisions of the ERA are as follows:

STATUTORY RIGHTS IN RELATION TO SUNDAY SHOP WORK

You have become employed as a shop worker and are or can be required under your contract of employment to do the Sunday work your contract provides for.

However, if you wish, you can give a notice, as described in the next paragraph, to your employer and you will then have the right not to work in or about a shop which is open once three months have passed from the date on which you gave the notice.

Your notice must –

      be in writing;
      be signed and dated by you;
      say that you object to Sunday working.

For three months after you give the notice, your employer can still require you to do all the Sunday work your contract provides for. After the three-month period has ended, you have the right to complain to an employment tribunal if, because of your refusal to work on Sundays on which the shop is open, your employer –

      dismisses you, or
      does something else detrimental to you, for example failing to promote you.

Once you have the rights described, you can surrender them only by giving your employer a further notice, signed and dated by you, saying that you wish to work on a Sunday or that you do not object to Sunday working and then agreeing with your employer to work on Sundays or on a particular Sunday.

Fig 16.2 Prescribed form of statement re Sunday shop work

- provisions under which an employer is not obliged to compensate the employee for loss of Sunday work, either in terms of extra hours or remuneration;
- provisions ensuring that an agreement between a shop worker and his or her employer cannot generally exclude the provisions of the ERA;
- provisions under which the dismissal of an employee for asserting a statutory right contained in the ERA is to be regarded as being automatically unfair.

The Deregulation and Contracting Out Act 1994 amended the Betting, Gaming and Lotteries Act 1963 to allow betting offices and bookmaking establishments to do business on Sundays. Workers are protected against unfair dismissal or victimisation if they object to working on Sunday. The provisions are largely the same as those set out above and are also contained in the ERA. They apply to workers regardless of age, hours of work or length of service.

Vicarious liability

Because of this principle of the law an employer is liable for damage caused to another person by his employee, **while the employee was carrying out his work** (or while he was in the course of employment, as it is called). The principle applies whether the injury was to an outsider or to a fellow employee (see further below). The employer is liable even though he was not in any way at fault and this rule, which seems at first sight to be unfair to the employer, is based upon **law** and **policy**.

So far as the law is concerned, employer and employee are regarded as **associated parties** in the business in which both are engaged. If the amount of work increases so that the owner of a business cannot do it all with his own hands, he must employ other hands and is in law responsible for the damage done by those hands as he would be for damage done by his own.

The point of policy is to provide the injured person with a defendant who is likely to be able to pay any damages which the court may award. An employer and the business generally profit from the employee's work and it is perhaps not entirely unreasonable that the employer should compen-sate those who are injured by the employee. The employer will normally insure against the risk of liability and of course the cost of that insurance is represented in the price at which the goods or services of the business are sold. Thus, in the end, the injured person is compensated by those members of the public who buy the goods or services.

It is worth noting here that under the Employers' Liability (Compulsory Insurance) Act 1969 an employer **must insure** himself against liability for bodily injury or disease sustained by employees and arising out of and in the course of their employment in Great Britain and so in effect in respect of injuries caused by his employees to fellow employees, but insurance is **not compulsory** (though highly advisable) in respect of injuries to outsiders.

Finally, it should be noted that the employee who actually caused the injury is always liable personally along with the employer, but of course the prime defendant is the employer because he has either insurance or other funds which the employee probably does not have.

The course of employment

Whether an employee was or was not acting in the course of employment when he brought about the injury for which the person injured wants to make the employer liable is a matter for the court to decide in each case. The decision is sometimes a difficult one to make and we may all from time to time disagree with a decision made by a judge in a particular case.

However, the following analysis of the cases gives some idea of the way in which the courts have dealt with this most important aspect of employers' liability.

1 **Acts outside of the contractual duties.** If the employee is engaged on a private matter personal to him, the employer will not be liable for injuries caused by the employee during this time.

Britt v *Galmoye & Nevill* (1928)
Nevill was employed by Galmoye as a van driver. Nevill wanted to take a friend to the theatre after he had finished work and Galmoye lent Nevill his private motor car for this purpose. Nevill, by negligence, injured Britt and Britt's action against Galmoye was based upon vicarious liability so that it was necessary to deal with the matter in course

of employment. The court decided that as the journey was not on Galmoye's business and Galmoye was not in control, he was not liable for Nevill's act.

Comment. (i) Britt's case is a rather obvious example of an act outside of the contract of service. However, sometimes the court is called upon to make a more difficult decision. In particular it should be noted that an employee does not make his employer liable by doing some act which is of benefit to the employer during the course of what is basically an outside activity. For example, in *Rayner* v *Mitchell* (1877) a van man employed by a brewer took, without permission, a van from his employer's stables in order to deliver a child's coffin at the home of a relative. While he was returning the van to the stables he picked up some empty beer barrels and was afterwards involved in an accident which injured Rayner. Rayner sued the van man's employer and it was held that the employer was not liable. The journey itself was unauthorised and was not converted into an authorised journey merely because the employee performed some small act for the benefit of his employer during the course of it.

(ii) In *Trotman* v *North Yorkshire CC* (1998) the Court of Appeal held that acts of sexual misconduct by a deputy headmaster on male pupils while on a school trip abroad was a personal act and an independant course of conduct that was outside the scope of his employment.

2 Unauthorised ways of performing the contractual duties. The employer may be liable in spite of the fact that the employee was acting improperly if the act was, even so, part of his contractual duties.

Century Insurance Co v Northern Ireland Road Transport Board (1942)

The driver of a petrol tanker was engaged in transferring petrol to an underground tank when he lit a cigarette and threw the match to the floor. This caused a fire and an explosion which did great damage, and the question of the liability of the Board, his employer, for that damage arose. The court decided that the employer was liable for the driver's negligence. His negligence was not independent of the contract of service but was a negligent way of discharging his actual duties under that contract of service.

3 Acts which the employer has forbidden the employee to do. Just because an employer has told his employee not to do a particular act does not always excuse the employer from vicarious liability if the employee causes damage when doing the forbidden act. There are two sorts of cases, as follows:

(a) *Where the act itself is forbidden.*

Rand (Joseph) Ltd v Craig (1919)

The defendants' employees were taking rubbish from a site and depositing it on the defendants' dump. They were working on a bonus scheme related to the number of loads per day which they dumped. The defendants had strictly forbidden their employees to tip the rubbish elsewhere than on the authorised dump. However, some of the employees deposited their loads on the claimants' property which was nearer. The defendants were sued on the basis that they were vicariously liable in trespass, the claimants arguing that the employees had general authority to cart and tip rubbish. The court decided that the defendants were not liable. The employees were employed to cart the rubbish from one definite place to another definite place. Shooting the rubbish on to the claimants' premises was a totally wrongful act not directly arising out of the duties that they were employed to perform.

Comment. A contrast is provided by *Rose* v *Plenty* (1976). Leslie Rose, aged 13, liked helping Mr Plenty, a milkman, to deliver the milk. Cooperative Retail Services Ltd, who employed Mr Plenty, expressly forbade their milkmen to take boys on their floats or to get boys to help them deliver the milk. On one occasion, while helping Mr Plenty, Leslie was sitting in the front of the float when his leg caught under the wheel. The accident was caused partly by Mr Plenty's negligence. The court decided that Mr Plenty had been acting in the course of his employment so that his employers were liable to compensate Leslie Rose for his injuries. There is really quite a difference in the facts of this case and those in *Rand*. Leslie Rose's presence on the milk float was connected with the delivery of the milk which was a reason connected with the employment and this seems to be why the court decided as it did.

(b) *Where the employer's instruction relates only to the way in which the contractual duty is to be done.* Obviously, perhaps, an employer cannot avoid liability by saying to his employees: 'Do your job in such a way as not to injure anyone.'

Limpus v London General Omnibus Co (1862)

The claimant's bus was overturned when the driver of the defendants' bus drove across it so as to be first at a bus stop to take all the passengers who were waiting. The defendants' driver admitted that the act was intentional and arose out of bad feeling between the two drivers. The defendants had issued strict instructions to their drivers that they were not to obstruct other omnibuses. The court decided that the defendants were liable. Their driver was acting within the scope of his employment at the time of the collision, and it did not matter that the defendants had expressly forbidden him to act as he did.

4 Employee's fraudulent acts. At first the courts would not make an employer liable for the fraudulent acts of his employee. Gradually, however, they began to accept that the employer could be liable, first in cases where the employee's fraud was committed for the employer's benefit, and later even in cases where the fraud was carried out by the employee entirely for his own ends, as the following case shows.

Lloyd v Grace, Smith & Co (1912)

Smith was a Liverpool solicitor and Lloyd was a widow who owned two properties at Ellesmere Port and had also lent money on mortgage. She was not satisfied with the income from these investments and she went to see Smith's managing clerk, Sandles, for advice. He told her to sell the properties and call in the mortgages, and reinvest the proceeds. At his request she signed two deeds which, unknown to her, transferred the properties and the mortgage to him. Sandles then mortgaged the properties and transferred the other mortgages for money and paid a private debt with the proceeds. The court decided that the firm of solicitors was vicariously liable for Sandles' fraudulent acts. An employer could be vicariously liable for a tort committed by an employee entirely for his own ends.

Comment. (i) This decision seems to contain at least some public policy and to be based on the principle that since someone must be the loser by reason of the fraud of the employee, it is more reasonable that the employer who engages and puts trust and confidence in the fraudulent employee should be the loser rather than an outsider.
(ii) Where the basis of a particular decision is public policy then circumstances can alter cases. When, as distinct from a 'consumer' situation as seen in the above case, the scenario is business the court may reach the conclusion that the act is within the course of employment but the fraud is not so that the employer is not liable for it. This was the attitude taken by the Court of Appeal in *Generale Bank Nederland NV v Export Credits Guarantee Department* (1997) where an employee of the Department had assisted in a fraudulent operation to obtain export guarantees which caused loss to the bank. The Department was not liable.

5 Employee's criminal acts. An employer may even be vicariously liable for a criminal act by his employee. The criminal act may be regarded as in the course of employment so that the employer will be liable at civil law for any loss or damage caused by the employee's criminal act.

Morris v C W Martin & Sons Ltd (1965)

The claimant sent a mink stole to a furrier for the purpose of cleaning. With the claimant's consent the furrier gave it to the defendants to clean. While it was in the possession of the defendants the fur was stolen by a person called Morrisey, who had been employed by the defendants for a few weeks only, though they had no grounds to suspect that he was dishonest. The claimant sued the defendants for damages for the tort of conversion. The county court judge held that the act of Morrisey, who had removed the stole by wrapping it around his body, was beyond the scope of his employment.

The Court of Appeal, however, decided that the defendants were liable to the claimant because Morrisey had been entrusted with the stole in the course of his employment.

Comment. (i) The above rule applies only in circumstances where the employee is entrusted with, or put in charge of, the goods by his employer.

The mere fact that the employee's employment gives him the opportunity to steal goods is not enough. Thus, in *Leesh River Tea Co v British India Steam Navigation Co* (1966) a person employed to unload tea from a ship stole a brass cover plate from the hold of the ship while he was unloading the tea and the court decided that he was not acting in the course of his employment on the grounds that his job had nothing to do with the cover plate.

Perhaps if the plate had been stolen by someone who was sent to clean it, then that person would have been acting within the course of employment and his employer might well have been liable.

(ii) The fraudulent or criminal act must be committed as part of the employment, that is as an act within the scope of employment. In *Heasmans v Clarity Cleaning* (1987) the Court of Appeal decided that the defendants were not liable when their employee, who was sent to the claimant's premises to clean phones, made unauthorised calls on them to the value of £1,400. He was employed to *clean* phones not to *use* them.

6 Corporations and the *ultra vires* rule. Where the employer is a corporation there are further difficulties as regards the corporation's vicarious liability, because the act which the employee does when he causes injury may be beyond the corporation's powers, or *ultra vires*, i.e. beyond the scope of what its constitution says it can do, though little if anything would be beyond the scope of a company which had adopted the 'one line objects clause' approach as a general commercial company (see further Chapter 6). This constitution may, as

we have seen, be a statute or a charter, as with a professional body, such as the Institute of Chartered Secretaries and Administrators, or the objects clause of the memorandum in the case of a registered company. It is necessary, therefore, to distinguish between those acts of employees which are within the company's powers (*intra vires*) and outside its powers (*ultra vires*).

(a) *Intra vires activities.* If an employee of a corporation injures someone by negligence while acting in the course of his employment in an *intra vires* activity, then the corporation is liable. Although it has been said that any wrongful act committed on behalf of a corporation must be *ultra vires* since the corporation has no authority in its constitution to commit wrongful acts, this view has not been accepted by the courts. Therefore, a corporation can have liability in law without capacity in law.

A corporation is liable, therefore, under the rule of vicarious liability, for injuries caused by its employees on *intra vires* activities. Thus, a bus company which is, obviously, authorised by its memorandum to run buses, will be liable if an employee injures a pedestrian while driving a bus along its routes.

(b) *Ultra vires activities.* A corporation will not be liable if one of its employees gets involved in an act which is *ultra vires* the corporation unless he has **express authority** from management to do the act.

Poulton v London & South Western Railway Co (1867)
The claimant was arrested by a station master for non-payment of carriage in respect of his horse. The defendants, who were the employers of the station master, had power to detain passengers for non-payment of their own fare, but for no other reason. The court decided that since there was no express authorisation of the arrest by the defendants, the station master was acting outside the scope of his employment and the defendants were not liable for the wrongful arrest.

Comment. (i) A contrast is provided by *Campbell* v *Paddington Borough Council* (1911). The members of the Council had passed a resolution authorising the erection of a stand in Burwood Place, London in order that members of the Council could view the funeral procession of King Edward VII passing along the Edgware Road. The claimant, who had premises in Burwood Place, often let

them so that people could view public processions passing along the Edgware Road. The Council's stand obstructed the view of the funeral procession from the claimant's house and she could not let the premises for that purpose. The court decided that the Council was liable. The fact that the erection of the stand was probably *ultra vires*, since there was no specific power in the Council's charter to put one up, did not matter. There had been authorisation by the Council resolution.

(ii) So far as **registered companies** are concerned, the Companies Act 1989 has made amendments to the Companies Act 1985 under which a company may alter its objects by special resolution, or be registered with objects, which state merely that it is to carry on business as a general commercial company so that it may carry on any trade or business whatsoever. The company also has power to do all such things as are incidental or conducive to that end without listing those powers.

Such a company will have effectively opted out of the *ultra vires* rule so that its employees are likely always to be engaged on *intra vires* activities so long as they are within the scope of their employment. The company will of course continue to escape liability where the employee is doing something he is not employed to do, as in *Heasmans* v *Clarity Cleaning* (1987) (above).

The old principles of *ultra vires* will continue to apply to charter and statutory companies.

Employer's defences

There are three main defences which an employer may have if he is sued under the rule of vicarious liability. These are set out below:

1   An exclusion clause in a contract or notice. Because of the Unfair Contract Terms Act 1977, an employer, like other people, cannot exclude or reduce his liability for **death or bodily injury** caused by his own negligence or that of his employees. As regards other types of damage, such as damage to property, an exemption clause in a contract or a notice will apply to exclude or reduce the liability, but only if the court thinks that it is **reasonable** that this should happen.

Thus, in the case of a dry-cleaning contract, if by the negligence of employees cleaning material is not properly removed so that the owner of the clothing contracts a skin disease, to which he is not especially susceptible, no exclusion clause in the contract for cleaning or in a notice in the shop can remove or restrict the employer's liability for this bodily harm.

However, if the clothing is, by reason of an employee's negligence, merely damaged and there is no resulting physical injury, then an exclusion clause or notice might operate to remove or restrict the liability of the employer if the judge thought it was reasonable for it to do so in the circumstances.

Although the Act gives no criteria for what is reasonable and it is a matter to be decided by the judge in each case, it would be generally true to say that the device of an exclusion clause in a contract or notice has lost a lot of its force as an employer's defence. (See further Chapter 9.)

As regards the position of the employee where the employer has taken an exemption clause in the contract, e.g. for damage to the other party's property while in the course of transit, then although such a clause may be effective to exempt the employer, it has not protected the employee who is not in privity of contract with the third party. Reference should now be made to the Contracts (Rights of Third Parties) Act 1999 under which the parties to the contract, i.e. the employer and the third party, may if they wish extend the exemption clause to the employee or the court may infer that this has been done unless the original parties have expressly excluded third party (i.e. the employee's) rights.

2 Voluntary assumption of risk. This defence is also referred to as *volenti non fit injuria* (to one who is willing no harm is done). This defence is most often tried in employment cases when employees sue their employers for injuries received at work. We will have a look at these cases later in this chapter. However, the defence is available to an employer when an outsider sues him on the basis of vicarious liability for injury caused by his employees.

Cutler v *United Dairies (London) Ltd* (1923)

The defendants' employee left the defendants' horse and van, two wheels only being properly chained, while he delivered milk. The horse, being startled by the noise coming from a river steamer, bolted down the road and into a meadow. It stopped in the meadow and was followed there by the employee who, being in an excited state, began to shout for help. The claimant, who had seen all of this, went to the employee's assistance and tried to hold the horse's head. The horse lunged and the claimant was injured. The claimant sued the defendants alleging negligence because apparently the horse was given to bolting and should not have been used on a milk round at all.

The court decided that in the circumstances the claimant voluntarily and freely assumed the risk. This was not an attempt to stop a runaway horse so that there was no sense of urgency to require the claimant to act as he did. He therefore knew of the risk and had had time to consider it and by implication must have agreed to incur it.

Comment. A different situation arises in what are known as the **rescue cases**. In these the claimant is injured while trying to save life or property which has been put in danger by the defendant's negligence. If the intervention is a reasonable thing to do for the saving of life or property, then this does not constitute an assumption of risk, nor does the defence of contributory negligence (see below) apply. Cutler, of course, was not effecting a rescue.

3 Contributory negligence. Sometimes when an injury occurs the person injured and the person causing the injury have both been negligent. In such a situation liability can be divided between the person injured and the person causing the injury.

The person injured can still claim damages but under the Law Reform (Contributory Negligence) Act 1945 they will be reduced according to how much the court thinks he was to blame. Thus, if the court thinks that A who has been injured by B's negligence is entitled to £1,000 but is 60 per cent to blame for the injury, it will deduct £600 from A's damages so that he will get only £400.

Again, this defence is most often used where an employee is suing his employer for injuries received at work and the employer claims that the employee was partly to blame and his damages should be reduced. This situation has yet to be looked at. However, an employer, A, who was sued as vicariously liable for injuries caused by employee B to a person who was not an employee, C, could, in the right circumstances, claim that the damages given to C should be reduced because of C's contributory negligence.

Employer's liability for injuries to his employees

In addition to the duties of an employer under the contract of service with which we have been dealing so far, an employee who is injured at work by a negligent act will want to sue his employer for damages. Under the Employers' Liability (Compulsory Insurance) Act 1969 an employer **must** insure himself in respect of liability for injuries caused to his employee where these arise from a negligent act.

These employee claims are brought on the basis of negligence by the employer and, because of the decision of the House of Lords in *Wilsons and Clyde Coal Co v English* (1938), the employer's duties towards his employees, i.e. the duty to take care which he owes them, can be set out under the headings which appear below.

Safe plant, appliances and premises

An employer has a duty to provide and maintain suitable plant, appliances, and premises.

Lovell v Blundells and Crompton & Co Ltd (1944)

Lovell was told by the defendants, who were his employers, to carry out an overhaul of a ship's boiler tubes. He could not reach some of the tubes so he got some planks for himself and from them he made up his own staging. The planks were unsound and collapsed, injuring Lovell. The defendants had not provided any form of staging, nor had they laid down any system of working.

The court decided that the employers were liable in negligence. They had failed to supply plant in a situation where there was an obvious requirement for it.

Comment. Having supplied plant, an employer will be liable if the employee is injured by it by reason of the employer's failure to inspect and maintain it and remedy defects. Thus, in *Baker v James Bros and Sons Ltd* (1921) Baker, who was a commercial traveller employed by the defendant, had to travel in a particular district taking orders and for this purpose the defendant supplied him with a car. The starting gear was defective and Baker complained to the defendants several times about this but nothing was done. On one occasion when Baker was out taking orders he was badly injured while trying to start the car with the starting handle. The court decided that Baker was entitled to damages. His employers had failed to maintain the car as they should. In the circumstances Baker could not be regarded as having consented to run the risk of injury, nor could he be regarded as guilty of contributory negligence.

The Employer's Liability (Defective Equipment) Act 1969 puts liability on an employer who provides defective equipment to an employee which causes that employee injury. The employer's liability is strict, which means that he is liable even though he was not himself negligent, as where the injury was caused by the negligence of the organisation which made the equipment. However, this does not affect the employer's right to claim that the injury was caused by the contributory negligence of the employee. Where the defect in the equipment is the fault of the manufacturer, the employer, having been sued for damages by the employee, can himself sue the manufacturer to recover from him any damages awarded to the employee. The employee can also sue the manufacturer direct if he chooses to do so.

Safe system of work

An employer is required to set up a safe way of working. It is also the duty of an employer to enforce the safe system having once set it up. Thus, where an employee may suffer damage to his eyes by flying sparks, as in welding, the employer must provide goggles or a face guard and introduce a system of supervision to ensure, as far as he can, that the protective equipment is being used by the relevant work force.

Sometimes the duty on the employer is a high one. For example, it was held in *Crouch v British Rail Engineering* (1988) that where the work which an employee does puts him **regularly** at risk of damage to the eyes then it is not enough to provide goggles from a central store at the workplace. Goggles must be given to the employee and form part of his tool kit which he carries with him. He should not be required to go and fetch goggles from the store each time the job he is doing requires him to protect his eyes by using goggles. His employer was held liable for damages because the employee, a maintenance engineer, was not given goggles 'into his hand'. His damages were not reduced because according to the court there was no contributory negligence (see below).

Employer's defences

1 Contributory negligence. Contributory negligence is available as a defence to an employer in a claim brought against him by an employee who says he has been injured because of his employer's negligence.

Cakebread v Hopping Brothers (Whetstone) Ltd (1947)

The employers of the claimant, who was engaged in a woodworking factory, had failed to see that the guard on a circular saw was properly adjusted and the claimant, who worked the saw, was injured as a result. However, it appeared that the claimant did not like working the machine with the guard properly adjusted and he had arranged with the foreman that the saw should be operated with an improperly adjusted guard. The court decided that the employer was in breach of his duty of care, but also that the claimant had failed to exercise the care of a prudent employee for his own safety and reduced his damages by 50 per cent.

2 Assumption of risk by the employee. This is unlikely to provide the employer with a successful defence these days since it is now the law that just because an employee **knows** of the risk he cannot for that reason be regarded as having **consented** to it.

Smith v Baker & Sons (1891)

Smith was employed by Baker & Sons to drill holes in some rock in a railway cutting. A crane, operated by fellow employees, often swung heavy stones over Smith's head while he was working on the rock face. Both Smith and his employers realised that there was a risk that the stones might fall, but the crane was nevertheless operated without any warning being given at the moment that it began to swing the stones over Smith's head. Smith was injured by a stone which fell from the crane because of the negligent strapping of the load.

The court decided that Smith had not voluntarily undertaken the risk of his employers' negligence and that his knowledge of the danger did not prevent him recovering damages.

Fatal accidents

If, as a result of the employer's negligence, an employee is killed in the course of his employment the personal representatives of the deceased have a claim on behalf of the estate under the Law Reform (Miscellaneous Provisions) Act 1934. In addition, under the Fatal Accidents Act 1976 certain dependant relatives, e.g. husband or wife and children, are entitled to claim in a personal capacity if they were dependent on the deceased for their living expenses.

HEALTH AND SAFETY AT WORK

Health and safety regulations

The general principles of health and safety and enforcement procedures are contained in the Health and Safety at Work Act 1974. However, the central core of provisions relating to health and safety at work are now to be found in six new sets of regulations which came into force at the beginning of 1993. They apply to work activity generally and, like the health and safety provisions which we have had since the Health and Safety at Work Act 1974 was passed into law, the regulations place duties on employers to protect their employees and in some cases others, e.g. members of the public who may be harmed by the work being carried out.

Self-employed persons also have duties under the regulations to protect themselves and others who might be affected by the work being done, and although we talk about 'employers' in this section of the book remember the expression also includes the self-employed.

The new regulations implement six EC Directives on health and safety at work. They were made under Art 118A of the Treaty of Rome which was added for this purpose. There is one set of regulations for each directive.

The duties in the new regulations are not absolutely new but they clarify and state more explicitly what the law is. Those who have followed previous health and safety law should not find the new rules unfamiliar. However, there are some new aspects, i.e. management of health and safety, manual handling of loads and the use of display screens. The regulations are considered below.

Management of Health and Safety at Work Regulations

The latest version of these regulations came into force on 29 December 1999. They set out the general duties of employers in regard to the management of health and safety as follows:

(a) Every employer is required to assess the risks to the health and safety of his employees and record the significant findings of the risk assessment together with means by which the employer controls them.

(b) Employers must make arrangements to implement health and safety measures to deal with the risks identified and put these into written form where there are five or more employees. A *written* risk assessment is not required if there are fewer than five employees.

(c) Competent safety advisers must be appointed to deal with the implementation of health and safety measures. These persons may come from within the organisation or from outside, and may recommend a health surveillance of employees if thought appropriate.

(d) Procedures must be put in place to deal with health and safety emergencies.

(e) Employees must be informed about arrangements for health and safety and be given adequate training. They must also be sufficiently competent at their jobs to avoid risk. Employers must give health and safety information to temporary workers.

(f) There must be co-operation with other employers sharing the same workplace.

The regulations also place duties on employees to follow health and safety instructions and report danger, and employers must consult employees' safety representatives and provide facilities for them.

An approved code of practice to accompany the 1999 regulations was published in March 2000.

Young people and new and expectant mothers

The regulations include provisions relating to what should be done to protect the health and safety at work of new and expectant mothers and young persons. A new or expectant mother is defined as an employee who is pregnant or who has given birth within the previous six months or who is breastfeeding. A young person means any person who has not attained the age of 18. The definition of 'child' where that word appears means a person who is not over compulsory school age. The key changes are as follows:

Young persons

- the main regulations as outlined above do not apply fully to young persons who are involved in occasional or short-term work on domestic service in a private household or a family business where the work is not harmful, dangerous or damaging to young people;
- there are provisions requiring employers to give certain information to the parents of a child they intend to employ, e.g. regarding the risks to health and safety identified by a risk assessment and the preventive and protective measures to be taken;

- there are additional requirements in regard to the risk assessment process in the case of young persons which must take account of, e.g., inexperience and immaturity.

New and expectant mothers

- a new regulation is added requiring assessment and avoidance of risks to health and safety from any processes or working conditions or physical, chemical or biological agents;
- there is a new regulation regarding night work under which the employer is required to operate a suspension from work at night upon receipt of a certificate from a medical practitioner or midwife that night work should not be undertaken for a specified period;
- a new regulation requires employers to pay particular attention in any risk assessment to the health and safety of new and expectant mothers.

Finally, although the main regulations are enforced under health and safety inspectorate arrangements and breach of any duty imposed by them does not of itself confer a right of action in any civil proceedings, the amendments to the main regulations set out above do reserve a right of civil action where there is a breach of duty in regard to the risks to new or expectant mothers and young persons.

Workplace (Health, Safety and Welfare) Regulations

These regulations tidy up and make more clear requirements formerly contained in statutes such as the Factories Act 1961 and the Offices, Shops and Railway Premises Act 1963. The regulations apply to all places of work, subject to some exceptions such as construction sites and fishing boats.

It is not necessary in a book of this nature to set out all the provisions in detail but in broad terms there are general requirements in four areas:

1 The working environment. These include provisions relating to temperature, and effective provision must be made for securing and maintaining a reasonable temperature in rooms where persons are employed other than for short periods. If the work being done does not involve serious physical effort, a temperature of not less than 16° C (60.8° F) after the first hour is reasonable. Incidentally, although we

have included the Fahrenheit temperature, there are now in force regulations implementing an EC Directive which require all legislation and other materials, such as guidance notes concerning health and safety, to be in metric units of measurement. A thermometer must be provided in a conspicuous place on each floor of the premises. There are some temperature exceptions such as rooms in which goods are stored which would deteriorate at 16° C. However, employees who work in such rooms must be provided with convenient, accessible and effective means of warming themselves.

As regards ventilation, every room in which persons are employed must be adequately ventilated and supplied with fresh or artificially purified air. There must also be suitable, sufficient lighting – either natural or artificial – in all parts of the premises. In addition, rooms in which people work must not be overcrowded.

2 **Safety.** Floors, passages and stairs must be of sound construction, properly maintained and kept free from obstruction and slippery substances. Handrails must be provided on stairways, and where a stairway is open on both sides there must be two handrails and both sides must be guarded to prevent persons slipping between the rails and the steps. All openings in floors must be fenced, except where the nature of the work makes fencing impracticable.

3 **Facilities.** Suitable and sufficient toilets must be provided. These must be kept clean and be properly maintained, lit and ventilated. Where there are male and female employees, separate toilets must be provided for each sex. Suitable and sufficient washing facilities must also be provided. This includes a supply of clean running hot and cold (or warm) water, soap and clean towels or other suitable means of drying. In this regard there is an approved code of practice which accompanies the regulations. It provides as follows:

Number of people at work	Number of WCs	Number of wash stations
1–5	1	1
6–25	2	2
26–50	3	3
51–75	4	4
76–100	5	5

The number of persons at work is to be taken as the likely maximum number in the workplace at any one time. Where men and women are employed, the calculation should be carried out separately for each sex.

An adequate supply of wholesome drinking water must be made available. If the supply is not piped, it must be contained in suitable vessels and must be renewed daily. If water is supplied other than by jet, a supply of disposable drinking vessels must be available, and if washable non-disposable vessels are used there must be a supply of clean water in which to rinse them.

Suitable and sufficient provision must be made for clothing which is not worn at work, and so far as is reasonably practicable arrangements must be made for drying the clothing.

Where reasonable opportunities exist for sitting during working hours, suitable sitting facilities must be made available, and those who sit to do their work must be provided with a seat together with a footrest if, for example, an employee is short-legged and cannot support his or her feet comfortably without one.

4 **Housekeeping.** All premises, furniture, furnishings and fittings must be kept clean and properly maintained and suitable drainage of the premises must be provided. It should be noted that other people connected with the workplace are involved, so that the owner of a building leased to one or more employers or self-employed people must ensure that requirements falling within his control are satisfied, as where the owner provides jointly used toilet facilities.

Health and Safety (Display Screen Equipment) Regulations

These regulations do not replace former legislation. They cover for the first time a new area of activity. The risks involved with work on display screens are not high but can lead to muscular problems, eye fatigue and mental stress.

The regulations apply where there are one or more employees who habitually use display screen equipment as a significant part of daily work. The employer's duties are to:

(a) assess display screen equipment workstations and reduce any risks which are discovered;

(b) ensure that workstations satisfy minimum requirements in terms of the display screen itself, the keyboard, desk and chair, working environment and task design and software;

(c) plan work on display screen equipment so that the user has breaks or changes of activity;

(d) provide information and training for display equipment users.

Users are also entitled to eye and eyesight tests and to special spectacles where normal ones cannot be used.

Provision and Use of Work Equipment Regulations

These regulations tidy up and bring together the law relating to equipment used at work. Instead of legislation relating to particular types of equipment in different industries, such as the Factories Act 1961 fencing provisions, the regulations place general duties on employers and list minimum requirements for work equipment to deal with selected hazards, regardless of the type of industry.

Some equipment may need to be upgraded and employers had until the end of 1996 to do this.

'Work equipment' is broadly defined to include everything from a hand tool, through all kinds of machines to a complete plant such as a refinery.

Safety in 'use' includes safety in starting, stopping, installing, dismantling, programming, setting, transporting, maintaining, servicing and cleaning. Specific requirements include the guarding of dangerous parts of machinery and replace previous provisions on this.

Manual Handling Operations Regulations

These apply to any manual handling operation which may cause injury at work. They cover not only the lifting of loads but also lowering, pushing, pulling, carrying or moving them, whether by hand or other bodily force.

Personal Protective Equipment at Work (PPE) Regulations

These regulations set out the principles to be followed in selecting, providing, maintaining and using PPE. They include protective clothing such as eye, foot and head protection, safety harnesses, life jackets and high-visibility clothing. The regulations cover maintenance cleaning and replacement, storage, proper use and training information, and instructions on use given to employees.

Directors' reports

Under the Health and Safety at Work Act 1974 the Secretary of State for Trade and Industry may make regulations under which the annual reports of company directors must contain information regarding arrangements in force during the year relating to the health, safety and welfare of employees. At the time of writing, no such regulations have been made.

Duties of employers and the self-employed to persons who are not their employees – generally

It is the duty of every employer to carry on his business in such a way as to make sure, so far as is reasonably practicable, that persons who are **not** his employees but who might be affected by the conduct of the business are not exposed to risks to their health or safety. This duty is placed also on self-employed persons.

A wide variety of people is covered, including customers in a shop, people who occupy the premises next door, and even members of the public who pass the workplace. It is a criminal offence for which the person at fault can be prosecuted, whether any one is injured or not, to run a business **negligently** or to create a **nuisance**.

Thus, if a customer in a shop trips over a trailing wire left by a maintenance man, there is the possibility of an action by the customer for damages for negligence, and the possibility, also, of a criminal prosecution. In a similar way, excess noise or vibration from premises on which the business is conducted may result in an action by a person who occupies premises next door for nuisance and there is also the possibility of a criminal prosecution.

R v Mara (1986)

This provides an illustration of the above provisions. In that case it was alleged that the director of a company was in breach of his duty, where machinery belonging to his cleaning and maintenance company was left at a store which his company was under contract to clean, and the cleaning company agreed that employees of the store could use the machinery for part of the cleaning, and one of the employees of the store was electrocuted because of a fault in the cable of one of the machines. The Court of Appeal held that the director concerned was in breach of his duty and dismissed his appeal from Warwick Crown Court where he had been fined £200.

The legal point was one of construction of the relevant provisions of the 1974 Act. Mr Mara claimed that when the electrocution took place his company was not conducting its undertaking at all; the only undertaking being conducted was that of the store whose employees were using the machine to clean their own premises.

The Court of Appeal did not accept this. Mr Mara's company had, as its undertaking, the provision of cleaning services. It appeared from the facts that the way it chose to carry out that undertaking, in this case, was to do the cleaning and also leave machines and other equipment on the store's premises with permission for employees of the store to use them and with the knowledge that they would in fact use them. The unsafe cable formed part of the equipment. The failure to remove or replace the cable was a clear breach by Mr Mara's company of its duty both to its own employees and also to the employees of the store.

Comment. The case shows the wide ambit of the relevant law. The liability of a director for offences by the company is set out in the 1974 Act which provides that where an offence is committed by a body corporate then its officers, e.g. directors and secretary, are also liable if the offence was committed with their consent or connivance. (See p 467.) There is also a civil claim for damages for this kind of breach. The above case was concerned solely with the criminal offence.

It should also be noted that the courts have, since March 1992, been allowed to impose fines of up to £20,000 for breaches of the relevant legislation. Furthermore, the Company Directors Disqualification Act 1986 applies if there is a prosecution of a director on indictment in the Crown Court (see Chapter 6). A director who is convicted of an indictable offence may be disqualified by the court, and this was done in *R* v *Chapman* (1992) at Lewes Crown Court where a director was convicted of an indictable offence under Health and Safety legislation arising out of the running of a dangerous quarry. He was fined £5,000 and disqualified from being a company director for two years.

Duties of employers and the self-employed to non-employees – premises

Certain duties are imposed upon employers and the self-employed in regard to people who are not employees but who come on to their business (not domestic) premises. The duty is to make sure, so far as is reasonably practicable, that the premises and the means of getting in and out of them, and any plant or substance on the premises, are safe and without risk to health. These duties also apply to a landlord who is letting business premises. Failure to comply with these duties may lead to prosecution.

Once again, a wide variety of people is covered, such as window-cleaners and painters, the employees of contractors maintaining lifts or installing central heating. The actual employer owes the duties of an employer to these people also, and must, for example, set up a safe system of working. However, the occupier of the premises owes the duties we have been looking at in regard to injuries received from defects in the premises or plant or a substance on them. Obviously, the occupier can assume that the employees of contractors will take proper steps, as trained people, to avoid the risks which are usually associated with the job.

Duties in regard to harmful emissions in the atmosphere

The Health and Safety at Work Act 1974 allows the Trade and Industry Secretary to control by regulations the emission into the atmosphere from premises of noxious or offensive substances and for making harmless and inoffensive such substances as may be emitted. The provisions are concerned only with air pollution. Other forms of pollution, such as the discharge of effluent into rivers, are not controlled by them.

The main regulations made so far under this head are entitled the Control of Substances Hazardous to Health Regulations 1994. These stay in place and are not absorbed into the main regulations already referred to.

General duties of those who make, import or supply articles of equipment or substances, or who erect or install equipment

This part of the 1974 Act creates the following duties:

1 To ensure, so far as is reasonably practicable, that the article, e.g. a machine, is so designed and constructed as to be safe and without risks to health when properly used or, in the case of a substance, e.g. cyanide, is safe and without risk to health when properly used.

2 To carry out or arrange for the carrying out of such testing and examination as may be necessary for the performance of the duty laid down in 1 above.

3 To take such steps as may be necessary to make sure that there is available as regards the use of the article or substance at work adequate information about the use for which it is designed or made and has been tested, and about any conditions necessary to make sure that when the article or substance is put to that use it will be safe and without risk to health.

All forms of supply are included and this part of the 1974 Act covers the supplying by way of sale, leasing, hire or hire-purchase.

As regards the installation and erection of equipment, the 1974 Act provides that it is the duty of any person who erects or installs any article for use at work in any premises where the article is to be used by people at work to make sure, as far as is reasonably practicable, that nothing about the way in which it is erected or installed makes it unsafe or a risk to health when properly used.

Under amendments made by the Consumer Protection Act 1987 the above general duties are extended to those who supply any article of fairground equipment.

Research, examination and testing

This part of the 1974 Act makes it the duty of any person who undertakes the design or manufacture of an article for use at work or the manufacture of a substance for use at work to carry out or arrange for the carrying out of any necessary research with a view to the discovery, and, so far as is reasonably practicable, the elimination or minimisation of any risks to health or safety to which the design, article or substance may give rise.

There is no need to repeat any testing, examination or research which has been done by someone else if it is reasonable to rely on the results of another's testing, examination or research. For example, those who lease goods are not required to go again through the manufacturer's testing, examination and research programmes.

If you design, manufacture, import or supply an article to someone else's specification or request, the Act says that if you have a **written undertaking** as part of the documentation of the contract from that person to take specified steps sufficient to ensure, so far as is reasonably practicable, that the article will be safe and without risk to health when properly used, then the written undertaking will relieve the designer, manufacturer, importer or supplier of liability to such an extent as is reasonable having regard to the terms of the undertaking.

General duties of employees at work

It is the duty of every employee while at work:

1 to take reasonable care for the health and safety of himself and of other persons who may be affected by his acts or omissions at work; and

2 as regards any duty or requirement put upon his employer or any other person by the relevant Acts of Parliament to cooperate with him so far as is necessary to enable that duty or requirement to be carried out or complied with. Therefore, if the employer is required to provide his workers with goggles, the workers have a duty to wear them.

Furthermore, the 1974 Act provides that no person shall intentionally or recklessly interfere with or misuse anything provided in the interests of health, safety or welfare, e.g. remove a safety guard from a machine. To do so is an offence for which the employee can be prosecuted.

These are useful sections which could enable an employer to enforce his safety policies. Some workers are reluctant to use safety equipment, such as machine guards, because they feel it slows them down or prevents the most efficient operation of the machine in terms of its production. If the employee's wages depend, because of the system of payment, upon his production, then it is even more difficult to gain his acceptance of safety devices which might affect production.

In this connection it should be noted that an employee's consent to a dangerous practice, or his willing participation in it, is no defence for an employer who is prosecuted under the Act.

Duty not to charge employees for things done or provided by the employer by law

The 1974 Act states that no employer shall levy or permit to be levied on any employee of his any charge in respect of anything done or provided by the employer as a result of the provisions of an Act of Parliament or statutory instrument. This would apply, for example, to personal protective clothing which an employer was required to provide by law. For example, in workplaces where there is a noise hazard from a woodworking machine, ear protectors must be provided and the employee must not be charged for them. The employee, in turn, must treat them properly and not misuse them.

The statutory duties and civil liability

The 1974 Act states that failure to comply with any of the duties considered above shall not be construed as conferring a right of action in civil proceedings. Thus, the Act creates no new civil liability although, as we have seen, amendments made to the Management of Health and Safety at Work Regulations do reserve rights in regard to new and expectant mothers and young persons in respect of infringements of provisions designed to protect them.

However, the ordinary action for negligence at common law remains available. If there is an action by an employee at common law, say for injuries received at work by what he alleges to be the employer's negligence, the employee can plead that the employer has been convicted under the Act and where this is so the employee's claim is near certain to succeed but will not inevitably do so. Therefore, where the employer has infringed the Act and this has caused injury to the employee, the Act is a relevant part of establishing the employee's case for damages at civil law.

Offences and civil claims for accidents at work are more likely to arise in a factory than in an office. However, the following are examples of accidents which can occur and medical conditions which can arise in an office environment:

(a) injury in a fire caused by a discarded cigarette or by an overloaded or defective electrical system;

(b) a fall or other injury caused by a defect in the premises, such as a dangerous and badly lit staircase;

(c) an electric shock caused by badly fitted or defective electrical equipment;

(d) injury caused by a defect in or careless use of equipment, such as a guillotine or stapler;

(e) a medical condition caused by defective or ill-designed chairs supplied to employees, particularly secretaries;

(f) eye strain and other conditions caused by exposure to VDU screens.

Many of the claims brought broadly under headings (e) and (f) above have been in regard to what is called repetitive strain injury.

It is also necessary to note the case of *Walker* v *Northumberland County Council* (1994) where damages, eventually settled out of court at £175,000, were awarded to Mr Walker when he suffered psychiatric damage because he was overworked by his employer. The employer was in breach of his duty to provide a safe system of work for the employee and was therefore liable in negligence for not doing so.

Civil claims – strict liability

Stark v *Post Office* (2000)

The Court of Appeal ruled that where the employer's equipment caused personal injury to an employee a claim by that employee for damages against the employer can succeed even though the employer has not been negligent in terms, for example, of its maintenance. Mr Stark was a postman. The Post Office provided him with a bicycle. During the course of his employment he was riding the bicycle when the front wheel locked sending him over the handlebars and causing him serious injuries. It was accepted that the bicycle had been maintained and that the defendants were not negligent. Even so, the court found that the employer was liable to Mr Stark since there is strict liability under health and safety legislation.

Comment. Despite the fact that the Post Office had a safe system of maintenance and repair, the claimant suceeded. A reasonable system for maintenance may no longer be an adequate defence. Employers faced with health and safety incidents should take note of the implications of this ruling.

Smoking in the workplace

It is also arguable that at common law an employer is at fault in requiring employees to work in an atmosphere containing heavy concentrations of cigarette or cigar smoke, although it may be possible to call medical evidence to challenge the existence or degree of the risks involved in 'passive smoking'. In fact, in *Bland* v *Stockport Metropolitan Borough Council* (1993), a woman who had been exposed to passive smoking from 1979 to 1990 when her employer implemented a no-smoking policy, received £15,000 damages for injury to her health, including, in particular, chronic bronchitis and sinusitis. There is, of course, a statutory duty now the new regulations apply. Certainly there is no implied contractual right to smoke at work and if an employee leaves because he or she is not allowed to smoke, there is no constructive dismissal (see *Dryden* v *Greater Glasgow Health Board* (1992)) and it may well be that a dismissal for infringement of a no-smoking rule properly communicated and agreed with staff would not be unfair.

More recently the Employment Appeal Tribunal has decided that the secretary in a solicitor's office who left because of discomfort caused at the workplace by colleagues who smoked was constructively dismissed (see *Waltons and Morse* v *Dorrington* (1997)). In previous passive smoking cases the complainant has suffered physical injury. However, in this case, the EAT, after ruling that it is an implied term in all employment contracts that the employer will provide and continue to monitor, as far as is reasonably practicable, a working environment which is reasonably suitable for employees to carry out their duties, then went on to comment that the right of an employee not to be required to sit in a smoky atmosphere affects the welfare of employees at work, even though employees who complain cannot necessarily prove that there has been any health and safety risk to them. It would appear that discomfort is enough.

Smoking in the workplace – a code of practice

Following consultation, the Health and Safety Commission has issued a code of practice on passive smoking under the Health and Safety at Work Act 1974. The code will have special force in that failure to follow it, though not in itself an offence,

could lead to a sucessful claim for damages under health and safety provisions by an employee who having suffered injury put it in evidence. The code is likely to lead to a total ban in smaller companies that find that they cannot afford the alternative measures in the code, such as segregated smoking rooms. Hotels, restaurants and bars continue with a voluntary code until 2002.

Drink and drugs in the workplace

Because of the duties of care placed upon them by statute and common law, employers must take reasonable steps to ensure that their workers are not under influence of drink or drugs where it would create a risk to the health and safety of others if the workers' performance was impaired in this way. Employees who are under the influence of drink or drugs – or who fail to report fellow workers who are – may also be in breach of their own common law or statutory duties of care.

Except for these rather general duties, there is little specific regulation in regard to drink and drugs in the workplace, though there is some regulation in regard to railways.

Abusive fellow workers – a health and safety risk

The decision of the EAT in *Harvest Press Ltd* v *McCaffrey* (1999) provides an unexpected application of s 100 (1)(d) of the Employment Rights Act 1996. This states that it is automatically unfair to dismiss an employee who has left his work because circumstances of danger of a serious nature appear imminent, which one normally associates with a health and safety risk. The EAT ruled that an employment tribunal's decision that the dismissal of McCaffrey after he left his work in the middle of a shift because of the abusive behaviour of a fellow worker was automatically unfair within s 100 (1)(d). The subsection had a wide scope and was without limitation and could cover any danger howsoever arising.

The Health and Safety Commission and the Health and Safety Executive

The 1974 Act establishes the above bodies and describes their powers. Briefly, the Commission is concerned to make codes of practice, assist and encourage research and the availability of information and training, to recommend to government areas in which new regulations are required and what they should be and, as we shall see below, to conduct enquiries.

The Executive is required, through its inspectors, to enforce the provisions of the Act throughout the country by covering all industries.

Investigations and inquiries

If there is, for example, a serious accident on a particular employer's premises, then this part of the Act may be brought into effect. It provides that whenever there has been any accident, occurrence, situation, or other matter of any sort which the Commission thinks it necessary or expedient to investigate, which includes the situation where new regulations might be required, the Commission may:

1 direct the Executive to investigate and report; or
2 authorise another person, e.g. someone with particular expertise, to investigate and report; or
3 direct an inquiry to be held if the Secretary of State agrees.

There is a provision that normally the inquiry is to be held in public and regulations made dealing with the conduct of inquiries include provisions giving the person conducting the inquiry powers of entry and inspection of premises, the power to summon witnesses to give evidence or produce documents, and the power to take evidence on oath and require the making of declarations as to the truth of statements made.

The Act also provides that the Commission may publish the report of the inquiry or part of it as it thinks fit.

The investigations and inquiries referred to above are, of course, a form of enforcement but in the main enforcement is through the powers conferred on the Commission and the Inspectorate.

The Commission

The Commission has the following general duties:

1 to assist and encourage health and safety measures;
2 to make arrangements for the carrying out of research, the publication of the results of research, and the provision of training and information in connection with these purposes, and

to encourage provision of training and research in the publication of information by others;
3 to make arrangements for an information and advisory service;
4 to submit recommendations for new regulations;
5 to direct the holding of investigations and inquiries.

The Inspectorate and its major powers

In order that there should be compliance with health and safety legislation, health and safety inspectors are given wide-ranging powers, for example to:

- enter premises;
- examine and investigate, take measurements, samples and photographs and make recordings;
- require any person whom they reasonably believe to be able to give information to answer questions and sign a declaration of the truth of those answers;
- require the production of, inspect and take copies of books or documents or entries in them;
- serve upon any person who is in control of particular activities an Improvement or Prohibition Notice (see below).

1 Improvement notices. The Act provides that if an inspector is of the opinion that a person is contravening one or more of the statutory provisions relating to health and safety or has done so in the past and the circumstances suggest he is likely to do so again, he may serve an improvement notice on him requiring the person concerned to put matters right within the period stated in the notice.

2 Prohibition notices. The Act also provides that if an inspector is of the opinion that activities as they are carried on or are about to be carried on involve a risk of serious personal injury, the inspector may serve a prohibition notice on the person who controls the activities. The notice must give the inspector's reasons for thinking that the activity is unsafe. When the notice has been served, the activity must cease immediately. It should be noted that improvement and prohibition orders may be issued in respect of offences under the provisions of the various health and safety regulations already considered. They have, for example, been served in regard

to service lifts (sometimes called dumb waiters) in restaurants, which can be overworked and not properly maintained; they have also been served in respect of dangerous staircases leading to kitchens in a restaurant, resulting in the restaurant being closed until the staircase has been put into good order.

Under the provisions of the Environmental and Safety Information Act 1988 the Health and Safety Executive is required to keep a register of improvement and prohibition notices which is available for inspection by the public. Such notices are not required to be registered where they would reveal a trade secret such as a secret manufacturing process.

3 Appeal against improvement or prohibition notice. There are rights of appeal against improvement and prohibition notices. The appeal is to an employment tribunal. An improvement notice is suspended until the appeal is heard or withdrawn and things can go on as before. A prohibition notice is not automatically suspended but may be if the person making the appeal asks for suspension and the tribunal so directs. Suspension is from the date of the tribunal's direction.

There is a right of appeal from the tribunal to the Divisional Court of the Queen's Bench, both against the making of either notice or against a refusal to suspend a prohibition notice.

4 Power to deal with cause of imminent danger. Under the 1974 Act an inspector has power to enter premises and remove from them any article which he has reasonable cause to believe is a cause of imminent danger or serious personal injury and cause it to be made harmless, whether by destruction or in some other way. This part of the 1974 Act requires the inspector to make a report giving his reasons for taking the article and to give a copy to a responsible person at the premises from which the article was removed and to the owner if the two are not the same, as where the owner has let his premises for industrial use.

5 Actions against inspectors – indemnity. It is possible to bring at common law an action for damages against an inspector who negligently issues an improvement, or more particularly, a prohibition, notice which causes loss to the person against whom it is issued. If the inspector loses his

case then the Executive is given power under the 1974 Act to indemnify him (i.e. make good) any damages, costs or expenses which he incurs.

6 Obtaining of information. The Act carries provisions under which the Commission or the Executive can obtain information which is needed for the discharge of their duties by the serving of a notice requiring the person concerned to supply that information within a specified time.

Offences due to the fault of another person

The Act provides that if an offence under the Act was the fault of some other person that other person is guilty of the offence and may be charged and convicted of it whether or not proceedings are taken against anyone else who is responsible.

The effect of this provision is that, for example, an executive of a company or other business organisation may be prosecuted rather than the company or other organisation where the Act was infringed because the executive himself was at fault. However, before blame can be passed on in this way the company or other organisation should have a very good system to ensure, for example, safety, which the executive did not in practice operate.

Offences by bodies corporate

This part of the Act also imposes potential liability upon the executive of a company but not because the person concerned was **directly** involved in a failure, for example, to operate a safety system, under the above provision, but where the offence was committed with his consent, connivance or neglect.

In effect, the section will enable members of boards, managers and company secretaries to be prosecuted where nothing has been done by management to prevent the commission of an offence under the Act or where with knowledge of its commission management has consented to, for example, a dangerous practice being carried on, or has connived at its being carried on, as where a blind eye has been turned on the wrongful activity.

Corporate killing

The Home Office has issued a consultation document containing the government's proposals on how the law on involuntary manslaughter might be reformed. Included in the document is a proposal for the creation of a new offence of corporate killing.

It has proved difficult to successfully prosecute companies and their officers for manslaughter, even though it has been clear that there have been management failures in safety matters resulting in a death or deaths. The problem under the present law is that prosecutions for corporate manslaughter can only be brought where a company through the controlling mind of one of its agents carries out an act that fulfils the requirements of the crime of manslaughter. It is necessary to identify the agent in order to carry the crime back to the company, and in all of the major disasters brought about by a failure of a company-supplied service – as in a ferry or train disaster – the effective acts of carelessness are diffused throughout the company's structure.

In *A-G's Reference* (*No 2 of 1999*) (2000) the Court of Appeal affirmed the principle, in regard to a finding of corporate manslaughter by gross negligence, that a corporation cannot be convicted unless there is evidence that establishes the guilt of an *identified human individual* for the same crime.

One of the few convictions is to be found in *R v OLL* (1994), a prosecution heard at Winchester Crown Court in 1994, where the managing director of an activity centre was sentenced to three years' imprisonment for manslaughter following the deaths of four teenagers in the Lyme Bay canoe disaster. Here there was no difficulty in establishing the controlling mind because the company was a 'one-man band'.

The consultation document, which contains the Law Commission's draft Bill on the matter, proposes: a new offence of corporate killing where 'management failure' meant that the conduct of the business fell 'far below what could reasonably be expected'; businesses found guilty of corporate killing will face unlimited fines and court orders to correct the cause of the accident; and directors convicted of corporate killing will face potential disqualification, although there is as yet no decision whether to make them criminally liable.

Codes of practice

Reference has already been made to certain ACAS codes of practice issued under what is now the ERA. However, codes of practice may also be issued in the field of health and safety by the Health and Safety Commission and, in particular, the Commission has issued a code and guidance notes relating to safety committees and the main regulations already considered.

Some general matters

The Act applies to agricultural workers on farms and agricultural holdings and to employees, e.g. lorry drivers, while working abroad. Part II of the Act is concerned with the Employment Medical Advisory Service and in particular paragraph 8 of the Third Schedule to the Act allows regulations to be made to require the making of arrangements for securing the health of persons at work, including arrangements for medical examinations and health surveys.

Part III of the Act (see now the Building Act 1984) is concerned with building regulations and seeks to secure the health, safety and welfare, and convenience of persons in or about buildings, and of others who may be affected by the buildings or other matters concerned with buildings. It is of interest mainly to builders, architects and surveyors and has not been dealt with here. In particular, however, the Act is concerned with the types of materials and components used and this is designed in particular to have effect on the 'towering inferno' problems in terms of fire which may result when certain materials are used in a building.

Employment protection in health and safety cases

Designated or acknowledged health and safety representatives must not be subjected to detriments, e.g. loss of overtime, for carrying out health and safety activities in the workplace. Dismissal or selection for redundancy for these reasons can lead to a complaint to a tribunal. These provisions apply to ordinary employees regardless of service who leave or refuse to return to the workplace because of a health hazard reasonably thought to exist.

Other statutory provisions

Apart from the Health and Safety at Work Act 1974 and the General Regulations relating to health and safety, three other areas are important in the general administration of business. They are set out below.

First aid

The Health and Safety (First Aid) Regulations 1981 (SI 1981/917) state that employers must determine what provision for first aid is required. A properly equipped first aid box must be provided in an appropriate place. If the business has a first aider, that person should have passed an approved course and be retested every three years. If there is no trained first aider, the regulations require that a person should be assigned to that function, the main duties of which are to take control if an accident occurs, to call an ambulance if required and to maintain the first aid box.

Reporting accidents

The Reporting of Injuries, Diseases and Dangerous Occurrences Regulations of 1995 (SI 1995/3163) require the reporting of accidents at work to the local environmental officer. Failure to make a report is a criminal offence.

Following a sucessful pilot scheme in Scotland, the Health and Safety Executive is setting up a central and national workplace accident and accident reporting system. All employers will use the same address and telephone facilities to report workplace accidents. The system is scheduled to be operational in 2001.

Fire precautions

Specific and detailed legal requirements relating to fire safety at work are laid down in the Fire Precautions Act 1971 and regulations made under it. In particular, regulations made under the 1971 Act make compulsory the inspection and issue of a fire certificate in respect of most workplaces where more than 20 people are employed or more than 10 persons are employed at any one time elsewhere than on the ground floor. Applications for a fire certificate must be made to the local fire authority. The detailed requirements are beyond the scope of a book of this nature and will not be considered further. However, new rules contained in regulations designed to comply with the EC Directives are relevant. The provisions appear below.

Fire Precautions (Workplace) Regulations 1997 (SI 1997/1840) (as amended). The regulations are currently in force and apply to premises which are used as a workplace by at least one person, as well as premises visited regularly by the public where people who are self-employed work. The major requirements are:

(a) employers must carry out an assessment of the fire risk using technical guidance from fire authorities;
(b) there must be emergency plans prepared for all purposes and these must be kept up to date;
(c) there must be appropriate fire escapes which are well maintained;
(d) premises must have fire-fighting equipment as well as fire warning and detection systems. Written records must be kept for any maintenance work carried out on these systems;
(e) all staff and self-employed persons must be given instructions and training in fire precautions. Written records must be kept of any instruction and training given.

The regulations are enforced by fire authorities, and such authorities can serve enforcement notices if safety is at risk. Failure to comply with an enforcement notice is a criminal offence which may lead to a fine and/or imprisonment of relevant management. Furthermore, an intentional or reckless breach of the provisions set out in the regulations is also an offence.

The Home Office has for some time now been working on a Bill to consolidate fire safety legislation.

The working time regulations (WTR)

The Working Time Regulations (SI 1998/1833) came into force on 1 October 1998. They enact the European Working Time Directive (93/104). From that date there are detailed rules which govern hours of work and entitlement to paid holidays, as set out in general terms below:

- a maximum 48-hour working week averaged over 17 weeks or 26 weeks in some cases (see below);
- at least three weeks paid annual leave, which rose to four weeks after 23 November 1999;

- a daily rest period of at least 11 consecutive hours in 24 hours;
- a weekly rest period of at least 24 hours in each seven-day period (this may be averaged over a two-week period, i.e. a worker is entitled to a period of 48 hours rest in 14 days or two periods of 24 hours rest in 14 days; the days off for weekly rest are in addition to paid annual leave);
- an in-work rest break of 20 minutes for those working more than six hours a day (this should not be taken at either the start or the end of a working day and should not overlap with a worker's daily rest period);
- rest breaks are not in addition to lunch breaks (it is up to the employer and the worker to agree between them whether breaks are paid; in many cases this will be decided by the terms of the existing contract);
- the normal hours of night workers should not exceed eight hours for each 24 hours with no averaging.

The Working Time Directive – no direct effect

In so far as employees may seek to exploit any differences that may emerge between the Directive and the UK regulations, the decision of the Court of appeal in *Gibson* v *East Riding of Yorkshire DC* (2000) is relevant. The Court of Appeal ruled that the directive was too vague to have direct effect in the UK so that the Working Time Regulations have supremacy over the Directive. The case has potentially at least a far-reaching effect since increasingly employment-related Directives are based on framework agreements and are similarly vague, such as the Part-time Worker Directive, so that the direct effect argument in cases brought against emanations of the state, such as central and local government authorities, may have little part to play in this area in future.

Who is a worker?

Generally speaking, a worker is a person employed under a contract of service, but the majority of agency workers will be included as will trainees who are engaged on work experience. The regulations also apply in part to domestic employees, though the working time limits do not apply, but

they are entitled to the rest breaks, rest periods and paid annual leave. Those who are genuinely self-employed are not covered.

Partners are not included since they own the firm, though salaried partners could be if, as is usually the case, such persons are regarded as employees.

What is working time?

Working time is defined by the WTR as when a worker is working at his employer's disposal and carrying out his duty or activities. Training time is included but, according to DTI Guidance, time when a worker is 'on call' but is otherwise free to pursue his own activities or is sleeping would not be working time. Lunch breaks spent at leisure would not be working time, but working lunches and working breakfasts would be. Travelling to and from a place of work is unlikely to be working time. The regulations usefully allow workers or their representatives and employers to make agreements to add to the definition of working time.

The latest government guide to the regulations (URN 00/633) (available from the DTI's orderline, tel: 0845 6000 925 and on their Internet site *http://www.dti.gov.uk/er/work_time_regs*) states that the government has previously advised that on-call time is not working time. However, an interim judgment in a recent ECJ case has suggested that on-call time where a worker is restricted to the workplace is working time but on-call time is not working time if a worker is free to pursue leisure activities. The guide will be updated apparently when a final judgment is reached. (The case is *SIMAP* v *Conselleria de Sanidad y consumo de la Generalitat Valencia*: C-308/98 (16 December 1999, unreported), ECJ. An Advocate-General's Opinion.)

The 48-hour week

The law does not say that employees cannot work more than 48 hours in any one week. The 48-hour limit is averaged over a 'reference period' which will generally be a 17-week rolling period in the absence of any other agreement. This gives a certain amount of flexibility for businesses to cope with surges in demand so long as the average over the whole reference period is not exceeded.

The reference period may be increased to 26 weeks if the worker is a special case as in hospital work or where there is a foreseeable surge of activity as in agriculture, tourism and postal services (see further, reg 21). The reference period can be increased to 52 weeks by a workforce agreement (see below) or by individual agreement with the employer (see below).

Barber v *RJB Mining (UK) Ltd* (1999)

The High Court judge in this case ruled that all contracts of employment should be read as providing that an employee should not work more than an average of 48 hours in any week during the 17-week working time reference period unless the relevant employee has opted out in writing. The judge also ruled that if the average hours are equalled or exceeded during the reference period, an employee may refuse to work *at all* during the remainder of the period until the working hours come down to the required level.

Mr Justice Gage gave his ruling in a case brought by five members of the pit deputies' union NACODS against RJB Mining, their employer. They had all been required to carry on working although they had all worked in excess of 816 hours in the 17-week reference period. The judge also granted them an injunction (breach of which by the employer could lead to sanctions of contempt of court) to the effect that they could refuse to work any more during a 17-week reference period where the 48-hour average had been equalled or exceeded.

Comment. The decision could present a number of employers with major problems, particularly in terms of staff in key areas. They could face the prospect of a number of workers being able to refuse to do any more work until their hours came down to the required level.

Paid annual leave

The right to paid annual leave arises after 13 weeks' employment. The entitlement is to three weeks leave rising incrementally to four weeks from 23 November 1999. This is not additional to contractual entitlements, so that taking contractual paid leave in a particular leave year counts against the worker's entitlement under the regulations. In the absence of any agreement, the employer can require a worker to take all or any of the leave at specified times, subject to giving the worker notice of at least twice the period of the leave to be taken. The worker is also required to give notice to the employer of the wish to take leave. The notice period must again be at least twice the period of leave to be taken.

A week's leave is to be equivalent to the time a worker would work in a week. A full-time worker working five days a week would be entitled to 20 days annual leave; a part-time worker working two days a week would have a right to 8 days annual leave. Where the work is expressed in hours, annual leave may be so expressed, e.g. a worker works 24 hours a week and gets 96 hours leave entitlement.

The leave must be taken in the year in which it is due and it cannot be replaced with a payment in lieu except on termination of employment.

The following additional points on paid annual leave are worth noting:

- the leave entitlement under the regulations is not additional to bank holidays, because there is no statutory right to take them;
- employers' can set the time that workers can take their leave, e.g. for a Christmas shutdown;
- if a worker's employment ends, he/she has a right to be paid for the leave time due but not taken;
- employers must ensure that their workers can take their leave, but they are not forced to see that they do.

The Working Time regulations came into force on 1 October 1998 and already the High Court has referred to the European Court of Justice for a preliminary ruling on the UK Regulations qualifying period of 13 weeks' service before a worker is entitled to paid annual leave (*R* v *Secretary of State for Trade and Industry, ex parte BECTU* (1999)).

The EC Working Time Directive provides that member states shall take all measures necessary to ensure that *every worker is entitled to paid annual leave.* This is subject to conditions for entitlement laid down by national legislation and/or practice. The ECJ is asked whether a member state is permitted to defer entitlement, as the UK has done, and if so, what would be regarded as a lawful and proportionate period of delay. In addition, the ECJ is asked to decide whether it is legitimate for a member state to take into account the cost for employers of conferring the rights on those workers who are employed for less than the qualifying period.

Length of night work

Night work is presumed to be work between 11 pm and 6 am unless otherwise defined by agreement.

Night workers must not work more than eight hours in 24 hours on average. This does not include overtime except guaranteed overtime. If night workers work fewer than 48 hours a week, they are not exceeding this limit and so no further action need be taken.

Excluded sectors

The regulations other than those parts which apply to young workers (see below) do not apply to workers who are employed in the following sectors:

- air transport;
- rail;
- rail transport;
- sea transport;
- inland waterway and lake transport;
- sea fishing; and
- other work at sea, e.g. offshore work in the oil and gas industry.

The regulations do not apply to the activities of doctors in training, but the European Commission brought forward proposals in regard to this sector. In fact, the Commission recommended that the 48-hour week should apply to junior doctors within seven years, but EU ministers have overruled this by agreeing to implementation in 13 years to give time to train additional doctors. A more recent compromise has reduced this figure to eight years. The regulations do not apply to the activities of specific services such as the police or the armed forces.

In this connection, an agreement has been reached between EU employers and employee organisations to extend the Working Time Directive to rail and maritime transport workers. The agreement in each area will now be converted into proposals for legislation to be ratified by the Council. This may lead to the amendment of the UK position where these areas of work are currently excluded from the working time provisions (see EC press release IP/98/855).

More recent compromises within the EU will give three years for implementation by the member states with the exception of doctors (see above).

Derogations

Employees whose working time is not measured or predetermined are exempt from the provisions relating to the 48-hour week, daily and weekly rest periods, rest breaks and limits on night work but not the holiday provisions. Examples given in the WTR include 'managing executives or other persons with autonomous decision making powers, family workers and ministers of religion'. This seems to be a very limited exception that will only cover individuals who can choose the hours which they work. It was not likely to cover professional staff who have core hours but work additional hours as required. Since the definition is not entirely clear, employers would be advised to make the position clear by agreement. A salaried partner, although a 'worker', may well be exempt under this head.

Under amendments made by the Working Time Regulations 1999 (SI 1999/3372) the position is that:

- the 48-hour limit does not apply where the employee's working time is not measured, as in the case of managers and other executives;
- the limit does not apply to those with pre-determined hours who *choose* to work beyond those limits. The pre-determined element must be 48 hours but any extra hours in the sense of overtime need not be counted. In these cases employers are not required to keep records of the hours worked but merely a record of those who have opted out.

Collective and workforce agreements

The regulations allow employers to modify or exclude the rules relating to night work, daily and weekly rest periods and rest breaks and extend the reference period in relation to the 48-hour week – *but not the 48-hour week itself* – by way of agreement as follows:

- A collective agreement between an independent trade union and the employer (or an employers' association).
- A workforce agreement with representatives of the relevant workforce *or if there are 20 workers or fewer the agreement may be with a majority of the workforce which obviates the need to elect worker representatives*. As regards worker representatives, these may be representatives elected for other purposes, e.g. health and safety consultation.
- For, as an example, technical reasons or reasons concerning the organisation of work, the 17-week averaging period may be extended by up to 52 weeks by a collective or workforce agreement.

- Individuals may also choose to agree with their employer to work in excess of the 48-hour weekly time limit. *This is all that an individual agreement can cover.*
- This individual agreement must be in writing and must allow the worker to bring the agreement to an end. The agreement may specify a notice period of up to three months and if no period of notice is specified only seven days notice by the employee is required. The worker must give written notice to the employer.
- In addition, a workforce agreement may apply to the whole of the workforce or to a group of workers within it.

These agreements can only last for a maximum of five years.

Records

The regulations should be referred to but in outline the position is as follows.

Weekly working time. An employer must keep adequate records to show that he has complied with the weekly working time limit. The records must be kept for two years. It is up to the employer to determine what records must be kept. Pay records may adequately demonstrate a worker's working hours.

Similar provisions apply in regard to records showing that the limits on night work are being complied with. Records need not be kept in regard to rest periods and in-work rest breaks nor in regard to paid annual leave.

Records are not required for those who have opted out, merely a record of those who have done must be kept and updated.

Compensatory rest

Employers who make use of the derogations or who enter into collective or workforce agreements must provide an equivalent period of rest or if this is not possible give appropriate health and safety protection. Thus, the regulations allow, through agreement, flexibility in the way rights are delivered but they do not allow those rights to be avoided.

Health and safety assessments

An employer must offer a free health assessment to any worker who is to become a night worker.

Employers must also give night workers the opportunity to have further assessments at regular intervals. A night worker is a person who normally works at least three hours a night.

Young (or adolescent) workers

The regulations also apply rights to persons over the minimum school leaving age but under 18. These are set out below:

- *Weekly working hours*: adult and young workers are treated the same.
- *Night work limit*: adult and young workers are treated the same.
- *Health assessments for night workers*: adolescent workers are entitled to a health and capacity assessment if they work during the period 10 pm to 6 am. Such an assessment for an adolescent worker differs in that it considers issues like physique, maturity and experience and takes into account the competence to undertake the night work that has been assigned.
- *Daily rest*: for young workers this is 12 hours of consecutive rest between each working day.
- *Weekly rest*: for young workers the general requirement is two days off per week.
- *In-work rest breaks*: For young workers the general provision is 30 minutes if the working day is longer than $4\frac{1}{2}$ hours. Rest breaks are not in addition to lunch breaks.
- *Paid annual leave*: adult and young workers are treated the same.

Young worker below school-leaving age

The Children (Protection at Work) (No 2) Regulations 2000 apply and amend the Children and Young Persons Act 1933 by limiting the number of hours young persons may be employed in any week in which they are required to attend school to 12. The EU's insistence on this requirement will seriously affect activities such as domestic newspaper distribution.

Enforcement and remedies

The weekly working time limit, the night work limit and health assessment for night workers are enforced by the Health and Safety Executive or local authority Environmental Health Officers. The usual criminal penalties for breach of health and safety law apply. In addition, workers who are not allowed to exercise their rights under the regulations or who are dismissed or subjected to a detriment – whether a pay cut, demotion or disciplinary action – for doing so will be entitled to present a complaint to an employment tribunal. In view of the possible abolition on the ceiling of awards for unfair dismissal, employment tribunal claims could be much more expensive than health and safety fines. The following case gives an example of a situation which gave rise to a claim.

Brown v Controlled Packaging Services (1999)

A fork-lift truck driver was told when interviewed for a job that he would have to work overtime on occasions. On commencing work, he discovered that the amount of overtime he was expected to do conflicted with an evening part-time job which he had. His manager indicated that his services were not required in the business if he did not sign the opting-out agreement. Mr Brown took this as a dismissal and left. He later claimed unfair dismissal. The tribunal ruled that the main reason for the dismissal was his refusal to sign the agreement and that his dismissal was automatically unfair.

DISCRIMINATION ON GROUNDS OF SEX, MARITAL STATUS OR RACE

Generally

The law relating to discrimination is to be found in the Sex Discrimination Acts 1975 and 1986, the Race Relations Act 1976, the Disability Discrimination Act 1995 and the Employment Act 1989. This legislation is *not* consolidated in the ERA. Before looking at the detail of the relevant legislation we will consider some of the more general provisions of the Employment Act 1989.

Section 1 provides that any legislation dealing with employment and vocational training passed before the Sex Discrimination Act 1975 is overridden by the 1989 Act unless specifically continued in force by that Act. The 1989 Act identifies certain discriminatory provisions and either removes or preserves them (see below). However, because there could be some discriminatory provisions in existing legislation which have not been identified, s 1 overrides them.

Section 2 supports s 1 by giving the Secretary of State power, by statutory instrument, to remove or amend any discriminatory legislation which may be discovered in the future. Section 1 overrides it unless and until it is discovered, and, for the avoidance of doubt, ss 2 and 6 allow the Secretary of State to repeal, or amend, or retain it, when it is discovered.

Section 3 amends s 51 of the Sex Discrimination Act 1975 which exempts acts of discrimination required by statute before 1975. Section 51 was a blanket provision and s 3 cuts it down so that it is still within the law to discriminate in regard to women if it is done to protect them in matters relating to pregnancy and maternity or to comply with those provisions of the Health and Safety at Work Act 1974 which relate to the protection of women.

The specific areas of protection are enacted by s 4 and are set out in Sch 1 to the 1989 Act. They include industrial processes which involve the use of lead and radiation. It is still within the law to discriminate against women workers in these areas because of the risk of foetal damage.

The provisions preventing women from returning to work in a factory within four weeks of childbirth are retained in force.

Section 7 repeals previous law so that women can now work in mines and quarries and clean machinery in factories. The prohibition on women lifting loads 'so heavy as to be likely to cause injury' remain but discrimination is removed by extending the prohibition to men.

In recruitment and selection of employees

The relevant provisions of the Sex Discrimination Acts 1975 and 1986, the Race Relations Act 1976 and the Disability Discrimination Act 1995 are set out below.

Offers of employment

It is unlawful for a person in relation to an employment by him at a place in England, Wales or Scotland and on British ships, aircraft and hovercraft to discriminate against men or women on grounds of sex, marital status, colour, race, disability, nationality or ethnic or national origins:

(a) in the arrangements he makes for the purpose of deciding who should be offered the job; or

(b) in the terms on which the job is offered; or

(c) by refusing or deliberately omitting to offer the job.

'Arrangements' is a wide expression covering a range of recruitment techniques, e.g. asking an employment agency to send only white applicants, or male applicants. Discrimination by employment agencies themselves is also covered.

A decision of the European Court is in point here, and has implications for UK employers. Elizabeth Dekker was refused a job at a youth centre in Holland. She was pregnant when she applied for the job and told the selection committee this. She claimed damages under a Dutch equal treatment law implementing EC Directive 76/207. The European Court decided (see *Dekker* v *Stichting Vormingscentrum etc.* (1991)) that since maternity could never concern anyone but a woman, to take the pregnancy into account in justifying the refusal of a job was direct discrimination on the grounds of sex. Mrs Dekker's claim succeeded. It should be noted that this case is not concerned with dismissal because of pregnancy, which is the concern of the ERA, but the refusal of a job because of pregnancy, which is not covered by that Act. *Dekker* is therefore a case of continuing relevance in that field. The question to be considered is whether the employer would also have rejected a job application from a man who had similar qualifications and experience and would shortly require a long absence from work. If not, there has been unlawful direct discrimination against the pregnant woman. It is not therefore impossible for, say, a small business to show that because of financial constraints a man heading for lengthy time off would not have been taken on, so avoiding an allegation of discrimination.

As regards the terms of the contract of employment, it is unlawful to discriminate against an employee on the grounds listed above in terms of the employment which is given to him or the terms of access to opportunities for promotion, transfer or training, or to any other benefit, facilities, or services, or subjecting him to any other detriment. Thus, it is unlawful to discriminate in regard to matters such as privileged loans, and mortgages by banks and building societies, and discounts on holidays given to employees of travel firms.

A person who takes on workers supplied by a third party, rather than employing them himself, is obliged by the Acts not to discriminate in the treatment of them or in the work they are allowed to do. This means that temporary staff supplied by an agency are covered by the anti-discrimination provisions.

The anti-discrimination provisions except disability are also extended to partnerships as regards failure to offer a partnership, or the terms on which it is offered including benefits, facilities and services. The provision regarding race (but not sex) discrimination applies only to firms of six or more partners, although there is a power in the legislation to reduce this number. The provision as it stands will allow race (but not sex) discrimination in the majority of medical practices but not, for example, in the major accounting and law firms.

Exceptions

There are some circumstances in which it is lawful to discriminate and these will now be considered.

1 Genuine occupational qualification. So far as sex discrimination is concerned, an employer may confine a job to a man where male sex is a 'genuine occupational qualification' (GOQ) for a particular job. This could arise, for example, for reasons of physiology as in modelling male clothes, or authenticity in entertainment, as where a part calls for an actor and not an actress. Sometimes a man will be required for reasons of decency or privacy, such as an attendant in a men's lavatory. Sometimes, too, where the job involves work outside the United Kingdom in a country whose laws and customs would make it difficult for a woman to carry out the job, being a male may be a GOQ. As regards marital status, it may be reasonable to discriminate in favour of a man or a woman where the job is one of two held by a married couple, as where a woman is a housekeeper living in with her husband who is employed as a gardener.

There are, of course, some situations where female sex would be a GOQ for a certain type of job, as the following case illustrates.

Sisley v *Britannia Security Systems* (1983)
The defendants employed women to work in a security control station. The claimant, a man, applied for a vacant job but was refused employment. It appeared that the

women worked 12-hour shifts with rest periods and that beds were provided for their use during such breaks. The women undressed to their underwear during these rest breaks. The claimant complained that by advertising for women the defendants were contravening the Sex Discrimination Act 1975. The defendants pleaded genuine occupational qualification, i.e. that women were required because the removal of the uniform during rest periods was incidental to the employment.

The Employment Appeal Tribunal accepted that defence. The defence of preservation of decency was, in the circumstances, a good one. It was reasonably incidental to the women's work that they should remove their clothing during rest periods.

Comment. However, s 27(4) of the 1975 Act imposes a duty on employers to take reasonable steps to avoid relying on the GOQ exceptions. Thus, in *Etam plc* v *Rowan* (1989) Steven Rowan applied for a vacancy as a sales assistant in Etam's shop in Glasgow which sold only women's and girls' clothing. He was not considered for the post because of his sex and complained to an employment tribunal. There was later an appeal by the employer to the Employment Appeal Tribunal (EAT). The EAT affirmed the employment tribunal's award of £500 to Mr Rowan. He had been discriminated against on the grounds of sex. The EAT found that he would have been able quite adequately to carry out the bulk of the job of sales assistant. Such parts as he could not carry out, such as attendance on women in fitting rooms for the purpose of measuring or otherwise assisting them, could easily have been done by other female sales assistants without causing any difficulty or inconvenience to the employer. It is also worth noting that in *Wylie* v *Dee & Co (Menswear) Ltd* (1978) a woman was refused employment in a men's tailoring establishment in which the rest of the staff were men because it was considered inappropriate for her to measure the inside legs of male customers. An employment tribunal decided that she had been discriminated against because those measurements could have been carried out by other male employees.

A further illustrative example from case law is provided by *Lasertop Ltd* v *Webster* (1997) which also reveals a gap in discrimination law. In that case a man's complaint of sex discrimination, made when he applied for an appointment as a sales staff/trainee manager at a women's health club and was told that only female staff would be employed, failed. The employer was entitled to rely on the defence that being a woman was a 'GOQ' for the post in order to preserve decency and/or privacy. The EAT ruled that it could not be said that the holding of the post, with duties that would involve showing prospective members around the premises, could be undertaken without inconvenience if the post-holder was a man.

A major point of interest in the case relates to the contention that a GOQ could not be applied because the relevant aspects of the job, i.e. those involving decency or privacy such as showing new members around saunas and changing rooms, could have been carried out by female staff. This argument failed because the business was recruiting for start-up staff at the particular branch and *at the time of refusal of the post* there were no female staff actually in employment there. Section 7(4) of the SDA states that the GOQ defence does not apply where the employer 'already has' (male) (female) employees capable of carrying out the GOQ duties. There would appear to be a gap in discrimination law in the sense that if the branch had been in operation the GOQ reference may not have applied, leaving the male applicant discriminated against.

As regards race, it is lawful to discriminate where there is a GOQ for the job as, for example, in the employment of a West Indian social worker or probation officer to deal with problems relating to young West Indians. Other instances are dramatic performances or other entertainment, artists or photographic models and employment in places serving food or drink to be purchased and consumed on the premises by the public. Thus, being Chinese is a GOQ for employment in a Chinese restaurant, but not necessarily in a 'take-away'.

2 Other major exceptions. These are as follows:

(a) *Private households.* Race discrimination is not unlawful where the employment is in a private household. Sex and marital discrimination is now unlawful even in private households (Sex Discrimination Act 1986). However, the 1986 Act provides that sex discrimination may take place where the job is likely to involve the holder of it doing his work or living in a private house and needs to be held by a man because objection might reasonably be taken to allowing the degree of physical or social contact with a person living in the house or acquiring the knowledge of intimate details of such a person's life.

(b) *Work outside Great Britain.* Discrimination legislation does not apply to work which is done wholly outside Great Britain. However, it does apply to work on a British ship, aircraft or hovercraft unless the work is wholly outside Great Britain.

As regards employment outside Great Britain, it should be borne in mind that under Art 39 of the Treaty of Rome, which is directly applicable, there must be no discrimination on grounds of nationality against workers from the EU member states so that discrimination legislation must be applied to protect them. Thus, in *Bossa* v *Nordstress* (1998) a person of Italian nationality living in Great Britain was not interviewed for aircraft cabin crew to be based in Italy. The EAT decided that his claim for racial discrimination must be heard. The decision means, in effect, that the employment outside Great Britain exclusion does not apply where the employment is in another European Union member state.

The previous rule that the UK discrimination provisions did not apply where the job was 'wholly or mainly' outside Great Britain was changed by the Equal Opportunities (Employment Legislation) (Territorial Limits) Regulations 1999, so that the job must now be wholly outside Great Britain. This strengthens workers' rights. Discrimination law applies even when the job is mainly outside Great Britain.

(c) *Special cases.* The anti-discriminatory rules apply to Crown appointments. However, certain public sector jobs are not entirely covered by the discrimination provisions, e.g. there may be discrimination as regards height in the police and prison services. The armed forces are given protection except where sex discrimination is necessary to ensure 'combat effectiveness'. The legal barriers to men becoming midwives have been removed.

Other special cases are set out in s 5 of the Employment Act 1989 under which the appointment of head teachers in schools and colleges may be restricted to members of a religious order where such a restriction is contained in the trust deed or other relevant instrument. Furthermore, a university professorship may be restricted to a man if there is a statutory requirement that the holder of the post should also be a canon. In practice this will apply only to certain professorships of Divinity. Finally, academic appointments in university colleges may be restricted to women where this was required when the 1989 Act came into force. In practice the provision applies to two colleges at Oxford – Somerville and St Hilda's, and to two at Cambridge – Lucy Cavendish and Newnham. The Secretary of State has power to remove these exemptions by statutory instrument.

(d) *Positive discrimination* is allowed in regard to any payments made or special conditions allowed in the training of single (or lone) parents. Thus payment of child care costs for single parents in the context of special training and employment and enterprise schemes does not amount to unlawful discrimination against married people under the 1975 Act.

Other exceptions also known as 'positive action' are designed to help women (and, less likely, men) compete on equal terms in the labour market. Thus an employer can run single sex training courses so as to equip women (or men) with skills for specific jobs in which they are under-represented. Selection must nevertheless always be made on merit. Similar arrangements may be made for under-represented racial groups.

Types of discrimination

There are two forms of discrimination as follows:

1 Direct discrimination, which occurs where an employer or prospective employer treats a person less favourably than another on grounds of sex, race, disability, or marital status, as where an employer refuses, on discriminatory grounds, to grant a suitably qualified person an interview for a job. In addition, the segregation of workers once in employment on discriminatory grounds is also unlawful direct discrimination.

Examples are provided by the following cases.

Coleman v Skyrail Oceanic Ltd (1981)

The claimant, Coleman, who was a female booking clerk for Skyrail, a travel agency, was dismissed after she married an employee of a rival agency. Skyrail feared that there might be leaks of information about charter flights and had assumed that her dismissal was not unreasonable since the husband was the breadwinner. The Employment Appeal Tribunal decided that the dismissal was reasonable on the basis that the husband was the breadwinner. However, there was an appeal to the Court of Appeal which decided that those provisions of the Sex Discrimination Act which dealt with direct discrimination and dismissal on grounds of sex had been infringed. The assumptions that husbands were bread winners and wives were not were based on sex and were discriminatory. The claimant's injury to her feelings was compensated by an award of £100 damages.

Comment. The claimant was also held to be unfairly dismissed having received no warning that she would be dismissed on marriage. The additional and discriminatory reason regarding the breadwinner cost the employer a further £100.

Johnson v Timber Tailors (Midlands) (1978)

When the claimant, a black Jamaican, applied for a job with the defendants as a wood machinist the defendants' works manager told him that he would be contacted in a couple of days to let him know whether or not he had been successful. Mr Johnson was not contacted and, after a number of unsuccessful attempts to get in touch with the works manager, was told that the vacancy had been filled. Another advertisement for wood machinists appeared in the paper on the same night as Mr Johnson was told that the vacancy had been filled. Nevertheless, Mr Johnson applied again for the job and was told that the vacancy was filled. About a week later he applied again and was again told that the job had been filled although a further advertisement had appeared for the job on that day. An employment tribunal decided that the evidence established that Mr Johnson had been discriminated against on the grounds of race.

Bloomberg Financial Markets v Cumandala (2000)

C applied for a post in Madrid but the company did not offer him the job because he wanted to return to London every weekend to see his wife. C was black and of Angolan nationality. He claimed marital and race discrimination. The EAT ruled that there was no marital discrimination. The employer simply felt that C could not give the necessary commitment to the job given the weekly commuting. The employer would have taken the same view if, for example, C had been a keen football fan and had wished to commute every weekend in the season to see his favourite team. However, in appointing a white person, the view had been expressed that he would 'fit in better'. The EAT ruled that there had, in consequence, been unlawful race discrimination in that aspect of the employment.

Comment. Shorter-distance commuting may result in a successful claim for marital discrimination in the case where an applicant wants to see his family at weekends.

Other examples. The following fact situations are offered as further examples of direct discrimination:

● A black clerk applies to a bank for a job. He is the only suitably qualified applicant. If he had been white, the interviewer would have appointed him. In the event, no appointment is made and it is decided to readvertise. The bank has directly discriminated against the black applicant. There can be a finding of direct discrimination against an employer even if he has no hostile motive.

● A firm wishes to appoint a woman to a post as senior manager. She will be dealing mainly with one particular client who says he would prefer not to work with a woman. The firm therefore appoints a man instead. This is direct discrimination.

● A company wishes to recruit a black woman as supervisor of a typing pool but there is a change of mind when some of the white employees object. This is direct racial discrimination.

2   Indirect discrimination, as where an employer has applied requirements or conditions to a job but the ability of some persons to comply because of sex, disability, marital status or race is considerably smaller and cannot be justified.

Examples are provided by the following cases.

Price v The Civil Service Commission (1977)

The Civil Service required candidates for the position of executive officer to be between $17\frac{1}{2}$ and 28 years. Belinda Price complained that this age bar constituted indirect sex discrimination against women because women between those ages were more likely than men to be temporarily out of the labour market having children or caring for children at home. The Employment Appeal Tribunal decided that the age bar was indirect discrimination against women. The court held that the words 'can comply' in the legislation must not be construed narrowly. It could be said that any female applicant could comply with the condition in the sense that she was not obliged to marry or have children, or to look after them – indeed, she might find someone else to look after them or, as a last resort, put them into care. If the legislation was construed in that way it was no doubt right to say that any female applicant could comply with the condition. However, in the view of the court, to construe the legislation in that way appeared to be wholly out of sympathy with the spirit and intention of the Act. A person should not be deemed to be able to do something merely because it was theoretically possible; it was necessary to decide whether it was possible for a person to do so in practice as distinct from theory.

Bohon-Mitchell v Council of Legal Education (1978)

The claimant, an overseas student, complained of discrimination in regard to a requirement of the defendants that a student would have to undergo a 21-month course, as opposed to a diploma of one year, to complete the academic stage of training for the Bar where he did not have a UK or Irish Republic university degree. This rule was regarded by an industrial tribunal to be discriminatory because the proportion of persons not from the UK or Irish Republic who could comply was considerably smaller than persons from the UK or Irish Republic who could and the rule was not justifiable on other grounds. The claimant satisfied the tribunal that there had been indirect discrimination.

Comment. The other side of the coin is illustrated by *Panesar* v *Nestlé Co Ltd* (1980) where an orthodox Sikh, who naturally wore a beard which was required by his religion, applied for a job in the defendants' chocolate factory. He was refused employment because the defendants applied a strict rule under which no beards or excessively long hair were allowed on the grounds of hygiene. The claimant made a complaint of indirect discrimination but the defendants said that the rule was justified. The Court of Appeal decided that as the defendants had supported their rule with scientific evidence there was in fact no discrimination.

A further example is offered. A company has a strict office rule under which women may not wear trousers in the office. A Muslim woman applies for a job with the company but is unable to comply with this rule because religion and custom require that she must cover her legs. Although religious discrimination as such is not forbidden the proportion of the members of her racial group who can comply with the requirement is considerably smaller than the proportion of other persons who can apply. There is therefore indirect discrimination.

Homosexuals and transsexuals

It is clear that neither the SDA 1975 nor the law of the EU covers discrimination on the grounds of sexual orientation as such. EU law does cover and prohibits discrimination that results from an employee's gender reassignment. The authority is the ruling of the ECJ in *P* v *S and Cornwall CC* (1996) where the court decided in favour of a transsexual who was dismissed after a sex change. The decision put the UK government under some pressure to clarify the law and the Sex Discrimination (Gender Reassignment) Regulations 1999 (SI 1999/1102) were introduced to cover discrimination on grounds of gender reassignment in employment and vocational training. There are no similar regulations applying to homosexuals.

The High Court did refer to the ECJ the question of whether sex discrimination might include homosexuals under the EC Equal Treatment Directive (see *R* v *Secretary of State for Defence, ex parte Perkins* (1997)). However, the ECJ first heard the case of a lesbian railway clerk who was denied free travel concessions for her female partner and ruled that the claim for sexual discrimination failed (see *Grant* v *South-West Trains Ltd* (1998)). The *Perkins* case was then withdrawn (see *R* v *Secretary of State for Defence, ex parte Perkins* (No 2) (1998).

Gay employees, however, can claim sexual discrimination as between themselves, as where they can show a discriminatory act based on gender, e.g. that the employer has treated a gay man less favourably than a lesbian woman would be treated (see *Smith* v *Gardner Merchant Ltd* (1996).

As regards developments, the EAT continues to rule against homosexuals, as in *Pearce* v *Governing Body of Mayfield School* (2000) where it decided that the verbal abuse of a lesbian teacher by pupils relating to her homosexuality did not amount to sexual discrimination under the SDA 1975 since the Act gave protection from discrimination on grounds of sex not sexual orientation.

However, the European Court of Human Rights has decided that certain members of the UK armed forces who were discharged because of their homosexuality had been subjected to a violation of their human rights (see *Lustig-Prean and Becket* v *United Kingdom* (1999)). The decision means that the armed forces have had to revise their policy on homosexuals, but the decision has no binding effect on private business but only on 'emanations of the state', such as public authorities.

Reform

The Employment Framework Directive has been approved by the EU governments. It requires the introduction of regulations on discrimination on grounds of sexual orientation. The Directive also improves the rights of older workers, of handicapped people and members of religious and ethnic minority groups.

Under the Directive EU governments must introduce laws preventing discrimination on grounds of sexual orientation or religious or ethnic grounds by 2003, and on the grounds of handicap and age by 2006. Sanctions for non-compliance will include compensation and reinstatement.

Workers with HIV or AIDS

Once again, there is no specific legislation prohibiting discrimination against employees with HIV or AIDS. Workers with a progressive condition, such as HIV or AIDS, are not deemed disabled until the disease is having a 'substantial effect' on the carrying out of day-to-day duties. Where the condition is not having this effect, there is no protection.

Remedies

Allegations of discrimination may be the subject of a complaint to an employment tribunal which may, among other things, award monetary compensation. Also, as we have seen, the Commission may apply to the courts for judicial review, as in *R v Secretary of State for Employment, ex parte Equal Opportunities Commission* (1994) where the application, if successful, would help in working towards the elimination of discrimination.

In addition, the Equal Opportunities Commission, which is responsible for keeping under review the working of sex discrimination legislation, including equal pay, and the Commission for Racial Equality, which has a similar function in terms of racial discrimination, may carry out formal investigations into firms where discrimination is alleged and may issue non-discrimination notices requiring the employer to comply with the relevant legislation.

The employer may appeal to an industrial tribunal within six weeks of service of the notice. If there is no appeal, or the industrial tribunal confirms the notice, then the employer must comply with it; if he does not the relevant Commission may ask the county court for an injunction which, if granted, will make an employer who ignores it in contempt of court and he may be fined and/or imprisoned for that offence.

The Commissions are also required to enter non-discrimination notices which have become final in a Register. Copies of the Register are kept in Manchester (Equal Opportunities Commission) and in London (Commission for Racial Equality), and are available for inspection to any person on payment of a fee and copies may also be obtained.

Under s 6 of the Sex Discrimination Act 1986 terms of contracts, collective agreements and organisational rules which are discriminatory on the grounds of sex, e.g. not employing women with children, or bonus schemes which exclude part-timers most of whom are women, are void. However, there was no mechanism for individuals to get a legal ruling on these provisions. As a result of an amendment to s 6 by what is now the ERA, job seekers, employees and prospective members of trade or professional organisations can now ask a tribunal to give a declaration that a term is void. The tribunal cannot amend the term. The parties must decide what should fill the gap.

The Disability Rights Commission has similar powers to the Equal Opportunities Commission and the Commission for Racial Equality.

So far as individuals affected are concerned, the most usual remedy for a successful complaint of discrimination is an order for payment of compensation to the victim. The tribunal can also make a recommendation as regards action the employer can take to remedy the situation which can lead to a further award of compensation if there is a failure to comply. Recommendations are, in practice, rarely made. Money compensation can include compensation for injured feelings and aggravated damages, and there is no overall limit.

Relationship between the Sex Discrimination Act and the Equal Pay Act

The two Acts do not overlap. Complaints of discrimination in regard to pay and other non-monetary matters governed by the contract of employment, such as hours of work, are dealt with under the Equal Pay Act and complaints of discrimination in regard, for example, to access to jobs are dealt with under the Sex Discrimination Act. A complaint to an employment tribunal need not be based from the beginning on one Act or the other. A tribunal is empowered to make a decision under whichever Act turns out to be relevant when all the facts are before it.

Discriminatory advertisements for employees

The sex discrimination and racial discrimination legislation make it unlawful to place advertisements for employees which are discriminatory unless they relate to a recognised exceptional case, as where, for example, there is a GOQ. Thus job descriptions such as 'waiter', 'salesgirl', 'stewardess' or 'girl friday' have largely disappeared from our newspapers and one now finds the descriptions 'waiter/waitress' or the expression 'male/female' as indicating that both sexes are eligible for employment. However, one still sees advertisements which are clearly intended to attract female applicants which, nevertheless, remain within the law, e.g. 'publishing director requires sophisticated PA/secretary with style and charm who can remain cool under pressure'.

Before legislation relating to discrimination came into force, advertisements in the UK were discriminatory mainly as regards sex, but obviously an advertisement which said 'Chinese only' would be unlawful unless there was a GOQ as, for example, there would be where the advertisement was for a waiter in a Chinese restaurant.

As regards sanctions, the placing of discriminatory advertisements may lead to the issue of a non-discrimination notice by the appropriate Commission; this, if not complied with, may lead to proceedings being taken by the Commission in an industrial tribunal. If the industrial tribunal accepts the contention of discrimination and yet the advertiser does not comply but continues to advertise in a discriminatory way, the Commission may take proceedings in the county court for, among other things, an injunction. If this is not complied with, the advertiser is in contempt of court and may be punished by a fine or imprisonment unless he complies.

In addition, it is a criminal offence to place a discriminatory advertisement and those who do so may be tried by magistrates and are subject to a fine. The person who publishes the advertisement, e.g. a newspaper proprietor, also commits a criminal offence. However, he may not know precisely that the advertisement is discriminatory. For example, without a knowledge of the advertiser's business, he cannot really know whether there is a GOQ or not. Accordingly, he is given a defence to any criminal charge if he can show that in publishing the advertisement:

(a) he relied on a statement by the person placing it to the effect that it was not unlawful and on the face of it might come within one of the exceptional cases; *and*

(b) it was reasonable for him to rely on that statement.

Age discrimination

The government has issued *Age Diversity in Employment*, which is a non-statutory code of practice to tackle age discrimination in employment, together with accompanying guidance for employers and illustrative case studies. Tribunals may choose to take it into account when considering, e.g., cases of unfair selection for redundancy. The code sets out good practice in the areas of recruitment, selection, promotion, training and development, redundancy and retirement.

The Disability Discrimination Act 1995

The recruitment implications of this Act are set out below.

Applicants for employment. It is unlawful under s 4 of the Act to discriminate against a disabled person:

- in the arrangements, including the advertisements, made for deciding who should be offered employment and its terms;
- by refusing to offer or deliberately not offering employment.

In other words, in deciding whom to interview, whom to give the employment to and the offer's terms, s 5 carries an employer's defence which allows discrimination if, but only if, the reason for it is both material to the circumstances of the case and substantial. Thus, less favourable treatment may be justified if the employer believes on reasonable grounds that the nature of the disability substantially affects the disabled person's ability to perform the required task(s).

It is also against the law for trade associations, trade unions and professional bodies to treat a disabled person less favourably than someone else.

The Act will receive further consideration later in this chapter, but it will suffice to say here that employers are required to make adjustments in the working conditions and workplace to accommodate disabled persons but cost may be taken into account in deciding what is reasonable (s 6).

Exceptions. The employment part of the Act does not apply to employers who employ fewer than 15 people but they will be encouraged to follow good practice guidelines. The government may lower this limit so as to include more employers following advice from the Disability Rights Commission. The Act does not apply to operational staff employed in the armed forces, the police or prison services, the fire services or to anyone employed on board ships, hovercraft or aeroplanes. Complaints must be made to an employment tribunal within three months of the act complained of. Remedies are considered later in this chapter.

Unlike the sex discrimination rules, there are no provisions in the Disability Discrimination Act 1995 that require a tribunal to take into account associated organisations, such as wholly owned subsidiaries, when calculating the number of employees (see *Hardie* v *CD Northern Ltd* (2000). There are, of course, no small-employer exemptions in the sex discrimination legislation but s 82 of the SDA 1975 does carry an employer definition that includes associated employers where this is relevant.

The Asylum and Immigration Act 1996

This Act is relevant in terms of recruitment and is now in force. It contains provisions designed to prevent illegal working by immigrants, overstayers and those breaching their immigration conditions. Under regulations made by the Secretary of State employers must take steps to check the existence (but not the authenticity) of documents such as birth certificates or certificates of registration or naturalisation to prevent illegal working. If such checks have been carried out and illegal employment takes place nevertheless the employer is not liable. Failure to check responsibility can result in a fine on the employer of up to a maximum of £5,000. In the case of a corporate employer, directors and other officers and management of the company may be similarly prosecuted if they have connived at the offence or it has been committed as a result of their neglect. There is no need to check existing employees. The Act does not apply to employees under the age of 16 or to self-employed or agency workers. Furthermore, employers are not required to check the status of employees who come to the organisation following a transfer of undertakings. Non EEA (European Economic Area) students must get permission from the local Jobcentre for a specific job, and as regards university students permission may be obtained from the Department for Education and Employment.

Other matters relevant to recruitment

Criminal records. The Home Office plans to give easier access to job applicants' criminal records. A White Paper sets out proposals for a new Criminal Records Agency that would charge job applicants for providing information to them about criminal records where the employer has asked for this. The provisions are in the Police Act 1997 which has received Royal Assent. The section relevant to the above matters is not yet in force. However, the government is proceeding with the setting up of the Criminal Records Bureau and has indicated that certificates relating to criminal records will be issued from July 2001.

Medical examinations. It was held in *Baker* v *Kaye* (1997) that a doctor retained by an employer to carry out pre-employment medical assessments on prospective employees owed a duty of care to those examined to take reasonable care in carrying out his examination and assessment of suitability for employment. If he fails to do so he may be sued by the prospective employee who is not, for medical reasons, offered the job.

The above decision was reversed by the Court of Appeal in the next case.

Kapfunde v *Abbey National plc* (1999)

K applied for a job with the defendants. She filled in a medical questionnaire which was considered by a doctor. He did not see K but concluded from the questionnaire that she would have a higher than usual level of absence. She did not get the job. It was held that Abbey National was not liable, even if the doctor's assessment could have been proved to have been negligent, because Abbey National did not employ him. As regards a claim against the doctor personally, it was held that, contrary to *Baker*, there was no special relationship leading to a duty of care. Commenting on *Baker*, the Court of Appeal said there was no duty of care in that case either even though the doctor did actually see the claimant in that case before making an assessment.

Additionally, it was held by the Court of Appeal in *Kapadia* v *Lambeth London Borough Council* (2000) that an employee cannot legally prevent disclosure of medical records to the employer as part of expert evidence at a tribunal. The claim was for disability discrimination and the employee had consented to a medical examination by the employer's medical expert.

Protection of children

The Protection of Children Act 1999 makes changes to the law with the object of creating a framework for identifying people who are unsuitable for work with children and to compel, or in some cases to allow, employers to access a single point for checking the names of people they propose to employ in a post involving the care of children. This will involve permitting checks against criminal records and two lists of people considered unsuitable for work with children. The Department of Health and the Department for Education and Employment will maintain the lists to be made via the Criminal Records Bureau, which is due to come into operation under Part V of the Police Act 1997.

Discrimination once in employment

We have already considered the law relating to discrimination in formation of the contract, i.e. in recruitment and selection, and in terms of remuneration, i.e. equal pay. Discrimination on termination of the contract will be dealt with later when we look at discriminatory dismissal. Here we are concerned with discrimination in the treatment of employees during the course of the contract of employment.

Discrimination on the grounds of sex or race. Under the sex and race discrimination legislation it is unlawful to discriminate against a person on grounds of sex or race as regards opportunities for promotion, training, or transfer to other positions, or in the provision of benefits, facilities or services, or by dismissal or by any other disadvantages. It was decided in *Porcelli v Strathclyde Regional Council* (1986) that sexual harassment which affects a woman's working conditions is contrary to ss 1(1) and 6(2)(b) of the Sex Discrimination Act 1975 under the general heading of subjection to a 'detriment' on the grounds of sex. There are many complaints to industrial tribunals about sexual harassment, mainly by women but sometimes by younger male employees complaining of sexual harassment by other male employees. Sexual harassment is actionable whether it is physical or verbal, whether it is aggressive or merely unwanted, and whether it involves threats or promises, e.g. of promotion in return for sexual

favours. Complaints can be brought by those still employed or by those who have resigned because of harassment. The employer is very often liable, since in the vast majority of cases the tribunal has not regarded the employee involved in harassing the other(s) as being beyond the scope of his employment, though the employer may have the 'reasonable steps' defence set out below.

Individuals are sometimes reluctant to bring proceedings for sexual harassment because of the inevitable publicity given to such proceedings by the media. However, there are provisions in the Employment Tribunals Act 1996 under which employment tribunals and the Employment Appeal Tribunal will remove from documents available to the public any information which might identify the alleged victim or other parties or witnesses. In addition, tribunals have a discretion to make a restricted reporting order forbidding media reporting on the application of one of the parties. The order is not automatically granted; application must be made. Transgression of such an order is punishable by a fine of up to £5,000. The provisions also extend to disability cases.

An illustrative example of a successful race discrimination case appears below.

Burton v De Vere Hotels Ltd (1997)

The appellants were two young Afro-Caribbean women. They were employed as casual waitresses at the Pennine Hotel, Derby. On the relevant occasion some 400 men, members and guests of the City of Derby Round Table, attended a dinner at the hotel, the speaker being Mr Bernard Manning.

The appellants heard Mr Manning making jokes about the sexual organs and sexual abilities of black men. He made racially offensive remarks to them and created an atmosphere which, said the EAT, probably encouraged some guests further to abuse them. The appellants brought complaints against their employer under the Race Relations Act 1976. Section 4 of that Act is relevant and provides that it is unlawful for a person in the case of a person employed by him to discriminate against that employee by subjecting him to detriment.

The employment tribunal found that the two employees had suffered the detriment of racial harassment but had been subjected to it by Mr Manning and the guests and not by the employers. There was an appeal to the EAT by the appellants. The EAT did not agree with the employment tribunal. The problem was to decide the extent of the duty of an employer to protect the employee from harassment by third parties. This involved an examination of the true meaning of the word 'subjecting' to detriment. In the EAT's view 'subjecting' connoted 'control'. A person subjected another to something if he caused or allowed that something to happen in circumstances where he could control whether it happened or not. Here the employer could, by good employment practice, have prevented the harassment or reduced the extent of it. Mrs Justice Smith said that the hotel manager ought to have warned his assistant managers to keep a lookout for Mr Manning and to withdraw the young waitresses if things became unpleasant. He did not do so because he did not give the matter a thought. He should have done.

If the assistant managers had been properly instructed, said the judge, the two young women would not have suffered any harassment. They might possibly have heard a few offensive words before they were withdrawn but that would have been all. Therefore, the employer 'subjected' the appellants to the racial harassment which they received from Mr Manning and the guests. The case was remitted to the employment tribunal for the assessment of compensation. It will be borne in mind that there is no cap on such compensation.

Comment. Of course, the employer will not always be in control. As the EAT said, the employer of a bus or train conductor might feel that an employee would face a genuine risk of racial harassment at times, and yet the prevention of such harassment would be largely beyond the control of the employer. All he could do would be to make his attitude to such behaviour known to the public and to offer his employee support if harassment occurred. However, where there is control there is likely to be liability if it is not exercised properly.

Most complaints of discrimination against employers relate to discrimination in relation to promotion, detrimental treatment or dismissal.

We have already noted that the law allows women to receive special treatment when they are pregnant and there is no discrimination where the sex or racial status of the employee is a genuine occupational qualification.

There are some exemptions in special cases, such as height in the case of police officers and prison officers, which have already been considered in the material relating to recruitment. The armed forces are now generally brought within the sex and racial discrimination provisions, though in regard to sex discrimination there is an exemption for acts done for the purpose of ensuring the 'combat effectiveness' of the armed forces.

There is also an exemption in respect of discriminatory training. An employer or a body responsible for training may provide training exclusively applicable to persons of a particular sex or racial group where the purpose is to enable them to take up work in situations where that sex or racial group is under-represented, but there may not be discrimination in terms of recruitment for such work. Trade unions may also take special action to attract members of particular sexual or racial groups into membership or to office in the union where there is under-representation (and see the somewhat similar provisions in regard to single parents already considered).

A major development in case law occurred in the decision of the EAT in *Falkirk Council* v *Whyte* (1997). The ruling appears to close a major loophole in the law. This relates to the fact that it has generally been held by tribunals that discrimination does not apply where the alleged discriminatory matter is expressed only as a *preference* for the job and not *a condition of employment or promotion.* However, in the *Whyte* case the EAT ruled that the operation of the relevant Acts is not avoided where it is clearly a decisive factor in appointment or promotion. In the case management training was said to be 'desirable' (though in the event vital to promotion), as also was 'supervisory experience'. There was an adverse effect on women applicants who had not had the opportunity to meet these qualifications.

Enforcement

As regards enforcement, if an unlawful act of discrimination is committed by an employee such as a personnel officer, the employer is held responsible for the act along with the employee unless the employer can show that he took all reasonable steps to prevent the employee from discriminating. If he can do this, only the employee is responsible.

Individual employees who believe that they have been discriminated against may make a complaint to an employment tribunal within three months of the act complained of. It is then the duty of a conciliation officer to see whether the complaint can be settled without going to a tribunal. If, however, the tribunal hears the complaint, it may make an order declaring the rights of the employer and the employee in regard to the complaint, the intention being that both parties will abide by the order for the future.

The tribunal may also give the employee monetary compensation, and there is no limit on the award in sex, race or disability cases, and may additionally recommend that the employer take, within a specified period, action appearing to the tribunal to be practicable for the purpose of obviating or reducing discrimination.

Lastly, the Sex Discrimination Act 1986 deals with discrimination in retirement age and provides that organisations with a compulsory retirement age will have to make sure it is the same for men and women. A woman who is forced to retire earlier than her male colleagues will be entitled to claim unfair dismissal.

None of the above rulings and provisions has at present any effect on the state retirement pension under which women retire at 60 and men at 65. The Pensions Act 1995 contains provisions to give a common retiring age of 65 for both men and women to be phased in from 2010 to 2020.

Discrimination against married persons

The anti-discriminatory provisions outlined in the previous section are applied also to discrimination against married persons. An employer must not treat a married person of either sex, on the ground of his or her marital status, less favourably than he treats or would treat an unmarried person of the same sex; e.g. there must not be a marriage bar attached to a particular employment, unless, of course, there is a GOQ (see *Bloomberg Financial Markets* v *Cumandala* (2000) above).

Homosexuals, transsexuals and workers with HIV or AIDS

These matters have already been considered in the section of this chapter relating to recruitment.

Victimisation in employment

Under the sex, racial and disability discrimination legislation it is unlawful to treat a person less favourably than another because that person asserted rights under the equal pay or other anti-discriminatory legislation relating to sex or race or has helped another person to assert such rights or has given information to the Equal Opportunities Commission or the Commission for Racial Equality, or it is thought that he or she might do so.

Damages can be awarded where victimisation has occurred. An example is to be found in *Cornelius* v *Manpower Services Commission* (1986) where the Commission refused to consider C for a permanent post for which she had applied because one of the references which she had supplied indicated that she was involved in an unresolved sexual harassment case.

Other examples not uncommon in business are pressuring an employee to drop a claim of discrimination and refusing holiday leave at the time desired by the employee. We have already considered the protection offered by the Public Interest Disclosure Act 1998 in regard to victimisation or dismissal following whistleblowing.

DISABILITY DISCRIMINATION

The Disability Discrimination Act 1995 applies. The main twin aims of the Act are to render unlawful discrimination when already in employment and when applying for a job and to provide a right of access to services, goods and facilities for the disabled. This section is concerned only with the employment aspects.

What is disability?

Section 1 defines a disabled person as a person who has a physical or mental impairment which has a substantial and long-term adverse effect on his or her ability to carry out normal day-to-day activities. Schedule 1 expands on this and states among other things that 'mental impairment' includes an impairment resulting from or consisting of a mental illness only if the illness is well recognised clinically. It also states that impairments which would have an effect on a person's ability but for medical treatment or some form of aid are included. Section 3 allows the Secretary of State to issue Guidance and there are various rule making powers to carry the definition further.

A variety of conditions can be brought under the general definition of physical and mental impairment. In *O'Neill* v *Symm & Co Ltd* (1998) the EAT accepted that chronic fatigue syndrome (ME) fell within the definition. The EAT has also accepted that employees who were suffering from depression were disabled persons under the Act (see *Kapadia* v *London Borough of Lambeth* (2000)). It is clear from the above decisions that employers should be especially cautious before they dismiss employees on the grounds of ill-health since the condition may be regarded as a 'disability' for the purposes of the 1995 Act. Medical reports should be obtained and the employer should consult with the employee to see whether any adjustments can be made in the work situation such as a transfer to a new post or by providing additional training or making modifications in the workplace or equipment. It is the need to take these steps that distinguishes dismissal for an unsatisfactory sickness record (which may be fair) from a disability dismissal leading to a claim for uncapped damages. In this connection, the Court of Appeal has rejected the idea that in a disability dismissal there can be a comparison between the treatment of a disabled person and a person suffering from long-term sickness (see *Clark* v *TDG Ltd (t/a Novacold)* (1999)).

Impairment of long-term effect

Schedule 1 applies and states that impairment is of long-term effect if it has lasted for 12 months, or is likely so to last, or is likely to last for life. A severe disfigurement is included. The effect on normal day-to-day activities is dealt with by a list in para 4 of Sch 1 which includes mobility, manual dexterity, physical coordination and lack of ability to lift or speak, see, hear, remember, concentrate, learn or understand or to perceive the risk of physical danger. Also included are those who have a progressive condition such as HIV resulting in impairment of ability provided the effect is currently substantial. Persons who were on the register of disabled persons kept under s 6 of the Disabled Persons (Employment) Act 1944 when the relevant provisions came into force are deemed disabled.

The Act also covers in s 2 'a person who has had a disability', even though he or she may no longer be disabled. This applies in regard to employment, services and discrimination in regard to premises and follows a government pledge that those with a history of disability should be covered.

Employees

Under s 4 it is unlawful for an employer to discriminate against a disabled employee:

- in the terms of employment and the opportunities for promotion, transfer, training or other benefits or by refusing the same;
- by dismissal or any other disadvantage.

This is firmed up as regards pensions by s 17 which makes clear that trustees and managers of occupational pension schemes are under a general duty not to discriminate against the disabled. This rule will be implied into the rules of occupational pension schemes. However, it is envisaged that pension benefits of disabled people might justifiably be less than those who are not disabled.

As regards insurance benefits, where an employer makes arrangements for employees with an insurance company for matters such as private health insurance, the insurance company will under s 18 act unlawfully if it treats a disabled person in a way which would be an act of discrimination if done by the insurance company to a member of the public generally. This covers refusal to insure and the levying of higher premiums unless justified as it may be if there are reasonable grounds for supposing that the disabled person represents a higher than normal risk.

Employer's defence

Section 5 which deals with the meaning of discrimination allows employer discrimination if, but only if, the reason is both material to the circumstances of the case and substantial. Thus, less favourable treatment may be *justified* if the employer believes on reasonable grounds that the nature of the disability substantially affects the disabled person's ability to perform the required task.

Reasonableness is of course related to practicability in terms of how useful the adjustments will be and the cost and the ability of the organisation to meet them. The value of the employee, which includes training, skill and service, is also a relevant factor. Thus a high cost adjustment might be required as reasonable for a long-serving managing director but not for a temporary cleaner.

In this regard, an employment tribunal accepted the defence of justification in *Kelly* v *Hampshire Constabulary* (1997). The claimant suffered from cerebral palsy and so needed help in various ways including eating and using the toilet. The employers offered him employment on the basis that they would try to make the necessary arrangements to accommodate him. The employers were later able to satisfy a tribunal that although they had made every effort to do this, it was impossible for them to accommodate him and because of this they were held not to have discriminated when the employment did not continue.

It is, or course, important that the employer be aware of the disability. See *O'Neill* v *Symm & Co Ltd* (1998), where the employers were not liable for the dismissal of an accounts clerk suffering from ME because they had not been aware of the nature of her illness and so could not have her treated her less favourably than an employee who did not have this disability. The dismissal was for the amount of sick leave taken and non-production of a doctor's certificate, which the contract of employment required. In addition, the employers had not infringed the requirement of the Act to take all reasonable steps to find out about the disability since in the circumstances of the case there was nothing to put the employers on inquiry. Where, however, the employer is aware of facts which put him on inquiry, the matter may be different.

H J Heinz v *Kenrick* (2000)

K was dismissed after a long period of sickness absence. His employers knew of his symptoms and that ME was a disability within the scope of the DDA 1995. They did not know, however, the exact nature of the reason behind his absence when they dismissed him. The EAT did not follow its earlier decision in *O'Neill* and in fact doubted it. The employers' lack of precise knowledge as to absence was no defence and K's dismissal was unlawful as a dismissal based on disability discrimination.

Comment. the result of this case in terms of employers is that where an employee has been absent for sickness for a reasonable amount of time and it appears that this will continue, it is prudent for the employer to start asking more questions about the reasons for that absence. Failure to do so could result in a disability claim where there is no cap on compensation by reason of the employer's own inaction or lack of knowledge.

Duty to make adjustments

Section 6 includes 12 examples of steps, e.g. altering working hours, acquiring or modifying equipment, arranging for training and providing supervision, an employer may have to take so as to comply with a new duty to make reasonable adjustments to working arrangements or the physical features of premises where these constitute a disadvantage to disabled persons. However, s 6 specifies that regard shall be had to the extent to which it is practical for the employer to take the steps involved, the financial and other costs to be incurred and the extent of any disruption to the employer's activities and his financial and other resources. Section 16 contains provisions relating to adjustments in leasehold premises. The tenant employer must seek the consent of the landlord. The latter must not withhold consent unreasonably.

Exemption for small businesses

Section 7(1) provides that nothing in Part II of the Act (Employment) shall apply to an employer who has fewer than 15 employees. The Secretary of State may substitute a lower number.

As we have seen, there are no provisions in the DDA 1995 that require the taking into account of employees of associated companies, such as wholly owned subsidiaries (see *Hardie* v *CD Northern Ltd* (2000).

Validity of agreements

Section 9 provides that any term in a contract of employment or other agreement is void if, e.g., it requires a person to do anything which would contravene Part II or prevent a complaint to an industrial tribunal unless in the latter case the exclusion is in writing and follows independent legal advice or the matter has been settled by reference to a conciliation officer.

Discrimination by other persons

An important provision is contained in s 12 which provides protection for disabled contract workers who work for an employment business. The hirer must not discriminate against them. Here the following case is instructive.

MHC Consulting Services Ltd v *Tansell* (1999)

T was employed by I Ltd which was a service company of which he was the sole shareholder. I Ltd offered T's computer services to third parties and I Ltd contracted with MHC, which in turn contracted with Abbey Life, the end user. T was, therefore, subject to the control of Abbey Life. T brought a disability discrimination claim against Abbey Life because it had rejected his services because of his disability. This caused MHC to do the same. The EAT had to interpret s 12 and decided that although T was not employed by Abbey Life, his remedy was against Abbey Life. Otherwise MHC, if the principal, could justify its actions by reference to the rejection by Abbey Life.

Comment. The case widens the scope of s 12 by allowing it to accommodate a series of contracts, the end user being the principal for the purposes of s 12. The reasoning may also apply to sex and race discrimination cases involving contract workers. The 'end user' interpretation tends to the view that those who benefit from the person's work are responsible for complying with the relevant legislation.

Victimisation

It also amounts to discrimination under the Act if someone is treated less favourably because they have brought, or given, evidence in claims under the Act, or merely made allegations that the Act has been infringed.

Enforcement

Under s 8 employment complaints are to be presented to an employment tribunal. Regulations allow a restricted reporting order where 'evidence of a personal nature' is likely to be heard.

The claim must be brought within three months of the act complained of and the tribunal may take any of the following steps as it considers just and equitable:

- make a declaration of the rights of the complainant as a basis for these to be adopted by the employer;
- order monetary compensation with no limit;
- recommend steps to be taken by the employer within a specified period to obviate or reduce the adverse effects of which the employee complains.

The services of ACAS can also be invoked with a view to settlement without a tribunal hearing.

There is no cap upon the compensation which may be awarded for disability discrimination. In *Kirk* v *British Sugar plc* Nottingham Employment Tribunal (December 1997/January 1998, unreported) a partially sighted employee who was able to prove that his defective eyesight was the dominant factor in his selection for redundancy was awarded £100,000. The scores he achieved in his assessment were influenced by his disability and were not an objective assessment based upon his past work performance. The tribunal accepted that a partially sighted person would have greater difficulties in obtaining employment and based the award on the finding that he would not get alternative employment for the rest of his working life of 15 years, less 20 per cent to take account of the risk that had he stayed on his eyesight might have deteriorated to the point where he could not continue.

Employers should note that the number of cases involving disability discrimination is increasing. In this area, as in so much of modern labour law, employers need to be aware of their duties and to be pro-active in respect of them.

In regard to compensation, it is important to note that the EAT has set aside an employment tribunal award of £1,500 compensation for injured feelings under the DDA 1995. It said that the tribunal, in error, had taken the employer's size and resources into account (see *Evans* v *Oaklands Nursing Home Group Ltd* (2000)). The EAT directed that there should be a fresh hearing with a clean sheet.

The EAT made a consistent ruling in a sex discrimination case (*Ministry of Defence* v *Cannock* (1994)), stating that an award for injury to feelings is based solely on principles of compensation which the claimant makes for it and must prove. The decision is not comforting for small employers, though there is exemption for the very small employer under discrimination legislation concerned with disability but not with sex.

Questionnaires

Disabled persons who think they have been subject to discrimination can serve questionnaires on the employer in the same way as for sex and race claims.

The Disability Rights Commission (DRC)

The Disability Rights Commission Act received the Royal Assent on 27 July 1999. It sets up the Disability Rights Commission which is now in operation.

The DRC will:

- work towards eliminating discrimination against disabled people;
- promote equal opportunities for disabled people;
- provide information and advice in particular to disabled people, employers and service providers;
- prepare codes of practice and encourage their use;
- review the working of the Disability Discrimination Act 1995;
- investigate discrimination and ensure compliance with the law;
- arrange for a conciliation service between service providers and disabled people to help resolve disputes on access to goods and services.

Illustrative case law – generally

1 An employment tribunal at Bury St Edmunds made what was one of the first decisions on the Disability Discrimination Act 1995 (see *Tarling* v *Wisdom Toothbrushes Ltd* (1997)). It appears that Mrs Barbara Tarling, aged 48, who has a club foot, brought a claim against her employers, Wisdom, alleging unfair dismissal at a toothbrush factory by reason of her disability. She had been employed at the Wisdom factory at Haverhill, Suffolk for 16 years but latterly she had suffered increasing pain in her legs and hips, leading to her not achieving her production targets. She was forced to take four weeks' sick leave and was dismissed on her return. The employment tribunal ruled that she should be reinstated and awarded her £1,200 compensation for injury to her feelings.

It seems that the company had failed to make reasonable adjustments in the workplace to accommodate Barbara Tarling's disability in that she might have been better able to perform her duties by using a special chair which Wisdom were advised by the Department for Education and Employment to use. However, that advice was not followed through and a series of 'ordinary' chairs were provided. The tribunal found that the special chair could have been obtained on free trial and that because of available assistance the cost to the employer might not have been more than £200. In the tribunal's view this 'was not something that would have caused a significant problem and was a reasonable step'.

2 An employment tribunal decided that an employer did not treat a disabled person less favourably when it expressed concern about the amount of his absence through sickness and reminded him that payments during sickness were at the employer's discretion (see *O'Dea* v *Bonart Ltd* (1997)).

Mr O'Dea was a registered disabled sales representative. His sickness absences amounted to 107 days over three years. His employer had expressed concern about this. Later it became clear that Mr O'Dea would need a further period of four months off for an operation. The employer informed him by letter that any sick pay would be discretionary. Mr O'Dea complained to an employment tribunal on the basis of unfavourable treatment for a reason relating to his disability contrary to s 5(1)(a) of the Disability Discrimination Act 1995.

The employment tribunal held that the employee was entitled to be concerned about the situation and it was reasonable for the employer to raise the issue of sickness absence with Mr O'Dea and to remind him of the discretionary nature of sickness payments. In addition, any implication in the letter that he would not necessarily receive sick pay for the forthcoming period of absence was justified under s 5(1)(b) of the 1995 Act as a proper exercise of the employer's discretion. Mr O'Dea's claim was dismissed.

Guidance

The Department for Education and Employment has issued guidance for employers on how to avoid discrimination against disabled people: see *Disability Discrimination Act 1995 – What Employers Need to Know*. A code of practice entitled 'The Code of Practice for the elimination of discrimination in the field of employment against disabled persons or persons who have a disability' can be purchased from the Stationery Office.

Policy statement

On the basis of the guidance, it is useful for employers to draw up a policy statement for staff regarding disability discrimination and how it should be dealt with.

Unfair dismissal and disability discrimination

The following table illustrates the contrast.

	Unfair dismissal	Disability discrimination
Service	One year's service before eligibility to claim	No minimum service necessary
Incapability	A valid reason for dismissal	Where incapability relates to disability, a claim for disability discrimination may be made
Compensation	Cap of £51,700	No cap on compensation

TERMINATION OF THE CONTRACT OF EMPLOYMENT

Unfair dismissal

Generally

Before a person can ask an industrial tribunal to consider a claim that another has unfairly dismissed him or her it is once again essential to establish that the relationship of employer and employee exists between them. In this connection the ERA provides that an employee is a person who works under a contract of service or apprenticeship, written or oral, express or implied.

An example of a case where a person failed in an unfair dismissal claim because he was unable to show that he was an employee is given below.

Massey v *Crown Life Insurance Co* (1978)

Mr Massey was employed by Crown Life as the manager of their Ilford branch from 1971 to 1973, the company paying him wages and deducting tax. In 1973, on the advice of his accountant, Mr Massey registered a business name of J R Massey and Associates and with that new name entered into an agreement with Crown Life under which he carried out the same duties as before but as a self-employed person. The Inland Revenue were content that he should change to be taxed under Schedule D as a self-employed person. His employment was terminated and he claimed to have been unfairly dismissed. The Court of Appeal decided that being self-employed he could not be unfairly dismissed.

In addition to showing that he is an employee, the claimant must satisfy an **age requirement**. The unfair dismissal provisions do not apply to the dismissal of an employee from any employment if the employee has on or before the effective date of termination attained the age which, in the undertaking in which he is employed, was the normal retiring age for an employee holding the position which he held, or, for both men and women, age 65.

However, such persons are not excluded where the dismissal is automatically unfair, e.g. for taking part in trade union activities. (See further later in this chapter.) There are two important developments to note here.

1 There have been allegations that the law as stated above is illegal as being contrary to EU law. This issue will not be settled until the ECJ rules in *Simpson* v *British Timken Ltd* (1998), where an equivalent provision in relation to redundancy is the subject of a reference to the ECJ.

2 There is no question of age discrimination where an employer enforces an early retirement provision in the contract of employment, even though that contract may contain an equal opportunities clause, provided that the contract contains a clause under which continuation in employment beyond the date of retirement is at the employer's discretion (see *Taylor* v *Secretary of State for Scotland* (2000)).

Continuous service – generally

As regards the period of employment, the unfair dismissal provisions do not apply to the dismissal of an employee from any employment if the employee has not completed at least one year's continuous employment ending with the effective date of termination of employment unless the dismissal is automatically unfair.

Automatically unfair dismissals

In the case of an automatically unfair dismissal, no length of service is required before a claim can be brought.

The reasons which make a dismissal automatically unfair can be listed as follows:

(a) trade union membership or activities including protected industrial action;

(b) not belonging to a trade union or particular union;

(c) pregnancy, maternity, parental or dependants leave;

(d) selection for redundancy on any of the above grounds;

(e) the transfer of the undertaking or a reason connected with it (unless there is an ETO). It should, however, be noted at this point that the one-year qualifying period does not apply where the complaint is based on dismissal for one of the automatically unfair reasons, though if the dismissal related to the transfer of an undertaking the one-year qualifying period does apply;

(f) asserting a statutory employment right under ERA 1996, s 104;

(g) in health and safety cases involving union safety representatives and now including being an employee safety representative or putting up for election to be one;

(h) performing the duties of a member-nominated trustee under the Pensions Act 1995;

(i) being an employee representative in redundancy consultation or putting up for election to be one (ERA 1996, s 103);

(j) refusing (in certain circumstances) to do shop or betting work on a Sunday;

(k) dismissal for exercising rights under the Working Time Regulations including rights as an employee representative in connection with workforce agreements (s 101(A), ERA 1996, as inserted by the regulations);

(l) dismissal for asserting rights under the National Minimum Wage Act 1998 (s 104(A), ERA 1996, as inserted by the NMW Act 1998);

(m) dismissal for asserting rights to time off for study or training under s 63A of the ERA 1996, as inserted by the Teaching and Higher Education Act 1998;

(n) dismissals of employees because they exercised or tried to exercise the right under s 19 of the Employment Relations Act 1999 to be accompanied at disciplinary and grievance hearings or because they accompanied a fellow worker to such a hearing;

(o) protection of whistleblowers under the Public Interest Disclosure Act 1998.

It should also be noted that employees have the right not to be dismissed, regardless of age or service, if the dismissal involves sex, racial or disability discrimination or victimisation.

Continuous service EC and other developments

On the issue of continuous service, an important development in case law should be noted. In *R v Secretary of State for Employment, ex parte Seymour-Smith* (1996) the Court of Appeal decided that the two-year rule before a claim for unfair dismissal can be brought was indirectly discriminatory against women. Fewer women than men could qualify because women workers tended to move in and out of the labour market more frequently than men, due to family commitments. The effect of this decision on private-sector employees, with whom we are mainly concerned, is that they may have a claim against the government for failing to implement the Equal Treatment Directive properly. They cannot sue their employers because only the state as an employer was involved in this case.

In *R v Secretary of State for Employment, ex parte Seymour-Smith and Another* (1997) the House of Lords discharged the declaration made by the Court of Appeal on the ground that (1) it did not help the employees concerned with the claim against their employers who are in the private sector, and to whom the Directive is not directly applicable; (2) the facts on which the declaration was based are not now the same. Since 1993 the gap between men and women who could qualify under the two-year rule has now narrowed; and (3) it would not enable the employees to make a claim against the state for incorrectly implementing the equal treatment directive, since such a claim would have to be brought against the Attorney-General and the issues would not necessarily be the same.

However, since the employees had also introduced incompatibility with Art 141 of the Treaty of Rome (Equal Pay) (which is directly applicable), the case was referred to the European Court of Justice for a ruling on the applicability of Art 141.

The ECJ decided in February 1999 not to give a ruling on the alleged discriminatory period of two years for claims for unfair dismissal. However, the House of Lords held that the period of two years' service was a form of indirect sexual discrimination since the proportion of men who could comply was greater than women, the latter, often because of domestic reasons, moving in and out of jobs. Nevertheless, the House of Lords felt the two-year period was justified as encouraging employers to recruit staff (see *R v Secretary of State for Employment, ex parte Seymour-Smith* (2000)).

The above litigation has been rendered ineffective since the Unfair Dismissal and Statement of Reasons for Dismissal (Variation of Qualifying Period) Order 1999 came into force for dismissals on or after 1 June 1999. It reduces the service period to one year. The only consequence of the litigation is that many claims held in abeyance and by persons with less than two years' service are now lost because the 1999 order is not retrospective.

It was decided in *Colley v Corkindale (t/a Corker's Lounge Bar)* (1996) that continuity of employment was not broken simply because the employee worked alternate weeks over the then two-year period.

The following are also ineligible and cannot claim:

1   Those on fixed contracts of one year or more, if they have agreed in writing, either in the contract or during its duration, to forgo the right to compensation.

The rules allowing contractual waiver of unfair dismissal claims was repealed by the Employment Relations Act 1999. Agreements in fixed-term contracts to exclude the unfair dismissal provisions are valid if entered into before 25 October 1999. The rules relating to the exclusion of redundancy rights in fixed-term contracts continue.

2   As regards dismissal during industrial action, the position is as follows:

- a worker dismissed while taking *unofficial industrial action* cannot claim unfair dismissal;
- the Employment Relations Act 1999 provides that a worker who is dismissed by reason of taking *official action* can claim unfair dismissal if the dismissal takes place within the period of eight weeks beginning with the day on which the worker first took part in industrial action. Dismissal during unofficial action is not protected nor is action that involves unlawful secondary action, even if official.

3   Certain other categories are excluded by the ERA, e.g. employees over retiring age and police officers. Members of the armed forces are now covered by the unfair dismissal provisions of the ERA provided they have first followed service redress procedures.

Pre-hearing reviews

If the complaint appears to be a frivolous one, the employer should ask the tribunal office to arrange a pre-hearing review. A chairman may or may not then agree to this. Alternatively, a chairman may order a pre-hearing review even if no one requests one.

No evidence is given at a pre-hearing review. However, the employer or his representative will have the opportunity to argue why the complaint against him is unfounded and is unlikely to succeed. If these arguments are accepted, the tribunal may be prepared to give a 'costs warning' to the complainant. The effect will be that he or she will then be at an increased risk of being ordered to pay the costs if the complainant goes to a hearing and is unsuccessful.

In theory, a 'costs warning' could be given to the respondent, if the defence as a whole or one particular line of defence which has been put forward appears unlikely to have any prospect of success. In practice, however, a 'costs warning' is rarely given to a respondent.

The pre-hearing assessment is not to be confused with the preliminary hearing. This is an informal hearing, commonly arranged in discrimination and other complicated cases. The purpose of it is to clarify the issues and sort out the procedure for the full hearing of the matter.

Rules allow a tribunal either on its own motion or that of the parties to hold a preliminary hearing on 'entitlement'. This allows the 'weeding out' of cases in which it has no jurisdiction.

A tribunal can at a pre-hearing review also require a party to deposit £150 as a condition of being allowed to proceed if a claim or a defence is weak. The deposit is not lost if the claim or defence is established at a hearing.

Reform

The government has announced changes to further control vexatious claims against employers. Tribunals will be given power to award costs against unreasonable litigants of up to £10,000. The current limit is £500. Also, the deposit that the tribunal may require in a case regarded as weak will go up from £150 to £500. However, legal aid (help at court) was extended to employment tribunals in Scotland from 15 January 2001, and may be extended to England and Wales. The change has been pushed ahead by human rights challenges to the lack of legal aid for tribunals.

Conciliation

The respondent employer may have good reason for fighting a particular claim all the way, for example where it could open the floodgates to similar claims. In general, however, he should be prepared to consider the possibility of settling a claim against him, so long as this can be done on reasonable terms. The main advantages of a settlement are:

(a) saving the costs of legal representation at the hearing;

(b) possible saving of a great deal of valuable time. Although many employment tribunal cases are concluded in one day, others last several days or even weeks during which employees, often senior employees, are taken away from their usual work while giving evidence or waiting to give evidence;

(c) avoiding unfavourable publicity;

(d) a public defeat is more likely than a settlement to damage morale within the organisation and to encourage further claims;

(e) it may be possible to settle the claim for substantially less than the amount which would be awarded by the employment tribunal.

There is a great deal to be said for negotiating through an ACAS (Advisory, Conciliation and Arbitration Service) conciliation officer. Anything said to or by the conciliation officer is privileged and cannot be disclosed or referred to at a tribunal hearing. Furthermore, the conciliation officer, being impartial, can take much of the heat out of the situation.

An ACAS conciliated settlement operates as a bar to proceeding or continuing with a range of tribunal complaints such as unfair dismissal (see Employment Tribunals Act 1996 and the ERA).

While there is no reason why the above procedure involving ACAS should not be followed it should be noted that the ERA provides for binding agreements not to bring or continue proceedings before an employment tribunal to be made between employer and employee even though ACAS is not involved. However, the term which precludes the employee's right to bring or continue with proceedings before an employment tribunal in regard to the dispute covered by it will only be enforceable if all of the following conditions are met:

● the employee must have received independent advice from a solicitor holding a practising certificate or a barrister who is in practice as such or employed to give legal advice;
● the advice must be covered by professional negligence insurance;
● the advice must make clear that the employee is giving up his right to go to a tribunal;
● the agreement must be in writing, identify the legal adviser and state that the conditions regulating a compromise agreement (as they are called) are satisfied.

A claim for a payment of money due under a compromise agreement can be enforced directly by a tribunal.

Dismissal – meaning of

An employee cannot claim unfair dismissal unless there has first been a dismissal recognised by law. We may consider the matter under the following headings:

1 **Actual dismissal.** This does not normally give rise to problems since most employees recognise the words of an actual dismissal, whether given orally or in writing.

A typical letter of dismissal appears below.

> **Dear Mr Bloggs,**
>
> I am sorry that you do not have the necessary aptitude to deal with the work which we have allocated to you. I hope you will be able to find other work elsewhere which is more in your line. As you will recall from your interview this morning, the company will not require your services after the 31st of this month.

2   Constructive dismissal. This occurs where it is the employee who leaves the job but he is compelled to do so by the conduct of the employer. In general terms the employer's conduct must be a fundamental breach so that it can be regarded as a repudiation of the contract. Thus, if a male employer were sexually to assault his female secretary, this would be a fundamental breach entitling her to leave and sue for her loss on the basis of constructive dismissal.

As regards illustrative case law, it was held by the EAT in *Greenaway Harrison Ltd* v *Wiles* (1994) that an employee who resigned after her employer threatened to give her due notice if she refused to agree to a change in her pattern of shifts, i.e. to a major change in the terms of her contract, was constructively dismissed. Again, in *Whitbread plc (t/a Thresher)* v *Gullyes* (1994) the EAT decided that an employee who resigned from a management position because her employer did not give her proper support where, among other things, the most experienced staff were transferred out of her branch without consultation, was constructively unfairly dismissed.

It is worth noting that the employer's breach that justifies the employee's action in leaving the job must, as we have seen, be a fundamental breach (or breach of a condition), in other words a repudiatory breach. As is the case with other contracts, such a breach cannot be relied upon unless accepted by the other party, in this case the employee. The employee should, therefore, make clear, such as in the letter of resignation, that the resignation results from the employer's breach, otherwise there may be difficulties in establishing constructive dismissal (see *Holland* v *Glendale Industries Ltd* (1998) where the employee's prime motive in resigning was to take early retirement). Nevertheless, the fact that there is no mention at the time of resignation that the employee regards it as a constructive dismissal is not an absolute bar to a claim.

3   Fixed-term contracts. When a fixed-term contract expires and is not renewed, there is a dismissal.

The rules allowing a contractual waiver of unfair dismissal claims was repealed by the Employment Relations Act 1999. Agreements to exclude unfair dismissal provisions entered into before 25 October 1999 continue to have effect and may still be met with in practice.

Dismissal – grounds for

If an employer is going to escape liability for unfair dismissal, he must show that he acted **reasonably** and, indeed, the ERA requires the employer to give his reasons for dismissal to the employee in writing.

It should be remembered that the question whether a dismissal is fair or not is a matter of **fact** for the particular tribunal hearing the case and one cannot predict with absolute accuracy what a particular tribunal will do on the facts of a particular case. Basically, when all is said and done, the ultimate question for a tribunal is: 'Was the dismissal fair and reasonable' in fact?

The ERA includes in the test of reasonableness required in determining whether a dismissal was fair, the 'size and administrative resources of the employer's undertaking'. This was included as a result of fear that the unfair dismissal laws were placing undue burdens on small firms and causing them not to engage new workers. The ERA also removes the burden of proof from the employer in showing reasonableness so that there is now no 'presumption of guilt' on the employer and the tribunal is left to decide whether or not the employer acted reasonably.

Reasonableness – an old test resurrected

The Employment Appeal Tribunal resurrected an old test for reasonableness in unfair dismissal cases (see below, *Haddon* v *Van den Bergh Foods Ltd* (1999)). At one time tribunals dealt with the general fairness test for dismissals under s 98(4) of the Employment Rights Acts 1996 by asking themselves what they would have done if they had been in the employer's place. However, the Court of Appeal in *British Leyland Ltd* v *Swift* (1981) said this was wrong and only if no reasonable employer would have dismissed the employee was the latter to be regarded as unfairly dismissed. There was, in other words, a band of reasonableness. This meant that in some cases the test of the perverse or harsh employer was applied, the tribunal saying in effect that although they would not have dismissed the employee in the circumstances, some employers might have done so, and so the dismissal was not unfair.

Haddon v *Van den Bergh Foods Ltd* (1999)

The claimant employee was to receive a long-service award half-way through his shift. He asked his immediate manager if he had to return to work after the award ceremony. The manager said 'yes' because of staff shortages. He then asked another manager who said he need not return to work. After the award he went home and did not tell his immediate manager. He was, in consequence, dismissed.

His claim for unfair dismissal was dismissed by an employment tribunal. His dismissal was within the band of reasonable responses (the perverse or harsh employer syndrome, no doubt). The EAT allowed Mr Haddon's appeal. The band of reasonable responses test was wrong: tribunals should test reasonableness by asking what they would have done in the circumstances and then see if the dismissal was in general terms equitable (as s 98(4) requires).

Reasonableness – an old test rejected

There was a quick response to *Haddon* by a differently constituted EAT in *Midland Bank* v *Madden* (2000) where the range of reasonable responses test was restored on the basis that *British Leyland* v *Swift*, being a Court of Appeal decision, could not be overruled by the EAT. This must be accepted. The remainder of the judgment in *Madden* in terms of the correct test was not well received in legal circles and is not dealt with here. However, the Court of Appeal has now heard an appeal in *Madden*. Van den Bergh Foods did not appeal. The Court of Appeal gave its judgment in the *Madden* case on 31 July 2000 along with an associated case (*Foley* v *Post Office; HSBC Bank plc* v *Madden* (2000)). The Court of Appeal endorsed a ruling by the EAT under Judge Peter Clark in *Beedell* v *West Ferry Printers* (2000), summarised below.

Beedell v *West Ferry Printers* (2000)

In this case the Court of Appeal ruled as follows:

1 The band of reasonable responses test must be applied and in considering whether a dismissal is reasonable the question that the tribunal must ask is –

> If no reasonable employer would have dismissed [the employee] then the dismissal is unfair. But if a reasonable employer might reasonably have dismissed [the employee] then the dismissal is fair...even though some other employers may not have dismissed [the employee].

2 The above test does not extend to the perverse employer who will presumably be regarded as unreasonable if his response is indeed perverse.

3 The tribunal must not substitute its own view for that of the employer either as to the reason for dismissal or as to its reasonableness.

4 In cases of dismissal the long established test in *British Home Stores Ltd* v *Burchell* (1978) must be applied. This contains a three part test:
   - In a misconduct case did the employer believe that the employee was guilty of misconduct?
   - Did the employer have reasonable grounds for that belief?
   - Had the employer carried out as much investigation into the matter as was reasonable in the circumstances? An employer who accepts the findings of an investigation too readily and uncritically will fail this part of the test.

Comment. the Court of Appeal's ruling in this case is good news for employers (tough but not perverse), particularly when recent reforms have unleashed an unfair dismissal boom. Employees may well find some rather harsh decisions by employers will be acceptable to tribunals. This is the practical effect of the *Madden* ruling. However, the need to adopt fair procedures remains important.

1 Potentially fair reasons. These are as follows:

(a) *Lack of capability or qualifications.* This would usually arise at the beginning of employment where it becomes clear at an early stage that the employee cannot do the job in terms of lack of skill or mental or physical health. It should be remembered that the longer a person is in employment the more difficult it is to establish lack of capability.

By way of illustration we can consider the case of *Alidair* v *Taylor* (1977). The pilot of an aircraft had made a faulty landing which damaged the aircraft. There was a board of inquiry which found that the faulty landing was due to a lack of flying knowledge on the part of the pilot, who was dismissed from his employment. It was decided that the employee had not been unfairly dismissed, the tribunal taking the view that where, as in this case, one failure to reach a high degree of skill could have serious consequences, an instant dismissal could be justified. As regards qualifications, this could occur where a new employee does not have the qualification claimed or fails to get a qualification which was a condition of employment, as in the case of legal and accounting trainees who fail to complete their examinations.

It would also apply if a qualification was lost as where a long-distance lorry driver lost his driving licence or a solicitor was struck off by the Law Society for some kind of conduct in breach of the rules of the Society.

(b) *Conduct.* This is always a difficult matter to deal with and much will depend upon the circumstances of the case. However, incompetence and neglect are relevant, as are disobedience and misconduct, e.g. by assaulting fellow employees. Immorality and habitual drunkenness could also be brought under this heading and so, it seems, can dress where this can be shown to affect adversely the way in which the contract of service is performed.

Boychuk v *H J Symonds (Holdings) Ltd* (1977)

Miss B was employed by S Ltd as an accounts audit clerk but her duties involved contact with the public from time to time. Miss B insisted on wearing badges which proclaimed the fact that she was a lesbian and from May 1976 she wore one or other of the following: (a) a lesbian symbol consisting of two circles with crosses (indicating women) joined together; (b) badges with the legends 'Gays against fascism' and 'Gay power'; (c) a badge with the legend 'Gay switchboard' with a telephone number on it and the words 'Information service for homosexual men and women'; (d) a badge with the word 'Dyke', indicating to the initiated that she was a lesbian.

These were eventually superseded by a white badge with the words 'Lesbians ignite' written in large letters on it. Nothing much had happened in regard to the wearing of the earlier badges but when she began wearing the 'Lesbians ignite' badge there were discussions about it between her and her employer. She was told she must remove it – which she was not willing to do – and if she did not she would be dismissed. She would not remove the badge and was dismissed on 16 August 1976 and then made a claim for compensation for unfair dismissal.

No complaint was made regarding the manner of her dismissal in terms, e.g. of proper warning. The straight question was whether her employers were entitled to dismiss her because she insisted on wearing the badge. An employment tribunal had decided that in all the circumstances the dismissal was fair because it was within an employer's discretion to instruct an employee not to wear a particular badge or symbol which could cause offence to customers and fellow employees. Miss B appealed to the Employment Appeal Tribunal which dismissed her appeal and said that her dismissal was fair. The EAT said

that there was no question of Miss B having been dismissed because she was lesbian or because of anything to do with her private life or private behaviour. Such a case would be entirely different and raise different questions. This was only a case where she had been dismissed because of her conduct at work. That, the EAT said, must be clearly understood.

Comment. (i) The decision does not mean that an employer by a foolish or unreasonable judgment of what could be expected to be offensive could impose some unreasonable restriction on an employee. However, the decision does mean that a reasonable employer, who is, after all, ultimately responsible for the interests of the business, is allowed to decide what, upon reflection or mature consideration, could be offensive to customers and fellow employees, and he need not wait to see whether the business would in fact be damaged before he takes steps in the matter.

(ii) In *Kowalski* v *The Berkeley Hotel* (1985) it was decided by the EAT that the dismissal of a pastry cook for fighting at work was fair although it was the first time he had done it. As regards smoking at work, it was decided in *Dryden* v *Greater Glasgow Health Board* (1992) that employees have no implied contractual right to smoke at work. If, as in Mrs Dryden's case, the employee leaves because he or she is not allowed to smoke there is no constructive dismissal. The employer in this case had offered counselling but without success.

Before an employee is dismissed for misconduct, the employer must be able to answer yes to each of the following questions:

(a) Does he believe the employee to be guilty of the misconduct in question? (It is self-evident that the dismissal must be unfair if he does not genuinely believe in the employee's guilt.)

(b) Does he have reasonable grounds for that belief?

(c) Has he, in order to form that belief, carried out all the investigations reasonably to be expected of him in the circumstances? Alternatively, has the employee admitted the misconduct?

(d) Has he given the employee a fair hearing, both on the question of whether he is guilty of the misconduct and on the question of the appropriate penalty, and has he taken fully into account what he or she has had to say?

(e) Is it reasonable, in the circumstances, for him to decide to dismiss the employee rather than to impose some lesser penalty, such as suspension?

So far as (b) is concerned, the question is whether the employer has reasonable grounds for his belief, having regard to the information which was then available to him or should have been available to him if he had investigated properly. It is immaterial if information which comes to light subsequently would have caused him to take a different view.

It was held by the EAT in *Boys and Girls Welfare Society* v *McDonald* (1996) that the questions set out above, called the *Burchell* guidelines (see *British Home Stores* v *Burchell* (1978)), are not *automatically applicable* in every complaint of unfair dismissal on the grounds of alleged misconduct. They give valuable guidance but it must always be borne in mind that the question of what is reasonable must always be decided in the words of s 98(4) of ERA 1996 which in summary provides that once a potentially fair reason has been established it is then necessary for a tribunal to consider whether the employer acted fairly in dismissing for that reason. There is no burden of proof on either the employer or employee. The matter is to be determined 'in accordance with equity and the substantial merits of the case'.

On the issue of reasonable grounds for belief, the Employment Appeal Tribunal has decided that an employee was fairly dismissed on the grounds of theft, even though the employer could not specifically prove loss of stock but had only a reasonable belief in the employee's guilt.

Francis v Boots the Chemists Ltd (1998)

The employee had been dismissed for misconduct on the grounds that he was involved in the theft of stock from the company's warehouse. He contended that his dismissal could not be regarded as fair on the sole basis of the employer's reasonable belief that he had been involved in theft unless a theft in terms of missing stock could be proved. Boots could not establish any specific loss from its stock records.

The EAT rejected the employee's contentions. Circumstantial evidence could be enough and there was such evidence in this case. It included the fact that a security guard saw the employee's car, identified by its registration number, being loaded with boxes at night at a Boots warehouse. The EAT held that the dismissal was fair.

Comment. The EAT stressed that tribunals should be wary of accepting as grounds for reasonable belief that a theft had taken place allegations put forward by a large employer who could not prove that theft because of inadequate records. There would usually be every reason to assume that a large company, such as Boots, running a warehouse would have records under which it would be possible to know whether stock had been moved unlawfully.

Misuse of the Internet as misconduct. Cases are coming before tribunals, as was expected, relating to dismissals for misuse of the Internet by employees at work. An employment tribunal found in the first case of its kind that an employee who had surfed the net during working hours had not been unfairly dismissed for doing so.

Franxhi v Focus Management Consultants (1999)

Lois Franxhi was alleged to have surfed the Internet for cheap holidays during working hours and her employers sacked her. She alleged that this was because she was pregnant. A director of the company stated that she had been using her computer to do nearly 150 searches on the Internet. She alleged that the total time amounted to 111 minutes over four days including two full lunch breaks. She also stated that the director concerned was aware of her searches and had even asked her how to access Liverpool Football Club's web page. His attitude changed, she said, when he discovered she was pregnant.

Nevertheless, the tribunal dismissed Mrs Franxhi's claims for unfair dismissal and sex discrimination, but a claim for wrongful dismissal by breach of contract for failure to give proper notice was upheld and a week's pay in lieu of notice awarded.

Drink and drugs as misconduct. An employee's use of drugs outside the workplace is unlikely to amount to a fair reason for dismissal nor will the mere fact that an employee concealed a drug problem when recruited. The employee's condition may, however, constitute a fair reason for dismissal if the employer believes on reasonable grounds that it makes the employee unsuitable for the position which he or she holds. It is advisable to have a policy on drink and drugs. If this is inserted into the employer's disciplinary rules, there will normally be no need to get the consent of employees, but they must be informed of the changes. Any attempt to make such rules a term or condition of employment would require the consent of the employees concerned.

(c) *Sickness and injury.* The possibilities here are as follows:

- The employee may, because of injury or illness, have become incapable of doing the job. Here a dismissal should be regarded as fair, provided that the employer has fully investigated the matter and discussed it with the employee and considered the possibility of alternative work.
- The employee may have repeated absences for minor illnesses. Here the employer should consult with the employee to indicate the problems being created and to see whether there is any assistance the employer can give. However, a fair dismissal may be made if the absences continue. *It is important for the employer to keep full written records of absence.* Any dismissal will certainly be unfair if it is based on a vague impression that the employee has been off work rather often.
- The employee may have a longer term absence with no prospect, it appears, of a return to work. Here the employer should have discussions with the employee on the lines set out above, and obtain medical reports with the employee's consent. The possibility of alternative work should be considered, but given adverse medical opinion and proper discussion with the employee, a dismissal may be fair.

It is important now in all sickness dismissal cases to consider the possibility of disability discrimination where the legal requirements may require more of the employer, e.g. adjustments in the workplace.

(d) *Redundancy.* Genuine redundancy is a defence. Where a person is redundant, his employer cannot be expected to continue the employment, although there are safeguards in the matter of **unfair selection for redundancy** and where there was no genuine redundancy situation or the employer failed to consult or failed to offer alternative employment where this was possible. As regards unfair selection for redundancy, a tribunal will expect a methodical approach, as by awarding each potentially redundant worker with points against various criteria dismissing those who score least. A consistent and objective process will usually justify a dismissal (*Williams and Others* v *Compair Maxam* (1982)).

(e) *Statutory restriction placed on employer or employee.* If, for example, the employer's business was found to be dangerous and was closed down under Act of Parliament or ministerial order, the employees would not be unfairly dismissed. Furthermore, a lorry driver who was banned from driving for 12 months could be dismissed fairly under this heading also.

(f) *Some other substantial reason.* An employer may on a wide variety of grounds which are not specified by legislation satisfy an employment tribunal that a dismissal was fair and reasonable.

Crime and suspicion of crime may be brought under this head, though if dismissal is based on suspicion of crime, the suspicion must be reasonable and in all cases the employee must be told that dismissal is contemplated and in the light of this information be allowed to give explanations and make representations against dismissal.

Where an employee has been charged with theft from the employer and is awaiting trial, the best course of action is to suspend rather than dismiss him, pending the verdict. Investigations which the employer must make, as part of establishing a fair dismissal, could be regarded as an interference with the course of justice. It is best, therefore, not to make them, but to suspend the employee.

The matter of fair or unfair dismissal depends also upon the terms of the contract. If the difficulty is that a particular employee is refusing to do work which involves him, say, spending nights away from home, then his dismissal is likely to be regarded as fair if there is an **express term** in his contract requiring this. Of course, the nature of the job may require it, as in the case of a long-distance lorry driver – where such a term would be implied if not expressed.

Employees who are in breach of contract are likely to be regarded as fairly dismissed. However, this is not an invariable rule. Thus a long-distance lorry driver who refused to take on a particular trip because his wife was ill and he had to look after the children would be unfairly dismissed (if dismissal took place) even though he was, strictly speaking, in breach of his contract.

One of the most common reasons for dismissal under this head is a *dismissal because of reorganisation.* The employer is entitled to reorganise the workforce and the terms and conditions under which they work in order to improve efficiency. An employee who does not cooperate with the changes can be fairly dismissed (*Lesney Products* v *Nolan* (1977)). It is enough if the employer can show that the reorganisation is for sound business reasons, but the reorganisation need not be essential in that, for instance, the business would not survive without it.

The overall requirement of reasonableness. In cases other than those where the dismissal is automatically unfair, there are two questions to be answered:

- Is the dismissal for one of the reasons recognised by law? (See above.)
- If so, did the employer act reasonably in dismissing in the circumstances?

As regards reasonableness, we have already considered the decisions in *Haddon* and *Maddon* to which reference may usefully be made again at this point. It should be borne in mind that the above cases are mainly concerned with *whether the tribunal should attempt to decide whether the employer's conduct is within the reasonable band of employer responses*. The answer is that the tribunal must do this and not substitute its own view. *Further guidance on reasonableness*, as such, appears below in the *Mills* case.

2 Grievance and disciplinary procedures are usually part of the contract. The employer must comply with them if he wishes to avoid liability. If a series of oral and written warnings is laid down, the procedure should be observed. However, reasonableness will always prevail.

No matter how good the employer's reason for dismissal may be there may still be a claim by the employee for unfair dismissal if the dismissal was 'unfair in all the circumstances'.

In *Whitbread & Co plc* v *Mills* (1988) the then President of the Employment Appeal Tribunal, Mr Justice Wood, gave guidance on the issue of whether an employer had acted reasonably as the law requires. In applying the guidance let us assume that the main reason for dismissal is the acceptable one of incompetence as in the case of a senior member of a publisher's staff who commissions books without proper market research so that they do not sell and the publisher is caused loss.

Having reached the conclusion that the incompetence is established, the employer must, according to Mr Justice Wood, satisfy a tribunal on four other matters, otherwise the dismissal might still be unfair, though the employee's compensation might be reduced for contributory fault (see below). The four matters are:

(a) Can the employer satisfy a tribunal that he complied with the pre-dismissal procedures which a reasonable employer could and should have applied in the circumstances of the case? If the tribunal finds that the employer has not acted reasonably in this regard, at the date of dismissal, then according to the decision in *Polkey* v *A E Dayton Services Ltd* (1987) it is not open to the tribunal to say that the procedures do not matter since it is clear that the employee was incompetent. The unfairness of the dismissal could still give the employee a successful claim.

Thus, the decision of the House of Lords in Polkey makes clear the importance of consultation in regard to the fairness of a dismissal. There may be grounds for dismissal but if there is no proper consultation the dismissal may still be unfair, though the compensation will generally be reduced if there were grounds for dismissal. However, it is not always necessary to consult, said the House of Lords: it depends on all the circumstances. Thus, in *Eclipse Blinds* v *Wright* (1992) Mrs Wright was dismissed because of poor health. The employer had received a medical report with her consent. It revealed that she was much more seriously ill than she thought, and rather than upset her in a consultation process the personnel officer wrote her a letter in sympathetic terms ending her employment on the grounds of incapability. The court decided that she was not unfairly dismissed even though there had been no proper consultation.

(b) Where there is a contractual appeal process, the employer must have carried it out in its essentials. A minor departure may sometimes be ignored but a total or substantial failure entitles a tribunal to find that the dismissal was unfair. Even though no contractual appeal process exists, it may nevertheless be reasonable, as was decided in *West Midlands Cooperative Society Ltd* v *Tipton* (1986), for some sort of appeal to be arranged since this is encouraged by the code of practice issued by the Advisory, Conciliation and Arbitration Service.

(c) Where conduct is the main reason, the employer must show, on a balance of probabilities, that at the time of the dismissal he believed the employee was guilty of misconduct and that in all the circumstances of the case it was reasonable for him to do so.

Williams v Royal Institution of Chartered Surveyors (1997)
Ms Williams had been employed by the Royal Institution for 11 years. She was a marketing manager with no disciplinary record. Her work was highly regarded. At the office Christmas party in 1995 she got seriously drunk but promised that it would not happen again. However, in July 1996 she concluded an agreement with a supplier and spent the rest of the afternoon with the supplier in the employer's bar where she drank alcohol. Later she was found sliding down the first floor banisters at the employer's premises. She fell and fractured her skull and knocked out a tooth. She agreed that she had not been sober but contended that she was only mildly drunk.

There was a disciplinary hearing and she was dismissed for misconduct. She complained to an employment tribunal of unfair dismissal, contending throughout that she did not have a drink problem. Her claim failed.

The tribunal was satisfied that her long period of service had been taken into account as well as her satisfactory work record. However, it accepted that her employer had been concerned that she could not be trusted again after failing to keep her promise. It was held that the employer's decision was within the scope of reasonable responses available to a reasonable employer.

(d) During the disciplinary hearings and the appeal process the employer must have been fair to the employee. In particular, the employee must have been heard and allowed to put his case properly or, if he was not at a certain stage of the procedures, this must have been corrected before dismissal.

The Employment Relations Act 1999 now gives employees the *right* to be accompanied by a trade union representative or a fellow employee. This means that an employer will no longer be able to exclude trade union officials from internal disciplinary hearings. The employee's request for a hearing must be reasonable. This will eliminate requests to set up a hearing straight away or within a very short space of time. But, on the other hand, if the employer's date for the hearing is not convenient for the employee, it must be changed to within five working days of the original date. The

accompanying person is entitled to paid time off and protection from dismissal for accompanying the companion worker. The worker has a right to address the hearing on behalf of his colleague and to confer with him, but is not permitted to answer questions on his behalf. Employers who infringe this right may be required to pay an employee up to two weeks' pay.

The above right to be accompanied by a trade union official applies *even where the employer does not recognise trade unions*. Trade union representatives may, therefore, offer their services in the hope of getting new members. Hearings will undoubtedly be lengthened and be more formal and since trade union representatives may well deal with the proceedings in an adversial way the internal hearing could well come to resemble a tribunal hearing. It may, therefore, be wise in future for the employer to ask a solicitor to be present at the hearings as adviser and to take notes of the proceedings as may be thought legally desirable. There is an ACAS code of practice on disciplinary and grievance procedures that includes guidance on the above statutory right.

3 **Employee's contributory fault.** This can reduce the compensation payable to the employee by such percentage as the tribunal thinks fit. Suppose an employee is often late for work and one morning his employer, who can stand it no more, sacks him. The dismissal is likely to be unfair in view of the lack of warning, but a tribunal would very probably reduce the worker's compensation to take account of the facts of the situation.

An example of case law in connection with contributory fault follows.

Optikinetics Ltd v Whooley (1999)
Mr Whooley was the head of the screen-printing department at Optikinetics. He was allowed to use the company's facilities for his private work, provided that this took place outside normal working hours and materials were paid for. There were one or two breaches and he was eventually summarily dismissed. He complained of unfair dismissal and the EAT upheld that complaint holding that the breaches were not sufficiently serious to justify summary dismissal. However, it reduced his compensation by 20 per cent to represent his contributory fault.

Principles of natural justice also apply; it is necessary to let the worker state his case before a decision to dismiss is taken. Furthermore, reasonable inquiry must be made to find the truth of the matter before reaching a decision. Failure to do this will tend to make the dismissal unfair.

4 **Unacceptable reasons for dismissal.** These are as follows:

(a) *Dismissal in connection with trade unions.* An employee will be regarded as automatically unfairly dismissed if the principal reason for the dismissal was that he was or proposed to become a member of a trade union which was independent of the employer; that he had taken part or proposed to take part in the activities of such a union at an appropriate time, i.e. outside working hours or within working hours with the consent of the employer; that he was not a member of any trade union or of a particular one or had refused or proposed to refuse to become or remain a member. Under the relevant provisions of the Trade Union and Labour Relations (Consolidation) Act 1992 all closed shop dismissals are now automatically unfair. Dismissal will also be automatically unfair if the employee is selected for redundancy on any of the above 'trade union' grounds.

The above trade union dismissals are contained in s 152 of the 1992 Act and are generally referred to as 'the s 152 reasons'.

(b) *Unfair selection for redundancy.* An employee dismissed for redundancy may complain that he has been unfairly selected for redundancy, as where the employer *has asked unreasonably* and, e.g., selected him because he is a member of a trade union or takes part in trade union activities, or where the employer has disregarded redundancy selection arrangements based, for example, on 'last in, first out', as is still commonly applied. Though it is a somewhat crude method of approach, it is sometimes found justifiable. Ideally, all employers should have proper redundancy agreements on the lines set out in the Department of Employment booklet *Dealing with Redundancies.*

However, even though there is in existence an agreed redundancy procedure, the employer may defend himself by showing a 'special reason' for departing from that procedure, e.g. because the person selected for redundancy lacks the skill and versatility of a junior employee who is retained.

There is, since the decision of the Employment Appeal Tribunal in *Williams* v *Compair Maxam* (1982), an overall standard of fairness also in redundancy arrangements. The standards laid down in the case require the giving of maximum notice; consultation with unions, if any; the taking of the views of more than one person as to who should be dismissed; a requirement to follow any laid down procedure, e.g. last in, first out; and finally, an effort to find the employees concerned alternative employment within the organisation. However, the EAT stated in *Meikle* v *McPhail (Charleston Arms)* (1983) that these guidelines would be applied less rigidly to the smaller business.

(c) *Strikes.* The position in this context has already been considered.

(d) *Dismissal in connection with pregnancy, childbirth, parental and dependants leave.* The relevant law has already been considered.

(e) *Pressure on employer to dismiss unfairly.* It is no defence for an employer to say that pressure was put upon him to dismiss an employee unfairly. So, if other workers put pressure on an employer to dismiss a non-union member so as, for example, to obtain a closed shop, the employer will have no defence to a claim for compensation for the dismissal if he gives in to that pressure. If an employer alleges that he was pressurised into dismissing an employee and that pressure was brought on him by a trade union or other person by the calling, organising, procuring or financing of industrial action, including a strike, or by the threat of such things, and the reason for the pressure was that the employee was not a member of the trade union, then the employer can join the trade union or other person as a party to the proceedings if he is sued by the dismissed worker for unfair dismissal. If the tribunal awards compensation, it can order that a person joined as a party to the proceedings should pay such amount of it as is just and equitable, and if necessary this can be a complete indemnity so that the employer will recover all the damages awarded against him from the union.

(f) *Transfer of business.* The Transfer of Undertakings (Protection of Employment) Regulations 1981 apply where there is a transfer of a business. Under the regulations, if a business or part of it is transferred and an employee is dismissed because of this, the dismissal will be treated as automatically unfair. Exceptionally, however, there is a service requirement here and one year's service with the transferor employer is required. This includes constructive dismissal and failure to renew a fixed-term contract (see *Collective Redundancies and Transfer of Undertakings (Protection of Employment) (Amendment) Regulations 1995*).

If the old employer dismissed before transfer, or the new employer dismissed after the transfer, either will have a defence if he can prove that the dismissal was for 'economic, technical, or organisational' reasons requiring a change in the workforce and that the dismissal was reasonable in all the circumstances of the case.

Meikle v McPhail (Charleston Arms) (1983)

After contracting to take over a public house and its employees, the new management decided that economies were essential and dismissed the barmaid. She complained to an employment tribunal on the grounds of unfair dismissal. Her case was based upon the fact that the 1981 regulations state that a dismissal is to be treated as unfair if the transfer of a business, or a reason connected with it, is the reason or principal reason for the dismissal. The pub's new management defended the claim under another provision in the 1981 regulations which states that a dismissal following a transfer of business is not to be regarded as automatically unfair where there was, as in this case, an economic reason for making changes in the workforce. If there is such a reason, unfairness must be established on grounds other than the mere transfer of the business.

The Employment Appeal Tribunal decided that the reason for dismissal was an economic one under the regulations and that the management had acted reasonably in the circumstances so that the barmaid's claim failed.

It should be noted that in *Gateway Hotels Ltd* v *Stewart* (1988) the Employment Appeal Tribunal decided that on a transfer of business dismissal of employees of the business transferred prior to the transfer at the insistence of the purchaser of the business is not an 'economic' reason within the regulations so that the dismissals are unfair.

The Collective Redundancies and Transfer of Undertakings (Protection of Employment (Amendment) Regulations (as amended by regulations of the same name in 1999) apply. These regulations are considered later in this chapter, but they do require consultation with unions or workers' representatives on a transfer of business. The provisions mirror those that relate to collective redundancies except that there is no limitation on the number of employees who will be affected by the transfer before a duty to consult arises. The employer will have to consult relevant unions or representatives, as described later in this chapter, even if only one person is transferred.

(g) *Health and safety dismissals and detriments.* The position with regard to these dismissals and detriments was noted earlier in this chapter.

(h) *Dismissal for asserting statutory right.* This protects employees regardless of service against dismissal for trying to enforce employment rights under the EPA that can be brought before a tribunal. Dismissal will be unfair even if the worker does not in fact have the right provided he has acted in good faith.

(i) *Dismissal for performing the duties of a member-nominated trustee of an occupational pension scheme.*

(j) *Dismissal for performing the duties of an employee representative in redundancy consultation or putting up for election to be one.*

Unfair dismissal and frustration of contract

In cases appearing before employment tribunals there is a certain interplay between the common law rules of frustration of contract (see Chapter 7) and the statutory provisions relating to unfair dismissal. At common law a contract of service is frustrated by incapacity, e.g. sickness, if that incapacity makes the contract substantially impossible of performance at a particularly vital time, or by a term of imprisonment (*see Hare* v *Murphy Bros* (1974)). If a contract has been so frustrated then a complaint of unfair dismissal is not available because the contract has been discharged on other grounds, i.e. by frustration. Thus termination of a contract of service by frustration prevents a claim for unfair dismissal.

It is, of course, necessary now in terms of the sickness or incapacity of an employee for the employer to be alert to the rules about disability discrimination, particularly where an adjustment to working conditions might enable an employee to do the job satisfactorily.

Remedies for unfair dismissal

These are as follows.

Conciliation. An employment tribunal will not hear a complaint until a conciliation officer has had a chance to see whether he can help, provided that he or she has been *requested* so to do by a party to the potential complaint. A copy of the complaint made to the employment tribunal will in such a situation be sent to a conciliation officer of the Advisory, Conciliation and Arbitration Service (ACAS) and, if he is unable to settle the complaint, nothing said by the employer or employee during the process of conciliation will be admissible in evidence before the tribunal.

The reference of cases to a conciliation officer has led to the settlement of some one-third of them before the tribunal hearing, but the parties do not have to become involved in this procedure.

ACAS arbitration and compromise agreement. The following provisions of the Employment Rights (Dispute Resolution) Act 1998 should be noted.

Part II of the Act contains provisions to allow parties to opt for their dispute to be resolved by independent binding arbitration and gives ACAS powers to pay for and provide an arbitration service for claims of unfair dismissal and unlawful discrimination.

Part II also contains provisions making changes to the law relating to compromise agreements. The parties to an individual employment rights dispute may conclude that dispute by reaching, for example, a financial settlement. For such an agreement to be binding, the parties must have settled after an ACAS-appointed conciliation officer has taken action, or, alternatively, the terms of the settlement must be contained in a private compromise agreement. Formerly, a compromise agreement that had not involved ACAS had to be made in circumstances where the employee had received independent legal advice from a qualified lawyer. The 1998 Act changed this to advice from any independent adviser, provided that advice is covered by an insurance policy or an indemnity provision for members of a profession or professional body (ss 9 and 10). This will allow trade unions, advice agencies and others – in addition to lawyers – to give relevant advice.

Other provisions of Part II allow ACAS-appointed conciliation officers to conciliate in claims relating to statutory redundancy payments where before they had no duty to conciliate, as they have in almost all other individual employment rights disputes (s 11).

There are also provisions that clarify, streamline and make more flexible current legislation under which employers and employer-recognised trade unions can, by making a dismissal procedures agreement, opt out of the statutory rules on unfair dismissals (s 12)

Other remedies. An employee who has been dismissed may:

(a) seek reinstatement or re-engagement; or
(b) claim compensation.

The power to order (a) above is discretionary and in practice rarely exercised. However, reinstatement means being taken back by the employer on exactly the same terms and seniority as before; re-engagement is being taken back but on different terms.

Calculations of compensation. The compensation for unfair dismissal is in four parts as follows:

(a) *Basic award* (maximum £7,200). This award is computed as a redundancy payment (see p 509 before reading on) except that there is no maximum age limit. Contributory fault of the employee is taken into account.

Example

Fred, a 35-year-old lorry driver employed for ten years earning £500 per week (take home £440), is unfairly dismissed. He did his best to get a comparable job but did not obtain one until one week before the tribunal hearing, to start two weeks after the tribunal hearing. Fred had a history of lateness for work and his contributory misconduct or fault is assessed at 25 per cent.

Fred's basic award: Fred is in category 22 years of age or over but under 41 years of age for redundancy which allows one week's *gross* pay for every year of service or (currently) £230, whichever is less.

10 x £240	£2,400	
Less: 25%	£600	
	£1, 800	= basic award

Before proceeding further with a study of the calculations, it should be noted that the basic award is based, as we have indicated, on *gross* pay, but the compensatory award is based on *net* pay. A cap of £51,700 is placed on compensatory awards, but this is removed for those who are unfairly dismissed for blowing the whistle on illegal practices or health and safety matters, and who are protected in terms of compensation against such dismissal by the Public Interest Disclosure Act 1998. There is no ceiling on such awards. This is because it was thought that some senior executives might have been deterred from whistleblowing since they would have most salary to lose if dismissed. The basic award is calculated, as we have indicated, with reference to a week's pay that is currently £240, but is automatically increased annually to a figure that is index-linked to the retail price index for September of each year. This is a maximum figure so that gross pay is the starting point, but if this exceeds £240, the figure of £240 applies.

There is a minimum basic award of £3,300 (currently) where the dismissal is due to trade union membership or activities, duties of a health and safety representative, trustee of an occupational pension scheme or employee representative, for consultation. This may be reduced for contributory fault.

The amount of the basic award is only two weeks' pay where a tribunal finds that the reason or principal reason for the dismissal was that the employee was redundant and then:

- he unreasonably refused or left suitable alternative employment; or
- his employment was renewed or he was re-engaged and he was not, therefore, considered dismissed (s 121, ERA 1996).

(b) *Compensatory award* (maximum £51,700). This consists of:

(i) estimated loss of wages, net of tax and other deductions to the date of the hearing, less any money earned between the date of the dismissal and the hearing;

(ii) estimated future losses;

(iii) loss of any benefits such as pension rights and expenses;

(iv) loss of statutory right. An award under this heading is given for loss of minimum notice entitlement. For example, Fred has been continuously employed for ten years. He was entitled to ten weeks' notice, which he did not get. He now has a new job but it will take him time to build up that entitlement again. A tribunal can award something for this. A nominal sum of £200 is commonly awarded. Once again, contributory fault is take into account.

It should be noted that a compensatory award is not linked to a redundancy payment as a basic award is. The figure of one week's pay of (currently) £240 does not apply. The calculation is based on actual net pay and is designed to compensate the worker for the financial loss suffered as a result of being dismissed. *The basic award is payable in all cases regardless of proved loss.* The following example assumes that Fred has been out of work for ten weeks before the tribunal hearing.

Fred's compensatory award:

		£
The loss up to the hearing	10 x £440	4,400
Loss up to time of starting new job	2 x £440	880
		5,280
Less 25%		1,320
		3,960
	£	
Loss of statutory rights	200	
Less 25%	50	150
		4,110

Fred's total award is therefore:	£
Basic	1,800
Compensatory	4,110
	5,910

If Fred has lost anything else, e.g. use of the employer's van at week ends and/or pension rights, these would be added to the compensatory award, after valuation, subject to 25 per cent discount for contributory fault.

Those on higher wages or salary may very well reach the maximum of £51,700 for the compensatory award. If the compensatory award calculated in accordance with the above example exceeds this amount (currently), then only £51,700 is awarded for the compensatory award element, though the basic award is payable in excess of this.

(c) *Additional award.* This is payable in addition to the above where an employer fails to comply with an order for reinstatement or re-engagement unless it is not practicable for him to do so. The amount of the additional award was varied by the Employment Relations Act 1999 s 33(2) and is now at one level, i.e. an amount not less than 26 weeks nor more than 52 weeks' pay subject to a weekly maximum of £240. The maximum awards are, therefore, £6,240 and £12,480.

(d) *Special award.* This was abolished by the Employment Relations Act 1999 s 33. Instead, the maximum compensatory award of £51,700 (currently) does not apply to cases that would previously have attracted a special award, i.e. where dismissal is on grounds of trade union membership or activities, or health and safety duties, and the employee has asked for reinstatement or re-engagement but the tribunal has refused to make such an order, generally on grounds of impractibility. In this type of situation it can make an award of uncapped money compensation instead.

Any employment or supplementary benefits received by the employee are deducted from any award made by a tribunal. However, the employer must pay the amount(s) in question over to the Department of Social Security.

As regards *ex gratia* payments that the employer may have made in connection with the dismissal as a leaving non-contractual gesture, credit will be given for this in fixing the amount of compensation if and only if the dismissal is in the context of being unfairly chosen for redundancy. This results from the provisions of the ERA 1996, as interpreted in *Boorman* v *Allmakes Ltd* (1995). If the dismissal is not in that context, the employee keeps the *ex gratia* payment in addition to any compensation.

Time limits. A claim for compensation against an employer must reach the tribunal within three months of the date of termination of employment.

A worker can claim while working out his notice but no award can be made until employment ends.

A tribunal can hear a claim after three months if the employee can prove that:

(a) it was not reasonably practicable for him to claim within three months;
(b) he did so as soon as he could in the circumstances.

Internal appeal procedures

Part III of the Employment Rights (Dispute Resolution) Act 1998 contains provisions relating to internal appeal procedures and unfair dismissal awards. They are intended to encourage more use to be made of internal procedures, which will hopefully increase the number of cases settled without recourse to a tribunal hearing.

A new s 127A is added to the ERA 1996. It provides that where a tribunal finds that an applicant was unfairly dismissed and (a) the employer has an internal procedure for appealing against dismissal, and (b) the applicant did not appeal under that procedure, the tribunal is to reduce the compensatory award by such an amount, if any, as it thinks is just and equitable.

Conversely, where the employer has an appeals procedure that the employee wishes to use, but the employer prevents the employee from appealing by use of it, the tribunal shall make a supplementary award to the employee of such amount, if any, as it thinks is just and equitable. However, s 127A (4) limits the reduction or the supplementary award to a maximum of two weeks' pay (s 13).

Discriminatory dismissals

In addition to legislation relating to unfair dismissal generally, the Sex Discrimination Act 1975, the Race Relations Act 1976 and the Disability Discrimination Act 1995 deal with complaints to employment tribunals for dismissal on the grounds of sex, marital status, race or disability. The nature and scope of these provisions has already been considered and it is only necessary to add here that there are provisions in the ERA which prevent double compensation being paid, once under discrimination legislation and once under the general unfair dismissal provisions of the ERA.

The previous cap on these awards was removed by the Sex Discrimination and Equal Pay (Remedies) Regulations 1993 and the Race Relations (Remedies) Act 1994. There is now no cap in contrast to claims for unfair dismissal as such.

Redundancy

The ERA gives an employee a right to compensation by way of a redundancy payment if he is dismissed because of a redundancy.

Meaning of redundancy

Under the ERA redundancy is **presumed** to occur where the services of employees are dispensed with because the employer ceases, or intends to cease, carrying on business, or to carry on business at the place where the employee was employed, or does not require so many employees to do work of a certain kind. Employees who have been laid off or kept on short time without pay for four consecutive weeks (or for six weeks in a period of 13 weeks) are entitled to end their employment and to seek a redundancy payment if there is no reasonable prospect that normal working will be resumed.

Where is the workplace?

The proper test for ascertaining whether an employee is or is not redundant is to see whether there has been a reduction of the employer's requirements for employees to do work at the place where the employee concerned **works in fact**. It is not correct to look at the contract of employment to see where the employee may be required to work.

High Table Ltd v Horst (1997)

In the above case the applicants were employed by HT as waitresses but had worked for several years at one company, i.e. Hill Samuel. HS informed HT that the services of the waitresses were no longer required and they were dismissed by HT on the grounds of redundancy. The waitresses complained that HT had not tried to redeploy them elsewhere, although they had mobility clauses in their contracts. Therefore, they alleged unfair dismissal. The matter eventually came before the Court of Appeal which decided that an employee's place of work was to be decided as much on the fact situation in the case as on the provisions of the contract of employment, otherwise mobility clauses might be used in genuine redundancy sit-

uations in favour of claims for unfair dismissal. The place of work in this case was Hill Samuel and the dismissals were for redundancy. The applicants' case failed.

A group redundancy test – contract and function

In deciding whether an employee is or is not redundant the tribunal may use a 'contract' test, i.e. has the work which the employee does under contract of employment diminished, or if he has been employed on other work has the requirement for that work diminished, i.e. a 'function' test. However, it has been suggested that a tribunal may in an appropriate case apply what may be called a 'group' redundancy test which may lead to what is known as a 'bumped' redundancy.

The following cases illustrate these principles.

Johnson v Peabody Trust (1996)

In 1977 Mr Johnson was employed as a labourer by the Peabody Trust which is a housing association owning more than 13,000 properties. By 1985 he had developed skills as a roofer and had been paid and promoted accordingly. From 1988 his written contract of employment stated that his employment was that of a roofer but it contained a clause which said: 'Where possible tradespersons will be expected to carry out multitrade operations.' In 1990 Peabody made some 30 painters and decorators redundant and in 1993 nine other employees from the works department were dismissed due to operating losses. Of the nine, Peabody decided that a roofer should be made redundant. Mr Johnson was dismissed.

In the three years before his dismissal Mr Johnson had done some roofing work but had also been engaged on bricklaying, painting, carpentry, tiling and plastering.

Mr Johnson, seeking, presumably, a higher award, claimed that there had not been a redundancy but that his dismissal was unfair. The case eventually reached the EAT.

Mr Johnson referred to what is now s 139(1)(b) of the Employment Rights Act 1996, which provides that a dismissal shall be taken to be by reason of redundancy if it is attributable wholly or mainly to the fact that the requirements of the employer's business 'for employees to carry out work of a particular kind … has ceased or diminished'. In this connection Mr Johnson pointed to the clause in his contract which stated that he would be required to carry out 'multitrade operations'. He pointed out that Peabody's requirements for all kinds of work, particularly plastering, had not diminished and submitted that no redundancy situation existed in this case.

The EAT said that the 'contract test' rather than the 'function test' should be applied in interpreting s 139. The proper approach was to look at whether there had been a cessation or diminution in the requirements of the business for the specific type of work which the employee could be asked to perform under his or her contract rather than for the work which the employee was actually doing at the time.

Applying the contract test in this case, the EAT held that Mr Johnson was employed under his contract as a roofer. The fact that he could be required to help on other work when roofing was not available did not alter this fact. Peabody could not require Mr Johnson to work on multi-trade operations if it had roofing work for him to do instead.

The EAT concluded that Mr Johnson had been made redundant rather than unfairly dismissed and his appeal failed.

Safeway Stores PLC v Burrell (1997)

In this case the EAT, which is not bound by its own decisions, rejected both the 'contract' and the 'function' tests. It decided in particular that in reaching conclusions as to whether there had been a diminution or cessation in the requirements of the employer's business for employees (not just the employee) to carry out work of a particular kind, or an expectation of such in the future, and the employee concerned was dismissed wholly or mainly because of this, there is a redundancy situation and it is irrelevant to consider the employee's contract of employment and its terms, or his functions. Mr Burrell was employed by Safeway as the manager of its petrol station at Penzance. A revision of the store's management structure was undertaken and the manager's job disappeared, to be replaced by the new post of petrol station controller at lower pay. Mr Burrell would not apply for this job because of that and was made redundant. A week after he left, a new description was issued for the post of controller which differed on paper to some extent from Mr Burrell's old job description. Mr Burrell later claimed he had been unfairly dismissed.

The employment tribunal found that he had been dismissed, but not for redundancy, and because of this the dismissal was unfair. Safeway had not shown that it was because of redundancy and therefore that defence failed. The employment tribunal held that the job Mr Burrell had been doing still had to be done; it was merely the job title which had been changed. Therefore, applying the function test, Mr Burrell was not redundant, though applying the contract test he was, since the post of manager no longer existed. The employment tribunal preferred the function test in this case. Safeway appealed to the EAT asking that the contract test be applied.

The EAT rejected both tests, going instead for a 'group' test which could lead to what is known as a 'bumped redundancy' situation.

The example given by the EAT may assist in understanding. An employee is employed to work as a fork-lift truck driver. He delivers materials to six production machines on the shopfloor. Each machine has its own operator. The employer decides that only five machines are required and one machine operator is now in excess of requirements. This is, under the ERA 1996, a redundancy situation. Selection for dismissal is made on the LIFO (last in, first out) rule. The test is made across the group of workers needed to produce the end product of the machines. The driver falls to be dismissed under this rule. His dismissal is for redundancy. Under both the contract and the function tests he was employed as a fork-lift truck driver and there is no diminution in the requirement for this work. However, there was a diminution in the requirement for machine operators and this caused the driver's dismissal, his job being taken over by one of the machine operators.

The decision seems rather more understandable and fair if, using, e.g., the LIFO rule, the most recent employee in a 'group' working towards the production of a particular article or articles is dismissed in a situation of diminution of work within the group.

However, in Church v Lancashire NHS Trust (1998) a different EAT decided against 'bumped' redundancies. The diminution or cessation of work must relate to the work carried out by the employee, contractually or functionally. So, in Safeway the machinist should be redundant. It is doubtful whether this case can stand with Murray (see below).

The attributable test

The House of Lords ruling in *Murray v Foyle Meats Ltd* (1999) would seem to have settled the matter of 'bumped' redundancies by accepting that they are legal and within the definition of redundancy. A redundancy dismissal is on the grounds of redundancy and is not an unfair dismissal if it is 'attributable' to a need for a reduction in the number of employees. The ruling affirms the decision in *Safeway Stores plc v Burrell* (1997). In the *Murray* case the Lord Chancellor said that for an employee to be regarded as redundant, two matters must be shown:

- that there is a state of affairs in the employer's business that meets the statutory definition of redundancy; and
- that the employee's dismissal is wholly or mainly *attributable* to that state of affairs.

In this context, therefore, a redundancy may be bumped. This will assist management in managing redundancies. In fact, in some cases now a person will be regarded as redundant not because his particular job has gone, *but because his redundancy arises out of the way in which his employer has managed the situation*. This will assist the employer to restructure the business, particularly where there is a group of workers of similar skills or unskilled. The *Murray* case saves the employer, in an appropriate situation, from a more expensive claim for unfair dismissal. The facts of *Murray* provide an example.

Murray v *Foyle Meats Ltd* (1999)

The abbatoir run by Foyle Meats fell short of work because of the BSE crisis. Some employees worked in the slaughterhouse and the rest in the slaughterhall. All the redundancies were taken from workers in the slaughterhall by management decision, and the members of the workforce remaining were redeployed. The House of Lords found that the slaughterhall redundancies were 'attributable' to the shortfall in cattle for slaughter and were not unfair dismissals.

There is a legal presumption that dismissal is on the ground of redundancy unless the employer proves the contrary.

Eligibility

In general terms, all those employed under a contract of service as employees are entitled to redundancy pay, including a person employed by his/her spouse. Furthermore, a volunteer for redundancy is not debarred from claiming. However, certain persons are excluded by statute or circumstances.

The main categories are listed below:

1 A domestic servant in a private household who is a close relative of the employer. The definition of 'close relative' for this purpose is father, mother, grandfather, grandmother, stepfather, stepmother, son, daughter, grandson, granddaughter, stepson, stepdaughter, brother, sister, halfbrother, or halfsister.

2 An employee who has not completed at least two years of continuous service since reaching the age of 18. Thus, any employee aged 19 or less on the relevant date of dismissal is automatically excluded.

These provisions remain unchanged under amendments made by the Unfair Dismissal etc. Order 1999. The order applies only to claims for unfair dismissal that, as we have seen, can be brought after only one year's service.

Alternate-week working does not break continuity either for redundancy or unfair dismissal claims (see *Colley* v *Corkindale t/a Corker's Lounge Bar* (1996).

3 Men and women who have reached retirement age. In this connection s 12 of the Employment Act 1989 removes a previous discriminatory feature which was that men could receive statutory redundancy payments up to age 65 but women only up to age 60. This anomaly remained even though the Sex Discrimination Act 1986 removed the right of employers to set discriminatory retiring ages. Where there is a 'normal retiring age' for the job in question which is below 65 and is the same for men and women, i.e. non-discriminatory, the entitlement of both sexes is restricted to that age. In all other cases women's entitlement is extended to age 65 in line with that of men.

4 Where, in the case of a fixed-term contract of two years or more, the employee has agreed in writing in the contract or at any stage of the contract to forgo his right to claim redundancy payment.

5 Employees who normally work outside Great Britain under their contract.

6 An employee who is dismissed for misconduct loses the right to a redundancy payment. In the circumstances of the *Boychuck* and *Kowalski* cases we can note that although these cases were brought for unfair dismissal, they were also situations in which the employees concerned would have lost the right to a redundancy payment if selected for redundancy.

7 Workers on strike can generally be dismissed by their employers without liability to make a redundancy payment. This applies even though the employer was short of work at the time of the strike so that a redundancy situation did exist. Where the strike takes place after a redundancy notice has been given, the employee concerned may still get part or all of his redundancy pay by applying to a tribunal which has a power under the ERA to make an award which is 'just and equi-

table', the amount being arrived at by the tribunal. The question is, did the strike come first? If it did then there may be a dismissal without liability of the employer to make a redundancy payment. If the strike came after the service of a redundancy notice the position is as stated above.

8 There are provisions for the statutory scheme to be excluded where an equally favourable voluntary scheme has been set up under a collective agreement between an employer and a trade union.

Offers of suitable employment

An employee who accepts an offer of suitable alternative employment with his employer is not entitled to a redundancy payment. Where a new offer is made, there is a trial period of four weeks following the making of the offer, during which the employer or the employee may end the contract while retaining all rights and liabilities under redundancy legislation. An employee who unreasonably refuses an offer of alternative employment is not entitled to a redundancy payment.

Fuller v *Stephanie Bowman* (1977)

F was employed as a secretary at SB's premises which were situated in Mayfair. These premises attracted a very high rent and rates so SB moved their offices to Soho. These premises were situated over a sex shop and F refused the offer of renewed employment at the same salary and she later brought a claim before an employment tribunal for a redundancy payment. The tribunal decided that the question of unreasonableness was a matter of fact for the tribunal and F's refusal to work over the sex shop was unreasonable so that she was not entitled to a redundancy payment.

In addition, it should be noted that in *North East Coast Ship Repairers* v *Secretary of State for Employment* (1978) the Employment Appeal Tribunal decided that an apprentice who, having completed the period of his apprenticeship, finds that the firm cannot provide him with work is not entitled to redundancy payment. This case has relevance for trainees and others completing contracts in order to obtain relevant practical experience.

As regards time limits, the employee must make a written claim to the employer or to an employment tribunal within six months from the end of the employment. If the employee does not do this,

an employment tribunal may extend the time for a further six months, making 12 months in all, but not longer, from the actual date of termination of the employment, provided that it can be shown that it is just and equitable having regard to the reasons put forward by the employee for late application and to all relevant circumstances.

Amount of redundancy payment

Those aged 41 to 65 receive one and a half weeks' pay (up to a maximum of £240 per week) for each year of service up to a maximum of 20 years. In other age groups the above provisions apply except that the week's pay changes, i.e. for those aged at least 22, but under 41, it is one week's pay, and for those aged 18, but under 22, it is half a week's pay. There is a maximum payment which is currently £7,200 ($20 \times 1\frac{1}{2} \times £240$).

For example, a man of 52 who is made redundant having been continuously employed for 18 years and earning £200 per week as gross salary at the time of his redundancy would be entitled to a redundancy payment as follows.

34 to 41 years =		
7 years at one week's pay	=	7 weeks
41 to 52 years =		
11 years at one and a half weeks' pay	=	$16\frac{1}{2}$ weeks
		$23\frac{1}{2}$ weeks

It follows, therefore, that the redundancy payment would be $23\frac{1}{2}$ weeks × £200 = £4,700.

Assume also the case of an employee aged 62 dismissed on the ground of redundancy. His normal retiring age would have been 65. He had been employed for 30 years. His gross weekly wage was more than £240. His redundancy payment will be based on his last 20 years' service and he will be entitled to the current maximum of £7,200 ($20 \times 1\frac{1}{2} \times £240$).

Employees over 64 have their redundancy payment reduced progressively so that for each complete month by which the age exceeds 64 on the Saturday of the week on which the contract ends, the normal entitlement is reduced by 1/12th. Thus, a man or woman aged 64 years and three months would have 3/12th of the award deducted. The rule relating to the reduction in women's redundancy pay is not changed by the retirement provisions referred to earlier in this chapter. Complaints by employees in respect of the right to redundancy payment, or questions as to its amount, may, as we have seen, be made to an employment tribunal which will make a declaration as to the employee's rights which form the basis on which payment can be recovered from the employer.

Procedure for handling redundancies

Any agreed formula should be followed, e.g. last in, first out. Selection procedures may also be based on poor work performance or attendance record and there is no requirement on the employer to determine reasons for this (*Dooley* v *Leyland Vehicles Ltd* (1986)). If there is no agreed procedure, the employer must decide after considering the pros and cons in each case. It should be noted that the dismissal may well be unfair if some reasonable system of selection is not followed. In this connection the Employment Appeal Tribunal decided in *Rogers* v *Vosper Thorneycroft* (UK) Ltd (1988) that 'last in first out' is a relevant system but merely asking for volunteers is not. There must be some criteria, though calling for volunteers is acceptable as a preliminary step in the matter of eventual selection. Everyone should, as far as possible, be allowed to express their views, e.g. through elected representatives, if any. Any attempt to relocate a redundant worker should be considered. Failure to do so can result in a finding of unfair dismissal unless, of course, there was no chance of finding suitable alternative work. Fairness in the search for alternative work involves looking at other companies within a group (see *Euroguard Ltd* v *Rycroft* (1993)).

Selecting, say, a white single woman or a West Indian single man to go, rather than a married white man with two children and a mortgage might appear to be humane. However, unless the decision is made on the basis of competence, experience, reliability, and so on, the dismissal is likely to be unfair and also a breach of the Sex Discrimination Act 1975 and/or the Race Relations Act 1976.

Consultation over collective redundancies

In regard to dismissals on or after 1 March 1996 the Collective Redundancies and Transfer of Undertakings (Protection of Employment) (Amendment) Regulations 1999 apply. The regulations substantially amend s 188 of the Trade Union and Labour Relations (Consolidation) Act 1992 as follows:

- The obligation to consult about redundancies now arises where the employer is proposing to dismiss as redundant 20 or more employees at one establishment within a period of 90 days or less. The class of 'affected employees' includes not only those who may be dismissed but also any employee affected by the proposed dismissals or who may be affected by measures taken in connection with those dismissals, e.g. changes in job specification.

  Even so, it will be found that the need to consult under the regulations does not apply to some 96 per cent of UK business (but see *Mugford* below).

- Where consultation is required, the employer must consult all those who are 'appropriate representatives'.

- Appropriate representatives of employees are:

  1 employee representatives elected by them; or
  2 if an independent trade union is recognised by the employer, representatives of the union.

  Where the employees elect representatives and belong to a recognised union the employer must consult the union or in any other case the elected representatives. It will be noted that the regulations extend the requirement to consult to non-union workplaces.

- Employee representatives may be elected by the employees for the specific purpose of consultation or while not having been specifically elected it is appropriate to consult them as where they are members of an existing works council or joint consultative committee. In all cases the employee representatives must be employed by the employer. No method of election is stipulated in the regulations which means that *ad hoc* procedures as and when a redundancy situation will arise are acceptable.

- Consultation must begin in good time as distinct from the earliest opportunity as was formerly required and in any case.

- Where the employer is proposing to dismiss 100 or more employees at one establishment within 90 days or less consultation must begin, as before, 90 days before the first dismissals take effect. In cases involving less than 100 but at least 20 employees consultation must begin at least 30 days before that date.

- Appropriate representatives must be given access to employees who are to be made redundant.

It should, of course, be borne in mind that fairness towards employees in a redundancy situation is always paramount if the matter goes to a tribunal asserting unfair dismissal (see *Williams* v *Compair Maxam* (1982)). Therefore, individual consultation may be required even where the numbers involved are less than 20 and even though, the numbers being more, there has been consultation with representatives. Thus, in *Mugford* v *Midland Bank plc* (1997) the EAT, in confirming that a particular employee had not in the circumstances been subject to unfairness, commented that if a person is selected for redundancy, individual consultation may become important in the circumstances of the case, even if the employer (as he had in this case) has conducted detailed consultation with what were in this case union representatives.

It is perhaps rather obvious that it would be direct discrimination not to consult an employee about redundancy because she is on maternity leave (see *McGuigan* v *T & G Baynes* (1999)). The same presumably applies to those on parental and dependants leave.

It should be noted:

- that consultation must cover employees who have volunteered for redundancy; and
- although consultation does not have to end in agreement it must always be properly conducted.

In addition, the EAT has ruled that even if the possibility of redundancy is only one of several alternatives available to an organisation there should nevertheless be consultation. In *Scotch Premier Meat Ltd* v *Burns* (2000) the possibilities were the sale of the business as a going concern or closing it and selling off the site as a development property. The latter alternative involved the loss of 155 jobs, and was the course eventually taken but without consultation. The EAT held that the employees were entitled to a protective award and this applied to those who had taken voluntary as well as compulsory redundancy.

Notice. The employer must start the consultation process by giving written notice to the appropriate representatives stating:

(a) the reasons for the proposals;
(b) the numbers and descriptions of employees whom it proposes to dismiss as redundant;
(c) the total number of employees of that description. In *MSF* v *GEC Ferranti (Defence Systems) Ltd* (1994) the EAT held that the statutory period for consulting with a trade union over proposed redundancies did not begin when the employer gave the union a notice which contained only a 'best estimate' of the redundancies;
(d) the proposed method of selecting the employees to be dismissed;
(e) the proposed method of carrying out the dismissal, including the period over which the dismissals are to take effect;
(f) the method of calculating any non-statutory redundancy payments.

Consultation must also include consideration of ways to avoid redundancies, to reduce the number to be dismissed and to mitigate the consequences of dismissals.

The employer must also, as part of the consultation process, consider any representations by the appropriate representatives.

The above obligations do not apply if the employees whom the employer proposes to dismiss fall into one of several specified categories. The most important of these categories, for practical purposes, are:

(a) employees who under their contract ordinarily work outside Great Britain;
(b) employees under a contract for a fixed term of three months or less or who have been engaged to carry out a specific task which is not expected to last for more than three months (unless in either case the employment has continued beyond the three months).
(c) employees who are employed under a fixed-term contract of two years or more (including a contract of apprenticeship for the same term) where the dismissal consists of the expiry of the term without renewal, provided that before the term expires the employee has agreed in writing to exclude any right to a redundancy payment in that event.

The employer must also be able to argue that there were special circumstances which made it not reasonably practicable for it to comply with the requirements. Even then, it must do whatever is reasonably practicable. If, for example, the employer is proposing to dismiss 25 employees and cannot give the full 30 days' notice required, it must give as much notice as possible.

The main practical consequence, if the requirements are not complied with, is that the union or any employee representative or any of those made redundant can apply to an employment tribunal for what is known as a 'protective award'. The effect of the award is that a protected period not longer than 90 days is specified and individual employees can then apply to have their remuneration paid for that period. The following example illustrates the position.

Example

A firm is proposing to dismiss 25 employees and fails to give notice to the appropriate representatives. The employment tribunal makes a protective award under which the protected period begins on the date when the first dismissal takes effect and runs for 30 days. Employees who are dismissed on that first date can claim remuneration for the whole of the 30-day period. Employees dismissed part-way through the protected period can claim remuneration for the balance of the period (subject in each case to the dismissal being for redundancy and not for some other reason).

Notifying the Secretary of State. The employer's other obligation is to notify the Department of Trade and Industry of proposed redundancies. The obligation is to give written notice to the Department:

(a) at least 90 days before the first dismissal takes effect, in the case of 100 or more redundancies;
(b) at least 30 days before the first dismissal takes effect, in the case of 20 or more redundancies.

The notice must be in a prescribed form available from local offices and the employer must give a copy to the relevant appropriate representatives.

If there are special circumstances which make it not reasonably practicable for the employer to comply with the requirements, it must do everything that is reasonably practicable. If the special circumstances prevent the full required notice being given, it must give as much notice as possible.

Failing to comply with the above requirements means that the employer can be prosecuted and fined.

The role of ACAS

The Advisory, Conciliation and Arbitration Service (ACAS) has now taken on redundancy pay entitlement as an issue on which it has a duty to conciliate. The Employment Rights (Dispute Resolution) Act 1998 confers a duty on ACAS to conciliate if a person puts an application to an employment tribunal concerning entitlement to redundancy pay.

Collective agreements on redundancy

The Secretary of State may, on application of the employer and the unions involved, make an order modifying the requirements of redundancy pay legislation if he is satisfied that there is a collective agreement which makes satisfactory alternative arrangements for dealing with redundancy. The provisions of the agreement must be 'on the whole at least as favourable' as the statutory provisions, and must include, in particular, arrangements allowing an employee to go to an independent arbitration or to make a complaint to an employment tribunal.

Other cases for redundancy payments – lay-off and short-time working

In general, the obligation to make a redundancy payment arises only if an employee has been dismissed by reasons of redundancy. There are, however, circumstances in which an employee who has not been dismissed can leave and claim a redundancy payment. In practice these cases tend to arise mainly in manufacturing industry. Accordingly, the relevant provisions will only be outlined and not set out in detail.

The employee's rights arise if he or she has been laid off or put on short time either for four consecutive weeks or for at least six weeks in any period of 13 weeks. Being laid off involves having no work and not being entitled to any remuneration; being on short time means that there is a fall in work resulting in remuneration for the week being less than half a week's pay.

Subject to time limits and several conditions, the employee can:

(a) give notice of intention to claim a redundancy payment in respect of lay-off or short time;

(b) give notice of termination of the contract of employment;

(c) claim a redundancy payment as if he or she had been dismissed by reason of redundancy.

There is provision for the employer to serve a counternotice if there is a reasonable expectation that the lay-off or short-time working will end within four weeks after the date of the employee's notice of intention to claim.

The above provisions can apply only to employees who are paid on an hourly basis. They do not even apply to these employees if their contract gives them the right to a guaranteed wage in the event of a lay-off or short-time working. Many employees are of course entitled to a weekly or monthly salary, so that the above provisions cannot come into play.

Other methods of termination of contract of service

Having considered the termination of the contract by unfair or discriminatory dismissal or redundancy, we must now turn to other ways in which the contract of service may be brought to an end. These are set out below.

By notice

A contract of service can be brought to an end by either party giving notice to the other, although, where the employer gives notice, even in accordance with the contract of service or under the statutory provisions of the ERA, he may still face a claim for unfair dismissal or a redundancy payment.

The most important practical aspect is the length of notice to be given by the parties, in particular the employer. The ERA contains statutory provisions in regard to **minimum** periods of notice and the only relevance of the express provisions of a particular contract of service on the matter are that a contract may provide for longer periods of notice than does the Act. Under the Act an employee is entitled to one week's notice after employment for one month or more; after two years' service the minimum entitlement is increased

to two weeks, and for each year of service after that it is increased by one week up to a maximum of 12 weeks' notice after 12 years' service.

An employee, once he has been employed for one month or more, must give his employer one week's notice, and the period of one week's notice applies for the duration of the contract so far as the employee is concerned, no matter how long he has served the employer.

Breach of the provisions relating to minimum periods of notice do not involve an employer in any penalty, but the rights conferred by the ERA will be taken into account in assessing the employer's liability for breach of contract. Thus, an employer who has dismissed his employee without due notice is generally liable for the wages due to the employee for the appropriate period of notice at the contract rate.

It should be noted that the ERA provisions regarding minimum periods of notice do not affect the common law rights of an employer to dismiss an employee at once without notice for misconduct, e.g. disobedience, neglect or drunkenness.

In practice, a contract of service is often terminated by a payment of wages or salary instead of notice and this is allowed by the ERA.

By agreement

As in any other contract, the parties to a contract of employment may end the contract by agreement. Thus, if employer and employee agree to new terms and conditions on, e.g., a promotion of the employee, the old agreement is discharged and a new one takes over.

An employee could agree to be 'bought off' by his employer under an agreement to discharge the existing contract of service. In this connection it should be noted that discharge of a contract of service by agreement is not a 'dismissal' for the purposes, e.g., of an unfair dismissal claim, but should a claim for unfair dismissal be brought by an employee who has been 'bought off', the tribunal concerned will want to see evidence of a genuine and fair agreement by employer and employee and may allow a claim of unfair dismissal if the discharging agreement is one-sided and biased in favour of the employer.

By passage of time

In the case of a fixed-term contract, as where an employee is engaged for, say, three years, the contract will terminate at the end of the three years though there may be provisions for notice within that period.

By frustration

A contract of service can, as we have already seen, be discharged by frustration – which could be incapacity, such as illness. However, other events can bring about the discharge of a contract of service by frustration, e.g. a term of imprisonment, as in *Hare* v *Murphy Bros* (1975) (see Chapter 7).

Furthermore, death of either employer or employee will discharge the contract by frustration from the date of the death so that, for example, the personal representatives of the employer are not required to continue with the contract. However, the employee has a claim for wages or salary due at the date of death.

Under the ERA claims for unfair dismissal arising before the employer's death survive and may be brought after the death of the employer against his estate. Claims for discrimination commenced by the deceased may be continued after the death by the personal representatives but they cannot bring a claim for discrimination after the death if the deceased had not commenced the claim in his lifetime (see *Lewisham and Guys Mental Health NHS Trust* v *Andrews* (2000)). There are no provisions in discrimination allowing this as there are in unfair dismissal and redundancy legislation. Furthermore, the death of a human employer is usually regarded as a 'dismissal' for redundancy purposes and the employee may make a claim against the employer's estate.

If the employee is re-engaged or the personal representatives renew his contract within four weeks of the employer's death, the employee is not regarded as having been dismissed, and there is no break in the continuity of service. Where an offer of renewal or re-engagement is refused on reasonable grounds by the employee, he is entitled to a redundancy payment. If he unreasonably refuses to renew his contract or accept a suitable offer of re-engagement, he is not entitled to such a payment.

Partnership dissolution

A person who is employed by a partnership which is dissolved is regarded as dismissed on dissolution of the firm. Under the ERA this is regarded as having occurred because of redundancy.

The dismissal is also regarded as wrongful at common law and there may be a claim by the employee for damages but these will be nominal only if the partnership business continues and the continuing partners offer new employment on the old terms (*Brace* v *Calder* (1895); see Chapter 7).

An ordinary partnership is dissolved whenever one partner dies or becomes bankrupt or leaves the firm for any reason.

Of course, if a firm or sole trader sells the business as a going concern, employees are transferred to the new employer automatically under the Transfer of Undertakings (Protection of Employment) Regulations 1981.

Appointment of an administrator

As we have seen, the object of administration orders is to allow a company to be put on a profitable basis if possible, or at least disposed of more profitably than would be the case if other forms of insolvency proceedings, such as liquidation, were used. On the appointment of an administrator, the company's executive and other directors are not dismissed but their powers of management are exercisable only if the administrator consents. He also has power to dismiss and appoint directors.

Since an administrator is made an agent of the company by the Insolvency Act 1986 when the court makes the administration order, employees are not automatically dismissed. In addition, an administrator who wishes to trade with the company and, for that purpose, to retain employees, may adopt their contracts of employment as may an administrative receiver.

The legal position has already been considered in Chapter 6.

If, of course, an administrator or administrative receiver dismisses an employee, that employee can make a claim for a redundancy payment.

Appointment of an administrative receiver

As we have seen, where a company has borrowed money and given security for the loan by charging its assets under a debenture, the debenture holders may, if, e.g., they are not paid interest on the loan, appoint a receiver and manager, now referred to as an administrative receiver. The most common appointment is by a bank in respect of an overdraft or loan facility to a company.

If the administrative receiver is appointed under the terms of the debenture, he is, under the Insolvency Act 1986, an agent of the company and where this is so employees of the company are not dismissed on his appointment and their employment is continuous for the purposes of employment legislation. Employees are, however, dismissed if the administrative receiver sells the undertaking or where continuance of the employees' contracts would be inconsistent with the appointment of a receiver as could be the case in regard to the contract of a managing director. However, even a managing director may not be regarded as dismissed where the receiver has a part-time appointment, as was the case in *Griffiths v Secretary of State for Social Services* (1973).

If the appointment is made by the court, the receiver is not the agent of the company but an officer of the court and his appointment terminates the contracts of all employees, and the continuity of their employment ceases and they have a claim for a redundancy payment. The receiver may, of course, continue the employment by offering what are in effect new contracts, but where this is so there is a break in the continuity in the employment for the purposes of employment legislation. The employees are now employed by the receiver and not by the company to which he has been appointed.

Company liquidation

The possibilities are as follows:

1 **A compulsory winding-up.** Here the court orders the winding-up of the company, usually on the petition of a creditor because it cannot pay his debt. The making of a compulsory winding-up order by the court may have the following effects according to the circumstances of the case:

(a) where the company's business ceases, the winding-up order will operate as a wrongful dismissal of employees;

(b) where the liquidator continues the business for the purposes of a more beneficial winding-up, as where he allows employees to continue with work in progress to make complete and more saleable products, he may be regarded as an agent of the company so that the employment continues or, alternatively, the court may regard the appointment of the liquidator as a giving of notice to the employee who then works out that notice under the liquidator. It is, however, the better view that employees may, if they so choose, regard themselves as dismissed because the company has ceased to employ them, the new contract being with the liquidator. In practice, if the liquidator continues to use the services of the employees and pays them, the Department of Trade and Industry treats the redundancy of the employees as occurring at the time of the eventual dismissal by the liquidator.

2 **A voluntary winding-up.** This commences on the resolution of the members and if the company's business ceases there is a dismissal of employees. If the company's business continues for a while the position would appear to be as set out in **1(b)** above.

Bankruptcy

The bankruptcy of a human employer, or indeed of the employee, does not automatically discharge the contract of service, though it will if there is a term to that effect in the agreement. Thus, the employment can continue, though in practical terms it may be impossible to pay employees' wages; in this case they will be discharged and be able to make a claim for redundancy payment and also in the bankruptcy for wages accrued due (in regard to which they have a preferential claim in the bankruptcy).

A trustee in bankruptcy cannot insist that an employee should continue in service because the contract is one of a personal nature. The bankruptcy of an employee will not normally affect the contract of service unless there is a term to that effect in the contract. Company directors provide a special case since the articles of most companies provide for termination of the office on becoming bankrupt (see Chapter 6).

Wrongful and summary dismissal at common law

In spite of the statutory right to claim **unfair** dismissal, there are a number of reasons why a claim for **wrongful** dismissal either before a tribunal or a court is useful, particularly to the highly paid.

Since 1994, employment tribunals can hear claims for wrongful dismissal with a damages cap of £25,000. Claims above this figure must be brought in the ordinary courts, though a claimant can bring a claim of up to £25,000 in the ordinary courts and is not forced to use an employment tribunal.

Some of the main reasons for preferring a wrongful dismissal claim are as follows:

- An employee who is dismissed may not have completed the one year's service required for an unfair dismissal claim or may be over normal retiring age. These bars do not apply to wrongful dismissal claims.
- The time limit – i.e. three months – for bringing claims of unfair dismissal may have expired. The period for wrongful dismissal, which is a common law claim, is six years from dismissal. However the three-month period applies to wrongful dismissal claims before an employment tribunal unless the tribunal decides that it was not 'reasonably practicable' for the complaint to be presented during that period.
- Awards for unfair dismissal may be reduced substantially by a sum representing the fault of the employee – e.g. late arrival at work. Damages for wrongful dismissal are not subject to a deduction for contributory fault.
- The damages for wrongful dismissal in the case, e.g., of a highly-paid person could well exceed the maximum amount of compensation available for unfair dismissal – where the compensatory award is currently a maximum of £51,700.

When does wrongful dismissal occur? The main situations of wrongful dismissal are as follows:

- Where the contract is of indefinite duration but terminable by notice, the termination of the contract without notice or with shorter notice than that to which the employee is entitled, and of course summary dismissal without any notice at all.

In *Sarker* v *South Tees Acute Hospital NHS Trust* (1997) the EAT held that where a person enters into a contract to work for an employer and the contract is terminated before work is due to begin, an employment tribunal may hear a claim for wrongful dismissal, the damages being based on the contractual period of notice which the claimant had not received. A claim for unfair dismissal could be brought in similar circumstances but it would have to be a case not requiring one year's service, e.g. a maternity dismissal.

- In the case of a fixed-term contract, termination before the fixed term expires.
- In the case of a contract to carry out a specific task, termination before the task is completed.
- Where the employer dismisses the employee on disciplinary grounds but does not follow a procedure laid down in the contract.
- Selection for redundancy in breach of a procedure set out in the contract.

When dismissal is justified. Various forms of misconduct will justify a dismissal. For example, in *Connor* v *Kwik Fit Insurance Services Ltd* (1996) the managing director of an insurance company, who had falsely declared when signing a professional indemnity insurance form that he had not been involved with any company that had been wound up, failed in a claim for wrongful dismissal. Again, in *Blayney* v *Colne Liberal Club* (1995) a bar steward's claim for wrongful dismissal failed. He had been summarily dismissed for failure to hand over the bar takings to his employer or to put them in the safe and hand over the safe keys. It is worth noting, however, that the odd and isolated bit of **bad work** will seldom justify dismissal. Thus, in *Meiszner* v *Hart Timber Preservation Ltd* (1999) Mr Meiszner was summarily dismissed, i.e. without notice, after six years in the job for doing a piece of poor work. There had only been one complaint previously about his work. The EAT found that he had been wrongfully dismissed.

Damages for wrongful dismissal. An award of damages is the most usual remedy for wrongful dismissal. The period by reference to which damages will be calculated is either:

- in the case of a contract of indefinite duration, the period between the date of wrongful dismissal and the earliest date on which the employer could lawfully have terminated the contract – generally the date required by the period of notice set out in the contract. If no such period is expressed in the contract, the court will imply a 'reasonable' period or the minimum period laid down in the ERA, whichever is the longer; or

- if the employee was employed under a fixed-term contract, the damages period will in general be the unexpired remainder of the fixed term, unless the employer could terminate the contract by notice before the fixed term expired, in which case the damages period will be the period of that notice.

Case law has laid down 'reasonable' periods of notice in the absence of specific provisions in the contract. These vary from three months for a company director (*James* v *Kent & Co Ltd* (1950)) to one week for a hairdresser's assistant (*Marulsens* v *Leon* (1919)) – though, according to length of service, the ERA periods, which may be longer in the latter case, could apply.

Heads of damage. No damages can be recovered for the manner of dismissal – e.g. for hurt feelings (see *Addis* v *Gramophone Co Ltd* (1909)). It is possible to recover damages known as 'stigma' damages because dismissal has made it difficult to obtain other work (see *Malik* v *BCCI* (1997)), but only where the claim is brought while the claimant is still working for the employer.

A claim may be made for loss of pension rights, share option rights and other fringe benefits such as a company car, but only to the extent that it was made available for private use.

Mitigation of loss. The ex-employee must take reasonable steps to find other suitable employment or become self-employed, otherwise damages will be reduced by the sum that could reasonably have been earned from new employment or self-employment during the damages period. The court will take into account the nature of any reference given to the employee and the difficulty a dismissed employer may have in finding other suitable work.

Damages are compensatory. If the employee had worked during the damages period, he would have received net, not gross, pay. Thus, under the common law rule set out in *BTC* v *Gourley* (1955) and later in *Beach* v *Reed Corrugated Cases Ltd* (1956), the court will deduct from the gross award a notional sum to represent income tax. Under the Income and Corporation Taxes Act 1988, the first £30,000 of the net award is tax free. If the net award exceeds that sum the balance will be taxed again in the ex-employee's hands. Therefore, the court will add a sum to the non-exempt balance to ensure that after payment of tax on the sum awarded, the ex-employee is left with an appropriate net sum (see *Shove* v *Downs Surgical plc* (1984)). For example, Fred, a managing director on a gross salary of £120,000 a year and with a contract giving him the right to receive six months' notice, is dismissed without notice. His net pay is calculated at £80,000 so he is awarded £40,000 for failure to give him notice. The first £30,000 of this sum is tax free but £10,000 will be taxed again as income for the year in which the damages are received, at his highest rate (currently 40 per cent). If Fred's tax liability on the £10,000 is estimated to be £4,000, the award will be £44,000, so that after payment of that tax, Fred ends up with £40,000.

RIGHTS AND REMEDIES ON DISMISSAL

These are as follows.

Written statement of reasons for dismissal

The employer is not at common law under any legal obligation to give written reasons at the time when an employee is dismissed, but there are very strong arguments in favour of doing so. If no reason at all is given, even orally, the dismissal will almost certainly be unfair. The main advantage of giving or confirming the reason in writing is that there may otherwise be a dispute as to what was said and the reason given for the dismissal.

It is very important that the reason for dismissal which is given to the employee, whether at the time or later, should be the true reason. For example, if an employee is being dismissed for incompetence, he should not be told that he is being made redundant, in order to be kind to him. If an employer gives a false reason, whether to be kind or otherwise, he will thereby be making it much more difficult to show what the true reason was in the event of employment tribunal proceedings.

If the employer does not give the reason in writing at the time of the dismissal, the employee may, subject to certain exceptions (see below), ask the employer for a written statement of reasons. The employer must give the written statement within 14 days after the request is made. The request itself need not be in writing.

The employee can make an employment tribunal application on one of the following grounds:

(a) that the employer has unreasonably refused to provide the written statement; or

(b) that the particulars given are inadequate or untrue.

If the employment tribunal finds against the employer on either of these grounds, it may declare what the reasons for dismissal were. It must also award the employee compensation equal to two weeks' gross pay.

The time limit within which the employee must make the tribunal application is three months from the effective date of termination of the employment.

Exceptions

A request for a written statement of reasons for dismissal is not always made with a view to unfair dismissal proceedings. The employee may need the statement in order to claim unemployment benefit. He or she may also require the statement in order to show it to a prospective employer, particularly where the dismissal was on a ground such as redundancy, which implies no fault on the part of the employee.

There are two main exceptions to the right to request a written statement of reasons. The right is not held by:

(a) employees who have less than one year's continuous employment full or part time at the effective date of termination of the employment;

(b) share fishermen and the police.

However, it should be noted that, as we have seen, the ERA gives all women, regardless of service or hours of work, a right to written reasons for dismissal if dismissed while pregnant or during the statutory maternity leave period regardless of whether or not they request them.

Employer's insolvency

If the employer is bankrupt or dies insolvent, or where the employer is a company and is in liquidation, the unpaid wages of an employee have priority as to payment but only to a maximum of £800 and limited to services rendered during the period of four months before the commencement of the insolvency. Any balance over £800 or four months ranks as an ordinary debt. Also preferential is accrued holiday remuneration payable to an employee on the termination of his employment before or because of the insolvency.

The Insolvency Act 1986 adds to the above preferential debts by including in the list sums owed in respect of statutory guaranteed payments, guaranteed payments during statutory time off, remuneration on suspension for medical grounds, or remuneration under a protective award given because of failure to consult properly on redundancy. Statutory sick pay is also a preferential debt.

It should also be noted that under the ERA an employee may, in the case of his employer's insolvency, make a claim on the National Insurance Fund rather than relying on the preferential payments procedure set out above. If the employee is paid from the National Insurance Fund, the Secretary of State for Trade and Industry may then claim in the employer's insolvency for the amount paid out of the National Insurance Fund; the claim is preferential to the extent that the employee paid would have been.

The limits of the employee's claim on the National Insurance Fund are as follows:

1 Arrears of pay for a period not exceeding eight weeks with a maximum of £240 per week.

2 Holiday pay with a limit of six weeks in the last 12 months of employment and a financial limit of £240 per week.

3 Payments instead of notice at a rate not exceeding £240 per week up to the statutory maximum entitlement of a particular employee under the ERA.

4 Payments outstanding in regard to an award by an industrial tribunal of compensation for unfair dismissal limited to the amount of the basic award.
5 Reimbursement of any fee or premium paid by an apprentice or articled clerk.
6 Unpaid contributions to a pension scheme.

The amount of £240 refers to the employee's gross wage.

There is no qualifying period before an employee becomes eligible and virtually all people in employment are entitled.

It should also be noted that claims on the National Insurance Fund were in the past not admitted unless the relevant insolvency practitioner gave the Department of Trade and Industry a statement of the amount due, though this could be waived and payments made if there was likely to be an unreasonable delay in providing the statement. The ERA now allows the Department, at its option, to make payments without a statement where it has adequate evidence, often from its own records, of the amounts due.

The equitable remedy of specific performance and injunction

A decree of specific performance is, as we have seen, an order of the court and constitutes an express instruction to a party to a contract to perform the actual obligations which he undertook under its terms. If the person who is subject to the order fails to comply with it, he is in contempt of court and potentially liable to be fined or imprisoned. For all practical purposes the remedy is not given to enforce performance of a contract of service, largely because the court cannot supervise that its order is being carried out. A judge would have to attend the place of work on a regular basis to see that the parties were implementing the contract.

An injunction is, as we have seen, an order of the court whereby an individual is required to refrain from the further doing of the act complained of. Again, a person who is subject to such an order and fails to comply with it is in contempt of court and the consequences set out above follow from the contempt. An injunction may be used to prevent many wrongful acts, e.g. the torts of trespass and nuisance, but in the context of contract the remedy will be granted to enforce a negative stipulation in a contract in a situation where it would be unjust to confine the claimant to damages. In a proper case an injunction may be used as an indirect method of enforcing a contract for personal services, such as a contract of employment; but in that case a clear negative stipulation is required. Reference should be made to *Warner Brothers* v *Nelson* (1937) in Chapter 7 as an illustration of the application of the negative stipulation rule and the developments in it in more recent times.

In this connection it should also be noted that s 236 of the Trade Union and Labour Relations (Consolidation) Act 1992, consolidating a former statutory provision dating from 1974, provides that no court shall by way of specific performance or an injunction compel an employee to do any work or attend any place for the doing of any work. Thus, the Act is in line with the judicial approach to specific performance, but to some extent out of line with the judicial approach to the granting of an injunction, though less so in more recent times. Thus, the availability of an injunction in cases involving contracts of service is subject to the provisions of the 1992 Act. It would seem that, on general principles, the granting of an injunction in the context of a contract of employment is no longer possible since statute law prevails over decisions of the judiciary.

Employee's breach of contract

An employer may sue his employees for damages for breach of the contract of service by the employee. Such claims are potentially available for, e.g., damage to the employer's property, as where machinery is damaged by negligent operation, as was the case in *Baster* v *London and County Printing Works* (1899), or for refusal to work resulting in damage by lost production, as was the case in *National Coal Board* v *Galley* (1958). Such claims are rare and impractical because of the fact that the employee will not, in most cases, be able to meet the claim, and also, perhaps more importantly, because they lead to industrial unrest. In these circumstances we do not pursue the matter further here.

QUESTIONS/ACTIVITIES

1 How is the relationship of employer and worker established?

2 In connection with the provisions for maternity leave and statutory maternity pay:
   (a) What is the maximum leave entitlement?
   (b) What is the amount of maternity pay?
   (c) For how long must the claimant have been continuously employed?

3 Des and Eric are both employed by a bus company. Des is a bus driver and Eric a conductor. Eric has always nursed an ambition to be a driver and Des has, on occasion, let Eric drive a bus around the depot before other employees turned up for work. Last week, while Eric was having a drive around the yard, he struck Des who was riding his motor bike around the yard at 60 mph.

   Discuss the liability of Eric and the bus company in regard to the injuries suffered by Des.

4 Monty signalled to a van driver of Python Ltd to stop and asked him to take him to the Grotty Towers Hotel. The hotel was some five miles away from the route which the driver would usually take in the course of his duties, but he nevertheless agreed to give Monty a lift to the hotel. When the driver had deviated a quarter mile from his authorised route, he carelessly collided with another vehicle and Monty was injured.

   As company secretary of Python Ltd, you have received a letter from a firm of solicitors representing Monty threatening legal action against Python Ltd. Your managing director asks you to draft a memorandum for him on the legal aspects of the case. Draft the memorandum.

5 You have recently been appointed the company secretary of Foundry Ltd. The following problems emerge at the first board meeting.
   (a) The members of the board are concerned as to whether they are taking appropriate steps to communicate with the employees as to how the company is fulfilling its obligations under Health and Safety legislation. You are asked to write an explanatory memorandum for the next board meeting as to the legal requirements and indicate the steps which the company should be taking.

   (b) It appears that Foundry Ltd employs 100 women and 50 men in an area where there is a large number of immigrant families. The managing director appears to have paid little or no attention to sex, race and equal pay legislation. The board, which is concerned about this, asks for an explanatory memorandum, again, for the next board meeting, summarising the main provisions of the relevant legislation and setting out procedures which the company should adopt to ensure that the law is complied with.

6 John is one of the employees of a firm in which you are a partner. He suffers badly from arthritis. He has been employed for ten years. However, he has had a number of absences of two to three weeks' duration over the past three years.

   John is employed as a shop assistant and the manager of the shop has just informed you that John has now been off work for eight weeks with arthritis and is still not fit to come back to work. The manager wants to write to John telling him that he is dismissed.

   Prepare a note for your next partnership meeting as to the legal position if John is dismissed.

7 Alan worked for ten years for Pleasant Ltd. It was taken over 18 months ago by Aggressive Ltd and Alan continued in his job. He has found the management of Aggressive Ltd to be very difficult and domineering. Amongst other things, the management has asked him to work in the stores issuing and accounting for equipment issued to Aggressive's employees. Alan feels that he has not been trained to do this and has given in his notice.

   Advise him as to his rights.

8 The company of which you are secretary makes components for cars. Business has fallen off lately and the board has decided that it will have to dismiss 120 employees during the next five weeks. Write an explanatory memorandum to the board regarding any legal requirements there may be in terms of:
   (a) notification of the redundancies;
   (b) selection of employees for redundancy;
   (c) amounts of compensation that may be involved;
   (d) the consultation requirements.

INDEX